# 수능직방

실수 없는 수능 듣기 만점 공략!

# Listening

## 수능 듣기 실전 모의고사 20회

LEVEL
3

## 저자 및 연구진

### 저자

**Jason Lee**

연세대학교 영어교육 석사
Jason Lee Academy 대표
www.jasonlee.co.kr
jasonlee@jasonlee.co.kr

### 연구

**Jason Lee Academy 연구원**

연구실장: 김희선
Ryan DeLaney 수석연구원: University of Southern Indiana/University of Cambridge(CELTA)
서지연 연구원: 한국외대 영어과(卒)
박주현 연구원: 고려대 영어교육 석사
박성우 연구원: 연세대 영어영문학 석사
백재민 연구원: 연세대 영어영문학 석사
박동준 연구원: 서울대 경영학과(卒)
박국일 연구원: Boston University(卒)
이민령 연구원: 고려대 경영학과
Taylor Lagieski 연구원: University of Montana/ University of Cambridge(CELTA)

### 감수

양유리 선생님: 연세대 영어교육 석사, 양천고 교사
김세리 선생님: 연세대 영어교육 석사, 화곡중 교사

### 평가

김동원(성균관대) 김정호(인제의대) 김효중(육군사관학교) 박찬슬(서울대) 이승혁(경희대)
이우진(제주의대) 이종식(서울시립대) 임재훈(연세대) 장정우(美미시간주립대) 조원우(연세대)
최진명(서울대) 탁우령(고려대) 황인찬(서울대)

# 수능직방 **Listening** LEVEL 3

**지은이**  Jason Lee
**펴낸이**  최회영
**영문교열**  윤은지, Eric Williams
**펴낸곳**  (주)웅진컴퍼스
**등록번호**  제22-2943호
**등록일자**  2006년 6월 16일
**주소**  서울특별시 서초구 강남대로39길 15-10 한라비발디스튜디오193 3층
**전화**  (02)3471-0096
**홈페이지**  http://www.wjcompass.com

**ISBN**  978-89-6697-891-5

10 9 8 7 6 5 4
20 19 18 17

Printed in Korea

# 이 책을 내며

**최근 수능 영어는 많은 변화를 겪고 있습니다.** 2013학년도까지 15년간 기본 틀을 유지하며 난이도만 조절해 오던 데서 벗어나 2014학년도에 갑자기 수준별 시험(A·B형)으로 출제되더니 2015학년도부터는 A·B형 구분을 없애고 다시 단일형으로 바뀌었습니다. 급기야 2018학년도 수능 시험부터는 절대평가로 바뀌게 되었습니다. **급변하는 대입 영어 정책에 수험생과 학부모의 마음이 무거운 상황에서, 수능 영어 어떻게 준비해야 할까요?**

'최적의 수능 대비'와 '실질적인 영어 실력 향상'이 동시에 가능한 교재로서 불철주야 연구와 노력을 다하여 수능직방 Voca 시리즈에 이어 이번에 수능직방 Listening 시리즈를 출간하게 되었습니다. 그 특징은 다음과 같습니다.

**첫째,** 평가원의 최신 수능 개편안 및 출제 방침, 그리고 수능 연계 EBS 교재를 활용한 출제 경향까지 과학적으로 철저히 분석·반영하였습니다. 즉, 코퍼스 언어학에 기반을 둔 Jason Lee Academy는 이번 수능직방 Listening 개발 과정에서도 고유의 특허 기술을 활용하여 수능·평가원 모의고사의 어휘 수준과 문장 수, 선택지 길이와 한 문장에서의 최대 어휘 수까지 분석·반영하였습니다.

**둘째,** EBS 수능 연계 교재 및 최근 7년간의 시·도 교육청 모의고사 듣기 평가에서 정답률이 낮았던 문항들(60% 이하)을 엄선하여 비슷한 난이도로 재구성하였습니다.

**셋째,** 모든 문제와 지문은 수능·평가원 출제 경험이 있는 학교 선생님들의 조언과 감수를 거쳐 **최신 수능이 요구하는 기준을 만족시키도록 구성**되었고, 앞으로 출제 가능성이 없는 유형은 배제하였습니다.

**넷째,** 학생 개인별 맞춤 학습, 완전학습이 가능하도록 3종의 음원(문제풀이용, 문항별, 실전보다 빠른 듣기용 MP3 음원)과 무료 Mobile App을 제공합니다.

**다섯째,** 실제 원어민의 대화, 담화에 가깝게 구성하여 수능 시험을 준비하면서 살아있는 영어 (Real English) 실력까지 갖출 수 있습니다. 국내 유명 어학원과 학교에서 강의 경력이 풍부한 원어민 선생님들이 교재 기획·개발 전 과정에 참여하였기 때문입니다.

저희 Jason Lee Academy 연구진과 웅진컴퍼스 모두의 열정과 노력이 여러분의 수능 만점과 영어 실력 향상이라는 결실로 이어지리라 확신합니다.

강남 Jason Lee Academy에서

# 수능 출제 경향 분석 및 대비 전략

## 🍃 수능 듣기의 역사

수능 영어에서 가장 큰 변화를 겪은 영역은 단언컨대 듣기 영역입니다. 1994학년 1차 수능 8문항을 시작으로 1996학년에 10문항, 1997학년 17문항으로 늘어났고, 1998학년 수능부터 2013학년까지 15년간은 거의 비슷한 유형과 포맷을 유지하였습니다. 하지만 2014학년 6월 평가원 모의고사부터 '외국어 영역'에서 '영어 영역'으로 이름도 바뀌고 A형, B형으로 수준별 시험을 치르게 되면서 수능 영어 시험에 많은 변화가 나타났습니다. 그중 듣기 영역이 문항 수와 구성 면에서 가장 큰 변화가 있었습니다. 17문항에서 22문항으로 증가하여, 듣기 비중이 기존 약 37.78%에서 약 48.89%로 대폭 상승하였습니다. TOEIC과 TEPS 등의 시험과 매우 유사한 '짧은 대화 응답'과 '한 지문 두 문항' 등과 같은 신유형이 나타났습니다. 하지만 야심 차게 시작된 수준별 시험은 난이도 조절 실패 등의 이유로 2014학년 수능이 처음이자 마지막 시험이 되었고 2015학년부터 다시 듣기 문항 수도 기존 17문항으로 돌아가게 되었습니다. 다만, 2014학년의 22문항 체제에서 문제 유형은 그대로 유지하되, 중복 유형을 줄여 17문항으로 만든 점은 주목할 만한 대목입니다.

## 🍃 NEW 통합형 수능 영어 듣기 출제 경향 분석 및 학습 전략

<u>우리가 준비해야 하는 수능 영어 듣기</u>는 크게 4가지, 세부적으로는 총 15가지 유형으로 구성되어 있습니다.

### 1. 대의 파악 (2014학년 5문항 → 2015학년 이후 3문항)

대화 · 담화를 듣고 전체적인 내용을 이해하거나 추론하는 능력을 측정합니다.

① 대화 · 담화 목적
② 대화 · 주제/요지
③ 대화 · 담화자 주장/의견
④ 대화자 심정/관계, 대화 장소 → 관계의 비중이 압도적으로 높음

**학습 전략**

◆ 대화 도입부를 들으면서 대화/담화가 일어나는 상황, 장소, 대화자 간의 관계를 유추해 본다.
◆ 대화자가 반복, 강조하는 핵심 단어 · 표현에 집중한다.
◆ 너무 광범위하거나 지엽적인 선택지는 피한다.

### 2. 세부 사항 (2014학년 9문항 → 2015학년 이후 7문항)

대화 · 담화의 핵심적 내용과 전개 방식에 비추어 제시된 특정 정보를 가급적 정확하고 신속하게 파악할 수 있는 능력을 측정합니다. 직접적으로 제시된 정보를 구체적인 사항에 초점을 맞추어 정확하게 파악하는 연습이 필요합니다.

① 그림 내용 일치/불일치 → 대부분 불일치 문제
② 한 일/할 일/부탁한 일
③ 5W1H 세부사항 → 6하 원칙 중 주로 '이유'를 묻는 유형으로 출제
④ 숫자 관련 정보 → 고난도 문항으로 출제
⑤ 대화 언급/불언급
⑥ 담화 내용 일치/불일치 → 주로 불일치로 출제
⑦ 도표 내용 일치/불일치

**학습 전략**

◆ 평소 들으며 내용을 메모하는 연습을 하자.
◆ 계산 문제는 넓은 공간에 식을 세우고 복잡한 식은 대화가 끝난 후 계산한다.
◆ 내용 일치/불일치 문제는 선택지 순서대로 나오기 때문에, 선택지를 미리 봐놓고 줄을 그어가며 푼다.

3. **간접 말하기 (2014학년 6문항 → 2015학년 이후 5문항)**

실제 일상생활에서 흔히 발생할 수 있는 의사소통 상황과
관련된 듣기 자료를 통해 이해한 바를 가상의 말하기 상황에
적용할 수 있는 능력을 측정합니다.

① 짧은 대화 응답
② 대화 응답
③ 담화 응답



◈ 교과서 주요 의사소통 기능 표현을 미리 익혀두자.
◈ 미리 선택지의 내용을 읽고 무슨 내용인지 파악한다.
  (대화/담화를 듣고 난 후 선택지 내용을 읽으면, 시간에 쫓겨
  다음 문제까지 영향을 받기 때문이다.)
◈ 선택지의 내용을 두 개 이상 모르면, 과감히 그 문제는 건너
  뛰고 다음 문제에 집중하자.

4. **복합 (2014학년 2문항 → 2015학년 이후 2문항)**

하나의 대화 · 담화문을 통해서 주로 전체적인 흐름 파악과 세부적인 내용 파악 능력을 동시에 측정하고자 출제합니다.

① 하나의 대화 · 담화문 2문항



◈ 대화/담화가 시작되기 전에, 문제와 선택지를 반드시 미리 읽어놔야 한다.
◈ 들으면서 본인만 알 수 있도록 최대한 간결하게 메모하는 습관을 평소 들여놔야 한다.
◈ 세부적인 내용은 처음에 놓쳤더라도 두 번째에서 만회할 기회가 있다. 포기하지 말자.
◈ 상위권의 경우, 한 번 들을 때 두 문제를 정확하게 맞힐 수 있도록 집중한다. 그래야 시간을 아껴서 독해에 더 투자할 수 있다.

## 🍃 수능 영어 듣기 만점 전략

1. **평소 매일 꾸준히 듣는 연습이 필요합니다.**
   노력에 비해 당장 실력이 늘지 않는 듯해도, 영어 실력은 결국 계단식으로 향상된다는 것을 기억하세요.

2. **안 들리는 원인을 파악하여 보완하세요.**
   자신이 자주 틀리는 문제 유형, 모르는 어휘, 취약점을 파악해서 보완하세요. 받아쓰기(Dictation) 및 오답 노트 작성이 도움이
   됩니다.

3. **들으면서 메모하는 연습을 해 보세요.**
   문장 전체를 꼼꼼히 받아 적기는 사실 쉽지 않은 일입니다. 따라서 나만의 전략을 세워 평소 최대한 간결히 메모하는 습관을
   들여야 합니다. 예를 들어, Studying English를 받아 적어야 한다면 다 적는 것이 아니라 Stu~g Eng~ 처럼 본인만이
   알아볼 수 있도록, 기호 또는 축약 등의 방법을 이용하면 유용합니다.

4. **실제 수능보다 빠른 속도로 듣는 연습을 하세요.**
   실제 시험 당일에는 심리적으로 위축되고 긴장한 탓에 자칫 속도가 빠르지 않음에도 불구하고 순간적으로 놓칠 수가 있습니다.
   따라서 평소 실제 수능보다 빠른 속도의 대화/담화문을 긴장감을 유지하며 듣는 연습을 하세요. 실전 감각을 키울 수 있습니다.

**❘ BONUS TIP ❘**

평가원 공식 발표에 따르면, 2014학년도 수준별 영어 A형을 끝으로 '지도를 활용한 길 찾기' 문항은 더는 출제되지 않습니다.
또한, 1997학년도 수능부터 2013학년도 수능까지 13번으로 출제되었던 '그림 상황에 맞는 대화를 고르기' 문제도 신수능에서는
더 이상 찾아보기 어렵습니다.

# 구성과 특징

## { Step 1 }

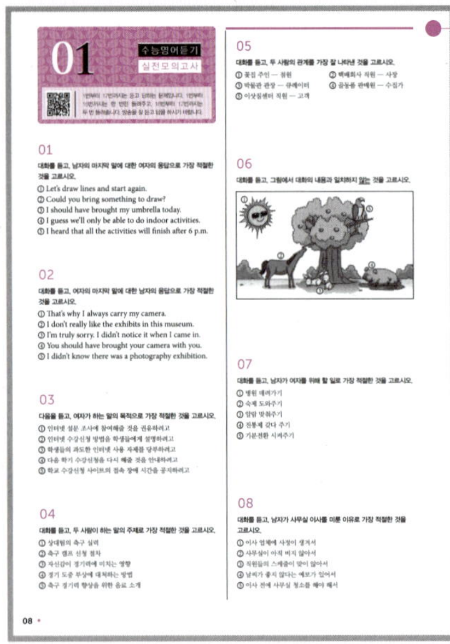

### 100% 수능 실전 모의고사

▶ **수능 최신 출제 경향 반영**: 평가원에서 제시한 수능 출제 방침과 수능 개편안을 최고의 연구·집필진이 철저히 분석, 반영하여 문항유형 및 배치, 어휘의 난이도와 script 길이까지 실전과 100% 동일하게 구성하였습니다.

▶ **바로 듣는 바로 푸는 QR Code 수록**: 언제 어디서나 자투리 시간에도 듣기 학습이 가능합니다.

## { Step 2 }

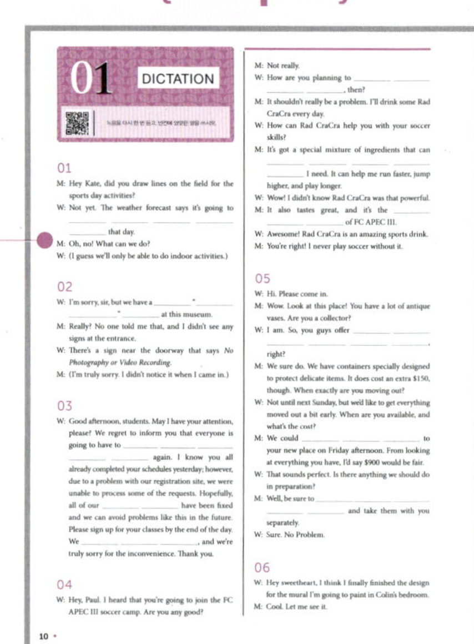

### Dictation (받아쓰기)

▶ **Lexical Chunk(의미 단위)별로 빈칸 구성**: 정답을 찾는 데 꼭 필요한 핵심 어구 및 수능 필수 어휘를 듣고 받아쓰는 연습을 통해, 해당 표현을 완전히 자신의 것으로 소화할 수 있고 수능 출제 포인트가 어디에 있는 지까지 파악하게 되어, 결국 수능 고득점으로 이어집니다.

▶ **문항별 MP3 음원 제공**: 자신이 틀린 문제, 다시 듣고 싶은 표현만 빠르게 찾아 학습할 수 있도록 문항별로 구분해둔 파일도 제공합니다.

## { Step 3 }

### 친절한 정답 및 해설

▶ **친절하고 상세한 정답 및 해설, 해석과 소재와 핵심 어휘까지 빠짐없이 수록**: 학습자 스스로 꼼꼼히 복습이 가능하도록 구성 하였습니다.

▶ **평가원 지침에 따라 분류한 수능 듣기 문제 유형**도 문항별로 친절히 표기해 놓았습니다. 자신이 자주 틀리는 문제 유형이 무엇인지 파악하고 부족한 점을 보완하는 데에 도움이 될 것입니다.

---

**완전학습을 위한 무료 제공**

＊ 용도별 MP3 음원 3종 (문제풀이용, 빠른 듣기용, 문항별)
www.wjcompass.com/sjlistening

＊ 수능직방 Listening 전용 Mobile App 제공
Apple App Store / Google Play Store 접속 후,
'수직리스닝'을 검색하세요.

# 목차



★ **책 속의 책**: 정답 및 해설
★ **무료 제공**: 수능직방 Listening 전용 Mobile App

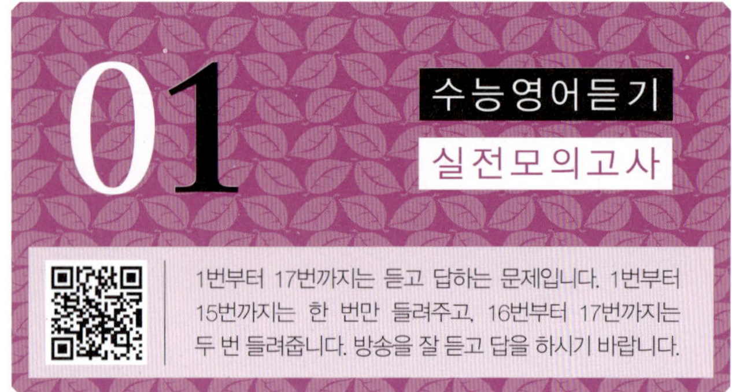



## 01

대화를 듣고, 남자의 마지막 말에 대한 여자의 응답으로 가장 적절한 것을 고르시오.

① Let's draw lines and start again.
② Could you bring something to draw?
③ I should have brought my umbrella today.
④ I guess we'll only be able to do indoor activities.
⑤ I heard that all the activities will finish after 6 p.m.

## 02

대화를 듣고, 여자의 마지막 말에 대한 남자의 응답으로 가장 적절한 것을 고르시오.

① That's why I always carry my camera.
② I don't really like the exhibits in this museum.
③ I'm truly sorry. I didn't notice it when I came in.
④ You should have brought your camera with you.
⑤ I didn't know there was a photography exhibition.

## 03

다음을 듣고, 여자가 하는 말의 목적으로 가장 적절한 것을 고르시오.

① 인터넷 설문 조사에 참여해줄 것을 권유하려고
② 인터넷 수강신청 방법을 학생들에게 설명하려고
③ 학생들의 과도한 인터넷 사용 자제를 당부하려고
④ 다음 학기 수강신청을 다시 해줄 것을 안내하려고
⑤ 학교 수강신청 사이트의 접속 장애 시간을 공지하려고

## 04

대화를 듣고, 두 사람이 하는 말의 주제로 가장 적절한 것을 고르시오.

① 상대팀의 축구 실력
② 축구 캠프 신청 절차
③ 자신감이 경기력에 미치는 영향
④ 경기 도중 부상에 대처하는 방법
⑤ 축구 경기력 향상을 위한 음료 소개

## 05

대화를 듣고, 두 사람의 관계를 가장 잘 나타낸 것을 고르시오.

① 꽃집 주인 — 점원
② 택배회사 직원 — 사장
③ 박물관 관장 — 큐레이터
④ 골동품 판매원 — 수집가
⑤ 이삿짐센터 직원 — 고객

## 06

대화를 듣고, 그림에서 대화의 내용과 일치하지 <u>않는</u> 것을 고르시오.

## 07

대화를 듣고, 남자가 여자를 위해 할 일로 가장 적절한 것을 고르시오.

① 병원 데려가기
② 숙제 도와주기
③ 알람 맞춰주기
④ 진통제 갖다 주기
⑤ 기분전환 시켜주기

## 08

대화를 듣고, 남자가 사무실 이사를 미룬 이유로 가장 적절한 것을 고르시오.

① 이사 업체에 사정이 생겨서
② 사무실이 아직 비지 않아서
③ 직원들의 스케줄이 맞지 않아서
④ 날씨가 좋지 않다는 예보가 있어서
⑤ 이사 전에 사무실 청소를 해야 해서

## 09

대화를 듣고, 여자가 지불할 총 금액을 고르시오.

① $90  ② $94  ③ $99  ④ $110  ⑤ $115

## 10

대화를 듣고, 현장학습에 관해 두 사람이 언급하지 <u>않은</u> 것을 고르시오.

① 활동 내용  ② 인원  ③ 날짜
④ 1인당 가격  ⑤ 당일 복장

## 11

Springfield Farmers' Market에 관한 다음 내용을 듣고, 일치하지 <u>않는</u> 것을 고르시오.

① Springfield Square에서 열린다.
② 신선한 유기농 농산물을 제공한다.
③ 다른 곳보다 가격이 더 저렴하다.
④ 매주 토요일과 일요일에 열린다.
⑤ 애완견은 데려올 수 없다.

## 12

다음 표를 보면서 대화를 듣고, 여자가 선택할 정수기를 고르시오.

**Quality Water Purifier Rentals**

|  | Ice | Hot Water | Energy Efficiency Rating | Monthly Rental Fee |
|---|---|---|---|---|
| ① | Yes | Yes | 1 | $50 |
| ② | No | Yes | 1 | $40 |
| ③ | Yes | No | 1 | $40 |
| ④ | No | Yes | 2 | $30 |
| ⑤ | No | No | 2 | $25 |

## 13

대화를 듣고, 여자의 마지막 말에 대한 남자의 응답으로 가장 적절한 것을 고르시오.

Man: _______________________________________

① I really want to be a professor of journalism.
② Even though journalism is quite boring, I still love it.
③ I think that high-quality journalists are rare these days.
④ I want to change my major, but my father won't let me.
⑤ I'd major in what I was more interested in if I were you.

## 14

대화를 듣고, 남자의 마지막 말에 대한 여자의 응답으로 가장 적절한 것을 고르시오.

Woman: _______________________________________

① Put everything in the garbage bin at school.
② You're right. I think everyone will be impressed.
③ No. I don't think it's that important to make it neater.
④ You can tell your teacher you've finished your project.
⑤ Try to find the most important message and make it clear.

## 15

다음 상황 설명을 듣고, Manny가 Katie에게 할 말로 가장 적절한 것을 고르시오.

Manny: _______________________________________

① Can I take a look at your guidebook, please?
② Did you double-check all of our reservations?
③ Everything's going to be fine. Let's just have fun.
④ Do you know what hotel we're staying at tonight?
⑤ I can't believe we're going to Bangkok. I'm so excited.

[16-17] 다음을 듣고, 물음에 답하시오.

## 16

남자가 하는 말의 주제로 가장 적절한 것은?

① Negative effects of distraction on study
② Health problems related to distractions
③ Various methods to study more effectively
④ Benefits of setting goals and rewarding yourself
⑤ Benefits of studying in a comfortable environment

## 17

언급된 장소가 <u>아닌</u> 것은?

① 교실  ② 자신의 방  ③ 공원
④ 카페  ⑤ 도서관

## 01

M: Hey Kate, did you draw lines on the field for the sports day activities?

W: Not yet. The weather forecast says it's going to __________ __________ __________ __________ __________ that day.

M: Oh, no! What can we do?

W: (I guess we'll only be able to do indoor activities.)

## 02

W: I'm sorry, sir, but we have a __________ "__________ __________" __________ at this museum.

M: Really? No one told me that, and I didn't see any signs at the entrance.

W: There's a sign near the doorway that says *No Photography or Video Recording*.

M: (I'm truly sorry. I didn't notice it when I came in.)

## 03

W: Good afternoon, students. May I have your attention, please? We regret to inform you that everyone is going to have to __________ __________ __________ __________ __________ again. I know you all already completed your schedules yesterday; however, due to a problem with our registration site, we were unable to process some of the requests. Hopefully, all of our __________ __________ have been fixed and we can avoid problems like this in the future. Please sign up for your classes by the end of the day. We __________ __________ __________, and we're truly sorry for the inconvenience. Thank you.

## 04

W: Hey, Paul. I heard that you're going to join the FC APEC III soccer camp. Are you any good?

M: Not really.

W: How are you planning to __________ __________ __________ __________, then?

M: It shouldn't really be a problem. I'll drink some Rad CraCra every day.

W: How can Rad CraCra help you with your soccer skills?

M: It's got a special mixture of ingredients that can __________ __________ __________ __________ __________ I need. It can help me run faster, jump higher, and play longer.

W: Wow! I didn't know Rad CraCra was that powerful.

M: It also tastes great, and it's the __________ __________ __________ of FC APEC III.

W: Awesome! Rad CraCra is an amazing sports drink.

M: You're right! I never play soccer without it.

## 05

W: Hi. Please come in.

M: Wow. Look at this place! You have a lot of antique vases. Are you a collector?

W: I am. So, you guys offer __________ __________ __________ __________ __________ __________, right?

M: We sure do. We have containers specially designed to protect delicate items. It does cost an extra $150, though. When exactly are you moving out?

W: Not until next Sunday, but we'd like to get everything moved out a bit early. When are you available, and what's the cost?

M: We could __________ __________ __________ to your new place on Friday afternoon. From looking at everything you have, I'd say $900 would be fair.

W: That sounds perfect. Is there anything we should do in preparation?

M: Well, be sure to __________ __________ __________ __________ __________ and take them with you separately.

W: Sure. No Problem.

## 06

W: Hey sweetheart, I think I finally finished the design for the mural I'm going to paint in Colin's bedroom.

M: Cool. Let me see it.

W: Sure. __________ __________ __________ __________

__________ __________ .

M: Well, the sun is pretty interesting. Those are some cool sunglasses, too.

W: Yeah. And the horse is eating grass from the ground.

M: That's cool. I guess that's an apple tree there. You did a great job drawing it.

W: Thanks. What do you think about the rabbits near the tree?

M: I think they look a little more like mice, but __________ __________ __________ __________ __________ __________ the wall. I like how the pig is playing in the mud.

W: Pigs love mud. You know, Colin also loves eagles, so I put one of those in the tree.

M: Neat. I'm sure he'll like it.

W: Well, I guess I should go to the art supply store and buy some paint.

M: Well, I'm really excited to see __________ __________ __________ __________ .

W: Me too, sweetheart.

## 07

M: Hey, is everything okay? You look stressed.

W: I have a big test next week that I should have been preparing for, but __________ __________ __________ __________ __________ __________ __________ a lot instead of studying. I'm worried that I won't do well.

M: Don't worry about it too much. You'll do fine if you start studying today.

W: I appreciate you saying that. It makes me feel a bit better. But still, all of this anxiety is making me hot.

M: That's strange. Let me take your temperature to make sure you don't __________ __________ __________ . [Pause] No, you're fine.

W: I want to take some pain medication anyway.

M: No, a pain pill won't help. If you want to be alert and able to study, you need to rest. You should __________ __________ __________ .

W: I can't nap now. I haven't finished this assignment yet.

M: You really look like you need to sleep. __________ __________ __________ __________ __________ . When you wake up, you'll be able to think more clearly and do better work.

W: Will you make sure to __________ __________ __________ __________ __________ ? I'm worried that if I fall asleep now, I'll sleep too long.

M: All right, I will. Now, go rest.

## 08

W: Good morning, Mr. Staller. We have everything ready to move to the new offices this weekend, right?

M: Didn't you hear? We're not moving in until next weekend.

W: Really? __________ __________ __________ __________ __________ __________ ?

M: I thought that it'd be best if we had the place thoroughly cleaned before we started over there.

W: Did you call the moving company to reschedule the move?

M: I did. __________ __________ __________ __________ the change of plans, though. They're actually going to be booked up next weekend.

W: Oh, no. What are we going to do if we can't find a moving company to replace them?

M: I'm not sure yet, but I thought about having the employees come in on Saturday to move everything out.

W: I really don't think they're going to like that.

M: You're probably right, but desperate times __________ __________ __________ __________ .

## 09

M: Hi. How can I help you today?

W: I'm shopping for a backpack for my son.

M: Well, you've come at the perfect time. We're running our back-to-school sale, and we're __________ __________ __________ __________ 40% off.

W: Awesome! Well, what's popular these days?

M: Well, this Spikey brand backpack is a big seller. It's priced at $50, but it's currently on sale for 20% off.

W: That's reasonable. I'll take it.

M: Great! Is there anything else I can help you with?

W: Well, my daughter could probably use a new backpack too. How much is that pink one over there?

M: That one is generally $60, but it's 10% off right now.

W: ___________ ___________ ___________ ___________,
   but I'm sure she'll love it. I'll take it.
M: All right. We can also make the bags ___________-
   ___________, if you'd like.
W: How much does that cost?
M: It's an additional $5 per bag.
W: That's okay. They're fine the way they are.


## 10

*[Telephone rings.]*
M: Good afternoon, this is Tafford Orchard.
W: Hello, I'm Mrs. Fink, the biology teacher at Paulson
   High School. ___________ ___________ ___________
   ___________ ___________ bringing my students to
   the orchard on a field trip.
M: I'm glad to hear that, Mrs. Fink. We offer half-day
   and full-day programs for students.
W: ___________ ___________-___________ ___________
   would be more appropriate for our needs, I think.
   What are some of the activities that you all do in
   these programs?
M: If the weather's nice, we usually take students out to
   pick apples and make apple cider.
W: That seems like something they'd like. I'd be bringing
   around 25 students. Do you have any openings on
   September 26th?
M: Yes, our schedule is open ___________ ___________
   ___________ ___________.
W: Excellent. I suppose I'd like to go ahead and make a
   reservation, then.
M: Okay. You said about 25 students on September
   26th, correct?
W: That's right. And that's for Paulson High School.
M: All right. You'll need to provide lunch for your
   students and ___________ ___________ ___________
   ___________ ___________ ___________.
W: Will do. Thanks for your help.


## 11

M: It's summer again, which means the return of the
   Springfield Farmers' Market. The market is located
   at Springfield Square and ___________ ___________
   ___________ ___________ some of ___________ ___________
   ___________ ___________ in the state. Why would
   you spend the extra money at the grocery store
   when you can buy directly from our local farmers
   for a fraction of the cost? Whether you're looking
   for watermelons, string beans, or fresh jams, our
   market has everything you need. We're ___________
   ___________ ___________ from noon until 7 p.m.
   and on Sundays from noon to 5. It's fun for the
   whole family. ___________ ___________ ___________
   ___________ ___________, so bring everyone down to
   the farmers' market this weekend.


## 12

M: Good evening, ma'am. What can I do for you?
W: Hi. I'm looking for a water purifier to rent for my
   office.
M: Well, you've come to the right place. We currently
   have five different models to choose from. I'll
   just need to ___________ ___________ ___________
   ___________ ___________ so we can find the perfect
   one for you.
W: That's fine. Ask away.
M: Okay. So, first off, what do you want this machine to
   do? Would you like it to make ice?
W: Well, that would be nice, but it doesn't have to. I do
   want it to make hot water, though.
M: All right. Now, as you might know, different purifiers
   use different amounts of energy. What kind of
   energy rating are you looking for?
W: We're an ___________ ___________ ___________,
   so I think we should go with the best rating possible.
M: I see. A lower number means it's more efficient. Just
   one more question: how much are you looking to
   spend per month?
W: We decided that $40 per month is the most
   ___________ ___________ ___________ ___________.
M: Then this is the model for you.
W: Perfect. I'll take it. Thank you for all your help.


## 13

W: Hey, I heard that you decided to ___________
   ___________ ___________.
M: Yeah, I really want to be a journalist.
W: That's cool. I guess ___________ ___________
   ___________ ___________?

M: That's right. I've loved writing since I was a child. Are you still going to major in anthropology?

W: No, I'm thinking about majoring in sociology.

M: __________ __________. You seemed pretty sure what you were going to major in the last time we talked.

W: Well, I realized I'm really interested in sociology as well. I don't know which one I want to study more.

M: What kind of job do you want when you graduate?

W: I really want to be a social worker, but my father says I should be an anthropology professor.

M: Ah. Isn't your father an anthropology professor?

W: Yeah. So which one do you think I should choose?

M: (I'd major in what I was more interested in if I were you.)

# 14

*[Knocking sound]*

M: Who's there?

W: Hey, Kevin. It's me.

M: Oh, hey Mom. Come on in. How's everything?

W: Not bad. What are you up to?

M: Just working on this project for science class. __________ __________ __________. Check it out.

W: *[Pause]* I'm not sure what I'm looking at here.

M: It's a battery made out of a potato. Pretty neat, huh?

W: Well, it is pretty interesting, but it seems a bit messy. There are wires everywhere. Can't you clean it up a little?

M: I know it's a bit complicated, but I __________ __________ __________ __________ __________ __________ __________ of how everything works. What do you think about the poster?

W: Well, when you're presenting something and trying to get others to understand, I think it's important to __________ __________ __________ __________ __________ __________.

M: Well, what do you think I should do, then?

W: (Try to find the most important message and make it clear.)

# 15

W: Manny and his girlfriend, Katie, __________ __________ __________ __________ through Southeast Asia. Neither of them had traveled abroad before, so they decided to prepare themselves rather than __________ __________ __________ __________ __________. Katie did most of the work to make arrangements. She found cheap accommodation and planned all of the routes. She also bought a Thai phrasebook so she could communicate with the locals. __________ __________ __________ __________ __________, they have finally arrived in Bangkok and are walking around The Grand Palace. Katie, however, is __________ __________ __________ __________ __________ __________ and is trying to think of new things to do. Manny wants to tell Katie that she shouldn't worry about planning and instead should enjoy the trip. In this situation, what would Manny most likely say to Katie?

Manny: (Everything's going to be fine. Let's enjoy our trip.)

# 16-17

W: Good morning, everyone. With final exams coming up, I'd like to __________ __________ __________ __________ __________ __________ effective study habits. Perhaps the first thing to consider when you study is finding the perfect place to concentrate. It needs to be quiet and comfortable, so it could be the classroom, your own room, a cafe, or the library. Second, it's important to __________ __________ when studying. Setting goals will help give you something to work towards as you study. You can also reward yourself with a treat when you reach the goals you have set for yourself. The third point I want to make is about resisting distraction. It's easy to __________ __________ by phones and other electronics these days, so make sure to __________ __________ __________ __________ __________, television, and other distracting devices before you start studying. Finally, recent studies have shown that some noises can be helpful for concentration. Droning noises, such as lights, white noise, rain, and the sounds of nature can help keep your mind sharp and relaxed. __________ __________ __________ __________ __________ while studying for next week's finals. Thank you for your time.

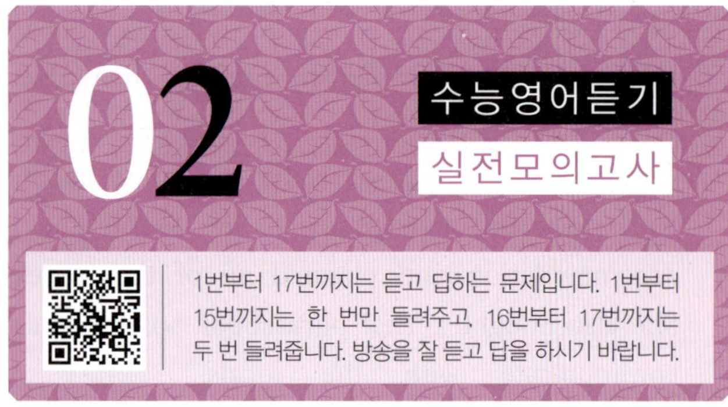


## 01

대화를 듣고, 남자의 마지막 말에 대한 여자의 응답으로 가장 적절한 것을 고르시오.

① I'll take hundreds and fifties, please.
② Would you like large or small bills?
③ I should exchange my money at the bank.
④ We don't allow you to exchange products here.
⑤ We can exchange it if you have the original receipt.

## 02

대화를 듣고, 여자의 마지막 말에 대한 남자의 응답으로 가장 적절한 것을 고르시오.

① I've never watched a documentary.
② It was certainly thought-provoking.
③ You can borrow it once I finish.
④ You know I haven't seen it yet.
⑤ I've read a few of his books.

## 03

다음을 듣고, 남자가 하는 말의 주제로 가장 적절한 것을 고르시오.

① 계절에 맞는 야외 운동법
② 날씨 변화에 따른 가구 배치법
③ 겨울에 몸을 따뜻하게 하는 방법
④ 일조량 부족으로 인한 우울증 대처법
⑤ 적절한 비타민 복용으로 활력 찾는 방법

## 04

대화를 듣고, 여자의 의견으로 가장 적절한 것을 고르시오.

① 야간에 차의 문단속을 철저히 하라.
② 차량 도난 신고는 가능한 한 빨리 해라.
③ 자동차에 경보장치를 반드시 설치하라.
④ 외출 시 집안에 전등을 하나 켜 두어라.
⑤ 경보장치보다는 밝고 좋은 곳에 주차하라.

## 05

대화를 듣고, 두 사람의 관계를 가장 잘 나타낸 것을 고르시오.

① 작가 — 성우
② 작곡가 — 리포터
③ 소설가 — 삽화가
④ 서점 주인 — 구직자
⑤ 도서 편집자 — 번역가

## 06

대화를 듣고, 그림에서 대화의 내용과 일치하지 <u>않는</u> 것을 고르시오.

## 07

대화를 듣고, 여자가 남자를 위해 할 일로 가장 적절한 것을 고르시오.

① 숙제 찾아주기
② 아침식사 챙겨주기
③ 선생님께 전화하기
④ 허가서 작성해주기
⑤ 학교에 태워다 주기

## 08

대화를 듣고, 남자가 기뻐하는 이유를 고르시오.

① 원하던 책을 사게 되어서
② 오디션 프로그램에 합격해서
③ 연락이 끊긴 친구에게 전화가 와서
④ 친한 친구가 TV에 출연하게 되어서
⑤ 오디션 프로그램을 방청하게 되어서

## 09

대화를 듣고, 두 사람이 지불할 총 금액을 고르시오.

① $29 ② $30 ③ $34 ④ $40 ⑤ $44

## 10

대화를 듣고, 신입 사원에 관해 두 사람이 언급하지 <u>않은</u> 것을 고르시오.

① 외국어 능력 ② 첫인상 ③ 전공
④ 자원봉사 이력 ⑤ 좌우명

## 11

Tarsier에 관한 다음 내용을 듣고, 일치하지 <u>않는</u> 것을 고르시오.

① 필리핀 군도의 남쪽 부근에 산다.
② 다 자란 안경원숭이는 어른 손바닥 크기이다.
③ 커다란 눈으로 유명하다.
④ 머리를 양쪽으로 180도 회전할 수 있다.
⑤ 낮에는 시력이 좋지만, 밤에는 잘 볼 수 없다.

## 12

다음 표를 보면서 대화를 듣고, 두 사람이 주문할 아기 침대를 고르시오.

**Infant Cribs**

| | Model | Cage Height | Mattress Included | Material | Price |
|---|---|---|---|---|---|
| ① | L-100 | Low | No | Plastic | $120 |
| ② | M-100 | Mid | Yes | Plastic | $140 |
| ③ | M-200 | Mid | Yes | Wood | $200 |
| ④ | H-100 | High | No | Wood | $180 |
| ⑤ | H-200 | High | Yes | Wood | $240 |

## 13

대화를 듣고, 남자의 마지막 말에 대한 여자의 응답으로 가장 적절한 것을 고르시오.

Woman: _______________________________

① They're charging way too much for admission.
② I'm glad that we decided to join the tour group.
③ I can see why so many people love Banksy's work.
④ It's rude to listen to audio while on an exhibition tour.
⑤ That way we can choose to listen to the explanation or not.

## 14

대화를 듣고, 여자의 마지막 말에 대한 남자의 응답으로 가장 적절한 것을 고르시오.

Man: _______________________________

① No problem. I'll get in touch and see if she has time.
② Sure. I'll look it over and get it back to you tomorrow.
③ That's fine, but I need to turn it in before this weekend.
④ It's great that you got a job with the school newspaper.
⑤ No, but I'll be sure to send you a copy of the school newspaper.

## 15

다음 상황 설명을 듣고, 교장 선생님이 Bill에게 할 말로 가장 적절한 것을 고르시오.

Mr. Thomas: Bill, _______________________________

① take a deep breath. You're going to do great.
② I'd like you to give the commencement speech.
③ I'm sure that you'll do great in your speech class.
④ congratulations on graduating from high school.
⑤ I'm sorry to hear that you won't be graduating this year.

[16-17] 다음을 듣고, 물음에 답하시오.

## 16

남자가 하는 말의 목적으로 가장 적절한 것은?

① 리조트의 새로운 시설들을 광고하려고
② 타지 음식 섭취의 위험을 알리려고
③ 다양한 해양 스포츠를 소개하려고
④ 세계 유명 맛집을 소개하려고
⑤ 좋은 휴양지를 홍보하려고

## 17

남자가 추천한 내용으로 언급되지 <u>않은</u> 것은?

① 스노클링 ② 채식 행사 ③ 음식 시식
④ 섬 방문 ⑤ 기념품 제작

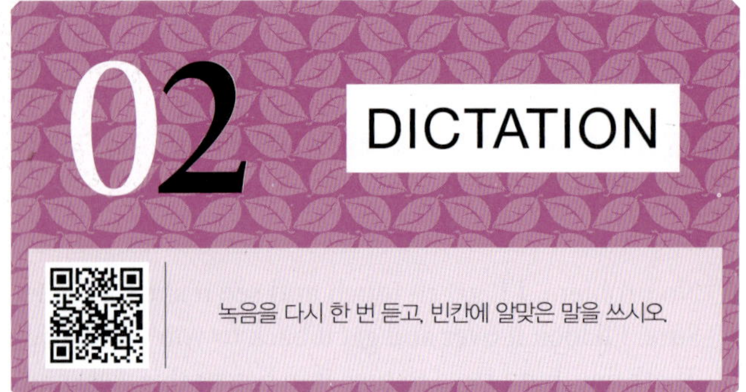



## 01

M: Hello. I have some leftover money that I'd like to exchange. ___________ ___________ ___________ ___________?

W: It's 119 yen to the dollar. How much are you looking to exchange?

M: I have 55,000 yen. Here you go.

W: (Would you like large or small bills?)

## 02

W: Conan, have you seen *Our History*, the new documentary on HBO?

M: Yeah, I watched it last night. It was really interesting to see ___________ ___________ ___________ on the history of mankind.

W: I thought so, too. It really ___________ ___________ ___________ ___________ ___________ ___________ ___________.

M: (It was certainly thought-provoking.)

## 03

M: Do you ever get moody or depressed during the winter season? If so, you might have what experts call "___________ ___________." This condition is quite common, as the human body receives vitamins from sunlight. Experts now say that up to 50% of people worldwide ___________ ___________ ___________ ___________ ___________. ___________ ___________ ___________ ___________ of vitamin D, experts suggest spending between 10 and 15 minutes outside each day. You can also organize your house to allow more sunlight to enter. ___________ ___________ ___________ ___________ ___________ ___________, spending time under a bright light can also help.

## 04

M: Krista, do you have an alarm on your car?

W: I don't. Why do you ask?

M: ___________ ___________ ___________ ___________ ___________ last night while I was out.

W: Oh, my. Did they take anything?

M: Luckily, there wasn't much to take. But they cut up my interior with knives. It seems like they just wanted to destroy property.

W: You must be pretty upset about that.

M: I am. That's why I'm thinking about ___________ ___________ ___________ ___________.

W: A good friend of mine had one and ended up taking it out because it would go off randomly. If people want to wreck your stuff, an alarm ___________ ___________ ___________ ___________ ___________.

M: Yeah, I suppose you're right. What should I do, then?

W: Well, my advice is to always ___________ ___________ ___________ ___________ ___________ ___________ ___________ ___________ or a nice part of town. Even if the parking space isn't the most convenient, it's better than the alternative.

M: You think that'll work?

W: I do. That's what I do, and I've never had a problem.

M: Okay. I'll do that from now on.

## 05

M: Hello. You must be Amelia Hawkins.

W: That's me. You're the great Jeffrey Martin. It's a pleasure to meet you, Mr. Martin.

M: The pleasure is all mine. Please, call me Jeffrey.

W: All right, Jeffrey. It's really great to get the chance to work with someone so famous.

M: Thanks. I've heard a lot about you too, Amelia. You're a real ___________ ___________ ___________ ___________.

W: Well, thank you. It's taken a lot of hard work to get where I am.

M: I understand. Have you read any of my books?

W: I've read them all. They're amazing. I recommend them to everyone I meet.

M: __________ __________, but I couldn't have written any of them without my lovely wife, Lola. She inspired me and pushed me to write them. She also told me that I should __________ __________ __________.

W: That's where I come in, huh?

M: That's right. I'm excited to have such a talented and beautiful voice __________ __________ __________ __________ __________.

W: I'll try my best, Jeffrey.

## 06

W: Dad, would you look at this photo? This is the stage for the performance I'm working on for the school talent show.

M: Cool, __________ __________ __________ __________ __________. What is the calendar for? The one on the back wall.

W: It's to show the passing of time.

M: What about that __________ __________ __________ __________ __________?

W: Most of the characters will use the window to talk to people offstage.

M: Okay, that's a good idea. I really like the sofa and the coffee table on the right side of the stage.

W: Thanks. I really like the sofa as well.

M: I assume the actors will sit and talk there quite often?

W: Yes, exactly.

M: I see there's __________ __________ __________ __________ __________ __________ __________ of the stage. It balances the sofa, but it doesn't look very inviting.

W: That's what I was hoping for, Dad.

M: It looks like __________ __________ __________ __________ __________ __________ __________. You did a good job.

W: I really appreciate that, Dad.

## 07

W: Peter, you're going to __________ __________ __________. Aren't you ready yet?

M: I'll be ready in a minute, Mom. I'm trying to __________ __________ __________ __________ for the field trip on Friday.

W: You gave it to me. Here you go.

M: This isn't the permission slip!

W: Well, I think I lost the original one, so __________ __________ __________ __________ __________.

M: I don't know if this will work, Mom.

W: It's okay. I'll give Mrs. Towns a call and explain.

M: Can you __________ __________ __________?

W: Okay. I'll call her now. You __________ __________ __________, though. Have a great day.

## 08

W: Where have you been, Alan?

M: I've been at the bookstore buying some books.

W: Is that all? Why do you look so happy?

M: Actually, I __________ __________ __________ __________ just a few minutes ago while I was on my back.

W: Oh? Who called?

M: You'd better sit down for this news. I __________ __________ __________ __________ see the audition program *Rising Star K* live at the studio in Seoul.

W: Wow, I know you've really been wanting to see that. Congratulations!

M: Thanks, Beth. I applied to be a member of the studio audience about six months ago, but there was no response at all. I had almost given up, so I really wasn't __________ __________ __________ __________ __________.

W: That's amazing. I know how hard it is to get that chance. Some of my friends applied to do something like that __________ __________ __________ __________, but nobody ever got called back. You're so lucky. So when are you going?

M: Next Friday. God, this is so great. I still can't believe it!

W: I envy you so much.

## 09

M: Hey sweetheart, what movie did you choose?

W: It took me a while, but I finally decided on this one.

M: *Windsor's List*, huh? __________ __________ __________ __________, but it's one of the greatest films of all time.

W: That's what I've heard. It was originally $30, but it's on sale for 50% off.

M: That's a great buy. What's that other movie you have?

W: Oh, this one? This is for Jake. It's called *The Light Crystal*. It's only $10.

M: I loved that movie when I was young. Oh, here's another version of it ___________ ___________ ___________ ___________ ___________ ___________.

W: That's cool. We should get that one. He really likes comics.

M: Yeah, but this one is ___________ ___________ ___________ ___________. It's $14.

W: That's still a great deal. Are you going to buy anything for yourself?

M: I can't find anything I want.

W: All right. Let's pay and go home.


## 10

W: Mr. Anderson, do you remember Randal Kim from the latest round of employee interviews?

M: Randal Kim? Ah, the one who ___________ ___________ ___________?

W: Yes, that's the one. My initial impression of him was very strong.

M: What was the most impressive thing about him?

W: Besides his language skills, he was very confident in his ability to work as part of a team.

M: I agree with you there. When he was interviewed, he looked confident and ___________ ___________ ___________ ___________ ___________ about contributing to the company.

W: One more thing that I liked about him was that he's done a lot of volunteer work for various organizations.

M: I saw that. He's done over 500 hours of volunteer work in Africa alone, ___________ ___________ ___________ ___________ ___________ ___________ ___________ ___________ ___________. He says his motto is, "If it is to be, it is up to me."

W: I think he'll be a valuable addition to our team.

M: I think you're right.


## 11

W: Good afternoon, ladies and gentlemen. Today, I want to talk a bit about an extraordinary little animal called the tarsier. This little guy is found in the southern part of the Philippines archipelago, namely on the islands of Bohol and Mindanao. Tarsiers are very small mammals. A fully grown tarsier can fit in the palm of your hand. ___________ ___________ ___________ ___________ ___________ ___________ its huge eyes. These eyes are locked into position, but the tarsier can rotate its head 180 degrees in either direction. What's more is that their eyes ___________ ___________ ___________ ___________ ___________. When there is minimal light, their pupils will expand to almost the size of the entire eye, allowing it to ___________ ___________ ___________ ___________ ___________ ___________ ___________ ___________ ___________ as in broad daylight. Isn't that fascinating? To learn more about tarsiers, I suggest catching a flight to the Philippines to see them for yourselves.


## 12

M: Hey sweetheart, what are you doing on the Internet?

W: I'm looking at cribs for our baby. She'll be here really soon, you know.

M: That's right. We should start thinking about buying things for her room. Did you find anything good?

W: Well, I think we should buy one of these five. This company gets great reviews because ___________ ___________ ___________-___________ ___________.

M: Well, let me take a look. *[Pause]* I think we should ___________ ___________ ___________ ___________-___________ ___________. That way we won't have to buy another one after she gets bigger.

W: Right. I think we should get one that includes a mattress as well. That way we won't have to buy one separately.

M: I agree.

W: What do you think about the material? Some of them are ___________ ___________ ___________, and others are made of plastic.

M: I think we should get a wooden one. It'll look better in her room.

W: Okay, that narrows it down to these two. Which do you think is better?

M: We're ___________ ___________ ___________ ___________ ___________, so let's go for the cheaper one.

W: Great. I'll go ahead and put in an order.

## 13

W: I can't believe we're finally here. I've been wanting to see some of Banksy's work for such a long time.

M: I can't believe he's __________ __________ __________ __________ in our city.

W: Let's go. I want to have plenty of time to look around before it closes.

M: We have to buy tickets first.

W: Okay. You know, $25 seems cheap for all the work he must've done.

M: Yeah, I'm sure __________ __________ __________ __________ __________.

W: Oh, look. There's a tour group that starts in a half hour. Should we wait and join that?

M: Well, if we join a group, we'll have to __________ __________ __________ __________. I'd rather take my time and enjoy the exhibition.

W: Really? I think it'd be interesting to learn more about the artist and his pieces.

M: Well, we can rent one of these __________ __________ __________. That seems interesting.

W: (That way we can choose to listen to the explanation or not.)

## 14

W: Hey, Mike. Are you busy? Do you have a couple of minutes?

M: I'm not too busy. What do you need?

W: Well, I've been trying to write this article for the school newspaper.

M: I always like reading your articles.

W: Yeah, I love writing. Anyway, I need someone to read over it and tell me what they think. I could use a bit of __________ __________.

M: But why would you want me to look over it?

W: Actually, I meant your sister. Didn't you say that she works for Kings and Queens Press?

M: She does, but she's __________ __________ __________ __________ __________ until next week.

W: Would it be possible for you to email it to her and __________ __________ __________ __________ __________ __________?

M: (No problem. I'll get in touch and see if she has time.)

## 15

W: Bill is a senior in high school and __________ __________ __________ __________ __________ __________ __________ __________ his graduating class. He's very intelligent and has an outgoing personality. Because of his hard work and popularity, the school's principal, Mr. Thomas, asked Bill to speak during the graduation ceremony. Bill gladly __________ __________ __________ and has been working hard on his speech. While Bill is a great student and an all-around nice guy, __________ __________ __________ __________ __________. Before the ceremony, Mr. Thomas notices that Bill is very nervous and would like to give him some __________ __________ __________. In this situation, what would Mr. Thomas most likely say to Bill?

Mr. Thomas: Bill, (take a deep breath. You're going to do great.)

## 16-17

M: Are you tired of taking the same old boring vacation to the same old beach every year? Try something different this year. Take an exotic vacation to beautiful Phuket. Located in southern Thailand, Phuket is an island that __________ __________ __________ __________ as well as your budget. The island brings in __________ __________ __________ __________ __________ every year who take in the culture, the exquisite seafood, and the countless beach activities. With some of the whitest sand in the world, Phuket has amazing opportunities to scuba-dive and snorkel. The numerous festivals, such as the vegetarian festival, will __________ __________ __________ and open your mind. Try the famous dish called *sum tam*, which is a mixture of papaya, carrots, spices, and other delicacies. It's a flavor __________ __________ __________ __________. If you're a little more adventurous, take a trip to Phi Phi Island, which is known for its rich greenery and powdered beaches. You can visit the sets of movies filmed here, such as *Blue Lagoon* and *The Beach*. So, book your trip now and come on out to beautiful Phuket!

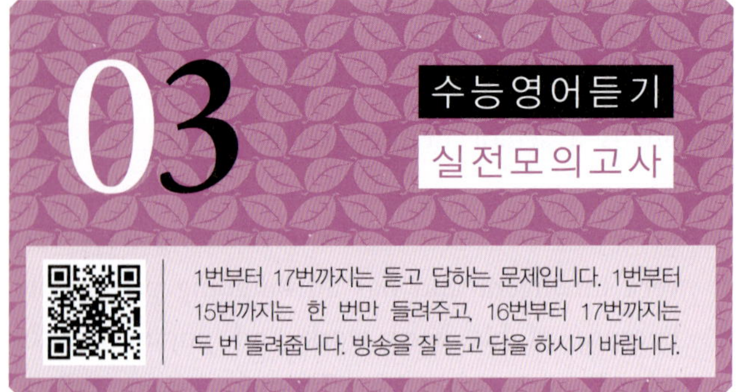

# 03

수능영어듣기

실전모의고사

1번부터 17번까지는 듣고 답하는 문제입니다. 1번부터 15번까지는 한 번만 들려주고, 16번부터 17번까지는 두 번 들려줍니다. 방송을 잘 듣고 답을 하시기 바랍니다.

## 01

대화를 듣고, 여자의 마지막 말에 대한 남자의 응답으로 가장 적절한 것을 고르시오.

① Are you sure about that? Okay, let's find it together.
② I'm sorry. I lost your cell phone outside the house.
③ You don't have to feel guilty. It's all my fault.
④ Don't worry. You can look for it at school.
⑤ I don't remember when I had it last.

## 02

대화를 듣고, 남자의 마지막 말에 대한 여자의 응답으로 가장 적절한 것을 고르시오.

① No problem. I'm always happy to help.
② Of course. I'll make extra copies of the report.
③ I've finished the report and I'm printing it now.
④ I told you I needed reports on the new employees.
⑤ My mistake. I'll print the correct reports right now.

## 03

다음을 듣고, 남자가 하는 말의 목적으로 가장 적절한 것을 고르시오.

① 여름철을 건강하게 보내는 방법을 소개하려고
② 효율적인 에너지 종류에 대해 소개하려고
③ 지구 온난화의 심각성을 인식시키려고
④ 악천후에 대비하는 방법을 알려주려고
⑤ 전기 절약을 위한 방법을 알려주려고

## 04

대화를 듣고, 스페인어 교육에 관한 여자의 의견으로 가장 적절한 것을 고르시오.

① 모국어와 외국어의 습득방식은 다르다.
② 습득에 대한 동기가 가장 중요하다.
③ 듣기와 말하기로 시작해야 한다.
④ 발음은 어릴 때 습득해야 한다.
⑤ 다양한 책을 많이 읽혀야 한다.

## 05

대화를 듣고, 여자의 심정으로 가장 적절한 것을 고르시오.

① calm and graceful
② elated and energetic
③ nervous and anxious
④ proud and determined
⑤ envious and upset

## 06

다음을 듣고, 포스터에서 남자가 하는 말의 내용과 일치하지 않는 것을 고르시오.

## 07

대화를 듣고, 여자가 남자에게 부탁한 일을 고르시오.

① 가족 사진 찾아주기
② 참가 신청서 제출하기
③ 신청서 작성 도와주기
④ Katie를 학교에서 데려오기
⑤ 아시아 문화에 대해 알려주기

## 08

대화를 듣고, 남자가 버스 여행에 가지 못하는 이유를 고르시오.

① 일을 해야 해서
② 차멀미가 심해서
③ 표가 너무 비싸서
④ 날씨가 좋지 않아서
⑤ 버스를 예약하지 못해서

## 09

대화를 듣고, 여자가 남자에게 송금할 금액을 고르시오.

① $65　　② $80　　③ $85　　④ $105　　⑤ $165

## 10

대화를 듣고, 북극 대륙 빙하에 관해 두 사람이 언급하지 <u>않은</u> 것을 고르시오.

① 지구에서 빙하의 역할
② 해빙을 막기 위한 사람들의 노력
③ 해수면의 높이에 끼치는 영향
④ 빙하가 녹는 것을 막는 방법
⑤ 다른 의견을 가진 과학자들

## 11

Brittany Spikes에 관한 다음 내용을 듣고, 일치하지 <u>않는</u> 것을 고르시오.

① 전통적인 미국 가정에서 태어났다.
② 7살 때 노래와 춤을 훈련받기 시작했다.
③ 그녀는 Mickey Mouse Club에 처음 출연했다.
④ 20살에 Hollywood 영화감독과 결혼했다.
⑤ 지금은 가수 활동을 하지 않고 있다.

## 12

다음 표를 보면서 대화를 듣고, 두 사람이 예약할 숙소를 고르시오.

**Guesthouses**

| | Name | Rate per Night | Location | Breakfast |
|---|---|---|---|---|
| ① | Beach Guesthouse | $60 | East Beach | X |
| ② | East Guesthouse | $75 | East Beach | O |
| ③ | Green Guesthouse | $55 | Downtown Area | X |
| ④ | Rainbow Guesthouse | $65 | Downtown Area | O |
| ⑤ | Seashore Guesthouse | $67 | East Beach | O |

## 13

대화를 듣고, 여자의 마지막 말에 대한 남자의 응답으로 가장 적절한 것을 고르시오.

Man: _______________________________________

① You worked hard and you earned that degree.
② I need some advice on how to intern at a hospital.
③ He is one of the most popular doctors at the school.
③ My mother is working overseas, so she couldn't make it.
⑤ I'm truly grateful, and I owe you so much for all your help.

## 14

대화를 듣고, 남자의 마지막 말에 대한 여자의 응답으로 가장 적절한 것을 고르시오.

Woman: _______________________________________

① Read this article. It's one of my favorites.
② That's fine. I can't wait to read your article.
③ I'm glad I've inspired you to become a writer.
④ I wish I could help you, but I'm not a journalist.
⑤ You really need to have it finished before tomorrow.

## 15

다음 상황 설명을 듣고, Craig이 Ms. Tate에게 할 말로 가장 적절한 것을 고르시오.

Craig: _______________________________________

① Your tires are thin and should be replaced immediately.
② It's clear you don't take good care of your bicycle.
③ I'm going to make sure the brakes work properly.
④ It looks like you replaced your tires last year.
⑤ Your bike looks to be in great shape.

[16-17] 다음을 듣고, 물음에 답하시오.

## 16

여자가 하는 말의 주제로 가장 적절한 것은?

① How different sports strain feet
② The benefits of stretching before exercising
③ Why different sports require different styles of shoes
④ The importance of wearing shoes while playing sports
⑤ The advantages and disadvantages of high-top sneakers

## 17

언급된 운동이 <u>아닌</u> 것은?

① running　　② tennis　　③ soccer
④ badminton　　⑤ basketball

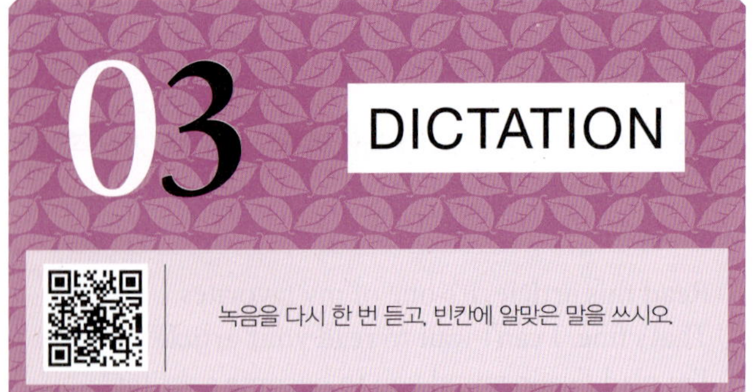



# 03 DICTATION

## 01

W: Dad, where's my cell phone? I can't find it.

M: Didn't you ____________ ____________ ____________ ____________? Why don't you look in your backpack first?

W: I didn't take it to school today. It must be here somewhere.

M: (Are you sure about that? Okay, let's find it together.)

## 02

M: Ingrid, did you find those reports I wanted?

W: I did. I printed them out for you. Here you go.

M: Thanks. *[Pause]* Wait a second. I don't need ____________ ____________ ____________ ____________. I need the reports on the new employees.

W: (My mistake. I'll print the correct reports right now.)

## 03

M: Good afternoon, everyone. These days we're using too much coal, gas, and electricity ____________ ____________ ____________ ____________ ____________ ____________. This summer, the most important issue is electricity. Because of global warming, summers are getting hotter and therefore we tend to use our air conditioners more often. However, this just adds to the problem. We need to seek out and practice ____________ ____________ ____________ ____________. If you're working in a place with abundant natural light, you should turn off the overhead lights. Also, wear short sleeves. Most businesses nowadays are adjusting their dress codes to ____________ ____________ ____________ attire. Finally, instead of using the air conditioning, ____________ ____________ ____________ windows to control the natural flow of air and use a fan if windows aren't available. Together we can make a difference in the environment and stay cool!

## 04

M: Ms. Hamilton, could you help me find a good Spanish book?

W: Sure. But why, Mr. Crowley? You're not a Spanish teacher.

M: My son Alfred has started to learn Spanish, and I'd like to help him study at home.

W: Okay. He is probably practicing his listening and speaking skills in class, right?

M: Yes, so I wanted to help him learn to read basic material in Spanish myself.

W: I think you should ____________ ____________ ____________ ____________ ____________ ____________ and speaking skills.

M: Really? But I thought reading was ____________ ____________ ____________ ____________ ____________ ____________ ____________.

W: Reading is important. But think about how your son learned to speak English. He started by listening and speaking.

M: You're right, but I think it's different now that he is older and ____________ ____________ ____________ ____________ ____________.

W: Actually, you'll learn a second or even a third language faster if you study the same way you learned your native language.

M: I see. Thanks a lot for your advice. I'll give it some more thought.

## 05

M: Hey, Sandra. Are you getting ready for your business trip to New York tomorrow?

W: I'm ready to go, but ____________, ____________ ____________ ____________ ____________ ____________ ____________.

M: Really? I thought you were really excited to travel to a new city.

W: Yeah, of course I want to see New York. But I have a really important meeting and a presentation as soon as I get there.

M: You're going to do great. You're great with presentations.

W: I appreciate that. However, the clients are German so I need to do it in their language. I'm nervous that ____________ ____________ ____________ ____________ ____________.

M: You'll be fine. They're aware that German isn't your first language, so even if you make a few mistakes it won't matter.

W: I understand that. I'm afraid because this is the most important presentation of my career. I need to do really well.

M: The most important thing is to relax. You're prepared for the meeting, so ____________ ____________ ____________ ____________ it for now and imagine you're headed to New York for a vacation.

W: Okay, I'll try. But it won't be easy.

## 06

M: Have you seen the new ad for the National Education Fund? The fund was created to give ____________ ____________ ____________ ____________ or children without families a way to pay for their education all the way through university. The title of the poster is *A Better Future for All*. In the center of the picture, there's a group of college graduates throwing their hats ____________ ____________ ____________. On the bottom of the poster are three more pictures. On the left is a happy child coloring in a kindergarten class. In the middle is a group of girls eating together on a bench. And on the right there is a picture of two young professionals holding hands. ____________ ____________ ____________ ____________ ____________ all the different types of people that can benefit from the National Education Fund.

## 07

M: Good morning, sweetheart. What are you up to?

W: I'm just ____________ ____________ ____________ ____________. It's for a homestay program at Katie's school.

M: A homestay program, huh? You mean like ____________ ____________ ____________, right?

W: That's right. Katie's school is hosting several students from another country.

M: That sounds interesting. And you want to house one of the students here?

W: I'm hoping to. It'll be a great experience for Katie, and for us.

M: I agree. So, what country are these students from?

W: Two are from Korea, and one is from Taiwan. It'll be nice for Katie to ____________ ____________ ____________ ____________ ____________ ____________ Asian lifestyle and culture.

M: I'd like to learn more about their culture as well. What can I do to help?

W: Well, we're going to need a family photo to send out with the application. Can you find the photo we had taken for Christmas last year?

M: Sure. I think I know where it is.

W: Great. Thank you.

## 08

W: Hey Dylan, Lilly and I are ____________ ____________ ____________ ____________ ____________ ____________ this weekend, and we were wondering if you wanted to join us.

M: That sounds great. I've been wanting to make it to the mountains this summer.

W: It's a long trip, though. ____________ ____________ ____________ ____________ ____________?

M: I used to get sick on buses when I was young, but I'm fine now. How much are tickets?

W: Well, I got three tickets from a friend who had to change her plans, so you don't have to pay anything.

M: Awesome!

W: Yeah. And I was worried about the forecast, but it looks like the weather will be beautiful.

M: That's great. So, what time does the bus depart on Saturday?

W: Saturday? It's actually leaving on Friday at noon.

M: Really? Oh, no. I have to ____________ ____________ ____________.

W: Oh, that's too bad. Lilly was really hoping you could come.

M: Well, maybe we can ____________ ____________ ____________ ____________ ____________. Thanks for the invitation, though.

## 09

*[Telephone rings.]*

M: Hello, this is the ticket office.

W: Hi. I'm calling about buying a ____________ ____________ ____________ ____________ ____________.

M: Sure. Are you interested in tickets for the LA Dodgers game or the Chicago Cubs one?

W: Both, actually. But how much are they?

M: The LA Dodgers tickets are $60 each, and the Chicago Cubs tickets are $80.

W: That's a bit pricier than I thought they would be. Are there any cheaper tickets?

M: I'm afraid not. These are the only tickets left for these games.

W: Fine, I'll just take one LA Dodgers ticket. I saw that you also sell the home team's banners. Do they come free with the tickets?

M: It's an extra $20 for the banner.

W: Okay, I guess I'll take the banner too. __________ __________ __________ __________ __________ __________?

M: Sorry, but shipping is an additional $5.

W: Okay. I'll transfer you the money as soon as I can.

## 10

W: Hey, Todd. Did you watch the documentary on the environment last night?

M: No, I missed it. What was the focus?

W: One of the main topics was the __________ __________ __________ __________ __________ __________.

M: Is it becoming a serious problem?

W: It is. You know, the ice caps act as a mirror which protects the Earth from overheating by reflecting the sun's rays.

M: Really? I didn't know that.

W: Yeah, most people don't. Since 2009, people have really __________ __________ __________ __________ __________ and trying to stop the melting.

M: That is really important, I suppose. Are they making progress?

W: Little by little, but they're still a long way off.

M: So, bigger problems may come from the melting?

W: Yes, exactly. It has a strong __________ __________ __________ __________ __________. Part of the problem is that it leads to __________ __________ __________ __________ __________ __________ of all the world's oceans, putting coastal cities around the world at risk of ending up underwater.

M: Oh, my. I've heard that most of the world's population lives on or near the coast.

W: Yes. However, some scientists believe the change is a part of a natural cycle. It's really hard to say who's right, but it's an important issue either way.

## 11

M: Good afternoon, everyone. I'd like to introduce one of the greatest performers of our time, Brittany Spikes. __________ __________ __________ to a traditional American family and named Bertha Beatrice. She started her vocal and dance training when she was seven. She first appeared on the Mickey Mouse Club, a children's talent show for up-and-coming young singers and dancers. She performed on the show until she was 16. During that time, she __________ __________ __________ __________ __________ for her flashy dance moves and winning smile. She married Hollywood movie director Albert Foster in May of 2001, when she was only 20 years old. Foster __________ __________ __________ __________ __________ the young performer and decided to get her into the music business. Today, Brittany __________ __________ __________ __________ and is delighting fans all around the world.

## 12

W: The school year is almost over. Amber's really excited about summer vacation.

M: I am too, actually. I think it would be nice to stay at a guesthouse nearby and just relax for a while.

W: That sounds wonderful.

M: Well, I've put together a list of guesthouses that I found on the Internet. How much do you think __________ __________ __________ __________ __________?

W: I think we should try to keep it under $70 a night if we can.

M: Okay, and among these locations, where would you most like to stay?

W: I'd like to __________ __________ __________ __________, if possible. It would be great if we could take our shoes off and walk around on a sandy beach.

M: All right. There are two guesthouses that seem to have everything we're looking for. Which one looks best to you?

W: Definitely the one that __________ __________. I don't want to do any cooking in the morning.

M: All right, great. I'll call them right now and make a reservation.

## 13

W: Congratulations ＿＿＿＿＿ ＿＿＿＿＿ ＿＿＿＿＿,
Dr. Nathan. I'm really proud of you.

M: I'm glad you could make it, Layla.

W: There's no way I'd miss my boyfriend's graduation.

M: I just really wish my mother could have been here,
too.

W: It's too bad that she missed it.

M: At least all my friends from med school showed up.

W: ＿＿＿＿＿ ＿＿＿＿＿ ＿＿＿＿＿ ＿＿＿＿＿
meet them.

M: You know, Layla, I don't think I would be here if I
hadn't met you.

W: Oh, come on! I didn't help you that much.

M: You really ＿＿＿＿＿ ＿＿＿＿＿ ＿＿＿＿＿
＿＿＿＿＿ ＿＿＿＿＿ ＿＿＿＿＿.

W: Don't mention it, Nathan. It really wasn't that big of
a deal.

M: (I'm truly grateful, and I owe you so much for all
your help.)

## 14

W: Hey Ms. Collins, do you have a minute?

W: Sure, Aron. What do you need?

M: Well, you know that literary nonfiction project you
assigned last week? Working on it ＿＿＿＿＿
＿＿＿＿＿ ＿＿＿＿＿. I think I want to be a
journalist.

W: That's great. I've always loved reading your work.

M: Thanks. ＿＿＿＿＿ ＿＿＿＿＿ ＿＿＿＿＿
＿＿＿＿＿ ＿＿＿＿＿ or short stories, but I think
writing nonfiction is interesting and fun. I'm having
a problem in the nonfiction project, though.

W: Oh, what is that?

M: Well, I know that the article is only supposed to be
500 words, but I don't think I can shorten it that
much.

W: So how many words have you written?

M: I've written almost 1,000 words. ＿＿＿＿＿
＿＿＿＿＿ ＿＿＿＿＿ ＿＿＿＿＿ ?

W: (That's fine. I can't wait to read your article.)

## 15

M: Craig is a bicycle repairman. He is tuning up Ms.
Tate's bike, which hasn't been tuned up in over a year
and is not riding smoothly. He finds ＿＿＿＿＿
＿＿＿＿＿ ＿＿＿＿＿ ＿＿＿＿＿ ＿＿＿＿＿
＿＿＿＿＿ ＿＿＿＿＿, pedals, and brakes. After
he oils each of those parts, they operate more
smoothly. He also discovers that the tread on the
tires is worn quite thin, so the tires ＿＿＿＿＿
＿＿＿＿＿ ＿＿＿＿＿ ＿＿＿＿＿. If Ms. Tate
continues to ride on these tires, they ＿＿＿＿＿
＿＿＿＿＿ ＿＿＿＿＿ ＿＿＿＿＿, which could
cause an accident. Craig wants to ＿＿＿＿＿
＿＿＿＿＿ ＿＿＿＿＿ to Ms. Tate. In this situation,
what would Craig most likely say to Ms. Tate?

Craig: (Your tires are thin and should be replaced
immediately.)

## 16-17

W: Each day, you put a great deal of stress on your feet.
It should come as no surprise that shoes are a very
important factor in relieving some of this stress,
especially for athletes. ＿＿＿＿＿ ＿＿＿＿＿
＿＿＿＿＿ can prevent serious injury while
supporting your ankles and feet. Different sports
will strain your feet in different ways. Therefore, you
need to choose shoes that are sufficient to whatever
activity you are participating in. For instance, if
you are a long-distance runner, you need to choose
shoes that cushion against the constant pounding
while ＿＿＿＿＿ ＿＿＿＿＿ ＿＿＿＿＿ ＿＿＿＿＿
＿＿＿＿＿. On the other hand, tennis and
badminton require a lot of movement from one side
to the other. If you play these sports, you're going
to want to look for shoes that support this kind of
movement. In regards to basketball, you ＿＿＿＿＿
＿＿＿＿＿ for jumping, running down the court,
and reversing direction. That's why high-top shoes
are necessary for basketball. As you can see, shoes
vary a great deal from sport to sport. ＿＿＿＿＿
＿＿＿＿＿ ＿＿＿＿＿ ＿＿＿＿＿ the next time
you're shopping for athletic shoes.

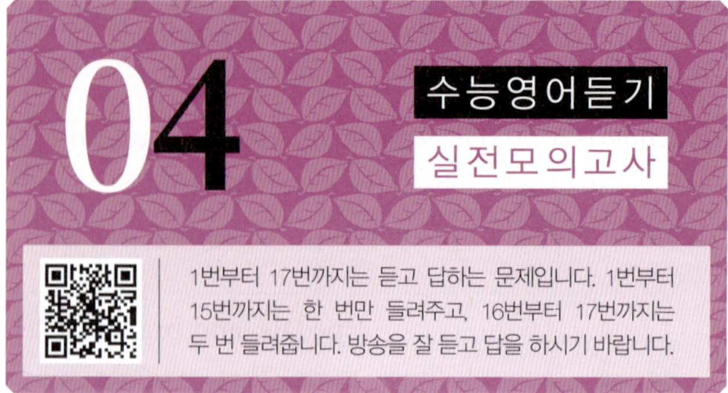


## 01

대화를 듣고, 남자의 마지막 말에 대한 여자의 응답으로 가장 적절한 것을 고르시오.

① It's a uPhone 6 with a black case.
② Well, I'm sure that I used it at work.
③ Don't worry. I'm sure you left it at home.
④ I thought so, too, but I already checked the bus.
⑤ I'll call your phone again to see if we can find it.

## 02

대화를 듣고, 여자의 마지막 말에 대한 남자의 응답으로 가장 적절한 것을 고르시오.

① I don't think so. It's not a useful example.
② If you say so, I'll use the same example.
③ I agree with you. This is a great report.
④ You're right. I'll correct it right now.
⑤ That's great. It really fits well here.

## 03

다음을 듣고, 여자가 하는 말의 목적으로 가장 적절한 것을 고르시오.

① 여름철 뱃놀이의 즐거움을 알려주려고
② 비상시 구명조끼의 사용법을 설명해 주려고
③ 배가 침몰할 때의 대처방법을 설명해 주려고
④ 안전한 뱃놀이를 위한 점검 항목들을 알려주려고
⑤ 여름철 물놀이 안전사고 예방교육에 대해 안내하려고

## 04

대화를 듣고, 남자의 의견으로 가장 적절한 것을 고르시오.

① 동물들은 훈련 받으면서 인간과 친밀해지고 교감하게 된다.
② 인간의 즐거움을 위해 동물을 훈련시키는 것은 옳지 않다.
③ 다치고 버려진 동물들에 대한 사람들의 배려가 필요하다.
④ 동물을 조련할 때 충분한 보상과 사랑을 주어야만 한다.
⑤ 동물 학대 및 유기에 대한 처벌을 보다 강화해야 한다.

## 05

대화를 듣고, 두 사람의 관계를 가장 잘 나타낸 것을 고르시오.

① 의사 — 간호사
② 경찰관 — 목격자
③ 영화 감독 — 배우
④ 구급 대원 — 신고자
⑤ 차량 정비사 — 고객

## 06

대화를 듣고, 그림에서 대화의 내용과 일치하지 <u>않는</u> 것을 고르시오.

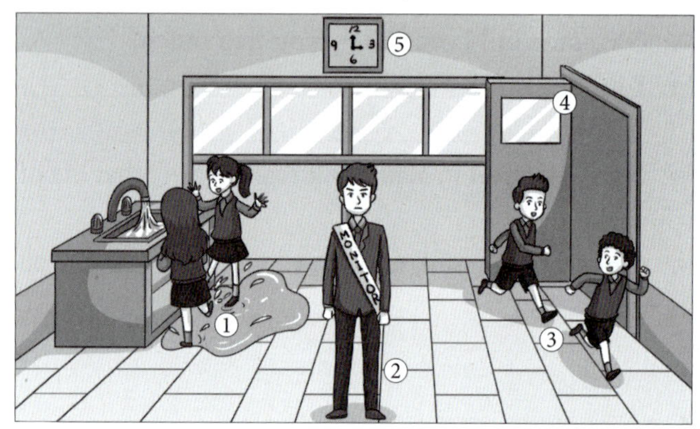

## 07

대화를 듣고, 남자가 여자를 위해 할 일로 가장 적절한 것을 고르시오.

① 자동차 빌려주기
② 캠핑 같이 가주기
③ 세일 기간 알아봐주기
④ 상점까지 차로 태워다 주기
⑤ 캠핑용 휴대 스토브 골라 주기

## 08

대화를 듣고, 여자가 육상 경기에 나갈 수 <u>없는</u> 이유를 고르시오.

① 아버지가 다치셔서
② 넘어져 발을 다쳐서
③ 여동생을 돌봐야 해서
④ 부모님이 안 된다 하셔서
⑤ 할아버지 댁을 방문해야 해서

## 09

대화를 듣고, 남자가 지불할 금액을 고르시오.

① $30 ② $40 ③ $50 ④ $60 ⑤ $80

## 10

대화를 듣고, 봉사활동에 관해 두 사람이 언급하지 않은 것을 고르시오.

① 활동 내용
② 봉사활동의 수혜자
③ 봉사 단체명
④ 봉사해 온 기간
⑤ 봉사를 통해 얻는 이점

## 11

Artists in August 행사에 관한 다음 내용을 듣고, 일치하지 않는 것을 고르시오.

① 16년간 개최되었다.
② 지역 예술가를 홍보하는 행사이다.
③ 입장료는 무료이다.
④ 기부금을 받는다.
⑤ 사진 작품을 볼 수 있다.

## 12

다음 표를 보면서 대화를 듣고, 여자가 선택한 드럼 키트 모델을 고르시오.

**River City Custom Drum Kits**

| | Model | Pieces | Custom Floor Tom | Price |
|---|---|---|---|---|
| ① | A | 3 | X | $600 |
| ② | B | 5 | X | $660 |
| ③ | C | 5 | O | $700 |
| ④ | D | 7 | X | $760 |
| ⑤ | E | 7 | O | $860 |

## 13

대화를 듣고, 여자의 마지막 말에 대한 남자의 응답으로 가장 적절한 것을 고르시오.

Man: ___________________________________

① You shouldn't leave work early to do yoga.
② Going to yoga every day must be pointless.
③ I really don't want to work overtime tonight.
④ I guess that's why you look so happy these days.
⑤ We should look for a place to practice yoga, then.

## 14

대화를 듣고, 남자의 마지막 말에 대한 여자의 응답으로 가장 적절한 것을 고르시오.

Woman: ___________________________________

① There's no need to worry. It won't rain that day.
② We really need to hurry. We have so much work.
③ We can finish the project before summer vacation.
④ Brilliant idea. I'm glad we're partners on this project.
⑤ Why would we do it in the gym? We can do it outside.

## 15

다음 상황 설명을 듣고, Pamela가 Malory에게 할 말로 가장 적절한 것을 고르시오.

Pamela: ___________________________________.

① Be careful when you talk to strangers on the phone.
② You should not play outside with your friends so often.
③ Finish your homework before you play computer games.
④ Being more active and outgoing can help you in your life.
⑤ Why don't you reduce the time you spend on the Internet?

[16-17] 다음을 듣고, 물음에 답하시오.

## 16

남자가 하는 말의 주제로 가장 적절한 것은?

① Tips for buying items for soccer
② Dangers of playing soccer at a park
③ Results of purchasing expensive items
④ The increasing popularity of the soccer camp
⑤ Various merits of playing soccer for teenagers

## 17

언급된 물건이 아닌 것은?

① 양말
② 축구화
③ 정강이 보호대
④ 반바지
⑤ 축구공

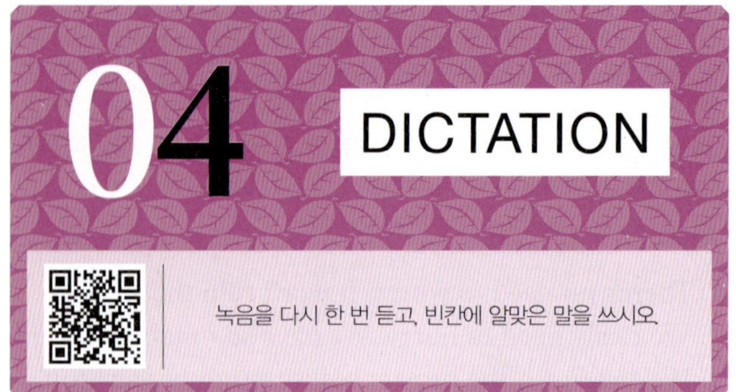

# 04 DICTATION



## 01

M: Hey Lucy, I've been calling you for hours. We ___________ ___________ ___________ ride the bus together.

W: Sorry about that. I lost my phone. I can't find it anywhere.

M: I've had that same problem before. Do you remember where you last had it?

W: (Well, I'm sure that I used it at work.)

## 02

W: I've finished going over your report, Edward.

M: How was it? Are there any problems with it, Ms. Jones?

W: There are no big mistakes. But it would be better to eliminate this example. ___________ ___________ ___________ the topic.

M: (You're right. I'll correct it right now.)

## 03

W: Hello. My name is Jenny Brown, and I'm an officer of the Minnesota Department of Water Safety. Today, I would like to share a few tips that everyone should keep in mind to ensure a safe and clean summer on our lakes and rivers. While boating or sailing, there are a few essential items that ___________ ___________ ___________ ___________ ___________ ___________. For example, the number of life vests on the boat should ___________ ___________ ___________ ___________ ___________ ___________, and every vessel should be equipped with a working fire extinguisher, a horn or whistle, and a spotlight. In addition to having these things on board, you should always make sure that your vessel's lights ___________ ___________ ___________ ___________. Following these tips whenever you are on the water will make the lakes and rivers safer and more fun for everyone. If you would like to learn more about water safety, please visit our website at *www.MNwaterfun.gov*. Thank you for your time, and have a great summer.

## 04

W: I'm thinking about going to the circus this weekend. You should come with me. I love watching the bears and the elephants ___________ ___________.

M: Thanks for the offer. But I don't think what the circus does to those animals is ethical.

W: What do you mean? I think it's a way for people to admire the intelligence and work of animals.

M: I've been reading a lot about the abuse ___________ ___________ ___________ ___________ ___________ ___________ ___________ ___________. Some animals are trained by being punished.

W: That might be true, but I've also heard that the animals have close, loving relationships with their trainers.

M: Maybe, but they're also locked in small cages and ___________ ___________ ___________ ___________.

W: I see. Well, don't you think that circuses can be a good experience for the animals if the conditions are good?

M: I really don't think so. I think that it's terrible for the animals to be harmed in order to entertain others.

W: I understand. Maybe I should reconsider supporting the circus.

## 05

M: Hello. Are you the one who had the accident and was ___________ ___________ ___________ ___________?

W: Yes, that's me. I think it might be something serious. I can't seem to walk.

M: All right. Well, hold still and try not to move. What happened?

W: ___________ ___________ ___________ ___________ ___________ on the sidewalk and hit me while I was walking.

M: That's terrible. Did you see what he looked like?

W: No, but I know he was wearing a helmet and a leather jacket.

M: Did you contact the police?

W: I didn't. I was in a daze.

M: I'll call them for you.

W: Thank you.

M: Anyway, I'm going to __________ __________ __________ __________ __________ to find out the extent of your injuries. First, I'm going to extend your leg like this. Does that hurt?

W: Ow! Yeah, it hurts.

M: Ma'am, I think you might have a broken leg. We're going to need to take you to the hospital to have it x-rayed.

## 06

W: Hey, Dad. Look at this poster I made for hallway safety at our school.

M: Looks pretty neat. What are those kids on the left doing?

W: They're playing with the sink, which is against the rules. Someone could slip in that puddle of water.

M: Who's the person wearing the sash?

W: That's the hallway monitor. They help __________ __________ __________, and students should always listen to them.

M: I see. Are those kids running in the hallway?

W: Yes, they are. I'm trying to show people __________ __________ __________ __________ __________ __________.

M: You're right. And it's also dangerous to leave doors open, huh?

W: Yeah. People can run into them and hurt themselves, so you should always keep them closed.

M: I like the round clock you put in the back. __________ __________ __________ __________.

W: Thanks, Dad. That's how all of the clocks in our school look.

M: Is it? Anyway, you did a great job.

## 07

W: Hey Charlie, it looks like Fat Panda Outfitters is having a big sale on outdoor gear.

M: I know. I stopped by there this morning and picked up a new pair of hiking boots. They have some great deals.

W: I'm going on a two-day hike next week, so I'm looking to __________ __________ __________ __________ __________.

M: You should get down there as soon as you can. There were a lot of people in the camping section.

W: I'll hurry, then. Oh, do you think I should buy a camp stove? It's my first hiking trip.

M: Well, you're probably going to need one to cook the food you bring. They're also __________ __________ __________ __________ and day trips to the mountains.

W: Okay. I guess I should buy one, then.

M: How are you going to get there? __________ __________ __________ __________ __________.

W: That's a good point. I'm not sure.

M: I suppose I could __________ __________ __________ __________. Today's my day off, and I don't really have any plans for the rest of the day.

W: That'd be great. I really appreciate it. I'm a bit busy now, though. Can we go after about 20 minutes?

M: That's fine. Let me know when you're ready.

## 08

M: Hi, Laura. What can I do for you today?

W: Well, Mr. Baker, I wanted to tell you that I can't go to the track meet this weekend.

M: What do you mean you can't go? It's two days away. __________ __________ __________ __________ __________ now.

W: I'm really sorry. I know you need me, but my parents have to go to my grandparents' house this weekend. __________ __________ __________ __________ __________.

M: I see. Is everything all right?

W: My grandfather fell in the bathroom and broke his hip. He __________ __________, so he can't leave his house for a while.

M: That's terrible. I'm sorry to hear that. So you're going to your grandparents' house?

W: No. My parents are going alone. I need to __________ __________ __________ __________ __________ while they're away.

M: I understand. It's really a shame, but don't worry about it. We'll sure miss you. I hope your grandfather gets well soon.

W: Thanks, Mr. Baker.

## 09

*[Telephone rings.]*

W: Thank you for calling Beachwood Resort. May I help you?

M: Yes. I'd like to ______________ ____________ ____________

____________ ____________ a room. ____________

____________ ____________ ____________?

W: Well, it's $60 on the weekends and $40 during the week.

M: Then ____________ ____________ ____________ ____________

____________ ____________ ____________ next Saturday, please.

W: Sure. And what's your name, sir?

M: Dennis Reynolds. Oh, I'd also like to make a reservation for two in the restaurant for brunch.

W: Sure. That'll be an additional $10 per person.

M: That's fine. I also have a coupon here for 50% off. The coupon code is XT750.

W: Let me check on that for you. *[Keyboard typing sound]* I'm sorry, but that ____________ ____________ ____________ to our rooms and not to the brunch.

M: That's fine. If I want to pay by card, should I give you the number now or can I wait until Saturday?

W: You can wait until Saturday if you'd like.

M: That's great. See you then.


## 10

W: Hey Louie, is now a good time for me to ask you some questions for that article I'm writing about your ____________ ____________ ____________ ____________ ____________?

M: Sure, Stacy. Ask away.

W: All right. What kind of things did you do as a volunteer?

M: Well, a lot of things. We helped ____________ ____________ ____________ ____________ ____________, and I helped organize the staff.

W: I see. So how many houses did you help build?

M: We had a large team, so we were able to build 32 houses in two months.

W: That's great. Did the migrant workers move into the houses immediately?

M: Yes. They were ____________ ____________ ____________ ____________ ____________, so they were quite excited to move into their new homes.

W: I bet they were. How long have you been doing this?

M: I've been working for this volunteer program since I was a freshman.

W: Really? So that's three years. Okay, one more question. What kind of benefits do you get from volunteering?

M: There are a lot of benefits, but most of all, I just like the feeling I get from helping others.

W: That's great. Thanks for your time, Louie.


## 11

M: Good afternoon, and welcome to our art gallery. I'm here to announce an upcoming event that I'm sure you'll be excited about. We here at the gallery would like to invite all of you to our annual Artists in August event. We have been holding this event ____________ ____________ ____________ ____________ ____________ ____________ ____________. We do it to ____________ ____________ ____________ and display their work in the gallery. Our city's artists are important to our community because they help beautify our parks and businesses as well as encourage creativity. Artists in August starts on August 17th this year and runs through the end of the month. ____________ ____________ ____________ ____________ is free. However, we recommend you ____________ ____________ ____________ ____________ to our foundation, which supports the local arts program. Please join us this year to see some of the area's finest paintings, drawings, and sculptures. Thank you for your time.


## 12

M: Good afternoon, ma'am. What can we do for you today?

W: I'm looking for a drum kit for my son's birthday. He wants to start a rock 'n' roll band.

M: All right. Well, we have five kits to choose from.

W: I'm not sure what's ____________ ____________ ____________ ____________ him. I was hoping you could help me with that.

M: Well, if he's going to be playing rock music, a three-piece kit won't be enough. You're going to want to look at the five- or seven-piece kits.

W: I see. He said something about wanting a kit that can ____________ ____________ ____________ ____________ ____________.

M: Then he'll want a floor tom. We ____________ ____________ ____________ ____________. You're going to want to choose between these two sets.

W: All right. Hmm… I don't want to spend more than $800, so I think this one will have to do.

M: Okay. I'll get it ready for you to take home.

W: Thanks.


## 13

M: Did you get a new boyfriend or something, Heather?

W: Haha! No. What makes you say that?

M: It just seems that you're much happier and full of energy these days.

W: Really? Well, I have felt really good lately, but ___________ ___________ ___________ ___________ ___________ ___________ ___________ .

M: Has anything else changed, then?

W: I ___________ ___________ ___________ recently. I've been going every night after work.

M: How long have you been practicing yoga?

W: Only about three months.

M: And it's not hard for you? I can't even touch my toes.

W: I had a hard time when I first started, but after a couple of weeks ___________ ___________ ___________ ___________ ___________ ___________ ___________ .

M: I heard that yoga also improves your cortisol levels, making it easier for you to ___________ ___________ ___________ .

W: I heard that, too. Anyway, I really love doing yoga every day. It gives me something to look forward to after work.

M: (I guess that's why you look so happy these days.)

## 14

W: ___________ ___________ ___________ ___________ ___________ summer vacation. What about you, Henry?

M: I'm really looking forward to it. But I'm a bit concerned we won't be able to finish our science project by then.

W: Relax. We don't have too much left to do.

M: I guess you're right. Hey, have you checked the weather for this week?

W: Yeah, it's supposed to be rainy and windy all week.

M: Really? Then how will we finish our project? We need to do our experiments outside.

W: You're right! Well, it looks like there's only a 50% chance of rain on Wednesday.

M: Well, we should ___________ ___________ ___________ ___________ that it won't rain on Wednesday. But we ___________ ___________ ___________ ___________ ___________ just in case.

W: Yeah. Do you have anything in mind?

M: We can probably use the gymnasium to do our experiments. Let's ask Mrs. Jones if that'll be okay.

W: (Brilliant idea. I'm glad we're partners on this project.)

## 15

W: Pamela went up to the school last night for parent-teacher conferences and met with her daughter's teacher. She was ___________ ___________ ___________ ___________ when the teacher told her that her daughter, Malory, is very shy and sensitive. The teacher said that Malory is a quiet child, who rarely runs at recess; she usually walks. Malory's teacher encouraged Pamela to try a few things to ___________ ___________ ___________ ___________ ___________ ___________ ___________ and energetic. She also recommended some websites with suggestions for increasing children's activity levels. Pamela thanked the teacher for her advice and went straight home to ___________ ___________ ___________ ___________ . Tonight, when Pamela was busy making dinner, the phone rang. She asked Malory to answer the call. Malory refused to answer the phone because she was so shy. Worrying that her daughter might miss something important one day, she has decided to give some advice to her daughter. What would Pamela most likely say to Malory in this situation?

Pamela: (Being more active and outgoing can help you in your life.)

## 16-17

M: Good afternoon, team. Today, we're going to talk about equipment. When you go into a sporting goods store, you might ___________ ___________ ___________ the massive amount of soccer equipment you can purchase. Everyone always asks me if they should purchase the most expensive goods. My answer is usually no. For example, there's no need to spend the extra money to buy those special space-age socks when the normal cheap ones work just as well. The most important items are, of course, the basic ones. You're going to need a pair of decent cleats, shin guards, socks, and a soccer ball. I believe that the most important item is a nice pair of cleats. You're going to want to make sure that they fit well and are durable enough to hold up for a long time. Another important item is your shin guards, as they are needed to ___________ ___________ ___________ ___________ ___________ . Remember, while the expensive items might look flashy and impress others, they're not really necessary for the game. I hope you have a great time at training camp.

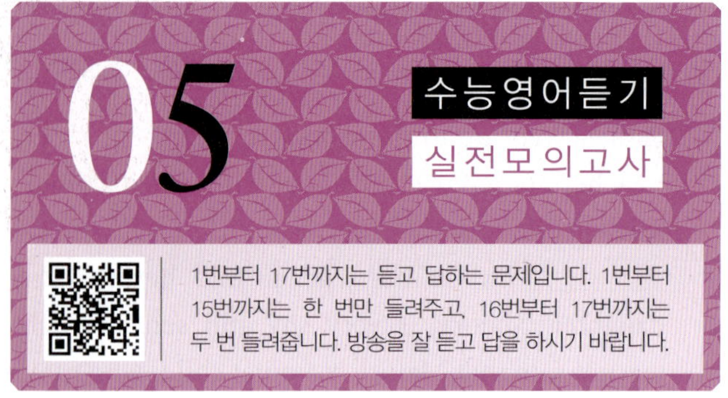



## 01

대화를 듣고, 여자의 마지막 말에 대한 남자의 응답으로 가장 적절한 것을 고르시오.

① I don't want to make a reservation just yet.
② Both of my kids have birthdays this month.
③ I hope to get a discount on the Disney tickets.
④ I've been meaning to talk to her about vacation.
⑤ Typically, we just go to the cabin and go fishing.

## 02

대화를 듣고, 남자의 마지막 말에 대한 여자의 응답으로 가장 적절한 것을 고르시오.

① About two kilometers away
② By taking the subway
③ Almost $100 each
④ About 15 minutes
⑤ Until about 9:30

## 03

다음을 듣고, 남자가 하는 말의 주제로 가장 적절한 것을 고르시오.

① 블로그 활성화를 위한 팁
② 블로그의 주제 선정 방법
③ 블로그 운영의 장점과 단점
④ 현대사회에서 블로그의 역할
⑤ 블로그를 통한 인간관계 형성법

## 04

대화를 듣고, 오락시설에 관한 여자의 의견으로 가장 적절한 것을 고르시오.

① 주말에는 예약 시스템의 운영을 중지해야 한다.
② 직원들은 고객 응대에 대한 교육을 받아야 한다.
③ 생일 파티 하는 팀들은 빨리 파티만 하고 나와야 한다.
④ 생일 파티 룸의 청결 상태 유지에 더 힘써야 한다.
⑤ 인원수에 따라 사용 시간을 다르게 줘야 한다.

## 05

대화를 듣고, 두 사람의 관계를 가장 잘 나타낸 것을 고르시오.

① 작가 — 리포터
② 기자 — 소설가
③ 감독 — 조명감독
④ 매니저 — 코디네이터
⑤ 배우 — 의상 디자이너

## 06

대화를 듣고, 그림에서 대화의 내용과 일치하지 <u>않는</u> 것을 고르시오.

## 07

대화를 듣고, 남자가 할 일로 가장 적절한 것을 고르시오.

① 도구 찾아오기
② 쓰레기 버려주기
③ 싱크대 청소하기
④ 고장 난 수도 고치기
⑤ 수돗물 필터 가져오기

## 08

대화를 듣고, 남자가 육상경기대회에 나가지 <u>못하는</u> 이유를 고르시오.

① 부상이 낫지 않아서
② 등록을 하지 못해서
③ 중간고사 기간과 겹쳐서
④ 부상 때문에 연습을 못해서
⑤ 인턴십 프로그램에 가입해서

## 09

대화를 듣고, 여자가 지불할 금액을 고르시오.

① $32   ② $40   ③ $48   ④ $52   ⑤ $54

## 10

대화를 듣고, 두 사람이 말하는 집에 관해 언급되지 <u>않은</u> 것을 고르시오.

① 침실과 화장실 개수
② 인근 학교 유무
③ 대중교통
④ 건축연도
⑤ 차고 유무

## 11

파쇄에 관한 다음 내용을 듣고, 일치하지 <u>않는</u> 것을 고르시오.

① 천연가스를 돌에서 추출하는 방법이다.
② 돌을 뭉쳐서 크게 만드는 방식을 이용한다.
③ 굉장히 쉽고 효율적인 방법이다.
④ 환경에 좋지 않은 영향을 끼친다.
⑤ 지진 활동의 원인으로도 의심된다.

## 12

다음 표를 보면서 대화를 듣고, 남자가 선택한 의사를 고르시오.

**Find a Doctor**

| | Doctor | Specialty | Years of Experience | Clinic Location |
|---|---|---|---|---|
| ① | Dr. Ryan Kebb | Allergies | 12 Years | Henderson County |
| ② | Dr. Jason Fecc | Eyes | 12 Years | Union County |
| ③ | Dr. Maro Kim | Allergies | 15 Years | Union County |
| ④ | Dr. Jeremy Paik | Eyes | 15 Years | Henderson County |
| ⑤ | Dr. Sarah Tortclud | Allergies | 10 Years | Henderson County |

## 13

대화를 듣고, 남자의 마지막 말에 대한 여자의 응답으로 가장 적절한 것을 고르시오.

Woman: ____________________________

① Not everyone can get into the publishing class.
② Me, too. I'd like to photograph all of the students.
③ I'm sure he'd allow you have a pet in class if you ask.
④ You're right. It took them most of the semester to finish it.
⑤ Yes. Students can also bring in their pets to show the class.

## 14

대화를 듣고, 여자의 마지막 말에 대한 남자의 응답으로 가장 적절한 것을 고르시오.

Man: ____________________________

① Nothing in particular. I'm just being lazy.
② It's okay. I can help you study for your test.
③ How is everything going with your friends?
④ I agree. Social science is my favorite subject.
⑤ Okay, I'll do my best to improve the situation.

## 15

다음 상황 설명을 듣고, Betty가 John에게 할 말로 가장 적절한 것을 고르시오.

Betty: ____________________________

① Did you know that I can fix your old phone?
② I heard a nearby church has a lot of used phones.
③ You should've gotten a new phone a long time ago.
④ Why don't you give me the phone, and I'll donate it?
⑤ Can you do me a favor and throw away that old phone?

[16-17] 다음을 듣고, 물음에 답하시오.

## 16

Arts Center Benefit의 목적으로 가장 적절한 것은?

① to raise money to benefit the Arts Center
② to seek artist donations for the Arts Center auction
③ to exhibit the artwork of students at Franklin College
④ to seek support for the construction of a new Arts Center
⑤ to provide free campus tours to members of the art community

## 17

계획 중인 행사로 언급되지 <u>않은</u> 것은?

① 사진 전시회   ② 작품 경매   ③ 재즈 밴드 공연
④ 유명인사 초대   ⑤ 많은 먹거리

## 01

W: __________ __________ __________ __________

with the service at Hotel Disney.

M: I was actually considering taking my kids there this weekend. Do you have the number for their reservation line?

W: I sure do. Is there any special reason you're going?

M: (Both of my kids have birthdays this month.)

## 02

M: Oh! We're never going to __________ __________

__________ __________ __________ __________

__________.

W: I'm sorry, but I didn't think traffic would be this bad at this time of night.

M: Yeah, downtown is always bad on Friday nights. How much time before it starts?

W: (About 15 minutes)

## 03

M: Technology moves fast these days, and one of the fastest-growing advances is in blogging. Blogging is a great way to tell others about your life and your interests. It's also a lot of fun. However, there are several things you should remember if you want your blog __________ __________ __________

__________ the millions of others. First, you should make it look interesting. Choose an __________

__________ __________ __________ __________

for your blog. Second, keep it focused on one topic. Too many different topics are distracting and will cause you to lose readers. Finally, it's important to interact with your audience. You should __________

__________ __________ __________ __________

__________ __________ left by readers. If you keep these tips in mind, I'm sure you'll attract more visitors to your blog.

## 04

M: Hey, Cindy. Did your son have a good time at his birthday party last Saturday?

W: No, it was awful. I'm so upset with the staff at the entertainment center.

M: Oh my! What happened?

W: When we arrived, they told us we had to wait for 30 minutes—even though I __________ __________

__________!

M: Well, I'm sure they're very busy during the summer months.

W: That makes sense. But then once we were seated, they told us __________ __________ __________

__________-__________ __________ __________!

M: Really? And two hours wasn't long enough for you?

W: No, it certainly wasn't. We had 15 kids to order for and get served so that they could eat. We also wanted them to have a chance to play games before we had cake and opened presents.

M: Well, they're probably trying to __________

__________ __________ __________ __________

__________.

W: Fine. But the time limit should be __________

__________ __________ __________ __________

__________ __________ __________.

M: So, did you talk to the management?

W: I did, but all they said was that it was company policy so there was nothing they could do. How rude!

## 05

M: Hey, Marie. I didn't think __________ __________

__________ __________ __________ __________.

W: Hey, Paul. I just had a quick talk with the director.

M: Oh. Are you __________ __________ __________

__________ again?

W: Yeah. Things didn't work out in Los Angeles.

M: I see. Have you ever done any modern work?

W: No. I've only done classics. So you're in *The Shape of Things*? What part are you playing?

M: I've __________ __________ __________ of Adam.

W: Wow, a leading role. That's pretty exciting. Congratulations.

M: Thanks, but it's pretty difficult to get everything just right.

W: I understand. I'm a bit nervous about my work, too. I know a lot about Shakespearean costumes, but not so much about modern fashion.

M: Well, you can watch the movie. I'm sure you can get some helpful tips from it.

W: You're right. I'm going to try to stay as __________ __________ __________ __________ as I can. I'll work on them this weekend. Anyway, I should be going. See you at dress rehearsal.

M: Bye, Marie.

## 06

M: Hey Laura, what's that you're looking at on your phone?

W: It's a photo my grandfather took during summer vacation last year.

M: That's cool. Let me see.

W: Sure. Here you go.

M: You guys went camping, huh? I love the mountains and the clouds. It looks so peaceful and relaxing.

W: Yeah. We rented an RV and took it to Walker Mountain.

M: I see. Is that you there in the back?

W: Yeah. __________ __________ __________ __________ __________ __________ __________ __________, so I was watching music videos.

M: Who's that in the RV?

W: That's my uncle. He's reading a book.

M: What about the woman in front of the car?

W: That's my mother. She was running from a spider that she saw.

M: And those kids playing with the dog? Who are they?

W: Those are my cousins. They brought their dog along on the trip.

M: So I'm guessing the man __________ __________ __________ __________ __________ __________ RV is your father.

W: That's right. He wanted to go to the mountain to relax, but I think the rest of us __________ __________ __________.

## 07

W: Our tap water is starting to __________ __________ __________ __________, don't you think?

M: I guess so. It's probably about time to change the filter.

W: Do we have any other filters?

M: I'm pretty sure we do. It seems like I bought some __________ __________ __________ __________ __________.

W: Well, I guess we can change it anytime, then.

M: We might as well do it right now.

W: All right. I'll go get a filter.

M: I'll go get it. I don't think you'll be able to find it.

W: __________ __________ __________ __________ __________ __________.

M: I don't think I'll need them.

W: Okay. I guess __________ __________ __________ __________ __________.

M: Great. I'll be right back.

## 08

W: Hey Stan, how's your shoulder doing?

M: It's feeling a lot better, thanks.

W: Great! So __________ __________ __________ __________ __________ again?

M: Yeah. I practiced a bit yesterday. I'm almost as good as I was before the injury.

W: Nice. I'm really looking forward to seeing you compete in the track meet this weekend.

M: Unfortunately, I'm not going to be able to.

W: Why not? Is it because you couldn't practice __________ __________ __________ __________ __________?

M: No. Actually, I forgot to sign up for this weekend's meet.

W: Oh, no! I guess you were busy and __________ __________ __________ __________.

M: That's right. I was stressed about midterm exams and forgot all about it.

W: __________ __________ __________. I missed registration for the summer internship program. The deadline was last week.

M: Sorry to hear that. Maybe we should buy planners so we can be more organized.

## 09

M: Good afternoon, miss. What can I do for you today?

W: Hello. __________ __________ __________ __________ __________ sweets for a company picnic tomorrow afternoon. How much are the cookies?

M: They're $2 apiece, but everything in the store is 20% off right now because we're about to close.

W: That's great. I'll take 20 cookies, then. Also, do you have any pies left?

M: Sure. We __________ __________ __________ __________ __________ __________ this afternoon. They'll be perfect for your picnic.

W: How  much  __________  __________  __________
__________?

M: They're $10 each.

W: Great. I'll take two of them.

M: Is there anything else I can get for you?

W: I think that's it. I also have this coupon for 10% off that I'd like to use.

M: I'm sorry, but we can't accept any coupons on discounted items.

W: That  makes  sense.  I'll  __________  __________
__________ __________ __________, then.

M: All right. So, you're going to take 20 cookies and two chess pies at a 20% discount, right?

W: That's right. Here's my card.


## 10

W: This is a recent photo of the home you asked me about, Mr. Anderson.

M: Nice. I really like the big backyard.

W: Yes, it's really pretty. The house also has three bedrooms and three bathrooms, and a beautiful garden out front.

M: Where is it located? Is it in a nice area?

W: It is. The neighborhood is very clean and safe. __________ __________ __________ __________,
__________.

M: I have two sons in middle school, so I'm glad to hear it's a good neighborhood. Are the schools nearby?

W: Yes. They're a short five-minute drive away. The house is on the school's bus route, as well.

M: That's wonderful. What about city buses or subways? __________ __________ __________ __________
__________ __________ __________?

W: Sure. The subway is about ten minutes away on foot.

M: Does the house have a garage? One car or two?

W: The house does __________ __________ __________
__________-__________ __________.

M: Great. Can we go take a look at the house now?

W: That shouldn't be a problem. Let me call the owner first __________ __________ __________.


## 11

W: One more thing, students. Before you leave, I'd like to talk to you for a moment about hydraulic fracking, or just 'fracking' for short. Fracking is a method for __________ __________ __________ __________ __________ using chemicals that break up rock that contains natural gas. The fracking method is very easy and quite __________-__________. However, there are certain environmental impacts associated with the process. For instance, fracking __________ __________ into  the  groundwater,  which  can __________ __________ __________ __________ __________. Fracking is also suspected of leading to seismic activity, such as earthquakes and tremors. We'll discuss fracking and its implications more in the next class.


## 12

M: My eyes are so itchy today. I guess __________ __________ __________ __________ __________ __________ again.

W: Yeah, __________ __________ __________ __________ in the spring, too. Why don't you see your allergist?

M: Well, I don't really have an allergist. Should I get one?

W: __________ __________ __________ __________ __________. Let's do a quick online search to find the right one for you. You don't need an eye doctor, right?

M: Yeah. My problem is with my allergies, so I don't think an eye doctor can help.

W: All right. This one has the most experience as an allergist. Why don't you call and __________ __________ __________ __________?

M: Okay. Wait a second! That doctor is all the way in Union County! It'll take me 45 minutes to get there.

W: I guess you're right. We should narrow our search to doctors in Henderson County. I guess these are the only two left.

M: All right. I'll go for the one that has more experience.

W: That'd be this one. I'll give you the phone number so you can make an appointment.

M: Great. Thanks for all of your help.


## 13

M: Hi, Chloe. What's that you're looking at?

W: Oh, hey Greg. It's __________ __________ __________ __________ __________ __________ __________ in our school.

M: A directory of animals? What for?

W: Well, our school actually has a lot of class pets. This shows all of the pets and what classrooms they're located in. Check it out.

M: That's cool. I didn't know the school had many pets. Who put this directory together?

W: Mr. Scott's publishing class assembled it, designed it, and printed it. Pretty neat, huh?

M: Yeah. So they did all of the work? Did they take the pictures of the pets, too?

W: Of course. They used Bailey's cell phone. The pictures __________ __________ __________ __________, huh?

M: Yes, they did. Wow, the sixth grade science teacher has a snake in his classroom? I had no idea.

W: __________ __________ __________ __________ __________, too. And did you know that Mr. Smith has a pet iguana?

M: Really? That's so cool. Anyway, it seems like the publishing class worked really hard on this pamphlet.

W: (You're right. It took them most of the semester to finish it.)

# 14

M: Hi, Ms. Diaz. I was told you wanted to see me?

W: Yes, Tom, I did. Why don't you have a seat?

M: Sure. *[Pause]* What did you want to see me about? Is everything all right?

W: Well, I'm becoming more and more __________ __________ __________ __________ in history. *[Mouse clicking sound]* Take a look at your most recent exam scores.

M: Hmm... Yeah, they don't look very good.

W: Right. But as you can see, your scores were going up until March. And then from there, __________ __________ __________ __________.

M: Yeah, I can see that.

W: Why do you think this is? Is everything all right at home?

M: *[Pause]* Well, to tell you the truth, I'm having some trouble with my friends and I haven't really __________ __________ __________ __________.

W: Well, Tom, you should work on figuring things out with your friends because I expect better scores __________ __________ __________ __________.

M: (Okay, I'll do my best to improve the situation.)

# 15

W: Betty goes to her friend John's house. While they're sitting in the living room having tea, Betty notices he has a new smartphone in his hand and an older one on the coffee table. He says he got the new smartphone because his old one wasn't very fast and didn't have enough memory. He says he's going to __________ __________ __________ __________ __________ __________ __________. Betty __________ and that John just wanted a new phone. Either way, she doesn't think he should just throw it away. Betty __________ __________ __________ __________ a local church that __________ __________ __________ __________ __________ to give to people who need them but can't afford them. She wants to tell John that he should give the phone to charity. What would Betty most likely say to John in this situation?

Betty: (Why don't you give me the phone, and I'll donate it?)

# 16-17

M: Good afternoon students, parents, and fellow staff members. I'd like to __________ __________ __________ __________ __________ an incredible evening on our campus. The Tenth Annual Franklin College Arts Center Benefit will be held on the campus fairgrounds on Saturday, August 15th. As always, the purpose of the benefit will be to raise the funds needed to support the Arts Center and create new programs that benefit our students as well as our community. As you all know, __________ __________ __________ __________ __________. It brings us together and __________ __________ __________ __________ __________ unimaginable ways. The benefit allows the community to give back to our program. Every penny raised will benefit the FC Arts Center fund. There are many different events being planned. As usual, we'll have our photography exhibition, an auction of some of our prized artwork, live performances by our talented campus jazz band, and, of course, lots of food. If you'd like to reserve tickets for our event, or if you can't make it and would like to donate money to our cause, visit our campus website and __________ __________ __________ __________ __________ __________. Thanks for listening.

1번부터 17번까지는 듣고 답하는 문제입니다. 1번부터 15번까지는 한 번만 들려주고, 16번부터 17번까지는 두 번 들려줍니다. 방송을 잘 듣고 답을 하시기 바랍니다.

## 01

대화를 듣고, 남자의 마지막 말에 대한 여자의 응답으로 가장 적절한 것을 고르시오.

① I think I'm going to sell the tickets.
② That's too bad. We'll try later today.
③ I can't remember where I left the tickets.
④ Don't worry. I already bought the tickets.
⑤ I'm really sorry. I'll get tickets for tomorrow.

## 02

대화를 듣고, 여자의 마지막 말에 대한 남자의 응답으로 가장 적절한 것을 고르시오.

① I wish we had spent more time in the museum.
② I've had a great time, but I sure am getting tired.
③ The park closes at sunset, so you can take your time.
④ This is the first stop on the tour, so you should hurry.
⑤ I'm sorry, but we can't. The butterfly garden is closed.

## 03

다음을 듣고, 남자가 하는 말의 목적으로 가장 적절한 것을 고르시오.

① 자원봉사 단체의 활동을 홍보하려고
② 오늘의 토크쇼 초대 손님을 소개하려고
③ 올해의 인물 선정 행사에 표를 모으려고
④ 행사지원을 위한 자원봉사자를 모집하려고
⑤ 올해의 인물에 대한 조사 결과를 발표하려고

## 04

대화를 듣고, 두 사람이 하는 말의 주제로 가장 적절한 것을 고르시오.

① 자가용 통근의 주의점
② 걷기 운동의 긍정적 효과
③ 버스 안에서의 예절 지키기
④ 버스로 통학하는 것의 장점
⑤ 버스가 지하철보다 좋은 이유

## 05

대화를 듣고, 두 사람의 관계를 가장 잘 나타낸 것을 고르시오.

① 학생 — 지도교사
② 면접관 — 신입사원
③ 학부모 — 교장 선생님
④ 취업상담원 — 구직자
⑤ 컴퓨터 프로그래머 — 고객

## 06

대화를 듣고, 그림에서 여자가 산 시계를 고르시오.

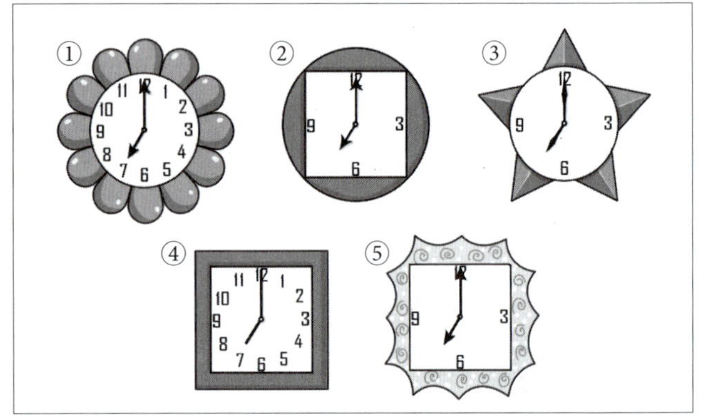

## 07

대화를 듣고, 남자가 할 일로 가장 적절한 것을 고르시오.

① 길 안내하기
② 책 주문하기
③ 책 가져다 주기
④ 컴퓨터로 책 찾아보기
⑤ 회원 카드 발급해 주기

## 08

대화를 듣고, 남자가 경기에 참가할 수 없는 이유를 고르시오.

① 연습량이 부족해서
② 병원에 입원해야 해서
③ 다른 팀으로 이적해서
④ 팀원과 심하게 다퉈서
⑤ 경기 중에 부상 당해서

## 09

대화를 듣고, 여자가 지불할 금액을 고르시오.

① $10  ② $15  ③ $20  ④ $24  ⑤ $30

## 10

대화를 듣고, 자선행사에 관해 두 사람이 언급하지 <u>않은</u> 것을 고르시오.

① 날짜  ② 슬로건  ③ 참가 방법
④ 장소  ⑤ 간식 제공 여부

## 11

Cherry Blossom Festival에 관한 다음 내용을 듣고, 일치하지 <u>않는</u> 것을 고르시오.

① 올해 네 번째로 열리는 축제이다.
② 축제는 매년 봄 같은 날짜에 열린다.
③ 아이들이 할 만한 활동도 계획되어 있다.
④ 주차를 하게 되면 입장료는 15달러이다.
⑤ 걸어서 입장하면 5달러만 내면 된다.

## 12

다음 표를 보면서 대화를 듣고, 여자가 구매할 중고 오토바이를 고르시오.

### 2016 Aladdin Used Motorcycle Sales

|   | Model | Year | Engine | Price |
| --- | --- | --- | --- | --- |
| ① | S-35 | 2007 | 300cc | $3,800 |
| ② | S-35 | 2009 | 400cc | $4,800 |
| ③ | K-350 | 2005 | 250cc | $2,500 |
| ④ | K-350 | 2008 | 350cc | $4,200 |
| ⑤ | K-350 | 2010 | 350cc | $7,200 |

## 13

대화를 듣고, 여자의 마지막 말에 대한 남자의 응답으로 가장 적절한 것을 고르시오.

Man: _______________________________________

① I'm going to need a ride from the bus station.
② Well, we'll postpone dinner until you get here.
③ I think you should buy tickets for the earlier bus.
④ Great. I should be at the station at around 7 o'clock.
⑤ No problem. I'll book you a ticket on the earlier bus.

## 14

대화를 듣고, 남자의 마지막 말에 대한 여자의 응답으로 가장 적절한 것을 고르시오.

Woman: _______________________________________

① Sure. The doorman will be there to help soon.
② That's no problem. You don't have to change rooms.
③ You can take care of the additional fee at checkout, sir.
④ I'll be sure to turn off the light outside your window, sir.
⑤ Of course. The front desk will give you a wake-up call at 7 a.m.

## 15

다음 상황 설명을 듣고, Leah가 Brody에게 할 말로 가장 적절한 것을 고르시오.

Leah: _______________________________________

① You should explain the storyline in more detail.
② You should beta test the game more before you present.
③ It's important to consult your programming team every day.
④ You could benefit by having someone else present the game.
⑤ It's important to provide more visual examples in the presentation.

[16-17] 다음을 듣고, 물음에 답하시오.

## 16

남자가 하는 말의 주제로 가장 적절한 것은?

① Mental and physical benefits of outdoor activities
② Tips on being safe and having fun while camping
③ What to bring on your family camping trip
④ Dangers of getting lost while camping
⑤ How to give first aid while camping

## 17

남자가 언급하지 <u>않은</u> 것은?

① 여분의 옷  ② 충분한 음식  ③ 구급상자
④ 청소  ⑤ 랜턴

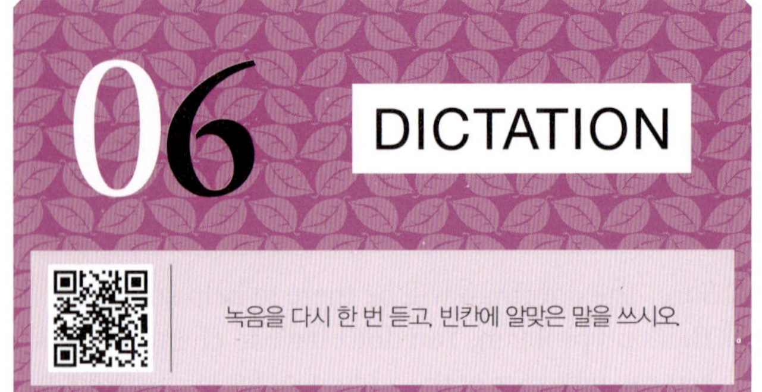


## 01

M: Honey, did you reserve tickets for today's baseball game?

W: Oh, that's right. I forgot. I'll do it now online.

M: I think it's too late. I saw online that __________ __________ __________ __________. You should have bought them sooner.

W: (I'm really sorry. I'll get tickets for tomorrow.)

## 02

W: This must be the butterfly garden I read about in the brochure.

M: That's right. It's also the end of our tour. __________ __________ __________ __________ __________, Mrs. Conn.

W: I did. Everything was beautiful. How long can I stay in the garden?

M: (The park closes at sunset, so you can take your time.)

## 03

M: Hi, everyone. I'm Michael Johnson. Thank you for joining us this morning for our program, "Student Volunteers." I'm sure all of you have taken, or at least know of, the survey __________ __________ __________ __________ __________ __________ __________ find out who is the most respected person in our country from the viewpoint of college students. Almost every year, the person chosen has been someone in a position of power, such as a successful entrepreneur or politician. But this year was quite different. College students voted for Amelia Henderson, someone who has been helping the less fortunate for many years. She has helped those in poor communities develop skills so they can find decent jobs. Her generosity and ambition has __________ __________ __________ __________ __________ __________ __________.

## 04

M: Hey, Rachel.

W: Good morning, Mr. Turner. Do you always take the bus to school in the morning?

M: Not every morning. I take it a couple of times a month. What about you?

W: I take it every morning. My mother __________ __________ __________ __________ __________ her car, but I prefer the bus.

M: Why's that?

W: __________ __________ __________ __________ __________ __________. Plus, because of expensive gas prices, it's also cheaper.

M: Well, that's quite thoughtful of you.

W: Well, I read that driving is ten times more expensive than taking the bus.

M: Is that right? That's a big difference.

W: It's also a great time for me to read the news and check my LookBook page on my smartphone.

M: I see. Well, I usually take the subway because __________ __________ __________ __________ __________ __________ __________ a little more.

W: I know what you mean. I really enjoy the short walk to my bus stop. It gives me the chance to think about my day. It's also great exercise.

M: That's a great way to think about it.

## 05

W: You must be Mr. Carter. How is everything going?

M: Well, honestly, I haven't been doing so well.

W: I'm sorry to hear that, but I'm here to help you __________ __________ __________ __________. Can you tell me anything about yourself that would be relevant?

M: I don't have any formal training, but I do know a lot about fixing motorcycles.

W: I see. What do you do when you have free time, Mr. Carter?

At this time, I would like to introduce Ms. Henderson, who we've invited here to speak with you all. She will share with us today why it's so important __________ __________ __________ __________ __________. Good morning, Ms. Henderson. Let me begin by saying __________ __________ __________ __________ to have you with us today.

M: I spend a lot of time building computers and doing a little bit of networking.

W: I see. So you like computers?

M: That's right. I grew up with computers. They were my only friends when I was young.

W: That's great. __________ __________ __________ __________ __________ or around others?

M: __________ __________ __________ __________ __________. I'm a bit of an introvert.

W: I see. Well, it looks like there's an opening at Computers Plus for a technician. I think it'd be suitable for someone like you.

M: I agree. Thanks for your help.

## 06

M: Hi. What can I do for you today?

W: I'm looking for a new clock for my kitchen. __________ __________ __________ __________ __________ __________?

M: We only have these five in stock at this time. How about this flower one? It's designed for the kitchen.

W: It looks a bit cheesy for me. My kitchen is very modern.

M: I see. Well, in that case, what about this square one? It's elegant and simple.

W: I'd __________ __________ __________ __________ __________ than that, even. I'd like it to have just four numbers instead of all twelve.

M: All right, so we have these three left. I guess you don't want this one because it's star-shaped and probably wouldn't __________ __________ __________ __________.

W: Yeah, and the square sun clock is a bit too loud for me.

M: Well, I guess this one would be best for you.

W: I think you're right. __________ __________ __________ __________.

M: All right.

## 07

M: Good morning. What can I do for you?

W: I'm looking for *Chocalat*.

M: Well, you're going to want to check the candy aisle. It's __________ __________ __________.

W: Oh, I don't mean candy. I'm looking for the book by that name.

M: Ah, __________ __________ __________ __________. Do you know the author's name?

W: I'm not sure. I just know it's about a woman who opens up a chocolate shop in France.

M: Give me a minute and I'll search for it on the computer. *[Keyboard typing sound]* Okay, __________ __________ __________ __________ __________ __________.

W: Great. How much is it?

M: It's $13.99. If you're a member of our rewards program, you can get 10% off.

W: Unfortunately, I'm not a member. I'll take the book anyway, though.

M: No problem. Let me go find it for you.

## 08

*[Cell phone rings.]*

W: Hey, Leo. You know, the team is pretty worried about you since you missed practice today.

M: Yeah, sorry I couldn't make it. Actually, what I called to talk to you about is the match tomorrow.

W: Oh, what's wrong?

M: Well, you're going to have to plan on me not playing tomorrow.

W: Really? But you're __________ __________ __________ __________ __________. We need you.

M: I'd love to play, but there's no way I'll be able to.

W: Are you going to tell me what happened?

M: Well, it's kind of embarrassing, but I was __________ __________ __________ __________ __________ and lost control and crashed into a wall.

W: That's awful! Are you okay?

M: I'm __________ __________ __________ __________ from the crash, but I feel all right. The doctors think that I should get x-rayed, though, and stay in the hospital overnight.

W: That's terrible news, but I guess __________ __________ __________ __________ __________. I hope you heal up soon.

M: Thanks.

## 09

M: Hello, how can I help you?

W: I'd like to __________ __________ __________ __________ __________.

M: Okay, what would you like?

W: A supreme pizza and garlic bread combo and some extra dipping sauce.

M: Sure, but the extra sauce is a dollar more.

W: That's fine. And do you sell chicken?

M: Yes, we do. We have fried chicken and buffalo wings. They're $5 each.

W: Great. I'd like to add one of each to my order.

M: Will that be everything today?

W: Yeah, that's everything. How much is the total?

M: All together, the supreme pizza and garlic bread combo with extra sauce and two orders of chicken comes to $30. Will you be using any coupons this evening?

W: Yes, actually. I have a coupon for a 20% discount on orders over $30.

M: Okay, great. Oh, __________ __________ __________ __________ __________ if you're paying with a VISA credit or debit card.

W: Yes, I know. I have my VISA debit card.


## 10

W: What's that flyer you're looking at, Tommy?

M: It's for a charity event to __________ __________ __________ __________ __________. It's on October 13th.

W: That's this coming Saturday, right?

M: That's right. They even have a slogan. It's "__________ __________ __________ to those without."

W: It seems that they could've __________ __________ __________ something more creative. Oh, this flyer says the event will be held at the new recreation center. Where is that?

M: It's right down the street. Do you know where the courthouse is? It's just across the street from that.

W: Ah, I've been wondering what that building is. I think we should join.

M: I agree. I always __________ __________ __________ __________ __________.

W: Me, too. And the advertisement says that they'll have free refreshments for the attendees.

M: Yep. Let's join and help the cause.


## 11

W: Good morning, ladies and gentlemen. Finally, spring has come again. Our cherry blossoms __________ __________ __________ __________! Take a deep breath of the fresh spring air and __________ __________ __________ __________ __________ __________ all the beauty of the blossoms. __________ __________ __________ __________ __________ __________ we will be hosting the Fourth Annual Cherry Blossom Festival! The festival dates change annually and this year will be April 20th through April 27th. We have some new activities planned for this year's festival, including more things for kids to enjoy! So get the whole family together and come out to enjoy our wonderful festival. There is so much to see and do that you'll wish you had more time! If you want to park your car on the festival grounds, the fee is $15, but if you choose to walk in, it's only $5. We look forward to seeing you soon!


## 12

M: Hello. May I help you?

W: Hi, I'm looking for a used motorcycle.

M: Do you __________ __________ __________ __________ __________ __________?

W: Yes. The S-35 and K-350 are my favorite models.

M: Okay. *[Mouse clicking sound]* Take a look at this list. We have five bikes available in those models.

W: Well, I don't want a motorcycle that's more than 10 years old.

M: The price of this K-350 is the cheapest of the five.

W: Nevertheless, I want one no more than 10 years old with an engine no bigger than 350cc.

M: All right. Can I ask __________ __________ __________ __________ __________ __________?

W: Less than $5,000.

M: That leaves you two choices.

W: Hmm. Although __________ __________ __________ __________ __________ __________ __________, I want the bike with the bigger engine. It'll be faster than the other one.

M: Great! Excellent choice!


## 13

*[Telephone rings.]*

W: Hey, Dad.

M: Oh, hey Kaitlyn. Are you on your way?

W: Not yet, but I'm at the station.

M: Nice. So, when is your bus leaving?

W: It's scheduled to leave a little after 3 o'clock. I'm going to have a snack at the cafe while I wait.

M: I see. Do you think __________ __________

__________ __________ __________ __________ to

have dinner with your grandparents at six?

W: I don't think so. It's Friday, so traffic is going to

be really bad __________ __________ __________

__________ __________ .

M: Why didn't you take the earlier bus?

W: I tried, but by the time I got to the station, all of the

__________ __________ __________ __________ .

M: Well, that's unfortunate. They're looking forward to

seeing you.

W: Yeah, I'd really like to be there in time for dinner,

but I'll probably arrive too late.

M: (Well, we'll postpone dinner until you get here.)

## 14

*[Phone rings.]*

W: This is the front desk. What can I do for you?

M: Hello. This is Dennis Reynolds in room 3D.

W: What can I do for you, Mr. Reynolds?

M: Listen, there's a street light outside my window. It's

far too bright. __________ __________ __________

__________ __________ __________ .

W: I'm sorry, Mr. Reynolds, but those lights have to

__________ __________ __________ __________

__________ .

M: I have to wake up early in the morning. I need

to sleep. __________ __________ __________

__________ .

W: Maybe I could switch you to a room on the other

side of the building. Would that be okay?

M: I suppose that'll work.

W: Great. We'll put you in room 4B on the second floor.

M: Is there any way I could get someone to help me

move my belongings?

W: (Sure. The doorman will be there to help soon.)

## 15

W: Brody has put the finishing touches on a presentation

because he wants to promote a new game to a

computer game company. He asks his good friend,

Leah, if he could practice his presentation with her

__________ __________ __________ __________

__________ __________ on it as well as some

constructive feedback. They meet in a cafe, where

he goes through his presentation. She likes the

idea of the game, but thinks that his presentation

has some problems. The story of the game seems

too complicated, and he doesn't have enough

screenshots. She notes that __________ __________

__________ __________ and not enough visual

information will __________ __________ __________

__________ __________ __________ . Brody wonders

what he can do to improve the presentation, and

asks Leah for advice. In this situation, what would

Leah most likely say to Brody?

Leah: (It's important to provide more visual examples

in the presentation.)

## 16-17

M: When living in the city, it might be hard to

__________ __________ __________ __________

__________ . However, many people have taken to

the outdoors in order to escape their city lives. In

particular, many hobbyists have taken up camping

as their leisure activity of choice. Getting outdoors

is great for your health, both mentally and physically.

However, there are __________ __________

__________ __________ __________ when going

on a camping trip. First of all, you're going to

want to be sure to bring an extra set of clothes.

This will keep you warm __________ __________

__________ __________ __________ __________

__________ or if you get your original clothes wet.

Second, make sure to bring enough food to last for

your whole trip. You might even want to pack extra

food in case you get lost while hiking around your

campsite. Third, be sure to pack a first-aid kit. As with

all outdoor activities, camping can be dangerous.

Also, be sure to clean up after yourself when leaving

your campsite. It's important that we keep our

environment clean. Finally, have fun. It's not a hobby

if you don't enjoy it. With these tips in mind, you're

sure to have a safe, fun time on your next camping

trip.

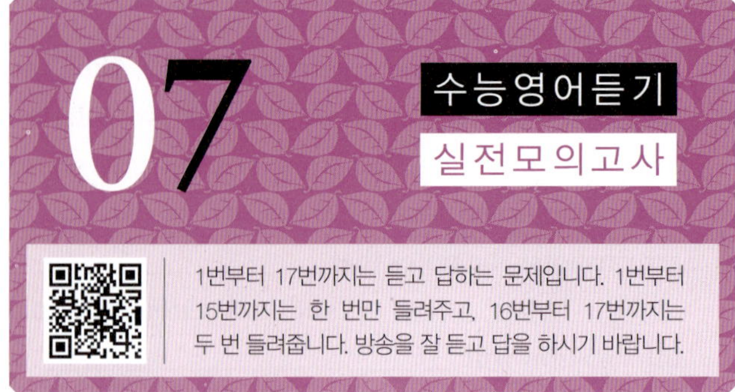



## 01

대화를 듣고, 여자의 마지막 말에 대한 남자의 응답으로 가장 적절한 것을 고르시오.

① There's an extra one in my car.
② I apologize for bothering you.
③ I'm not sure I understand.
④ I should prepare better.
⑤ Yes, you definitely will.

## 02

대화를 듣고, 남자의 마지막 말에 대한 여자의 응답으로 가장 적절한 것을 고르시오.

① That's okay. I already had dinner.
② There's none left. I ate it all last night.
③ All right. I know a great Italian restaurant.
④ Put the leftovers in the refrigerator, please.
⑤ I love pizza, but I don't think they sell it here.

## 03

다음을 듣고, 여자가 하는 말의 주제로 가장 적절한 것을 고르시오.

① 식초를 이용한 블랙베리의 신선도 유지법
② 세균을 없앨 수 있는 식기류 세척 요령
③ 신선한 블랙베리를 고르는 법
④ 과일에 세균이 많은 이유
⑤ 간편한 블랙베리 요리법

## 04

대화를 듣고, 남자의 의견으로 가장 적절한 것을 고르시오.
① 온라인에서 젊은이들의 은어 사용은 심각한 수준이다.
② 은어를 사용하면 매우 무례한 사람처럼 보일 수 있다.
③ 은어 사용을 통해 젊은 사람들과 가까워 질 수 있다.
④ 은어 사용은 젊은이들이 소속감을 갖도록 해준다.
⑤ 대중매체에서 은어의 사용을 자제해야 한다.

## 05

대화를 듣고, 두 사람의 관계를 가장 잘 나타낸 것을 고르시오.
① police officer — victim
② taxi driver — pedestrian
③ reporter — soccer coach
④ insurance agent — client
⑤ medical doctor — athlete

## 06

대화를 듣고, 그림에서 대화의 내용과 일치하지 <u>않는</u> 것을 고르시오.

## 07

대화를 듣고, 남자가 여자를 위해 할 일로 가장 적절한 것을 고르시오.
① to make survey questions
② to reserve two baseball tickets
③ to hand in her two term papers
④ to give advice about her book report
⑤ to ask people to complete the survey

## 08

대화를 듣고, 남자가 회의에 참석할 수 <u>없는</u> 이유를 고르시오.
① 사무실을 이전해야 해서
② 가족 모임이 잡혀 있어서
③ 촬영을 위한 출장을 가야 해서
④ 다른 다큐멘터리를 상영해야 해서
⑤ 아직 다큐멘터리 주제를 못 정해서

## 09

대화를 듣고, 여자가 지불할 총 금액을 고르시오.

① $60    ② $70    ③ $80    ④ $90    ⑤ $100

## 10

대화를 듣고, 남자가 사고 싶어 하는 정장에 관해 두 사람이 언급하지 <u>않은</u> 것을 고르시오.

① 매장 이름    ② 매장 위치    ③ 사이즈
④ 색상    ⑤ 가격

## 11

Bellington University에서 열릴 겨울 캠프에 관한 다음 내용을 듣고, 일치하지 <u>않는</u> 것을 고르시오.

① 캠프는 1월 2일부터 8일까지 열린다.
② 참가자들은 캠프 기간 동안 캠퍼스 내에서 생활한다.
③ 캠프 참가비는 무료이고 고등학생 누구나 참가 가능하다.
④ 미술이나 정보 통신 교사로부터 추천서를 받아야 한다.
⑤ 학교 홈페이지에서 지원서를 작성하면 된다.

## 12

다음 표를 보면서 대화를 듣고, 여자가 선택한 Flat Screen TV 모델을 고르시오.

**Flat Screen TVs**

| | Model | Price | Brand | 3D | Color |
|---|---|---|---|---|---|
| ① | LD40 | $570 | LD | X | Silver |
| ② | LD50 | $630 | LD | O | Black |
| ③ | S400 | $510 | Solo | X | Silver |
| ④ | S401 | $540 | Solo | O | Silver |
| ⑤ | S500 | $570 | Solo | O | Black |

## 13

대화를 듣고, 여자의 마지막 말에 대한 남자의 응답으로 가장 적절한 것을 고르시오.

Man: ___________________________

① I really don't want to get allergy shots.
② Yes. He can't go back to school until he is better.
③ He's not going to like that, but it'll help in the long run.
④ I think we should take him to the doctor for a checkup.
⑤ I'm happy that you're out of the hospital and back home.

## 14

대화를 듣고, 남자의 마지막 말에 대한 여자의 응답으로 가장 적절한 것을 고르시오.

Woman: ___________________________

① Okay. I guess it's this fish's lucky day.
② We should go fishing together on Saturday.
③ If the water is too polluted, the fish will die.
④ I think Mom should use this one to make dinner.
⑤ I agree. The bigger fish are much harder to measure.

## 15

다음 상황 설명을 듣고, Peter가 Dr. Goldberg에게 할 말로 가장 적절한 것을 고르시오.

Peter: ___________________________

① I don't think I can make a bigger roller coaster.
② I think I should rework some of the design flaws.
③ I really didn't expect to win the engineering contest.
④ I really enjoy studying engineering at this university.
⑤ Congratulations on winning the engineering contest.

[16-17] 다음을 듣고, 물음에 답하시오.

## 16

여자가 하는 말의 주제로 가장 적절한 것은?

① Defining characteristics of international English
② Changes in the English language throughout history
③ How English is becoming the international language
④ Differences in the English language among native speakers
⑤ Differences in pronunciation of American and British English

## 17

여자가 언급하지 <u>않은</u> 것은?

① 발음    ② 억양    ③ 강세
④ 어휘    ⑤ 철자

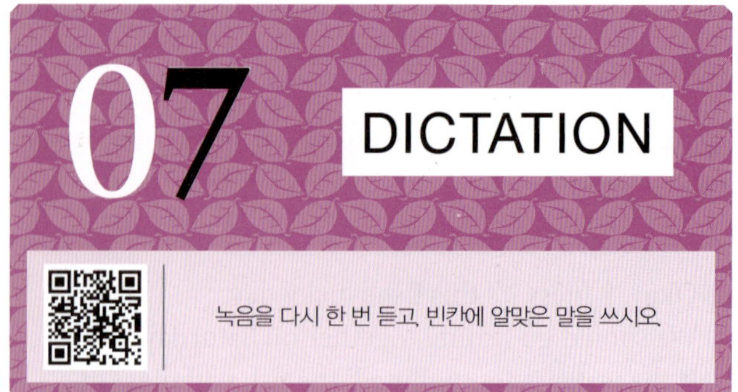



녹음을 다시 한 번 듣고, 빈칸에 알맞은 말을 쓰시오

## 01

W: Wow! The temperature has really dropped. ____________ ____________ ____________ ____________ .

M: You should have worn some warmer clothes. Do you want my coat?

W: No, that's all right. You'll be cold too without it.

M: (There's an extra one in my car.)

## 02

M: Hey, Lisa. You don't look so well. Is everything all right?

W: I had a really busy day at school, Dad. ____________ ____________ . What's for dinner?

M: Well, I haven't prepared anything, but I think there's ____________ ____________ in the refrigerator.

W: (There's none left. I ate it all last night.)

## 03

W: It's springtime, which means it's almost time to enjoy fresh fruits like blackberries. I used to have problems with ____________ ____________ ____________ ____________ , but then a friend showed me an easy way to maximize shelf life. Simply by using a solution of water and vinegar, you can greatly ____________ ____________ ____________ of fresh berries. The process is so simple that anyone can do it. First, wash the berries in a mixture of equal parts vinegar and water. Let the berries soak for about five minutes while the vinegar does its work on the bacteria. Finally, just ____________ ____________ ____________ ____________ in the sink to rid them of any remaining vinegar. The secret is that the mixture has killed any bacteria that might eat away at the berries' freshness. ____________ ____________ ____________ ____________ is strong enough to kill the bacteria, but vinegar is still safe to use in the home and even to consume. Using this tip, you can keep berries fresh for weeks longer than you could otherwise.

## 04

M: Ms. May, are you okay? You look upset. What's the matter?

W: I feel as if I was a foreigner in my own land.

M: Why do you feel that way?

W: Well, I was on the subway this morning on my way here, and there was a group of young people sitting across from me. I didn't understand half of what they were talking about.

M: You mean they were using slang?

W: Exactly. I'm not sure what they were saying, but ____________ ____________ ____________ ____________ ____________ .

M: Yeah, I think many adults find that young people's language sounds impolite, but perhaps ____________ ____________ ____________ ____________ ____________ ____________ they could get closer to the young people.

W: I don't understand.

M: They might see you as someone ____________ ____________ ____________ ____________ ____________ if they hear you use their slang once in a while.

W: Oh, yeah. I get it.

M: Sometimes I ask my kids to teach me some of their slang, or I ask them about something I heard on TV.

W: I wasn't aware that you felt ____________ ____________ ____________ ____________ ____________ was such a big deal.

M: I think it helps my relationship with them.

## 05

W: Phillip, can you hear me? Are you okay?

M: I think so. Ah, my neck. It really hurts.

W: Yeah. Don't move. We're going to ____________ ____________ ____________ ____________ . So, do you remember what happened?

M: The last thing I remember, I was going for a pass and someone on the other team ____________ ____________ ____________ ____________ . I fell on my shoulder, and my head hit the ground.

W: Do you remember anything after that?

M: I remember that I tried to walk, but I ____________ ____________ . I think I fell back to the ground, maybe. I don't remember anything else until waking up here in the locker room.

W: I think you might have a concussion, Phillip.

M: Really? Is that bad?

W: Well, it's certainly not good. We're going to do some tests to see how serious it was.

M: Thank you. I really appreciate your help.

W: No problem. That's my job.

## 06

M: Hey Carrie, you did a great job preparing the table for the picnic.

W: Thanks, Bob. I'm worried ___________ ___________ ___________ ___________ ___________ for everyone, though.

M: I'm sure it will be plenty. Anyway, I like how you decorated the table with flowers in the middle.

W: I picked them from the garden. I also made pasta for the vegetarians. I put it closest to the diners.

M: It looks delicious. I see that you also made chicken for us meat eaters.

W: That's right. Do you think that the corn is ___________ ___________ ___________ ___________ ___________?

M: Yeah, maybe you should bring it closer to the front. Say, where are the drinks?

W: ___________ ___________ ___________ ___________ for the drinks.

M: I see. And it seems you put together a healthy dessert for the guests.

W: Yes. Fruit is great for picnics in the summertime and isn't ___________ ___________ ___________ ___________ or pie.

M: I agree. By the way, thanks for inviting me.

W: No problem, Bob. I'm glad you could come.

## 07

M: Hi, Catherine. I have two tickets to the baseball game this Friday. Would you like to go with me?

W: I'd love to, but I'm afraid I can't. I have two ___________ ___________ ___________ ___________ ___________.

M: What are they? Can you go with me if I help you finish writing them?

W: Of course. One is a book report on a novel, and the other is an analysis report on how smartphones have ___________ ___________ ___________ ___________ ___________.

M: How's your book report going?

W: I think it'll be done by tomorrow. The problem is the second report.

M: Have you ___________ ___________ ___________ on the effects of the smartphone?

W: Yes, but I don't think it's possible to give it to enough people in such a short time. Could you help me with that?

M: Sure. ___________ ___________ ___________ ___________ ___________ ___________ ___________. Then you'll go to the baseball game with me this Friday, right?

W: Yes, I promise. Thanks a million.

## 08

*[Telephone rings.]*

M: Hello? This is Dan Brown.

W: Good afternoon, Mr. Brown. This is Claudia from Global Media.

M: Hi, Claudia. What can I do for you today?

W: I talked to my bosses about the conversation that we had last week about you working with our company.

M: So you're calling to tell me you ___________ ___________ ___________ ___________ on the nature documentary, then?

W: That's right. We were wondering if you'd still be interested in producing it.

M: That'd be great. I'd love to.

W: Thank you. I'd like to ___________ ___________ ___________ with you and the other producers we've lined up in the near future. Is Thursday at 7 p.m. okay with you?

M: I can't make it that day. ___________ ___________ ___________ ___________ ___________ I've just finished up. How about Friday at noon?

W: I'm sorry, but one of the producers will be out of town on Friday and won't be back until the 14th.

M: Well, in that case, could you possibly have the meeting without me? You can brief me on it at a later date.

W: I think that'll work. I'll just need to confirm. Talk to you again soon, Mr. Brown.

## 09

M: Good afternoon. How can I help you today?

W: Hi. I'm looking for a pair of tennis rackets for my nephews. They're twins, and they have a birthday coming up.

M: Sure. How old are they going to be?

W: They'll be turning ten. Do you have anything for children that young?

M: Absolutely. ___________ ___________ ___________ at this black racket. It's $70.

W: Wow! That's a bit too much.

M: Well, it's made of titanium alloy and ___________ ___________ ___________ ___________. What's your budget?

W: I'm looking to spend around $60 each.

M: If you absolutely won't go above that, then what about these aluminum rackets? The blue one is $20 ___________ ___________ ___________ ___________ ___________ you just saw, and the red one is only $40.

W: They both like blue, so I think I'll get that one for both of them.

M: Great choice!

W: You take credit cards, right?

M: Absolutely. I'll walk you ___________ ___________ ___________ ___________ ___________ ___________.

## 10

M: Hey Mom, you know, I'm getting pretty excited about graduation.

W: Yeah, your father mentioned that this morning. He said you've been looking for a new suit.

M: I have, and I found a great one down at Bowtie Suits. You know where that is, right?

W: Of course. ___________ ___________ ___________ ___________ ___________ on Fourth Street. What kind of suit have you found?

M: It's formal, but not too formal. The cut is great. I think ___________ ___________ ___________ ___________ ___________.

W: That sounds nice. Is it a black suit or a navy blue one?

M: It's a very dark navy blue. It almost ___________ ___________.

W: What's the price?

M: It's on sale for $300. Not too bad, huh?

W: That's a little more ___________ ___________ ___________ ___________. Let's go to the shop today. I want you to ___________ ___________ ___________ for me.

M: Sure. When will you have time to take me?

W: Let's wait until your father comes home. We can all go together.

## 11

M: Good afternoon, everyone. I'd like to talk to you all about a new program we are offering at Bellington University this winter. Bellington University will offer a one-week camp focusing on acting and directing. The camp will be held from January 2nd to January 8th, and students who sign up will ___________ ___________ ___________ ___________ ___________. There is no fee to sign up, but the number of students allowed to participate is limited. Because of the limited space, only high school juniors and seniors who hold at least a B average ___________ ___________ ___________ ___________ ___________. Also, for those eligible students who are interested, you must also ___________ ___________ ___________ ___________ ___________ from your fine arts or communications teacher. You can sign up by ___________ ___________ ___________ ___________ on our school's homepage.

## 12

M: Good evening, ma'am. What can we do for you today?

W: Hi. I'm looking for a new TV. The one I have is really outdated. It's got tubes.

M: Wow. I haven't seen one of those in a while. Well, we have quite a variety of flat-screen TVs in stock. ___________ ___________ ___________?

W: I don't want to ___________ ___________ ___________ ___________ ___________ ___________.

M: Is there a specific brand you have in mind?

W: I've read a lot of online reviews, and it seems that Solo makes great products.

M: They certainly do. We carry Solo at this location. Would you prefer one with 3D capabilities or without?

W: The reviews say that the 3D TVs are remarkable. I'd like one of those, if it's in my budget.

M: We have two that ___________ ___________ ___________. They come in black or silver.

W: I'd ___________ ___________ ___________ ___________. That way it would match my cable box.

M: Great. If you wait right here, I'll go in the back and get one out of the stockroom.

W: That'd be wonderful. Thank you for your help.

## 13

M: Hey, sweetheart. Did you take Mike to the doctor?

W: I did. It seems like he has some serious issues with his stomach.

M: Is that right? I know he's been complaining a lot about __________ __________ __________ __________ __________.

W: Yeah, the doctor said that he might have food allergies. They're known to __________ __________ __________.

M: Wow! It never seemed to bother him when he was younger.

W: Well, the doctor said that sometimes people can get allergies later in life.

M: So what can we do now?

W: We need to watch what he eats. He should __________ __________ __________ __________ __________ like rice and beans for now.

M: And he's going to do that for the rest of his life?

W: No, just until he gets an allergy test. The doctor __________ __________ as well.

M: (He's not going to like that, but it'll help in the long run.)

# 14

W: Hey Dad, why are you __________ __________ __________ __________?

M: Well, we don't want to keep the small ones.

W: Why not? We can still eat them.

M: Well, the small fish need more time to grow. There won't be any fish in the lake if we keep them all.

W: Can I help? I like playing with fish.

M: Sure. Pick up a fish and __________ __________ __________ __________ __________ __________.

W: How long should it be?

M: If it's under 25 centimeters, you should throw it back. It's actually __________ __________ __________ to keep any fish smaller than that.

W: Really? So __________ __________ __________ __________ __________ for keeping small fish?

M: That's right. Oh, you're going to have to let that one go. It's way too small.

W: (Okay. I guess it's this fish's lucky day.)

# 15

M: Peter is a physics major. His university opened up an engineering contest for students, and Peter decided to __________ __________ __________ __________ __________ to enter into the contest. After weeks of researching famous roller coasters around the world, he finally came up with an idea and built a finished product. Now at the contest, his model roller coaster has just finished up a strong performance and wowed the audience. The dean of the department, Dr. Goldberg, __________ __________ __________ and commends Peter for his effort. He informs Peter that other professors feel the same way, and so Peter is going to __________ __________ __________ __________ in the engineering contest. Peter is delighted by Dr. Goldberg's response and can't believe that he has been chosen as the contest's winner. In this situation, what would Peter most likely say to Dr. Goldberg?

Peter: (I really didn't expect to win the engineering contest.)

# 16-17

W: Good afternoon, everyone. Today, we're going to __________ __________ __________ __________ __________. According to a respected news authority based in London, there are around two billion people in the world who can speak English. In fact, there are about four times more non-native speakers of English than there are native English speakers. There are even __________ __________ __________ __________ for those who speak it as their first language. For instance, there are American English, Canadian English, British English, and Australian English. The differences between these are usually matters of pronunciation, intonation, and vocabulary. Oftentimes there are __________ __________ __________ __________, especially between American English and British English. Words like *color* and *colour* or *favorite* and *favourite* are primary examples of these differences. Canadian English is __________ __________ __________ American and British English, but it definitely borrows more from the American side. To get a better idea of the differences in these native English countries, have a look at the handout I have provided. *[Pause]* Now, during our break I would like for each of you to think of other countries that speak the same language as one another and list any differences between them. Thanks for listening, everyone. We'll see you all after the break.

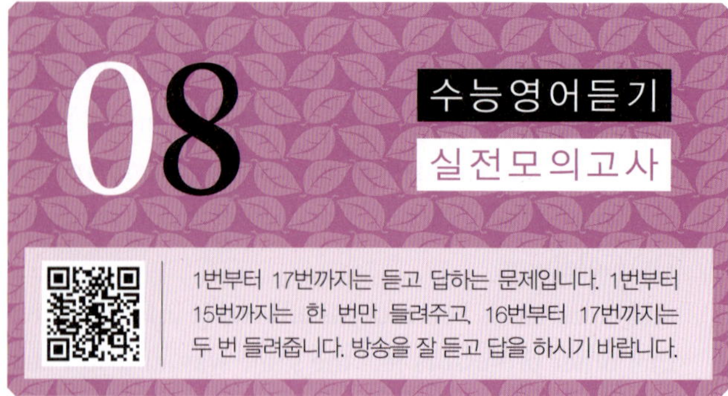



## 01

대화를 듣고, 여자의 마지막 말에 대한 남자의 응답으로 가장 적절한 것을 고르시오.

① You should be thankful that you've already performed.
② I thought my routine was better than the others.
③ Don't judge your ability based on other people.
④ My routine was really good compared to yours.
⑤ The show will start in just under an hour.

## 02

대화를 듣고, 남자의 마지막 말에 대한 여자의 응답으로 가장 적절한 것을 고르시오.

① All right. I'll just take some of the seashells with me.
② I'm having a hard time remembering that place.
③ Oh, now I see. I'll put them back right away.
④ That's great! I'll go get more to bring home.
⑤ I really hope we can visit here again soon.

## 03

다음을 듣고, 남자가 하는 말의 주제로 가장 적절한 것을 고르시오.

① 친환경적인 생활 습관
② 잘못된 환경 보호 운동
③ 대중교통 이용의 필요성
④ 전자제품의 효율성 문제
⑤ 삶의 질 향상을 위한 녹색주거공간

## 04

대화를 듣고, 새 도서관 건립에 관한 여자의 의견으로 가장 적절한 것을 고르시오.

① 새 도서관에 필요한 예산을 확보해야 한다.
② 신축 도서관의 건립 예정 위치를 바꿔야 한다.
③ 현 도서관의 전면부를 살려서 새로 지어야 한다.
④ 전통 양식 건물의 구조를 모방하여 설계해야 한다.
⑤ 현재 도서관은 역사적 건축물이므로 신축하면 안 된다.

## 05

대화를 듣고, 두 사람의 관계를 가장 잘 나타낸 것을 고르시오.

① 운전 연수 강사 — 수강생
② 주차 요원 — 건물 관리인
③ 보험회사 직원 — 차량 소유주
④ 자동차 정비사 — 정비 의뢰인
⑤ 자동차 판매원 — 자동차 구매자

## 06

대화를 듣고, 그림에서 대화의 내용과 일치하지 <u>않는</u> 것을 고르시오.

## 07

대화를 듣고, 여자가 할 일로 가장 적절한 것을 고르시오.

① 등산화 빌리기
② 준비 운동하기
③ 가방에서 물 빼기
④ 등산스틱 가져오기
⑤ 빠진 것 없는지 확인하기

## 08

대화를 듣고, 여자가 인터넷을 <u>끊은</u> 이유를 고르시오.

① 컴퓨터가 고장 나서
② 이용 요금이 비싸서
③ 성적이 많이 떨어져서
④ 수업 낙제가 우려되어서
⑤ 명의 도용이 걱정되어서

## 09

대화를 듣고, 남자가 지불할 총 금액을 고르시오.

① $280　　② $312　　③ $320　　④ $350　　⑤ $390

## 10

대화를 듣고, 신혼부부가 주의해야 할 재정적 조언으로 언급되지 <u>않은</u> 것을 고르시오.

① 저축 늘리기　　　　　　② 소비 줄이기
③ 계좌 개설하기　　　　　④ 배우자의 계좌 개설하기
⑤ 보험 가입하기

## 11

Fantasy Film Festival에 관한 다음 내용을 듣고, 일치하지 <u>않는</u> 것을 고르시오.

① 2012년부터 매년 열리는 행사이다.
② 올해는 새로운 장소에서 열릴 것이다.
③ 입장권은 온라인으로만 구매 가능하다.
④ 축제 입장 가격은 1인당 60달러이다.
⑤ 10명 이상의 그룹은 할인받을 수 있다.

## 12

다음 표를 보면서 대화를 듣고, 여자가 선택할 프로그램을 고르시오.

### Maro Hotel Special Activities

| | Program | Time | Fee |
|---|---|---|---|
| ① | Cooking Class | 9:00 a.m. / 1:00 p.m. | Adults: $10<br>Children under 10: Free |
| ② | Singing Lesson | 10:00 a.m. / 2:00 p.m. | Adults: $10<br>Children under 10: $5 |
| ③ | Dancing Class | 10:00 a.m. / 3:00 p.m. | Adults: $5<br>Children under 10: Free |
| ④ | Yoga Class | 11:00 a.m. / 12:00 p.m. | Free |
| ⑤ | Drawing Lesson | 2:00 p.m. / 5:00 p.m. | Only Children under 10: Free |

## 13

대화를 듣고, 여자의 마지막 말에 대한 남자의 응답으로 가장 적절한 것을 고르시오.

Man: ________________________________

① He should jump high off his right foot.
② I think you can block anything he shoots at you.
③ Don't worry. If you work hard, you can score on him.
④ I see what you mean. I think I can find a way to score on him.
⑤ I'm sorry, but I don't think you'll be able to win Saturday's match.

## 14

대화를 듣고, 남자의 마지막 말에 대한 여자의 응답으로 가장 적절한 것을 고르시오.

Woman: ________________________________

① So holding hands seems to lower stress in couples.
② I don't think they should show affection in public.
③ No wonder I get stressed when we hold hands.
④ It sounds like they had a nice afternoon.
⑤ They got married very recently.

## 15

다음 상황 설명을 듣고, Jason이 Ryan에게 할 말로 가장 적절한 것을 고르시오.

Jason: Ryan, ________________________________

① would you like to be my roommate?
② could you please be quieter during the week?
③ is it okay if I join one of your parties sometime?
④ will you teach me how to play that computer game?
⑤ how about playing in the computer game tournament?

[16-17] 다음을 듣고, 물음에 답하시오.

## 16

남자가 하는 말의 주제로 가장 적절한 것은?

① Tips for decreasing snoring
② Physiological causes of snoring
③ Natural ways to get rid of insomnia
④ How snoring affects your day-to-day life
⑤ Finding the most suitable sleeping position

## 17

피해야 할 것으로 언급되지 <u>않은</u> 것은?

① 비만　　　　② 수면제　　　　③ 유제품
④ 흡연　　　　⑤ 야식

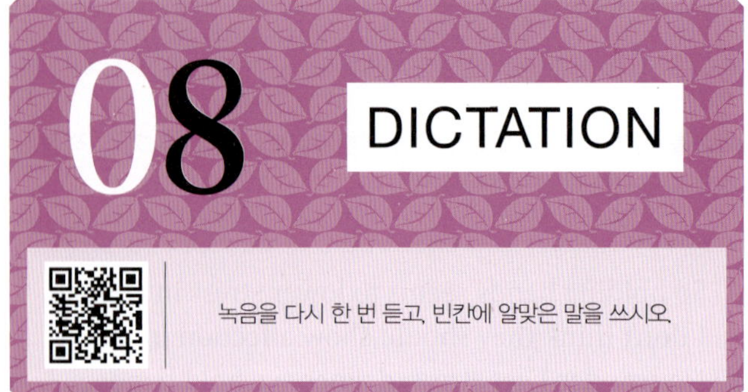


## 01

W: Aiden, I'm really nervous. I don't know if I can do this.

M: Of course you can! You know all the moves, and __________ __________ __________ __________.

W: Yeah, but all of the other dancers did really awesome routines.

M: (Don't judge your ability based on other people.)

## 02

M: Lillian! You need to leave the shells on the beach. You can't __________ __________ __________ __________.

W: But there are so many. Why can't I just take a few?

M: Just imagine if everyone who came to the beach took "just a few."

W: (Oh, now I see. I'll put them back right away.)

## 03

M: It is becoming very important to __________ __________ __________ __________. In addition to the expense of energy, recent environmental problems caused by pollution have led many people around the country to a new, more conscientious way of life. There are some things you can do to help. For example, you should only use your car when it's absolutely necessary. When it's not, you should __________ __________ __________ __________ __________ __________ __________ of transportation, such as travel by bicycle, bus, or train. If you're not using an electronic device, be sure to unplug it. Your computers and televisions use power when they are plugged in even if they're not turned on. __________ __________ __________ __________ __________ of energy used when washing your laundry if you use cold water. Bring your own bags to the supermarket to reduce landfill waste, and try to avoid disposable items, such as paper cups or plates. __________ __________ __________ and join millions of others in going green.

## 04

W: Tom, have you heard about the city's plan to tear down the old library?

M: Yes, I did. But I also heard that they have plans to build a new library in its place.

W: It's really too bad. The current building is a __________ __________.

M: That's true, but __________ __________ __________ __________ __________ for all of the new material.

W: That's a good point. We need a new library. The old one is far too inconvenient.

M: Certainly. It's really hot in the summer and freezing in the winter.

W: A new building would definitely solve those problems, but they should at least save the front of the original building.

M: That's a really wonderful idea. The front of the building is so beautiful.

W: Yeah, and then we would have a modern building on the inside with an antique look on the outside.

M: Exactly. That way we can __________ __________ __________ __________ __________.

## 05

M: __________ __________ __________ __________, Mrs. Allen. Here's your key.

W: Thanks. Wait… This is just a remote. Where's the actual key?

M: All new Mondo cars come with a smart key. As long as this is in your pocket, you can unlock your car by pressing the button on the door handle.

W: Let's give it a try. [Pause] That's really cool, but how can I start the car?

M: As long as the smart key is in the car, all you have to do is press the Start button.

W: Wow! This is quite convenient. __________ __________ __________ __________.

M: Right! Also, you can never lock your keys in the car. If the key is in the car, the door won't lock.

W: That's great because I can get __________ __________ __________ __________. Is there anything else I should know?

M: I think that's it. Thanks again for buying from us. Don't hesitate to call us if you have any problems with the car.

W: Thanks for your help.

## 06

M: Hey Beth, check out this poster I made for the fruit stand at the farmers' market.

W: It looks great, Jerry. I like the slogan. "Hungry for apples?"

M: I thought that up myself.

W: I had no idea you were so creative. Is the apple on the left a drawing? It looks so real.

M: It took me a long time to draw that. What do you think of the name of our fruit stand? It isn't too boring, is it?

W: Well, it seems all right to me.

M: But "Jerry's Fruit Stand" seems so plain. I should __________ __________ __________ __________ __________.

W: It's fine. Maybe the font should be a little bigger, though. The slogan __________ __________ __________ __________ __________ on the poster.

M: You're right. I'll resize the fonts before I print it. I also drew a picture of my son holding some apples.

W: That's so cute. And the drawing of you carrying a basket full of apples __________ __________ __________ as well.

M: You think so? I think my head looks too big.

W: Not at all. This will be perfect for the fruit stand.

## 07

M: Hey, Lucy. I made it.

W: Hey, Bobby. Thanks for coming early. It's a great day for a hike, huh?

M: It sure is. I like your boots.

W: Thanks, but they're not mine. I borrowed them from my cousin.

M: That's cool. So, __________ __________ __________ __________ __________?

W: I'm ready, but I should warn you: it's been a while since I've been hiking.

M: That's all right. __________ __________ __________ __________. Let's make sure we have everything before we go.

W: I think I have everything I need. __________ __________ __________ __________ __________ __________ __________.

M: That's okay. We might need it. Did you bring your hiking sticks?

W: Oh, I guess I must've left them in the car. I'll go get them.

M: All right. I'll wait here.

## 08

M: Did you see the new Gamebox PC? It looks amazing.

W: Wow! It does look great! Look at the graphics!

M: I'd love to buy it, but I just got a new computer last year. I haven't paid it off yet.

W: Yeah, why would you buy a new PC when the one you have still works well?

M: You're right, but this new computer is just __________ __________ __________ __________ __________. It could run all of the newest games.

W: You'll probably fail some of your classes, though. __________ __________ __________ __________ __________.

M: Haha. Maybe you're right. Is that why you haven't upgraded your computer in so long?

W: Actually, I got rid of my Internet altogether. I'm afraid of getting my identity stolen.

M: I heard that it's getting riskier to use computers. I can't stay away, though. I love playing games.

W: Yeah, but __________ __________ __________ __________ __________ __________.

M: I understand __________ __________ __________ __________.

## 09

W: Hello. Welcome to Frank's Home Appliances. Is there anything I can help you with today?

M: Well, our washing machine just broke, so I'm looking for a new one.

W: All right. Well, we have a __________ __________ __________ __________ __________. How much are you looking to spend?

M: I'd like to spend less than $400.

W: Sure. Let's see what's in the clearance section. This one is nice. It was originally $500, but it has a little bit of cosmetic damage so we marked it down to $350.

M: Looks great. I'll take it.

W: Oh! And if you got a leaflet from our shop, there's a coupon for an additional 20% off.

M: Yeah, I saw that and I cut out the coupon. Here you go. Do you deliver?

W: We sure do. Delivery is free, but we do __________ __________ __________ __________. That's an additional $40.

M: Well, it's probably better that you install it. I don't know if I can.

W: Okay.

## 10

W: Jiho, now that you and Kate are getting married, you both need to be more careful about what you do financially.

M: Yes, I know. We have a responsibility to each other, and all of our decisions will impact more than just ourselves.

W: Exactly. You both should start __________ __________ __________ __________ __________, because you're definitely going to need it.

M: That's good advice. I'll open a savings account right away.

W: Good. And she should, too. Once you're married, your accounts will be shared.

M: She's a student right now, and __________ __________ __________ __________-__________, so she doesn't have much money to put into an account.

W: __________ __________ __________ __________ that will need to be paid? Or rent?

M: No, she doesn't.

W: Then she should be able to save most of what she makes, at least for a while, until you both are comfortable.

M: All right. I'll talk to her and see how she feels about it.

W: That's a good idea. I'm glad to hear it.

## 11

W: Good morning, everyone. __________ __________ __________ __________ __________ __________ of the annual Fantasy Film Festival. The Fantasy Film Festival has grown since 2012. Last year, we had to deny a lot of visitors entrance to the festival because our location was not big enough. Fortunately, we have found a new location that is much bigger but still __________ __________ __________ __________ __________ __________ locations used in years past. I can assure you that your friends and family

will not be turned away, and a much larger audience will view your films. Because we're expecting more visitors than in the past, we have moved our ticket sales online. You can still get them at the box office, but it may be more convenient to buy them from our website: *www.fantasyfilms.com*. The price for a single admission ticket is $60, and __________ __________ __________ __________ __________ of ten or more.

## 12

M: This is the front desk. What can I do for you?

W: Hi. __________ __________ __________ about the rain today. We __________ __________ __________ __________ __________, but it looks like we'll be staying inside instead. I understand you have some activities here at the hotel that might keep us entertained.

M: Sure. We __________ __________ __________ __________ __________ the day.

W: Well, we're going to see a movie next door at 11 a.m. I think it runs for one hour and a half.

M: I see. Well, how about a cooking class? Today's lesson is how to make croissants.

W: That sounds interesting, but I really don't think my daughter would enjoy it much. __________ __________ __________ __________ __________.

M: Well, we offer two children's drawing lessons in the afternoon. Perhaps your daughter would be interested in that.

W: She might, but it's only for children, right? We're looking for something the whole family can enjoy.

M: All right. Well, there are a couple of other options. Does the cost of the activity matter?

W: Well, since it's our last day of vacation, we're running a little low on money. I don't want to spend more than $15 for my husband, my daughter, and myself.

M: I understand. Well, I have the perfect activity for you and your family.

## 13

W: What's up, captain?

M: Just watching some FC Barcelona videos. I don't know if we'll be able to beat them on Saturday.

W: Really? But your team is __________ __________ __________ __________ __________. I'm sure you'll be able to win.

M: Their goalie is much too strong. He can __________
__________ __________ __________ just about any
ball __________ __________ him.

W: That might be so, but after you find his weakness,
you'll __________ __________ __________
__________ __________ .

M: Hah! And what's his weakness?

W: If you look very carefully, you can see what part of
the goal he has trouble defending.

M: *[Pause]* Well, I'm still not seeing anything.

W: Look at the way he moves his body. He's shifting his
weight to his left side and jumping to his right.

M: You're right!

W: Now look again. He's doing a similar movement
__________ __________ __________ __________
__________ . If I were you, I'd shoot at the left corner.

M: (I see what you mean. I think I can find a way to
score on him.)

# 14

W: What are you reading, dear?

M: This really interesting study __________ __________
__________ .

W: A recent one?

M: Yep.

W: What kind of contact?

M: Things like holding hands and __________ __________
__________ __________ married couples.

W: That sounds really interesting. Tell me more.

M: Well, the study focused on two groups of married
couples. In one group, couples were asked to take a
walk while holding hands.

W: So the other group took a walk without holding
hands?

M: Exactly. After the walk, the couples sat down
with the researchers and were asked to discuss
__________ __________ __________ __________
__________ __________ __________ together after
getting married.

W: What were the results?

M: The couples that spent the afternoon holding hands
__________ __________ __________ __________
__________ than the other group while telling their
stories.

W: (So holding hands seems to lower stress in couples.)

# 15

W: After winning a major FPS tournament, Jason
finally __________ __________ __________ __________
buy a house. He found a place with two bedrooms
and asked his friend, Ryan, to be his roommate.
Everything was __________ __________
__________ . Jason enjoyed having someone to play
computer games with, and Ryan liked living away
from his parents. However, after Jason started
studying in university, the __________ __________
__________ __________ __________ . Now, Ryan
stays up late playing games and sometimes has loud
parties during the week. It's __________ __________
__________ __________ Jason, who has to study
every night and wake up for class early every
morning. Jason wants to talk about this noise problem
with Ryan. In this situation, what would Jason most
likely say to Ryan?

Jason: Ryan, (could you please be quieter during the
week?)

# 16-17

M: Good morning, listeners. Have you or your loved
one ever experienced __________ __________
__________ __________ due to snoring? Well,
__________ __________ __________ __________
__________ __________ snoring can lead to poor
sleep quality, tiredness during the day, health
problems, and relationship problems with your
partner. It really caused some problems for me
in my thirties. My wife would complain about
her sleepless nights due to my snoring. I started
researching snoring and found some tips online
that helped me stop. The first tip I followed was
to lose weight. Being overweight can create fatty
tissue in the back of your throat, which can lead to
frequent, loud snoring. You should also __________
__________ __________ __________ . They cause
the muscles in the throat to relax, which interferes with
breathing. Caffeine, dairy products, and late-night
meals should also be avoided before bedtime. Finally,
try sleeping on your side instead of your back. When
you sleep on your back, __________ __________
__________ __________ __________ __________
__________ . When you sleep on your side, it
doesn't. If you follow all of these tips, I'm sure you'll
make your partner and yourself happier.

# 09

1번부터 17번까지는 듣고 답하는 문제입니다. 1번부터 15번까지는 한 번만 들려주고, 16번부터 17번까지는 두 번 들려줍니다. 방송을 잘 듣고 답을 하시기 바랍니다.

## 01

대화를 듣고, 남자의 마지막 말에 대한 여자의 응답으로 가장 적절한 것을 고르시오.

① I don't like eating at home.
② It'll be a while before I finish.
③ Sure. I'll help you finish the report.
④ That's fine. I'll wait until you're done.
⑤ The delivery man brought the food quickly.

## 02

대화를 듣고, 여자의 마지막 말에 대한 남자의 응답으로 가장 적절한 것을 고르시오.

① We have to sit in assigned seats.
② Sorry, but I have other plans tonight.
③ It's sold out, so there aren't any tickets left.
④ No problem. You can have these two tickets.
⑤ Let's get there early so we can sit near the front.

## 03

다음을 듣고, 남자가 하는 말의 요지로 가장 적절한 것을 고르시오.

① 직원들의 조기 출근 제도가 필요하다.
② 출퇴근용 통근버스의 수와 노선을 늘려야 한다.
③ 직원들의 근무환경 개선이 가장 시급한 문제이다.
④ 생산성 증대는 직원들의 자율성 보장에서 비롯된다.
⑤ 생산성을 증가시키는 재택근무 제도를 개발해야 한다.

## 04

대화를 듣고, 두 사람이 하는 말의 주제로 가장 적절한 것을 고르시오.

① 친한 친구 사이에서도 말을 가려서 해야 한다.
② 상대방의 동의를 구하지 않고 사진을 촬영해서는 안 된다.
③ 소셜 네트워킹 사이트에서 바르고 고운 말을 사용해야 한다.
④ 소셜 네트워킹 사이트에서 익명으로 남을 비방해서는 안 된다.
⑤ 소셜 네트워킹 사이트 이용 시 서로의 사생활 보호에 주의해야 한다.

## 05

대화를 듣고, 두 사람의 관계를 가장 잘 나타낸 것을 고르시오.

① 모델 — 매니저
② 호텔 직원 — 투숙객
③ 옷 가게 점원 — 고객
④ 여행 가이드 — 관광객
⑤ 비행기 승무원 — 승객

## 06

대화를 듣고, 그림에서 대화의 내용과 일치하지 <u>않는</u> 것을 고르시오.

## 07

대화를 듣고, 여자가 남자를 위해 할 일로 가장 적절한 것을 고르시오.

① 좋은 트레이너 소개시켜 주기
② 비타민과 영양보충제 주기
③ 영화 티켓 대신 예매하기
④ 영화 보고 커피 사주기
⑤ 남자와 함께 운동하기

## 08

대화를 듣고, 여자가 회계사가 된 이유를 고르시오.

① 학창 시절 매우 좋아했던 경제 선생님 때문에
② 대학 졸업 후 아버지의 조언을 받아들여서
③ 안정적이고 매력적인 직업이라 생각돼서
④ 대학교에서 인상 깊게 들은 강의 때문에
⑤ 원래 숫자 다루는 일을 좋아했기 때문에

## 09

대화를 듣고, 여자가 선물을 사기 위해 부담하기로 한 금액을 고르시오.

① $22    ② $24    ③ $26    ④ $48    ⑤ $60

## 10

대화를 듣고, 남자의 후원 활동에 관해 두 사람이 언급하지 <u>않은</u> 것을 고르시오.

① 동물을 입양한 지역    ② 입양한 동물 이름
③ 후원해 온 기간    ④ 입양하게 된 계기
⑤ 후원하는 방법

## 11

토네이도 대처법에 관한 다음 내용을 듣고, 일치하지 <u>않는</u> 것을 고르시오.

① 경보가 울리면 지하실로 대피한다.
② 수건이나 이불로 자신을 덮는다.
③ 창문에서 떨어져 있어야 한다.
④ 정전을 대비해서 휴대폰을 챙긴다.
⑤ 기상 상태를 주시한다.

## 12

다음 표를 보면서 대화를 듣고, 두 사람이 택한 관광 코스를 고르시오.

### Bus Tour Guide

| | Program | Time of Departure | Price | Location of Departure |
|---|---|---|---|---|
| ① | Garden Tour | 9:00 a.m. / 1:00 p.m. / 5:00 p.m. | $40 | Central Station |
| ② | Museum Tour | 9:00 a.m. / 11.00 a.m. / 1:00 p.m. | $30 | Central Station |
| ③ | Shopping Tour | 9:30 a.m. / 12:30 p.m. / 3:30 p.m. | $20 | West Terminal |
| ④ | City Tour | 9:00 a.m. to 7:00 p.m. Every Hour | $50 | Central Station |
| ⑤ | Castle Tour | 10:00 a.m. (Once a Day) | $70 | West Terminal |

## 13

대화를 듣고, 여자의 마지막 말에 대한 남자의 응답으로 가장 적절한 것을 고르시오.

Man: _______________________________

① Let's test our rocket right now!
② Sorry. You should find a new partner.
③ I don't think we have enough supplies.
④ Let's use the Internet to get some ideas.
⑤ I think playing with rockets is dangerous.

## 14

대화를 듣고, 남자의 마지막 말에 대한 여자의 응답으로 가장 적절한 것을 고르시오.

Woman: _______________________________

① Maybe you still can, but for now you need to rest.
② I agree. You know your body better than anyone.
③ Yeah, I think you should consult another doctor.
④ Wow! I didn't know you were so good at tennis.
⑤ You should hurry. Otherwise you'll miss out.

## 15

다음 상황 설명을 듣고, Andrew가 사서에게 할 말로 가장 적절한 것을 고르시오.

Andrew: _______________________________

① I promise I'll return the DVD on time.
② It's late because I couldn't find the DVD.
③ I'd like to check this DVD out for longer, please.
④ I'd like to be a librarian in the future. Could you help me?
⑤ Someone stole the original DVD, so I bought a replacement.

[16-17] 다음을 듣고, 물음에 답하시오.

## 16

남자가 하는 말의 목적으로 가장 적절한 것은?

① to convince people to donate money
② to find a new job in a recruiting company
③ to recruit people with shipping experience
④ to talk about the benefits of working abroad
⑤ to discuss the challenges of working overseas

## 17

남자가 언급한 내용이 <u>아닌</u> 것은?

① He worked for a shipping company.
② He saw the Leaning Tower of Pisa.
③ He met lots of fascinating people.
④ He traveled the world with his friends.
⑤ He had lunch with the owner of a company.

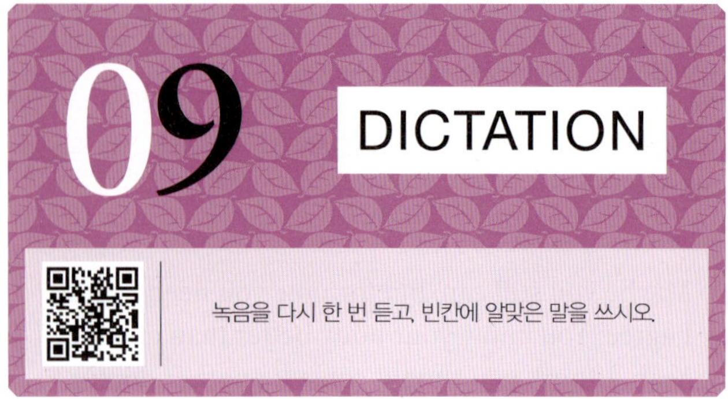



## 01

M: Hey Stacy, it's getting late. ____________ ____________

____________ ____________ ____________ ____________

and head home.

W: I can't tonight, Tyler. I really need to finish this report before tomorrow morning.

M: If you're almost finished, I can wait for you.

W: (It'll be a while before I finish.)

## 02

W: Hey George, my boss gave me two tickets to the basketball game tonight. ____________ ____________

____________ ____________ ____________.

M: Sure. That sounds great. ____________ ____________

____________ ____________?

W: They're in the fan section, so we can sit anywhere.

M: (Let's get there early so we can sit near the front.)

## 03

M: Good morning, everyone. I would like to talk to you all today about ____________ ____________ ____________

____________. In the past, ____________ ____________

____________ ____________ ____________ the employee coming to work in the morning and working all day under the close watch of his or her supervisor. But have you ever thought about the amount of time that's wasted commuting every morning, or how the stress of that commute could diminish the employee's energy before they even arrive at work? I'd like to see all of you employers develop a system that allows all or some of your employees to ____________

____________ ____________ ____________ ____________.

By eliminating the stress brought on by the daily commute, you'll allow your employees to put more energy into their tasks. Allowing your employees to work at home will ____________ ____________

____________ ____________ to you in the end.

## 04

M: Have you seen the photo of Daryl that Scott ____________ ____________ LookBook yesterday?

W: Yeah, I did see it.

M: Did you think it was funny?

W: Yes, it was quite humorous. But I think Daryl might be upset at Scott for posting it.

M: What do you mean?

W: Daryl looks very silly in the photo.

M: Oh, I understand. You think Daryl will be upset if he sees the photo and knows other people saw it. I suppose I would be angry, too.

W: Exactly. I just think Scott ____________ ____________

____________ Daryl if it was okay to post it.

M: I agree with you. Social networking sites like LookBook can be very useful for networking and ____________ ____________ ____________ ____________

____________ ____________, but they can also compromise people's privacy.

W: Yeah. I really enjoyed those kinds of sites in the beginning, but soon I realized how quickly ____________ ____________ ____________ ____________.

M: Right. ____________ ____________ ____________ ____________

____________ when posting anything on social networking sites.

## 05

W: Good morning. I'm Lilly Jones. I'm sorry I'm late. ____________ ____________ ____________ ____________ by a couple of hours.

M: No problem, Mrs. Jones. Welcome to Alaska. I'm Joseph, but my friends call me Joey. I'll be your guide.

W: It's a pleasure to meet you, Joey. Have all the others already arrived?

M: Yes, the rest of the group has arrived. They're waiting in the lounge. You should probably ____________ ____________ ____________ ____________ in the restroom. Alaska isn't as warm as Florida.

W: Can't it wait until we get to the hotel?

M: I'd really recommend doing it now. We're going to stop by the traditional Inuit fish market before we go to the hotel. It's quite cold there.

W: All right, I guess that means I should change my clothes.

M: And by the way, there's been a change of plans. ____________ ____________ ____________ ____________

____________ ____________ a lot of snow at the ski resort, so we're going to Denali National Park instead.

W: That's a shame, but it's okay. I've heard the park is beautiful.

M: I apologize nonetheless. Thank you for understanding.

## 06

M: Oh, isn't this a picture from one of your birthday parties?

W: It is. It was my seventh birthday. I remember because _________ _________ _________ _________ _________ all seven candles on the cake.

M: Are those your friends next to you in the picture?

W: Yes, that's Jessica and Tim. They were my best friends at the time. I wonder what they're doing now.

M: I love the birthday hats. All of you look adorable.

W: It's a really cute photo. You can see that all of the hats are a little different. My friends have stripes on theirs, and I have polka dots on mine.

M: I see that. You also have three balloons behind you.

W: Yes, my parents _________ _________ _________ _________ the room.

M: That's nice. _________ _________ _________ _________ _________ _________ Tim look delicious.

W: Actually, he ate one of the muffins just before we took this picture. I remember being very mad.

M: Really? In the picture you all look very happy.

## 07

W: Larry, do you have a minute?

M: I'm actually headed to the gym right now. I have a personal training appointment at noon.

W: Oh, that's right. I forgot. You have your personal training appointments every Monday and Wednesday, right? Do you like it?

M: Yeah, I really do. My trainer is very knowledgeable, and he _________ _________ _________ _________ _________ .

W: That sounds great. _________ _________ _________ _________ _________ _________ _________ ? If you have time, we should go see the new *Iron Man* movie.

M: Well, I was planning on going to the health store to _________ _________ _________ _________ _________ _________ .

W: Oh, I have a lot at home. In fact, depending on what kind you need, _________ _________ _________ . You can come take a look, and I'll give you what you need.

M: Really? Wow, that'd be great. Then yeah, we can go to the movie.

W: Great. I actually won two free tickets at our office yesterday.

M: Perfect. We can watch the movie, then I'll come check out the supplements, and I'll treat you to coffee afterwards.

## 08

W: Hey, Paul. It's me, Lori Townsend. We went to school together at Markwell High School. Do you remember me?

M: Yes, of course. How's everything with you?

W: Everything is great. I just started a job as an accountant for Green Tree Financial. What about you?

M: I'm still in school. I'm _________ _________ _________ _________ at Transylvania University.

W: Is that right? What are you studying? Everyone thought you were going to be a big singer in high school.

M: Well, my interests have actually changed a bit since then. Now I'm studying political science.

W: That's awesome. Why did you choose political science?

M: Well, _________ _________ _________ _________ politics since the last election. What about you? Why did you become an accountant?

W: Do you remember our economics teacher in high school, Mrs. Lee?

M: Yeah, she was great. She was so charismatic and funny.

W: _________ _________ _________ _________ . She and I became good friends after high school, and _________ _________ _________ _________ _________ _________ .

M: Really? That's cool.

## 09

W: Hey, I just realized that Mom's birthday is this weekend.

M: I totally forgot! What do you think we should get her?

W: Well, I was at the mall earlier and I saw a necklace that I know she'll love.

M: Really? Is it expensive?

W: Not too bad. It's only $60 with a 20% discount.

M: _________ _________ _________ _________ _________ . I only have $22. Is there anything we can buy that's cheaper than the necklace?

W: Well, I did see some earrings, but I really think she'll love the necklace.

M: But it's $48, right? I don't have enough money __________ __________ __________ __________ __________.

W: I guess you can give me your $22 and __________ __________ __________ __________ __________ __________.

M: Great. Thanks.

## 10

W: Hi, Max. What're you up to?

M: I'm just reading about this elephant I adopted in Africa. Look at this picture.

W: An elephant, huh? That's really cool. What's his name?

M: It's Chang.

W: So, you adopted him __________ __________ __________ __________ or something?

M: That's right. I recently watched a documentary about poaching and elephant abuse in Africa. __________ __________ __________ __________ __________ __________, so I decided that I'd do what I could to help.

W: That's nice of you. So what're you doing to help Chang?

M: Well, I found a wildlife sanctuary that takes care of these animals, and that's where he lives. I send them money every month.

W: How much do you send?

M: Well, I can send as much as I want, but it's usually not more than $30 a month. Would you like to __________ __________ __________ __________ __________?

W: It sounds great and all, but __________ __________ __________ __________ __________ at the moment.

M: That's all right. Maybe you can help when you have some money to spare.

## 11

M: Good afternoon, everyone. Thank you for coming to our town hall meeting. My name is Jerry Mills, and I'm the chief of the Milford Fire Department. As you know, __________ __________ __________ __________ __________. I'd like to go over some tips that will help you keep safe in the event of a tornado. First, when you hear a tornado siren, __________ __________ __________ __________ __________. If you don't have a basement, go

into a bathroom and cover yourself with towels, blankets, or a mattress. Stay away from windows and sharp objects. Do not go outside during severe weather. It might be wise to keep a battery-powered radio handy __________ __________ __________ __________ __________ __________. That way you can stay current on the weather conditions. If you follow these helpful tips during a tornado, you can stay safe. Thank you for your time.

## 12

M: Oh, no. We missed the nine o'clock Garden Tour bus!

W: That's too bad. What time is the next one?

M: According to the tour schedule, they run every four hours. We can't wait that long.

W: Here's __________ __________ __________ __________ __________ __________. What do you think of this one?

M: Christine, did you already forget that we've been on that tour?

W: Oh, right. Then how about the tour that leaves at 10 o'clock? It's 9:10 now, so __________ __________ __________ __________ __________ to catch that one.

M: It costs too much. __________ __________ __________ __________ __________ more than $50 per person.

W: Okay. There's a tour that departs in 20 minutes. Let's take that one.

M: It leaves from West Terminal. It would take us at least 30 minutes to get there from here.

W: Then it looks like we have only one choice. I guess we'll have to wait a while for the next bus.

M: __________ __________ __________ __________ __________ __________ by walking around Central Station.

W: Sounds like a plan.

## 13

W: Hey, Luke. Have you heard about the "Space Shooters" competition?

M: I haven't. What's that?

W: It's an event for __________ __________ __________ __________ __________.

M: So, what can you tell me about it?

W: Students have to work together to build a working miniature rocket to __________ __________ __________ __________ __________. It seems like something you'd be interested in.

M: You're right! I love making model rockets. My father and I used to build them all the time when I was younger.

W: Then you should be great at it! Would you like to be my partner?

M: That sounds great, but __________ __________ __________ __________ __________. I don't know if __________ __________ __________ __________ the other students.

W: You'll be great! Let's do it together.

M: Hmm… Okay. We're a team. Where do you think we should start?

W: How about researching some rocket designs?

M: (Let's use the Internet to get some ideas.)

# 14

W: Owen, I was shocked to hear that you're in the hospital. Is everything all right?

M: I'm fine. I just hurt my knee playing tennis. Thanks for coming to see me though, Nora.

W: When I heard you were here, I downloaded some songs I thought you'd like. Let me send them to your phone. Maybe it'll help you keep from getting too bored.

M: __________ __________ __________ __________ __________.

W: So, how did you hurt your knee?

M: During practice this morning, I jumped up for the ball and it twisted as I landed.

W: Ouch! Is it serious?

M: No. The doctor said __________ __________ __________ __________ __________, but I should stay off of it for a couple of days.

W: Then you should listen to him and __________ __________ __________ __________ __________ __________.

M: But I need to continue my training if I want to compete in the tournament this coming fall.

W: I don't think that's such a good idea. If you hurt it more, you may never be able to play tennis again.

M: My doctor said the same thing. I really want to win that tournament, though.

W: (Maybe you still can, but for now you need to rest.)

# 15

W: Andrew checked out a DVD from the Hudson Public Library. However, when he was getting ready to return it a week later, he realized that __________ __________ __________. He believes that __________ __________ __________. However, the library's policy states that he should buy a new copy to replace the one that went missing. Andrew buys a new DVD from the department store, and takes it to the library. The librarian realizes that the DVD doesn't have a library sticker on it. She says that she can't check in the DVD and that Andrew must have __________ __________ __________. Andrew wants to explain himself. In this situation, what would Andrew most likely say to the librarian?

Andrew: (Someone stole the original DVD, so I bought a replacement.)

# 16-17

M: Good afternoon, ladies and gentlemen. My name is George Wondell, and I'm happy that you've joined me for my seminar here at the San Jose State Job Fair. I'd like to talk to you about __________ __________. Have you ever thought about the opportunities that come with working in another country? Let me tell you my story. After I graduated from high school, I went to a job fair much like this one. An international shipping company was hiring and took me on as a deckhand. This was my chance to see the world and __________ __________ __________. I got to travel to many beautiful and interesting places. I saw the Eiffel Tower, the Leaning Tower of Pisa, and many other famous landmarks. I also met a lot of interesting people along the way and made friends wherever I went. One day, I met a man who owned a company that recruits people from around the world to work __________ __________ __________ __________ __________. We had lunch, and I told him stories about my travels. He found them so interesting that he offered me a job speaking __________ __________ __________ __________ __________ at seminars and job fairs like this one. Working overseas was the experience of a lifetime. It opens doors and provides opportunities that you won't find anywhere else. If you'd like more information, please visit our booth. Thank you for listening.

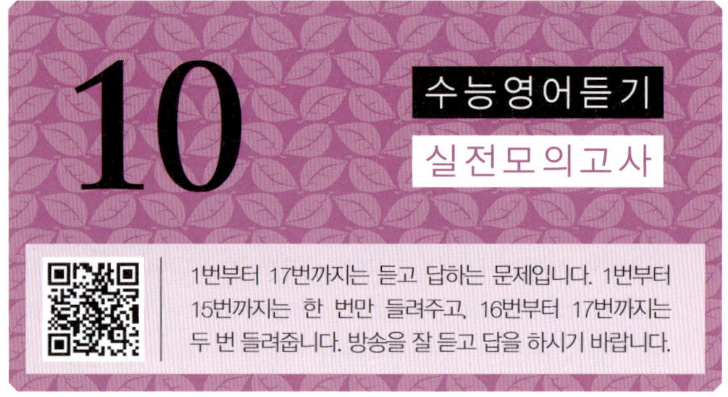


## 01

대화를 듣고, 여자의 마지막 말에 대한 남자의 응답으로 가장 적절한 것을 고르시오.

① Did you try to turn the headlights off?
② I think we should give them a call immediately.
③ I think so. Maybe you should answer the phone.
④ Leave your phone number and they'll call you later.
⑤ You're right. I think it's time to change the headlights.

## 02

대화를 듣고, 남자의 마지막 말에 대한 여자의 응답으로 가장 적절한 것을 고르시오.

① We need to buy another trash bin.
② I'm okay. The water is still too cold.
③ I appreciate all that you have done for us.
④ It only takes an hour to pick up the garbage.
⑤ Some people just don't care about the environment.

## 03

다음을 듣고, 남자가 하는 말의 목적으로 가장 적절한 것을 고르시오.

① 예술 축제 행사의 후원을 부탁하려고
② 예술 축제 행사의 개최 장소를 논의하려고
③ 예술 축제 행사의 기획 의도를 설명하려고
④ 예술 축제 개최를 위한 설문 참여를 부탁하려고
⑤ 예술 축제 행사를 위한 자원봉사자를 모집하려고

## 04

대화를 듣고, 두 사람이 하는 말의 주제로 가장 적절한 것을 고르시오.

① 방과후 운동이 아침운동보다 효과적인 이유
② 다양한 방과후 운동과목 신설의 필요성
③ 운동과 수업시간 집중력과의 상관관계
④ 학생들의 운동량을 늘리기 위한 방안
⑤ 운동 부족으로 인한 비만 학생 증가

## 05

대화를 듣고, 두 사람의 관계를 가장 잘 나타낸 것을 고르시오.

① customer — clerk
② journalist — cook
③ reporter — editor
④ photographer — model
⑤ interviewer — applicant

## 06

대화를 듣고, 그림에서 대화의 내용과 일치하지 <u>않는</u> 것을 고르시오.

## 07

대화를 듣고, 남자가 여자를 위해 할 일로 가장 적절한 것을 고르시오.

① 유리병 사기
② 집안일 도와주기
③ 차와 향신료 사기
④ 슈퍼마켓 함께 가기
⑤ 친구한테 병 받으러 가기

## 08

대화를 듣고, 남자가 어제 회의에 참석하지 <u>못한</u> 이유를 고르시오.

① 아내의 사무실에 들렀다 오느라
② 걸어오느라 시간이 많이 걸려서
③ 아내를 병원에 데려다 주느라
④ 넘어져서 다쳤기 때문에
⑤ 교통체증과 주차 때문에

## 09

대화를 듣고, 여자가 지불할 금액을 고르시오.

① $12　　② $16　　③ $21　　④ $22　　⑤ $25

## 10

대화를 듣고, 전시회에 관해 두 사람이 언급하지 않은 것을 고르시오.

① 전시회 주제　　　　　② 전시회 기간
③ 장소 대여 비용　　　④ 홍보 포스터
⑤ 정식 초대장

## 11

Ricardo's on the Boardwalk에 관한 다음 내용을 듣고, 일치하지 않는 것을 고르시오.

① 시내에서 5분 가량 떨어진 곳에 있다.
② 건물 완공에 거의 2년이 걸렸다.
③ 옥외에서는 호수 전망을 볼 수 있다.
④ 매일 평일 저녁에 재즈 공연이 있다.
⑤ 현지에서 재배된 식품만을 사용한다.

## 12

다음 표를 보면서 대화를 듣고, 남자가 선택한 축구화를 고르시오.

| | Brands | Type | Material | Price |
|---|---|---|---|---|
| ① | AP-101 | Offensive | Cloth | $30 |
| ② | AP-102 | Defensive | Plastic | $50 |
| ③ | EC-201 | All-Purpose | Cloth | $60 |
| ④ | EC-202 | All-Purpose | Plastic | $90 |
| ⑤ | PE-300 | All-Purpose | Plastic | $120 |

## 13

대화를 듣고, 여자의 마지막 말에 대한 남자의 응답으로 가장 적절한 것을 고르시오.

Man: _______________________________

① Thanks for the tip. It's very helpful.
② This is my first time traveling to Thailand.
③ I finally got my flight confirmation to Bangkok.
④ I can get these souvenirs for much cheaper there.
⑤ That's a good idea. I've spent a lot of money here.

## 14

대화를 듣고, 남자의 마지막 말에 대한 여자의 응답으로 가장 적절한 것을 고르시오.

Woman: _______________________________

① You're wrong. I really love eating desserts.
② Everybody loves to eat churros at an F1 race.
③ I don't want anything from the concession stand.
④ I think we should go to the F1 race this weekend.
⑤ No thanks. I don't want to eat anything that sweet.

## 15

다음 상황 설명을 듣고, Kristen이 Gavin에게 할 말로 가장 적절한 것을 고르시오.

Kristen: Gavin, _______________________________

① the weather should be perfect for hiking tomorrow.
② you're going to need a set of dry clothes for our hike.
③ I've prepared some of your favorite snacks for our hike.
④ I think we should reschedule the hike for next weekend.
⑤ it will take longer to get to the top of the mountain in the rain.

[16-17] 다음을 듣고, 물음에 답하시오.

## 16

남자가 하는 말의 주제로 가장 적절한 것은?

① Benefits of cooking meals at home
② How to choose the freshest produce
③ Advice on how to save money on food
④ How to create delicious and healthy meals
⑤ Cheap and easy food recipes for busy people

## 17

남자가 언급한 식품이 아닌 것은?

① 즉석 요리 제품　　② 제철 농산물　　③ 통조림
④ 냉동식품　　　　　⑤ 스파게티

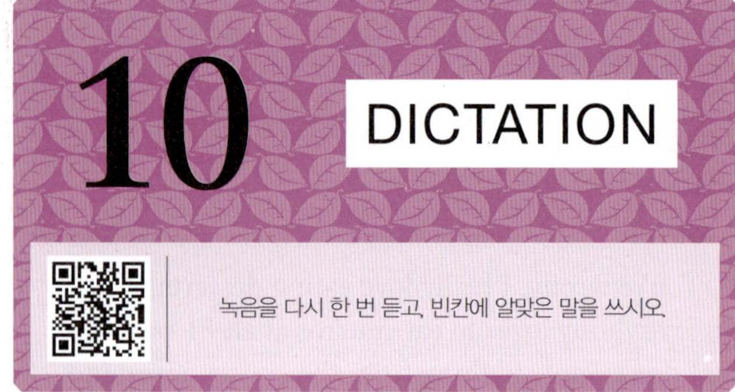



## 01

W: Look, Dad. Someone left their headlights on. I don't see anyone else around the car.

M: I guess they __________ __________ __________ __________ __________. Is the door locked?

W: Yes. But here's their phone number.

M: (I think we should give them a call immediately.)

## 02

M: Mary, if you're hot, why don't you __________ __________ __________ __________ and put your feet in the water? It's nice and cool.

W: That sounds lovely. [Pause] Eww! Is that garbage floating in the water?

M: It is. I'll never understand how __________ __________ __________ __________ __________. It's so easy to just throw it away.

W: (Some people just don't care about the environment.)

## 03

M: Thank you all for coming to tonight's booster's meeting. The Boosters Board has an art festival planned for the spring of 2016, and we would like all of your help in making it a successful event. The art festival has been a great event for our school in the past, and we would like this year's event to be our most successful ever. We are looking for as much __________ __________ __________ __________ __________ as possible on matters like these: Should we __________ __________ __________ __________ __________ or elsewhere? Should we have live music? Should we invite other school districts to join or not? We would appreciate it if you would answer these questions and a few others that are on the questionnaires being passed out now. It won't take long to __________ __________ __________, and all of your answers and opinions will be very useful. This is a community event, so we want to hear from all of you. Please __________ __________ __________ __________ __________ __________ when you've finished.

## 04

W: Mr. Baker, I don't think that students at our school are __________ __________ __________ __________ __________ __________.

M: I agree with that, but what can we do to help?

W: Maybe we should provide an extra exercise program.

M: You mean like an after-school class?

W: Well, I was actually thinking that we could do it in the mornings.

M: __________ __________ __________ __________ __________?

W: Before school starts in the morning, we can have students do some simple exercises in the courtyard.

M: That seems like a pretty good idea, but I don't think you'd want to make them tired before school even starts.

W: I've read that exercise in the morning actually has the opposite effect. It can help students with their focus and concentration.

M: Does it? Anyway, I've heard that some schools are __________ __________-__________ __________ to encourage students to be more active.

W: I think that's a great idea, too.

M: Well, __________ __________ __________ __________ __________ __________ and see if they work.

## 05

W: Thanks for meeting with me, Mr. Gaines.

M: Thanks for having me.

W: I'd first like to congratulate you on Gaines' Eatery being named Austin's top restaurant of 2015.

M: Thanks. I appreciate it. But I couldn't __________ __________ __________ __________. The members of my crew are the real heroes.

W: So, Mr. Gaines, I have a few questions I'd like to ask you. First, when did you decide to get into the restaurant business?

M: Well, when I was young, my father owned a small bakery on Second Street. It was there that I really gained an appreciation for the business.

W: That's great. And what is the most difficult part of your job?

M: I sometimes __________ __________ __________
__________ __________ __________ during the
dinner rush. It gets stressful, but my crew really
helps ease the chaos.

W: What do you do in your free time?

M: The work never ends for me. When I'm not at work,
I'm usually __________ __________ __________
and testing new methods.

W: It sounds like you take your work very seriously.
Do you mind if we get a couple of photos of you
__________ __________ __________ __________
__________?

M: Sure. No problem.

## 06

W: How's your advertisement coming along, Patrick?

M: I think I'm almost finished. Have a look.

W: I'm impressed. The slogan 'Need Energy?'
__________ __________ __________ __________
__________ __________. The bold capital letters are
so bright and full of energy.

M: That's what I was going for. I also put this arrow
__________ __________ __________ __________ to
show forward movement.

W: That's a great idea.

M: Also, to catch people's attention, I included a can of
Rad CraCra with hands, and it's waving __________
__________ __________ __________ __________
__________.

W: That's a nice touch. I also like the soccer player
kicking the ball.

M: That's Phil Phillips, the spokesmodel for the drink.

W: It's also cool that you put some __________
__________ __________ __________ __________.
That's really important to some people these days.

## 07

*[Telephone rings.]*

M: Hello?

W: Hi, Bill. It's me.

M: Hi there, honey. What's going on?

W: __________ __________ __________ __________
you're still at the office.

M: I am still here, yes. I'll be leaving fairly soon, though.

W: Okay, that's great. Would you mind stopping by the
supermarket __________ __________ __________
__________?

M: Sure. What do you need me to pick up?

W: Well, I helped out my friend Rachel yesterday with
some errands she needed to take care of.

M: Yes. I remember you telling me about that.

W: She gave me a box of assorted teas and spices,
and I need __________ __________ __________
__________ __________ __________ __________.

M: That was nice of her to give you a gift, and it's a great
idea to put them in jars. What type of jars are you
thinking about?

W: Just some small glass jars with screw-on lids.
You know, __________ __________ __________
__________ __________-__________.

M: All right, I got it. I'll give you a call again when I get
to the supermarket.

## 08

M: Here you go, Amanda. I got you some tea.

W: Thanks a lot, Nathan. So, where were you yesterday?
You __________ __________ __________.

M: I was late getting to work because my wife had an
accident.

W: Oh my! Is everything okay?

M: Yes, everything is fine. She just slipped and fell in
the bathroom.

W: That's terrible. I can see why you were late.

M: Well, that's not all. I decided to drive to work because
I thought it would save time.

W: Oh. You usually __________ __________ __________
__________ __________, don't you?

M: Yeah, I do. I thought I could get to the office quicker
if I drove, but __________ __________ __________
it takes longer because of __________ __________
__________ __________.

W: Yes, I know. I never drive because it takes so long to
get here.

M: Well, since I'm new to the area, I __________
__________ __________ __________ __________
__________. I should have asked somebody.

W: It's all right. So your wife is okay?

M: Yeah, she just hurt her ankle. Thank god it was
nothing more serious.

## 09

M: Good morning, Mrs. Crocker. What can I get for
you today?

W: Well, I'm looking to make my famous cherry cake
for a family reunion this afternoon.

M: All right. I have just what you need. These Washington cherries came in this morning. They're $6 a pound.

W: Perfect. I'll take two pounds. I think a pineapple would be great for the reunion, as well. How much are they running?

M: They're $10 a piece.

W: That's a bit too expensive. __________ __________ __________ __________ __________ __________ get half of one?

M: Sure. That's not a problem.

W: __________ __________ __________ __________ __________ of a full pineapple, right?

M: Well, it's actually $6 for half a pineapple, but since you're a regular customer, I'll give it to you for $5.

W: Thanks. I'd also like a gallon of lemonade.

M: It's $4 a gallon. But you can __________ __________ __________ __________ __________ if you spend more than $25.

W: That's all right. I'll just take the two pounds of cherries, half a pineapple, and a gallon of lemonade. __________ __________ __________ __________ __________, right?

M: Sure. Thank you, Mrs. Crocker.

## 10

W: Hey, Mr. Wise. I've been thinking what if we __________ __________ __________ for the photography contest this spring.

M: That's a great idea. We can show people in our town our students' hard work.

W: That's right. But we need to think of __________ __________ __________ __________ __________ __________. What do you think about nature photography?

M: That sounds good to me. Hey, I think we might be able to reserve some space in the exhibition room of the downtown library.

W: You think so? How much will it cost?

M: Well, I know some people on the library board. I think we might be able to __________ __________ __________ __________ __________. I'll check to see if it's available.

W: Great. I'll __________ __________ __________ __________ __________ so that we can promote the exhibit around town.

M: Good idea. What do you think about formal invitations for the parents?

W: I don't really think that'll be necessary. I think the posters and __________ __________ __________ __________ __________ __________.

M: I see. Well, I guess we should get to work.

## 11

M: This fall, we're bringing you the finest dining experiences the city has to offer. Ricardo's on the Boardwalk is the perfect restaurant for any dining situation. It's located on Scales Lake, situated __________ __________ __________ __________ __________. The construction of our magnificent restaurant has taken almost two years, but we're finally ready to open our doors. Our open-air dining room offers an incredible view of the lake, and our upstairs lounge houses local jazz talent __________ __________ __________ __________ __________ __________. You can enjoy a meal and drinks while listening to the best jazz the area has to offer. We also have a more family-friendly dining area to cater to your young ones. Our establishment employs only the finest chefs, and __________ __________ __________ __________ __________ __________. If you're looking for a memorable dining experience, look no further than Ricardo's on the Boardwalk, opening this fall.

## 12

W: Welcome to Owen Sports. What can I help you with today?

M: I'm looking for a new set of soccer cleats. Do you have any recommendations?

W: Here's a list of our products. Do you play defense or offense?

M: These cleats are actually for my son, and he likes to __________ __________ __________.

W: I see. Well, perhaps the all-purpose cleats would better suit him.

M: That sounds good. Would you recommend plastic or cloth?

W: I'd recommend the plastic ones. Plastic is __________ __________ __________, so they'll last longer.

M: All right. I'll take the plastic ones. So I have two options: the cheaper pair or the more expensive one.

W: Those are more expensive because they're new for this season.

M: I don't think my son will care if they're the newest model or not. I'll __________ __________ __________ __________ in size 5.

W: Great choice. I'll ring them up for you at the front register.
M: Sounds good. Thank you for your help.

## 13

W: Good morning, Stan. What's new?
M: Well, I'm trying to ___________ ___________ ___________ to visit Thailand this summer.
W: Really? What part of Thailand are you going to? I went there last winter, you know.
M: Yeah, I'm going there because of what you said about it. Did you stay around Bangkok or did you make it to the beaches?
W: I stayed in Bangkok for a couple of days, and then I went to Phi Phi Island. You've got to get to the beaches. They're incredible.
M: Yeah, I don't think I'll care too much for the big city. ___________ ___________ ___________ ___________ ___________ to give me about traveling there?
W: Well, you should haggle on prices everywhere you go.
M: Really? Is everything there expensive?
W: No. everything is quite cheap, but ___________ ___________ ___________ ___________ ___________. You can almost always bargain.
M: I see. So I should always argue about the price.
W: Yeah. Most of the time you can get souvenirs for about ___________ ___________ ___________ ___________ ___________ they initially quote you.
M: (Thanks for the tip. It's very helpful.)

## 14

M: Are you excited to watch your first F1 race?
W: I'm really excited. Let's buy some snacks at the ___________ ___________ before we sit down.
M: Sure. I'm kind of ___________ ___________ ___________ ___________ ___________ ___________. Oh, look. They have cotton candy.
W: You like cotton candy? That's a snack for kids.
M: Maybe you're right, but this is an F1 race and cotton candy is a fun treat.
W: I guess so. I just think a grown man ___________ ___________ ___________ ___________ ___________.
M: Okay. What about some churros? I love churros, too.
W: You've got to be kidding. Churros are ___________ ___________. Can't we get a couple of hotdogs and a hamburger, like normal people?
M: Oh, come on! Have a churro.

W: (No thanks. I don't want to eat anything that sweet.)

## 15

W: Kristen and her family are planning to ___________ ___________ ___________ ___________ ___________ on Saturday. Her son, Gavin, is especially excited to go because he loves the outdoors. Kristen has been preparing for the hike all week, and she has even prepared some of Gavin's favorite snacks. However, Kristen ___________ ___________ ___________ ___________ on Friday night and realizes that it's calling for an 80% chance of rain. In fact, the forecast predicts that a series of storms will be in the area throughout the weekend. ___________ ___________ ___________ ___________ ___________, the National Weather Service is urging people to stay in their homes. Kristen thinks that it'll be best if they ___________ ___________ ___________ ___________ ___________ ___________. In this situation, what would Kristen most likely say to Gavin?
Kristen: Gavin, (I think we should reschedule the hike for next weekend.)

## 16-17

M: Cooking every day can be costly and time-consuming. People these days are always on the go and don't have time to cook for themselves. I'm here to provide tips to save you money and time on food. First, buy food items in bulk. It's cheaper to buy items in bulk than it is to purchase them individually. Second, avoid brand names and buy store-brand goods. Brand-name products often contain the same ingredients as store-brand ones, but are much more expensive. Third, buy produce only when ___________ ___________ ___________. Canned or frozen food can be substituted when produce is out of season and therefore expensive. Also, be sure to ___________ ___________ ___________ ___________ and sales. You can save a lot of money by using coupons and ___________ ___________ ___________ ___________. Finally, cook in bulk. I know it may be boring, but bringing your lunch to work every day will save you loads of money. For example, you can dedicate some time on Sunday night to cooking lunch for the week. Spaghetti is a great, cost-effective dish that can be reheated and eaten all week. Changing your lifestyle to save money can be difficult, but it's certainly worthwhile.

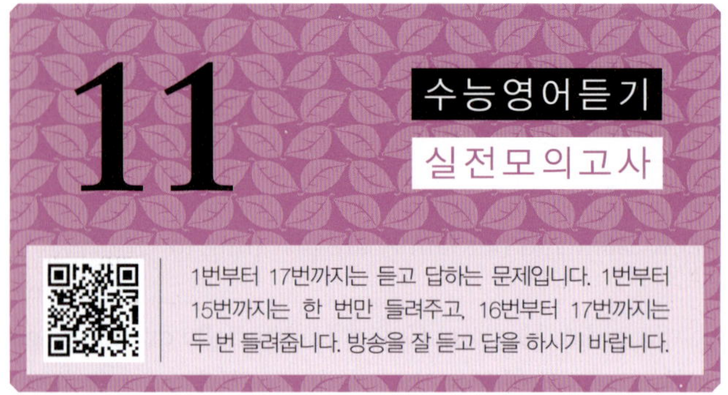


## 01

대화를 듣고, 여자의 마지막 말에 대한 남자의 응답으로 가장 적절한 것을 고르시오.

① Of course. I'm ready for the meeting now.
② I'm sorry, but I'm not sure how to get there.
③ Yes. Give me directions to your office, please.
④ No. I just got off at the wrong subway station.
⑤ The office is in the tall building across the street.

## 02

대화를 듣고, 남자의 마지막 말에 대한 여자의 응답으로 가장 적절한 것을 고르시오.

① You should take better care of your eyes.
② You don't have to get your eyes tested now.
③ You won't be able to break the habit that way.
④ You need to wait a while before you read a book.
⑤ You should consider using the computer more often.

## 03

다음을 듣고, 여자가 하는 말의 주제로 가장 적절한 것을 고르시오.

① 온라인 쇼핑의 부정적인 측면
② 온라인 쇼핑이 증가하게 된 원인
③ 믿을 만한 온라인 쇼핑 사이트 찾는 법
④ 오프라인 쇼핑과 온라인 쇼핑의 비교
⑤ 온라인 쇼핑의 판매 전략

## 04

대화를 듣고, 남자의 의견으로 가장 적절한 것을 고르시오.

① 자선 단체에서 파는 신발을 구입하라.
② 용도에 맞는 신발을 구입해서 신어라.
③ 새로 사지 말고 헌 신발을 수선해서 신어라.
④ 헌 신발을 버리지 말고 자선 단체에 기부하라.
⑤ 직접 상점에 가지 말고 인터넷 쇼핑몰을 이용하라.

## 05

대화를 듣고, 두 사람의 관계를 가장 잘 나타낸 것을 고르시오.

① 교수 — 학생　　　　② 봉사자 — 리포터
③ 면접관 — 구직자　　④ 사회자 — 출연자
⑤ 과학자 — 피실험자

## 06

대화를 듣고, 그림에서 대화의 내용과 일치하지 <u>않는</u> 것을 고르시오.

## 07

대화를 듣고, 남자가 할 일로 가장 적절한 것을 고르시오.

① 지구 온난화에 대해 조사하기
② 시 대회를 위한 야구 연습하기
③ 친구가 보고서 쓰는 것 도와주기
④ 도서관에 가서 영화 DVD 찾아보기
⑤ 지난주에 빌린 영화 DVD 반납하기

## 08

대화를 듣고, 남자가 일일 캠프 관리자로 일하는 이유를 고르시오.

① 다른 일보다 보수가 많은 편이라서
② 스트레스는 받지만 보람을 느껴서
③ 자연을 즐기며 일할 수 있어서
④ 아이들과 지내는 것이 좋아서
⑤ 근무 시간이 규칙적이라서

## 09

대화를 듣고, 남자가 지불할 총 금액을 고르시오.

① $48　　② $54　　③ $55　　④ $60　　⑤ $66

## 10

대화를 듣고, 섬에 관해 두 사람이 언급하지 <u>않은</u> 것을 고르시오.

① 위치　　　　　② 날씨　　　　　③ 숙박 비용
④ 현지 가이드　　⑤ 할 만한 것들

## 11

Mobile Device Photo Contest에 관한 다음 내용을 듣고,
일치하지 <u>않는</u> 것을 고르시오.

① 16세 이하의 아이들만 참가할 수 있다.
② 출품작은 세 주제 중 하나를 담아야 한다.
③ 우승자는 각 분야를 합쳐서 단 한 명이다.
④ 참가자는 부모님의 동의를 받아야만 한다.
⑤ 이번 주 목요일 정오부터 등록을 시작한다.

## 12

다음 표를 보면서 대화를 듣고, 두 사람이 주문할 공룡 장난감 모델을
고르시오.

**Dinosaur Toys**

| | Type | Price | Material | Size |
|---|---|---|---|---|
| ① | Tyrannosaurus Rcx | $220 | Plastic | Two Feet |
| ② | Triceratops | $150 | Plastic | Two Feet |
| ③ | Tyrannosaurus Rex | $150 | Wood | Two Feet |
| ④ | Triceratops | $100 | Wood | One Foot |
| ⑤ | Tyrannosaurus Rex | $150 | Wood | One Foot |

## 13

대화를 듣고, 여자의 마지막 말에 대한 남자의 응답으로 가장 적절한
것을 고르시오.

Man: ______________________________

① How about joining our X-Fit club?
② Do you know any gyms that I can go to?
③ You look like you've lost some weight, too.
④ I think it's a lot better if you exercise alone.
⑤ You should be careful when exercising alone.

## 14

대화를 듣고, 남자의 마지막 말에 대한 여자의 응답으로 가장 적절한
것을 고르시오.

Woman: ______________________________

① She must have helped you decide well.
② She suggested I try something different.
③ She considers the interest of all students.
④ She refused to help me find a new major.
⑤ She used to help students choose majors.

## 15

다음 상황 설명을 듣고, Katie가 Joseph에게 할 말로 가장 적절한
것을 고르시오.

Katie: ______________________________

① Isn't there someone else you can help?
② I couldn't join the all-state choir competition.
③ I'm really excited about joining the talent show.
④ You should forget about including a musical act.
⑤ Could you give me a little time to think about it?

[16-17] 다음을 듣고, 물음에 답하시오.

## 16

여자가 하는 말의 목적으로 가장 적절한 것은?

① to repair couples' relationships through music
① to invite married couples to the music program
③ to promote conversation between a husband and wife
④ to teach the importance of healthy marital relationships
⑤ to introduce a topic of conversation for married
　 couples

## 17

최근 실험에 언급된 부부들이 대화를 나누는 주당 평균 시간은?

① 6분　　　　② 14분　　　　③ 16분
④ 30분　　　　⑤ 1시간

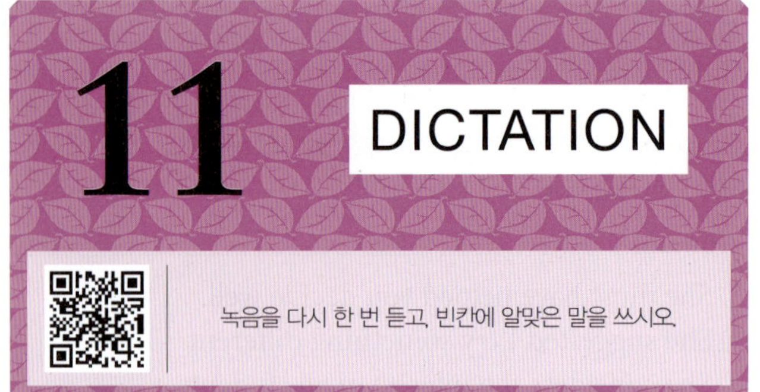


## 01

W: Good afternoon. What can I do for you today?

M: Hi. I'm Thomas Moore. I __________ __________ __________ __________ __________ __________ __________. I'm sorry I'm late.

W: No problem, Mr. Moore. Was it difficult to find our office?

M: (No. I just got off at the wrong subway station.)

## 02

M: It's hard for me to see the words on the blackboard clearly.

W: Are you serious? __________ __________ __________ __________ __________ __________. What happened?

M: Lately I've gotten into the bad habit of playing computer games too much.

W: (You should take better care of your eyes.)

## 03

W: Did you know that you can shop for groceries online? Online grocery shopping has become quite popular in recent years. Buying online __________ __________ __________ __________ __________ __________ __________, tablets, or computers, which saves them the time it takes to go to the market. Shopping online can also save money. But beware— there are __________ __________ __________ __________. Most of the items are cheaper because they are stored in bulk in a warehouse instead of in a store, but the problem is that these warehouses are often left unattended and so there is little supervision of the goods. This could lead to __________ __________ __________ by infestation or improper storage methods. Some consumers have reported getting rotten fruit delivered to their homes. When they want to __________ __________ __________, all they can do is send an email and hope for a response. Buying online is a great way to __________ __________ __________ __________, but you should restrict the products you buy online to those that do not suffer negative consequences when they're neglected.

## 04

M: __________ __________ __________ __________, Amy?

W: I'm off to the mall to shop for some new sandals.

M: The sandals you have on now seem fine.

W: Actually, the soles are __________ __________ __________ __________.

M: Are you going to __________ __________ __________ after you buy new ones?

W: Probably. Why?

M: Instead of throwing them away, you should consider giving them to the Good Will Foundation. They'll give them to someone who needs them.

W: Really? But I don't know where the Good Will Foundation is located.

M: Don't worry about that. Just go to their website and look up the nearest donation center.

W: Do I need to repair my old shoes before I donate them?

M: Nope. They'll __________ __________ __________ __________ __________ for you. They'll even repair the soles.

W: That's really cool. I'll definitely donate them after I buy new ones, then.

M: Great! I'm glad to hear it!

## 05

W: Thank you for joining our program, Professor Marsh.

M: Thanks for having me.

W: Well, let's __________ __________ __________ __________. First off, what do you think will be the next breakthrough technology?

M: Well, as you might be aware, power is a huge problem in our country. Not only is our current power infrastructure inefficient, but it's also polluting our air, land, and water.

W: That's right. You always hear about __________ __________ __________ __________ __________. It's even worse in less developed countries.

M: Right. We need to develop alternative energy sources and abandon our traditional methods.

W: What technology is __________ __________ __________ __________?

M: Solar cells. They're the future.

W: Do they have any benefit over other ___________ ___________ ___________, like wind power or hydroelectric?

M: Absolutely. Most of the developed world has access to sunlight, but not everyone is close to a river, and even fewer can harness the wind. Solar power is also becoming a lot cheaper.

W: Well, there you have it, folks. Solar power is the future. Thank you for sharing, Professor Marsh.

M: No problem. I'm always happy to speak to your viewers.

## 06

M: Hey Rose, what's that you're looking at?

W: This? Oh, it's just a ___________ ___________ for the stadium's new cafe. Take a look.

M: It looks pretty fun. Is that a bakery in the back left?

W: Yeah. And next to that is a snack bar.

M: Those ___________ ___________ ___________. And is that a DJ in the cafe?

W: Yeah, it is. It seems a little bit strange to have a DJ in a cafe, though. Don't you think?

M: I agree. This certainly doesn't seem like a normal cafe.

W: Yeah. They also have some entertainment for children outside of the cafe.

M: I see that. Is that a clown?

W: It looks like it. He's ___________ ___________ ___________ ___________ ___________ there.

M: Yeah, I see the staff helping him prepare the balloons. It's a strange cafe, but I think it'll be a success.

W: I sure hope so. Its grand opening is just before this Sunday's concert.

## 07

M: Hey Rachel, could you help me with something?

W: Sure, Peter. What's up?

M: Well, ___________ ___________ ___________ ___________ ___________, I wasn't in class on Thursday.

W: Right. You were playing baseball in the city tournament. How'd you all do?

M: We did great. We're ___________ ___________ ___________ ___________ ___________ ___________.

W: That's great. Your team is really talented this year. You all have been practicing hard. I bet you guys win it all.

M: I hope so. Anyway, did you finish your report on global warming for Mr. Smith's class?

W: I did. Have you finished yours?

M: Well, I'd like to work on it, but I can't seem to find the movie ___________ ___________ ___________ ___________ ___________ ___________.

W: Right. You're talking about *A Troublesome Fact*, right?

M: That's the one.

W: Have you checked the library? They must ___________ ___________ ___________ ___________ ___________ ___________.

M: I didn't think about checking the library. I'll head over there right now.

## 08

W: Hey, what are you going to do this summer?

M: I was thinking of working at the school ___________ ___________ ___________ ___________ ___________ ___________.

W: That sounds interesting.

M: I've been doing it every summer ___________ ___________ ___________ ___________ ___________, actually.

W: Wow, I didn't know that. What's the job like?

M: It's pretty easy. I teach the kids and lead them in whatever fun things we have planned for the day.

W: Is it a fairly relaxed environment?

M: Yeah, it really is. The hours ___________ ___________ ___________ ___________ ___________ ___________ ___________ ___________ the activities, but everyone is really cool about staying late or arriving early. There's very little stress.

W: How about your pay?

M: It's average for a camp supervisor, but it's definitely ___________ ___________ ___________ ___________. But I don't really care too much about the money.

W: Why have you been working there for so long?

M: It's really my ideal job. I get to be outside every day to ___________ ___________, and all of the work is very hands-on.

## 09

W: Well, that's it. ___________ ___________ ___________ ___________ ___________.

M: Thank you so much. My hair looks much better. I'm going to look great at the company party tonight.

W: I ___________ ___________ ___________ ___________ ___________.

M: That's good to hear. I'll be sure to recommend you to all of my friends.

W: Thank you. That'll be $25 for the haircut. Would you like to purchase any hair care products today?

M: Absolutely. I'll take some of your styling wax. How much is it?

W: The wax is $20. How about shampoo? Our aloe-infused shampoo is great for your hair type.

M: I'll take a bottle of that, too.

W: Great. It runs $15 a bottle. __________ __________ __________ __________ for you?

M: Yes. Hey, didn't you mention some kind of discount for first-time visitors?

W: Right. Since you're __________ __________-__________ __________, you get a 10% discount on your total.

M: That's great. Here's my card.

## 10

M: Hey Sally, I'm thinking about taking a trip to somewhere warmer this winter. Do you have any suggestions?

W: Sure. There's __________ __________ __________ __________ __________ __________ __________ all the time called Tybee Island. I'm sure you'll love it.

M: Tybee Island? I've never heard of that. Where is it?

W: It's in Georgia, near Savannah.

M: I see. __________ __________ __________ __________ __________?

W: Well, that area of the country is very beautiful. The colonial-style houses are lovely, and the beach is quite stunning.

M: What's the weather like at that time of year?

W: It's not too hot, but it might be too cold to go swimming.

M: That's cool. I don't swim much anyway. How much do the hotels in the area usually run?

W: Well, you can __________ __________ __________ __________ for about 700 dollars a week. A three-bedroom condo would be perfect for your family, I think.

M: That sounds fair. I'd definitely like to tour some of the more historic places. Do they offer tours?

W: Absolutely. There are several history tours you can join. They __________ __________ __________ __________ you can take in the evening.

M: That sounds awesome. I'm going to start researching Tybee Island immediately.

## 11

M: We are proud to announce the entry dates for our world-famous Mobile Device Photo Contest. The idea is to give young people creative license with their smartphones or tablets. Contestants must be 16 years of age or younger to enter. __________ __________ __________ __________ and wish to participate should __________ __________ that fall into one of the following categories: architecture, nature, or commerce. We will choose __________ __________ __________ __________ __________ __________, and the winners will receive a cash prize of $500. Remember, each contestant must have __________ __________ __________ __________ to enter the contest. Online registration will open this Thursday at noon on our website: *www.mdphoto.com*. Entries must be submitted by October 15th, 2016.

## 12

M: Hey darling, what's that you're looking at?

W: I'm just browsing the Internet for a gift for Jake. You know his birthday is coming up, right?

M: Of course. What do you have in mind?

W: Well, __________ __________ __________ dinosaurs now, so I figured a toy triceratops would be cool. Look at this one. It's really cute.

M: Yeah, that might work, but he told me his favorite dinosaur is a tyrannosaurus rex.

W: I see. Well, I found a list of this website's top dinosaur toys. How much are we looking to spend?

M: I don't think __________ __________ __________ __________ __________ $200.

W: Okay. How about the material? I think we should get a wooden one. Plastic is __________ __________.

M: I think so, too. What size do you think we should get?

W: Well, I think that two feet is too big. Don't you?

M: I agree. Well, it looks like we've found the one we want. Go ahead and place the order.

W: All right. __________ __________ __________ __________ __________ before his birthday.

## 13

M: Hey, Laura. It's been a while. How's everything with you?

W: Everything's great. You look like you've changed a bit __________ __________ __________ __________ __________.

M: I have. I've __________ __________ __________ __________ weight from dieting and exercise.

W: That's cool. What kind of exercises are you doing?

M: I play soccer a bit, but I also do an X-Fit program __________ __________ __________ __________.

W: X-Fit? I was doing the Lunacy program at home, but I didn't like it.

M: That's one of those home video programs, huh? I tried one of those. I quit after three days.

W: So, what's so different about X-Fit?

M: Well, X-Fit is a routine you do with other people. We meet at a gym and do our routine.

W: I see. I guess exercising alone isn't very motivating.

M: Right. When you're with a group, __________ __________ __________ __________ __________ to try harder. It's really fun.

W: I think I should start exercising again, but I don't really want to do it alone.

M: (How about joining our X-Fit club?)

# 14

M: __________ __________ __________ __________ __________ __________, Sabrina. I don't know what I should do.

W: Really? I think your major is a lot more interesting than some of the other ones at the university.

M: I do the same things every day. I don't really learn much. I just don't think that computer science is for me.

W: Have you __________ __________ __________ __________ __________ about it?

M: No. She wasn't too helpful the last time I spoke to her. Plus, she's really busy speaking to new students because it's the __________ __________ __________ __________.

W: That may be true, but if you don't talk to her, you'll be stuck doing something you don't like __________ __________ __________ __________ __________.

M: I don't want to waste her time. I'm not sure what other major I'd enjoy.

W: I think that's something your advisor can help you decide. I wasn't sure __________ __________ __________ __________, but my advisor changed all of that.

M: Really? What did she do for you?

W: (She suggested I try something different.)

# 15

M: Joseph is __________ __________ __________ __________ __________ that takes place at the end of the school year. He has a magic act, a dancing act, and a juggling act, but he'd really like to find a musician to play in the show. He remembers that Katie was a finalist in last year's state choir competition. Joseph calls Katie and __________ __________ __________. She declines his request because she's too busy preparing for her exams to practice. However, Joseph is persistent and keeps trying to __________ __________ __________ __________ __________ __________. He tells her that she's the only person who can balance the show. Katie __________ __________ __________ __________, but can't make up her mind. In this situation, what would Katie most likely say to Joseph?

Katie: (Could you give me a little time to think about it?)

# 16-17

W: Good evening. This is *Sunday Evening Classics*, and I'm your host, Lauren Bell. Before we start tonight, I want to talk a little bit about married couples and communication. An experiment was conducted recently to calculate the __________ __________ __________ between a husband and wife, and the results might surprise you. The average person might assume that an average married couple would talk to each other quite often. But one psychologist found that couples speak far less than __________ __________ __________. Keep in mind that the number I'm about to give you is for a week, not a day. It's sixteen minutes! Shocking, isn't it? If you consider yourself a part of an average couple, then try __________ __________ __________ 14 minutes more per week to bring the total amount of time to 30 minutes of conversation. Then try to have 30 minutes of conversation every day. Will it help your relationship? We think so. __________ __________ __________ __________ or even just trivial conversation is very important for couples. So, in the interest of all the couples out there, I want to play *The Modern Love Song* by Scotty McGee. Enjoy!

1번부터 17번까지는 듣고 답하는 문제입니다. 1번부터 15번까지는 한 번만 들려주고, 16번부터 17번까지는 두 번 들려줍니다. 방송을 잘 듣고 답을 하시기 바랍니다.

## 01

대화를 듣고, 남자의 마지막 말에 대한 여자의 응답으로 가장 적절한 것을 고르시오.

① All of his music was so inspiring.
② It's going to be at the state theater.
③ I appreciate the advice. Thank you.
④ Oh, I won't be able to make it then.
⑤ Make sure you take a lot of pictures.

## 02

대화를 듣고, 여자의 마지막 말에 대한 남자의 응답으로 가장 적절한 것을 고르시오.

① It should be less than $20.
② The price for admission is $10.
③ You should pay me back soon.
④ I think the gallery closes at 9 p.m.
⑤ I might be late because of bad traffic.

## 03

다음을 듣고, 남자가 하는 말의 주제로 가장 적절한 것을 고르시오.

① 창의성을 키우는 방법
② 뇌 활동을 자극하는 방법
③ 기분과 창의성의 상관관계
④ 지식이 창의성에 주는 영향
⑤ 뇌 활동을 활발히 하는 음식

## 04

대화를 듣고, 여자의 의견으로 가장 적절한 것을 고르시오.

① 아이에게 자신이 가지고 논 장난감을 정리하도록 해야 한다.
② 아이들은 장난감을 통해 또래와의 상호작용을 배워 나간다.
③ 아이들의 노는 방과 공부방을 따로 분리해 주어야 한다.
④ 장난감이 많으면 아이들의 자율성 강화에 도움이 된다.
⑤ 너무 많은 장난감은 아이들의 상상력에 방해가 된다.

## 05

대화를 듣고, 두 사람의 관계를 가장 잘 나타낸 것을 고르시오.

① 코치 — 골키퍼
② 기자 — 축구감독
③ 축구선수 — 축구팬
④ 물리치료사 — 운동선수
⑤ 경기 해설자 — 현장 진행자

## 06

대화를 듣고, 그림에서 대화의 내용과 일치하지 <u>않는</u> 것을 고르시오.

## 07

대화를 듣고, 여자가 남자에게 부탁한 일을 고르시오.

① 졸업 연설 후보자들의 지원서 받기
② 졸업 연설 후보자들과 대화하기
③ 졸업 연설 후보자 추천하기
④ 졸업 연설 후보자 추리기
⑤ 졸업 연설 대본 작성하기

## 08

대화를 듣고, 남자가 놀이공원에 갈 수 <u>없는</u> 이유를 고르시오.

① 딸의 여름캠프를 등록해야 해서
② 딸의 숙제를 도와주어야 해서
③ 회사 출장과 날짜가 겹쳐서
④ 가족 모임이 있어서
⑤ 부모님 생신이라서

## 09

대화를 듣고, 여자가 지불할 금액을 고르시오.

① $365　　② $405　　③ $450　　④ $500　　⑤ $550

## 10

대화를 듣고, 헌혈에 관해 두 사람이 언급하지 <u>않은</u> 것을 고르시오.

① 나이　　　　　② 체중　　　　　③ 혈액형
④ 맥박　　　　　⑤ 체온

## 11

Franklin 대학교 '행진 악단 오디션'에 관한 다음 내용을 듣고, 일치하지 <u>않는</u> 것을 고르시오.

① 접수 날짜는 9월 25일에서 30일까지이다.
② 기성곡과 창작곡 모두 연주 가능하다.
③ 최소 10분간 연주를 해야 한다.
④ 연주할 곡의 악보도 첨부해야 한다.
⑤ 악단의 정원은 100명이다.

## 12

다음 표를 보면서 대화를 듣고, 남자가 선택한 파티를 고르시오.

### Party Room Packages

| | Party Packages | Maximum Number of Children | Time (minutes) | Price | Number of Large Pizzas |
|---|---|---|---|---|---|
| ① | A | 15 | 100 | $220 | 2 |
| ② | B | 15 | 90 | $180 | 2 |
| ③ | C | 15 | 90 | $170 | 1 |
| ④ | D | 15 | 70 | $170 | 2 |
| ⑤ | E | 13 | 70 | $160 | 1 |

## 13

대화를 듣고, 여자의 마지막 말에 대한 남자의 응답으로 가장 적절한 것을 고르시오.

Man: _______________________________

① You should have picked your son up earlier.
② It might be too dark for the students to study.
③ I'll see what I can do about keeping the lights on.
④ Don't worry. I'll have the lights repaired tomorrow.
⑤ Raymond should be more careful, so he doesn't get hurt.

## 14

대화를 듣고, 남자의 마지막 말에 대한 여자의 응답으로 가장 적절한 것을 고르시오.

Woman: _______________________________

① How much does this purse cost?
② You shouldn't waste old products.
③ I don't know how to make a purse.
④ I would, but I'm not very good with my hands.
⑤ My art teacher enjoys woodworking as a hobby.

## 15

다음 상황 설명을 듣고, Stella가 Clara에게 할 말로 가장 적절한 것을 고르시오.

Stella: _______________________________

① You shouldn't tell Grandpa you don't like his gift.
② I think that we should go and visit Grandpa soon.
③ Please don't tell Grandpa that I gave you this shirt.
④ This T-shirt is too small. Please send it back to Grandpa.
⑤ Will you take Grandpa to the store to exchange this shirt?

[16-17] 다음을 듣고, 물음에 답하시오.

## 16

여자가 하는 말의 목적으로 가장 적절한 것은?

① 저축의 필요성을 강조하려고
② 상품 판매 전략을 안내하려고
③ 돈을 절약하는 방법을 알려주려고
④ 새로운 온라인 쇼핑몰을 홍보하려고
⑤ 합리적 소비의 중요성을 설명하려고

## 17

여자가 언급하지 <u>않은</u> 것은?

① 대중교통 이용　　　　　② 상점 평면도 의식
③ 온라인 쇼핑 이용　　　　④ 물 여과기 사용
⑤ 가계부 작성

## 01

M: Aren't you a huge Elvis fan? Did you see that there's a new Elvis exhibition coming to town?

W: I did! I just read about it this morning. I'm really excited.

M: Yeah, I am too. ___________ ___________ ___________ ___________ ___________ ___________ ___________ exactly?

W: (It's going to be at the state theater.)

## 02

W: Hi. I need to go to the art gallery downtown. How long will it take?

M: Well, ___________ ___________ ___________ ___________ ___________ the traffic isn't so congested. It should take about a half hour.

W: That's not bad. Do you know how much it'll cost to take a taxi?

M: (It should be less than $20.)

## 03

M: Hi everyone, and good morning. I'd like to talk to you all today about a really interesting study that has just come out from the University of Minnesota. The study ___________ ___________ ___________ ___________ ___________ happiness and creativity. The researchers took three groups of people and placed them in different scenarios. The first group was sent to an amusement park. The second group was sent to a theater to watch a horror movie, and the third group was sent to a pottery museum. After each group returned, the researchers ___________ ___________ ___________ ___________. As it turns out, the group of people who went to the amusement park did far better on the test than the other two groups. This result leads the researchers to believe that when we are happy, our brains can access more previously obtained knowledge and utilize this knowledge to create. Therefore, happy people are more creative because of their ability to ___________ ___________

___________ ___________ and, out of them, form something new.

## 04

W: Hey, look at Tommy's playroom. His parents really bought him a lot of toys, huh?

M: Yeah. And you should see his bedroom. ___________ ___________ ___________ ___________ ___________ in there.

W: I read an article about how fewer toys can help children develop different skills.

M: Really? I've never heard that before. I figured ___________ ___________ ___________, ___________ ___________.

W: Well, some toys are great for helping children grow and learn, but too many can actually be harmful.

M: Hmm… I wonder why that is.

W: The article said that too many toys can really ___________ ___________ ___________ ___________ ___________.

M: Oh? How so?

W: Kids with fewer toys have to use their imagination more than kids with more toys. They have to be more creative when they're playing.

M: ___________ ___________ ___________ ___________ ___________. I didn't really have too many toys growing up. I had to make my own toys or invent games instead.

## 05

W: Did you see the match between Liverpool and Manchester City on Saturday?

M: Yeah, I saw it.

W: What did you think of Liverpool?

M: They played great. They had a lot of ___________ ___________ ___________ ___________, but they ___________ ___________ ___________ ___________ ___________.

W: Yeah. It was a very close game. ___________ ___________ ___________ ___________ ___________ ___________.

M: Yep. Manchester City managed to hold them off. Their goalie did an amazing job.

W: I agree. So, what kind of strategy are you going to use against Liverpool when you play them next week?

M: We're going to have to ___________ ___________ ___________ to keep those shots away. We've also been reworking some of our offensive plays, so hopefully they'll produce some results.

W: We're excited to watch the match. Is there anything you'd like to say to the soccer fans watching this interview?

M: Thank you for all your support and for watching us grow in the league. We're looking forward to winning this next match.

W: We appreciate you taking the time to do this interview, Charlie. This is Susan Peters with BCC News signing off.

## 06

*[Cell phone rings.]*

M: Hey, Megan.

W: Sam? I was wondering if you could help me out with something.

M: Sure I can. What's up?

W: Well, I'm trying to sell my car and I thought using social media, like Twitter, would help get the word out.

M: Yeah, that's a great idea. I have a lot of followers on Twitter. You want me to __________ __________ __________ __________ __________ of your car?

W: That would be wonderful. The car is a Wasp 2015 Special Edition and has about 20,000 miles on it.

M: Does it have a sunroof?

W: Yes, the special edition comes standard with a sunroof.

M: I see. And are there any other features that are included with the special edition?

W: Yes, there are pinstripes along the sides.

M: Is that all?

W: It also has star-shaped wheels.

M: All right. Is there any damage to the car?

W: There's __________ __________ __________ __________ __________ __________ __________, but __________ __________ __________ __________ __________ my asking price. Other than that, I've taken good care of it and have all of the service records.

M: Okay, got it. I'll put the description up on Twitter right away.

W: Thanks a lot, Sam.

## 07

M: Hey, Amanda.

W: Hi, John. Come in, please.

M: I wanted to know if you needed any help deciding __________ __________ __________ __________ __________ __________ this year.

W: Yes, that would be great. I've narrowed it down to 15 candidates.

M: Okay. So what would you like me to do with these students?

W: I was hoping you could meet with them and just have a conversation with each one. I want you to find out __________ __________ __________ __________ __________ and what message they'd like to share with their classmates if they had the chance.

M: What should I do after meeting with them?

W: You and I will meet again, and I'd like for you to give me the details of what each student had to say along with your general impression of them.

M: All right, I can do that. But it may be difficult to meet with all of them because everyone's schedule is so different.

W: I think __________ __________ __________ __________ __________, John.

M: I appreciate your confidence in me. All right, __________ __________ __________.

W: Thanks, John. Let me know when you've finished so we can talk about it.

## 08

W: Hey Joe, where are you going?

M: __________ __________ __________ __________ the museum with my daughter. She's got an assignment about ancient Egypt that she has to do over summer vacation.

W: Homework over vacation, huh? That's rough. So, what else is she going to do this summer?

M: Well, we have her __________ __________ __________ __________ __________ at Lake Totanka. Why?

W: My boss gave me eight tickets to the Holidayland Amusement Park. I'm taking my family and was wondering if you wanted to join us.

M: That would be awesome. When are you going?

W: Next Sunday, the 20th.

M: Next Sunday, huh? Well, I'd love to, but we can't. We're going to my parents' house next weekend.

W: __________ __________ __________.

M: Yeah, we can't really reschedule because __________ __________ __________ __________ __________. It's going to be a pretty big party.

W: I see. Well, maybe some other time.

M: Sure. Thanks for the invitation.

## 09

M: How can I help you today?

W: I'm trying to decide on which monitor to buy.

M: Do you need one __________ __________ __________ __________ __________?

W: Well, what's the difference?

M: A professional monitor has an ultra-high-definition screen for areas like video editing and graphic design.

W: How about the one for general purposes? What are general purposes, anyway?

M: General purposes include emailing, word processing, and watching the occasional movie on your computer.

W: Okay. __________ __________ __________ graphic design or video production, but I'd still like a nice screen.

M: Of course. All of our monitors have really nice pictures, but you'll save some money by going with one of the general purpose monitors.

W: All right. How much are they?

M: The original price is $500, but __________ __________ __________ __________, so you'll get a 10% discount.

W: Wow, that's a good deal. Can I combine that with the coupon I got from your website?

M: Absolutely. That's why we have them.

W: That's great. So I get an additional __________ __________ __________ __________ __________ __________?

M: That's correct. I'll be right back with your monitor.

## 10

M: Hi. I've decided that I want to donate blood. This is my first time, though, so I'm a bit nervous.

W: That's okay. We'll __________ __________ __________ __________ __________. But I have a few questions I need to ask you. First, how old are you?

M: I'm 17. Is that going to be a problem?

W: Well, there is a limited age range we can allow, but it's between 16 and 69 years old, so you're fine.

M: Great. What other requirements do you have?

W: Men have to __________ __________ __________ __________ __________, and women have to be over 45 kilograms. It looks like you'll be fine there.

M: For sure. What else?

W: You should also have a steady resting pulse between 50 and 100 beats per minute. Also, __________ __________ __________ __________ __________?

M: I haven't. If I were sick, I couldn't give blood?

W: Right. You can't donate if your body temperature is above 37.5 degrees Celsius.

M: I see. I guess it's really important to be in good health __________ __________ __________ __________ __________.

## 11

M: Good afternoon, students. The Franklin College marching band tryouts are coming up, and we're

opening registration from the 10th to the 15th of September, __________ __________ __________ __________ __________ __________ from the 25th to the 30th. Any musician who would like to try out is welcome to play pieces that they've written or pieces published by others. We would like each contestant to play for at least 10 minutes. With your registration, you must also __________ __________ __________ __________ about your experience as well as the sheet music for the piece that you will play. Our professional judges will determine __________ __________ __________ __________ __________ __________. The band will be limited to 100 members. I hope that any of you who are interested in joining our award-winning marching band will register and try out. Thank you for listening.

## 12

W: Good afternoon, sir. What can I help you with?

M: Hi. I'm trying to __________ __________ __________ __________ my son's baseball team. Do you have any openings for Saturday afternoon?

W: Sure. It looks like we'll have something available at 2 p.m. We offer several different packages. Take a look at the brochure.

M: Well, there are 15 children on his team. Do all of the packages provide pizza?

W: They do. How long do you want to __________ __________ __________ __________? We have three options.

M: This is the last time they'll see each other, so I think a longer party would be nice.

W: You should probably book the room for either 90 or 100 minutes, then.

M: That sounds great, but I don't want to __________ __________ __________ __________ __________.

W: Well, there are two different packages that will __________ __________ __________. One includes two large pizzas and drinks. The other comes with only one large pizza and drinks.

M: I think we'll go with the one with two pizzas.

W: All right, sir. __________ __________ __________ __________ the party room at two o'clock on Saturday.

## 13

*[Telephone rings.]*

M: Good morning, St. Paul High School. This is Vice Principal Jones.

W: Hi, Mr. Jones. This is Grace Conroy, Raymond's mom. I'd like to talk to you for a minute about a problem on your campus.

M: Sure. What's the problem?

W: Well, I was picking my son up from the library last night and I noticed that it was __________ __________ __________ __________ __________ __________ .

M: I'm sorry, but we usually turn off all of the campus lights after nine. __________ __________ __________ __________ __________ __________ .

W: I understand. Conserving energy is important. But don't you think there's a safety concern here? Someone could fall and get hurt.

M: I didn't realize it was that big of an issue.

W: Also, lights might __________ __________ __________ __________ .

M: (I'll see what I can do about keeping the lights on.)

## 14

M: Hey Amelia, I made something for you.

W: A purse? I've been wanting a new one. You didn't really make it yourself, did you?

M: Well, I did most of the work. My art teacher helped me a little bit. __________ __________ __________ __________ __________ .

W: That's interesting. Did you __________ __________ __________ __________ __________ yourself?

M: Actually, I joined the Greenback Club at school. We learn how to repurpose old things.

W: That's really cool. What do you mean by "repurpose old things"?

M: We take old, unused things and use them to make new products—like this purse.

W: Sounds like an interesting club. This purse looks like it was hard to make.

M: Not really. In fact, most of our projects are really easy. In our next meeting, we're going to learn how to make drinking glasses __________ __________ __________ __________ .

W: Sounds really cool. How do you do that?

M: The instructor will show us when we meet. You should come along.

W: (I would, but I'm not very good with my hands.)

## 15

M: A package has just arrived for Stella. It's from her grandfather, who Stella doesn't get the opportunity to see very often. After opening the package and reading the very touching note, Stella is delighted to see that her grandfather has sent her a Taylor Swift T-shirt. However, after __________ __________ __________ , Stella realizes that the shirt is a bit too small for her. She considers sending it back to her grandfather and asking him to __________ __________ __________ __________ __________ __________ . However, after some deliberation, she realizes that it wouldn't be easy for her grandfather to exchange the shirt and send her another. Instead, she __________ __________ __________ __________ __________ __________ __________ , Clara. Clara also loves Taylor Swift and __________ __________ __________ __________ __________ , but Stella doesn't want her grandfather to know that she gave it to her sister. In this situation, what would Stella most likely say to Clara?

Stella: (Please don't tell Grandpa that I gave you this shirt.)

## 16-17

W: Good evening, everyone. My name is Mary Anne Baker, and I work for Baker Financial. I'd like to talk to you today about ways you can save money in your day-to-day life. First of all, transportation can be expensive. If you __________ __________ __________ __________ __________ taking a taxi to work each day, you can save a lot of money by taking the bus or subway. Try to change your sleeping pattern so that you wake up earlier. Secondly, the floor plans of stores are set up to maximize what you buy. Have you ever wondered why the everyday goods that you need most, such as eggs and milk, are located in the back of the store? It's so that you walk through the store and see all of the other products on sale. Be conscious of these strategies and resist impulse purchases. Third, __________ __________ __________ __________ __________ . Shopping online can save you money, as you can compare prices very easily and find the best deals. Finally, try to __________ __________ __________ __________ . Instead of spending a dollar or two on water every day, invest in a water filter and fill a bottle before you leave the house. If you follow these simple tips, I'm sure you'll save money and live a more fulfilling life. Thanks for listening.

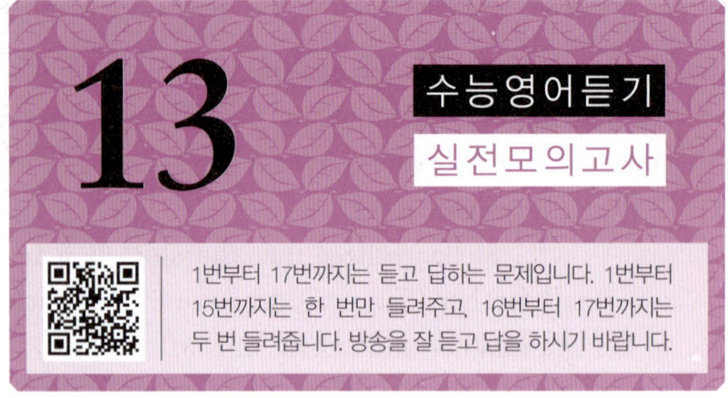


## 01

대화를 듣고, 여자의 마지막 말에 대한 남자의 응답으로 가장 적절한 것을 고르시오.

① The mattress is very stiff and uncomfortable.
② Actually, we don't have any rooms available.
③ I can't remember your room number.
④ I'd like to be connected to room 305.
⑤ Please leave your things with us.

## 02

대화를 듣고, 남자의 마지막 말에 대한 여자의 응답으로 가장 적절한 것을 고르시오.

① When are you going to leave?
② That's right. The festival is on Saturday.
③ Thanks a lot. I'm really excited about it.
④ We need to hurry. The party starts in 10 minutes.
⑤ That's a great idea. I think he'll appreciate the surprise.

## 03

다음을 듣고, 남자가 하는 말의 목적으로 가장 적절한 것을 고르시오.

① 의사결정에 필요한 지식을 소개하려고
② 학생들이 학교에서 하는 활동들을 알리려고
③ 전문 분야의 지식을 공유하도록 요청하려고
④ 경제적으로 힘든 학생들을 돕도록 부탁하려고
⑤ 경험을 통한 배경지식의 중요성을 강조하려고

## 04

대화를 듣고, 두 사람이 하는 말의 주제로 가장 적절한 것을 고르시오.

① 식품 안전 교육의 중요성
② 좋은 육류를 선택하는 기준
③ 영양성분 표시 라벨을 보는 법
④ 건강한 다이어트 식단 짜는 방법
⑤ 식료품 영양성분 표시제의 필요성

## 05

대화를 듣고, 두 사람의 관계를 가장 잘 나타낸 것을 고르시오.

① 간호사 — 환자 보호자    ② 학부모 — 체육 교사
③ 학생 — 보건 교사    ④ 구직자 — 면접관
⑤ 의사 — 환자

## 06

대화를 듣고, 그림에서 대화의 내용과 일치하지 <u>않는</u> 것을 고르시오.

## 07

대화를 듣고, 여자가 남자를 위해 할 일로 가장 적절한 것을 고르시오.

① 플래시 드라이브 사용법 알려주기
② 스마트폰으로 파일 전송해 주기
③ 더 좋은 제품 추천해주기
④ 사이트 주소 알려주기
⑤ 물건 대신 주문하기

## 08

대화를 듣고, 여자가 독서 클럽 모임에 참석할 수 <u>없는</u> 이유를 고르시오.

① 책을 잃어버려서
② 남편을 도와주어야 해서
③ 책을 다 읽고 갈 수 없어서
④ 중요한 발표를 준비해야 해서
⑤ 아들의 영어 선생님과 만나야 해서

## 09

대화를 듣고, 여자가 지불할 금액을 고르시오.

① $108  ② $117  ③ $130  ④ $135  ⑤ $150

## 10

대화를 듣고, Pear Computers 인턴 프로그램에 관해 두 사람이 언급하지 <u>않은</u> 것을 고르시오.

① 근무 장소  ② 지원 기한  ③ 지원 자격
④ 근무 기간  ⑤ 경비 지급

## 11

Environmental Edge Photography Contest에 관한 다음 내용을 듣고, 일치하지 <u>않는</u> 것을 고르시오.

① 전국의 학생들이 참여할 수 있다.
② 컬러 또는 흑백사진으로 제출 가능하다.
③ 이메일로 제출한 출품사진은 허용되지 않는다.
④ 우승자는 제출 마감일로부터 약 2주 후 발표된다.
⑤ 세 편의 우수사진을 선정하여 시상한다.

## 12

다음 표를 보면서 대화를 듣고, 두 사람이 살 냉장고를 고르시오.

**Refrigerators on Sale**

|   | Model | Price | Storage (liters) | Type | Warranty (years) |
|---|---|---|---|---|---|
| ① | A | $1,300 | 1,000 | Four-door | 10 |
| ② | B | $1,000 | 950 | Four-door | 5 |
| ③ | C | $900 | 800 | Four-door | 10 |
| ④ | D | $800 | 800 | Two-door | 10 |
| ⑤ | E | $600 | 650 | Two-door | 5 |

## 13

대화를 듣고, 여자의 마지막 말에 대한 남자의 응답으로 가장 적절한 것을 고르시오.

Man: _______________________________

① Sure. I'd love to read your version.
② Don't consider the theme. Focus on content.
③ I think you'll really enjoy reading the original.
④ I'm going to need the author's permission first.
⑤ No. After you finish, you should write a review.

## 14

대화를 듣고, 남자의 마지막 말에 대한 여자의 응답으로 가장 적절한 것을 고르시오.

Woman: _______________________________

① I think I should go see a doctor.
② We should plant some bamboo outside.
③ I'll go to the florist and buy some today.
④ You have to water the bamboo every day.
⑤ You should drink eight cups of water daily.

## 15

다음 상황 설명을 듣고, Paul이 담당자에게 할 말로 가장 적절한 것을 고르시오.

Paul: _______________________________

① The problem is fixed. Thanks for all of your help.
② Thank you, but I already have an Internet provider.
③ Please send someone over to fix my Internet as soon as possible.
④ I'd like to know how I can become a customer service representative.
⑤ I'm sorry about your problem. We will send someone over to look at it.

[16-17] 다음을 듣고, 물음에 답하시오.

## 16

남자가 하는 말의 주제로 가장 적절한 것은?

① Parental roles in child health care
② Long-lasting impacts of childhood habits
③ Advantages of playing outside for children
④ Importance of close parent-child relationships
⑤ Activities to develop children's willingness to take risks

## 17

비타민 D와 관련된 질병으로 언급되지 <u>않은</u> 것은?

① 우울증  ② 심장병  ③ 당뇨병
④ 피부병  ⑤ 비만

## 01

W: Good morning, sir. How can I help you?

M: Well, __________ __________ __________ __________ __________ __________ __________ my room.

W: All right. So what exactly is the problem?

M: (The mattress is very stiff and uncomfortable.)

## 02

M: Hey, Julia. Did you hear the news? Owen is __________ __________ __________ Hong Kong next week.

W: I heard. I'm really excited to hear about his time there.

M: Let's go and meet him at the airport when he arrives.

W: (That's a great idea. I think he'll appreciate the surprise.)

## 03

M: Hi, everyone! Thank you all so much for continuing to show interest in our school. One of the things we really focus on is preparing and encouraging your children __________ __________ __________ __________ __________ __________ __________.

So, now I want to introduce you all to one of our meaningful new programs. I'm sure most of you have heard the saying, "Knowledge is power." However, what's the point of having knowledge if it cannot be shared? Some of you here can __________ __________ __________. We want to encourage you to __________ __________ __________ __________ __________ __________ __________ __________. If you would like to participate and share with us, you can come to school next Wednesday. Sharing just a little of what you know can make a big difference in our students' lives.

## 04

W: I thought __________ DICTATION __________ __________ __________, Roy.

M: I am. Why do you ask?

W: Well, you just ordered that chicken salad with cheese and ranch dressing. If you're on a diet, the Asian salad would be a better choice.

M: Really? What's the difference?

W: Look at the nutritional information.

M: Ah, I see. The chicken salad has a lot more calories than the Asian salad. In fact, it has as many calories as a cheeseburger combo.

W: Right. It might seem healthy because it's a salad, but it's actually just as bad for you as a greasy sandwich.

M: I see. It's good that they have the information available for me to see. __________ __________ __________ __________ __________ on all food products. That way we can make better, healthier choices.

W: I agree. In some countries, __________ __________ __________ __________ on all food and drinks.

M: Really? I had no idea.

W: Yeah. For example, in the U.S., they have to include detailed information on meat. They even have to include the percentage of fat.

M: I wish our country would adopt the same policy. It'd make it easier for people like me to eat healthy.

W: Right. __________ __________ __________ __________ __________ __________ __________ __________ to see which one contained more fat, calories, or sodium.

## 05

M: Mrs. Tomlin, you asked to speak with me?

W: Yes, Alex. Come on in and have a seat. I just heard you had your appendix removed.

M: __________ __________ __________ __________ a couple of weeks ago. It was very sudden.

W: They are usually quite sudden. Are you feeling okay now?

M: I feel much better. It was a little scary when it happened, though.

W: Did you tell your P.E. teacher about it?

M: Yeah. He suggested __________ __________ __________ __________ for a week or two.

W: Are there any other problems you're dealing with?

M: Not really. I'm just nervous about my stomach area ever since the operation.

W: That's understandable. I think __________ __________ __________ __________ __________, but in the meantime just take it easy and relax.

M: Thanks for the advice. I'll definitely be doing more studying and less playing for the time being.

W: Well, perhaps that's a good thing. You'll be back outside playing in no time. Don't worry.

M: I appreciate your kindness. I should get back to class now.

## 06

M: Hey Katie, didn't you go to the Soccer Hall of Fame last weekend?

W: I did. Check out this picture that I took there.

M: Wow! ___________ ___________ ___________ ___________. Those posters on the wall are interesting. Why is the guy on the left wearing gloves and a different uniform?

W: Well, the goalkeeper always wears a different uniform so ___________ ___________ ___________ ___________ ___________ ___________ the other players.

M: Who's the player in the poster next to him? He looks very serious.

W: That's the legendary CF, or center forward, Conor James.

M: I see. Who is that guy taking a selfie with his smartphone?

W: That's my dad. He was really excited to ___________ ___________ ___________ ___________ ___________. Behind him, there's a statue of a famous coach.

M: That's cool. I guess that must be your brother and mom on the right.

W: You're right. My little brother had to use the restroom. He really didn't enjoy the trip.

M: Well, it seems like your father was having a great time, at least.

## 07

W: Hey Aaron, do you have ___________ ___________ ___________ ___________ ___________?

M: I do. If you have a flash drive handy, I can transfer them over to it.

W: I just bought one. Here you go.

M: Is this really a flash drive? It's a bit big, don't you think?

W: Yeah, it's new. On one end it has a regular USB plug, and on the other end it has a micro USB plug.

M: That's awesome. I guess that way you can ___________ ___________ ___________ ___________ quite easily.

W: That's right. This is the first time I've used it, though.

M: It seems like it works great. It transferred all of the files very quickly. Is there anything else you need for the presentation?

W: I have everything we need. I think we'll be ready for tomorrow.

M: All right. Oh, by the way, where did you get that flash drive? I think I want to pick one up for myself.

W: I bought it online. I'll ___________ ___________ ___________ ___________ ___________ for you.

M: That'd be great. Thanks.

## 08

M: Hey Susan, the book club meeting is tomorrow. Have you finished the book?

W: I haven't. What about you?

M: I finished it over the weekend. I couldn't put it down. It was so ___________ ___________ ___________. I really think you're going to enjoy the ending.

W: I don't think ___________ ___________ ___________ ___________ ___________ ___________ ___________ ___________. I think I left it on the train yesterday.

M: You can borrow my book if you'd like.

W: That'd be great. The meeting is at 8 tomorrow, right?

M: No, it actually starts at 6 this week.

W: Really? I'm not going ___________ ___________ ___________ ___________ ___________ ___________, then.

M: Why not? It's a pretty short book. I think you'll be able to finish it by then.

W: It's not that. I have a meeting with my son's English teacher tomorrow.

M: Can't your husband go?

W: He would, but ___________ ___________ ___________ ___________ ___________ all week. He has an important presentation on Friday.

M: I see. Well, I'll tell everyone you said hello.

W: Thanks.

## 09

M: Welcome to the gift shop. ___________ ___________ ___________ ___________ ___________ ___________.

W: I did. What an amazing finish!

M: It sure was. What can I do for you today?

W: ___________ ___________ ___________ ___________ ___________ ___________.

M: We have all kinds of souvenirs, such as t-shirts, jerseys, hats, and bumper stickers.

W: How much for a jersey?

M: Well, the adult jerseys are $30 and the child-sized jerseys are $25.

W: All right. I guess ___________ ___________ ___________ ___________ ___________ and two for children, please.

M: Sure. Is that all?

W: I think I'd like some hats as well. How much do they run?

M: They're $20 apiece.

W: Okay. I'll take two hats.

M: Great. If you still have your ticket stub, you can ___________ ___________ ___________ ___________ ___________ ___________ .

W: Sure, it's right here.

M: So, we have two adult jerseys, two child jerseys, and two hats with a 10% discount off your total.

W: That's right. Here's my card.

## 10

W: Hey, did you see that they opened registration for the summer internship program at Pear Computers?

M: Really? I didn't know they were looking for interns.

W: Yeah. I thought that you'd be interested in it since you want to study computer science. It'd be a great opportunity for you.

M: Definitely. Do you know ___________ ___________ ___________ ___________ ___________ ?

W: You'll be working in the labs at their company, so you'll have to spend the summer in California.

M: That sounds awesome. Do you think they'll accept me?

W: I think so. You're already quite ___________ ___________ ___________ ___________ ___________ , so you have the right qualifications.

M: Great! How long is the internship for?

W: They said that it's a two-month program.

M: Perfect. ___________ ___________ ___________ ___________ ___________ this internship, right?

W: Right. You'll also have to ___________ ___________ ___________ ___________ ___________ and travel costs.

M: Well, that is a drawback. But I think I'm interested anyway. I'm going to register as soon as I get home.

## 11

W: Good morning, students. I'd like to take some time to talk about the Environmental Edge Photography Contest. ___________ ___________ ___________ ___________ ___________ ___________ , and students around the country are encouraged to participate. The theme of this year's contest is environmental awareness. Photo entries should ___________ ___________ ___________ ___________ highlight environmental issues. ___________ ___________ ___________ ___________ ___________ ___________ , and in landscape orientation. All entries should be submitted to Mr. Lopez before May 15th. ___________ ___________ ___________ ___________ ___________ ___________ . Environmental Edge will announce the winners of the contest on June 1st. The top three photos in the country will receive prizes. We know there is plenty of talent in our school, and we encourage you to participate. You can find more information ___________ ___________ ___________ ___________ . Thank you for listening.

## 12

M: Look at this flyer, honey. There's a big sale on refrigerators this week.

W: Really? That's great, because we need to get a new one.

M: The flyer shows several models. How much do you think we should spend?

W: Well, I don't want to ___________ ___________ ___________ ___________ ___________ ___________ .

M: All right. Then how about these models?

W: Hmm.... I'd like one with at least 700 liters of storage.

M: I agree. ___________ ___________ ___________ ___________ ___________ would be good. That way all of our food would fit in easily. Should we get one with two doors or four?

W: I don't like two-door models. I think it's easier to ___________ ___________ in a four-door refrigerator.

M: Then there are two models we can choose from.

W: Oh, I think a warranty is pretty important, especially for appliances.

M: Okay. Then let's ___________ ___________ ___________ ___________ ___________ ___________ ___________ .

W: Great!

## 13

M: Rachel, did you finish watching *The Babbit*?

W: Yeah, Dad, I did. Why did you want me to watch it?

M: Didn't you like it?

W: It was okay. It had too much of a happy Hollywood ending for me, though.

M: It's quite different from the book, huh?

W: Yeah. The book had such a ___________ ___________ ___________ ___________ . I thought that the movie would be the same.

M: I thought so, too. So, did you like the movie or the book better?

W: I really __________ __________ __________ __________ __________ __________. The original story was too dark, and the movie was so unrealistic and happy.

M: Well, what would make you like the story more?

W: I guess I'd like it to be a happier story throughout but not so unrealistic.

M: I think you should __________ __________ __________ __________, then.

W: What do you mean? You want me to __________ __________ __________?

M: (Sure. I'd love to read your version.)

## 14

W: Hey, Lenny. What's up?

M: Oh, hey Sam. Are you okay? You look pretty tired.

W: I'm fine, but I've been having a hard time sleeping the past couple of weeks. The weather makes the air in my room too dry.

M: I see. Well, you could get a humidifier. I also heard that keeping plants in your room can __________ __________ __________ __________ __________.

W: I'm pretty irresponsible, so I'll probably forget to water them and __________ __________ __________ __________.

M: Well, there are some plants that don't need that much attention. You could get some of those.

W: Really? Like what?

M: You can put bamboo in a jar of water and __________ __________ __________ __________.

W: That seems easy enough.

M: Yeah. I have some bamboo plants in my room and I only have to water them when the jar is empty, which is about once a month.

W: I like the way bamboo looks, too.

M: I think bamboo would make __________ __________ __________ __________ __________. You should try it.

W: (I'll go to the florist and buy some today.)

## 15

M: Paul is working on an important assignment for his history class. However, while he's researching on his computer, the Internet goes out. He calls his Internet provider's customer service line to report the problem. He __________ __________ __________ __________ as it is late and there are no customer service representatives available. After a 15-minute wait, __________ __________ __________ __________ __________ __________ and tells Paul that he should try unplugging his modem and plugging it back in. He follows the representative's instructions, but it doesn't fix the problem. He __________ __________ __________ get his Internet fixed because his assignment is due tomorrow. In this situation, what would Paul most likely say to the customer service representative?

Paul: (Please send someone over to fix my Internet as soon as possible.)

## 16-17

M: Good afternoon, parents. I'd like to welcome you today to my seminar on children's health. My name is Dr. Jeffrey Day, and I've been a pediatrician for almost 30 years. Let's talk about children between the ages of 3 and 12. This age range is critical in the development of children. This is the timeframe within which __________ __________ __________ __________, become more physical, develop problem-solving skills, and __________ __________ __________ that will follow them for the rest of their lives. This is why I recommend that every parent urge their children to __________ __________ __________ __________ __________ __________. There are amazing benefits to playing outside. Children will have the chance to meet new friends and create lasting childhood relationships. They'll also build a sense of confidence by taking risks and playing outdoor games. Now, playing outside isn't always safe, but creating a willingness in a child to take risks and engage themselves in risky behaviors gives the child an opportunity to learn new skills and __________ __________ __________ __________. Lastly, playing outdoors provides children with vitamin D, which is essential to healthy development. This vitamin is known to help children battle depression, heart disease, diabetes, and obesity. So, please, I urge you parents to get your children outside. It'll be beneficial for you as well.

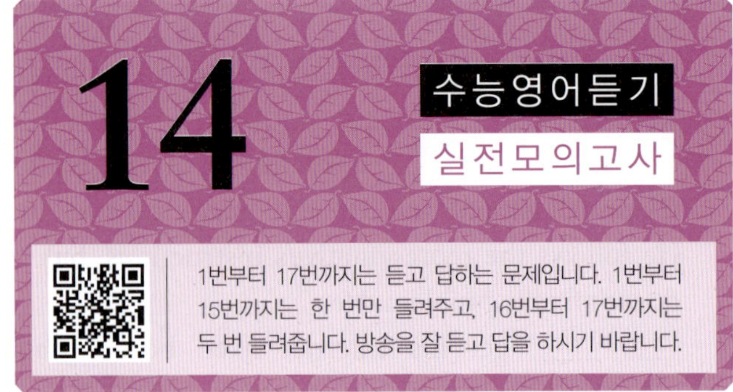


## 01

대화를 듣고, 남자의 마지막 말에 대한 여자의 응답으로 가장 적절한 것을 고르시오.

① I'll call the electric company and ask about the bill.
② I'll ask the repairman to look at our air conditioner.
③ Sure. Turn on the air conditioner when it's hot inside.
④ You shouldn't unplug appliances when you're using them.
⑤ Right. I guess we should turn it off when we leave the house.

## 02

대화를 듣고, 여자의 마지막 말에 대한 남자의 응답으로 가장 적절한 것을 고르시오.

① I agree. Let's order the book online.
② I know. That's why the book is easy to read.
③ Let's go to the library to check out the book.
④ I'll lend you my DVD. It's very interesting.
⑤ No. Once I finish reading this book, I'll watch the movie.

## 03

다음을 듣고, 여자가 하는 말의 주제로 가장 적절한 것을 고르시오.

① 인간관계 생성과 유지의 중요성
② 인간관계가 성공에 미치는 영향
③ 인간관계에 유사성이 미치는 영향
④ 인간관계에서 갈등을 해결하는 방법
⑤ 인종과 성별을 초월한 관계 형성의 필요성

## 04

대화를 듣고, 남자의 의견으로 가장 적절한 것을 고르시오.

① 출입문을 회전문으로 바꿔야 한다.
② 입구 쪽에 추가 난방기를 설치해야 한다.
③ 직원들에게 더 따뜻한 옷을 제공해야 한다.
④ 프런트 데스크에서 객실 온도를 체크해야 한다.
⑤ 에너지를 절약하기 위해 난방을 약하게 해야 한다.

## 05

대화를 듣고, 두 사람이 대화하고 있는 장소로 가장 적절한 곳을 고르시오.

① hospital
② restaurant
③ classroom
④ TV studio
⑤ grocery store

## 06

대화를 듣고, 그림에서 대화의 내용과 일치하지 <u>않는</u> 것을 고르시오.

## 07

대화를 듣고, 여자가 남자를 위해 할 일로 가장 적절한 것을 고르시오.

① 새 셔츠 사다 주기
② 야구경기 보러 오기
③ 친구에게 부탁해 주기
④ 학교로 셔츠 가져다 주기
⑤ 경기장에 아빠 모시고 오기

## 08

대화를 듣고, 남자가 화가 난 이유를 고르시오.

① 수집한 자료를 분실해서
② 발표 수업을 잘하지 못해서
③ 조원들이 모임에 나오지 않아서
④ 마음에 드는 배역을 맡지 못해서
⑤ 원하는 친구와 팀을 이루지 못해서

## 09

대화를 듣고, 여자가 지불할 금액을 고르시오.

① $70　　② $80　　③ $90　　④ $100　　⑤ $110

## 10

대화를 듣고, 인턴십 프로그램에 관해 두 사람이 언급하지 <u>않은</u> 것을 고르시오.

① 출시된 게임　　　　　② 모집 인원
③ 모집 분야　　　　　④ 남자의 지원 분야
⑤ 지원 자격

## 11

Campus tour에 관한 다음 내용을 듣고, 일치하지 <u>않는</u> 것을 고르시오.

① 학교 학생들이 안내한다.
② 학교 생활에 대해 알려준다.
③ 투어의 첫 부분은 1시에 시작한다.
④ 점심은 학교 식당에서 먹는다.
⑤ 학생회의 연극이 진행된다.

## 12

다음 표를 보면서 대화를 듣고, 여자가 선택할 프로그램을 고르시오.

**Sustainable Living Programs**

| | Program | Organic Gardening (in groups) | Vegan Cooking (individually) | Lunch (provided) | Price |
|---|---|---|---|---|---|
| ① | A | Yes | Yes | Yes | $50 |
| ② | B | Yes | Yes | No | $40 |
| ③ | C | Yes | No | Yes | $30 |
| ④ | D | No | Yes | Yes | $30 |
| ⑤ | E | Yes | No | No | $25 |

## 13

대화를 듣고, 여자의 마지막 말에 대한 남자의 응답으로 가장 적절한 것을 고르시오.

Man: _______________________________

① I'm not really sure why you need me to email it.
② No problem. I'll send the file as soon as it's ready.
③ You're welcome. I'll be sure to write your letter tonight.
④ I'm really sorry, but I think I've misplaced the document.
⑤ Sure. My email address is gwilson@northwestacademy.edu.

## 14

대화를 듣고, 남자의 마지막 말에 대한 여자의 응답으로 가장 적절한 것을 고르시오.

Woman: _______________________________

① Of course. We need all the help we can get.
② We can find different volunteer work if you want.
③ You can teach me how to get along with children.
④ It's important to the children that you sing with them.
⑤ Playing games and singing helps them be more social.

## 15

다음 상황 설명을 듣고, Sarah가 Ryan에게 할 말로 가장 적절한 것을 고르시오.

Sarah: _______________________________

① It's not easy to find a job in journalism these days.
② I thought it was your dream to work at Hush-Hush.
③ You shouldn't have accepted Courier Crossing's offer.
④ I don't do this work for the money. I do it because I really like it.
⑤ Good choice. Some things in life are more important than money.

[16-17] 다음을 듣고, 물음에 답하시오.

## 16

남자가 하는 말의 목적으로 가장 적절한 것은?

① to advertise for community businesses
② to promote the sale of Parents' Day kits
③ to introduce parents to members of the faculty
④ to inform parents of upcoming university events
⑤ to recruit volunteers to sell welcome kits to parents

## 17

쿠폰이 있는 곳으로 언급되지 <u>않은</u> 것은?

① 카페　　　　② 제과점　　　　③ 볼링장
④ 식당　　　　⑤ 수영장

# 14 DICTATION

녹음을 다시 한 번 듣고, 빈칸에 알맞은 말을 쓰시오.

## 01

M: Whoa! Look at our power bill for this month. It's almost $500.

W: Wow! That's far too expensive. I'll call the electric company. There must be some mistake.

M: I doubt they made a mistake. You know, we've been __________ __________ __________ __________ a lot this summer.

W: (Right. I guess we should turn it off when we leave the house.)

## 02

W: What are you doing, Liam? __________ __________ __________ __________ __________ __________ __________ .

M: I'm reading Yann Martel's *Life of Pi*. It is so interesting that I can't stop reading.

W: Did you see the movie first? It's a great movie.

M: (No. Once I finish reading this book, I'll watch the movie.)

## 03

W: Good morning, class. Last time, we discussed how important it is for us to create and __________ __________ and how that affects our overall success. In today's class, we'll talk about the truth in the old saying, "Birds of a feather flock together." As humans, we tend to __________ __________ __________ __________ __________ . Most people make friends with people who are of the same age, race, or gender. Take your classmates, for example. You're much __________ __________ __________ __________ __________ with those classmates that you share certain characteristics with. Some of these characteristics might include your interests or hobbies. Now, of course these rules aren't across the board. Some people date or marry __________ __________ __________ __________ . However, these relationships typically form out of shared values or education.

## 04

M: Sarah, what's the matter? Are you all right?

W: __________ __________ __________ __________ and a stuffy nose. I think I'm sick.

M: You should wear some warmer clothes.

W: You're right, I should. It gets quite cold in here.

M: I can relate. I've worked at a front desk before. I always hated the cold.

W: Yeah, the cold air always follows people in as they enter the building.

M: Perhaps if we __________ __________ __________ , we can stop the cold from entering.

W: I don't think we need a new door. Wouldn't it __________ __________ __________ to just buy another heater?

M: No, a new door would be more effective. If we __________ __________ __________ __________ system, it'll greatly reduce the amount of cold air that enters the building.

W: Really? How does that work?

M: __________ __________ __________ __________ in the door and can't get in because the door is spinning.

W: That sounds great! I hope it works.

## 05

M: Welcome back, Dr. Delgado.

W: Thank you for having me. It's a pleasure to be here.

M: Great. Let's begin our program. First, I'd like you to give the audience a quick health tip.

W: Sure. You know, everyone is always on the go these days. That can be bad for your health.

M: Right. So what can someone who's always on the go do __________ __________ __________ ?

W: A good breakfast is the key to health. Breakfast is skipped more than any other meal. No one has time to make it. But with just a couple of basic ingredients, __________ __________ __________ __________ __________ __________ .

M: What sort of ingredients are we talking about?

W: Protein shakes are a great way to get your day started. All you need is protein powder and milk.

M: What about fruit or other ingredients?

W: Good thinking. To __________ __________ __________ __________ __________ __________ , you can add fruits such as bananas or strawberries. I like to add spinach to mine __________ __________ __________ __________ .

M: Spinach in a shake, huh? That doesn't sound very tasty. I guess the nutrition is the point, right? Thank you, Dr. Delgado. We'll be back after the commercial break.

## 06

W: Hey Ryan, I just finished up the poster for the FPS World Championship. What do you think?

M: ___________ ___________ ___________ ___________! I like what you did with the title at the top. It looks like a banner.

W: Thanks. I also put the time and date on the left side.

M: I see that. Did we get a confirmation on that date and time?

W: We did. The gaming association confirmed it this morning.

M: Awesome. That gives us ___________ ___________ ___________ ___________ ___________. I see that you left the box for the place blank.

W: Yeah. We're still ___________ ___________ ___________ ___________ ___________ to have the event at the stadium, so it hasn't exactly been confirmed yet. How about the picture of you and Jason on the right?

M: Not my best picture, but I like how you put it together.

W: (laughs)

M: I also like the picture of the mascot, "Dinosaur", at the bottom. What's that it's saying?

W: It says, "___________ ___________ ___________ ___________!"

## 07

*[Telephone rings.]*

W: Hello?

M: Hey, Mom. Thank goodness you're home. I need your help with something.

W: What's the matter, Andrew?

M: I'm sure ___________ ___________ we have a big baseball game tonight?

W: Of course. Your father and I had ___________ ___________ ___________ ___________ ___________ ___________.

M: That's great, but I forgot my jersey at the house this morning.

W: Oh, Andrew. Why are you so forgetful? Do you have time to come get it after school?

M: I don't. We have a pre-game dinner after classes, and then we go straight to the field.

W: Is there anyone you know who can ___________ ___________ ___________ ___________ and pick it up for you?

M: Not that I know of. Everyone is pretty busy after school on Fridays. Would you please ___________ ___________ ___________ ___________ ___________ for me?

W: Yes, I suppose I can do that.

M: Thank you so much, Mom.

W: No problem, honey. See you soon.

## 08

W: Daniel, you look so angry. What happened?

M: Never mind. ___________ ___________ ___________ ___________. I just feel tired.

W: Come on. Tell me ___________ ___________ ___________ and you'll feel better.

M: Well, Jeremy, Jane, Selena, and I were scheduled to meet to prepare for our presentation for English class this morning.

W: Oh, right. My group met yesterday to assign members their parts for the presentation.

M: We were also planning to divide up our presentation and start collecting materials for it.

W: So, ___________ ___________ ___________ ___________ ___________?

M: Jeremy and Selena didn't show up.

W: Well, maybe they had a good reason.

M: Nope. They both said they just forgot about it. I'm so upset. How could they be so irresponsible?

W: Well, calm down. You still have lots of time to prepare for the presentation. I'm sure they're sorry.

M: Well, I'm not so sure. Anyway, I'm going to go home and rest for a while.

## 09

*[Telephone rings.]*

M: Walker Mountain Campgrounds. What can I do for you today?

W: Hi. My family is looking to come to your campground for our vacation next month. ___________ ___________ ___________ ___________?

M: It's $35, and that includes one vehicle spot.

W: Well, we're going to ___________ ___________ ___________ ___________.

M: In that case, it'll be an additional $10 per night.

W: All right. I'd like to make a reservation for two nights, the 14th and 15th of August. My name is Minnie Martin.

M: All right, Mrs. Martin. Is there anything else I can do for you?

W: Oh, do you provide water and electricity at your campsites?

M: We do. However, __________ __________ __________ __________ water and electricity. Campsites with water hookups are an additional $5 per night, and ones with electricity are an additional $10 per night.

W: Okay. I don't think we'll need the water, but we'll __________ __________ __________ __________, please.

M: All right, two nights at a two-car campsite with electricity. I've made your reservation. We'll see you next month.

## 10

W: Hey Johnny, did you get my email?

M: I haven't checked it yet. What was it about?

W: There's a __________ __________ __________ at RD Games.

M: That's cool. They put out some great games.

W: That's right. They released *Counterclockwise* and *Super Doctor Brothers*.

M: Yeah, I love those games.

W: They're great. Anyway, they __________ __________ __________ __________ __________ __________, character design, and beta testing.

M: Awesome! I know a bit about programming, but I'd love to __________ __________ __________ __________. What kind of qualifications are they looking for?

W: Well, they're just looking for someone who has taken a couple of game design classes and has a love for creating fun and interesting games.

M: I've taken a few game design classes and, as you know, I really love gaming.

W: I think they'll take you on. You're quite popular around the gaming community.

M: I'll go apply right away. I appreciate you telling me about this.

## 11

W: Hello, everyone. I'm Mrs. Jones, the vice principal here at Williams Academy, and I'd like to welcome you to our prestigious school. Today, we're going

to give potential students the chance to visit our campus and __________ __________ __________.
Your guides are going to be students from the school who are going to __________ __________ __________ __________-__________ __________ of life at our establishment. They will also detail all of our educational programs and give you some history of the campus. The first part of the tour __________ __________ __________ __________. I'll meet you all at noon in our school's cafeteria for lunch. Then at one o'clock, we'll head to the auditorium, where our student council will __________ __________ __________. That will be followed by a short presentation. After the presentation, the student council will take any questions you might have about our school. I really hope you enjoy your day, and we thank you for coming.

## 12

M: Hey Brittney, didn't you say you __________ __________ __________ __________ __________ this year?

W: I am. I think I'm going to become a vegan. Why?

M: Well, I found this flyer for some classes they're offering at the community college this summer. You should take one.

W: Really? That'd be great. *[Pause]* The organic gardening classes seem interesting.

M: Well, do you also want to learn how to cook vegan food?

W: That does sound cool. I get to __________ __________ __________ __________ __________ in class, right?

M: That's right. You can also bring what you cook back home for me to try.

W: Awesome. I'll take that class as well, then.

M: Great. Then we're down to two programs you can take. Do you want them to provide you with lunch?

W: I don't really think that'll be necessary, since I'll be cooking there. I can eat the food I cook, right? It's also $10 cheaper.

M: All right. I think we found the perfect program for you.

## 13

W: Hi, Mr. Wilson.

M: Hey, Margaret. What's up?

W: Not a whole lot. I was just wondering if you finished up my __________ __________ __________.
I need to turn in my university application __________ __________ __________ __________ __________ __________.

M: Right. I finished it up on Monday. It must be somewhere around here. Give me a minute.

W: Take your time.

M: *[Pause]* Oh, here it is. I spent a lot of time writing it. You were one of my favorite students, you know.

W: Thanks. It looks great, Mr. Wilson. Is there any way I can get the file?

M: Absolutely. Do you need it for backup or something?

W: Well, all of the university applications __________ __________ __________ these days. So I have to email it to them.

M: I can scan it so that you have a version with my signature.

W: That sounds great. Could you __________ __________ __________ __________ after you've scanned it?

M: Sure. Just write down your email address on this sheet of scrap paper.

W: All right. Thank you for all your help, Mr. Wilson.

M: (No problem. I'll send the file as soon as it's ready.)

## 14

M: Hey, Hailey. __________ __________ __________ __________ __________ today?

W: I had a great time. I played games and sang songs with all the children.

M: That's nice. But I really don't know how you can __________ __________ __________ __________ __________.

W: It's easy, really. Children are a lot of fun to be around.

M: I'd really love to __________ __________ __________ __________, but I don't know if I should.

W: Why not?

M: Well, I don't think that children like me.

W: Why do you think so? You're usually so kind and energetic.

M: I'm not a very good singer, and I don't think I __________ __________ to play games with them. __________ __________ __________ __________ __________ __________ is make their lunch.

W: Well, I think you can volunteer to do that. Let's go together next time.

M: Do you really think I can be of help?

W: (Of course. We need all the help we can get.)

## 15

M: Ryan, a journalism student at Uptown University, will graduate at the end of this semester. He has been working hard to find a job after graduation and receives __________ __________ __________ __________ - __________ __________.
The first offer is from Courier Crossing, a large newspaper in a big city. The other is from Hush-Hush, __________ __________ __________ __________.
Courier Crossing offers him a great salary and job security, but it would force him to move away from his hometown. Hush-Hush has a much lower salary, but he won't have to leave his family and friends. __________ __________ __________, Ryan finally decides to accept the Hush-Hush offer. He meets his classmate Sarah in the hallway and tells her what he has decided. Sarah understands why Ryan made this decision and __________ __________ __________ __________ __________ __________. In this situation, what would Sarah most likely say to Ryan?

Sarah: (Good choice. Some things in life are more important than money.)

## 16-17

M: Good afternoon, parents. We'd like to welcome you to Franklin University's annual Parents' Day. Because you're parents of the students at this fine university, we are offering you the chance to buy our Parents' Day kits, which have been a tradition here at the university __________ __________ __________ __________ 1927. In this kit, you'll find bumper stickers, pens, and key chains for you and your loved ones. Members of our student government have also baked homemade cookies for you to enjoy during this year's festivals. Our Parents' Day kits are created by student organizations and community businesses. On top of helping create these kits, these businesses have also put together a coupon booklet with a $200 value. In these booklets you'll find __________ __________ __________ Franklin City Cafe, Rainbow Bakery, Echo Lanes Bowling Alley, and The Downtown Diner. All of the proceeds for the Parents' Day kits are used to benefit campus-wide events such as Spring Fest and our annual Talent Contest. If you would like to __________ __________ __________ __________ __________ __________ __________ __________, come to the front desk of the visitor's center. Thank you for attending Parent's Day at our wonderful campus.

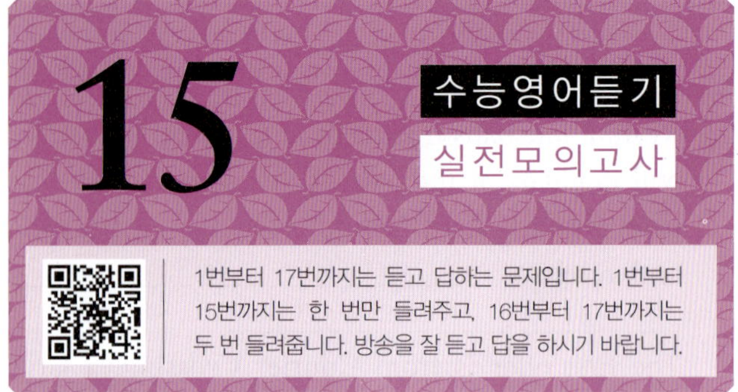

1번부터 17번까지는 듣고 답하는 문제입니다. 1번부터 15번까지는 한 번만 들려주고, 16번부터 17번까지는 두 번 들려줍니다. 방송을 잘 듣고 답을 하시기 바랍니다.

## 01

대화를 듣고, 여자의 마지막 말에 대한 남자의 응답으로 가장 적절한 것을 고르시오.

① That's nice! That way I can cancel my order.
② That's a great idea. Jane is a wonderful baker.
③ It really wouldn't be a problem if I baked a cake.
④ That's a good idea, but I've already chosen a cake.
⑤ It's really a shame that she can't make it to the banquet.

## 02

대화를 듣고, 남자의 마지막 말에 대한 여자의 응답으로 가장 적절한 것을 고르시오.

① Sorry, but Southback jackets are too expensive.
② I just washed it, so it's hanging up now.
③ I'll bring some extra gloves just in case.
④ You can borrow your dad's ski pants.
⑤ No, you shouldn't go skiing there.

## 03

다음을 듣고, 남자가 강의하는 내용의 주제로 가장 적절한 것을 고르시오.

① A lot of exercise can be unhealthy.
② Talk to a nutritionist about your diet.
③ Find ways to exercise in your daily life.
④ Diet and exercise at the same time.
⑤ Make time to exercise every day.

## 04

대화를 듣고, 여자의 의견으로 가장 적절한 것을 고르시오.

① 장난감에 대해 가지고 있는 성 고정관념을 없애야 한다.
② 건전한 장난감을 통해 창의성과 지능을 발달 시킬 수 있다.
③ 장난감을 고를 때 가장 중요하게 고려할 부분은 안전성이다.
④ 성에 맞는 장난감을 이용한 역할놀이는 사회성을 발달시킨다.
⑤ 아이들에게 고정관념을 심어줄 수 있는 장난감은 피해야 한다.

## 05

대화를 듣고, 두 사람이 대화하고 있는 장소로 가장 적절한 곳을 고르시오.

① 길거리　　　② 박물관　　　③ 음식점
④ 방송국　　　⑤ 잡지사

## 06

대화를 듣고, 그림에서 대화의 내용과 일치하지 <u>않는</u> 것을 고르시오.

## 07

대화를 듣고, 여자가 남자를 위해 할 일로 가장 적절한 것을 고르시오.

① to show him around the city
② to help him find an apartment
③ to ask about on-campus housing
④ to clean the house before the party
⑤ to help him fill out his college application

## 08

대화를 듣고, 남자가 아침에 일찍 일어난 이유를 고르시오.

① 아침 식사를 하기 위해서
② 아빠와 하이킹을 가기 위해서
③ 친구와 영화를 보러 가기 위해서
④ 일찍 깨기로 한 자신과의 약속 때문에
⑤ 엄마한테 등산용 지팡이를 빌리기 위해서

## 09

대화를 듣고, 남자가 지불할 금액을 고르시오.

① $30　　② $40　　③ $45　　④ $50　　⑤ $60

## 10

대화를 듣고, 남자가 참여한 자원봉사 활동에 관해 두 사람이 언급하지 않은 것을 고르시오.

① 봉사 장소　　② 봉사 기간　　③ 주최 기관
④ 활동 내용　　⑤ 신청 방법

## 11

Field hockey에 관한 다음 내용을 듣고, 일치하지 않는 것을 고르시오.

① 캐나다와 미국에서 가장 인기 있는 운동이다.
② 인도와 파키스탄에서 전국민이 즐기는 스포츠이다.
③ 필드하키는 아이스하키와 거의 비슷하다.
④ 골키퍼는 몸의 어떤 부분으로든 공을 만질 수 있다.
⑤ 선수들은 스틱의 평평한 부분으로 공을 쳐야 한다.

## 12

다음 표를 보면서 대화를 듣고, 여자가 선택한 모델을 고르시오.

**Bird Rental Cars**

| | Model | Type | Rental Fee (per day) | Capacity (persons) | Number of Vehicles Available |
|---|---|---|---|---|---|
| ① | Magpie | Economy | 60 | 4 | 3 |
| ② | Jay | Economy | 65 | 4 | 2 |
| ③ | Swift | Family | 70 | 5 | 1 |
| ④ | Raven | Luxury | 75 | 7 | 0 |
| ⑤ | Woodpecker | Minivan | 80 | 7 | 2 |

## 13

대화를 듣고, 남자의 마지막 말에 대한 여자의 응답으로 가장 적절한 것을 고르시오.

Woman: _______________________________

① This was a big help. Now I have an idea for a topic.
② I think you should focus on completing the graph.
③ You must have misinterpreted the assignment.
④ I don't understand what your report is about.
⑤ Sure. I'd love to help you with your project.

## 14

대화를 듣고, 여자의 마지막 말에 대한 남자의 응답으로 가장 적절한 것을 고르시오.

Man: _______________________________

① Why don't you turn on the humidifier?
② You should see a doctor about your stuffy nose.
③ I can't seem to find the one that you want online.
④ You're right. Dry air is also very bad for your skin.
⑤ We can run the shower in the bathroom for a while.

## 15

다음 상황 설명을 듣고, Jack이 Charles에게 할 말로 가장 적절한 것을 고르시오.

Jack: _______________________________

① I can't believe we actually won the game today!
② What's wrong with you? You let them score again!
③ You need to try harder. We're going to lose this game.
④ We all make mistakes. You're going to do fine in the game.
⑤ The season is almost over. Just play hard for one more game.

[16-17] 다음을 듣고, 물음에 답하시오.

## 16

남자가 하는 말의 주제로 가장 적절한 것은?

① How animals find their way back home
② Animal senses that aren't found in humans
③ Methods that animals use to identify their prey
④ Benefits of performing scientific research on animals
⑤ Animals that use electromagnetic fields for navigation

## 17

언급된 동물이 아닌 것은?

① 비둘기　　② 연어　　③ 박쥐
④ 바다거북　　⑤ 상어

## 01

W: Hey Evan, have you __________ __________ __________ the banquet this evening?

M: I've finished most of the preparations, but I can't decide on __________ __________ __________ __________ __________ __________.

W: Why don't you ask Jane? She said that she could help out.

M: (That's a great idea. Jane is a wonderful baker.)

## 02

M: Hey Mom, I'm __________ __________ with my friends tonight at Walker Mountain.

W: __________ __________ __________ __________ __________ tonight. Be sure you take your scarf and beanie.

M: All right. I can't find my Southback jacket. Have you seen it?

W: (I just washed it, so it's hanging up now.)

## 03

M: Have you exercised today? Everyone knows that exercise is good for your health. But perhaps you feel like you're too busy and simply don't have the time or energy to get to a fitness center. So, what is someone like you to do? __________ __________ __________ __________ __________ __________ your gym. For instance, if you can, you should walk to the post office or grocery store instead of driving, or use a push lawn mower to cut the grass. __________ __________ __________ __________ __________ people who stay active for most of the day will use 10 percent more energy than people who use a gym for 60 minutes a day but do not stay active otherwise. It's easier and better for __________ __________ __________ __________ __________ __________ __________. This also helps make weight loss goals easier to meet. So, what kinds of activities in your daily life could also be exercise?

## 04

M: Hey, Katie. Did you do your Christmas shopping yet?

W: I sure did. I bought a concert DVD for my father, a flowerpot for my mother, and some action figures for my cousin.

M: That's cool. I loved action figures when I was young. I'm sure he'll love them.

W: Why do you think my cousin is a boy?

M: You mean you bought action figures for your cousin who's a girl?

W: I did. She actually __________ __________ __________ __________ __________.

M: Hmm… I thought that only boys played with action figures. Girls play with dolls.

W: I thought so, too. I was confused about it at first, but after seeing how much she enjoys them I've really opened my mind up __________ __________ __________.

M: What are "gender stereotypes?"

W: It's what society __________ __________ __________ __________ __________ __________ __________ __________. I think it's okay for boys to play with girls' toys and vice versa.

M: That's something that I've never thought about before.

W: I hadn't either, but my cousin really made me consider it.

## 05

W: Wow! This place is really busy. Is someone famous here? Look at all the cameramen.

M: I think they must be from the local news station.

W: What's so special about this place?

M: This place is very famous for its spaghetti. It's the owner's family's secret recipe. __________ __________ __________ __________ __________ his great grandmother.

W: Wow! So this place is pretty old, huh?

M: Yeah, it's been in the family for four generations. I heard it's almost 100 years old.

W: That's pretty incredible. I'm going to have to try that spaghetti.

M: I've heard such great things about it. Look! I think that's the owner over there, getting interviewed.

W: __________ __________ __________ __________ __________. He must be nervous.

M: __________ __________ __________ __________ if you were being interviewed?

## 06

W: Hey Taylor, what is that you're looking at?

M: It's a photo of the party room where we're going to welcome Ryan and Sarah to our facility. __________ __________ __________ __________ __________.

W: Cool. It's going to be a great time.

M: For sure. So, what do you think about the room?

W: It looks great. The banner on the back wall is huge!

M: Yeah, I thought it was going to be smaller, but I think it looks nice. What do you think of the balloon __________ __________ __________ __________?

W: I think it's a nice touch. I like that "Welcome" was written on it. Are the three tables on the left side for food?

M: No. We're not having a buffet. Those are for guests and Sarah's supporters.

W: So the table in the middle with the wine bottles must be for Sarah and Ryan.

M: That's right. I thought __________ __________ __________ __________ __________ __________ __________ in the center of the room.

W: I'm sure they'll love it. What's the podium under the balloon for?

M: That's for our guest speakers. Several of Sarah's friends and family members would like to speak to show their support.

W: That sounds lovely.

## 07

*[Cell phone rings.]*

W: Hello?

M: Hey, Alice. I am calling to share some good news with you.

W: Good news? Did you get into the college you wanted?

M: I did! I just got home and __________ __________ __________ __________ __________ in the mailbox from Princeton!

W: That is so wonderful. I never doubted it for a minute. Congratulations!

M: Thank you so much. Alice, I was wondering if you would help me with something.

W: Of course. How can I help?

M: Well, it's just that I don't have a lot of time and there are so many things I need to do before classes start and I can't seem to find a place to stay.

W: Would you like me to look at apartments for you?

M: That would be great. You've lived in the area for so long that I know __________ __________ __________ __________ __________.

W: Sure, it actually sounds like fun. __________ __________ __________ __________ __________ __________ __________ __________?

M: I'd like a one bedroom apartment. I'm not looking for anything too big, but I want more space than a studio.

W: All right, I'll call you back as soon as I've found a couple of good options for you.

M: You're the best. Thank you again for helping me out.

W: It's my pleasure.

## 08

M: Good morning, sis. What're you cooking?

W: I'm cooking an omelet. You're up early. I figured you'd be sleeping since __________ __________ __________ __________ __________ last night.

M: Yeah, I was out celebrating the end of the school year with my friends.

W: I'm sure you're tired. You should get some more sleep. It's the first day of summer vacation.

M: That'd be nice, but I promised Dad I'd __________ __________ __________ with him today.

W: Now I see why you got up so early.

M: You should come with us. __________ __________ __________ __________ __________ __________ __________ sometimes. I don't know what to talk about with him.

W: I'd like to help and all, but I already have plans. I'm going to see a movie with Brandon.

M: Oh. No, that's fine. Hey, do you know where Mom is? I need to borrow her hiking sticks.

W: She ran to the grocery store, but she should be back soon.

M: All right. I guess I'll wait for her instead of looking myself.

## 09

W: Oh, hello. What can I do for you today?

M: Well, I want to buy a souvenir for my girlfriend. She was quite upset that she couldn't come on this trip with me.

W: I see. Well, __________ __________ __________ __________ __________ __________?

M: I want something that she can use every day, but something that __________ __________ __________.

W: How about this traditional Thai lantern? It's only $20.

M: I like it, but don't you think it's a little small? __________ __________ __________ __________ __________ __________?

W: That one is $40. It was handcrafted by tribesmen in the northern part of the country.

M: It's beautiful. Okay, I'll take the bigger lantern.

W: Sure. How about something for your mother or grandmother? They would like these traditional fans. They're only $5 each. Also, if you spend more than $45, I'll take 10% off your total.

M: They are nice. I'll take two of them. Is there any way you could giftwrap these?

W: I'm sorry, but __________ __________ __________ __________ __________ here.

M: No problem.


## 10

W: Hey, Kyle. How was your summer vacation?

M: It was great. I spent some time in Nepal as a volunteer.

W: That's awesome. How long did you stay?

M: 27 days.

W: Wow! __________ __________ __________ __________ __________ __________ __________.

M: Yeah, but I wish I could've stayed longer.

W: So, what kinds of things did you do there?

M: Well, as you know, __________ __________ __________ __________ __________ a few months ago. I helped take __________ __________ __________ __________ in the hospital and delivered food and water to the outskirts.

W: That's great. You must feel good about yourself. Were all the volunteers from America?

M: No, there was actually only one other American in our volunteer group. The rest came from all around the world.

W: I see. I might want to __________ __________ __________ __________ __________ __________ __________. How do I go about applying?

M: I'll email you some information. You have to sign up on their website and choose what kind of volunteer program you want to participate in.

W: That sounds easy. Thanks.


## 11

M: Are you interested in unique sports? If so, then you should check out field hockey. Field hockey is played all around the world, but is less popular in Canada and the United States, __________ __________ __________ __________. However, field hockey is much more popular worldwide. In fact, it is the national sport of both India and Pakistan. Field hockey is almost identical to ice hockey, except that __________ __________ __________ __________ __________ __________ __________. During play, goalkeepers are the only players who are allowed to touch the ball with any part of their body, while field players must play the ball __________ __________ __________ __________ __________ __________ __________. This sport is a great alternative to ice hockey because it is much less expensive to start playing and you don't need a rink to play, __________ __________ __________ __________ __________ most of the world. If you're looking for something new to try, you should look for a field hockey club in your area!


## 12

M: Welcome to Bird Rental Cars. My name is Gabe. What can I do for you today?

W: Hi. I'd like to rent a car, please.

M: No problem. What kind of car would you like?

W: Well, we're going on a family vacation, so we're going to need something a bit big. There are five of us going on the trip.

M: Okay. In that case, you're going to want to take one bigger than __________ __________-__________ __________.

W: We also have a lot of luggage. So we'll probably need one that's quite large.

M: I'd recommend taking one of our minivans, then. It has ample space and is very comfortable on long trips.

W: The minivan is a little pricey. What about a Raven? __________ __________ __________ __________ __________, and it's cheaper.

M: I'm sorry, but none of those are __________ __________ __________ __________.

W: Well, I guess I'll have to spend the extra money and take this one.

M: Great choice, ma'am.


## 13

M: Hey Lucy, did you finish the assignment that Mr. Miller gave us?

W: I didn't get a chance to work on it last night. It's a big assignment, and I have no idea ____________ ____________ ____________.

M: You'd better start soon. It's due on Thursday, you know.

W: Yeah, I just don't know what to choose for my topic.

M: Take a look at my report. It's not finished, but maybe it can help you decide.

W: *[Pause]* This is really interesting. I didn't know that ____________ ____________ ____________ ____________ ____________ ____________ ____________ ____________ ____________.

M: Yeah. I used a line graph to ____________ ____________ ____________ ____________ ____________.

W: You did a great job with it. It must've taken you a while to organize all of the data.

M: Yeah, it did take a bit of work to choose my topic, but once I decided, it got a whole lot easier.

W: What did you do after you chose your topic?

M: I focused on finding as many sources of data as I could.

W: (This was a big help. Now I have an idea for a topic.)


# 14

M: Hey, sweetheart. I heard you coughing. Are you all right?

W: My throat is a bit dry. I think it's because of the weather.

M: Yeah, ____________ ____________ ____________ ____________ ____________. I think our apartment is too dry.

W: Maybe ____________ ____________ ____________ ____________ ____________.

M: I think so. I've been thinking about buying one for the last couple of weeks.

W: I looked at a couple when I was at the store earlier. I found one that I like.

M: Really? You should've bought it.

W: I didn't realize how badly we needed it.

M: I'll go to the store now and pick one up.

W: They must be closed by now. I bet we can find ____________ ____________ ____________ ____________ ____________ ____________.

M: Yeah, but if we order from the Internet, it'll take a couple of days to arrive. I'll stop by the store tomorrow and buy one.

W: But we're suffering now. What do we do until then?

M: (We can run the shower in the bathroom for a while.)


# 15

W: Charles and Jack have been chosen as co-captains of JLA's soccer team. The first game is coming up soon, and their team practices for about two hours every day. Charles is the team's goalie, but lately he ____________ ____________ ____________ ____________ ____________ ____________ during practice. His team and his school are counting on him ____________ ____________ ____________ ____________ ____________ ____________ ____________. Charles is ____________ ____________ ____________ ____________ from his teammates and tells Jack that he wants to quit the team. Jack wants to reassure Charles that he'll do fine, and that nobody is perfect. In this situation, what would Jack most likely say to Charles?

Jack: (We all make mistakes. You're going to do fine in the game.)


# 16-17

M: I'd like to welcome you all to West Town Zoo. My name is Frank Berger, and I'm a zoologist. I'd like to talk to you today about senses in nature. Everyone knows that ____________ ____________ ____________ ____________ ____________: sight, smell, touch, taste, and sound. What about animals? Do they have the same senses as humans? Some animals have stronger senses than humans, and some even have senses that humans don't have. Take the pigeon, for example. Pigeons are in tune with the Earth's magnetic fields. They can find their way home ____________ ____________ ____________ ____________ ____________ ____________. That's why the homing pigeon was used to send messages in the past. Salmon also use the ____________ ____________ ____________ to find their way back to their birthplace to lay eggs. Sea turtles use a similar technique to return to the beaches where they were born. Some snakes, particularly vipers, have infrared vision, which they use to ____________ ____________ ____________. Sharks can sense electricity from muscle contractions in their prey. The animal kingdom is truly magnificent. Let's take a look at some of these amazing animals.

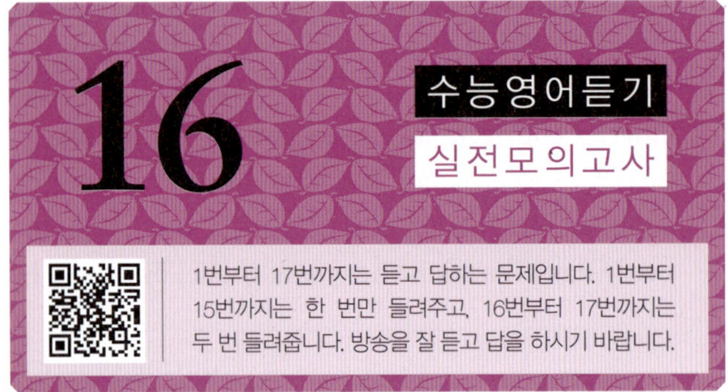



## 01

대화를 듣고, 여자의 마지막 말에 대한 남자의 응답으로 가장 적절한 것을 고르시오.

① I really enjoyed the movie. I highly recommend it.
② You should see if you can check it out at the library.
③ No problem. I won't have time to watch it until Saturday.
④ You've already watched it. I didn't expect to get it back this fast.
⑤ I'm really sorry, but I need to keep the DVD for a couple more days.

## 02

대화를 듣고, 남자의 마지막 말에 대한 여자의 응답으로 가장 적절한 것을 고르시오.

① Why don't you give me a hand with this?
② I actually have to go to a meeting now.
③ I was never very good at social studies.
④ You always give really good advice.
⑤ Sure, come back at around 3 p.m.

## 03

다음을 듣고, 남자가 하는 말의 목적으로 가장 적절한 것을 고르시오.

① 천문대의 관측 프로그램에 대해 안내하려고
② 신설된 천문대의 개관행사를 소개하려고
③ 천문대 관람 시 질서유지를 부탁하려고
④ 천문대 안내원의 채용을 공고하려고
⑤ 천문대 오는 길을 안내해 주려고

## 04

대화를 듣고, 두 사람이 하는 말의 주제로 가장 적절한 것을 고르시오.

① 성에 따른 생체 리듬 비교
② 생체 리듬이 서로 다른 이유
③ 생체 리듬에 따른 학습 능률
④ 집중력 향상에 좋은 수학 수업
⑤ 성적향상을 위한 시간 관리 방법

## 05

대화를 듣고, 두 사람의 관계를 가장 잘 나타낸 것을 고르시오.

① 기자 — 배우
② 학생 — 교수
③ 승무원 — 승객
④ 여행객 — 럭비팀선수
⑤ 식당 종업원 — 손님

## 06

대화를 듣고, 그림에서 대화의 내용과 일치하지 <u>않는</u> 것을 고르시오.

## 07

대화를 듣고, 남자가 여자에게 부탁한 일로 가장 적절한 것을 고르시오.

① to celebrate a holiday
② to put together a collage
③ to buy a new digital camera
④ to reserve the party room
⑤ to buy something special

## 08

대화를 듣고, 여자가 집에 가려고 하는 이유를 고르시오.

① 친구와 말다툼을 하게 되어서
② 동생을 집에 데려다 줘야 해서
③ 아빠의 부탁으로 동생을 돌보기 위해
④ 내일까지 마쳐야 할 학교 숙제가 있어서
⑤ 편의점에서 필요한 것을 사다 주기 위해

## 09

대화를 듣고, 여자가 지불할 총 금액을 고르시오.

① $240  ② $260  ③ $300  ④ $420  ⑤ $450

## 10

대화를 듣고, 총회의 일정에 관해 두 사람이 언급하지 <u>않은</u> 것을 고르시오.

① 부의장님의 연설  ② 남자의 발표
③ 청중과의 대화  ④ Paul Stevenson과의 회의
⑤ 점심식사

## 11

My Little Organics에 관한 다음 내용을 듣고, 일치하지 <u>않는</u> 것을 고르시오.

① 장갑은 참가자가 가져와야 한다.
② 강좌는 일주일에 네 차례 열린다.
③ 수강할 수 있는 연령에 제한이 있다.
④ 10명이 넘으면 강좌 예약을 해준다.
⑤ 수업료는 한 회당 15달러이다.

## 12

다음 표를 보면서 대화를 듣고, 두 사람이 선택할 서비스를 고르시오.

**Office Cleaning Service**

| | Package | Window Cleaning | Floor Waxing | Thorough / Express | Cost (per floor) |
|---|---|---|---|---|---|
| ① | A | X | O | Express | $200 |
| ② | B | X | O | Thorough | $300 |
| ③ | C | O | O | Express | $400 |
| ④ | D | O | X | Thorough | $400 |
| ⑤ | E | O | O | Thorough | $500 |

## 13

대화를 듣고, 여자의 마지막 말에 대한 남자의 응답으로 가장 적절한 것을 고르시오.

Man: _______________________________

① I think we should hurry because they'll close soon.
② We should finish up our work before we eat.
③ I'm trying not to eat anything after 8 p.m.
④ I think they're renovating the restaurant.
⑤ They have the best fish tacos in the city.

## 14

대화를 듣고, 남자의 마지막 말에 대한 여자의 응답으로 가장 적절한 것을 고르시오.

Woman: _______________________________

① Put yourself in their shoes before you make any judgments.
② I'm not really interested in the forces behind decision-making.
③ What a disappointment. I'll never attend one of his lectures again.
④ I didn't care much for the topic, but the lecturer was really interesting.
⑤ I agree completely. I wish more people had the dedication that they have.

## 15

다음 상황 설명을 듣고, Mike가 Mr. Smith에게 할 말로 가장 적절한 것을 고르시오.

Mike: Mr. Smith, _______________________________

① is everything going well for you at Jefferson Academy?
② what song are we going to perform for the festival?
③ I'm ready for our performance at the festival.
④ could you help me with the music routine?
⑤ I'd like to be in charge of the performance.

[16-17] 다음을 듣고, 물음에 답하시오.

## 16

남자가 하는 말의 목적으로 가장 적절한 것은?

① 대입 추천서 작성을 위한 웹사이트 개통을 알리려고
② 온라인을 통한 대입 지원서 접수 방법을 공지하려고
③ 대입을 위한 상담 시 질문 사항들을 알려주려고
④ 대입에 필요한 서류의 작성요령을 설명하려고
⑤ 대입을 위한 추천서의 중요성을 알려주려고

## 17

웹사이트에서 학생들이 할 수 있는 것으로 언급되지 <u>않은</u> 것은?

① 자기소개서 등록  ② 선생님과 상담 예약
③ 자기소개서 샘플 참조  ④ 지원 대학의 경쟁률 확인
⑤ 필요한 서류에 관한 정보 수집

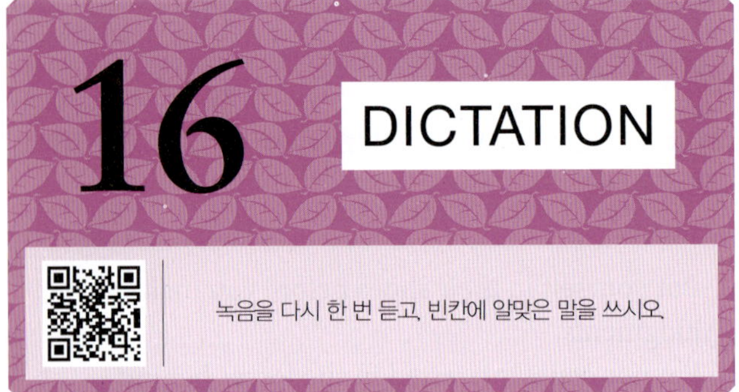


## 01

W: Hey Dylan, do you need that DVD that you let me borrow last week?

M: Well, I don't need it now but I'm planning on watching it this weekend.

W: ______________ ____________ ____________ ____________ ____________ to watch it yet. Is it okay if I return it to you on Thursday?

M: (No problem. I won't have time to watch it until Saturday.)

## 02

M: Would you mind if ____________ ____________ ____________ ____________ ____________ ____________ on my social studies project, Ms. Wilson?

W: I wouldn't mind, Tim, but I'm in the middle of ____________ ____________ ____________ right now.

M: Then can I come back later today?

W: (Sure, come back at around 3 p.m.)

## 03

M: Would you like to check out the Milky Way and all of your favorite constellations? Then make the Lone Star Observatory the destination for your next weekend trip. We are open from May 31st to October 1st this year, Wednesdays through Sundays from 1 p.m. to 8:30 p.m. All programs offered at the Lone Star Observatory are ____________ ____________ ____________ ____________ and are completely free— you don't even need to make a reservation. During the afternoon, you can check out the sun and view several different telescope displays. In the evening hours, visitors have the chance to view the night sky, ____________ ____________ ____________ ____________ ____________ ____________. To make your visit more enjoyable, we always have an astronomer available to guide you on a short tour of the observatory. We hope to see you this summer!

## 04

W: Bill, you seem to have more energy in the morning than later in the day.

M: I do. I really struggled this afternoon. I couldn't concentrate in Mrs. Field's math class.

W: Really? I thought you really enjoyed her class.

M: I do, but I just don't have any energy in the afternoon. I can't focus on anything.

W: I think it's a matter of biological rhythm. ____________ ____________ ____________ ____________ in the afternoon, but I never have any energy in the morning.

M: So ____________ ____________ ____________ ____________ ____________ ____________ ____________ ____________.

W: That's right. You're a morning person.

M: So, you must be an afternoon person.

W: Exactly. Everyone's biological clock is a little different.

M: That's so cool!

W: Yeah, I think so too. Everyone should study ____________ ____________ ____________ ____________ ____________ ____________ in order to benefit the most from their studies.

M: I agree. I should try to study more in the morning.

## 05

W: Good evening. What can I get you to drink?

M: Just a glass of water, please.

W: Sure. *[Pause]* Here you are. Oh! Aren't you a rugby player?

M: That's correct. I'm the captain of the national team.

W: I thought so. It's great to meet you. I'm a big fan.

M: Is that right? Well, ____________ ____________ ____________ ____________ ____________.

W: It's amazing that I get to ____________ ____________. We don't have too many celebrity passengers. I heard you're going to the United States to play in a tournament. This is that trip, right?

M: You're right. We'll be in the US for a little over a month.

W: I'm really looking forward to watching the match on TV. If you need anything, please ____________ ____________ ____________ ____________.

M: Thank you. So, how long before ____________ ____________ ____________ in Los Angeles?

W: Well, it's already five o'clock, so we should be there in about four hours.

M: Okay. Hey, I'd like some peanuts if you have any.

W: Sure. I have a bag right here. I hope you enjoy your flight.

## 06

W: Hey! What's that you're looking at, Jeff?

M: I'm just going over some photos from last weekend. I ___________ ___________ ___________ ___________.

W: That sounds like a lot of fun. Is that your family in the picture?

M: It sure is.

W: Who are those people sleeping under the tree?

M: I'm not sure. Just some people we didn't know who were also at the park. Anyway, that's my mother reading a book on the bench.

W: I see. The man ___________ ___________ ___________ ___________ must be your father.

M: That's right. My father and I love playing games in the park.

W: You two really look a lot alike.

M: That's not the first time I've heard that.

W: Who's the guy on the left manning the barbecue?

M: That's my grandfather. He's ___________ ___________ ___________ ___________.

W: Who else do we have here? I see your sister, Emma, on the bike, but who is that chasing after her?

M: That's my cousin. She and my sister get along well, so ___________ ___________ ___________ ___________.

W: They're adorable.

M: They really are. I love picnics. I want to go back next weekend.

## 07

W: Hey Nate, you know it's Mom and Dad's anniversary this weekend, right?

M: I'd totally forgotten about it. ___________ ___________ ___________ ___________.

W: It's a big one. They'll have been married for 30 years. I think we should do something big for it.

M: I'm not really good with gifts. Maybe we could go in on something together and make it something big and special.

W: I'm thinking a surprise party would be better.

M: I like that idea. We should ___________ ___________ ___________ ___________ ___________. Do you know any good restaurants for parties?

W: Well, their favorite restaurant is Turoni's Pasta.

M: I love that place. Could you ___________ ___________ ___________ ___________ for Saturday?

W: I'll look into it. Don't you think we should do something else for them, too?

M: How about making a collage with pictures of them throughout the years?

W: I think that's a great idea. They'll love it.

## 08

W: Hey Logan, I'm really sorry but I can't go with you to the library.

M: Really? We're almost there. What's wrong?

W: Well, my dad just called and he's expecting me to ___________ ___________ ___________ ___________ ___________ today.

M: So you need to head home now?

W: Very soon. I have to pick up a couple of things for my brother before I go home.

M: Why don't you go to ABC Supermarket? ___________ ___________ ___________ ___________.

W: That would be convenient, but my brother really loves Jojo's Pizza. He's already ordered something from there. I just need to ___________ ___________ ___________.

M: Their pizza is amazing. I'll head there with you. I'd love a slice of pepperoni.

W: That's great. I'd enjoy the company.

M: I also need to pick up a couple of drinks.

W: ___________ ___________ ___________ ___________ right next door to Jojo's. They should have what you're looking for.

M: I'm sure they do. Let's go.

## 09

M: Hello. What can I do for you today?

W: Hi. ___________ ___________ ___________ ___________ some folding chairs.

M: Great. But it's much cheaper to buy a table set. This table comes with two free chairs. It's usually $500, but I think I can get you 40% off.

W: That's a bit on the expensive side. Do you think you can come down a bit?

M: That's about ___________ ___________ ___________ ___________ ___________.

W: I really only need the chairs. How much are those over there?

M: Those are $150 each. If you buy a set of four, though, we can give you 30% off.

W: I'm only looking to ___________ ___________ ___________.

M: We can still give you 20% off the original price.

W: Great! I'll go with those then, please. Do you
_________ _________ _________ _________?

M: We sure do. It's an additional $20, though.

W: That's no problem. I'd like to set up a delivery for Saturday afternoon, please.

## 10

W: Hey, Stan. It's hard to believe that the convention is today.

M: Yeah, _________ _________ _________. Even after all these months of preparation, I'm still nervous.

W: Relax. I'm sure everything will be fine.

M: I know, but I still want to _________ _________ _________ _________ again.

W: All right. We're sending the vice president up to talk first, right?

M: Yes. He's going to be the first speaker. Then it'll be time for me to _________ _________ _________ _________.

W: Yeah. You're meeting with Paul Stevenson afterwards, right?

M: That's right. Did you _________ _________ _________ _________ _________ with his secretary?

W: I did. Oh, I almost forgot. I spoke with Mary this morning, and she wanted to make some changes to your presentation. She gave me a list of notes. What do you think?

M: She's great at her job, so I trust her.

W: All right. Let's go to lunch at the convention center.

## 11

W: Welcome to the DIY Science Museum! This summer we are going to introduce a new and exciting program called 'My Little Organics'. We will have skilled instructors on hand to teach participants how to _________ _________ _________ _________ _________ and vegetables using inexpensive techniques and minimal space. We'll provide all of the material you need for the class, but you should bring your own gloves. _________ _________ _________ _________ _________ _________ _________—on Monday, Wednesday, and Friday evenings at 7 p.m., and on Sunday afternoons at 2 p.m. This program is available _________ _________ _________ _________ _________, and we also reserve class times for groups of over 10. There is a one-time $15 fee to join the 'My Little Organics' class, and we _________ _________ _________ _________ _________ for group classes. If you would like to learn more about the 'My Little Organics' program, you can visit us on the web or give us a call at 555-251-8956.

## 12

W: Hey Jeff, what're you looking at?

M: At prices from different office cleaning companies. This place is really _________ _________ _________ _________.

W: I agree. So have you found one that you like?

M: Well, this one seems to have the best deals and guarantees.

W: Let's take a look. *[Pause]* Oh, so I guess you want to _________ _________ _________ _________ and the floors waxed.

M: Well, I'm not really sure. What do you think?

W: We definitely need the windows cleaned.

M: Absolutely. What do you think about the floors? They probably need to be waxed, right?

W: I don't think they've been waxed since we moved into this office, so yes, I would think so.

M: Well, then we have these _________ _________ _________ _________ _________.

W: What's the difference between "thorough" and "express"?

M: "Thorough" means that they're done more carefully and the quality is better. For example, they offer some special treatment that protects the floors.

W: I see. It's a bit more expensive than _________ _________ _________ _________, though.

M: Right. Well, we haven't had the windows or the floors done since we've been here, so maybe we should go for the more expensive package.

W: I agree.

M: Great. I'll give them a call and set up a date.

## 13

W: Wow! Look at the time! I think it's about time to finish up for the day.

M: That's what I was thinking. _________ _________ _________ _________ _________ _________.

W: Sounds great. What are you in the mood for?

M: How about Johnny Burgers?

W: I'm __________ __________ __________ __________
__________ __________ a burger right now.

M: Well, it's quite late, so we don't have many choices.

W: How about Mexican food? I know a great late-night Mexican restaurant near here.

M: __________ __________ __________ __________
__________ Walking Taco's, right?

W: That's the one. I think they're open 24 hours.

M: Oh, but I __________ __________ __________
today and they were closed.

W: Really? Why?

M: (I think they're renovating the restaurant.)


# 14

W: Hey, Blake. Do you mind if I sit next to you?

M: Not at all. __________ __________ __________ __________.

W: Thanks. So, what's that you're working on?

M: I'm writing a report for my psychology class about Malcolm George's Ed Talk yesterday. Did you get a chance to see it?

W: Yeah, I was there. That was really an amazing lecture about choice, wasn't it?

M: It sure was. He had some very interesting insights.

W: Yeah, the lecture __________ __________ __________
Barry Schwartz.

M: He's the guy who wrote *The Right Choice*, right?

W: That's right. You really know your psychologists, Blake.

M: Well, __________ __________ __________ __________
the forces behind decision-making. It's something I've studied __________ __________.

W: You know, we __________ __________ __________
__________ __________ __________. Not too many people know Malcolm George and Barry Schwartz.

M: I think they're very important to psychology because they've dedicated a lot of time to understanding why people make the decisions they do.

W: (I agree completely. I wish more people had the dedication that they have.)


# 15

W: Mike recently moved to Charlestown and started studying at Jefferson Academy. He likes living in Charlestown and __________ __________ __________
all of the other students at school, but he has __________ __________ __________ __________
__________. The school is having their annual Spring Sprung Festival, and he is the only student in his class that __________ __________ __________
__________ __________. All of the other students have had months of practice but Mike, because he is new to the school, has only had a couple of weeks. He wants to practice after school, but he's going to need some help. Mr. Smith __________ __________
__________ __________ the performance and Mike would like to ask him for help. In this situation, what would Mike most likely say to Mr. Smith?

Mike: Mr. Smith, (could you help me with the music routine?)


# 16-17

M: Good morning, students of Middle Brook High School. This is your academic advisor, Michael Manson. A lot of you are seniors and will be spending most of your free time getting ready for college entrance exams and essay writing. Don't forget, while you are putting all of your documents together, to include a recommendation letter from one or more of your current teachers. Keep in mind that these letters take time to write and that your letter is probably not the only one your teacher will be writing. So, before you approach your teacher with the request, __________ __________ __________
__________ __________ __________ about yourself. We have set up a webpage that makes doing this quick and easy. Simply __________ __________
__________ __________ __________ and click the "Academic Guidance" link in the upper right hand corner of the home page. From there, you will be guided through a step-by-step process where you can upload a personal statement and other information that will make it much easier for your teacher to write your letter of recommendation. After you have finished the online process, your teacher will begin the task of writing your letter of recommendation. __________ __________ __________ __________
__________ __________, you can also use the webpage to make a one-on-one appointment with your teacher to talk about the letter and any other questions you may have regarding the writing process. If you need help writing your personal statement, you can view samples. There is also information on other required documents. If you need further assistance, please __________ __________
__________ __________ __________ __________.

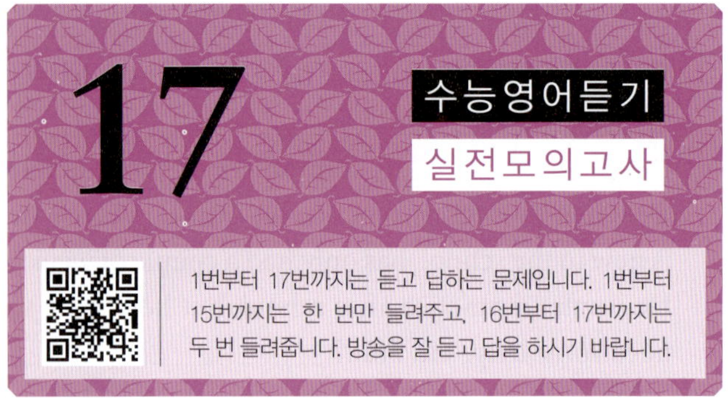


## 01

대화를 듣고, 여자의 마지막 말에 대한 남자의 응답으로 가장 적절한 것을 고르시오.

① Sure. I'll get them ready for you now.
② All right. I'll give them to you on Monday.
③ I haven't chosen a topic for the debate yet.
④ I don't really know too much about debate. Sorry.
⑤ No problem. You can go ahead and turn it in today.

## 02

대화를 듣고, 남자의 마지막 말에 대한 여자의 응답으로 가장 적절한 것을 고르시오.

① I understand why you're so interested in this project.
② I'm going to use them to make some bird feeders.
③ Let's use them for your science project.
④ I'll throw away all of these old bottles.
⑤ You should always recycle old bottles.

## 03

다음을 듣고, 남자가 하는 말의 목적으로 가장 적절한 것을 고르시오.

① 학생들의 학생회장 선거 투표를 촉구하려고
② 선거 관리에 필요한 자원봉사자를 모집하려고
③ 학생회장 선거의 투표율이 낮은 이유를 설명하려고
④ 학생회장 선거에 공식적인 출마를 선언하려고
⑤ 학생들에게 공정한 선거 운동을 장려하려고

## 04

대화를 듣고, 두 사람이 하는 말의 주제로 가장 적절한 것을 고르시오.

① 등산 장비 구입 계획
② 추천할 만한 등산 코스
③ 등산 시 불을 피우는 요령
④ 안전한 등산을 위한 유의 사항
⑤ 등산 시 길을 잃었을 때 대처방안

## 05

대화를 듣고, 두 사람의 관계를 가장 잘 나타낸 것을 고르시오.

① 피고 — 검사　　　　② 앵커 — 기자
③ 검찰 — 특파원　　　④ 리포터 — 행인
⑤ 배심원 — 변호사

## 06

대화를 듣고, 그림에서 대화의 내용과 일치하지 <u>않는</u> 것을 고르시오.

## 07

대화를 듣고, 남자가 할 일로 가장 적절한 것을 고르시오.

① 캠프 활동을 위한 준비물 사러 가기
② 캠프 활동을 위한 책 찾아보기
③ 영어공부를 위한 책 사러 가기
④ 대출한 도서 반납하기
⑤ 영어캠프 신청하기

## 08

대화를 듣고, 남자의 관심 진로 분야가 바뀐 이유를 고르시오.

① 선생님의 조언 때문에
② 즐겨보던 TV쇼 때문에
③ 인상 깊게 읽은 책 때문에
④ 경제전반에 관한 관심 때문에
⑤ 토론을 하면서 생각이 바뀌어서

## 09

대화를 듣고, 남자가 지불할 금액을 고르시오.

① \$500　　② \$540　　③ \$580　　④ \$600　　⑤ \$640

## 10

대화를 듣고, 여자가 언급하지 <u>않은</u> 것을 고르시오.

① 지원동기
② 자격증 취득 시기
③ 근무 경력
④ 전 직장을 그만 둔 이유
⑤ 희망 보수

## 11

Angel Mounds Historic Park의 행사에 관한 다음 내용을 듣고, 일치하지 <u>않는</u> 것을 고르시오.

① 첫 번째 행사는 3월 마지막 주에 열릴 것이다.
② 원주민의 날 행사에서 투어는 4시간이 소요된다.
③ 원주민의 날 행사에서는 원주민 전통 음식을 먹어볼 수 있다.
④ 4월 17일에 열리는 행사는 어린이들을 위한 행사이다.
⑤ 어린이날 행사에서는 온 가족이 즐길 수 있는 행사가 많다.

## 12

다음 표를 보면서 대화를 듣고, 여자가 수강할 강좌를 고르시오.

**Film Editing Class**

| | Level | Teacher | Maximum Number | Time |
|---|---|---|---|---|
| ① | Intermediate | Liam | 20 | Morning |
| ② | Advanced A | Michael | 10 | Evening |
| ③ | Advanced B | Michael | 10 | Morning |
| ④ | Advanced C | Michael | 15 | Morning |
| ⑤ | Advanced D | Liam | 15 | Evening |

## 13

대화를 듣고, 여자의 마지막 말에 대한 남자의 응답으로 가장 적절한 것을 고르시오.

Man: ________________________________

① She'll be glad to help you out with your novel.
② You're right. She should arrive to work on time.
③ Well, I don't think so. I don't really care for her novels.
④ I'll bring this to her attention and give her a warning.
⑤ I don't know. I think writing novels is very time consuming.

## 14

대화를 듣고, 남자의 마지막 말에 대한 여자의 응답으로 가장 적절한 것을 고르시오.

Woman: ________________________________

① Don't worry. I'm sure you can go to the next match.
② That's no problem. I can take your father to the match.
③ No. I was really surprised by how well they performed.
④ I'm worried that my father won't let me go to the match.
⑤ Yeah. I wish my father was as interested in soccer as yours is.

## 15

다음 상황 설명을 듣고, Mrs. Towns가 James에게 할 말로 가장 적절한 것을 고르시오.

Mrs. Towns: ________________________________

① I heard that you're very popular at this school.
② You should talk to your friends about your problems.
③ Why have you been missing so many classes these days?
④ I'm concerned about your behavior. Is everything all right?
⑤ I was wondering about extracurricular events at this school.

[16-17] 다음을 듣고, 물음에 답하시오.

## 16

남자가 하는 말의 주제로 가장 적절한 것은?

① The symptoms of malaria sufferers
② The insect problem in tropical areas
③ The diseases passed on by mosquitoes
④ The medication used in malaria treatment
⑤ The methods to prevent mosquito infestation

## 17

ABCD 접근법에 관해 언급되지 <u>않은</u> 것은? [3점]

① 감염 위험에 대해 인식하기
② 모기 물림을 예방하기
③ 위험 지역은 방문하지 않기
④ 약 복용이 필요한지 확인하기
⑤ 유사증상이 있을 경우 즉시 진단 받기

## 01

W: Hey, Mr. Nelson. I'm sorry, but I won't be able to come to class on Monday.

M: That's okay. I know that you have the ___________ ___________ ___________ to attend.

W: That's right. Is there any way I can get Monday's assignments today?

M: (Sure. I'll get them ready for you now.)

## 02

M: What are you going to do with those old plastic bottles?

W: I'm going through them all and choosing ones I want to ___________ ___________ ___________ ___________ ___________ I've been thinking about.

M: Cool! What kind of project did you have in mind?

W: (I'm going to use them to make some bird feeders.)

## 03

M: Hello, everyone. I'm Tony Brown, your ___________ ___________ ___________ and a junior in the Fine Arts School. As you've probably guessed, I'm here to speak with you about the upcoming election for student body president. First, I want to ___________ ___________ ___________ ___________, and that's voter turnout. Last year it was only 28%. Can you believe it? Because of ___________ ___________ ___________ ___________, life on campus has been anything but satisfactory. Would you like to see the libraries outfitted with up-to-date facilities? Would you like to have a wider variety of food to choose from in the school cafeteria? If you would like these and many other changes to take place, please do your part and vote. Always remember that ___________ ___________ ___________ ___________, and together we can make school a better place for all of us.

## 04

W: I'm thinking about hiking Steven's Peak this weekend.

M: I had no idea you liked hiking, Laura.

W: It's a new hobby of mine, so actually I'm ___________ ___________ ___________ ___________ ___________ ___________ ___________. Do you have any?

M: Sure. First of all, you really want to ___________ ___________ ___________. It's the most important consideration. For instance, you should always make sure you have enough daylight to get all the way down the mountain.

W: I already know that.

M: Of course you do. And, ___________ ___________ ___________ ___________ ___________ ___________ and can't make it back, you want to carry a flashlight and a lighter or some matches.

W: Aha. If I get lost, that will help me start a fire to ___________ ___________.

M: Fires can also be used to signal others in case you get lost.

W: I'd never thought of that before. Do you have any other advice?

M: You should also carry a first-aid kit. As they say, " ___________ ___________ ___________ ___________."

W: Okay. I'll be sure to pack one before I leave. Thanks for the help.

M: No problem. I hope you enjoy your hike. Steven's Peak is beautiful this time of year.

## 05

W: We ___________ ___________ ___________ coming from the Clinton Town Courthouse. Let's get some answers from our reporter on the scene, Ron Berger. Good evening, Ron.

M: Hello, Stacy. I'm here at the Clinton Town Courthouse, where the jury has finally ___________ ___________ ___________ ___________ the trial of Pat Parker, the millionaire businessman accused of handing out bribes to government officials.

W: I know the citizens of our town are curious to hear the results. What did they decide, Ron?

M: In a stunning turn of events, Pat Parker has been ___________ ___________ ___________ of bribery. It's a shock to us all.

W: Wow! That is a surprise. So the jury found him not guilty on all counts?

M: That's right. They decided that the prosecution didn't provide enough evidence to convict Parker.

W: Do you have a statement from the prosecution?

M: Yes, they're going to ___________ ___________ ___________.

W: That's interesting. We'll look forward to hearing how it goes. Thank you for the report, Ron. *[Pause]* That was Channel 2's Ron Berger reporting from Clinton Town Courthouse on the jury finding Pat Parker not guilty on several counts of bribery. We'll be back with analysis of this shocking news after __________ __________ __________ __________.

## 06

W: Nolan, have you been to the library?
M: I have. Are you looking for Meagan? She was in there reading when I went in.
W: Was there anyone else in the library, or was Meagan the only person there?
M: There were a few other people. Gianna was also there __________ __________ __________.
W: I believe I just saw Kathy __________ __________ __________ __________ a half hour ago. Was she there?
M: Yes, I saw her. She was arranging all of the returned books, so I'm guessing she's either volunteering or got a part-time job there.
W: She's working there to __________ __________ __________.
M: It would be a good way to gain experience.
W: What about Nancy? Did you see her? I hope she was there studying—her grades are not very good these days.
M: I did see Nancy. __________ __________ __________ __________ __________ __________.
W: That's really good to know.
M: And William was at one of the computers reading something.
W: Okay. Actually, I need to do some research for a project. I hope there is another computer available.
M: I think there was.

## 07

M: Hey, Emma! Where are you headed?
W: Hi, Ian! I'm just headed to the bookstore.
M: Really? Me, too! I need to __________ __________ __________ __________ __________ __________ __________ next week.
W: That sounds great. What skill level are you looking for?
M: Most of the students will be advanced, with a few intermediate ones mixed in.
W: Sounds like you have your work cut out for you. __________ __________ __________ __________ to teach both levels?
M: Yeah, it will be. I'm hoping to just use the books as study guides and get ideas for activities that can be useful to both levels at the same time.

W: That is a cool idea. It'll make the camp really fun and original.
M: I hope so. I definitely want the students to learn something special at my camp.
W: __________ __________ __________ __________ __________ and have backup ideas in case things don't go as planned. I am sure you'll do a great job!
M: Thanks for saying that.

## 08

M: Hey Patty, I've just heard that you're the school's new debate champion. Congratulations!
W: Thanks, Tommy.
M: What was the final debate about?
W: I debated the pro side in the argument about whether the European Union is beneficial to its members. I studied so hard for it.
M: So, you're pretty informed about the topic. Do you really agree that the EU is beneficial to member states, then?
W: I do. It really helps poorer European nations by __________ __________ __________ __________ and allowing their residents to freely work in other countries. Then they send the money back to their families, so that money from outside begins to circulate around their home country.
M: Huh. So, do you think you'll use your debate skills in the future?
W: I think so. I really want to be a lawyer when I'm older.
M: Really?
W: Yeah, I've always liked lawyer shows on TV. __________ __________ __________ __________ __________, right?
M: I used to be, but these days I'm studying to be a banker. I guess they're kind of related.
W: Yeah, money and law __________ __________-__________-__________. What made you change your mind?
M: I __________ __________ __________ __________ __________ __________ who made a lot of money trading stocks. He followed his dream and lived an interesting life. I loved it so much that I decided I want to model my life after his.
W: That's really cool, Tommy.

## 09

*[Telephone rings.]*
W: Good morning. This is Backwoods Orchard.
M: Hello. This is Mr. Lewis at Vanguard High School. I'm looking to __________ __________ __________ __________ for my students.

W: All right, Mr. Lewis. Would you like to do a half-day tour or a full-day one?

M: What's the _____________ _____________?

W: Well, the half-day tour runs $20 per participant, and the full-day trip is $30 each.

M: I guess we'll book the full-day trip for 20 students on October 13th.

W: All right. Let me make sure we have an opening that day. *[Clicking sounds]* It looks like we should _____________ _____________ _____________ _____________ _____________.

M: Great.

W: Groups of 20 or more people get a 10% discount _____________ _____________ _____________ _____________ _____________ _____________.

M: Is there a charge for teachers?

W: It's $40 for adults; however, for teachers who _____________ _____________ _____________ _____________ _____________, that fee is waived.

M: Great. Would you like my credit card information now, or can I give it to you when I get there?

W: You can pay when you get here.

M: Sounds good. Thanks a lot.

## 10

W: Hi, I'm Nora Stenson. It's a pleasure to meet you.

M: I'm John Ramstad. It's nice to meet you, too.

W: I'd like to start by asking you a few questions. First, _____________ _____________ _____________ _____________ _____________ _____________ at our day camp for kids?

M: Well… I'd like to work with kids outdoors in the summertime, and your day camp is the most popular one in the area. It seems like a high-quality organization, and I'd really like to be a part of it.

W: Great to hear. Okay, so when did you receive your CPR and general care certificates?

M: I got them both about nine months ago.

W: And _____________ _____________ _____________ _____________ _____________ _____________?

M: I have three years of experience as a camp counselor. I worked for Little Acorns Day Camp for a year and then at Young Explorers Day Camp for the last two years.

W: Why did you decide to quit your job at Young Explorers Day Camp?

M: I didn't agree with the curriculum there, and I found _____________ _____________ _____________ _____________ _____________ _____________.

W: Okay, thanks for your time. We will _____________ _____________ _____________ _____________ _____________ _____________.

## 11

W: Good afternoon. My name is Eston Cotton, and I'm the curator for Angel Mounds Historic Park. This spring we're going to _____________ _____________ _____________ _____________. The first takes place the last weekend of March. It's our annual Native American Days event. In this event, we'll learn how Native Americans lived, _____________ _____________ _____________ _____________ _____________ _____________ homes, and how they hunted. The full tour _____________ _____________ _____________ _____________, so be sure to make reservations and come early. The other event, which takes place on April 17th, is the Children's Day event. In this event, children can learn Native American dances, _____________ _____________ _____________ _____________, and try traditional Native American foods. There are also many other family-friendly events on that day. We hope to see you at this year's events. Thank you for your time.

## 12

M: Hi. How can I help you this morning?

W: I'd like to _____________ _____________ _____________ _____________ _____________ _____________ _____________.

M: Sure, I can help you with that. Will this be the first time you've had a class here?

W: No, actually. I've taken a couple of other courses through your program in the past.

M: Were those courses in film editing?

W: No, but in the same general discipline. They were film production and directing.

M: Okay, then I think you'd be fine _____________ _____________ _____________ _____________ _____________ in film editing. Sound okay to you?

W: Yeah, I think so.

M: Okay, we have a few options to choose from.

W: Is it possible to get into one of Michael's classes? I've heard he's a great teacher.

M: Michael teaches three courses at your level. Two of those have a 10-student limit, and the other has a 15-student limit. You can choose a morning or evening session.

W: Okay, I'd like to _____________ _____________ _____________ _____________ _____________ _____________ _____________.

M: Morning or evening?

W: Morning, please.

M: Okay, great. You're on the list.

## 13

W: Hey, Mr. Green. Do you have a couple of minutes?

M: Sure. What's up?

W: Well, I need to talk to you about Karen.

M: All right. What about Karen?

W: ________ ________ ________ ________ . I think that she's a great employee, but she seems to be distracted at work these days.

M: I'm not sure I know what you mean.

W: I don't know if she told you, but she's actually a pretty well-known novelist.

M: Is that right? I had no idea. So, what's the problem?

W: I think she works on her writing a lot at work and neglects her duties here at the office. She's ________ ________ ________ ________ ________ ________ ________ .

M: That's definitely troubling. She should be ________ ________ ________ ________ when she's at the office.

W: I agree. What do you think we should do?

M: (I'll bring this to her attention and give her a warning.)

## 14

W: Hey Devin, what's that you're doing on the computer?

M: I'm waiting until the tickets for the soccer match go on sale.

W: ________ ________ ________ ________ ________ .

M: I really need a ticket in the standing section, but I need to click the button ________ ________ ________ ________ ________ ________ .

W: Really? What match is it?

M: FC Barcelona is playing Real Madrid. It should be an amazing game.

W: I guess the tickets aren't for you, right?

M: You're right. They're for my father. ________ ________ ________ ________ of FC Barcelona, and the match is on his birthday.

W: That's an amazing idea for a gift for him.

M: Yeah, he's been talking about this soccer match for months. He's been really excited about it.

W: That kind of ________ ________ ________ ________ ________ . I was really excited about the match against Real Madrid, but my parents wouldn't ________ ________ ________ ________ ________ .

M: That's a shame. I'm sure you were upset about it.

W: (Yeah. I wish my father was as interested in soccer as yours is.)

## 15

W: James is a popular and outgoing student. He's always very active in extracurricular events and holds ________ ________ ________ ________ ________ . He has many friends and is admired by most of the students and teachers at the school. Recently, however, James has begun ________ ________ ________ ________ while the other students are in the cafeteria for lunch. His teachers have also noticed that he's ________ ________ ________ ________ . The school counselor, Mrs. Towns, has been notified of James' bizarre behavior. Mrs. Towns is worried that James' problems will get worse, and she decides to talk to James to address his problem. In this situation, what would Mrs. Towns most likely say to James?

Mrs. Towns: (I'm concerned about your behavior. Is everything all right?)

## 16-17

M: In our last class we discussed how some insects can be carriers of disease. Today we're going to talk about an insect I'm sure you're all familiar with, the mosquito. A mosquito's bite can cause more problems than just a temporary itch. In fact, mosquitoes kill more people throughout the world than all other animals combined. They do this ________ ________ ________ from one person to another. Some of these diseases, such as dengue fever and malaria, can be fatal. Dengue fever is incredibly dangerous for children and the elderly and, ________ ________ ________ , can cause death. Malaria, which affects about 200 million people worldwide every year, can be treated with medication. These diseases are especially common in tropical areas because mosquitoes are so prevalent in those areas. If you ________ ________ ________ ________ , take the ABCD approach. A is for awareness of the risks of contracting malaria. B is for bite prevention and ________ ________ ________ ________ ________ . C is for checking whether taking malaria tablets is necessary. And D is for diagnosis. If you start showing the symptoms of malaria or dengue fever, you should seek medical treatment immediately.

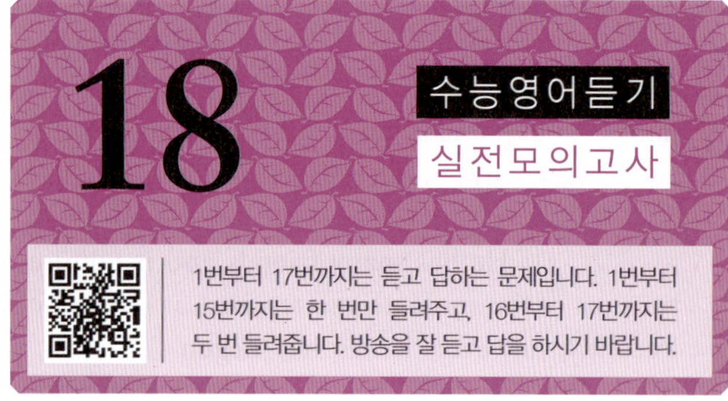



## 01

대화를 듣고, 여자의 마지막 말에 대한 남자의 응답으로 가장 적절한 것을 고르시오.

① I enjoy joining clubs at school.
② Since I was in the fourth grade.
③ I'd like to join your writing club.
④ I used to write for about two hours a week.
⑤ I was better at writing in elementary school.

## 02

대화를 듣고, 남자의 마지막 말에 대한 여자의 응답으로 가장 적절한 것을 고르시오.

① Can you find my cell phone?
② I've been cleaning the house all day.
③ You should call it and listen for the ring.
④ What kind of cell phone are you looking for?
⑤ I haven't called anyone on my cell phone today.

## 03

다음을 듣고, 남자가 하는 말의 요지로 가장 적절한 것을 고르시오.

① 가계부를 작성을 해야 한다.
② 환경 운동에 관심을 가져야 한다.
③ 환경친화적인 물건을 구입해야 한다.
④ 쓰레기 분리수거를 철저히 해야 한다.
⑤ 자신의 경제 능력에 맞게 쇼핑할 필요가 있다.

## 04

대화를 듣고, 두 사람이 하는 말의 주제로 가장 적절한 것을 고르시오.

① 저널리즘 이해의 필요성
② 협동과제 참석에 관한 제안
③ 새로운 수업방식에 대한 대안
④ 사교기술 향상을 위한 방법
⑤ 인터뷰 숙제에 대한 조언

## 05

대화를 듣고, 두 사람의 관계를 가장 잘 나타낸 것을 고르시오.

① 사장 — 비서
② 세탁소 주인 — 고객
③ 식당 지배인 — 손님
④ 패션모델 — 디자이너
⑤ 백화점 직원 — 수선공

## 06

대화를 듣고, 그림에서 대화의 내용과 일치하지 <u>않는</u> 것을 고르시오.

## 07

대화를 듣고, 여자가 남자를 위해 할 일로 가장 적절한 것을 고르시오.

① to meet an instructor
② to pay for a membership
③ to sign up for personal training
④ to assist him in choosing activities
⑤ to ask about annual sporting events

## 08

대화를 듣고, 여자가 학교를 휴학하려는 이유를 고르시오.

① 등록금을 내기 힘들어서
② 다른 공부를 해보고 싶어서
③ 가족이 이민을 가게 되어서
④ 해외로 봉사활동을 가기 위해
⑤ 해외 오지 여행을 하고 싶어서

## 09

대화를 듣고, 여자가 지불할 금액을 고르시오.

① $10　　② $24　　③ $32　　④ $36　　⑤ $40

## 10

대화를 듣고, speech contest에 관해 두 사람이 언급하지 <u>않은</u> 것을 고르시오.

① 개최 일자　　② 참가 자격　　③ 개최 장소
④ 신청 마감일　　⑤ 연설 제한시간

## 11

미술관 견학 안내에 관한 다음 내용을 듣고, 일치하지 <u>않는</u> 것을 고르시오.

① 미술관을 견학 하는 동안 자녀와 함께 다녀라.
② 자녀 스스로 미술 작품을 즐기게 하라.
③ 자녀에게 작품에 대한 해석을 해 주지 마라.
④ 자녀에게 미술관의 투어가이드처럼 행동하게 하라.
⑤ 방문했을 때 최대한 많은 작품을 보여 주어라.

## 12

다음 표를 보면서 대화를 듣고, 두 사람이 선택한 제품을 고르시오.

**Toasters**

| | Model | Price | Capacity | Digital Display | Color |
|---|---|---|---|---|---|
| ① | A | $49 | 2 Slices | X | Black |
| ② | B | $69 | 4 Slices | X | White |
| ③ | C | $89 | 4 Slices | O | White |
| ④ | D | $119 | 6 Slices | X | Black |
| ⑤ | E | $149 | 6 Slices | O | Brushed Steel |

## 13

대화를 듣고, 남자의 마지막 말에 대한 여자의 응답으로 가장 적절한 것을 고르시오.

Woman: _______________________

① Great. I'm really looking forward to working here.
② I noticed that you studied journalism in university.
③ We think you'll be a perfect fit for this company.
④ I've published books for ESL BEST in the past.
⑤ I've always wanted to be an ESL teacher.

## 14

대화를 듣고, 여자의 마지막 말에 대한 남자의 응답으로 가장 적절한 것을 고르시오.

Man: _______________________

① I forgot to do my homework last night, so I couldn't practice playing the piano.
② I might give that a try. There are a lot of TV shows I'd like to catch up on.
③ Staying up-to-date on my TV shows is more important than anything else.
④ I don't play many sports these days because of TV shows.
⑤ We can watch TV shows together if you'd like.

## 15

다음 상황 설명을 듣고, Jane의 어머니가 Jane에게 할 말로 가장 적절한 것을 고르시오.

Jane's mother: Jane, _______________________

① no one likes to be spoken poorly about when they're not around.
② why are you so negative towards everyone you meet at school?
③ why don't you stop hanging out with Olivia for a few weeks?
④ you need to look at all the options before choosing a club.
⑤ moving to a new school can make you feel lonely.

[16-17] 다음을 듣고, 물음에 답하시오.

## 16

여자가 하는 말의 주제로 가장 적절한 것은?

① Benefits of eating vegetables regularly
② The dangers of eating processed foods
③ Foods that are harmful to a child's health
④ Tips to change your children's eating habits
⑤ Creative ways to spruce up a children's party

## 17

언급된 음식이 <u>아닌</u> 것은?

① broccoli　　② carrots　　③ oatmeal
④ spinach　　⑤ tomatoes

## 01

W: Hey Austin, I heard that you ___________ ___________ ___________ ___________. Do you write a lot?

M: Well, I'd like to write more, but right now I only have about an hour a week to do it.

W: ___________ ___________ ___________ ___________ ___________ ___________ ___________ writing?

M: (Since I was in the fourth grade.)

## 02

M: Hey Mom, you haven't seen my cell phone lying around, have you?

W: I haven't, and I just cleaned the kitchen. Do you think ___________ ___________ ___________ ___________ ___________?

M: I think so. I've searched everywhere, but ___________ ___________ ___________ ___________ ___________ ___________.

W: (You should call it and listen for the ring.)

## 03

M: The past few years have seen young people like you making more purchases on their own than ever before. I would like to remind you, though, that everything you buy affects the world around you. No matter what you buy, it will most likely ___________ ___________ ___________ ___________ the environment because just about every product comes from the Earth. Even your cool new uPhone is made with materials that came directly from the ground. What you can do to help is ___________ ___________ ___________ ___________ ___________—buy what you need instead of what you want. Whenever you make a purchase, you should spend some time making sure it is ___________ ___________. Doing this little bit of research will help protect our planet now and for generations to come. It's easy but smart, and you'll help make the world we live in a better place for everyone.

## 04

M: How are you doing in Mr. Smith's class, Katie?

W: Well, at the beginning of the semester it was really difficult for me to ___________ ___________ ___________ ___________ ___________.

M: I understand. I was struggling, too.

W: Now, though, I think that all of the extra homework is a great way to learn about publishing and journalism.

M: Yeah, it's an interesting way of teaching, but I don't think it's very effective for me. It's hard for me to stay interested in the homework.

W: I noticed that you haven't been doing so well on your homework. I haven't seen many of your pieces in the school newspaper.

M: Well, ___________ ___________ ___________ ___________ ___________ ___________ ___________ other students and faculty at the school.

W: I was the same way at first, but after I ___________ ___________ ___________ ___________ of talking to others, my social skills have really improved.

M: I see. I guess ___________ ___________ ___________ ___________ ___________ ___________ and start asking for interviews.

W: You should. I think it will really help you enjoy the class more.

## 05

M: Hello.

W: Good afternoon. What can I do for you today?

M: Well, I bought these dress pants at the mall last weekend and they're a little long for me, so I need to get them hemmed.

W: All right. Let me ___________ ___________ ___________, and then we can alter them for you. Do you want them to run a little high or touch your shoes?

M: I usually wear my pants a little high.

W: All right. No problem.

M: I also have this shirt I want you to take a look at.

W: What seems to be the problem?

M: Well, I was eating at an Italian restaurant last week and I spilled spaghetti sauce on it.

W: ___________ ___________ ___________ ___________ ___________ ___________ ___________ ___________.

M: Well, after I spilled the spaghetti sauce, I got wine on it. Is there any way you can ___________ ___________ ___________?

W: Red wine stains are difficult to get out, but I think we can do it.

M: Thanks. So, when can I pick them up? I'd like to wear the pants to a formal dinner on Saturday.

W: I'll do my best to get them ready by then. Why don't you give me a call on Thursday and I'll tell you if they'll be ready?

M: That sounds great. Thanks.

## 06

M: Hey, you're finally back from vacation.

W: Yeah. I'm glad to be back, but I already miss the beach.

M: I understand. Which beach did you go to?

W: St. Petersburg Beach. It was really nice. I took a photo. Check it out.

M: *[Pause]* Wow. It looks lovely. I really like the hat you're wearing.

W: Thanks. My mother bought it for me. __________ __________ __________ __________ __________ __________ __________ __________, though.

M: Is that your husband?

W: Yeah, he's taking a nap under the parasol. He spent most of the vacation relaxing.

M: That must be your son, Billy, building the sandcastle.

W: He's quite creative. __________ __________ __________ every day.

M: Who's that on the raft in the water?

W: That's my father-in-law, William. He and his wife actually own the condo we stayed in.

M: Those must be the condos in the background.

W: That's right. We stayed in the center building on the 7th floor.

M: Well, __________ __________ __________ __________ your vacation. I need one soon.

W: I can't wait to go back.

## 07

W: Good afternoon. What can I do for you?

M: Hi, there. I'm thinking of joining some sporting activities.

W: Okay, great. __________ __________ __________ __________ __________ __________?

M: No, actually I'm not.

W: That's okay. Did you have __________ __________ __________ __________ __________?

M: Not really. I'm not sure what's best for me.

W: Okay. Well, this is a list of all the sporting activities we have planned for this summer. You can see that we offer both indoor and outdoor activities.

M: Wow, there are a lot of activities to choose from.

W: Right. So __________ __________ __________ __________ __________ __________ all of the activities and choose the one that works for you.

M: Can you give me some help?

W: With choosing an activity?

M: Yeah. I'd like to join at least two activities, but __________ __________ __________ __________ __________ __________.

W: Let's look at the list together, and I'll try to help you.

M: That would be great. Thanks so much.

## 08

W: Good afternoon, professor.

M: Amelia, come on in and have a seat. What can I do for you today?

W: There's something important I'd like to discuss with you.

M: Sure. What is it?

W: Well, this is hard to say, but I think that __________ __________ __________ __________ __________ __________ __________.

M: Really? Why? You've always been such a great student.

W: Thanks. I'd just like to __________ __________ __________ __________ __________ __________ __________ in the outside world.

M: Like what?

W: Like volunteer. I've decided to go abroad and help those who need it.

M: That's very kind of you. What country are you thinking of going to?

W: There was a __________ __________ __________ __________ recently. I'd like to go there and help them.

M: I think that will be good for you. You can always come back and study when you're finished. Good luck with everything, Amelia.

W: Thank you for understanding, professor.

## 09

M: Welcome to Poptastic's Gourmet Popcorn. What can I do for you?

W: How much is a large bag of caramel popcorn?

M: It'll be $10 a bag.

W: __________ __________ __________. I'll take 4 bags, please.

M: Sure. And if you sign up for our mailing list, we'll give you a 10% discount. It only takes a few minutes to complete the form.

W: Is that right? Okay, I'd like to sign up. *[Pause]* I'm finished. Here you go.

M: Let's take a look at this. Okay. Your email address is mashimaro@leemail.com?

W: That's right. __________ __________ __________ __________ __________ __________?

M: Sure. We offer a 20% discount during the month of your birthday. Hey! It says on the form you just filled out that your birthday is tomorrow!

W: That's right. Would you like to see my ID?

M: That's okay. I trust you. Well, we can't give 2 discounts at the same time, so we'll give you the larger discount.

W: That's great. __________ __________ __________ __________ __________?

## 10

W: Hey Andrew, I saw this __________ __________ __________ __________ in the hallway and thought that you might be interested.

M: Oh, it's about the speech contest. Do you mind if I look at the flyer?

W: Not at all. So, do you think you'll be ready by September 22nd?

M: I think so, but I'm a bit worried. You know it's open to all students. __________ __________ __________ __________ __________. Do you plan on registering?

W: I'm thinking about it. I don't think I'd do very well, but I could use it to __________ __________ __________ __________ __________.

M: That's for sure. You're interested in famous speeches, aren't you?

W: Definitely. That's why it'd be good for me. I'd like to be a politician one day. Are you going to register?

M: Sure. __________ __________ __________ __________ __________ Walker Auditorium. That's pretty close.

W: Yeah. We can ride our bikes there. We should register soon, though. The deadline is this Friday.

M: Let's go to my house and use my computer to register.

W: Great idea.

## 11

W: Good afternoon, everyone. Welcome to the Center City Art Museum. I'm here to give you some advice on the best way for your kids to get the most from their visit to the museum. First of all, make sure your kids are always with you. If they __________ __________ __________, they can easily get lost and scared. However, __________ __________ __________ __________ __________ __________ __________ __________. It's not a good idea to quiz them or try to interpret the art for them. __________ __________ __________ __________ __________, and ask them what their favorite piece was and why. You can even give your kids a map of the museum and a list of artwork and __________ __________ __________ __________ __________ __________ for you. This'll allow them to see the whole museum and feel like __________ __________ __________. It's not so important to see all of the artwork in one visit. We're open all year long, so there is plenty of time for multiple visits.

## 12

W: Sweetheart, Christmas is coming up soon. What are we going to get for your parents?

M: Well, Mom did say that __________ __________ __________ __________ __________. Let's look for one of those.

W: All right, but I don't think we should spend more than $140.

M: I agree. We still have a lot of other gifts to shop for.

W: Right. Anyway, what size do you think we should buy?

M: I think a two-slice toaster is a bit too small. Mom would definitely want a bigger one.

W: For sure. Let's get a 4- or 6-slice one. Do you know what the digital display is for?

M: It lets you use timers and see how long it will take to finish toasting your bread. I don't really think it's necessary, though. __________ __________ __________ __________ __________ for Mom to use.

W: I agree. Check out this black one. It looks so sleek and modern.

M: I think it'd look great in our kitchen, but __________ __________ __________ __________ __________ __________.

W: Okay. Let's go with that color, then.

M: I think this one is perfect. Let's buy it.

## 13

M: Welcome to JLA. We are excited to work with a native English speaker with so much teaching experience.

W: Thank you. I'm really excited to be a part of the JLA team.

M: I see you've been an ESL instructor here in Korea for almost four years now.

W: Yes. I've always enjoyed teaching, and being here in Seoul has been an amazing experience.

M: _________ _________ _________ _________ on ESL books before?

W: I haven't, but I'm enthusiastic about starting a new project.

M: I'm glad to hear it. Actually, we have another native speaker working with us. _________ _________ _________.

W: Really? I'd like to meet him. I'm sure _________ _________ _________ _________ _________ _________.

M: I'm sure you do. He'll be here shortly. You can meet him then.

W: So how many books have you published so far?

M: We've only published five books so far, but we're working with ESL BEST on a few new projects.

W: (Great. I'm really looking forward to working here.)

## 14

M: Stephanie, how many hours of television do you watch every week?

W: I usually watch TV for about twenty hours a week.

M: Really? Wow, you watch a lot of TV!

W: Yeah, I usually watch between three and four hours of TV a day.

M: Four hours a day? I don't have the time to watch that much TV. I have to study and practice playing the piano after school.

W: I have a lot to do, too, Steve. But I _________ _________ _________ _________ _________.

M: How do you possibly have that much time to waste?

W: Well, I only watch the TV shows that I like. I do my homework and other things in between the shows.

M: I guess that's one way of doing it. It still seems like _________ _________ _________ _________ _________ _________.

W: Time you enjoy is not wasted time.

M: That's a good point. But I still don't understand how you get everything done.

W: I usually schedule my other activities around my TV schedule. I always _________ _________ _________ _________-_________ _________ and prioritize my responsibilities before television time.

M: (I might give that a try. There are a lot of TV shows I'd like to catch up on.)

## 15

W: Jane and Olivia have always been really close friends and do everything together. Unfortunately, they've been arguing recently over very simple things, like _________ _________ _________ _________ _________ _________ _________ _________ _________ _________. Jane always tries to avoid the arguments, but they continue to argue anyway, so Jane talks to her mother about this situation. Jane's mother believes the arguments are happening because the _________ _________ _________ _________ _________ _________ _________ _________. She thinks they should take some time _________ _________ _________ _________, and she wants to suggest that Jane and Olivia _________ _________ _________ _________ _________ _________. What would Jane's mother most likely say in this situation?

Jane's mother: Jane, (why don't you stop hanging out with Olivia for a few weeks?)

## 16-17

W: Do you have any fussy eaters in your family? Is every day at the dinner table a battle because your child won't eat vegetables or other healthy foods? Well, forcing your child to eat food that he or she dislikes can have a negative emotional impact. Sensible parents are patient about ushering their children into _________ _________ _________. I'd like to provide you with some tips that helped me change my children's habits. First, decorate your child's food to _________ _________ _________ _________. For example, shape the vegetables on their plate to make them look like a smiley face. Broccoli makes a great nose, carrot slices look great as eyes, and a slice of potato can smile up at your child. Second, _________ _________ _________ _________ _________ _________. Try putting a couple of drops of blue and red food coloring in your child's oatmeal to give it a vibrant appearance. Third, you can cut your child's fruits and vegetables into shapes such as stars, hearts, or letters. You can even spell out their name. Finally, I find that I can sometimes _________ _________ _________ _________ _________ _________ _________ _________. Spinach, for example, is packed with nutrients and is easy to hide in a pizza or even in cookies and brownies. If you use your mind and a bit of creativity, you'll have your children eating healthily in no time.

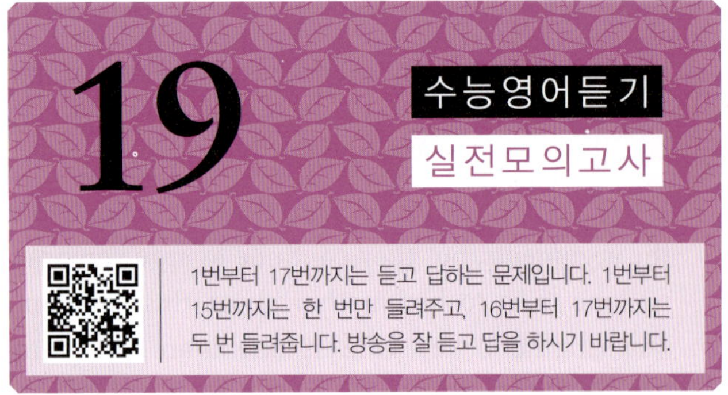


1번부터 17번까지는 듣고 답하는 문제입니다. 1번부터 15번까지는 한 번만 들려주고, 16번부터 17번까지는 두 번 들려줍니다. 방송을 잘 듣고 답을 하시기 바랍니다.

## 01

대화를 듣고, 여자의 마지막 말에 대한 남자의 응답으로 가장 적절한 것을 고르시오.

① You will have another chance.
② I wish you could have seen it.
③ Wow, that's great! I don't believe it!
④ No problem. You can practice more.
⑤ Don't forget about your assignment.

## 02

대화를 듣고, 남자의 마지막 말에 대한 여자의 응답으로 가장 적절한 것을 고르시오.

① I'd like to, but I can't. I have plans this weekend.
② Yeah. It wasn't easy getting tickets for the opera.
③ It's great that you and your wife will see the opera.
④ Don't worry about it. I know how to get to the theater.
⑤ It looks like you can still book tickets for next weekend.

## 03

다음을 듣고, 여자가 하는 말의 목적으로 가장 적절한 것을 고르시오.

① 운동의 중요성을 강조하려고
② 휘트니스 센터를 홍보하려고
③ 개인 트레이너 모집을 안내하려고
④ 휘트니스 센터의 이전을 알려주려고
⑤ 휘트니스 센터의 리모델링을 공지하려고

## 04

대화를 듣고, 두 사람이 하는 말의 주제로 가장 적절한 것을 고르시오.

① 소셜 미디어 사이트의 효과적인 사용 방법
② 학생들 사이에서 소셜 미디어 사이트의 인기
③ 학생들의 소셜 미디어에 대한 중독의 심각성
④ 소셜 미디어 사이트가 학생들에게 끼치는 다양한 영향
⑤ 소셜 미디어 사이트가 학생들의 정서 발달에 끼치는 영향

## 05

대화를 듣고, 두 사람의 관계를 가장 잘 나타낸 것을 고르시오.

① 인테리어 업자 — 고객
② 청소업체 사장 — 직원
③ 택배 회사 직원 — 의뢰인
④ 페인트 가게 주인 — 고객
⑤ 부동산 중개업자 — 건물주

## 06

대화를 듣고, 그림에서 대화의 내용과 일치하지 <u>않는</u> 것을 고르시오.

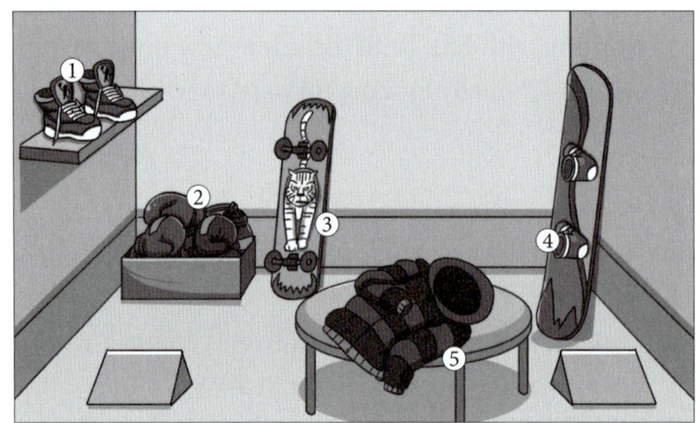

## 07

대화를 듣고, 남자가 여자를 위해 할 일로 가장 적절한 것을 고르시오.

① 아들을 데려와 주기
② 워터 파크에 같이 가기
③ 여행을 위한 쇼핑 같이 하기
④ 크루즈 여행 예약하기
⑤ 보고서 작성 도와주기

## 08

대화를 듣고, 여자가 도서관에 온 이유를 고르시오.

① 친구를 도와주기 위해서
② 역사책을 반납하기 위해서
③ 기말고사 공부를 하기 위해서
④ 보고서 작성을 하기 위해서
⑤ 조별 과제를 하기 위해

## 09

대화를 듣고, 여자가 지불할 총 금액을 고르시오.

① $25　　② $40　　③ $51　　④ $61　　⑤ $70

## 10

대화를 듣고, 팔라완 섬에 관해 두 사람이 언급하지 <u>않은</u> 것을 고르시오.

① 팔라완 섬의 문화
② 팔라완 섬의 날씨
③ 사람들이 팔라완 섬을 찾는 이유
④ 팔라완 섬을 처음 대중화시킨 사람들
⑤ 팔라완 섬에서 인기 있는 마을

## 11

Busan International Film Festival에 관한 다음 내용을 듣고, 일치하지 <u>않는</u> 것을 고르시오.

① 매년 부산 해운대에서 열린다.
② 1996년 9월 처음으로 개최되었다.
③ 주로 유럽의 저예산 영화들을 소개한다.
④ 젊은 사람들에게 호소력이 있다.
⑤ 2011년 영구적 장소로 옮겼다.

## 12

다음 표를 보면서 대화를 듣고, 여자가 선택한 스캐너 모델을 고르시오.

### Scanner Rental Service

| | Model＼Feature | Color Scan | Rental Fee per Month | Fax | Printer |
|---|---|---|---|---|---|
| ① | TL-2 | X | $25 | O | X |
| ② | TL-3 | O | $27 | X | O |
| ③ | D-3 | O | $30 | O | X |
| ④ | D-5 | O | $32 | X | O |
| ⑤ | D-7 | O | $40 | O | O |

## 13

대화를 듣고, 여자의 마지막 말에 대한 남자의 응답으로 가장 적절한 것을 고르시오.

Man: _______________________

① All right. I'll send my application in immediately, then.
② I guess you're right. I'll ask my computer science professor.
③ Thanks. Please let me know when you've finished the letter.
④ I really appreciate you taking the time to fill out the application.
⑤ That's not a problem. I'll finish writing it by the end of the week.

## 14

대화를 듣고, 남자의 마지막 말에 대한 여자의 응답으로 가장 적절한 것을 고르시오.

Woman: _______________________

① Well, I don't really remember much from my time there.
② I've lost contact with all of my relatives in my hometown.
③ No. I didn't take any pictures when I went there for Christmas.
④ Of course. I'll show you some of the ones we took on the farm.
⑤ Sure. I have a lot of photos of you from when you were a baby.

## 15

다음 상황 설명을 듣고, Mike가 아빠에게 할 말로 가장 적절한 것을 고르시오.

Mike: Dad, _______________________

① I don't think you realize how much I worry about you.
② my friends really appreciate you letting me go out with them.
③ I'm really happy that we get to spend so much time together.
④ it's time that you treat me like an adult. I'm not a kid anymore.
⑤ how about you and Mom spend more time together on the weekends?

[16-17] 다음을 듣고, 물음에 답하시오.

## 16

남자가 하는 말의 목적으로 가장 적절한 것은?

① to fight against animal testing for cosmetics
② to caution the public on the effects of poverty
③ to introduce new techniques of raising livestock
④ to explain the benefits of raising domesticated animals
⑤ to inform people about a way they can help the poor

## 17

다음 중 소가 제공하는 것으로 언급되지 <u>않은</u> 것은?

① 우유　　② 치즈　　③ 비료
④ 고기　　⑤ 새끼

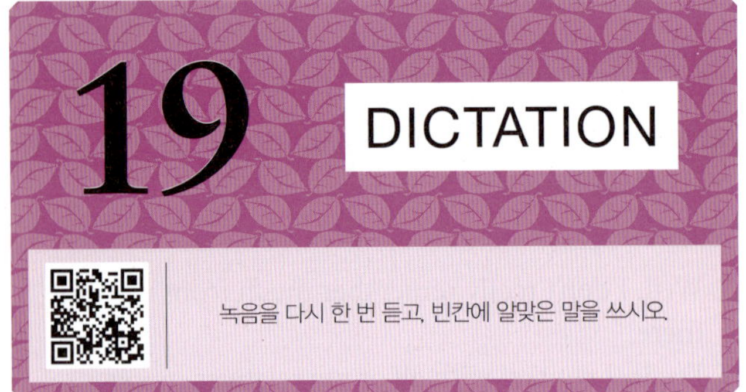




## 01

W: Did you see last night's game? It was really good! You want to know ___________ __________, Steven?

M: I'm guessing the North Stars __________ __________ __________. Our team always loses to them.

W: Nope! We won last night!

M: (Wow, that's great! I don't believe it!)

## 02

M: Hey, Linda. Can you check to see if there are any tickets left for the opera this weekend?

W: Give me a second. [Pause] Well, it looks like they're sold out.

M: Really? I wish I had bought tickets last week. My wife __________ __________ __________ __________ __________.

W: (It looks like you can still book tickets for next weekend.)

## 03

W: How are you feeling today? You might have noticed some people in the office today who were especially energetic. You may have also noticed people who seemed down or depressed for no specific reason. Which group would you place yourself in? If it's the second group you belong to, then __________ __________ __________ __________ __________ Heavenly Fitness for a free consultation? Heavenly Fitness is a state-of-the-art fitness center for functional strength training and overall wellness. We have 15 __________ __________ __________ that will help you come up with an exercise program specific to your individual needs. What's more, all of the facilities, including the locker rooms and bathrooms, are brand-new, and our workout equipment is all __________-__________-__________ __________. If you want to get more out of your life, then stop by Heavenly Fitness today.

## 04

W: Hey, Joshua. What are you listening to? Anything interesting?

M: Hi, Ann. I'm listening to a podcast online.

W: Oh yeah? What's it about?

M: It's about social media. They're saying that by 2018, almost every child in America 8 years old and up will have some sort of social media profile. How do you feel about that?

W: Well, I believe social media sites can be of __________ __________ __________ and teach children lessons about online security.

M: Okay, but don't you think social media sites can __________ __________ __________ __________ in many ways?

W: In what ways?

M: I've read reports of dangerous people __________ __________ __________ __________ so they can chat with minors. There are also people who __________ __________ __________ __________ __________ to gain personal information, like phone numbers and addresses.

W: Yeah, I guess that is pretty scary.

M: Also, while social media sites can be educational, they can be very distracting for students who use them to talk with friends instead of to share homework and ideas.

## 05

W: Sir, did you take a look at the contract?

M: I did. But I found a couple of things I'd like to change.

W: Oh really? What changes did you want to make?

M: The first is about the __________ __________. We originally wanted a sauna and a hot tub, but we now want two hot tubs.

W: That should be fine, but it's going to cost extra.

M: Cost doesn't matter. __________ __________ __________ when it's complete.

W: Sure. So, what else would you like to change?

M: I originally said I wanted __________ __________ __________ __________ __________ __________ __________ __________, but we decided to go with white instead.

W: That's no problem. I'll __________ __________ __________ on red paint and order some white. Was there anything else?

M: Nope. That's it. I can't wait to see it when it's finished.

W: It's going to look great. By the way, when does it need to be finished?

M: Well, training starts in August, so we'd like to ___________ ___________ ___________ ___________ ___________ ___________.

## 06

M: This sporting goods store ___________ ___________ ___________ ___________.

W: You're right. You know, Uncle Jesse's birthday is coming up. Maybe we should get him something from here.

M: That's a great idea. What about those sneakers on the shelf? He plays a lot of basketball this time of year.

W: That sounds like a pretty good idea, but I don't know ___________ ___________ ___________ ___________. Do you?

M: Nope.

W: What about a pair of boxing gloves? They have plenty of them in that box in the corner.

M: I think he likes watching boxing, but he doesn't really box much.

W: Yeah, I guess you're right. That long skateboard is pretty awesome. Look at the design on the bottom.

M: Yeah, that is cool. It has a tiger on it. I think it's a bit too pricey for us, though.

W: You're right. That snowboard in the corner is probably ___________ ___________ ___________ ___________ ___________ as well.

M: Yeah. Hey, look on the table! Maybe we should get him one of those basketball jerseys.

W: That's a great idea! That's his favorite team, the Indiana Pacers. I think he'll love one.

M: I do, too.

## 07

M: The weather is great today. I wish we could go to Wally's Waterland.

W: That name brings back memories. I used to go there a lot when I was younger.

M: Yeah, me too. ___________ ___________ ___________ ___________ ___________ ___________ ___________, until I was just too tired.

W: I really liked the wave pool as well.

M: It was always a good time, but there were always so many people there.

W: Yeah, but it was still more fun than ___________ ___________ ___________ ___________ ___________.

M: I suppose you're right. We should get back to work, though.

W: Do you think we'll be finished with work early today?

M: I'm not sure. Why?

W: I'm supposed to pick up my son from a friend's house and go shopping for our cruise next week, but I feel like ___________ ___________ ___________ ___________ ___________ ___________ ___________.

M: Well, I'll be done with my work soon, and I'll ___________ ___________ ___________ ___________ ___________ this afternoon.

W: That's so nice of you, Greg. I really appreciate it.

M: Don't mention it. Someday I'll ___________ ___________ ___________ ___________ ___________, too.

## 08

M: Good morning, Melissa. What're you doing in the library?

W: Hey, Norman. I've got a lot of work to do. What about you? ___________ ___________ ___________ ___________ on a Sunday?

M: I need to do some research for my biology paper about plant reproduction. It's due on Tuesday.

W: I see. Sounds difficult, but you're very studious, so I'm sure you'll do well.

M: Thanks. Oh, by the way, you're looking a bit ___________ ___________ ___________. Is everything okay?

W: I'm fine. I just have a little cold. I should be resting, but I've been having trouble sleeping the past few nights.

M: I see. I suppose you're pretty ___________ ___________ ___________ ___________ ___________ next week, huh?

W: You're right. I always seem to get sick before exam week. Plus, I have a history exam that's worth 40% of my grade.

M: ___________ ___________ ___________. I can help you study if you want.

W: That's all right. Thanks anyway.

M: No problem. I hope everything works out for you.

## 09

M: Good afternoon. How can I help you today?

W: I need to ___________ ___________ ___________ ___________ ___________ ___________.

M: Okay, we have a standard vacuum cleaning for $10 or a deluxe shampooing for $25.

W: Which do you think is best? The carpet __________ __________ __________ __________ __________.

M: I'd recommend the shampooing. That way you'll have a fresh, clean carpet going into the spring and summer.

W: Okay. I'll go with that, then. I'd also like the outside of the car washed.

M: Sure. The exterior wash is $15.

W: Okay, that's fine. Oh, and I need to __________ __________ __________ __________.

M: No problem. Wheel cleaning is usually $30, but I'll give you a 30% discount because you're getting the exterior wash and the carpet cleaned.

W: Wow, that's great. When should I __________ __________ __________ __________ __________ the car?

M: It'll be ready to go in about 45 minutes.

## 10

W: Tom, what are you up to?

M: I'm reading a story in this travel magazine about Palawan, in the Philippines.

W: Palawan? What's the story?

M: It's about how the island came to be such a popular tourist destination.

W: __________ __________ __________ __________ __________ __________. It's probably one of those places only experienced travelers would enjoy, right?

M: Not according to this story. It says, "Palawan's culture is so different from the rest of the Philippines and Southeast Asia, and __________ __________ __________ __________ __________, __________ people from all over started flocking there on vacation."

W: But how did Palawan first get popularized?

M: Well, a few years ago the island __________ __________ __________ __________ __________ __________ looking for the next great dive.

W: Really? But now it's not just for divers, huh?

M: Not at all. There are things to do for everyone. The town of El Nido __________ __________ __________ __________, __________ __________ __________ __________, giving it a very mellow atmosphere.

W: It sounds really cool. I'll have to google it later and check it out.

M: You should. Let me know what you think.

## 11

W: Do you know about the Busan International Film Festival, held annually near Haeundae Beach in Busan, South Korea? It's one of the most important film festivals in Asia. __________ __________ __________ __________ __________ __________ __________ __________ from September 13th to September 21st, 1996. That was also the first international film festival in Korea. The focus of the BIFF is __________ __________ __________ and first-time directors, especially those from Asian countries. __________ __________ __________ is the appeal of the festival to young people, in terms of both the large, youthful audience it attracts and its efforts to develop and __________ __________ __________. In 1999, the Busan Promotion Plan was established to connect new directors to funding sources. The 16th BIFF in 2011 saw the festival move to a new permanent home, the Busan Cinema Center.

## 12

M: Hello. What can I do for you this afternoon?

W: I need to rent a color scanner. Do you have any available?

M: Yes, we can help you with that. We have four different models you can choose from. __________ __________ __________ __________ __________ __________. It shows all of the different models. The most popular one right now is the D-7.

W: Okay, what can you tell me about it?

M: Well, it'll give you really high quality scanning for $40 a month.

W: Actually, $40 is a bit too expensive for my budget. I want to spend $35 a month at the most.

M: That's fine. __________ __________ __________ the D-5 model because it provides great scanning for $32 a month.

W: All right, that __________ __________ __________ __________ __________. Are there any other features I should know about?

M: Sure. The D-5 can also be used as a normal printer that you can hook up wirelessly to your computer.

W: I have enough printers in my office; __________ __________ __________ __________ is a fax machine.

M: Then I believe this model is right for you.

W: I'll take it.

## 13

M: Hey Mrs. Towns, can you spare a couple of minutes?

W: Of course, Richard. What can I do for you today?

M: I'm looking to __________ __________ __________ __________ __________ __________ at Pear Computers. Do you think I have the qualifications to get accepted?

W: I think so. You've really __________ __________ in all of your classes and extracurricular activities this year.

M: Yeah, but I'm not sure if I have __________ __________ __________ __________ __________ __________.

W: You're kidding, right? You're exactly what they're looking for in an intern. Anyway, it couldn't hurt to at least try.

M: Thanks for the words of encouragement, Mrs. Towns. Oh, by the way, is there any way you could __________ __________ __________ __________ for me? It's one of the requirements for the internship.

W: I'd love to, but I think that it might look better if someone more qualified wrote one for you.

M: (I guess you're right. I'll ask my computer science professor.)

## 14

M: Hey Mom, did you see the moon tonight? It's huge!

W: Yeah, it is. It's the biggest full moon of the year. It's called the 'harvest moon'.

M: Why is it called that?

W: Well, it's the moon that's closest to the autumnal equinox. It's __________ __________ __________ __________ __________ __________ harvest crops late into the night.

M: How do you know all this?

W: Well, you know __________ __________ __________ __________ __________ __________, right?

M: Yeah, I remember you telling me about that.

W: Well, I used to help out on the family farm when I was young.

M: Oh, right. Does your family still live out there?

W: Yes, a lot of them still do.

M: Do you still __________ __________ __________ __________ __________?

W: Of course. I write letters to my Aunt Lucinda every few months. I just received a letter from her last week.

M: When was the last time you went to visit your hometown?

W: I went back for Christmas about ten years ago. It was great to visit with them.

M: It sounds like an interesting place. Do you have any photos from when you were young?

W: (Of course. I'll show you some of the ones we took on the farm. )

## 15

M: Mike, a 17 year-old high school student, has very loving parents that treat him well. However, Mike recently __________ __________ __________ __________ __________ his parents. He feels like he's old enough to live his life the way he'd like to live it, but his parents still treat him __________ __________ __________ __________ __________.

While his friends are out on Friday hanging out in Internet cafes playing computer games, Mike is usually stuck at home with his parents playing board games and watching old movies. Last weekend, Mike __________ __________ __________ from his parents to go to a concert with some of his friends. They refused, of course. He then asked his father to give him a reason why he couldn't go; his father said that the concert would finish too late. Mike believes his parents are too strict and __________ __________ __________ __________ __________ __________. He decides to talk about this with his father. In this situation, what would Mike most likely say to his father?

Mike: Dad, (it's time that you treat me like an adult. I'm not a kid anymore.)

## 16-17

M: Hi. I'm Noah Redman, Founder of Animals for Joy. When I was young, my father __________ __________ __________ __________. He gave them to families that really needed them. You may be wondering why my father would give cows to families in need. Well, owning livestock is like __________ __________ __________ __________ __________. The milk, cheese, and other products from these cows can be sold, and the income can be used for school, home improvements, debt relief—simply put, for a better life. Cows also naturally __________ __________ for future crops. They reproduce as well, which is like growing a business. If the family you help chooses to __________ __________ __________ __________ __________ __________ __________ __________ __________ and this trend continues throughout the community, soon you will find that poverty in the community has decreased. Please show your support for Animals for Joy by donating online. To do so, visit our website at *www.animals4joy.org.* Thank you in advance for your time and support.

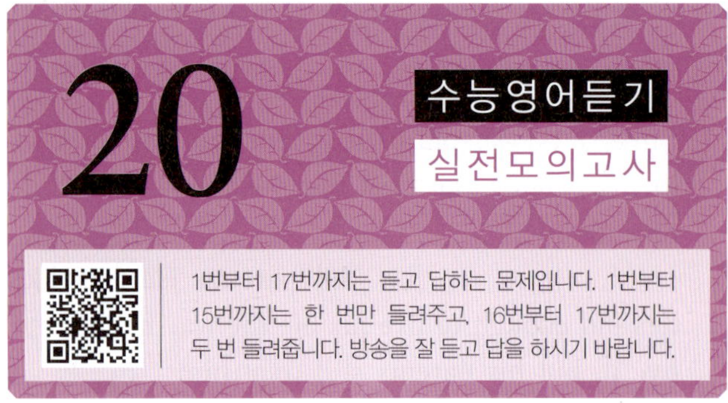



## 01

대화를 듣고, 여자의 마지막 말에 대한 남자의 응답으로 가장 적절한 것을 고르시오.

① Why do I have to get up early?
② You know, the library is closed today.
③ Oh, you shouldn't have woken me up early.
④ Is that true? Then I need to get up and get ready.
⑤ I can't believe it. I think sixteen is old enough to go there alone.

## 02

대화를 듣고, 남자의 마지막 말에 대한 여자의 응답으로 가장 적절한 것을 고르시오.

① Me, too. Fall is my favorite season.
② I think it's too cold to walk outside.
③ Thank you, but I think I'm busy next week.
④ Sounds great! That's just what I wanted to say.
⑤ Thanks for inviting me, but I've already had dinner.

## 03

다음을 듣고, 남자가 하는 말의 목적으로 가장 적절한 것을 고르시오.

① 동파 발생 시 대처요령을 알려주려고
② 정전 사태 대비 훈련 계획을 알리려고
③ 교내에서의 에너지 절약 방법을 교육하려고
④ 동파 방지를 위해 창문을 닫고 다닐 것을 요청하려고
⑤ 난방을 위한 대체 에너지 개발의 필요성을 강조하려고

## 04

대화를 듣고, 두 사람이 하는 말의 주제로 가장 적절한 것을 고르시오.

① 인터넷 사기를 피하는 방법
② 제품 사용 후기의 작성 요령
③ 가격비교 사이트 이용의 필요성
④ 품질 보증서를 보관해야 하는 이유
⑤ 중고거래에서 좋은 물건 고르는 법

## 05

대화를 듣고, 두 사람이 대화하고 있는 장소로 가장 적절한 곳을 고르시오.

① supermarket
② culinary school
③ commercial kitchen
④ office building
⑤ coffee shop

## 06

대화를 듣고, 그림에서 대화의 내용과 일치하지 <u>않는</u> 것을 고르시오.

## 07

대화를 듣고, 여자가 남자를 위해 오후에 할 일로 가장 적절한 것을 고르시오.

① 시험공부 도와주기
② 병문안 같이 가주기
③ 수영 팀에 등록해주기
④ 병원에 차로 데려다 주기
⑤ 도서관에서 책 빌려다 주기

## 08

대화를 듣고, 여자가 아르바이트를 할 수 <u>없는</u> 이유를 고르시오.

① 건강상태가 좋지 않아서
② 학교 권투부에 가입해서
③ 부모님이 허락하시지 않아서
④ 지금 하는 일이 마음에 안 들어서
⑤ 스페인으로 수학여행을 가기 위해서

## 09

대화를 듣고, 여자가 지불할 금액을 고르시오.

① $980   ② $1,020   ③ $1,050   ④ $1,110   ⑤ $1,120

## 10

대화를 듣고, 전시회에 관해 두 사람이 언급하지 <u>않은</u> 것을 고르시오.

① 참가 예술가 수　　　　② 작품의 수
③ 시작하게 된 계기　　　④ 기금마련의 목적
⑤ 전시 기간

## 11

Aspiring Writers Summer Camp에 관한 다음 내용을 듣고, 일치하지 <u>않는</u> 것을 고르시오.

① 캠프의 기간은 일주일이다.
② 글쓰기를 위한 다양한 프로그램이 있다.
③ 매년 초청 작가가 방문한다.
④ 한 달 전에 신청하면 할인을 받을 수 있다.
⑤ 신청서는 학교 홈페이지에서 받으면 된다.

## 12

다음 표를 보면서 대화를 듣고, 남자가 선택할 가방의 모델을 고르시오.

### Rickshaw Bags

| | Model | Size | Style | Material | Price |
|---|---|---|---|---|---|
| ① | A | Small | Satchel | Waxed Canvas | $170 |
| ② | B | Small | Messenger | Waxed Canvas | $190 |
| ③ | C | Small | Messenger | Leather | $210 |
| ④ | D | Large | Satchel | Waxed Canvas | $220 |
| ⑤ | E | Large | Messenger | Leather | $240 |

## 13

대화를 듣고, 남자의 마지막 말에 대한 여자의 응답으로 가장 적절한 것을 고르시오.

Woman: _______________________________

① We should organize a school talent show.
② I don't think they should do it like that.
③ You can't go to the school's talent show.
④ Ribbons aren't as expensive as medals.
⑤ If that's the case, why not get medals?

## 14

대화를 듣고, 여자의 마지막 말에 대한 남자의 응답으로 가장 적절한 것을 고르시오.

Man: _______________________________

① That's right. What brand do you usually drink?
② Right. Caffeine can help you be more productive.
③ Yes, I remember. Let's go out and have a couple of colas.
④ Yeah. It's really hard for me to kick my caffeine addiction.
⑤ Exactly. I think you should drink less cola and more water.

## 15

다음 상황 설명을 듣고, Seha가 Laura에게 할 말로 가장 적절한 것을 고르시오.

Seha: _______________________________

① Don't worry. You'll do better next time.
② That's okay. I'll go home and get my charger.
③ That too bad. Why don't you buy a new one?
④ You can use mine. I'm not using it right now.
⑤ It's really nice of you to let me use your computer.

[16-17] 다음을 듣고, 물음에 답하시오.

## 16

남자가 하는 말의 주제로 가장 적절한 것은?

① 즉각적인 보도의 중요성
② 최근 언론계에서 일어난 캠페인
③ 시대별 언론인들의 다양한 역할
④ 대중 매체에 대한 지역별 선호도
⑤ 보도에 사용되는 대중 매체의 변화

## 17

언급된 매체가 <u>아닌</u> 것은?

① newspaper　　② poster　　③ radio
④ television　　⑤ social media

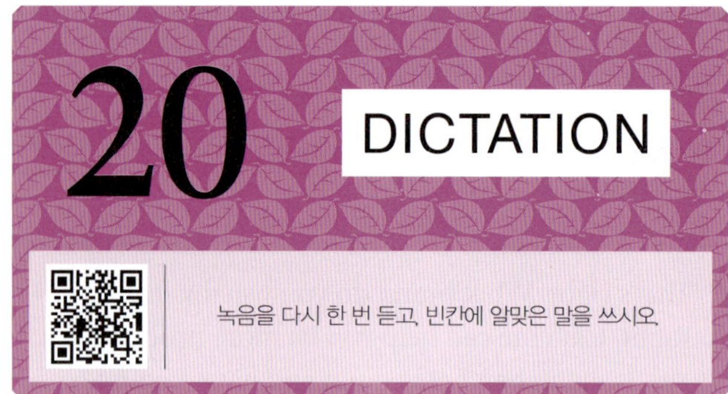





## 01

W: Hunter, wake up! __________ __________ __________ go to the library today.

M: Mom, I'm going to the library tomorrow. Today's the sixteenth.

W: Are you so busy that __________ __________ __________ __________ __________ __________ ? Today's the seventeenth.

M: (Is that true? Then I need to get up and get ready.)

## 02

M: Autumn is my favorite season. I like the autumn breeze.

W: I agree with you. __________ __________ __________ __________ __________ __________ __________ , __________ .

M: Another great thing about autumn is the red leaves. __________ __________ __________ __________ __________ __________ to enjoy the autumn leaves today?

W: (Sounds great! That's just what I wanted to say.)

## 03

M: Please excuse the interruption, everyone. This is your principal. I'm sure you all recall the pipes in our school freezing last winter. I doubt something like that will happen again, but just in case, I'd like to remind students and faculty to close all windows when you leave a classroom, especially at the end of the day. Our school has an automatic heating system, but it will fail if windows are left open. If __________ __________ __________ __________ __________ __________ , the classroom will get too cold and the heating system can't __________ __________ __________ __________ __________ . When a pipe freezes, it can cause the water supply to get backed up, and if this happens over the weekend when no one is here for a couple of days,

those backed-up pipes can burst and __________ __________ __________ __________ . This situation is easily preventable if everyone does their part by simply closing the windows.

## 04

W: Hey Carl, did you hear about Mark?

M: No. What happened?

W: Well, he's been searching for a used phone. He finally found an aPhone 5 that he liked for a great price online. He sent the money to the seller, but never received the product.

M: Well, __________ __________ __________ __________ __________ ?

W: Of course he did, but that so-called "company" had posted fake contact information.

M: Well, I guess he got scammed. __________ __________ __________ __________ __________ __________ .

W: It's got me worried because I've been looking to buy a used laptop.

M: You know, it's pretty easy to find out if a company is trustworthy or not.

W: Really? How can I check?

M: Well, if the seller is a company, a simple online search should tell you about their history.

W: That sounds easy enough to do.

M: Right. You can also ask the seller questions about your purchase, such as its delivery date and __________ __________ __________ __________ .

W: I guess I'll take your advice. Thanks, Carl.

## 05

M: Hi, there. My name is Larry.

W: Hello, Larry. My name is Tammy Smith. I assume you're the new intern.

M: It's a pleasure to make your acquaintance, Tammy.

W: It's a pleasure meeting you as well. We should get started because we have a lot of work.

M: Okay. How can I help?

W: First, put on some rubber gloves and a hairnet to protect your skin and __________ __________ __________ __________ __________ __________ . Then go to the storage room and get some potatoes.

M: All right. [Pause] Here you are.

W: Now peel the potatoes as quickly as you can. There's a banquet scheduled to start in about an hour.

M: Okay. How many patrons are we expecting?

W: There should be around 80 to 90 customers.

M: Got it. When will the head chef be coming in?

W: He's coming soon. Be sure to have all the potatoes peeled __________ __________ __________ __________ __________.

## 06

M: Hey Mom, check out this poster I made for the Earth Day Fair at our school.

W: That's pretty cool. What kind of things are you doing at your school for Earth Day?

M: We're going to talk about our environment and how we can help it.

W: Oh, cool. Are you going to talk about __________ __________, like the people are doing on the left side of the poster?

M: That's right. We're going to see a demonstration about how to plant trees. I also put a sun at the top because __________ __________ __________ __________ __________.

W: That makes sense. I guess that's why you also put the wind turbines next to the road.

M: Right. Wind can also give us energy. You know, I thought that they all had four blades but all the ones I saw on the Internet only had three.

W: Who's that riding a bike?

M: That's my friend, Frank. __________ __________ __________ __________ __________ is also a great way to help the environment.

W: That's right. What are the two kids at the bottom right doing?

M: They're cleaning garbage up from the roadside.

W: I guess we should all do our part to __________ __________ __________ __________ __________ __________.

M: That's right, Mom. Oh, I really think we should start recycling more.

W: All right. We can start today.

## 07

W: Bill, have you heard from Nancy?

M: I haven't. She wasn't in class this morning. Is everything all right?

W: __________ __________ __________ __________ __________ __________ last night and broke her arm.

M: Oh, that's terrible. Will she be okay?

W: Yeah, she'll be fine. But she __________ __________ __________ __________ __________ __________ __________ team this year.

M: That's bad news. Is she still in the hospital?

W: Yes. Do you want to go there with me this afternoon?

M: I can't today. I have a lot of studying to do for my science exam next week. Maybe I'll give her a call.

W: I could help you study. I did well on the exam last year. __________ __________ __________, and it would give us a chance to hang out more.

M: That sounds great. I could really use the help. So, do you want to come to the library and meet me after you visit the hospital?

W: Sure. That works for me. Should I just give you a call after I see Nancy?

M: Sure. Give her my best regards, please.

## 08

W: Hey Arthur, did you watch the boxing match last night?

M: I sure did. The champion defended his title. It was a great fight.

W: Yeah, it was fantastic. Hey, you're pretty good at boxing. You should __________ __________ __________ __________ __________.

M: I'd like to, but I can't.

W: Why not?

M: I have a part-time job at the theater after school.

W: Oh. Are you saving money for something?

M: Yeah. I really want to go on the school trip to Spain over summer vacation.

W: Yeah, that does sound cool. I'd love to get a part-time job, but my parents won't let me. They think __________ __________ __________ __________ __________.

M: Well, they might be right. I don't have enough time to study these days. My math scores are starting to drop.

W: You should probably quit your job and focus __________ __________ __________ __________.

M: Right. I think my grades are more important. Besides, I can work when I'm older.

W: Yeah, you're right.

## 09

M: Hi. Welcome to Big Al's Furniture Outlet. What can I do for you folks today?

W: Hi. My husband and I are looking at this bedroom set. How much is it?

M: This is one of our __________ __________ __________. It's $900, and it includes the bed frame, the dresser, the nightstand, and the desk.

W: Not a bad deal. I really like it.

M: It's one of our top sellers, and you're in luck because we just __________ __________ __________ 10% off its normal price of $1,000.

W: That's great. We'll take it. Is there any way we can add another nightstand?

M: That shouldn't be a problem. Would you like a matching one?

W: Absolutely. How much is it?

M: It's normally $150 on its own, but since you're buying the set, I'll give you another one at a 20% discount.

W: Great. Also, we don't have a truck to move all of this. __________ __________ __________ __________ __________?

M: Sure. Normally we charge an $80 delivery fee, but you're in luck. That fee doesn't apply to purchases over $1,000.

W: That's fine. We're going to take the bedroom set with another nightstand, then.

## 10

W: Hello. I'm Lori from CBC.

M: Nice to meet you, Lori. I'm Stan, and I'm here to answer any questions you might have about the event.

W: Thanks. Well, first I'd like to say that you've __________ __________ __________ __________ __________ __________.

M: Thank you. There are artists from 15 countries displaying their work here. There are more than 150 pieces.

W: Wow, that's quite impressive. __________ __________ __________ __________ __________ __________ to start this exhibition?

M: I've been interested in art my whole life, especially art from Latin America. I modeled this exhibition after one I saw in Boston a couple of years ago.

W: What exactly are you raising money for in this event?

M: Latin America has fallen on hard times. Money raised at this event will help __________ __________- __________ __________ __________.

W: I see. How long will the exhibition last?

M: All of the pieces will be on display until the end of the month.

W: That's great to know. Thank you for your time, Stan.

## 11

W: Good afternoon, students. I'd like to announce the registration for the Aspiring Writers Summer Camp. This week-long camp presents future writers with a chance to participate in a variety of programs. The programs __________ __________ __________ __________ __________ __________ in everything from creative writing to non-fiction. Each year we have a guest author speak to our students, and this year we're happy to reveal that George Martins will speak and take questions from the attendees. __________ __________ __________ at this time. If you apply before Friday, you can get our __________-__________ __________. The camp fills up quickly, so sign up as soon as you can. Application forms can be found on the school's website. Thank you for listening.

## 12

W: Hey Andrew, did you see this flyer? Rickshaw Bags at the mall is having a sale this week.

M: That's awesome! You know, I really need a new bag. I start university in the fall.

W: That's right. I think one of these would be perfect for you. Which one do you like?

M: Well, I don't think I'll need that much space and I don't like bulky bags, so I think a small one would be better.

W: I noticed that. The bag you have now isn't very big.

M: Right. But __________ __________ __________ __________ __________?

W: I don't know. Would you rather carry it on your shoulder or __________ __________ __________?

M: Across my chest. I guess the messenger bag is a better fit for me, then.

W: Well, __________ __________ __________ __________ __________. Would you rather have a leather bag or a waxed canvas one?

M: Well, I like to be stylish, so __________ __________ __________ __________ __________.

W: That one is a bit more expensive. Is that okay?

M: Yeah, that's not a problem. I'm going to go to the mall and pick one up right away.

## 13

W: Hey, I heard that the school is holding a talent show __________ __________ __________ __________ __________.

M: Yeah, they have one every year. I'm actually organizing this year's one.

W: Really? __________ __________ __________ __________ __________ __________?

M: I like to try new things, and I'd never organized an event before.

W: That's cool. What do you have to do?

M: Well, first of all, I have to find people to participate in the show. I also need to choose some prizes for the winners.

W: That seems easy enough. What kinds of prizes did you have in mind?

M: Originally I was thinking about __________ __________ __________ __________, but it turns out they're way too expensive.

W: Hmm… what about ribbons for the winners?

M: I was really looking for something a little more valuable that they can hold on to and treasure for a long time.

W: (If that's the case, why not get medals?)

## 14

M: Hey, are you going to get another cup of diet cola?

W: Yeah. Would you like me to get you anything while I'm in the kitchen?

M: I'm fine, thanks. How many colas have you had today?

W: __________ __________ __________ __________ __________ __________. Why?

M: I think you drink too much cola. Don't you think it's bad for you?

W: Well, this is diet cola, so it's actually much healthier for me.

M: You think so?

W: There isn't any sugar in it, so __________ __________ __________ __________ __________ __________ __________.

M: That's true, but…

W: But what? Do you think that drinking diet cola is bad for you?

M: Well, it might be true that it's better for you than regular cola, but drinking so much of it must be bad for your body. __________ __________ __________ you're consuming.

W: I guess you're probably right. Like the old saying goes, "__________ __________ __________."

M: (Exactly. I think you should drink less cola and more water.)

## 15

M: Seha is attending a seminar at Jason Lee Academy. He's waiting for his turn to give a presentation about California, which __________ __________ __________ __________ __________. While waiting, Seha notices Laura sitting next to him. She is frantically looking through her bag for something. She looks very worried. Seha asks her about her problem. She says that __________ __________ __________ __________ __________ and she left the charger at home. __________ __________ __________ __________ __________ __________ __________, and she won't be able to give her presentation without a computer. Seha is sympathetic to Laura and would like to help. He wants to offer to let Laura borrow his computer. In this situation, what would Seha most likely say to Laura?

Seha: (You can use mine. I'm not using it right now.)

## 16-17

M: In last week's class, we discussed journalism's importance to society. Today we're going to __________ __________ __________ __________ used to get messages to the public. The first one we'll talk about is the printing press, which gave rise to the newspaper. For the first time in history, information could be presented to the public on a regular basis. Literate people in major cities around the world could hear about significant events __________ __________ __________ __________. The newspaper was the primary source of news for nearly three hundred years, until the first radio news broadcast. Journalists were suddenly given __________ __________ __________ __________ __________ __________ to a large audience instantly. Television soon followed radio and gave journalism a much more visual medium. Finally, the information age gave rise to Internet journalism, which is quickly becoming the primary source of news throughout the world. Internet users can now read articles, listen to sound bites, and watch videos almost instantaneously. Social media, such as Twitter, brought about immediate reporting. Journalists can now broadcast their reports __________ __________ __________ __________.

Now I'd like to talk about other changes in journalism that have occurred within your lifetime.

MEMO

# 수능직방



실수 없는 수능 듣기 만점 공략!

# Listening

수능 듣기 실전 모의고사 20회

정답 및 해설

# 목차

# 01 수능영어듣기 실전모의고사

| 01 ④ | 02 ③ | 03 ④ | 04 ⑤ | 05 ⑤ | 06 ② |
| 07 ③ | 08 ⑤ | 09 ② | 10 ④ | 11 ⑤ | 12 ② |
| 13 ⑤ | 14 ⑤ | 15 ③ | 16 ③ | 17 ③ | |

## 01 짧은 대화의 응답

**소재** 운동회 준비

**듣기 대본 해석**

남: Kate. 운동장에 운동회 날 행사를 위한 선을 그렸니?
여: 아니 아직. 그런데 일기 예보에서 그날 하루 종일 비가 심하게 올 거래.
남: 오, 안돼! 어떡하지?
여: ④ 내 생각엔 실내 활동만 할 수 있을 것 같아.

**어휘**

**weather forecast** 일기 예보　〈문제〉 **indoor** *a.* 실내의

**정답** ④

**문제풀이**

여자가 운동회 날 비가 많이 올 거라는 예보를 말하자 남자는 어떻게 하냐고 물었으므로 여자의 대답으로 가장 적절한 말은 ④ '내 생각엔 실내 활동만 할 수 있을 것 같아.'이다.

**오답 보기 해석**

① 선을 그리고 다시 시작하자.
② 그릴 것 좀 가져다 줄 수 있니?
③ 오늘 우산을 가져왔어야 했는데.
⑤ 모든 행사는 저녁 6시 이후에 끝난다고 들었어.

**총 어휘 수** 46

## 02 짧은 대화의 응답

**소재** 박물관 내 사진 촬영 금지

**듣기 대본 해석**

여: 죄송하지만, 이 박물관에는 엄격한 "사진 촬영 금지" 방침이 있습니다.
남: 정말이요? 아무도 저에게 그것을 말해주지 않았고, 저는 입구에서 어떠한 표지판도 못 봤는데요.
여: 입구 근처에 "사진이나 비디오 촬영 금지"라는 표지판이 있어요.
남: ③ 정말로 죄송해요. 제가 들어올 때 알아채지 못했습니다.

**어휘**

**strict** *a.* 엄격한　**policy** *n.* 정책, 방침　**entrance** *n.* 입구
**doorway** *n.* 출입구

**정답** ③

**문제풀이**

남자가 박물관 내 사진 촬영 금지에 대한 어떤 말이나 표지판이 없었다고 하자 여자는 입구에 표지판이 있다고 말했으므로 적절한 남자의 응답은 ③ '정말로 죄송해요. 제가 들어올 때 알아채지 못했습니다.'이다.

**오답 보기 해석**

① 그래서 전 늘 카메라를 가지고 다니죠.
② 이 박물관의 전시품이 별로 맘에 안 드네요.
④ 당신은 당신의 카메라를 가져왔어야 했어요.
⑤ 저는 사진 전시회가 있었는지 몰랐어요.

**총 어휘 수** 53

## 03 담화 목적

**소재** 다음 학기 수강 재신청 안내

**듣기 대본 해석**

여: 학생 여러분. 안녕하세요. 잠시 주목해 주시겠어요? 유감스럽게도 학생 여러분 모두 다음 학기에 들을 강의들을 다시 신청해야 한다는 사실을 알려드립니다. 어제 여러분 모두 스케줄을 완성한 것을 알고 있지만 수강신청 사이트의 문제로 신청 몇 개를 처리할 수 없었습니다. 기술적인 문제들은 모두 해결되어 차후에 이런 문제가 다시 발생할 일이 없길 바랍니다. 오늘까지 강의 신청을 해주시기 바랍니다. 협조해주셔서 감사드리고 불편을 끼쳐 죄송합니다. 감사합니다.

**어휘**

**register** *v.* 등록하다, 신청하다　**cooperation** *n.* 협조, 협력
**inconvenience** *n.* 불편

**정답** ④

**문제풀이**

수강신청 사이트의 문제로 어제 했던 수강신청 몇 개가 처리되지 않았기 때문에 오늘까지 다시 신청을 해달라고 말하고 있으므로 여자가 하는 말의 목적은 ④ '다음 학기 수강신청을 다시 해줄 것을 안내하려고'이다.

**총 어휘 수** 98

## 04 대화 주제

**소재** 스포츠 음료 섭취를 통한 경쟁력 확보

**듣기 대본 해석**

여: Paul. 네가 이번에 FC APEC Ⅲ 축구 캠프에 참여할 거라고 들었어. 축구 잘해?
남: 잘 못해.
여: 그럼 다른 참가자들과 어떻게 경쟁하려고 그래?
남: 큰 문제는 안 될 거야. 매일 Rad CraCra를 조금 마실 거야.
여: Rad CraCra가 어떻게 너의 축구 실력을 향상시켜?
남: 내가 필요한 힘을 그 특별한 혼합물(Rad CraCra)이 줄 수 있어. 내가 더 빨리 뛰고, 더 높이 뛰고, 더 오래 뛸 수 있게 도와줘.
여: 우와! 난 Rad CraCra가 그렇게 강력한지 몰랐어.
남: 맛도 좋고 FC APEC Ⅲ의 공식 스포츠 음료야.
여: 최고네! Rad CraCra는 대단한 스포츠 음료야.
남: 맞아! 난 이거 없이는 절대 축구 안 해.

**어휘**

**compete** *v.* 경쟁하다　**mixture** *n.* 혼합물　**boost** *n.* 증가

**정답** ⑤

**문제풀이**

여자는 축구를 잘하지 못하면서 축구 캠프에 참여하려는 남자에게 어떻게 경쟁할 것인지를 물었고, 남자는 축구 실력을 향상시키기 위해 스포츠 음료(Rad CraCra)를 섭취할 것이라고 이야기하고 있으므로, 정답은 ⑤ '축구 경기력 향상을 위한 음료 소개'이다.

**총 어휘 수** 120

## 05 대화자의 관계 파악

**소재** 이삿짐센터에 의뢰하는 대화

**듣기 대본 해석**

여: 안녕하세요. 들어오세요.
남: 우와. 여기를 봐요! 골동품인 꽃병들이 많네요. 수집가세요?

여: 맞아요. 그러니까 그쪽 회사는 부서지기 쉬운 물건들을 위해 특별한 서비스를
　　제공해 주시는 거죠?
남: 맞습니다. 조심히 다뤄야 할 물건들을 보호하기 위해 특별히 만들어진
　　용기가 있습니다. 다만, 추가로 150달러를 받습니다. 정확히 언제 이사
　　가시나요?
여: 다음 주 일요일이요. 근데 더 일찍 짐을 다 옮기려고요. 언제 시간 가능하시고
　　비용은 얼마 정도 드나요?
남: 금요일 오후까지 모든 짐을 옮겨드릴 수 있어요. 갖고 계신 것들을 보면
　　900달러가 적당한 것 같네요.
여: 좋네요. 미리 준비해둬야 할 것들 있나요?
남: 글쎄요, 귀중품은 따로 싸서 직접 챙겨가시기 바랍니다.
여: 네, 알겠습니다.

### 어휘

**antique** *a.* 골동품인, 고대의　*n.* 골동품　　**fragile** *a.* 부서지기 쉬운, 섬세한
**delicate** *a.* 연약한, 다치기 쉬운　　**ship** *v.* 싣다, 짐을 옮기다　*n.* 배
**valuables** *n.* 귀중품

### 정답 ⑤

### 문제풀이

두 사람의 대화에서 이사 가는 날짜와 부서지기 쉬운 물건에 대한 관리, 비용
등을 이야기 하는 것으로 보아 여자가 이삿짐센터에 의뢰하는 상황임을 알
수 있으므로 두 사람의 관계는 ⑤ '이삿짐센터 직원 ― 고객'으로 볼 수 있다.

### 총 어휘 수 134


## 06 그림의 세부 내용 파악

### 소재 아이 방에 그릴 벽화

### 듣기 대본 해석

여: 여보, 드디어 Colin 방에 그릴 벽화 디자인을 완성한 것 같아.
남: 좋네. 나도 볼래.
여: 응. 어떤지 좀 말해 줘.
남: 일단 태양이 좀 흥미롭네. 멋진 선글라스도 쓰고 있어.
여: 맞아. 그리고 저 말은 땅에 있는 풀을 뜯어 먹고 있어.
남: 좋네. 저기 있는 건 사과나무겠네. 이거 그림 진짜 잘 그렸다.
여: 고마워. 나무 주변에 있는 토끼들은 어때?
남: 좀 더 쥐같이 생겼는데 벽에다가 그리면 훨씬 알아보기 쉬울 거야. 돼지가
　　진흙탕에서 노는 것도 맘에 들어.
여: 돼지들은 진흙을 진짜 좋아해 당신도 알다시피. Colin이 독수리를 좋아해서
　　나무에도 한 마리 그려 놨어.
남: 예쁘네. Colin이 분명히 좋아할 거야.
여: 그럼 이제 미술 용품 가게에 가서 페인트 좀 사야겠다.
남: 음, 결과물이 어떻게 나올지 정말 기대된다.
여: 나도 여보.

### 어휘

**mural** *n.* 벽화　　**art supply store** 미술 도구를 파는 가게
**turn out** 모습을 드러내다, 나타나다

### 정답 ②

### 문제풀이

말이 땅에 있는 풀을 뜯어 먹고 있다고 했는데, 그림에서는 나무에 있는 사과를
먹고 있으므로 정답은 ②번이다.

### 총 어휘 수 160


## 07 할 일

### 소재 휴식의 필요성

### 듣기 대본 해석

남: 괜찮니? 기분이 안 좋아 보이는구나.
여: 다음 주에 큰 시험이 있어서 제가 준비를 열심히 했었어야 했는데 공부
　　대신 친구들과 너무 어울려 놀았어요. 시험을 잘 못 볼까 걱정이 돼요.
남: 그거에 대해 너무 걱정하지 마. 만약 네가 오늘 공부를 시작한다면 시험을
　　잘 볼 거야.
여: 그렇게 말씀해 주셔서 감사해요. 기분이 좀 나아져요. 하지만 이 불안감이
　　저를 덥게 만드네요.
남: 이상하구나. 네가 열이 나지 않는지 보기 위해 체온을 재 보마. [잠시 후]
　　괜찮아.
여: 어쨌든 진통제를 좀 먹고 싶어요.
남: 아니, 진통제는 도움이 안 돼. 네가 정신을 차리고 공부를 하고 싶으면,
　　휴식을 취해야 해. 낮잠을 자야 한다.
여: 지금 낮잠 잘 수는 없어요. 아직 이 숙제도 마치지 못했어요.
남: 너는 정말 잠이 필요한 것처럼 보이는구나. 올라가서 누우렴. 깼을 때 너는
　　더 정신이 맑아지고 숙제를 더 잘 할 수 있을 거야.
여: 알람을 맞춰 주시겠어요? 만약 지금 낮잠을 자면 제가 너무 길게 잘까
　　걱정돼요.
남: 그래, 그럴게. 이제 쉬러 가렴.

### 어휘

**hang out with** ～와 시간을 보내다　　**fever** *n.* 열　　**medication** *n.*
약　　**pain pill** 진통제　　**alert** *a.* 정신을 바짝 차린　　**assignment** *n.*
과제

### 정답 ③

### 문제풀이

남자는 두통이 있는 여자에게 일단 낮잠을 자면서 쉬고 일어나서 공부하기를
권하고 있다. 여자는 낮잠을 오래 잘까 걱정하며 알람을 맞춰달라고 부탁하고
있으므로 남자가 여자를 위해 할 일은 ③ '알람 맞춰주기'이다.

### 총 어휘 수 195


## 08 이유

### 소재 사무실 청소로 인해 미뤄진 이사

### 듣기 대본 해석

여: 안녕하세요 Staller 씨. 이번 주말에 새로운 사무실로 옮길 준비가 되었죠,
　　맞죠?
남: 못 들으셨어요? 다음 주 주말까지는 옮기지 않습니다.
여: 정말이요? 왜 갑자기 계획이 바뀌었죠?
남: 우리가 그곳에 옮겨 시작하기 전에 철저히 청소를 해놓는 것이 좋다고
　　생각했어요.
여: 이사 업체에 다시 스케줄을 잡아야 한다고 전화해 줬나요?
남: 그랬죠. 그들은 계획이 바뀐 것에 대해 좋아하지 않았어요. 사실 다음 주말에
　　이미 일정이 예약되어 있거든요.
여: 오, 이런. 우리가 만약 그들을 대체할 이사 업체를 찾지 못하면 어떻게 하죠?
남: 아직 확실하지는 않지만 토요일에 직원들이 모두 나와 짐을 빼주도록
　　생각하고 있어요.
여: 그들이 그 생각을 좋아할 것 같진 않군요.
남: 당신 말이 아마 맞을 거예요. 하지만 궁여지책이 필요한 절박한 시기거든요.

### 어휘

**replace** *v.* 교체하다, 대신하다　　**desperate** *a.* 필사적인, 절박한
**measure** *n.* 조치

### 정답 ⑤

대화의 앞부분에서 여자가 왜 사무실 옮기는 계획이 바뀌었냐고 물었을 때 남자가 옮겨서 새로 시작하기 전에 철저히 청소하는 것이 좋다고 생각했다고 했으므로 정답은 ⑤ '이사 전에 사무실 청소를 해야 해서'이다.

**총 어휘 수** 138

# 09 숫자

**소재** 아들과 딸의 가방 구매하기

**듣기 대본 해석**

남: 안녕하세요. 어떻게 도와드릴까요?

여: 아들 가방 사려고요.

남: 아, 딱 좋을 때 오셨네요. 지금 개학 시즌이라 할인을 최대 40퍼센트까지 해드리고 있어요.

여: 좋네요! 요즘 제일 잘 나가는 가방이 뭐예요?

남: 음, 이 Spikey 상표 가방이 굉장히 잘 팔려요. 50달러로 가격이 책정되었지만 지금 20퍼센트 할인 중이에요.

여: 괜찮네요. 살게요.

남: 알겠습니다! 더 필요한 것 있으세요?

여: 우리 딸도 새 가방 하나 사주면 좋겠네요. 저 핑크색 가방은 얼마예요?

남: 그건 원래 60달러인데, 지금 10퍼센트 할인해 드려요.

여: 좀 비싸지만 딸 아이가 분명 좋아할 거예요. 살게요.

남: 알겠습니다. 원하시면 가방을 방수로 해드릴 수도 있어요.

여: 얼만데요?

남: 가방당 추가로 5달러가 들어요.

여: 괜찮아요. 그냥 이대로 가져갈게요.

**어휘**

**back-to-school** *a.* 신학기의, 개학의    **popular** *a.* 인기 많은
**pricey** *a.* 값비싼    **water-resistant** *a.* 방수의, 물이 잘 스며들지 않는

**정답** ②

**문제풀이**

아들의 가방은 50달러인데 20퍼센트 할인하므로 40달러, 딸의 가방은 60달러인데 10퍼센트 할인되어 54달러이다. 방수 처리는 하지 않는다고 했으므로 총 40+54=94달러가 되어 정답은 ② '$94'이다.

**총 어휘 수** 153

# 10 언급 유무

**소재** 과수원으로의 현장학습

**듣기 대본 해석**

*[전화벨이 울린다.]*

남: 안녕하세요. Tafford 과수원입니다.

여: 여보세요, 저는 Paulson 고등학교에 있는 생물 선생님인 Fink예요. 제 학생들을 과수원으로 현장학습 데려가는 것에 대해 알아보려고 전화했습니다.

남: 그 말을 들으니 기쁘네요, Fink 선생님. 저희는 학생들을 위한 반나절 동안, 그리고 하루 종일 하는 프로그램이 있어요.

여: 반나절 프로그램이 더 적절할 것 같아요. 이런 프로그램에서 해주시는 활동들은 무엇인가요?

남: 날씨가 좋으면, 저희는 주로 학생들을 데리고 나가서 사과를 따고 사과주스를 만들어요.

여: 학생들이 좋아할 것 같네요. 저는 학생 약 25명을 데려가려고요. 9월 26일에 자리가 있나요?

남: 네, 저희 스케줄은 그 주 내내 비어 있어요.

여: 좋아요. 그러면 그때로 예약할게요.

남: 네. 9월 26일에 약 25명이라고 하셨죠?

여: 맞아요. 그리고 Paulson 고등학교예요.

남: 알겠어요. 학생들에게 점심을 제공하셔야 하고 학생들이 편한 복장을 입도록 말해주세요.

여: 그럴게요. 도와주셔서 감사해요.

**어휘**

**orchard** *n.* 과수원    **inquire** *v.* 묻다, 알아보다

**정답** ④

**문제풀이**

대화에서 과수원에서의 활동 내용(사과 따서 주스 만들기), 인원(25명), 현장학습의 날짜(9월 26일), 당일 복장(편한 복장)에 관한 언급은 있지만 1인당 가격에 대한 언급은 없었으므로 정답은 ④ '1인당 가격'이다.

**총 어휘 수** 171

# 11 내용 일치 · 불일치

**소재** 유기농 농산물 시장에 대한 안내

**듣기 대본 해석**

남: 여름이 돌아왔고 Springfield 농산물 시장도 돌아왔습니다. 이 시장은 Springfield Square에 위치하고 있으며, 방문객들에게 주에서 가장 신선한 유기농 농산물을 기꺼이 제공해드립니다. 더 저렴한 가격에 지역 농부들로부터 직접 구매할 수 있는데 왜 굳이 돈을 더 내고 마트를 가나요? 수박이든, 줄기콩이든, 신선한 잼이든 우리 시장은 당신이 필요한 모든 것을 팔고 있습니다. 매주 토요일 정오부터 오후 7시, 일요일에는 정오부터 오후 5시까지 열려 있습니다. 가족 모두에게 즐거운 경험이 될 수 있습니다. 애완동물도 환영이므로, 이번 주말에 모두를 데리고 농산물 시장을 방문하세요.

**어휘**

**produce** *n.* 생산물, 농산물    **fraction** *n.* 부분, 일부

**정답** ⑤

**문제풀이**

담화의 마지막 부분에서 애완동물도 환영이라고 말했으므로 내용과 일치하지 않는 것은 ⑤ '애완견은 데려올 수 없다.'이다.

**총 어휘 수** 112

# 12 도표

**소재** 정수기 선택하기

**듣기 대본 해석**

남: 안녕하세요. 무엇을 도와드릴까요?

여: 안녕하세요. 사무실에 놓을 정수기를 대여하려고요.

남: 맞게 찾아 오셨습니다. 지금 다섯 가지 모델 중에서 고를 수 있어요. 당신에게 꼭 맞는 정수기를 찾기 위해 질문을 몇 가지 할게요.

여: 네. 물어보세요.

남: 네. 먼저 이 정수기의 기능으로 어떤 것을 원하세요? 얼음을 만들길 원하세요?

여: 그러면 좋지만 꼭 그럴 필요는 없어요. 그렇지만, 뜨거운 물은 나왔으면 좋겠어요.

남: 알겠습니다. 자, 아시다시피 정수기가 다르면 쓰는 에너지의 양도 달라요. 에너지 효율 등급을 몇으로 찾고 계신가요?

여: 우리 회사는 친환경적인 회사라서 가장 좋은 등급이 좋을 것 같아요.

남: 알겠습니다. 낮은 숫자가 더 효율적인 것을 의미합니다. 자, 이제 마지막 질문입니다. 정수기에 한 달에 얼마 정도 쓰실 생각이신가요?

여: 한 달에 40달러가 우리가 지불하고자 하는 최대치인 것으로 결정했습니다.

남: 그러면 이 모델이 좋을 겁니다.
여: 좋네요. 살게요. 도와주셔서 감사합니다.

**어휘**
**look for** ~을 찾다    **water purifier** 정수기    **energy rating**
에너지 효율 등급

**정답** ②

**문제풀이**
여자가 제빙 기능은 꼭 필요하지 않지만 뜨거운 물을 만드는 기능은 원한다고
했으므로 ③, ⑤번을 제외한 나머지 중 에너지 등급이 더 낮으면서 40달러
이하인 것을 고르면 정답은 ②번이다.

**총 어휘 수** 189

## 13 긴 대화의 응답

**소재** 원하는 전공 정하기

**듣기 대본 해석**
여: 안녕. 네가 전공으로 언론학을 공부할 거라고 들었어.
남: 응. 난 언론인이 되고 싶어.
여: 멋지다. 네가 글쓰기에 흥미가 있는 것 같은 걸?
남: 맞아. 어릴 적부터 글쓰기를 좋아했어. 아직도 인류학을 전공할 예정이니?
여: 아니. 사회학을 공부할까 생각 중이야.
남: 잠깐. 지난번 우리가 얘기했을 때는 네가 무엇을 전공할지 확실해 보였던
    것 같은데.
여: 글쎄. 내가 사회학에도 정말 관심이 많다는 것을 깨달았어. 어떤 걸 더
    공부하고 싶은지 모르겠어.
남: 졸업하면 어떤 직업을 갖고 싶은데?
여: 난 사회복지사가 정말 되고 싶은데 우리 아빠는 내가 인류학 교수가 되길
    원하셔.
남: 아. 너의 아버지는 인류학 교수 아니셨니?
여: 맞아. 그러면 넌 내가 어떤 것을 선택해야 한다고 생각해?
남: ⑤ 내가 너라면, 내게 좀 더 흥미 있는 것을 전공할 거야.

**어휘**
**journalism** *n.* 언론학    **anthropology** *n.* 인류학    **sociology** *n.*
사회학    **social worker** 사회복지사

**정답** ⑤

**문제풀이**
사회학과 인류학 중 어떤 것을 전공해야 할지 고민하는 여자에게 남자는
⑤ '내가 너라면, 내게 좀 더 흥미 있는 것을 전공할 거야.'라고 응답하는 것이
가장 자연스럽다.

**오답 보기 해석**
① 난 정말 언론학 교수가 되고 싶어.
② 언론학이 좀 지루하지만, 난 여전히 좋아해.
③ 내 생각엔 높은 수준의 언론인이 요즘 드문 것 같아.
④ 난 전공을 바꾸고 싶은데 아빠가 허락하지 않으실 거야.

**총 어휘 수** 147

## 14 긴 대화의 응답

**소재** 과학 수업 과제 정리

**듣기 대본 해석**
*[똑똑 두드리는 소리]*
남: 거기 누구예요?
여: 나야, Kevin.

남: 아, 엄마. 어서 들어오세요. 요즘 어때요?
여: 나쁘지 않아. 뭐하고 있니?
남: 과학 시간을 위한 학습 과제를 하고 있어요. 내일이 마감이에요. 한번 보세요.
여: *[잠시 후]* 여기 내가 보고 있는 것이 뭔지 모르겠구나.
남: 감자로 만들어진 배터리예요. 꽤 훌륭하죠?
여: 음. 재미있긴 한데 좀 지저분한 것 같구나. 여기저기에 선들이 있구나. 좀
    깔끔하게 할 수 있겠니?
남: 저도 조금 복잡한 거 알아요. 대신에 과정과 모든 것이 어떻게 작동하는지를
    설명하기 위해서 이 포스터까지 만들었어요. 포스터에 대해 어떻게 생각
    하세요?
여: 음. 네가 무언가를 발표하고 다른 사람들을 이해시키려고 할 때는 가능한
    단순하게 만드는 게 중요한 것 같구나.
남: 그럼 제가 어떻게 해야 할까요?
여: ⑤ 가장 중요한 메시지를 찾고 그것을 명확하게 하려고 노력하렴.

**어휘**
**messy** *a.* 지저분한    〈문제〉 **impressed** *a.* 감동을 받은

**정답** ⑤

**문제풀이**
아들이 엄마에게 과학 과제인 감자 배터리를 보여주었고 엄마는 지저분해
보이니 조금 깔끔하게 만들 것을 조언했다. 이어서 설명 포스터에 대한 엄마의
생각은 단순하게 만드는 것이 중요하다고 했기 때문에 아들의 질문에는
⑤ '가장 중요한 메시지를 찾고 그것을 명확하게 하려고 노력하렴.'으로 대답하는
것이 적절하다.

**오답 보기 해석**
① 모든 것을 학교에 있는 쓰레기통에 넣으렴.
② 네가 옳아. 나도 모든 사람들이 감동받을 거라고 생각해.
③ 아니야. 나는 그것을 좀 더 깔끔하게 만드는 것이 그렇게 중요하다고 생각하지
   않아.
④ 선생님께 너의 프로젝트를 다 끝냈다고 말해도 좋아.

**총 어휘 수** 147

## 15 상황에 적절한 말

**소재** 방콕 여행 계획

**듣기 대본 해석**
여: Manny와 그의 여자친구인 Katie는 동남 아시아 배낭여행을 가려고 준비를
    했습니다. 둘 다 이전에 해외로 여행을 간 적이 없어서, 그들은 여행사를
    통해서 가기보다 직접 준비해서 가기로 결정했습니다. Katie가 준비를
    위해 대부분의 일을 했습니다. 그녀는 값싼 숙박을 찾았고 모든 경로를 다
    계획했습니다. 그녀는 현지인과 의사소통할 수 있도록 태국어 회화책도
    샀습니다. 모든 준비 이후에, 그들은 마침내 방콕에 도착했고, Grand Palace
    주위를 걷고 있습니다. 그러나 Katie는 여전히 그들의 여행 계획에 대해
    강박감을 갖고, 새로 할 일을 생각해내고 있습니다. Manny는 Katie에게
    계획 짜는 것을 걱정하지 말고 대신에 여행을 즐기라고 말하고 싶어 합니다.
    이 상황에서 Manny가 Katie에게 할 말로 적절한 것은 무엇입니까?
Manny: ③ 모든 것이 괜찮을 거야. 재미있게 놀자.

**어휘**
**make arrangements** 준비하다    **accommodation** *n.* 숙박
**phrasebook** *n.* (여행객 등을 위한) 상용 회화집    **local** *n.* 현지인, 주민
**obsess** *v.* ~에 집착하게 하다, ~에 강박감을 갖다

**정답** ③

**문제풀이**
방콕 여행 가기 전과 도착한 후에도 여행 계획에만 집착하는 여자친구 Katie에게
Manny가 할 말로 가장 적절한 것은 ③ '모든 것이 괜찮을 거야. 재미있게
놀자.'이다.

오답 보기 해석
① 내가 너의 안내책자를 봐도 될까?
② 모든 예약을 다시 한번 확인했니?
④ 오늘 밤에 우리가 어느 호텔에 머무를지 아니?
⑤ 우리가 방콕에 간다는 사실을 믿을 수 없어. 너무 신나.

**총 어휘 수** 138

# 16 담화 주제 / 17 세부 내용 파악

**소재** 효과적인 공부 습관

**듣기 대본 해석**

남: 여러분 안녕하세요. 기말고사가 다가오는 시점에서 효과적인 공부 습관에 대해서 좀 얘기해 보려고 합니다. 아마도 공부를 할 때 첫 번째로 고려해야 할 것은 집중할 수 있는 최적의 공간을 찾는 것입니다. 조용하고 편해야 하며 이는 교실, 자신의 방, 카페, 또는 도서관이 될 수 있습니다. 두 번째, 공부를 할 때는 목표를 세우는 것이 중요합니다. 목표를 세우는 것은 무언가를 향해 공부할 수 있게끔 도와줍니다. 그리고 자신이 세워놓은 목표들을 다 이뤘을 때 자기 자신한테 상을 줄 수도 있습니다. 제가 말하고 싶은 세 번째 습관은 방해를 받지 않으려고 하는 것입니다. 요즘에는 휴대폰이나 다른 전자기기로 인해 방해를 받기 쉬운데, 그러므로 공부를 할 때는 휴대폰, 텔레비전, 그리고 방해될 만한 다른 전자기기는 반드시 꺼놔야 합니다. 마지막으로 최근 연구 결과 어떤 소리들은 집중력 향상에 오히려 도움을 줄 수 있다고 합니다. 전등, 백색소음, 빗소리, 그리고 자연의 소리와 같이 단조로운 소리들은 정신을 맑게 하고 평온하게 해줍니다. 다음 주 기말고사 공부를 할 때 이러한 조언들을 기억하시길 바랍니다. 감사합니다.

**어휘**

**effective** *a.* 효과적인  **habit** *n.* 습관  **consider** *v.* 고려하다  **concentrate** *v.* 집중하다  **comfortable** *a.* 편한, 쾌적한  **reward** *v.* 상을 주다 *n.* 상  **treat** *v.* 다루다, 대하다 *n.* 특별한 것, 선물  **resist** *v.* 저항하다  **distraction** *n.* 집중을 방해하는 것  **electronics** *n.* 전자기기  **drone** *v.* 웅웅거리는 소리를 내다 *n.* 웅웅거리는 소리, 단조로운 소리

**정답** 16 ③  17 ③

**문제풀이**

16 남자는 학습 최적의 공간, 목표 수립, 방해물을 멀리하는 것 등 효과적인 학습 방법에 대해 이야기하고 있으므로 정답은 ③ '공부를 더 효과적으로 할 수 있는 여러 가지 방법'이다.

17 조용하고 편한 최적의 학습 공간으로 교실, 자신의 방, 카페, 도서관은 언급되었지만 공원은 언급되지 않았으므로 정답은 ③ '공원'이다.

**오답 보기 해석**

16
① 주의 산만이 공부에 미치는 부정적 영향
② 주의 산만과 관련된 건강 문제
④ 목표를 세우고 스스로 보상하는 것의 이점
⑤ 편안한 환경에서 공부하는 것의 이점

**총 어휘 수** 188

| 01 ② | 02 ② | 03 ④ | 04 ⑤ | 05 ① | 06 ⑤ |
|------|------|------|------|------|------|
| 07 ③ | 08 ⑤ | 09 ① | 10 ③ | 11 ⑤ | 12 ③ |
| 13 ⑤ | 14 ① | 15 ① | 16 ⑤ | 17 ⑤ | |

## 01 짧은 대화의 응답

**소재** 환전하기

**듣기 대본 해석**

남: 안녕하세요. 환전하고 싶은 남은 돈이 있는데요. 환율이 어떻게 되죠?
여: 달러당 119엔입니다. 얼마나 환전하려고 하시죠?
남: 55,000엔 가지고 있어요. 여기 있습니다.
여: ② 고액권을 원하세요, 소액권을 원하세요?

**어휘**

**leftover money** 남은 돈　**exchange rate** 환율
〈문제〉 **large bill** 고액권　**small bill** 소액권

**정답** ②

**문제풀이**

남자가 환전을 원하면서 돈을 내밀었을 때, 여자는 어떻게 바꾸길 원하는지 묻는 것이 적절하므로 정답은 ② '고액권을 원하세요, 소액권을 원하세요?'이다.

**오답 보기 해석**

① 100엔과 50엔짜리로 주세요.
③ 저는 은행에서 돈을 환전해야 해요.
④ 여기서 상품을 교환하실 수 없습니다.
⑤ 영수증 원본이 있으시면 교환해 드릴 수 있습니다.

**총 어휘 수** 43

## 02 짧은 대화의 응답

**소재** 다큐멘터리의 감상

**듣기 대본 해석**

여: Conan, HBO에서 방영하는 새 다큐멘터리 Our History 봤어?
남: 응. 어젯밤에 봤어. 인류의 역사에 관한 다른 관점을 보게 되어 정말 흥미로웠어.
여: 나도 그렇게 생각해. 어떤 역사가 진실인지 궁금하게 만들지.
남: ② 확실히 많은 생각이 들게 하더라.

**어휘**

**perspective** *n.* 관점　〈문제〉 **thought-provoking** *a.* 생각하게 하는, 시사하는 바가 많은

**정답** ②

**문제풀이**

여자가 다큐멘터리를 보고 어떤 역사가 진실인지 궁금해졌다고 말했으므로 남자의 응답은 그에 동조하는 ② '확실히 많은 생각이 들게 하더라.'가 가장 적절하다.

**오답 보기 해석**

① 난 다큐멘터리를 본 적이 없어.
③ 내가 다 본 후에 빌릴 수 있어.
④ 너는 내가 그것을 아직 안 본 것 알잖아.
⑤ 나는 그가 쓴 책들 중 몇 권을 읽었어.

**총 어휘 수** 48

## 03 담화 주제

**소재** 일조량 부족으로 인한 우울증을 피하는 방법

**듣기 대본 해석**

남: 겨울철에 뚱해지거나 우울해진 적 있으신가요? 만약 있다면 당신은 전문가들이 말하는 '계절성 우울증'을 앓고 있을 지도 모릅니다. 이 질환은 사람의 몸이 햇빛으로부터 비타민을 받기 때문에 꽤나 흔합니다. 현재 전문가들이 말하기를 전 세계 사람들의 50퍼센트가 비타민D 결핍을 겪고 있다고 합니다. 충분한 양의 비타민D를 얻기 위해서 전문가들은 하루에 10분에서 15분을 야외에 있는 것을 추천합니다. 또, 집을 재배치해서 햇빛을 더 잘 들게 하는 방법도 있습니다. 이것이 가능하지 못하다면 밝은 빛 아래에서 시간을 보내는 것도 도움이 될 수 있습니다.

**어휘**

**moody** *a.* 뚱한, 기분 변화가 심한　**depression** *n.* 우울증
**deficiency** *n.* 결핍　**adequate** *a.* 충분한

**정답** ④

**문제풀이**

겨울철에 일조량 부족으로 오는 우울증을 피하기 위한 방법을 설명해 주고 있으므로 남자가 하는 말의 주제는 ④ '일조량 부족으로 인한 우울증 대처법'이다.

**총 어휘 수** 95

## 04 의견

**소재** 자동차 경보장치 설치

**듣기 대본 해석**

남: Krista, 차에 경보장치 있어요?
여: 없어요. 왜 물었어요?
남: 어젯밤에 제가 나간 사이에 누군가 제 차에 침입했었어요.
여: 오, 저런. 무엇을 가져갔나요?
남: 다행히도 가져갈 것은 별로 없었어요. 하지만 그들이 칼로 내부를 잘라놨어요. 그들은 단지 재산을 파손하고 싶었던 것 같아요.
여: 당신 그것 때문에 굉장히 화났겠네요.
남: 네. 그래서 제가 경보장치 설치에 대해 생각하게 된 거예요.
여: 제 친한 친구가 하나 가지고 있는데, 그것이 아무 때나 울려서 결국 떼어버렸어요. 사람들이 당신의 물건을 파손하려 할 때 경보장치로는 그들을 멈추지 못할 거예요.
남: 네, 당신 말이 맞는 것 같아요. 그럼 저는 무엇을 해야 하죠?
여: 음, 항상 당신의 차를 밝은 곳이나 동네에서 좋은 지역에 주차하세요. 주차 공간이 가장 편리하지 않더라도 경보장치보다는 나을 거예요.
남: 그게 효과가 있을 거라고 생각해요?
여: 네. 저도 그렇게 하는데 한 번도 문제가 생기지 않았어요.
남: 좋아요. 이제부터 그렇게 할게요.

**어휘**

**break into** 침입하다, (차문을) 억지로 열다　**property** *n.* 재산
**install** *v.* 설치하다　**go off** (경보기 등이) 울리다
**randomly** *ad.* 닥치는 대로, 임의로　**wreck** *v.* 망가뜨리다, 파괴하다
**convenient** *a.* 편리한　**alternative** *n.* 대안, 선택 가능한 것

**정답** ⑤

**문제풀이**

여자는 자동차 경보장치의 설치를 생각하고 있는 남자에게 경보장치를 설치했다가 제대로 작동하지 않아서 떼어버린 친구의 이야기를 해주면서 대신 밝고 좋은 곳에 주차를 해두라고 조언하고 있다. 따라서 정답은 ⑤ '경보장치보다는 밝고 좋은 곳에 주차하라.'이다.

**총 어휘 수** 174

## 05  대화자의 관계 파악

**소재** 작가와 성우의 만남

**듣기 대본 해석**

남: 안녕하세요. 당신이 Amelia Hawkins 씨군요.

여: 맞아요. 당신이 그 유명한 Jeffrey Martin 씨군요. 만나서 반갑습니다. Martin 씨.

남: 저야말로 만나서 반갑습니다. 편하게 Jeffrey라고 불러주세요.

여: 알겠습니다. Jeffrey. 이렇게 유명한 사람과 일할 수 있는 건 정말 영광이에요.

남: 감사합니다. 저도 얘기 많이 들었습니다. Amelia 씨. 이 분야에서 진정한 전문가시라고요.

여: 감사합니다. 이 자리에 오기까지 정말 많은 노력이 들었어요.

남: 이해합니다. 제 책을 읽어 본 적 있으신가요?

여: 다 읽어 봤어요. 정말 훌륭해요. 만나는 사람마다 추천해주고 있어요.

남: 과찬이세요. 근데 제 사랑스러운 아내 Lola 없이는 절대 그 어떤 책들도 쓰지 못했을 거예요. 그녀는 제가 그것들을 쓰도록 영감을 주었고 응원해 주었답니다. 제 이야기들을 녹음본으로 만들어 보라고 하기도 했고요.

여: 그걸 제가 하는 거군요?

남: 맞아요. 이렇게 훌륭하고 아름다운 목소리가 제 작품에 생명력을 불어 넣어 줄 것을 생각하니 기대됩니다.

여: 최선을 다 할게요, Jeffrey.

**어휘**

**pleasure** *n.* 기쁨, 즐거움    **professional** *n.* 전문가  *a.* 전문의
**field** *n.* 분야, 들판, 밭    **recommend** *v.* 추천하다
**I'm flattered** 과찬이세요, 영광이에요    **inspire** *v.* 영감을 주다
**record** *v.* 녹음하다    **talented** *a.* 재능이 있는, 훌륭한
**bring ~ to life** ~에 생기(활기)를 불어넣다

**정답** ①

**문제풀이**

남자는 책을 썼다고 했으므로 작가임을 알 수 있고, 여자는 남자의 이야기를 녹음본으로 만드는 작업을 자신의 목소리로 한다고 했으므로 성우임을 알 수 있다. 따라서 정답은 ① '작가 — 성우'이다.

**총 어휘 수** 161


## 06  그림의 세부 내용 파악

**소재** 학교 장기자랑을 위한 무대

**듣기 대본 해석**

여: 아빠, 이 사진 좀 보실래요? 이게 학교 장기자랑을 위해 제가 작업하고 있는 무대예요.

남: 멋지구나. 어디 보자. 달력이 왜 있는 거지? 뒷벽에 있는 것 말이야.

여: 그건 시간의 흐름을 보여주기 위한 거예요.

남: 달력 옆에 창문은 뭐니?

여: 대부분의 등장인물들이 무대 밖에 있는 사람들과 말하기 위해 창문을 이용할 거예요.

남: 그래, 좋은 생각이구나. 무대의 오른쪽에 있는 소파와 커피 테이블이 정말 좋구나.

여: 고마워요. 저도 소파가 좋아요.

남: 꽤 자주 배우들이 거기에 앉아서 이야기할 것 같은데?

여: 네, 맞아요.

남: 무대의 다른 쪽에 쓰러진 나무가 보이네. 그 나무가 소파와 균형을 유지하지만. 그건 매력적이지 않게 보여.

여: 그게 제가 원하는 거예요, 아빠.

남: 네가 그것에 많은 공을 들인 것 같구나. 정말 잘했어.

여: 정말 감사해요, 아빠.

**어휘**

**assume** *v.* 추정하다, 가정하다    **inviting** *a.* 매력적인

**정답** ⑤

**문제풀이**

무대의 오른쪽에 소파와 커피 테이블이 있고 다른 쪽에는 쓰러진 나무(a fallen tree)가 있다고 했는데 그림에서는 쓰러지지 않은 나무가 있으므로 정답은 ⑤번이다.

**총 어휘 수** 162


## 07  할 일

**소재** 수학여행 허가서

**듣기 대본 해석**

여: Peter, 버스 놓치겠다. 준비 다 안 됐어?

남: 금방 가요, 엄마. 금요일에 가는 수학여행 허가서 찾고 있어요.

여: 나한테 줬잖아. 자, 여기.

남: 이건 허가서가 아니에요!

여: 내가 원본을 잃어버린 것 같아서 그냥 쪽지로 썼어.

남: 이걸 받아줄지 모르겠어요, 엄마.

여: 괜찮아. Towns 선생님께 전화해서 설명할게.

남: 지금 전화해 줄 수 있어요?

여: 알겠어. 지금 전화할게. 너 지금 가야 되잖아. 좋은 하루 보내.

**어휘**

**miss** *v.* 놓치다    **permission slip** 허가서    **field trip** 수학여행
**note** *n.* 쪽지

**정답** ③

**문제풀이**

대화의 마지막 부분에서 남자는 여자에게 전화해 줄 수 있는지를 물었고 여자는 지금 전화하겠다고 했으므로 정답은 ③ '선생님께 전화하기'이다.

**총 어휘 수** 95


## 08  이유

**소재** 오디션 프로그램의 방청

**듣기 대본 해석**

여: 어디 다녀왔니, Alan?

남: 책 몇 권을 사러 서점에 다녀왔어.

여: 그게 다야? 왜 그렇게 기뻐 보이니?

남: 실은, 서점에서 돌아오다가 몇 분 전에 전화 한 통을 받았어.

여: 오? 누가 전화했는데?

남: 이 소식을 들으려면 좀 앉는 게 좋겠어. 나 오디션 프로그램 Rising Star K를 서울에 있는 스튜디오에 가서 볼 기회가 생겼어.

여: 와, 네가 그거 정말 보고 싶어 했던 걸 내가 잘 아는데. 축하해!

남: 고마워, Beth. 대략 6개월 전에 그 방청권을 신청했는데, 아무런 응답이 없었거든. 그래서 거의 포기하고 전화가 올 거라고 기대하고 있지 않았어.

여: 그것 참 놀랍다. 그 기회를 잡기가 얼마나 어려운지 알고 있어. 내 친구들 몇 명도 상당히 오래 전에 너랑 비슷하게 신청했었는데, 아무도 너처럼 전화를 받지 못했어. 그러면 언제 보러 가?

남: 다음 주 금요일. 세상에, 이건 정말로 엄청나. 아직도 믿을 수 없어!

여: 네가 너무 부럽다.

**어휘**

**studio** *n.* 스튜디오, 방송실, 촬영소    **apply to** ~에 신청하다, 지원하다
**envy** *v.* 부러워하다

정답 ⑤

**문제풀이**
남자는 6개월 전에 방청 신청을 했던 오디션 프로그램에서 연락이 와서 프로그램을 보러 가게 되었다고 기뻐하고 있으므로 정답은 ⑤ '오디션 프로그램을 방청하게 되어서'이다.

**총 어휘 수** 173


# 09　숫자

**소재** 영화 고르기

**듣기 대본 해석**
남: 여보, 무슨 영화 골랐어?
여: 좀 걸리긴 했는데 드디어 이걸로 골랐어.
남: Windsor's List? 그거 정말 우울하게 만드는 영화인데 최고 명작들 중 하나야.
여: 나도 그렇다고 들었어. 원래 가격은 30달러였는데 50퍼센트 할인 중이야.
남: 잘 골랐네. 당신이 들고 있는 다른 영화는 뭐야?
여: 아, 이거? 이건 Jake 거야. The Light Crystal이라는 영화야. 10달러밖에 안 해.
남: 나 어렸을 때 그 영화 많이 좋아했는데. 오, 여기 만화책이랑 같이 있는 다른 버전이 있어.
여: 좋네. 그걸 사는 게 좋겠다. 그는 만화책 무척 좋아하잖아.
남: 응. 근데 이게 4달러 더 비싸. 14달러야.
여: 그래도 괜찮네. 당신 거는 안 사?
남: 원하는 게 없어.
여: 알겠어. 그럼 계산하고 집에 가자.

**어휘**
**depressing** *a.* 우울하게 만드는　　**version** *n.* 버전, 판

**정답** ①

**문제풀이**
처음 고른 Windsor's List는 30달러인데 50퍼센트 할인을 한다고 했으므로 15달러이고, 두 번째 고른 The Light Crystal은 만화책과 같이 있는 것이 14달러이므로 두 사람이 지불할 총액은 ① '$29'이다.

**총 어휘 수** 146


# 10　언급 유무

**소재** 신입사원

**듣기 대본 해석**
여: Anderson 씨, 가장 최근에 했던 사원 면접 때 있었던 Randal Kim을 기억하세요?
남: Randal Kim이요? 아, 여러 언어를 구사했던 사람이요?
여: 네, 그 사람이에요. 그에 대한 나의 첫인상은 매우 강했어요.
남: 그에게 가장 인상적인 것이 뭐였죠?
여: 언어 능력 외에 그는 팀 일원으로서의 능력에 매우 자신감이 있었어요.
남: 저도 그 점에 동의해요. 그를 인터뷰했을 때, 그는 자신감 있어 보이고 아주 동기 부여가 되어 있고 회사에 기여하는 데 열정적으로 보였어요.
여: 제가 그에 대해 좋았던 또 다른 한 가지는 그가 다양한 조직에서 자원봉사를 많이 해왔다는 거예요.
남: 저도 그것을 봤어요. 그는 중국과 폴란드에서 보낸 시간은 말할 것도 없고 아프리카에서 혼자 500시간 이상 자원봉사를 했더군요. 그가 말하길 그의 좌우명은 "뭔가를 하고 싶다면, 그것은 나에게 달려 있다."라고 했어요.
여: 제 생각에는 그가 우리 팀의 중요한 멤버가 될 것 같아요.
남: 저도 그렇게 생각해요.

**어휘**
**initial** *a.* 처음의, 초기의　　**impression** *n.* 인상　　**confident** *a.* 자신감 있는　　**motivated** *a.* 동기가 부여된　　**enthusiastic** *a.* 열정적인　　**contribute** *v.* 기여하다　　**not to mention** ~은 말할 것도 없고

**정답** ③

**문제풀이**
남자와 여자는 채용 면접을 본 사람에 대해 이야기하고 있는데, 그의 외국어 능력, 첫인상, 자원봉사 이력, 좌우명에 대해서는 언급했지만 전공에 대한 언급은 하지 않았으므로 정답은 ③ '전공'이다.

**총 어휘 수** 156


# 11　내용 일치 · 불일치

**소재** 안경원숭이의 특징

**듣기 대본 해석**
여: 안녕하세요, 신사 숙녀 여러분. 오늘 저는 안경원숭이라고 불리는 특별한 작은 동물에 대해 조금 이야기하고 싶습니다. 이 작은 녀석은 필리핀 군도의 남쪽 부근 즉, 보홀섬과 민다나오섬에서 발견됩니다. 안경원숭이는 아주 작은 포유동물입니다. 다 자란 안경원숭이는 여러분의 손바닥에 딱 맞습니다. 안경원숭이를 유명하게 만드는 것은 그것의 커다란 눈입니다. 이 눈은 자리에 고정되어 있지만 안경원숭이는 머리를 양쪽 방향으로 180도 돌릴 수 있습니다. 더 놀라운 것은 안경원숭이의 눈은 믿을 수 없는 야간 시력을 가지고 있다는 것입니다. 최소한의 불빛이 있을 때, 한밤중에도 대낮처럼 잘 볼 수 있게 하기 위해 안경원숭이의 동공은 거의 눈의 크기만큼 확대됩니다. 정말 흥미롭지 않으요? 안경원숭이에 대해 더 알고 싶으시면 필리핀으로 가는 비행기를 타고 가셔서 직접 안경원숭이를 보시기를 제안합니다.

**어휘**
**extraordinary** *a.* 특별한, 보기 드문　　**archipelago** *n.* 군도　　**namely** *ad.* 즉, 다시 말해　　**mammal** *n.* 포유동물　　**palm** *n.* 손바닥　　**incredible** *a.* 믿을 수 없는　　**expand** *v.* 확장하다, 확대하다

**정답** ⑤

**문제풀이**
안경원숭이의 눈은 최소한의 불빛만 있어도 동공이 크게 확대되어 한밤중에도 낮처럼 볼 수 있다고 했으므로 내용과 일치하지 않는 것은 ⑤ '낮에는 시력이 좋지만, 밤에는 잘 볼 수 없다.'이다.

**총 어휘 수** 152


# 12　도표

**소재** 아기 침대 고르기

**듣기 대본 해석**
남: 여보, 인터넷으로 뭐해?
여: 우리 아기를 위한 침대를 보고 있어. 알다시피 곧 태어나잖아.
남: 맞아. 아기 방에 놓을 것을 생각해 봐야겠어. 좋은 것 찾았어?
여: 음, 이 다섯 개 중에 고르는 게 좋을 거 같아. 이 회사가 질 좋은 침대를 많이 만들기 때문에 평이 좋아.
남: 어디 보자. [잠시 후] 낮은 것은 빼는 게 좋겠어. 그래야 아기가 커졌을 때 새로 안 사도 되니까.
여: 맞아. 매트리스도 포함하는 게 좋을 것 같아. 그럼 따로 안 사도 되잖아.
남: 동감이야.
여: 재질은 어떻게 할까? 어떤 것들은 나무로 만들어졌고 다른 건 플라스틱이야.
남: 나무로 하는 게 나을 것 같아. 방이랑 잘 어울릴 거야.
여: 응. 그럼 이 두 개로 선택이 좁혀졌어. 어떤 것이 나은 것 같아?

남: 예산이 좀 빠듯하니까 더 싼 걸로 하자.
여: 좋아. 바로 주문할게.

**어휘**

**crib** *n.* 아기 침대   **review** *n.* 논평, 평가   **mattress** *n.* 매트리스
**budget** *n.* 예산, 비용

**정답** ③

**문제풀이**

남자와 여자가 아기 침대를 고르는 상황이다. 둘은 높이가 낮은 것은 빼자고
했으므로 ②~⑤번이 해당되는데 매트리스가 포함된 것으로 하자고 했으므로
④번은 제외된다. 또한, 이들은 나무로 된 침대를 골랐으므로 ③, ⑤번이 남는데
그 중 더 싼 것으로 하자고 했으므로 두 사람이 선택한 침대는 ③번이다.

**총 어휘 수** 183


# 13   긴 대화의 응답

**소재** 유명 화가의 작품 전시회

**듣기 대본 해석**

남: 우리가 드디어 여기 있다는 게 믿어지지 않아. Banksy의 작품을 예전부터
　　정말 보고 싶었어.
남: 그가 우리 도시에서 이렇게 전시회를 한다는 게 믿겨지지가 않아.
여: 가자. 닫기 전에 충분히 둘러볼 시간이 있으면 좋겠어.
남: 먼저 표를 사야지.
여: 응. 근데 그가 만든 작품에 비해서 25달러는 좀 싼 것 같아.
남: 응. 분명히 그만큼의 값어치를 충분히 할 거야.
여: 어, 봐봐. 30분 후에 시작하는 투어 그룹이 있어. 기다려서 그 모임이랑
　　갈까?
남: 근데 그룹으로 가면 그들의 속도에 맞춰야 되잖아. 난 내가 원하는 대로
　　시간을 갖고 전시회를 즐기고 싶어.
여: 난 화가랑 작품들에 대해서 좀 더 배우는 게 재미있을 것 같아.
남: 그럼 오디오 안내 장치를 하나 빌리면 되겠네. 재미있겠다.
여: ⑤ 그렇게 하면 우리가 설명을 들을지 말지 선택할 수 있겠네.

**어휘**

**exhibition** *n.* 전시회   **pace** *n.* 속도, 걸음   **device** *n.* 장치
〈문제〉**admission** *n.* 입장, 입장료

**정답** ⑤

**문제풀이**

여자는 투어 그룹에 들어가서 설명을 듣고 싶어하지만 남자는 원하지 않는
상황에서 남자가 오디오 안내 장치를 빌리자고 제안했으므로 그에 적절한
여자의 대답은 ⑤ '그렇게 하면 우리가 설명을 들을지 말지 선택할 수 있겠네.'이다.

**오답 보기 해석**

① 그들은 입장료로 너무 많은 돈을 받아.
② 우리가 투어 그룹에 합류하게 돼서 기뻐.
③ 나는 왜 그렇게 많은 사람들이 Banksy의 작품을 사랑하는지 알겠어.
④ 전시회 투어 동안 오디오를 듣는 것은 예의 없는 거야.

**총 어휘 수** 153


# 14   긴 대화의 응답

**소재** 자신이 쓴 글에 대한 조언 부탁

**듣기 대본 해석**

여: Mike. 바빠? 시간 좀 있어?
남: 그렇게 바쁘지는 않아. 뭐 필요한 거 있어?
여: 학교 신문에 이 글을 실으려고 하고 있거든.

남: 난 네 글 읽는 거 좋아해.
여: 응. 난 쓰는 거 좋아해. 하여튼, 내 글을 읽고 어떤지 말해 줄 사람이 필요해.
　　건설적인 비판도 해주면 더 좋을 것 같아.
남: 근데 왜 나한테 봐달라고 하는 거야?
여: 실은, 너희 누나 말하는 거야. 그녀가 Kings and Queens 신문사에서
　　일한다고 하지 않았어?
남: 그렇긴 한데 다음 주까지 출장 가 있어.
여: 내 글을 너희 누나한테 이메일로 보내서 읽어봐 달라고 하면 안 될까?
남: ① 문제없어. 내가 누나한테 연락해서 그녀가 시간이 되는지 알아볼게.

**어휘**

**article** *n.* 글, 기사   **constructive** *a.* 건설적인, 적극적인
**criticism** *n.* 비판   **press** *n.* 신문사, 언론사

**정답** ①

**문제풀이**

여자는 남자의 누나에게 자기 글을 이메일로 보내서 검토해주기를 부탁하고
있는 상황이므로 여자의 질문에 대한 남자의 적절한 답은 ① '문제없어. 내가
누나한테 연락해서 그녀가 시간이 되는지 알아볼게.'이다.

**오답 보기 해석**

② 물론이야. 내가 그것을 검토해서 내일 너한테 돌려줄게.
③ 괜찮긴 하지만 나는 이번 주말 전에 그것을 제출해야 해.
④ 네가 학교 신문과 관련된 일을 얻어서 잘됐어.
⑤ 아니. 그렇지만 내가 너한테 학교 신문 한 부를 꼭 줄게.

**총 어휘 수** 132


# 15   상황에 적절한 말

**소재** 졸업식 연설

**듣기 대본 해석**

여: Bill은 고등학교 3학년 학생이고 졸업반에서 가장 인기 있는 학생들 중
　　한 명입니다. 그는 굉장히 똑똑하고 외향적인 성격을 갖고 있습니다. 그의
　　많은 노력과 인기로 인해 학교의 교장인 Thomas 선생님은 Bill에게
　　졸업식 때 연설을 부탁했습니다. Bill은 기뻐하면서 이 제안을 받아들였고
　　연설에 많은 노력을 들여 왔습니다. Bill은 훌륭한 학생이고 여러모로 좋은
　　사람이지만 사람들 앞에서 말하는 것에 어려움을 겪습니다. 졸업식 전에
　　Thomas 선생님은 Bill이 긴장하고 있는 것을 발견하고 그에게 격려의 말
　　몇 마디를 하고 싶어 합니다. 이러한 상황에서 Thomas 선생님이 Bill에게
　　할 말로 가장 적절한 것은 무엇일까요?
Mr. Thomas: Bill, ① 숨을 깊이 들이쉬렴. 너는 잘할 거야.

**어휘**

**senior** *n.* 졸업반 학생, 상급생   **principal** *n.* 교장 선생님   **notice** *v.*
알아차리다   **encouragement** *n.* 격려   〈문제〉**commencement**
*n.* 졸업식, 학위 수여식, 시작

**정답** ①

**문제풀이**

교장 선생님은 졸업식 연설을 앞두고 긴장하고 있는 Bill에게 격려의 말을 해주고
싶어하는 상황이므로 편안하게 긴장을 풀어주고 격려해 주는 내용인 ① '숨을
깊이 들이쉬렴. 너는 잘할 거야.'가 정답이다.

**오답 보기 해석**

② 나는 네가 졸업식 연설을 해주었으면 좋겠구나.
③ 나는 네가 연설 수업에서 잘할 거라고 확신해.
④ 고등학교 졸업을 축하해.
⑤ 네가 올해 졸업을 못 한다니 유감이구나.

**총 어휘 수** 118

**소재**  휴가 가기 좋은 관광지 푸켓 소개

### 듣기 대본 해석

남: 매년 똑같은 해변가에 똑같은 여행을 가는 게 지겨우십니까? 올해는 새로운 것을 해보세요. 아름다운 푸켓으로 이국적인 여행을 해보세요. 푸켓은 태국 남쪽에 위치한 섬으로 여러분의 호기심뿐만 아니라 예산도 충족시켜주는 곳입니다. 이 섬에는 매년 푸켓의 문화, 훌륭한 해산물, 그리고 셀 수 없이 많은 해변가 활동들을 체험하는 수많은 관광객들이 찾아옵니다. 세상에서 가장 흰 모래를 갖고 있는 곳들 중 하나로 푸켓은 스쿠버 다이빙과 스노클링을 할 멋진 기회를 제공합니다. 채식 행사와 같은 수 많은 축제들이 여러분의 호기심을 충족하고 마음을 열어줄 것입니다. 파파야, 당근, 향신료, 그리고 다른 진미들을 사용하여 만든 유명한 요리 sum tam을 드셔보세요. 잊을 수 없는 맛일 겁니다. 좀 더 모험을 즐기는 사람이라면 무성한 화초와 고운 해변가로 유명한 Phi Phi섬에 가보세요. Blue Lagoon과 The Beach 같은 영화들을 촬영한 세트장에도 들러 보실 수 있습니다. 지금 바로 여행 계획 잡으시고 아름다운 푸켓으로 오세요!

### 어휘

**exotic** *a.* 이국적인    **cater** *v.* 음식을 공급하다, 충족시키다
**budget** *n.* 예산, 비용    **exquisite** *a.* 매우 아름다운, 정교한
**delicacy** *n.* 진미, 별미, 여림, 연약함    **adventurous** *a.* 대담한, 모험을 즐기는    **greenery** *n.* 화초    **powdered** *a.* 고운, 가루로 만든

### 정답  16 ⑤   17 ⑤

### 문제풀이

16 푸켓에서 즐길 수 있는 다양한 즐길 거리와 먹거리, 볼거리들을 소개하며 여행을 하러 오라고 하는 것으로 보아 남자가 하는 말의 목적으로 가장 적절한 것은 ⑤ '좋은 휴양지를 홍보하려고'이다.

17 남자는 스노클링, 채식 행사(vegetarian festival), 음식 시식(sum tam), 유명한 Phi Phi섬 방문을 언급했으나, 기념품에 대해서는 언급하지 않았으므로 정답은 ⑤ '기념품 제작'이다.

### 총 어휘 수  180



01  What's the exchange rate

02  a different perspective / makes you wonder which history is true

03  seasonal depression / suffer from vitamin D deficiency / To get an adequate amount / If this is not a possibility

04  My car was broken into / getting an alarm installed / isn't going to stop them / park your car in a well-lit area

05  professional in this field / I'm flattered / record my stories / bring my work to life

06  let me take a look / window next to the calendar / a fallen tree on the other side / you put a lot of thought into this

07  miss the bus / find my permission slip / I just wrote a note / call her now / need to leave

08  got a phone call / won a chance to go / expecting to get the call / quite a while ago

09  That's a really depressing movie / that comes with a comic book / four dollars more expensive

10  spoke several languages / seemed very motivated and enthusiastic / not to mention his time in China and Poland

11  What makes the tarsier famous is / provide tarsiers with incredible night vision / see just as well in the middle of the night

12  they make high-quality cribs / rule out the low-height one / made of wood / kind of on a budget

13  putting on an exhibition / it'll be worth every penny / move at their pace / audio tour devices

14  constructive criticism / out of town on business / ask her to look it over

15  one of the most popular students in / accepted the offer / he struggles with public speaking / words of encouragement

16-17  caters to your curiosities / hundreds of thousands of visitors / satisfy your curiosities / you won't soon forget

# 03 수능영어듣기 실전모의고사

| 01 ① | 02 ⑤ | 03 ⑤ | 04 ③ | 05 ③ | 06 ④ |
| 07 ① | 08 ① | 09 ③ | 10 ④ | 11 ⑤ | 12 ⑤ |
| 13 ⑤ | 14 ② | 15 ① | 16 ③ | 17 ③ | |

## 01 짧은 대화의 응답

**소재** 휴대폰 분실

**듣기 대본 해석**

여: 아빠, 제 휴대폰 어디 있어요? 찾을 수가 없네요.
남: 학교에 가져가지 않았니? 가방 안에 있는지 먼저 보지 그래?
여: 오늘 학교에 가져가지 않았어요. 분명 여기 어딘가에 있어요.
남: ① 확실하니? 그렇다면, 같이 찾아보자꾸나.

**어휘**

〈문제〉 **guilty** *a.* 죄책감이 드는　　**fault** *n.* 잘못, 책임

**정답** ①

**문제풀이**

휴대폰을 찾고 있는 딸이 학교에 휴대폰을 가져가지 않았고 분명 여기 있을 거라고 말하는 데에 대한 아빠의 적절한 응답은 ① '확실하니? 그렇다면, 같이 찾아보자꾸나.'이다.

**오답 보기 해석**

② 미안해. 집 밖에서 네 휴대폰을 잃어버렸어.
③ 네가 죄책감을 느낄 필요는 없어. 다 내 잘못이야.
④ 걱정 마. 그것을 학교에서 찾을 수 있을 거야.
⑤ 내가 그것을 언제 마지막으로 갖고 있었는지 기억이 안 나.

**총 어휘 수** 45

## 02 짧은 대화의 응답

**소재** 보고서 준비

**듣기 대본 해석**

남: Ingrid, 제가 원하는 보고서 찾았어요?
여: 네. 제가 출력했어요. 여기 있어요.
남: 고마워요. *[잠시 후]* 잠시만요. 저는 직원 생산성에 관한 보고서는 필요하지 않아요. 저는 신입사원에 관한 보고서가 필요해요.
여: ⑤ 제가 실수했네요. 지금 당장 올바른 보고서를 출력할게요.

**어휘**

**print out** 인쇄하다, 출력하다　　**employee** *n.* 종업원, 고용인
**productivity** *n.* 생산성　　〈문제〉 **correct** *a.* 올바른, 적절한

**정답** ⑤

**문제풀이**

남자가 다른 보고서가 필요하다고 말했으므로 그에 적절한 여자의 응답은 ⑤ '제가 실수했네요. 지금 당장 올바른 보고서를 출력할게요.'이다.

**오답 보기 해석**

① 문제없어요. 도와주게 되어서 항상 기뻐요.
② 물론이죠. 저는 여분의 보고서를 만들 거예요.
③ 제가 보고서를 끝냈고 지금 출력하는 중이에요.
④ 제가 신입사원에 관한 보고서가 필요하다고 당신한테 말했잖아요.

**총 어휘 수** 47

## 03 담화 목적

**소재** 전기 절약 방법

**듣기 대본 해석**

남: 여러분, 안녕하세요. 요즘 우리는 우리의 에너지 수요를 실컷 만족시키기 위해 너무 많은 석탄, 가스, 전기를 사용하고 있습니다. 이번 여름, 가장 중요한 주제는 전기입니다. 지구 온난화 때문에, 여름이 점점 더워지고 있어서 우리는 에어컨을 더 자주 켜는 경향이 있습니다. 그러나, 이는 문제를 가중시킬 뿐입니다. 우리는 시원함을 유지할 대안을 찾아 실천해야 합니다. 만약에 여러분이 자연광이 충분한 곳에서 일하고 있다면, 여러분은 머리 위의 불을 꺼야 합니다. 또한, 짧은 옷을 입으세요. 요즘 대부분의 회사들은 더 시원한 복장을 입을 수 있도록 복장 규정을 조절하고 있습니다. 마지막으로, 에어컨을 사용하는 대신에, 공기의 자연스러운 흐름을 조절하기 위해 창문을 이용하도록 노력하시고, 창문을 이용할 수 없다면 선풍기를 사용하도록 하세요. 우리 함께 환경에서 변화를 만들어서 시원함을 유지합시다!

**어휘**

**satiate** *v.* 실컷 만족시키다　　**alternative** *n.* 대안, 선택 가능한 것
**abundant** *a.* 풍부한　　**adjust** *v.* 조절하다　　**attire** *n.* 의복, 복장
**utilize** *v.* 활용하다, 이용하다

**정답** ⑤

**문제풀이**

남자는 요즘 에어컨의 잦은 사용이 문제가 됨을 지적하면서 시원함을 유지할 대안을 찾고 노력해야 한다고 말하며 전기 절약의 방법을 알려주고 있다. 따라서 남자가 말하는 목적으로 가장 적절한 것은 ⑤ '전기 절약을 위한 방법을 알려주려고'이다.

**총 어휘 수** 138

## 04 의견

**소재** 어린이 스페인어 교육

**듣기 대본 해석**

남: Hamilton 선생님, 좋은 스페인어 책 찾는 것을 도와주시겠어요?
여: 물론이죠. 그런데 왜요, Crowley 선생님? 선생님은 스페인어 교사가 아니잖아요.
남: 제 아들인 Alfred가 스페인어를 배우기 시작해서 제가 집에서 그 애 공부를 도와주고 싶어서요.
여: 좋아요. 그 애는 아마 수업시간에 듣기와 말하기를 연습하고 있을 거예요, 맞나요?
남: 네, 그래서 저는 그 애가 스페인어로 기본 교재 읽기를 배우는 걸 직접 도와주고 싶어요.
여: 제 생각에는 선생님께서 계속 그의 듣기와 말하기 실력에 집중하셔야 할 것 같아요.
남: 정말이요? 그렇지만 제 생각에는 읽기가 새로운 언어를 배우는 첫 번째 단계인 것 같은데요.
여: 읽기는 중요합니다. 하지만 선생님 아들이 영어로 말하기를 어떻게 배웠는지 생각해보세요. 그 애는 듣기와 말하기로 시작했잖아요.
남: 맞아요, 하지만 그 애는 더 나이가 들었고 언어의 기본을 이해하니까 그건 지금과는 다르다고 생각해요.
여: 사실, 모국어를 배우는 것과 같은 방법으로 공부한다면, 제 2언어 심지어 제 3언어조차 더 빨리 배우게 될 거예요.
남: 알겠어요. 조언 고마워요. 제가 조금 더 생각해 볼게요.

**어휘**

**second language** 제 2언어(모국어 외에 학교에서나 일을 위해 배워서 사용하는 언어)　　**native language** 모국어

**정답** ③

**문제풀이**

여자는 영어를 어떻게 배웠는지 생각해보라며 다른 언어 습득도 모국어를 배우듯이 듣기와 말하기로 접근해야 한다고 말하고 있으므로 정답은 ③ '듣기와 말하기로 시작해야 한다.'이다.

**총 어휘 수** 166


## 05 심정 파악

**소재** 프레젠테이션을 앞둔 걱정

**듣기 대본 해석**

남: 안녕, Sandra. 내일 뉴욕으로 가는 출장 준비는 하고 있니?

여: 갈 준비는 됐지만, 솔직히 내가 가지 않아도 된다면 좋겠어.

남: 정말? 나는 네가 새로운 도시로 여행가게 되어서 정말 좋아할 거라고 생각했는데.

여: 응, 물론 뉴욕은 보고 싶지. 그런데 내가 거기에 도착하자마자 중요한 회의와 프레젠테이션을 하거든.

남: 너는 잘 할거야. 프레젠테이션 잘 하잖아.

여: 고마워. 하지만 고객들이 독일인이라 난 독일어를 써야 해. 내가 엉망으로 할까 봐 걱정돼.

남: 괜찮을 거야. 그들은 독일어가 너의 모국어가 아닌 것을 아니까 만약 네가 작은 실수를 하더라도 문제가 되지는 않을 거야.

여: 나도 그건 이해해. 이건 내 경력에 가장 중요한 프레젠테이션이라 걱정되네. 나 정말 잘해야 해.

남: 가장 중요한 건 긴장을 푸는 거야. 회의 준비가 되었으니 지금은 그것에 대해 잊으려고 해보고 네가 휴가를 위해 뉴욕으로 떠난다고 상상을 해봐.

여: 좋아. 해보겠지만 쉽지는 않을 것 같아.

**어휘**

**mess up** 엉망으로 만들다   **matter** *v.* 중요하다, 문제되다
〈문제〉 **elated** *a.* 신이 난   **anxious** *a.* 불안해하는, 염려하는
**determined** *a.* 단호한, 완강한   **envious** *a.* 부러워하는   **upset** *a.*
속상한, 마음이 상한

**정답** ③

**문제풀이**

여자는 뉴욕으로 출장을 가는데 도착하자마자 아주 중요한 회의와 프레젠테이션이 있고, 그것을 독일어로 해야 해서 망치게 될까 봐 걱정하고 있다. 따라서 여자의 심정은 ③ '불안해하고 걱정하는'이 적절하다.

**오답 보기 해석**

① 조용하고 우아한
② 신이 나고 활기 넘치는
④ 의기양양하고 단호한
⑤ 부러워하고 화가 난

**총 어휘 수** 180


## 06 그림의 세부 내용 파악

**소재** National Education Fund의 포스터

**듣기 대본 해석**

남: National Education Fund를 위해 만들어진 새 광고를 본 적 있습니까? 그 기금은 수입이 적은 성인이나 가족이 없는 아이들에게 대학까지 모든 교육을 위한 비용을 지불해 주기 위해 만든 것입니다. 포스터의 제목은, "모두를 위한 더 나은 미래"입니다. 그림의 중간에 공중으로 자신들의 모자를 던지는 대학 졸업생들이 있습니다. 포스터의 아랫부분에는 세 개의 그림이 더 있습니다. 왼쪽에는 유치원 교실에서 색칠을 하고 있는 행복한 아이가 있습니다. 중간에는 벤치에 앉아 함께 식사하고 있는 소녀들이 있습니다. 그리고 오른쪽에는 두 젊은 전문가들이 손을 맞잡고 있는 사진이 있습니다.

이 포스터는 National Education Fund로부터 혜택을 받을 수 있는 모든 다른 종류의 사람들을 보여주려 하고 있습니다.

**어휘**

**income** *n.* 소득, 수입   **graduate** *n.* 대학 졸업생   **benefit from**
~로부터 이익을 얻다

**정답** ④

**문제풀이**

포스터의 중간 부분에는 모자를 공중으로 던지는 졸업생들이, 아랫부분에는 세 개의 그림이 있다고 했다. 세 그림 중 왼쪽에는 유치원 교실에서 색칠하는 아이가, 가운데는 벤치에 앉아 어떤 것을 먹고 있는 소녀들이, 오른쪽에는 두 젊은 전문가들이 손을 맞잡고 있는 사진이 있다고 했는데, 가운데 그림은 소녀들이 책을 읽고 있으므로 ④번이 내용과 일치하지 않는다.

**총 어휘 수** 134


## 07 부탁한 일

**소재** 교환학생 홈스테이

**듣기 대본 해석**

남: 좋은 아침이에요 여보, 당신, 뭐하고 있어요?

여: 이 지원서를 작성하고 있어요. Katie의 학교에서 하는 홈스테이 프로그램에 낼 거예요.

남: 홈스테이 프로그램이라고요? 외국 교환학생 같은 거 맞죠?

여: 맞아요. Katie네 학교가 다른 나라에서 온 몇몇 학생들을 초대할 예정이거든요.

남: 재미있겠는데요. 그리고 당신은 그 학생들 중 한 명을 여기에 머물게 하고 싶은 거죠?

여: 그러고 싶어요. Katie와 우리에게 멋진 경험이 될 거예요.

남: 맞아요. 그런데, 이 학생들은 어느 나라에서 오는 거예요?

여: 두 명은 한국에서 오고, 한 명은 대만에서 와요. Katie가 아시아의 생활 방식과 문화에 대해서 배울 기회를 가지게 돼서 좋을 거예요.

남: 나도 그 사람들의 문화에 대해서 더 많이 배우고 싶어요. 내가 도와줄 수 있는 게 뭐예요?

여: 음, 신청서와 함께 보낼 가족 사진이 필요할 거예요. 작년 크리스마스 때 찍은 사진 찾아줄 수 있어요?

남: 네, 어디 있는지 알 것 같아요.

여: 좋아요, 고마워요.

**어휘**

**fill out** 작성하다, 기입하다   **application** *n.* 지원(서), 신청(서)   **host**
*v.* 주최하다

**정답** ①

**문제풀이**

대화의 끝부분에서 여자는 남자에게 작년 크리스마스 때 찍은 가족 사진을 찾아달라고 부탁했으므로 정답은 ① '가족 사진 찾아주기'이다.

**총 어휘 수** 157


## 08 이유

**소재** 버스 여행

**듣기 대본 해석**

여: Dylan, 이번 주에 Lilly랑 내가 함께 산으로 버스 여행가기로 했는데 너도 같이 갈 수 있는지 궁금해.

남: 좋을 것 같아. 이번 여름에 산으로 가고 싶었거든.

여: 근데 긴 여행일 거야. 너 차멀미 한 적 있어?

남: 어렸을 적엔 버스 탈 때 멀미를 하기도 했는데 지금은 괜찮아. 표가 얼마지?

여: 내 친구가 계획이 바뀌는 바람에 내가 표 세 장을 얻었어. 그래서 돈을 낼 필요가 없어.
남: 멋지다!
여: 응. 날씨 예보 때문에 걱정했었는데 날씨도 좋을 것 같아.
남: 잘됐다. 토요일 몇 시에 출발하니?
여: 토요일? 실은 금요일 정오에 출발해.
남: 정말? 오, 이런. 나 금요일에는 일해야 해.
여: 아, 아쉽다. Lilly가 너와 함께 가기를 정말로 원했는데.
남: 다음 번에 같이 갈 수 있겠지. 그래도 초대해줘서 고마워.

**어휘**

**carsick** *a.* 차멀미를 하는　　**forecast** *n.* 예측, 예보　　**depart** *v.* 떠나다, 출발하다

**정답** ①

**문제풀이**

대화의 마지막 부분에서 여자가 금요일 정오에 출발한다고 하자 남자는 금요일에는 일을 해야 한다고 했으므로 남자가 여행에 가지 못하는 이유는 ① '일을 해야 해서'이다.

**총 어휘 수** 160


# 09　숫자

**소재** 야구 경기 표와 배너 구매

**듣기 대본 해석**

*[전화벨이 울린다.]*
남: 여보세요, 매표소입니다.
여: 안녕하세요, 곧 있을 경기의 표를 사는 것 때문에 전화드렸어요.
남: 그렇군요. LA Dodgers 경기의 표와 Chicago Cubs 경기의 표 중 어느 것을 사려고 하나요?
여: 사실 둘 다요. 근데 얼마죠?
남: LA Dodgers 표는 60달러이고 Chicago Cubs 표는 80달러입니다.
여: 제가 생각했던 것보다 비싸네요. 더 싼 표는 없나요?
남: 죄송해요. 이 경기들 표는 남은 게 이것들 밖에 없어요.
여: 그렇군요. LA Dodgers 표만 하나 살게요. 홈팀의 배너들을 파는 것도 봤는데, 표와 함께 무료로 오나요?
남: 배너는 20달러를 추가로 내셔야 합니다.
여: 네, 그럼 배너도 같이 살게요. 배송비는 가격에 포함된 건가요?
남: 죄송하지만 배송비로 5달러를 따로 내셔야 합니다.
여: 알겠어요. 돈은 최대한 빨리 입금해 드릴게요.

**어휘**

**upcoming** *a.* 다가오는, 곧 있을　　**banner** *n.* 배너, 현수막
**shipping** *n.* 배송　　**transfer** *v.* 옮기다, 이송하다

**정답** ③

**문제풀이**

여자는 60달러짜리 LA Dodgers 표 한 장과 20달러짜리 현수막을 구매하였고, 배송비 5달러를 추가로 지불해야 하므로 총 송금할 금액은 ③ '$85'이다.

**총 어휘 수** 145


# 10　언급 유무

**소재** 북극의 빙하

**듣기 대본 해석**

여: Todd, 어젯밤에 환경에 대한 다큐멘터리 봤어요?
남: 아니요, 놓쳤어요. 무엇에 대한 거였죠?
여: 주요 주제 중 하나가 북극의 빙하가 녹고 있다는 거였어요.

남: 심각한 문제가 되고 있죠?
여: 그래요. 얼음이 태양 광선을 반사함으로써 지구가 과열되는 것을 막아 주는 거울과 같은 작용을 하거든요.
남: 정말이요? 나는 그런지 몰랐어요.
여: 네, 대부분의 사람들이 몰라요. 2009년 이후로, 사람들은 의식을 높이려 많이 노력했고 녹는 것을 막으려고 해왔어요.
남: 그건 정말 중요한 일인 것 같아요. 진전이 있었나요?
여: 조금씩이요, 그래도 갈 길이 멀어요.
남: 그래서 더 큰 문제가 녹는 것 때문에 생기는 거죠?
여: 네, 맞아요. 그것은 지구 기후에 큰 영향을 주지요. 이것이 전 세계 바다의 수면이 높아지게 만들어서 해변가의 도시들이 결국 물에 잠기게 될 위험에 처해 있다는 것도 문제의 일부예요.
남: 오, 이런. 세계 인구의 대부분이 해안이나 근처에 살고 있다고 들었어요.
여: 네 하지만 그 변화가 자연스러운 순환의 한 부분이라고 믿는 몇몇 과학자들도 있어요. 누가 옳은지 말하는 것은 어려운 일이지만 어느 쪽이든 확실히 중요한 문제죠.

**어휘**

**polar** *a.* 극지의　　**ice cap** 빙원(만년설)　　**reflect** *v.* 반사하다
**make progress** 진행하다, 전진하다　　**coastal** *a.* 해안의
**at risk** 위험에 처한

**정답** ④

**문제풀이**

지구에서 빙하의 역할, 해빙을 막기 위한 사람들의 노력, 해수면의 높이에 주는 영향, 다른 의견을 가진 과학자들에 대해서는 언급되었지만 빙하가 녹는 것을 막는 방법에 대한 언급은 없으므로 정답은 ④ '빙하가 녹는 것을 막는 방법'이다.

**총 어휘 수** 202


# 11　내용 일치 · 불일치

**소재** 가수 Brittany Spikes에 대한 소개

**듣기 대본 해석**

남: 안녕하세요, 여러분. 저는 우리 시대 가장 위대한 가수 중 한 명인 Brittany Spikes를 소개하려 합니다. 그녀는 전형적인 미국 가정에서 태어났고 Bertha Beatrice로 불렸습니다. 그녀가 7살이 되었을 때 노래와 춤을 훈련받기 시작했습니다. 그녀는 떠오르는 어린 가수와 댄서들을 위한 어린이 탤런트 쇼, Mickey Mouse Club에 처음 출연했습니다. 그녀는 16살이 될 때까지 쇼에서 공연했습니다. 그 동안 그녀는 화려한 댄스 동작과 애교 있는 미소로 많은 인기를 얻었습니다. 그녀는 겨우 20살이 되었을 때 Hollywood 영화감독 Albert Foster와 2001년 5월에 결혼했습니다. Foster는 그녀의 젊은 가수로서 밝은 미래를 보았고 음악 사업에 그녀를 투입시키기로 결정했습니다. 오늘날, Brittany는 여전히 차트 정상에 있고 전 세계의 팬들에게 기쁨을 주고 있습니다.

**어휘**

**up-and-coming** *a.* 전도유망한, 떠오르는　　**gain popularity** 인기를 얻다　　**flashy** *a.* 화려한　　**winning** *a.* 애교 있는, 마음을 끄는
**delight** *v.* 기쁨을 주다

**정답** ⑤

**문제풀이**

Brittany는 결혼을 한 후, 음악 사업에 투입되었고, 여전히 차트 정상에 있다고 했으므로 일치하지 않는 것은 ⑤ '지금은 가수 활동을 하지 않고 있다.'이다.

**총 어휘 수** 135

## 12 도표

**소재** 숙소 정하기

**듣기 대본 해석**

여: 학기가 거의 끝났네요. Amber가 여름 방학 때문에 대단히 들떠 있어요.

남: 사실 나도 그래요. 가까운 게스트 하우스에 머물면서 잠시 휴식을 취했으면 좋겠어요.

여: 좋을 것 같아요.

남: 좋아요, 내가 인터넷에서 찾아서 숙소 목록을 만들었어요. 우리가 하루 당 지출할 수 있는 금액이 얼마죠?

여: 가능하면 하루에 70달러가 넘지 않도록 노력해야 할 것 같아요.

남: 네, 이 지역 중에 당신은 어디서 묵었으면 좋겠어요?

여: 저는 가능하면 바다 옆에 묵었으면 좋겠어요. 우리가 신발을 벗어놓고 모래 해변을 걸을 수 있다면 멋있을 것 같아요.

남: 알았어요. 우리가 찾는 모든 것을 갖춘 것 같은 숙소가 두 개 있네요. 어디가 당신한테 제일 좋아 보여요?

여: 물론 아침 식사가 포함된 곳이죠. 아침엔 어떤 요리도 하지 싶지 않아요.

남: 좋아요. 내가 바로 전화해서 예약할게요.

**어휘**

**guesthouse** *n.* 여행자용 숙소　　**sandy** *a.* 모래로 뒤덮인
**make a reservation** 예약하다

**정답** ⑤

**문제풀이**

하루에 70달러가 넘지 않았으면 좋겠다고 했으므로 ②번이 제외되고, 바다 옆에 묵었으면 좋겠다고 했으므로 ①번과 ⑤번으로 좁혀지는데 아침 식사가 포함되었으면 좋겠다고 했으므로 정답은 ⑤번이다.

**총 어휘 수** 163


## 13 긴 대화의 응답

**소재** 졸업식에서의 인사

**듣기 대본 해석**

여: 졸업을 축하해, Dr. Nathan. 네가 자랑스러워.

남: 네가 와줘서 기뻐, Layla.

여: 남자친구 졸업식을 놓칠 리가 없잖아.

남: 어머니도 여기 오셨으면 정말 좋았을 텐데.

여: 어머님이 졸업식을 놓쳐서 정말 안 됐어.

남: 어쨌든 모든 의대 친구들이 모두 와줬어.

여: 그들을 빨리 만나보고 싶다.

남: 있잖아, Layla, 너를 안 만났더라면 난 지금 여기에 있지 못했을 거야.

여: 오, 아니야! 그렇게 많이 도와주지도 않았는걸.

남: 내가 최선을 다할 수 있도록 영감을 줬어.

여: 천만에, Nathan. 별로 대단한 것도 아니었는데.

남: ⑤ 난 진심으로 고마워. 그리고 네 도움에 대해 너한테 신세를 많이 졌어.

**어휘**

**graduation** *n.* 졸업식　　**be proud of** ~을 자랑스러워하다
**make it** 해내다, 성공하다　　**show up** 나타나다　　**inspire** *v.* 영감을 주다　　〈문제〉**owe** *v.* ~덕분이다, 신세를 지다

**정답** ⑤

**문제풀이**

남자가 여자에게 졸업하는 데 도움을 줬다며 고마움을 표하고 있는 상황이므로 남자의 응답은 ⑤ '난 진심으로 고마워. 그리고 네 모든 도움에 대해 너한테 신세를 많이 졌어.'가 적절하다.

**오답 보기 해석**

① 너는 열심히 했고 그 학위를 받았어.

② 나는 병원에서 인턴을 어떻게 하는지에 대한 조언이 좀 필요해.

③ 그는 우리 학교에서 가장 인기 있는 의사 선생님 중 한 분이셔.

④ 어머니는 외국에서 일하고 계셔서 오실 수가 없었어.

**총 어휘 수** 117


## 14 긴 대화의 응답

**소재** 저널리스트가 되고 싶은 학생

**듣기 대본 해석**

남: Collins 선생님, 시간 좀 있으세요?

여: 그래, Aron. 무슨 일이니?

남: 음, 지난 주에 내 주신 실화 문학 프로젝트 아시죠? 그걸 하면서 영감을 많이 얻었어요. 저는 저널리스트가 되고 싶어요.

여: 잘 됐네. 난 늘 너의 작품을 읽는 걸 좋아했단다.

남: 감사해요. 시나 단편소설 쓰는 건 별로인데 실화에 대해 쓰는 건 굉장히 흥미롭고 재미있어요. 그런데 제 실화 문학 프로젝트에 문제가 하나 있어요.

여: 오, 그게 뭔데?

남: 음, 그 글이 500자여야 되는 건 알지만 그 정도로 못 줄일 것 같아요.

여: 그럼 몇 자를 썼니?

남: 거의 1,000자 썼어요. 괜찮을까요?

여: ② 괜찮아. 네 글을 빨리 읽고 싶구나.

**어휘**

**literary** *a.* 문학의　　**inspire** *v.* 영감을 주다　　**journalist** *n.* 저널리스트, 기자　　**be into** ~에 관심이 많다　　**article** *n.* 글, 기사

**정답** ②

**문제풀이**

여자가 내 준 과제가 500자여야 하는데 남자는 자신의 글이 1,000자가 되었다며 괜찮은지 물었으므로 그에 적절한 대답은 ② '괜찮아. 네 글을 빨리 읽고 싶구나.'이다.

**오답 보기 해석**

① 이 기사를 읽어봐. 내가 제일 좋아하는 것 중 하나야.

③ 내가 너에게 작가가 되도록 영감을 주었다니 기쁘구나.

④ 내가 너를 도와주고 싶지만 나는 저널리스트가 아니야.

⑤ 닌 내일 전에 그것을 꼭 마쳐야 해.

**총 어휘 수** 126


## 15 상황에 적절한 말

**소재** 자전거 타이어 교체

**듣기 대본 해석**

남: Craig은 자전거 정비공입니다. 그는 Tate 부인의 자전거를 손보고 있는데 그 자전거는 일 년 이상 손을 보지 않아서 부드럽게 나가지 않습니다. 그는 체인, 페달과 브레이크에 녹이 많이 슨 것을 알았습니다. 이 부분에 기름칠을 하자 이들이 좀 더 부드럽게 작동했습니다. 그는 또한 타이어의 접지면이 꽤 얇게 닳아서 교체할 필요가 있다는 걸 발견했습니다. 만약에 Tale 부인이 이 바퀴들로 계속 탄다면 바퀴들이 닳아 구멍이 나고, 이는 사고를 유발할 수도 있습니다. Craig은 Tate 부인에게 해결책을 추천하고 싶습니다. 이런 상황에서, Craig은 Tate 부인에게 뭐하고 말할 것 같은가요?

Craig: ① 타이어가 너무 낡아서 즉시 교체하셔야 합니다.

**어휘**

**rust** *n.* 녹　　**tread** *n.* (타이어의) 접지면　　**wear** *v.* 닳다, 해어지다
〈문제〉**properly** *ad.* 제대로, 적절히

정답 ①

**문제풀이**

자전거 정비공인 Craig은 Tate 부인의 자전거의 여러 부분을 손 본 후, 타이어 교체 시기가 지나서 너무 닳아 있음을 발견했고 해결책을 Tate 부인에게 추천 하고자 하므로 정답은 ① '타이어가 너무 낡아서 즉시 교체하셔야 합니다.'이다.

**오답 보기 해석**

② 자전거를 제대로 관리하지 않으신 게 분명해요.
③ 브레이크가 제대로 작동하도록 확실히 할게요.
④ 작년에 타이어를 교체하신 것 같네요.
⑤ 당신 자전거가 상태가 좋아 보이네요.

**총 어휘 수** 118

# 16 담화 주제 / 17 세부 내용 파악

**소재** 스포츠 종류에 따른 신발 선택의 필요성

**듣기 대본 해석**

여: 매일 당신의 발은 스트레스를 많이 받습니다. 이러한 스트레스를 풀어주는 데에 신발이, 특히 운동 선수들에게, 매우 중요한 작용을 한다는 것은 놀랄 일도 아닙니다. 적절한 신발을 신는 것은 당신의 발목과 발을 지탱해 주면서 부상을 방지할 수 있습니다. 다른 운동들은 발에 다른 방식으로 긴장을 줍니다. 그러므로 당신이 참여하는 운동에 적절한 신발을 골라야 합니다. 예를 들어, 장거리 육상 선수는 발 뒤꿈치를 받쳐주면서 계속되는 쿵쿵거림에 쿠션을 제공해주는 신발을 골라야 합니다. 반면에 테니스와 배드민턴은 이쪽과 저쪽으로 많이 움직여야 합니다. 만약 당신이 이러한 스포츠를 한다면, 이런 활동을 도와줄 수 있는 신발을 찾아야 합니다. 농구에서는 점프하고, 코트에서 뛰고 방향 전환을 하기 위해 안정감이 요구됩니다. 그렇기 때문에 농구에는 하이탑 신발이 필요합니다. 보시다시피 신발은 종목에 따라 달라집니다. 다음 번에 운동화를 사려고 할 때 이 점을 기억해 두는 것이 좋을 것입니다.

**어휘**

**factor** *n.* 요인    **suitable** *a.* 적합한    **strain** *n.* 부담, 압박    *v.* (근육 등에) 무리를 주다    **sufficient** *a.* 충분한    **constant** *a.* 끊임없는, 거듭되는    **pound** *v.* 치다, 쿵쿵거리다    **in regards to** ~에 관해서    **stability** *n.* 안정, 안정성    **vary from ~ to** ~에서 ~까지 다양하다

**정답** 16 ③  17 ③

**문제풀이**

16 여자는 운동에 따라 발에 다른 방식으로 긴장을 주기 때문에 각 운동에 맞게 다른 신발을 신어야 한다고 말하고 있으므로 여자가 하는 말의 주제는 ③ '다른 운동 종목에 다른 스타일의 신발이 필요한 이유'이다.

17 여자는 달리기, 테니스, 배드민턴, 농구는 언급했지만 축구는 언급하지 않았으므로 정답은 ③ '축구'이다.

**오답 보기 해석**

16
① 스포츠의 종류에 따라 어떻게 발에 긴장을 주는가
② 운동 전 스트레칭의 이점
④ 운동할 때 신발을 신는 것의 중요성
⑤ 하이탑 운동화의 장점과 단점

17
① 달리기
② 테니스
④ 배드민턴
⑤ 농구

**총 어휘 수** 183

| | | | | | |
|---|---|---|---|---|---|
| 01 ② | 02 ④ | 03 ④ | 04 ② | 05 ④ | 06 ⑤ |
| 07 ④ | 08 ③ | 09 ③ | 10 ③ | 11 ⑤ | 12 ③ |
| 13 ④ | 14 ④ | 15 ④ | 16 ① | 17 ④ | |

## 01 짧은 대화의 응답

**소재** 잃어버린 전화기

**듣기 대본 해석**

남: Lucy, 내가 너한테 계속 전화 했었어. 우리 버스 함께 타기로 했었잖아.
여: 미안해. 나 전화기를 잃어버렸어. 어디에서도 그것을 찾을 수가 없어.
남: 나도 이전에 똑같은 문제가 있었어. 네가 마지막으로 전화기를 가지고 있었던 곳을 기억하니?
여: ② 음, 직장에서 사용한 건 확실해.

**어휘**

**be supposed to V** ∼하기로 되어 있다　　**anywhere** *ad.* 어디에서도

**정답** ②

**문제풀이**

남자가 여자에게 전화기를 마지막으로 사용한 장소를 기억하는지를 물었으므로 적절한 응답은 ② '음, 직장에서 사용한 건 확실해.'이다.

**오답 보기 해석**

① 그것은 검정색 케이스가 있는 uPhone 6야.
③ 걱정하지 마. 나는 네가 그것을 집에 두고 왔다는 것을 확신해.
④ 나도 그렇게 생각했지만, 난 이미 버스를 확인했어.
⑤ 우리가 그것을 찾을 수 있는지 알아보기 위해 내가 다시 네 전화기에 전화해 볼게.

**총 어휘 수** 51

## 02 짧은 대화의 응답

**소새** 리포트 수정

**듣기 내본 해석**

여: Edward, 너의 리포트 검토를 끝냈단다.
남: 어떤가요? 리포트에 어떤 문제가 있나요, Jones 선생님?
여: 큰 실수는 없어. 하지만 이 예시는 삭제하는 게 좋겠다. 주제랑 관련이 없어.
남: ④ 맞아요. 바로 수정할게요.

**어휘**

**eliminate** *v.* 없애다, 제거하다　　**irrelevant** *a.* 관련이 없는
〈문제〉 **fit well** 잘 어울리다, 잘 맞다

**정답** ④

**문제풀이**

여자는 남자의 리포트 검토를 끝낸 후 예시를 삭제하는 것이 좋겠다는 충고를 하였다. 이에 대해 적절한 대답은 ④ '맞아요. 바로 수정할게요.'이다.

**오답 보기 해석**

① 전 그렇게 생각하지 않아요. 그건 유용한 예시가 아니에요.
② 그렇다면, 같은 예시를 사용할게요.
③ 동의해요. 그건 좋은 리포트예요.
⑤ 훌륭해요. 이곳에 딱 맞네요.

**총 어휘 수** 44

## 03 담화 목적

**소재** 안전한 뱃놀이를 위한 조언

**듣기 대본 해석**

여: 안녕하세요. 제 이름은 Jenny Brown이며 Minnesota주 수상 안전과의 관리자입니다. 오늘 저는 저희 호수와 강에서 안전하고 깨끗한 여름을 보내기 위해 모두가 명심해야 할 사항들을 공유하고자 합니다. 뱃놀이를 하는 동안, 배 위에 항상 있어야 하는 몇 가지 필수적인 물품들이 있습니다. 예를 들어, 배에 있는 구명조끼의 수는 배의 최대 승객 수용인원과 같아야 하고, 모든 배에는 제대로 작동하는 소화기, 경적이나 호각, 그리고 조명이 구비되어 있어야 합니다. 이러한 장비들을 배에 구비하는 것뿐만 아니라, 조명이 잘 작동하는지 항상 확인해야 합니다. 여러분이 물 위에 있을 때 이런 조언들을 잘 따르면 모두가 호수와 강에서 더 안전하고 재미있게 즐기실 수 있습니다. 수상 안전에 대해 더 많은 것을 알고 싶으시면 저희 웹사이트 www.MNwaterfun.gov를 방문하세요. 시간 내 주셔서 감사 드리며 멋진 여름 보내시기 바랍니다.

**어휘**

**tip** *n.* 조언　　**ensure** *v.* 보장하다　　**essential** *a.* 필수적인
**on board** 승선하여, 탑승하여　　**life vest** 구명조끼　　**vessel** *n.* 배
**capacity** *n.* 용량, 수용력　　**be equipped with** ∼을 구비하다
**fire extinguisher** 소화기　　**horn** *n.* 경적, 뿔나팔　　**spotlight** *n.* 조명

**정답** ④

**문제풀이**

여름철 호수나 강에서 뱃놀이를 할 때 안전을 위해 점검하고 지켜야 할 사항들을 조언하고 있다. 따라서 여자가 하는 말의 목적은 ④ '안전한 뱃놀이를 위한 점검 항목들을 알려주려고'가 된다.

**총 어휘 수** 164

## 04 의견

**소재** 인간의 즐거움을 위한 동물의 사용

**듣기 대본 해석**

여: 이번 주말에 서커스 갈 생각이야 같이 가자. 곰이링 코끼리가 재주 부리는 거 부는 게 재미있어.
남: 물어봐 줘서 고미워. 근네 서커스가 그 동물들에게 하는 싯이 윤리적인지 모르겠어.
여: 무슨 말이야? 난 그게 사람들이 동물들의 지능과 노력에 감탄할 수 있는 방법이라고 생각하는데.
남: 서커스단에 있는 동물들이 당하는 학대에 대해서 요즘 많이 읽어왔어. 어떤 동물들은 처벌 받으면서 훈련을 받아.
여: 그게 사실일지 몰라도 동물들이 사육사랑 가깝고 긴밀한 관계를 갖고 있다고도 들었어.
남: 아마 그럴지도, 하지만 동물들은 작은 우리에 갇혀 있고 억지로 사람들을 즐겁게 해줘야 돼.
여: 그렇구나. 글쎄, 조건만 괜찮으면 서커스도 동물들에게 좋은 경험이 될 수 있다고 생각하지 않아?
남: 아니, 그렇게 생각하지 않아. 사람들을 즐겁게 해주기 위해서 동물들이 학대를 받는 것은 정말 잔인한 거라고 생각해.
어: 일겠어. 니도 서커스를 지지하는 걸 다시 생각해 봐야겠어.

**어휘**

**ethical** *a.* 윤리적인, 도덕적인　　**abuse** *v.* 학대하다, 폭력을 가하다
**victim** *n.* 피해자, 희생자　　**entertain** *v.* 즐겁게 해 주다

**정답** ②

문제풀이
남자는 인간의 즐거움을 위해 동물을 훈련시키고 가두어 두는 것은 윤리적이지 않고 학대하는 것이라고 생각하고 있으므로 남자의 의견으로 적절한 것은 ② '인간의 즐거움을 위해 동물을 훈련시키는 것은 옳지 않다.'이다.

**총 어휘 수** 165

## 05  대화자의 관계 파악

**소재** 오토바이 사고를 당한 피해자와 구급대원의 대화

**듣기 대본 해석**
남: 안녕하세요. 당신이 사고가 나서 도움을 필요로 하시던 분인가요?
여: 네, 저 맞아요. 좀 심각한 것 같아요. 걸을 수가 없어요.
남: 알겠습니다. 일단 가만히 계시고 움직이지 마세요. 무슨 일이 있었나요?
여: 오토바이를 탄 어떤 사람이 인도로 와서 제가 걷고 있는데 치고 갔어요.
남: 정말 끔찍하네요. 어떻게 생겼는지 혹시 보셨나요?
여: 아뇨. 근데 헬멧과 가죽재킷을 입고 있었어요.
남: 경찰에는 연락하셨나요?
여: 아뇨. 정신이 없었어요.
남: 제가 경찰에 전화하도록 하겠습니다.
여: 감사합니다.
남: 그건 그렇고, 부상이 얼마나 심한지 알기 위해 몇 가지 테스트를 하겠습니다. 먼저 다리를 이렇게 뻗게 할겁니다. 아프세요?
여: 아야! 네, 아파요.
남: 저기, 아무래도 다리가 부러진 것 같습니다. 엑스레이를 찍기 위해 병원으로 이송해 드려야겠습니다.

**어휘**
**assistance** *n.* 도움    **still** *a.* 가만히 있는, 정지한    **leather** *n.* 가죽
**contact** *v.* 연락하다    **extent** *n.* 정도    **extend** *v.* 뻗다

**정답** ④

**문제풀이**
여자는 오토바이 뺑소니를 당했고, 남자가 부상 정도를 확인하고 있는 것으로 보아 두 사람은 ④ '구급 대원 — 신고자' 관계임을 알 수 있다.

**총 어휘 수** 154

## 06  그림의 세부 내용 파악

**소재** 복도 안전 포스터

**듣기 대본 해석**
여: 아빠. 제가 만든 우리 학교 복도 안전 포스터를 좀 보세요.
남: 잘 그렸네. 왼쪽에 있는 아이들은 뭐 하고 있는 거야?
여: 세면대에서 놀고 있는데 그건 규칙에 위반되는 행동이에요. 저 물웅덩이에 누가 미끄러질지도 몰라요.
남: 띠를 두르고 있는 사람은 누구야?
여: 복도 감독관이에요. 규칙을 집행하는 데에 도움을 주고 학생들은 항상 그들의 말을 들어야 해요.
남: 그렇구나. 이 애들은 복도에서 뛰고 있는 거야?
여: 네, 맞아요. 사람들한테 학교에서 하면 안 되는 것들을 보여주려고요.
남: 맞아. 그리고 문을 열어 놓는 것도 위험한 거지?
여: 네. 사람들이 가다가 부딪혀서 다칠 수 있으니까 문을 항상 닫고 다녀야 돼요.
남: 뒤쪽에 있는 둥그런 시계가 맘에 들어. 추가적으로 잘 넣은 것 같아.
여: 고마워요, 아빠. 우리 학교에 있는 시계들은 다 저렇게 생겼어요.
남: 그러니? 하여튼 아주 잘 그렸네.

**어휘**
**hallway** *n.* 복도    **slip** *v.* 미끄러지다    **puddle** *n.* 웅덩이
**monitor** *n.* 감독관    **enforce** *v.* 집행하다, 강요하다

**정답** ⑤

**문제풀이**
대화의 마지막 부분에서 남자가 둥그런 시계가 마음에 든다고 했는데, 그림에는 네모 모양의 시계가 걸려 있으므로 정답은 ⑤번이다.

**총 어휘 수** 149

## 07  할 일

**소재** 야외활동 장비 대 바겐세일

**듣기 대본 해석**
여: Charlie, Fat Panda Outfitters에서 야외활동 장비를 크게 세일하는 거 같던데.
남: 알아. 오늘 아침에 거기 잠시 들러서 새 하이킹화를 샀어. 좋은 제품들이 많아.
여: 나는 다음 주에 이틀 동안 하이킹을 갈 거라서, 캠핑 장비를 살까 생각 중이야.
남: 거기에 가능한 빨리 가야 해. 캠핑 장비 구역에는 많은 사람들이 있었어.
여: 그러면 서둘러야겠네. 오, 내가 캠핑용 휴대 스토브를 사야 한다고 생각하니? 이번이 나의 첫 번째 여행이라서 말이야.
남: 글쎄, 네가 가지고 간 음식을 요리하기 위해서는 아마도 캠프용 휴대 스토브가 필요할 거야. 피크닉 가거나 산에 당일 여행 갈 때는 그게 또 꽤 유용하거든.
여: 알았어. 그렇다면 하나 사야겠네.
남: 거기에 어떻게 갈 거야? 너의 차는 정비소에 있잖아.
여: 좋은 지적이야. 거기에 어떻게 갈지 잘 모르겠네.
남: 내가 너를 태워 줄 수 있을 것 같은데. 오늘은 내가 쉬는 날이고, 하루 종일 별다른 계획이 없어.
여: 그렇게 하면 좋지. 정말로 고마워. 그런데 내가 지금 약간 바쁘거든. 우리 20분쯤 후에 갈까?
남: 좋아. 준비되면 알려줘.

**어휘**
**pick up** (싼값으로, 우연히) ~을 사다    **stock up** ~을 사서 비축하다
**handy** *a.* 유용한, 가까운 곳에 있는    **day trip** 당일여행    **day off** (근무, 일을) 쉬는 날

**정답** ④

**문제풀이**
여자가 야외활동 장비를 세일하는 상점에 가려고 하는데 차가 수리소에 있다. 남자는 자신이 태워줄 수 있다고 했으므로 남자가 여자를 위해 할 일은 ④ '상점까지 차로 태워다 주기'이다.

**총 어휘 수** 200

## 08  이유

**소재** 육상 경기에 나갈 수 없는 이유

**듣기 대본 해석**
남: 안녕, Laura. 오늘의 용건은 뭐니?
여: 음. Baker 선생님. 이번 주말에 육상 경기에 나갈 수 없다는 것을 말씀 드리고 싶어서요.
남: 나갈 수 없다는 것이 무슨 말이니? 이틀 밖에 안 남았어. 지금은 대신할 사람도 구할 수 없어.
여: 정말로 죄송해요. 저를 필요로 하시는 것은 알지만 이번 주말에 저의 부모님께서 조부모님 댁에 가야 해요. 좀 긴급 상황이에요.
남: 알았어. 괜찮은 거니?
여: 제 할아버지께서 욕실에서 넘어져서 엉덩이를 다쳤어요. 할아버지께서는 수술을 받으셔서 얼마 동안은 집을 떠날 수가 없어요.
남: 안됐구나. 유감이야. 그럼 너도 조부모님 댁에 갈 거니?

여: 아니요. 부모님만 가셔요. 저는 부모님께서 안 계실 때 저의 어린 여동생을
　　돌봐야 해요.
남: 알았어. 정말로 안타깝네. 그렇지만 걱정하지는 마. 우리는 네가 분명히
　　그리울 거야. 할아버지께서 쾌차하시길 바라마.
여: 감사해요, Baker 선생님.

### 어휘
**track meet** 육상경기대회　　**replacement** *n.* 교체, 대신할 사람
**emergency** *n.* 응급 상황, 비상　　**have surgery** 수술 받다

### 정답 ③

### 문제풀이
여자는 부모님이 할아버지 댁에 가시는 동안 여동생을 돌봐야 해서 육상 경기에
나갈 수 없는 상황이다. 따라서 정답은 ③ '여동생을 돌봐야 해서'이다.

### 총 어휘 수 153


# 09　숫자

**소재** 리조트 숙박과 브런치 예약

### 듣기 대본 해석
*[전화벨이 울린다.]*
여: Beachwood Resort에 전화해 주셔서 감사합니다. 무엇을 도와드릴까요?
남: 네. 방을 예약하고 싶은데요. 하루 요금이 어떻게 되죠?
여: 주말에는 60달러이고, 주중에는 40달러예요.
남: 그러면 다음 주 토요일에 방을 예약하고 싶어요.
여: 네. 성함이 어떻게 되시나요?
남: Dennis Reynolds예요. 아, 그리고 식당에 브런치 예약을 두 명 하고 싶어요.
여: 네. 한 사람당 10달러를 추가하셔야 합니다.
남: 좋아요. 제가 여기 50퍼센트 할인 쿠폰도 있어요. 쿠폰 코드는 XT750
　　이에요.
여: 제가 한번 확인해 볼게요. *[키보드 치는 소리]* 죄송하지만, 그 쿠폰은 방에는
　　사용 가능하지만 브런치에는 사용 가능하지 않네요.
남: 괜찮아요. 제가 카드로 돈을 지불하고 싶으면 지금 카드번호를 드려야
　　하나요, 아니면 토요일까지 기다려도 되나요?
여: 원하시면 토요일까지 기다리셔도 됩니다.
남: 좋아요. 그럼 토요일에 뵙겠습니다.

### 어휘
**set up a reservation** 예약하다　　**rate** *n.* 요금　　**apply** *v.* 적용되다,
해당되다

### 정답 ③

### 문제풀이
토요일에 방을 예약하므로 주말 요금이 적용되어 60달러이고, 브런치를 2명
예약하여 20달러가 추가된다. 남자는 숙박요금에만 50퍼센트 할인이 적용되는
쿠폰을 가지고 있으므로 총 지불할 금액은 숙박요금 30달러와 브런치 2인
20달러를 합한 ③ '$50'이다.

### 총 어휘 수 153


# 10　언급 유무

**소재** 이주 노동자들을 위해 집을 짓는 자원봉사

### 듣기 대본 해석
여: 안녕, Louie. 지금 시간이 괜찮으면 너의 여름 자원봉사에 대해서 내가 쓰고
　　있는 기사를 위해 몇 가지 질문을 해도 될까?
남: 물론이야, Stacy. 물어봐.
여: 좋아. 자원봉사자로서 무슨 일들을 했어?
남: 많은 일들을 했어. 이주 노동자들을 위해 집을 짓는 것을 도와주고 스태프진을
　　구성하는 것을 도왔어.

여: 알겠어. 얼마나 많은 집을 짓는 것을 도왔는데?
남: 우린 큰 팀을 가지고 있어서 2달 안에 32채의 집을 지을 수 있었어.
여: 멋지다. 이주 노동자들이 바로 집으로 들어갔어?
남: 응. 원래 낡은 판자집에서 살고 있었어서, 새 집으로 들어간다니 아주 신나
　　하더라고.
여: 분명 그랬을 거야. 이 일을 얼마나 오랫동안 한 거야?
남: 이 자원봉사 프로그램에서 대학교 1학년 때부터 일해 왔어.
여: 정말? 그러면 3년이 됐네. 좋아. 질문 하나만 더. 자원봉사를 해서 어떤
　　이점이 있어?
남: 많은 이점이 있는데, 무엇보다도, 난 다른 사람들을 도움으로써 생기는
　　감정이 좋아.
여: 잘됐구나. 시간 내줘서 고마워, Louie.

### 어휘
**migrant** *n.* 이주자　　**organize** *v.* 조직하다, 정리하다　　**originally**
*ad.* 원래, 본래　　**rickety** *a.* 곧 부서질 듯한　　**shack** *n.* 판잣집

### 정답 ③

### 문제풀이
두 사람은 봉사활동에 관한 활동 내용, 봉사활동의 수혜자, 봉사해 온 기간,
봉사를 통해 얻는 이점에 관해 언급했지만 ③ '봉사 단체명'은 언급하지 않았다.

### 총 어휘 수 184


# 11　내용 일치 · 불일치

**소재** 미술관의 연간 행사 소개

### 듣기 대본 해석
남: 안녕하세요, 저희 미술관에 오신 것을 환영합니다. 저는 여러분께서 좋아하실
　　거라고 확신하는, 곧 있을 행사에 대해서 말씀드리고자 이 자리에 있습니다.
　　여기 미술관에 있는 저희들은 매년 열리는 8월의 예술인 행사에 여러분
　　모두를 초대하고자 합니다. 지난 16년간 매년 8월에 이 행사를 개최해
　　왔습니다. 저희는 지역 예술가들을 홍보하기 위해 이 행사를 개최하고,
　　미술관에 그들의 작품을 전시합니다. 우리 시의 예술가들은 창의성을 고무
　　시킬 뿐만 아니라 공원 및 사업체들을 아름답게 가꾸도록 돕기 때문에
　　우리 지역사회에 중요합니다. 이 행사는 8월 17일에 시작하여 월말까지
　　계속됩니다. 본 행사의 입장료는 무료입니다. 하지만 저희는 지역 예술
　　프로그램을 지원하는 저희 재단에 소액의 기부를 해주시길 추천합니다. 올해
　　행사에 참여하셔서 이 지역 최고 수준의 회화, 소묘, 조각 작품들 일부를
　　관람하세요. 시간 내주셔서 감사합니다.

### 어휘
**upcoming** *a.* 다가오는, 곧 있을　　**annual** *a.* 매년의, 연례의
**promote** *v.* 홍보하다　　**beautify** *v.* 아름답게 하다, 꾸미다
**modest** *a.* 많지 않은, 수수한, 겸손한　　**foundation** *n.* 재단

### 정답 ⑤

### 문제풀이
남자는 행사에 참여하여 이 지역의 회화, 소묘, 조각 작품들을 관람하라고 했으므로
내용과 일치하지 않는 것은 ⑤ '사진 작품을 볼 수 있다.'이다.

### 총 어휘 수 150


# 12　도표

**소재** 드럼 키트 구매

### 듣기 대본 해석
남: 안녕하세요, 부인. 무엇을 도와드릴까요?
여: 아들 생일 선물로 줄 드럼 키트를 찾고 있어요. 그는 로큰롤 밴드를 시작하고
　　싶어하거든요.

남: 좋습니다. 일단, 저희는 다섯 가지 키트가 있습니다.
여: 무엇이 그에게 가장 적합한지 모르겠네요. 도와주셨으면 하는데요.
남: 록음악을 한다면 3피스 키트는 충분하지 않아요. 5피스 아니면 7피스
  키트를 원할 거예요.
여: 네. 깊은 베이스 사운드를 만들 수 있는 키트를 원하는 것 같던데요.
남: 그러면 아드님이 플로어 톰을 원할 것 같군요. 저희는 그것도 제공합니다.
  이 두 세트 중에서 고르셔야 할 것 같은데요.
여: 네. 음... 800달러 이상은 쓰기를 원하지 않으니까. 그렇다면 이것을 선택
  해야겠네요.
남: 네. 집으로 가져가실 수 있게 준비하겠습니다.
여: 고맙습니다.

### 어휘
**suitable** *a.* 적합한

### 정답 ③

### 문제풀이
5피스 또는 7피스 키트를 원한다고 했으므로 ②~⑤번 중에 골라야 하는데
플로어 톰을 원한다고 했으므로 ③, ⑤번이 남게 된다. 그리고 800달러 이상은
쓰고 싶지 않다고 했으므로 정답은 ③번이다.

**총 어휘 수** 152


## 13  긴 대화의 응답

**소재** 퇴근 후 요가

### 듣기 대본 해석
남: 새로운 남자친구 또는 비슷한 관계가 생겼어요, Heather?
여: 하하! 아니요. 왜 그렇게 말한 거예요?
남: 요즘 훨씬 행복해 보이고 에너지가 충만해 보이는 것 같아서요.
여: 정말이요? 음. 제가 최근에 기분이 정말 좋지만, 제 삶에 새로운 사람이
  있는 건 아니에요.
남: 그럼 어떤 다른 변화가 생겼어요?
여: 최근에 요가를 시작했어요. 일 끝나고 매일 밤 가거든요.
남: 요가를 연습한 지 얼마나 됐어요?
여: 겨우 3개월이요.
남: 당신한테 어렵진 않아요? 저는 제 발가락에조차 닿을 수가 없어요.
여: 저도 처음 시작했을 때는 어려웠지만, 몇 주 지나니 훨씬 더 유연해졌어요.
남: 요가가 코티솔 수준을 향상시켜, 병을 물리치는 것을 더 쉽게 해준다고
  들었어요.
여: 저도 그렇게 들었어요. 어쨌든, 저는 매일 요가를 하는 것이 정말 좋아요.
  요가는 퇴근 후에 기대할 만한 뭔가를 주거든요.
남: ④ 요즘 당신이 그렇게 행복해 보이는 이유가 그것인 것 같군요.

### 어휘
**limber** *a.* 유연한    **improve** *v.* 개선하다, 향상시키다
**cortisol** *n.* 코티솔 (부신 피질에서 생기는 스테로이드 호르몬의 일종)
**look forward to** ~을 기대하다

### 정답 ④

### 문제풀이
남자는 여자가 요즘 행복하고 에너지가 충만해 보이는 이유를 묻고 여자는 퇴
근 후 하고 있는 요가 덕분이라고 말하고 있다. 요가가 퇴근 후 뭔가를 기대하
게 만들어 준다는 여자의 말에 대한 적절한 응답은 ④ '요즘 당신이 그렇게 행
복해 보이는 이유가 그것인 것 같군요.'이다.

### 오답 보기 해석
① 요가를 하기 위해 일찍 퇴근하면 안 돼요.
② 매일 요가를 가는 것은 할 가치가 없음이 분명해요.
③ 저는 오늘 밤 정말로 초과근무를 하고 싶지 않아요.
⑤ 그러면 우리 요가를 연습할 장소를 찾아야겠어요.

**총 어휘 수** 157


## 14  긴 대화의 응답

**소재** 프로젝트 실험 준비와 일기 예보

### 듣기 대본 해석
여: 여름 방학 때까지 기다릴 수 없어. 넌 어때, Henry?
남: 나도 정말 방학을 고대하고 있어. 하지만 난 우리가 그때까지 우리 과학
  프로젝트를 마칠 수 없을까 봐 좀 걱정이 돼.
여: 안심해. 우리 할 일이 그렇게 많이 남지 않았어.
남: 네 말이 맞는 것 같아. 근데, 이번 주 날씨를 확인해 봤어?
여: 응, 이번 주 내내 비가 오고 바람이 불 예정이야.
남: 정말? 그러면 우리 프로젝트를 어떻게 마치지? 우리는 실험을 밖에서 해야
  하는데.
여: 맞아! 음, 수요일에는 비 올 확률이 50퍼센트밖에 안 되는 것 같아.
남: 그럼, 우리 수요일에 비가 오지 않도록 행운을 빌어야겠어. 하지만 만약을
  대비해서 예비 계획도 세워둬야 해.
여: 그래. 그런데 생각해 둔 거 있어?
남: 아마도 우리 실험을 하기 위해 체육관을 사용할 수 있을 거야. 그게 괜찮을지
  Jones 선생님께 여쭤보자.
여: ④ 훌륭한 생각이야. 우리가 이 프로젝트의 파트너라서 좋아.

### 어휘
**look forward to** ~을 기대하다    **concerned** *a.* 걱정하는
**be supposed to V** ~하기로 되어 있다    **experiment** *n.* 실험
**keep one's fingers crossed** 행운을 빌다    **backup** *n.* 예비, 백업
**just in case** 만약을 대비해서, 혹시 모르니까    **gymnasium** *n.* 체육관
〈문제〉 **brilliant** *a.* 훌륭한, 멋진

### 정답 ④

### 문제풀이
두 사람은 과학 프로젝트에 관해 대화를 나누던 중 이번 주에 야외에서 실험을
해야 하는데 일주일 내내 비가 온다는 예보가 있다고 했다. 강수확률이 적은
수요일에 비가 오지 않도록 바라고, 예비 계획으로 체육관에서 실험을 할 수
있을지 알아보는 남자의 말에 대한 여자의 응답은 ④ '훌륭한 생각이야. 우리가
이 프로젝트의 파트너라서 좋아.'가 가장 적절하다.

### 오답 보기 해석
① 걱정할 필요 없어. 그날 비가 오지 않을 거야.
② 우리 정말 서두를 필요가 있어. 일이 너무 많아.
③ 우리 여름 방학 전에 프로젝트를 끝낼 수 있어.
⑤ 우리가 왜 실험을 체육관에서 해야 하지? 우리는 밖에서 할 수 있어.

**총 어휘 수** 152


## 15  상황에 적절한 말

**소재** 수줍음이 많고 소극적인 딸

### 듣기 대본 해석
여: Pamela는 지난 밤에 학부모-교사 상담을 하러 학교에 갔고 그녀 딸의
  선생님을 만났습니다. 그녀는 자신의 딸인 Malory가 매우 수줍음이 많고,
  예민하다는 선생님의 말에 전혀 놀라지 않았습니다. 선생님은 Malory가
  휴식 시간에 거의 뛰지 않고 걷기만 하는 조용한 아이라고 말했습니다.
  Malory의 선생님은 딸을 좀 더 활동적이고 에너지 넘치게 만들기 위해 몇
  가지를 시도해 보라고 Pamela를 격려했습니다. 또한, 선생님은 Malory의
  활동 수준을 올리기 위한 제안들이 많이 있는 웹사이트를 추천해주었습니다.
  Pamela는 선생님의 조언에 감사해하고 바로 집에 와서 웹사이트를 확인
  했습니다. 밤에, Pamela는 저녁을 준비하느라 바빴는데 전화가 울렸고,
  그녀는 Malory에게 전화를 받으라고 부탁했습니다. Malory는 자신이 너무
  부끄럼이 많기 때문에 전화 받기를 거절합니다. 그녀의 딸이 언젠가 중요한
  것을 놓칠까 걱정하면서 그녀는 딸에게 조언을 하기로 결심합니다. 이런
  상황에서 Pamela가 Malory에게 어떤 말을 할 것 같은가요?
Pamela: ④ 좀 더 적극적이고 활동적인 것이 네 삶에 있어서 도움이 될 거야.

## 어휘

**conference** *n.* 의논, 회의    **at recess** 휴식 시간에    **active** *a.* 생기 있는, 활발한

## 정답 ④

## 문제풀이

수줍음이 많고 조용한 딸 Malory에게 Pamela는 좀 더 생기 있고 활동적으로 생활하라고 말해주고 싶어하므로 정답은 ④ '좀 더 적극적이고 활동적인 것이 네 삶에 있어서 도움이 될 거야.'이다.

## 오답 보기 해석

① 전화로 낯선 이와 이야기할 땐 주의하렴.
② 친구랑 밖에서 그렇게 자주 놀면 안돼.
③ 컴퓨터 게임을 하기 전에 네 숙제를 마치렴.
⑤ 네가 인터넷 하는 데 쓰는 시간을 좀 줄이는 게 어떠니?

**총 어휘 수** 172

# 16 담화 주제 / 17 세부 내용 파악

**소재** 축구 용품 구입 요령

## 듣기 대본 해석

남: 안녕하세요, 팀 여러분. 오늘 우리는 운동용품에 대해서 이야기를 나눌 것입니다. 운동용품점에 들어가면 살 수 있는 축구 용품이 너무 많아서 당황할 수 있습니다. 사람들은 항상 내게 가장 비싼 용품을 사야 하는지 물어봅니다. 저는 보통 아니라고 대답합니다. 예를 들어 평범하고 싼 양말들도 충분히 좋은데 굳이 돈을 더 들여서 특별하고 멋져 보이는(초현대적인) 양말을 살 필요는 없죠. 가장 중요한 용품은 물론 기본적인 용품입니다. 꽤 쓸만한 축구화, 정강이 보호대, 양말, 그리고 축구공이 필요할 것입니다. 저는 가장 중요한 용품을 좋은 축구화라고 생각합니다. 축구화가 잘 맞고 오래갈 수 있도록 내구성이 좋은지 확인하는 것이 좋을 것입니다. 또 다른 중요한 용품은 다리 부상을 막아주는 정강이 보호대입니다. 비싼 용품들이 멋져 보이고 남들에게 깊은 인상을 줄 수도 있지만 경기를 뛰는 데는 그렇게 필요하지 않다는 것을 기억하세요. 훈련 캠프에서 좋은 시간을 보내기 바랍니다.

## 어휘

**equipment** *n.* 장비, 용품    **overwhelmed** *a.* 압도된, 당황한    **massive** *a.* 거대한    **space-age** *a.* 초현대적인    **decent** *a.* 괜찮은, 제대로 된    **shin** *n.* 정강이    **durable** *a.* 내구성이 있는    **flashy** *a.* 호화로운, 멋진    **impress** *v.* 깊은 인상을 주다

## 정답 16 ① 17 ④

## 문제풀이

16 남자는 수많은 축구 용품 중에서 반드시 비싼 것을 살 필요가 없으며, 기본적인 용품들이 중요하다는 등 축구 용품 구매 시 요령에 대해 말하고 있으므로 주제로 가장 적절한 것은 ① '축구 용품을 사기 위한 조언'이다.

17 남자는 양말, 축구화, 정강이 보호대, 축구공을 가장 중요한 기본용품의 예로 언급하였으나 바지는 언급하지 않았으므로 정답은 ④ '반바지'이다.

## 오답 보기 해석

16
② 공원에서 축구 하는 것의 위험성
③ 비싼 물품 구입의 결과
④ 축구 캠프의 늘어가는 인기
⑤ 축구를 하는 것이 청소년에게 주는 다양한 이점들

**총 어휘 수** 181

## DICTATION ANSWERS

01 were supposed to

02 It's irrelevant to

03 should always be kept on board / equal the vessel's maximum passenger capacity / are in working order

04 performing tricks / the animals in the circus are victim to / forced to entertain people

05 in need of assistance / Someone was riding their motorcycle / run a couple of tests

06 enforce the rules / what they shouldn't do at school / It's a great addition

07 stock up on camping gear / quite handy for picnics / Your car is in the shop / give you a ride

08 We can't find a replacement / It's kind of an emergency / had surgery / look after my little sister

09 set up a reservation for / What are your daily rates / I'd like to book a room for / coupon only applies

10 volunteering over the summer / build houses for migrant workers / originally living in rickety shacks

11 every August for the past sixteen years / promote area artists / Entry to the event / make a modest donation

12 the most suitable for / make some deep bass sounds / offer those as well

13 there's no new man in my life / took up yoga / I noticed I was much more limber / fight off sickness

14 I just can't wait until / keep our fingers crossed / should have a backup plan

15 not shocked at all / get her daughter to be more active / check out the websites

16-17 be overwhelmed by / protect your legs from injury

# 05 수능영어듣기 실전모의고사

| | | | | | |
|---|---|---|---|---|---|
| 01 ② | 02 ④ | 03 ① | 04 ⑤ | 05 ⑤ | 06 ② |
| 07 ⑤ | 08 ② | 09 ④ | 10 ④ | 11 ② | 12 ① |
| 13 ④ | 14 ⑤ | 15 ④ | 16 ① | 17 ④ | |

## 01 짧은 대화의 응답

**소재** 호텔 예약

**듣기 대본 해석**

여: 디즈니 호텔의 서비스에 정말 감동받았어요.
남: 사실 저도 이번 주말에 아이들을 데려갈까 생각 중이에요. 거기 예약 담당 전화번호 알아요?
여: 네, 물론이죠. 거기 가려는 특별한 이유라도 있나요?
남: ② 두 아이들 모두 생일이 이번 달이에요.

**어휘**

**impressed** *a.* 감동을 받은　〈문제〉**typically** *ad.* 보통, 일반적으로

**정답** ②

**문제풀이**

남자는 이번 주말에 디즈니 호텔에 갈까 한다며 여자에게 예약 전화번호를 알고 있는지 물었고, 여자는 안다고 대답하며 왜 가는지 이유를 물었다. 남자는 왜 가는지 대답해야 하는 상황이므로 ② '두 아이들 모두 생일이 이번 달이에요.'가 정답이다.

**오답 보기 해석**

① 전 아직 예약하고 싶지 않아요.
③ 전 디즈니 티켓을 할인 받길 바라요.
④ 그녀에게 휴가에 대해 이야기하려고 했어요.
⑤ 보통 우리는 오두막에 가서 낚시를 해요.

**총 어휘 수** 47

## 02 짧은 대화의 응답

**소재** 연극 관람하러 가는 길의 교통 정체

**듣기 대본 해석**

남: 외 연극 제 시간에 못 갈 것 같은데.
여: 미안. 저녁 이 시간에 차가 이렇게 막힐 줄은 몰랐어.
남: 응. 도심지는 금요일 밤에 항상 막히지. 시작하려면 얼마나 남았어?
여: ④ 약 15분쯤.

**어휘**

**on time** 제 시간에, 늦지 않고

**정답** ④

**문제풀이**

남자가 연극이 시작하려면 얼마나 남았는지 물었으므로 가장 적절한 여자의 대답은 ④ '약 15분쯤.'이다.

**오답 보기 해석**

① 약 2킬로미터 정도 떨어져 있어.
② 지하철 타고.
③ 장당 거의 100달러야.
⑤ 거의 9시 30분까지.

**총 어휘 수** 45

## 03 담화 주제

**소재** 블로그 방문자수 늘리는 방법

**듣기 대본 해석**

남: 기술은 요즘 빠르게 발전하고 있고 가장 빠르게 발전하고 있는 것들 중 하나가 블로깅입니다. 블로깅은 다른 사람들에게 자신의 생활과 관심사에 대해 알릴 수 있는 좋은 방법입니다. 또한 재미있기도 합니다. 그러나 수백만 개의 블로그들에서 여러분의 블로그가 돋보이기 위해 알아둬야 할 것들이 있습니다. 먼저 블로그가 흥미로워 보이도록 만들어야 합니다. 멋진 디자인과 색조를 고르세요. 두 번째, 블로그를 한 주제에 집중시키세요. 너무 많은 주제를 다루는 것은 집중력을 분산시키고 블로그 독자들을 잃게 할 것입니다. 마지막으로 독자들과 소통을 하세요. 블로그에 독자들이 남기는 댓글에 답을 하는 데 시간을 들이세요. 이러한 것들을 염두에 둔다면 당신의 블로그에 더 많은 사람들을 끌어들일 수 있습니다.

**어휘**

**stand out** 돋보이다　**attractive** *a.* 매혹적인, 멋진　**color scheme** 색조　**distracting** *a.* 집중력을 분산시키는　**respond to** ~에 응답하다

**정답** ①

**문제풀이**

남자는 세 가지 방법을 제시하며 그렇게 하면 블로그에 더 많은 사람들을 끌어들일 수 있다고 했으므로 남자가 하는 말의 주제는 ① '블로그 활성화를 위한 팁'이다.

**총 어휘 수** 128

## 04 의견

**소재** 오락시설에서의 시간 제한 규정에 대한 불만

**듣기 대본 해석**

남: 안녕하세요, Cindy. 지난 토요일 당신 아들 생일 파티에서 아들이 즐거운 시간을 보냈나요?
여: 아니요, 끔찍했어요. 저는 오락시설에서 직원 때문에 너무 화났어요.
남: 이런! 무슨 일이 있었어요?
여: 우리가 도착했을 때 그들은 우리한테 30분을 기다려야 한다고 말했어요. 저는 예약을 했는데도 말이죠!
남: 음, 그들이 여름에는 매우 바쁘다는 건 확실해요.
여: 그렇긴 해요. 하지만 우리가 앉고 나서 그들이 우리한테 두 시간 제한이 있다고 말했어요!
남: 정말이요? 그리고 두 시간이 당신에게는 충분하지 않았나요?
여: 네, 확실히 충분치 않았죠. 우리는 15명의 아이들을 위해 음식을 주문하고, 음식을 받아서 아이들이 먹을 수 있도록 해야 했어요. 또한, 케이크를 먹고 선물을 열기 전에, 아이들이 모두 게임을 할 기회를 주기를 원했어요.
남: 음, 그들은 아마 가능한 많은 고객을 수용하려 했나 보네요.
여: 좋아요. 그렇지만 시간 제한은 고객이 데려간 아이들의 수가 몇 명인지에 기반을 두어야 한다고요.
남: 그래서, 관리팀에 이야기하셨어요?
여: 말했죠. 하지만 그들은 그것이 회사 방침이어서 그들이 해줄 수 있는 것은 아무것도 없다고 말했어요. 정말 무례했어요!

**어휘**

**accommodate** *v.* 수용하다　**based on** ~에 근거하여　**policy** *n.* 정책, 방침

**정답** ⑤

**문제풀이**

여자는 아들의 생일 파티를 위해 간 오락시설에서 예약을 했는데도 30분을 기다렸다 들어갔고 자리에 앉자 두 시간의 시간 제한이 있다고 한 것에 불만을 표현하면서 인원이 많은 만큼 시간이 길었어야 한다고 말했으므로 정답은 ⑤ '인원수에 따라 사용 시간을 다르게 줘야 한다.'이다.

**총 어휘 수** 180

# 05 대화자의 관계 파악

**소재** 배우와 의상 디자이너와의 대화

**듣기 대본 해석**

남: 안녕하세요, Marie. 여기서 다시 볼 줄 몰랐어요.
여: 안녕하세요, Paul. 방금 감독님과 이야기 좀 나눴어요.
남: 오, 저희와 다시 작업을 하실 것을 고려 중이신가요?
여: 네, LA에서의 일이 잘 풀리지 않았어요.
남: 그렇군요. 전에 현대극 해보신 적 있으신가요?
여: 아니요, 저는 고전극만 해봤어요. 그러면 당신은 The Shape of Things 공연에 참여하나요? 어떤 역을 맡고 계신가요?
남: Adam 역할을 맡았어요.
여: 와, 주연을 맡으셨네요. 정말 흥분되겠어요. 축하해요.
남: 고마워요. 하지만 일을 잘 해내기가 정말 어렵네요.
여: 이해해요. 저도 제 일에 대해 약간 긴장돼요. 전 셰익스피어 풍의 의상에 대해 많이 알고 있지만 현대 패션에 관해서는 잘 몰라요.
남: 음, 영화를 볼 수 있어요. 제 생각엔 영화를 통해 도움이 될만한 조언들을 얻을 수 있을 거예요.
여: 맞아요. 제가 할 수 있는 한 본래의 의상에 가장 가깝도록 유지할 거예요. 이번 주말에 작업하려고요. 그럼, 전 이제 가봐야 해요. 다음 드레스 리허설 때 봐요.
남: 잘 가요, Marie.

**어휘**

**director** *n.* 감독  **role** *n.* 역할, 배역  **costuming** *n.* 의상(재료)
**dress rehearsal** 총연습

**정답** ⑤

**문제풀이**

여자가 어떤 역할을 맡았는지 물었을 때 남자는 Adam 역할을 맡았다고 하는 것으로 보아 배우임을 알 수 있고, 여자는 의상에 대해 공부하고 작업한다고 하는 것으로 보아 의상 디자이너임을 알 수 있다. 따라서 정답은 ⑤ '배우 ― 의상 디자이너'이다.

**총 어휘 수** 163


# 06 그림의 세부 내용 파악

**소재** 가족들과 함께 갔던 캠핑

**듣기 대본 해석**

남: 안녕, Laura. 네가 핸드폰으로 보고 있는 것은 뭐야?
여: 작년 여름 방학에 우리 할아버지께서 찍어주신 사진이야.
남: 멋지다. 나도 보여줘.
여: 물론. 여기 있어.
남: 너희 캠핑 간 거구나, 그렇지? 난 저 산과 구름이 마음에 들어. 정말 평화롭고 편안해 보인다.
여: 맞아. 우리는 RV를 빌려서 Walker Mountain에 갔었어.
남: 그렇구나. 뒤에 있는 저 사람이 너지?
여: 응. 나는 야외에는 별로 관심이 없어서 뮤직 비디오를 보고 있었어.
남: RV 안에는 누구야?
여: 우리 삼촌이야. 삼촌은 책을 읽고 계셔.
남: 차 앞에 있는 저 여성은 누구셔?
여: 우리 엄마야. 엄마는 거미를 발견하고 도망치고 있어.
남: 그리고 개랑 놀고 있는 저 아이들은? 이 애들은 누구야?
여: 내 사촌들이야. 그들이 자기들 개를 여행에 데려왔어.
남: 그럼 RV에서 짐을 꺼내 옮기는 남자가 너희 아버지겠네.
여: 맞아. 그는 쉬기 위해 산에 가고 싶어하셨지만, 내 생각엔 우리가 아버지를 기분 좋지 않게 만들었던 것 같아.

**어휘**

**RV** *n.* 레저 차량  **RV=recreational vehicle, camping car라는 말은 잘 쓰지 않습니다.*
**care for** ~를 좋아하다  **miserable** *a.* 비참한, 기분이 좋지 않은

**정답** ②

**문제풀이**

대화에서 차 안에 있는 사람은 삼촌이고 책을 읽고 계시다고 했는데 그림에서는 낮잠을 자고 있으므로 정답은 ②번이다.

**총 어휘 수** 174


# 07 할 일

**소재** 수돗물 필터 교체하기

**듣기 대본 해석**

여: 수돗물 맛이 이상해지는 것 같아, 그렇지 않아?
남: 그런 것 같아. 필터를 갈 때가 된 것 같아.
여: 다른 필터는 없어?
남: 있을 걸. 몇 달 전에 몇 개 사 놓은 것 같아.
여: 그럼 아무 때나 갈면 되겠네.
남: 지금 당장 가는 것이 좋을 것 같은데.
여: 알겠어. 지금 필터 갖고 올게.
남: 내가 갈게. 너 못 찾을 것 같아.
여: 도구 가져오는 것 잊지마.
남: 필요 없을 것 같은데.
여: 알겠어. 그럼 난 싱크대를 청소할게.
남: 그래. 금방 올게.

**어휘**

**tap water** 수돗물  **might as well** ~하는 편이 낫다

**정답** ⑤

**문제풀이**

여자가 수돗물 필터를 가져오겠다고 하자 남자는 자신이 가져오겠다고 했으므로 남자가 할 일은 ⑤ '수돗물 필터 가져오기'이다.

**총 어휘 수** 108


# 08 이유

**소재** 등록을 놓쳐서 출전하지 못하게 된 육상경기대회

**듣기 대본 해석**

여: 안녕, Stan. 어깨 어때?
남: 훨씬 더 좋아졌어. 고마워.
여: 잘됐네! 그럼 다시 창 던질 수 있는 거야?
남: 응. 어제 좀 연습했어. 거의 부상 전만큼 좋아졌어.
여: 좋네. 이번 주말에 육상경기대회에서 네가 시합하는 게 정말 기대되네.
남: 불행하게도 나갈 수 없을 것 같아.
여: 왜 안 돼? 어깨 다친 동안 연습을 못해서?
남: 아니. 사실은 주말 경기에 등록하는 걸 깜빡 했어.
여: 저런! 바빠서 잊어버린 것 같은데.
남: 맞아. 중간고사 때문에 너무 스트레스를 받아서 까맣게 잊고 있었어.
여: 그랬구나. 난 여름 인턴십 프로그램에 등록하는 것 놓쳤어. 마감일이 저번 주였거든.
남: 안타깝네. 아마도 우리는 플래너를 사서 좀 더 계획성 있게 해야 할 것 같아.

**어휘**

**javelin** *n.* 창  **injury** *n.* 부상  **track meet** 육상경기대회
**slip one's mind** (깜빡) 잊어 버리다  **registration** *n.* 등록
**organized** *a.* 정리된, 계획성 있는

정답 ②

**문제풀이**

남자는 중간고사 때문에 스트레스를 받아서 주말 경기에 등록하는 것을 잊었다고 했으므로 남자가 육상경기에 나가지 못하는 이유는 ② '등록을 하지 못해서'이다.

**총 어휘 수** 139


# 09  숫자

**소재** 회사 소풍 간식 사기

**듣기 대본 해석**

남: 안녕하세요. 오늘은 무엇을 도와드릴까요?

여: 안녕하세요. 내일 오후에 갈 회사 소풍 간식 좀 사려고요. 이 쿠키들은 얼마예요?

남: 한 개당 2달러인데 곧 닫을 거라서 지금 가게에 있는 건 모두 20퍼센트 할인해 드려요.

여: 좋네요. 그러면 쿠키 20개 살게요. 그리고 파이도 남았나요?

남: 그럼요. 오후에 체스 파이를 좀 만들었어요. 소풍에 안성맞춤일 거예요.

여: 얼마 정도 하나요?

남: 하나 당 10달러입니다.

여: 좋네요. 두 개 살게요.

남: 다른 것 또 필요하세요?

여: 그게 다인 것 같아요. 10퍼센트 할인 쿠폰도 있는데 쓸게요.

남: 죄송하지만 이미 할인된 상품에 대해서는 쿠폰을 받지 않습니다.

여: 그렇군요. 그럼 다음 번에 쓸게요.

남: 알겠습니다. 그럼 쿠키 20개랑 파이 2개를 20퍼센트 할인된 가격으로 가져가시는 겁니다, 맞죠?

여: 맞아요. 여기 카드요.

**어휘**

**apiece** *ad.* 각각, 하나에    **batch** *n.* 한 회분    **discounted** *a.* 할인된

정답 ③

**문제풀이**

쿠키는 하나당 2달러이고 20개이므로 40달러, 체스 파이는 하나당 10달러인데 2개이므로 20달러로 합계는 60달러이고 여기서 20퍼센트 할인이 된다고 했으므로 정답은 ③ '$48'이다.

**총 어휘 수** 162


# 10  언급 유무

**소재** 새로 구입한 집에 대한 문의

**듣기 대본 해석**

여: 이것이 당신이 저에게 문의했던 집의 최근 사진이에요, Anderson 씨.

남: 좋네요. 저는 큰 뒷마당이 너무 마음에 들어요.

여: 네, 뒷마당이 정말 예뻐요. 방 세 개와 세 개의 화장실 그리고 앞에 아름다운 정원이 있어요.

남: 위치가 어디죠? 좋은 지역 내에 있나요?

여: 그래요, 근처가 아주 깨끗하고 안전해요. 교통량도 그리 많지 않아요.

남: 저는 중학생인 두 아들이 있어서 근처가 좋다고 들으니 기쁘네요. 근처에 학교가 있나요?

여: 네, 학교는 차로 5분 거리에 있습니다. 집도 학교버스의 노선에 있어요.

남: 훌륭해요. 시내버스나 지하철은 어때요? 지하철역이 걸어갈 수 있는 거리에 있나요?

여: 물론이죠. 지하철은 걸어서 십분 정도 거리에 있어요.

남: 집에 차고는 있나요? 차 한 대 아니면 두 대가 가능해요?

여: 두 대 세울 수 있는 차고가 붙어 있습니다.

남: 좋아요. 지금 집을 보러 갈 수 있을까요?

여: 문제 없을 거예요. 확실히 하기 위해 먼저 집주인한테 전화해 볼게요.

**어휘**

**neighborhood** *n.* 인근, 근처    **garage** *n.* 차고    **attach** *v.* 붙이다, 첨부하다

정답 ④

**문제풀이**

대화에서 침실과 화장실 개수, 인근 학교 유무, 대중교통, 차고 유무에 대한 언급은 있었지만 집이 언제 지어졌는지에 대해서는 언급한 적이 없으므로 정답은 ④ '건축연도'이다.

**총 어휘 수** 169


# 11  내용 일치 · 불일치

**소재** 파쇄

**듣기 대본 해석**

여: 학생 여러분, 하나가 더 있습니다. 가시기 전에 여러분에게 수압 파쇄, 줄여서 '파쇄'에 대해서 잠시 동안 이야기해보려고 합니다. 파쇄는 천연가스를 포함하고 있는 돌을 깨는 특정 화학물질을 이용하여 돌로부터 천연가스를 추출해 내는 방법입니다. 파쇄 방법은 광장히 쉽고 비용 효율적입니다. 그러나 그 과정에서 환경에 끼치는 안 좋은 영향들이 있습니다. 예를 들어 파쇄는 지하수에 화학물을 넣는데 이는 인근 주민들의 수돗물을 오염시킬 수 있습니다. 파쇄는 지진이나 미진과 같은 지진 활동을 초래하는 것으로도 의심됩니다. 파쇄와 그 영향들을 다음 시간에 더 자세하게 얘기 나눠볼게요.

**어휘**

**hydraulic fracking** 수압 파쇄    **extract** *v.* 추출하다    **chemical** *n.* 화학물질    **cost-effective** *a.* 비용 효율이 높은    **associated with** ~와 관련된    **tap water** 수돗물    **seismic activity** 지진 활동    **tremor** *n.* 미진    **implication** *n.* 영향, 결과

정답 ②

**문제풀이**

파쇄는 천연가스를 갖고 있는 돌을 부수는 특정한 화학물을 이용한다고 했으므로 내용과 일치하지 않는 것은 ② '돌을 뭉쳐서 크게 만드는 방식을 이용한다.'이다.

**총 어휘 수** 103


# 12  도표

**소재** 자신에게 맞는 의사 선택하기

**듣기 대본 해석**

남: 오늘 눈이 너무 간지러워. 그 철이 다시 돌아왔나 봐.

여: 응, 나도 봄에 알레르기가 아주 심해. 알레르기 전문 의사에게 상담 받는 건 어때?

남: 사실 날 봐주는 알레르기 의사가 없어. 한 명 만나볼까?

여: 날 봐주는 의사는 광장히 도움이 돼. 인터넷으로 빠르게 검색해서 너에게 맞는 의사를 찾자. 안과 의사는 필요 없는 거지?

남: 응. 알레르기 때문에 그런 거니까 안과 의사는 도움이 안 될 것 같아.

여: 알겠어. 이 사람이 알레르기 전문의로서 제일 경험이 많아. 전화해서 예약하지 그래?

남: 응. 잠깐! 이 의사는 Union County에 있잖아! 가는 데 45분이 걸릴 거야.

여: 그렇네. Henderson County에 있는 의사들로 선택지를 줄여보자. 이 둘밖에 안 남았네.

남: 그렇구나. 경험이 더 많은 사람으로 할래.

여: 그럼 이 사람이네. 예약할 수 있게 전화번호 줄게.
남: 좋아. 도와줘서 고마워.

**어휘**
**itchy** *a.* 간지러운　　**allergy** *n.* 알레르기　　**allergist** *n.* 알레르기 전문
의사　　**county** *n.* 군

**정답** ①

**문제풀이**
안과 의사는 필요 없고 알레르기 의사로 해야 한다고 했고 Henderson
County에 있는 의사로 한다고 했으므로 ①번과 ⑤번이 남는다. 그 중에 경험이
많은 의사로 하겠다고 했으므로 정답은 ①번이다.

**총 어휘 수** 180


## 13　긴 대화의 응답

**소재** 출판교실에서 제작한 애완동물에 관한 팜플렛

**듣기 대본 해석**
남: 안녕, Chloe. 네가 보고 있는 것이 뭐니?
여: 아, Greg. 이것은 우리 학교에 있는 모든 동물들의 안내책자야.
남: 동물 안내책자? 뭐 하러?
여: 음, 우리 학교는 사실 교실에서 키우는 애완동물이 많아. 이건 모든 애완동물과
　　애완동물이 어느 교실에 있는지를 보여줘. 한번 확인해봐.
남: 멋진데. 학교에 애완동물이 많이 있는지 몰랐네. 누가 이 안내책자를
　　만들었어?
여: Scott 선생님의 출판교실이 자료를 모으고 디자인하고 인쇄해서 만들었어.
　　꽤 깔끔해. 그렇지?
남: 그래. 그러니까 그들이 이 모든 일을 다 했다고? 그들은 애완동물 사진까지
　　다 찍었니?
여: 물론이지. 그들은 Bailey의 휴대폰을 사용했어. 사진이 정말 잘 나왔어.
　　그렇지?
남: 그래, 잘 나왔네. 우와, 6학년 과학 선생님의 교실에는 뱀이 있어? 나는
　　몰랐어.
여: 나도 금시초문이었어. 그리고 너 Smith 선생님께서 이구아나를 애완동물로
　　기르시는 것 알아?
남: 진짜? 정말 멋지다. 어쨌든 출판교실이 이 팜플렛에 상당히 애쓴 것 같구나.
여: ④ 맞아. 그들이 팜플렛을 완성시키는 데 학기의 내무문이 걸렸어.

**어휘**
**directory** *n.* 안내책자　　**assemble** *v.* 모으다, 조립하다
〈문제〉 **semester** *n.* 학기

**정답** ④

**문제풀이**
남자와 여자는 출판교실에서 제작한 애완동물에 관한 팜플렛을 보면서 새로운
사실을 알게 되고 사진도 잘 나왔다고 말하면서 마지막에 이 팜플렛에 상당히
애를 쓴 것 같다고 했으므로 그에 적절한 대답은 ④ '맞아. 그들이 팜플렛을
완성시키는 데 학기의 대부분이 걸렸어.'이다.

**오답 보기 해석**
① 모든 사람들이 출판교실에 들어 갈 수 있는 것은 아니야.
② 나도, 나는 모든 학생들의 사진을 찍고 싶어.
③ 만약 네가 요청한다면 그는 네가 교실에서 애완동물 기르는 것을 허락하실
　　거라고 확신해.
⑤ 그래, 학생들은 그들의 학급 학생들에게 보여주기 위해 애완동물을 데려올
　　수도 있어.

**총 어휘 수** 177


## 14　긴 대화의 응답

**소재** 역사 성적 상담

**듣기 대본 해석**
남: 안녕하세요, Diaz 선생님. 선생님께서 저를 보기 원하신다고 들었는데요?
여: 그래, Tom, 내가 그랬어. 앉을래?
남: 네. [잠시 후] 무슨 일로 저를 보고 싶다고 하셨나요? 무슨 일이 있나요?
여: 음, 나는 너의 역사 성적이 점점 더 걱정이 된단다. [마우스 클릭하는 소리]
　　가장 최근의 시험 점수를 보렴.
남: 음... 네. 점수가 좋지 않네요.
여: 맞아. 그런데 3월까진 점수가 계속 올라갔어. 그러고 나서 그때부터 꾸준히
　　떨어졌구나.
남: 네, 그러네요.
여: 왜 그렇다고 생각하니? 집에 무슨 일 있니?
남: [잠시 후] 음. 사실대로 말하면, 저는 친구들과 충돌이 좀 있었는데 최근에는
　　저도 저 같이 느껴지지가 않았어요.
여: 자, Tom. 나는 지금부터 더 나은 점수를 기대하기 때문에 네가 친구들 사이에
　　일을 잘 해결하는 데 노력해야 해.
남: ⑤ 네, 상황이 나아지도록 최선을 다할게요.

**어휘**
**steadily** *ad.* 꾸준히　　**figure ~ out** ~을 이해하다, 알아내다
〈문제〉 **improve** *v.* 개선하다, 향상시키다

**정답** ⑤

**문제풀이**
남자의 역사 성적이 몇 달째 떨어진 것을 걱정하며 격려 및 조언을 해주는
여자에게 남자는 자신의 의지를 표현하는 것이 자연스럽다. 따라서 가장 적절한
대답으로는 ⑤ '네, 상황이 나아지도록 최선을 다할게요.'이다.

**오답 보기 해석**
① 특별한 건 없어요. 단지 제가 게을러서요.
② 좋아요. 제가 당신의 시험 공부를 도울게요.
③ 친구분들과 어떻게 지내세요?
④ 저도 동의해요. 사회과학은 제가 가장 좋아하는 과목이에요.

**총 어휘 수** 151


## 15　상황에 적절한 말

**소재** 오래된 스마트폰 처리

**듣기 대본 해석**
여: Betty는 친구인 John의 집에 갑니다. 그들이 거실에서 차를 마시며 앉아
　　있는 동안 Betty는 그가 새 스마트폰을 손에 쥐고 있고 예전 스마트폰은
　　탁자 위에 놓여있다는 것을 알아챕니다. 그는 그의 예전 스마트폰이 그다지
　　빠르지 않고 메모리가 충분하지 않아 새 스마트폰을 샀다고 말합니다. 그는
　　오래된 스마트폰을 쓰레기통에 버릴 것이라고 말합니다. Betty는 그렇게
　　하는 것은 말도 안 되는 일이고 그가 단지 새 폰을 원했다고 생각합니다. 어느
　　쪽이든, 그녀는 그가 그것을 그냥 버리면 안 된다고 생각합니다. Betty는
　　전자기기가 필요하지만 살 여유가 없는 사람들에게 주기 위해 필요하지
　　않은 전자기기를 모아 재디자인하는 지역 교회에 관한 기사를 읽은 것을
　　기억합니다. 그녀는 John에게 그가 자선단체에 폰을 주어야 한다고 말하고
　　싶습니다. 이 상황에서 Betty가 John에게 무슨 말을 할 것 같은가요?
Betty: ④ 그 폰을 나에게 주면 내가 그것을 기증하는 것은 어떠니?

**어휘**
**notice** *v.* 알아채다　　**nonsense** *n.* 어처구니없는 말이나 글
**either way** 둘 중에 어느 쪽이든　　**electronics** *n.* 전자기기　　**can't**
**afford something** ~을 살 여유가 없다　　**charity** *n.* 자선, 자선단체
〈문제〉 **donate** *v.* 기부하다

**정답** ④

## 문제풀이

Betty는 John이 쓰던 오래된 스마트폰을 버리는 것보다는 필요하지 않은 전자기기를 모아 개선해서 필요하지만 살 여유가 없는 사람들에게 주는 지역 교회에 기증하는 것이 낫다는 생각을 John에게 전하려 하므로 답은 ④ '그 폰을 나에게 주면 내가 그것을 기증하는 것은 어떠니?'이다.

## 오답 보기 해석

① 너는 내가 너의 오래된 폰을 고칠 수 있다는 것을 알았니?
② 근처 교회에 중고폰이 많다고 들었어.
③ 너는 오래 전에 새 폰을 샀어야 했어.
⑤ 저 오래된 폰을 좀 버려 줄래?

**총 어휘 수** 151

# 16 담화 목적 / 17 세부 내용 파악

**소재** Arts Center Benefit 자선행사

## 듣기 대본 해석

남: 안녕하세요 학생, 학부모, 그리고 직원 여러분. 여러분을 우리 캠퍼스의 황홀한 저녁에 초대합니다. 열 번째 연례 Franklin 대학 Arts Center Benefit이 8월 15일 토요일 우리 캠퍼스 박람회 장소에서 개최됩니다. 언제나 그렇듯이 자선 행사의 목적은 예술 센터를 지원하고 우리 학생들뿐만 아니라 지역사회에도 혜택을 줄 수 있는 새로운 프로그램들을 만들기 위한 자금을 마련하기 위함입니다. 모두가 아시다시피, 예술은 지역사회에 중요한 요소입니다. 예술은 우리를 하나로 묶어주고 상상도 할 수 없는 방법으로 우리의 마음과 영혼을 길러줍니다. 자선 행사는 지역사회가 우리 프로그램에 받은 것을 갚을 수 있게 해줍니다. 이 행사에서 나온 모든 수익금은 FC 예술 센터의 자금에 도움을 줄 것입니다. 다양한 이벤트들이 계획되고 있는데요, 여느 때처럼 사진 전시회, 특별하게 여겨지는 작품들의 경매, 훌륭한 우리 학교 재즈 밴드의 공연, 그리고 당연히 많은 먹거리들이 준비되어 있습니다. 행사의 표를 예매하고 싶거나 행사에는 참여하지 못하지만 기부를 하고 싶은 분들은 우리 학교 홈페이지를 방문하여 자선 행사 링크를 눌러 주세요. 감사합니다.

## 어휘

**incredible** *a.* 믿을 수 없는 놀라운　**benefit** *n.* 이득, 자선 행사
**fund** *n.* 기금, 자금 *v.* 자금을 모으다　**vital** *a.* 필수적인　**cultivate** *v.*
경작하다, 기르다　**exhibition** *n.* 전시회　**auction** *n.* 경매
**donate** *v.* 기부하다

## 정답 16 ① 17 ④

## 문제풀이

16 담화의 중간 부분에서 행사의 목적이 FC 예술 센터 지원과 프로그램 개발을 위한 것이라고 했으므로 Arts Center Benefit의 목적은 ① '아트 센터에 도움을 줄 자금을 모으려고'이다.

17 이벤트로는 사진 전시회, 작품 경매, 재즈 밴드 공연, 그리고 많은 먹거리가 있다고 했으므로 언급되지 않은 것은 ④ '유명인사 초대'이다.

## 오답 보기 해석

16
② 아트 센터 경매를 위한 예술가들의 기부를 찾기 위해
③ Franklin 대학교 학생들의 작품을 전시하기 위해
④ 새로운 아트 센터의 건축을 위한 후원을 마련하기 위해
⑤ 예술 공동체 회원들에게 무료 캠퍼스 투어를 제공하기 위해

**총 어휘 수** 191

## DICTATION ANSWERS

01 I was really impressed

02 make it to the play on time

03 to stand out from / attractive design and color scheme / take the time to respond to comments

04 had a reservation / there was a two-hour time limit / accommodate as many customers as possible / based on how many kids a customer brings

05 I'd ever see you here again / considering working with us / got the role / true to the original costuming

06 I really don't care for the outdoors much / getting the luggage out of the / made him miserable

07 taste a little strange / a couple of months back / Don't forget to bring your tools / I'll clean the sink out

08 you can throw a javelin / while your shoulder was injured / it slipped your mind / I can relate

09 I'm looking to buy some / baked a batch of chess pies / are they running for / save it for next time

10 There isn't much traffic, either / Are there any stations within walking distance / have an attached two-car garage / to be sure

11 extracting natural gas from rock / cost-effective / inserts chemicals / pollute nearby residents' tap water

12 it's that time of the year / I get bad allergies / Mine is a real help / set up an appointment

13 a directory of all of the animals / turned out really well / That was news to me

14 concerned about your grades / they've been steadily falling / felt like myself lately / from here on out

15 throw the old one in the garbage / thinks this is nonsense / remembers reading an article about / collects unwanted electronics and refurbishes them

16-17 invite each of you to / art is vital to a community / cultivates our minds and souls in / click the link for the benefit

| | | | | | |
|---|---|---|---|---|---|
| 01 ⑤ | 02 ③ | 03 ② | 04 ④ | 05 ④ | 06 ② |
| 07 ③ | 08 ② | 09 ④ | 10 ③ | 11 ② | 12 ④ |
| 13 ② | 14 ① | 15 ⑤ | 16 ② | 17 ⑤ | |

## 01 짧은 대화의 응답

**소재** 야구경기 예매

**듣기 대본 해석**

남: 여보, 오늘 야구경기 티켓 예매했어?

여: 아, 맞다. 깜박했어. 지금 온라인으로 할게.

남: 너무 늦은 것 같은데. 온라인에서 표가 매진된 걸 봤어. 더 일찍 샀어야 했는데.

여: ⑤ 정말 미안해. 내일 경기 표 예매할게.

**어휘**

**sold out** (표가) 매진된, 다 팔린

**정답** ⑤

**문제풀이**

예매하는 것을 깜박했는데 표가 매진되었다는 내용이다. 더 일찍 샀어야 했다는 남자의 말에 적절한 대답은 ⑤ '정말 미안해. 내일 경기 표 예매할게.'이다.

**오답 보기 해석**

① 나 이 표를 팔 생각이야.

② 안됐구나. 오늘 나중에 해보자.

③ 표를 어디다가 뒀는지 기억이 안 나.

④ 걱정하지 마. 벌써 표 샀어.

**총 어휘 수** 46

## 02 짧은 대화의 응답

**소재** 나비정원 방문

**듣기 대본 해석**

여: 여기가 안내책자에서 본 나비정원이 분명해요.

남: 맞아요. 우리 여행의 끝이기도 하죠. 즐거운 시간 보냈길 바라요, Conn 부인.

여: 네. 모든 것이 아름다웠어요. 정원에서 얼마나 있을 수 있죠?

남: ③ 공원이 해질 때 닫으니까 여유를 가지세요.

**어휘**

**brochure** *n.* 안내책자

**정답** ③

**문제풀이**

여자가 정원에서 얼마나 있을 수 있냐고 물었으므로 남자의 적절한 대답은 ③ '공원이 해질 때 닫으니까 여유를 가지세요.'이다.

**오답 보기 해석**

① 우리가 박물관에서 더 많은 시간을 보냈으면 좋았을 것 같네요.

② 좋은 시간을 보냈는데 확실히 피곤하네요.

④ 여기가 여행에서 처음 멈추는 곳이니까 서둘러야 합니다.

⑤ 미안한데 그럴 수 없어요. 나비정원이 문을 닫았거든요.

**총 어휘 수** 52

## 03 담화 목적

**소재** 토크쇼 손님 소개

**듣기 대본 해석**

남: 안녕하세요, 여러분. 저는 Michael Johnson이고 오늘 아침 우리 프로그램인 Student Volunteers에 참여해 주셔서 감사합니다. 대학생들의 관점에서 우리 나라에서 가장 존경 받는 사람이 누구인지 알아보기 위해 우리가 실시한 조사에 여러분이 참여했거나 적어도 그것에 대해 알고 계시리라고 확신합니다. 거의 매년 선택된 사람은 성공한 사업가나 정치가 같은 힘 있는 사람이었습니다. 하지만 올해는 꽤 다릅니다. 학생들은 수년 동안 불우한 이웃을 도와준 사람인 Amelia Henderson에 투표했습니다. 그녀는 빈민 지역사회에서 불우한 이웃들이 기술을 배우도록 도와서 그들이 제대로 된 직장을 찾을 수 있게 해주었습니다. 그녀의 너그러움과 포부는 우리 학생들에게 강하고 긍정적인 영향을 주었습니다. 이 시점에서 저는 우리 모두와 이야기하기 위해 오늘 초대된 Henderson 씨를 소개하고자 합니다. 그녀는 왜 불우한 사람들을 돕는 것이 중요한지를 오늘 우리와 이야기를 나눌 것입니다. 안녕하세요, Henderson 씨. 오늘 우리가 당신과 함께하게 되어서 너무나 행운이라고 말하며 시작할게요.

**어휘**

**survey** *n.* 조사    **conduct** *v.* 수행하다    **in an attempt to V** ∼하기 위하여, ∼하려는 시도로    **entrepreneur** *n.* 사업가, 기업가    **decent** *a.* 괜찮은, 제대로 된    **generosity** *n.* 너그러움    **ambition** *n.* 야망, 포부    **in need** 어려움에 처한, 궁핍한

**정답** ②

**문제풀이**

대학생들 사이에서 존경 받은 인물로 선정된 인물을 초청해 소개하고 있으므로 정답은 ② '오늘의 토크쇼 초대 손님을 소개하려고'이다.

**총 어휘 수** 180

## 04 대화 주제

**소재** 버스를 이용한 통학

**듣기 대본 해석**

남: 안녕, Rachel.

여: 좋은 아침이에요, Turner 선생님. 아침에 항상 학교에 버스를 타고 가시나요?

남: 매일 아침은 아니고 한 날에 두어 번 정도 타. 너는 어떠니?

여: 저는 매일 아침 타요. 엄마가 항상 차로 태워다 주신다고 하지만, 저는 버스가 더 좋아요.

남: 왜?

여: 저는 환경에 특별히 관심이 있어요. 게다가 비싼 기름값 때문에 그것이 더 싸기도 하고요.

남: 와, 참 훌륭하구나.

여: 음, 저는 버스를 타는 것보다 차를 타는 것이 열 배 더 비싸다고 읽었어요.

남: 정말? 큰 차이구나.

여: 또 스마트폰으로 뉴스를 읽고 제 LookBook 페이지를 확인할 수 있는 훌륭한 시간이죠.

남: 그렇구나. 음, 나는 조금 더 걸을 수 있는 기회가 생기기 때문에 보통 지하철을 타.

여: 무슨 말씀이신지 알겠어요. 서는 버스 정류장까지 짧게 걸어가는 것을 광장히 즐겨요. 그것은 저에게 저의 하루에 대해 생각할 기회를 줘요. 그것은 또한 좋은 운동이에요.

남: 그렇게 생각하는 것도 좋네.

**어휘**

**prefer** *v.* 더 좋아하다    **environmentally** *ad.* 환경적으로    **conscious** *a.* 의식하는    **thoughtful** *a.* 사려 깊은

**정답** ④

문제풀이
여자는 환경과 기름값, 시간 활용의 예를 들면서 버스로 통학할 때의 좋은 점을
말하고 있으므로 두 사람의 대화 주제는 ④ '버스로 통학하는 것의 장점'이다.

총 어휘 수 171


# 05  대화자의 관계 파악

소재  구직자와 직업 상담

듣기 대본 해석
여: Carter 씨군요. 어떻게 지내세요?
남: 음, 솔직히, 상황이 좋지는 않아요.
여: 유감이군요. 하지만 제가 당신의 상황이 호전되도록 도우러 왔어요. 당신과
   관련된 소개를 좀 해주시겠어요?
남: 정식 훈련을 받지는 않았지만 오토바이를 고치는 것에 대해 많은 것을
   알고 있어요.
여: 그렇군요. 여가시간에 무엇을 하시나요?
남: 컴퓨터 설계나 약간의 네트워킹을 하며 많은 시간을 보내요.
여: 알겠습니다. 컴퓨터를 좋아하시는군요?
남: 맞습니다. 저는 컴퓨터와 함께 자랐어요. 제가 어렸을 때 그것이 유일한
   친구였거든요.
여: 좋습니다. 혼자 일하시길 원하시나요, 아니면 여러 명이 함께 하는 것이
   좋으신가요?
남: 혼자 일하는 것이 낫겠군요. 약간 내성적이어서요.
여: 알겠습니다. Computers Plus에 기술자를 위한 자리가 있는 것 같군요.
   당신 같은 분에게 잘 맞는 자리인 것 같아요.
남: 동의합니다. 도와주셔서 감사합니다.

어휘
**relevant** *a.* 관련 있는, 적절한    **introvert** *n.* 내향적인 사람
**opening** *n.* (사람을 쓸 수 있는) 빈자리(공석)    **suitable** *a.* 적합한

정답 ④

문제풀이
여자는 남자에 대해 묻고, 남자는 자신의 능력과 기술, 원하는 일에 대해 대답해
주고 있다. 대화의 마지막 부분에서 여자가 남자에게 기술자를 위한 자리가 있다고
추천해주는 것으로 보아 두 사람의 관계는 ④ '취업 상담원 — 구직자'가 가장
적절하다.

총 어휘 수 159


# 06  그림의 세부 내용 파악

소재  시계 구입

듣기 대본 해석
남: 안녕하세요. 뭘 도와드릴까요?
여: 부엌에 놓을 새 시계를 찾고 있어요. 어떤 것들이 있죠?
남: 현재는 이 다섯 개만 재고로 가지고 있습니다. 이 꽃 모양은 어떤가요?
   부엌용으로 디자인된 건데요.
여: 저한테는 약간 싸구려같이 보이는데요. 제 부엌은 굉장히 현대식이거든요.
남: 알겠습니다. 그런 경우라면 이 사각형 모양은 어떤가요? 우아하고 단순하죠.
여: 전 이보다 더 단순한 게 좋은데요. 숫자가 12개 전부 있는 것 보다 4개만
   있으면 좋겠어요.
남: 알겠습니다. 그럼 3개가 남았네요. 이건 맘에 안 들어 하실 것 같은데 별
   모양이어서 손님의 부엌 장식용으로 아마도 어울리지 않을 것 같아요.
여: 네, 그리고 사각형 해 모양 시계는 저한테는 좀 요란한 것 같네요.
남: 네, 그럼 이게 가장 좋을 것 같네요.
여: 그런 것 같아요. 그걸로 할게요.
남: 좋습니다.

어휘
**in stock** 재고로 있는    **cheesy** *a.* 싸구려의, 값싼    **elegant** *a.* 우아한
**fit** *v.* 어울리다, 맞다    **loud** *a.* (색깔·무늬 등이) 야단스러운, 야한

정답 ②

문제풀이
꽃 모양은 싫다고 했고 숫자가 모두 써있는 것도 원하지 않는다고 했으므로
②, ③, ⑤번이 남는데 별 모양과 해 모양도 안 어울릴 거라고 했으므로 정답은
②번이다.

총 어휘 수 150


# 07  할 일

소재  손님이 찾는 책 가져다 주기

듣기 대본 해석
남: 안녕하세요. 무엇을 도와드릴까요?
여: *Chocolat*를 찾고 있어요.
남: 사탕 구역을 찾아보세요. 계산대 쪽에 있어요.
여: 아, 사탕을 말하는 게 아니에요. 그 이름으로 된 책을 찾고 있어요.
남: 아, 찾으시는 것 있는 것 같아요. 작가 이름 혹시 아세요?
여: 잘 모르겠어요. 프랑스에서 초콜릿 가게를 여는 여자에 관한 얘기란 것만
   알아요.
남: 잠시만 기다려 주시면 제가 컴퓨터로 찾아 드릴게요. *[키보드 치는 소리]*
   네, 재고에 한 권 있네요.
여: 좋네요. 얼마예요?
남: 13.99달러입니다. 저희 혜택 프로그램 회원이시면 10퍼센트 할인받으실
   수 있으세요.
여: 안타깝게도 회원이 아니네요. 그래도 책 살게요.
남: 알겠습니다. 찾아서 갖고 올게요.

어휘
**aisle** *n.* 통로, 구역    **register** *n.* 계산대    **in stock** 재고로

정답 ③

문제풀이
남자는 여자가 찾는 책의 재고가 있는지 알아봐 주었고 여자가 책을 사겠다고
했으므로 남자는 책을 찾아서 가져오겠다고 했다. 따라서 남자가 할 일은
③ '책 가져다 주기'이다.

총 어휘 수 129


# 08  이유

소재  경기에 참가 못하는 이유

듣기 대본 해석
*[휴대폰이 울린다.]*
여: 안녕, Leo. 너도 알다시피, 네가 오늘 연습에 빠져서 팀원들이 다 걱정하고
   있어.
남: 응, 미안해. 연습에 갈 수 없었어. 사실 내가 전화한 건 내일 경기에 관해
   얘기하기 위해서야.
여: 오, 무슨 일인데?
남: 그게 넌 내가 내일 못 뛸 걸 고려해야 할 것 같아.
여: 정말? 하지만 넌 우리의 가장 뛰어난 선수인걸. 우린 네가 필요해.
남: 나도 뛰고 싶은데 그럴 수가 없어.
여: 무슨 일이 있었는지 말해줄래?
남: 그게 좀 창피한 게, 내 차 타고 자랑하다가 자제력을 잃고 벽에 부딪혔어.
여: 큰일이네! 괜찮아?
남: 사고 때문에 멍이 좀 들긴 했는데 괜찮아. 근데 의사들이 엑스레이 찍고
   오늘 하루는 병원에서 지내는 게 좋을 것 같대.

여: 큰일이네. 근데 어쩔 수 없지. 빨리 다 나았으면 좋겠다.
남: 고마워.

**어휘**

**match** *n.* 경기　**embarrassing** *a.* 난처한, 창피한　**show off**
과시하다, 자랑하다　**crash into** ~와 충돌하다　**bruised** *a.* 멍든,
타박상을 입은

**정답** ②

**문제풀이**
남자는 차를 타고 자랑하다가 다친 나머지 하루 동안 병원에 입원할 처지에
놓여 내일 경기에 나갈 수 없게 되었다. 그러므로 정답은 ② '병원에 입원해야
해서'이다.

**총 어휘 수** 154

## 09　숫자

**소재** 피자 주문하기

**듣기 대본 해석**
남: 안녕하세요. 무엇을 도와드릴까요?
여: 배달 주문을 하고 싶어요.
남: 네, 어떤 것을 원하세요?
여: 슈프림 피자와 마늘빵 콤보와 디핑소스를 추가로 더 받고 싶어요.
남: 물론이죠. 그렇지만 추가 소스는 1달러를 더 내셔야 해요.
여: 좋아요. 닭고기도 있나요?
남: 네, 있어요. 후라이드 치킨과 버팔로윙이 있어요. 각각 5달러입니다.
여: 좋아요. 제가 주문한 것에 각각 하나씩 추가할게요.
남: 오늘은 그것이 전부인가요?
여: 네, 그게 전부예요. 모두 얼마죠?
남: 모두 합쳐서, 슈프림 피자와 마늘빵 콤보, 소스 추가와 치킨 두 개 추가해서
　　30달러입니다. 오늘 쿠폰을 사용하실 건가요?
여: 네, 30달러 이상 사용시 20퍼센트 할인되는 쿠폰이 있어요.
남: 네, 좋아요. 이 쿠폰은 손님께서 VISA 신용카드 혹은 직불카드로 결제하실
　　경우에만 가능합니다.
여: 네, 알아요. 전 VISA 직불카드를 가지고 있어요.

**어휘**

**make an order** 주문하다　**delivery** *n.* 배송, 배달　**valid** *a.* 유효한
**credit card** 신용카드　**debit card** 직불카드

**정답** ④

**문제풀이**
여자가 주문한 전체 금액이 30달러라고 했는데, 30달러 이상 주문 시 사용
가능한 20퍼센트 할인 쿠폰이 있다고 했으므로 30달러에 20퍼센트 할인을
적용하면 24달러가 된다. 따라서 답은 ④ '$24'이다.

**총 어휘 수** 153

## 10　언급 유무

**소재** 노숙자 보호소를 위한 자선행사

**듣기 대본 해석**
여: 네가 보고 있는 그 전단지는 뭐야, Tommy?
남: 지역 노숙자 보호소에 도움을 주기 위한 자선행사에 관한 거야. 행사가
　　10월 13일야.
여: 다가오는 토요일이네, 맞지?
남: 맞아. 그들은 슬로건도 있어. 슬로건은 "생활필수품이 없는 사람들에게
　　그것들을 줍시다"야.

여: 그들은 좀 더 창의적인 뭔가를 생각해 낼 수 없었나 보다. 오, 이 전단지에
　　행사가 새로운 레크레이션 센터에서 열릴 거라고 써 있네. 거기가 어디지?
남: 길 바로 아래야. 너 법원 청사가 어디에 있는지 알지? 그것은 법원 청사로부터
　　바로 길 건너편에 있어.
여: 아, 그게 무슨 건물인지 궁금했었어. 우리도 참가해야 한다고 생각해.
남: 맞아. 난 불우한 사람들을 돕는 것을 언제나 좋아해.
여: 나도 그래. 그리고 광고에 참석자들을 위해 무료 다과를 준다고 나와 있네.
남: 그래. 가서 도와주자.

**어휘**

**benefit** *v.* ~에게 이익을 가져다 주다, 이익을 얻다
**basic necessities** 기본적 필수품　**come up with** 생각해 내다
**courthouse** *n.* 법원 청사　**advertisement** *n.* 광고
**refreshments** *n.* 다과, 음식　**attendee** *n.* 참석자

**정답** ③

**문제풀이**
대화에서 자선행사의 날짜, 슬로건, 장소, 간식 제공 여부에 대한 언급은 있었지만
참가 방법에 관한 언급은 없으므로 정답은 ③ '참가 방법'이다.

**총 어휘 수** 131

## 11　내용 일치 · 불일치

**소재** 벚꽃 축제 안내

**듣기 대본 해석**
여: 좋은 아침입니다. 신사 숙녀 여러분. 드디어 봄이 다시 왔습니다. 벚꽃이
　　활짝 폈어요! 상쾌한 봄 공기를 깊이 들이마시고 여러분의 눈을 아름다운
　　꽃들에게 돌려보세요. 저희는 해마다 열리는 네 번째 벚꽃 축제의 개최를
　　발표하게 되어 더없이 기쁩니다! 축제 날짜는 해마다 바뀌는데 올해는
　　4월 20일부터 4월 27일까지입니다. 올해 축제에는 어린이들이 즐길만한
　　것들을 포함하여 새로운 활동들이 계획되어 있습니다! 그러니 가족 모두가
　　오셔서 멋진 축제를 즐겨주세요. 볼 것과 할 것이 너무 많아서 여러분은
　　시간이 더 있었으면 하실 겁니다! 만약 여러분이 축제 장소에 차를 주차하기
　　원하시면 요금은 15달러이지만 걸어서 오신다면 5달러입니다. 여러분
　　모두를 곧 뵙고 싶습니다!

**어휘**

**announce** *v.* 발표하다, 알리다　**blossom** *n.* 꽃　**in full bloom**
만발하여　**annual** *a.* 매년의, 연례의

**정답** ②

**문제풀이**
벚꽃 축제의 날짜는 해마다 바뀐다고 되어 있으므로 내용과 일치하지 않는 것은
② '축제는 매년 봄 같은 날짜에 열린다.'이다.

**총 어휘 수** 148

## 12　도표

**소재** 중고 오토바이 선택

**듣기 대본 해석**
남: 안녕하세요. 도와드릴까요?
여: 안녕하세요. 중고 오토바이를 찾고 있는데요.
남: 생각하고 계신 특정 모델이 있나요?
여: 네, S-35과 K-350이 가장 좋아하는 모델이에요.
남: 알겠습니다. [마우스 클릭 소리] 이 목록을 보세요. 그 모델 종류는 5종을
　　보유하고 있어요.
여: 음, 10년이 넘은 오토바이는 원하지 않아요.

남: 글쎄요, 하지만 이 K-350의 가격이 다섯 개 중 가장 저렴한데요.
여: 하지만 그래도 10년보다 오래되지 않았으면서 350cc보다 크지 않은
　　모델을 원해요.
남: 알겠습니다. 가격은 어느 정도 보고 계시는지 물어도 될까요?
여: 5,000달러 미만이요.
남: 그렇다면 두 가지 선택이 남는군요.
여: 흠, 비록 가격차가 약간 있지만 더 큰 엔진을 가진 오토바이를 원해요. 다른
　　것보다 더 빠를 테니까요.
남: 좋아요! 훌륭한 선택입니다!

### 어휘
**available** *a.* 이용할 수 있는

### 정답 ④

### 문제풀이
10년 넘은 기종은 원하지 않는다고 했으므로 ③번은 제외된다. 또한 350cc
이하가 아니기 때문에 ②번도 제외되고 가격이 5,000달러 이상인 ⑤번도
제외된다. 남아있는 ①번과 ④번 중 더 큰 엔진을 가진 것은 ④번이다.

**총 어휘 수** 129


## 13　긴 대화의 응답

**소재** 할아버지, 할머니와의 저녁 식사

### 듣기 대본 해석
*[전화벨이 울린다.]*
여: 아빠, 저예요.
남: 그래 Kaitlyn. 오는 중이야?
여: 아직이요. 근데 터미널에 도착했어요.
남: 그렇구나. 버스는 언제 출발해?
여: 3시 좀 지나서 출발 예정이에요. 기다리는 동안 카페에서 간식 사먹으려고요.
남: 그래. 할머니, 할아버지랑 저녁 먹으러 여기 6시까지 올 수 있겠어?
여: 아니요. 오늘 금요일이라 차가 많이 막혀서 도시 벗어나는 데 좀 걸릴 것
　　같아요.
남: 왜 좀 더 이른 시간의 버스를 타지 않았니?
여: 그러려고 했는데 터미널에 도착했을 때 표가 다 팔렸었어요.
남: 그래. 안됐구나. 그분들이 너 많이 보고 싶어 하셔.
여: 네, 저도 시간에 맞춰서 저녁 식사 같이 하고 싶은데 너무 늦게 도착할 것
　　같네요.
남: ② 그럼, 네가 도착할 때까지 우리가 저녁 식사를 미룰게.

### 어휘
**in time** 시간 맞춰　　**traffic** *n.* 교통(량)　　**sold out** (표가) 매진된
〈문제〉**postpone** *v.* 연기하다, 미루다

### 정답 ②

### 문제풀이
저녁 식사 약속 시간이 6시인데 여자가 너무 늦게 도착할 것 같다고 걱정하고
있으므로 아빠가 마지막에 할 말로 적절한 것은 ② '그럼, 네가 도착할 때까지
우리가 저녁 식사를 미룰게.'이다.

### 오답 보기 해석
① 나는 버스 정류장에서 차편이 필요할 거야.
③ 네가 더 이른 시간 버스표를 사야 할 것 같아.
④ 좋아. 나는 7시경에 역에 있을 거야.
⑤ 문제 없어. 내가 더 이른 시간의 버스 표를 예약해줄게.

**총 어휘 수** 142


## 14　긴 대화의 응답

**소재** 창 밖 가로등으로 인한 방 옮기기

### 듣기 대본 해석
*[전화벨이 울린다.]*
여: 안내 데스크입니다. 무엇을 도와드릴까요?
남: 안녕하세요. 3D 방의 Dennis Reynolds입니다.
여: 무엇을 도와드릴까요, Reynolds 씨?
남: 그게, 제 창 밖에 가로등이 있어요. 근데 너무 밝아요. 켜져 있는 채로는 잘
　　수가 없네요.
여: Reynolds 씨, 죄송하지만 그 가로등들은 안전상의 문제 때문에 켜져
　　있어야 합니다.
남: 아침 일찍 일어나야 하거든요. 전 잠을 자야 해요. 정말 거슬리네요.
여: 그럼 건물 반대편에 있는 방으로 옮겨 드릴게요. 괜찮을까요?
남: 그러면 되겠네요.
여: 알겠습니다. 2층의 4B방으로 옮겨 드릴게요.
남: 제 짐을 누군가가 같이 옮겨 줄 수 있을까요?
여: ① 물론이죠. 안내원이 곧 도우러 갈 겁니다.

### 어휘
**purpose** *n.* 목적　　**nuisance** *n.* 성가신 것, 귀찮은 것　　**belongings**
*n.* 소유물

### 정답 ①

### 문제풀이
남자가 창 밖 가로등이 너무 밝아 잠을 잘 수 없다며 가로등을 꺼달라고 하자
방을 바꿔주는 상황인데, 마지막에 남자가 짐을 옮겨줄 수 있냐고 물었으므로
그에 적절한 대답은 ① '물론이죠. 안내원이 곧 도우러 갈 겁니다.'이다.

### 오답 보기 해석
② 문제 없어요. 손님은 방을 바꾸실 필요가 없습니다.
③ 체크아웃 때 추가 요금을 처리하실 수 있습니다, 손님.
④ 제가 반드시 창문 밖에 있는 등을 끄겠습니다, 손님.
⑤ 물론이죠. 안내 데스크에서 아침 7시에 모닝콜을 해드릴게요.

**총 어휘 수** 133


## 15　상황에 적절한 말

**소재** 효과적인 프레젠테이션 준비

### 듣기 대본 해석
여: Brody는 새로운 게임에 대해 컴퓨터 게임 회사에 홍보하기 위해 프레젠
　　테이션의 마무리 작업을 합니다. 그는 좋은 친구인 Leah에게 건설적인
　　피드백뿐만 아니라 프레젠테이션에 대한 그녀의 의견을 얻기 위해 그녀와
　　프레젠테이션을 연습할 수 있는지 묻습니다. 그들은 카페에서 만나고, 거기서
　　그는 그의 프레젠테이션을 살펴봅니다. 그녀는 게임의 아이디어는 좋아
　　하지만 그의 프레젠테이션에 문제가 좀 있다고 생각합니다. 게임의 스토리가
　　좀 복잡해 보이는 것 같고 스크린샷이 충분하지 않습니다. 그녀는 너무
　　많은 언어적 정보와 충분하지 않은 시각적 정보가 회사의 임원들을 지루하게
　　할 거라고 지적합니다. Brody는 프레젠테이션을 개선하기 위해 무엇을
　　해야 할지 궁금해서 Leah에게 조언을 구합니다. 이런 상황에서 Leah는
　　Brody에게 뭐라고 말할까요?
Leah: ⑤ 프레젠테이션에 더 많은 시각적 예들을 제공하는 것이 중요해.

### 어휘
**constructive** *a.* 건설적인　　**go through** ~을 살펴보다, 조사하다
**complicated** *a.* 복잡한　　**verbal** *a.* 언어의, 구두의　　**executive** *n.*
경영진, 임원　　〈문제〉**in detail** 상세하게　　**beta test** (신제품에 대한)
베타 테스트　　**consult** *v.* 상담하다　　**benefit** *v.* ~에게 이익을 가져다
주다, 이익을 얻다

### 정답 ⑤

Leah는 Brody가 만든 프레젠테이션의 아이디어는 좋지만 언어적인 정보가 너무 많고 시각적 정보가 부족하다고 지적했으므로 프레젠테이션을 개선하기 위해 할 말로는 ⑤ '프레젠테이션에 더 많은 시각적 예들을 제공하는 것이 중요해.'가 가장 적절하다.

오답 보기 해석
① 스토리라인을 좀 더 자세하게 설명해야 해.
② 네가 발표하기 전에 게임의 베타테스트를 더 해야 해.
③ 매일 너의 프로그래밍 팀과 상담하는 것이 중요해.
④ 다른 사람이 게임을 발표하게 하는 것이 너한테 도움이 될 거야.

총 어휘 수 145


# 16 담화 주제 / 17 세부 내용 파악

소재 즐거운 캠핑을 위한 조언

듣기 대본 해석
남: 도시에서 살 때 밖으로 나와 자연을 즐기는 것이 쉽지 않습니다. 하지만 많은 사람들이 도시 생활에서 탈출하기 위해서 야외로 나갑니다. 특히 취미에 열심인 많은 사람들이 캠핑을 레저활동으로 선택하고 있습니다. 야외로 나가는 것은 정신적, 신체적 건강에 좋습니다. 하지만 캠핑을 갈 때 몇 가지 조심해야 할 것이 있습니다. 첫째로, 여러분은 여분의 옷을 꼭 챙기는 것이 좋을 것입니다. 기온이 갑자기 떨어지거나 원래 입고 간 옷이 젖었을 때 여러분을 따뜻하게 해 줄 것입니다. 둘째로, 여러분의 여행을 위해 충분한 음식을 가져가세요. 야영지 주변에서 하이킹을 하는 동안 만약 길을 잃어버릴 경우에 대비해 추가로 음식을 싸가는 것도 좋습니다. 셋째, 구급상자를 가져가세요. 다른 모든 야외활동과 마찬가지로, 캠핑은 위험할 수 있습니다. 또한, 야영지를 떠날 때는 뒷정리를 하세요. 우리의 환경을 깨끗하게 지키는 것이 중요합니다. 마지막으로, 즐거운 시간을 보내세요. 재미가 없다면 취미가 아닙니다. 이런 조언들을 염두에 둔다면 여러분께서는 다음 캠핑에서 안전하고 재미있는 시간을 보내실 수 있으실 겁니다.

어휘
outdoor *a.* 옥외의, 야외의    precaution *n.* 예방 조치
first-aid kit 구급상자

정답 16 ②  17 ⑤

문제풀이
16 안전하고 즐거운 캠핑을 위해 챙겨야 할 것들과 캠핑에 가서 그리고 캠핑이 끝난 후에 할 것들을 이야기하고 있으므로 정답은 ② '캠핑 동안 안전하고 즐겁게 놀기 위한 조언'이다.

17 캠핑 갈 때 가져가야 할 것으로 여분의 옷, 충분한 음식, 구급상자를 언급했고, 캠핑 후 뒷정리를 깨끗하게 청소해야 한다고 말했지만 랜턴에 관한 언급은 하지 않았으므로 정답은 ⑤ '랜턴'이다.

오답 보기 해석
16
① 야외 활동의 정신적, 신체적 장점들.
③ 가족 캠핑 때 가져가야 할 것들
④ 캠핑하는 동안 길을 잃어버릴 위험성
⑤ 캠핑하는 동안 응급치료 하는 방법

총 어휘 수 204


## DICTATION ANSWERS

01 they're all sold out

02 I hope you enjoyed yourself

03 that we conducted in an attempt to / had a strong positive impact on our students / to help those in need / how fortunate we are

04 always offers to take me in / I like to be environmentally conscious / it gives me the chance to walk

05 turn your life around / Do you prefer being alone / I'd much rather be alone

06 What do you have in stock / prefer one a little simpler / fit your kitchen's decor / I'll take that one

07 near the register / we probably have that / so we have one copy in stock

08 the best player we've got / showing off in my car / a little bruised up / we'll have to deal with it

09 make an order for delivery / this coupon is only valid

10 benefit the local homeless shelter / Give basic necessities / come up with / enjoy helping those less fortunate

11 are in full bloom / let your eyes take in / We couldn't be happier to announce that

12 have any particular model in mind / how much you're looking to pay / there's a little difference in price

13 you'll make it here in time / getting out of the city / tickets were sold out

14 I can't sleep with it on / stay on for safety purposes / It's really a nuisance

15 in order to get her opinion / too much verbal information / bore the executives of the company

16-17 get out and enjoy nature / several precautions you should take / if there's a sudden drop in temperature

# 07

| 01 ① | 02 ② | 03 ① | 04 ③ | 05 ⑤ | 06 ④ |
| 07 ⑤ | 08 ④ | 09 ⑤ | 10 ③ | 11 ③ | 12 ⑤ |
| 13 ③ | 14 ① | 15 ③ | 16 ④ | 17 ③ | |

## 01 짧은 대화의 응답

**소재** 옷 빌려주기

**듣기 대본 해석**

여: 왜! 기온이 많이 떨어졌어. 얼어버릴 것 같아.

남: 좀 더 따뜻한 옷을 입었어야 했는데. 내 코트 입을래?

여: 아니, 괜찮아. 너도 코트가 없으면 추울 거야.

남: ① 난 차에 여분 코트가 있어.

**어휘**

**freeze** *v.* 얼다, 얼리다　〈문제〉 **bother** *v.* 귀찮게 하다

**정답** ①

**문제풀이**

여자가 춥다고 하자 자기 코트를 입으라는 남자에게, 남자도 추울 테니 괜찮다고 말한다. 이때 남자의 응답으로 가장 적절한 것은 ① '난 차에 여분 코트가 있어.'이다.

**오답 보기 해석**

② 귀찮게 한 거 사과할게.

③ 내가 이해를 못한 것 같아.

④ 난 더 잘 준비해야 해.

⑤ 그래, 넌 틀림없이 그럴 거야.

**총 어휘 수** 39

## 02 짧은 대화의 응답

**소재** 배가 많이 고픈 딸

**듣기 대본 해석**

남: 안녕, Lisa. 너 얼굴빛이 안 좋아 보이네. 괜찮아?

여: 학교에서 오늘 정말 바빴어요, 아빠. 배고파 죽겠어요. 저녁은 뭐예요?

남: 음, 아직 어떤 것도 준비가 안 되었지만, 냉장고에 남은 피자가 있을 거야.

여: ② 남은 것이 없어요. 지난밤에 제가 다 먹었어요.

**어휘**

**starve** *v.* 굶주리다　**leftover** *n.* 남은 음식 *a.* 먹다 남은, 나머지의

**refrigerator** *n.* 냉장고

**정답** ②

**문제풀이**

냉장고에 남은 피자가 있을 거라는 아빠의 말에 적절한 응답은 ② '남은 것이 없어요. 지난밤에 제가 다 먹었어요.'이다.

**오답 보기 해석**

① 괜찮아요. 이미 저녁 먹었어요.

③ 알았어요. 제가 좋은 이탈리아 식당을 알아요.

④ 남은 것을 냉장고에 넣어 주세요.

⑤ 저는 피자를 좋아하지만 여기서 팔지 않을 것 같은데요.

**총 어휘 수** 49

## 03 담화 주제

**소재** 식초를 이용한 블랙베리의 신선함 유지법

**듣기 대본 해석**

여: 봄이 왔습니다. 블랙베리와 같은 신선한 과일을 즐길 때가 온 겁니다. 저는 블랙베리를 신선하게 유지하는 것이 어려웠지만, 한 친구가 보존 기간을 최대화할 수 있는 쉬운 방법을 알려주었습니다. 간단하게 물과 식초로 된 용액을 사용함으로써, 여러분은 신선한 블랙베리의 기한을 크게 늘릴 수 있습니다. 과정은 아주 간단해서 누구라도 할 수 있습니다. 우선 블랙베리를 식초와 물을 반반 섞은 것으로 씻으세요. 식초가 세균을 죽일 수 있도록 블랙베리를 약 5분 동안 담가주세요. 마지막으로 남아있는 식초를 제거하기 위해 싱크대에서 블랙베리를 헹구기만 하시면 됩니다. 그 비결은 블랙베리의 신선도를 해칠 수 있는 세균을 죽이는 것입니다. 식초의 산성은 세균을 죽이기에 충분히 강하지만, 식초는 가정에서 사용하기에 안전하며 먹어도 됩니다. 이 조언을 따르면, 여러분은 이렇게 하지 않았을 때보다 몇 주 더 오랫동안 신선한 블랙베리를 즐기실 수 있습니다.

**어휘**

**maximize** *v.* 극대화하다　**shelf life** (식품 등의) 보존 기간, 유통기한

**solution** *n.* 용액, 해결　**vinegar** *n.* 식초　**extend** *v.* 더 길게 늘이다

**soak** *v.* 담그다, 담기다　**rinse** *v.* 씻다　**acidity** *n.* 신맛, 산성

**정답** ①

**문제풀이**

여자는 세균을 죽이는 식초를 물과 반반씩 섞은 용액에 블랙베리를 일정 시간 담근 후에 헹굼으로써 그냥 보관했을 때보다 장기간 신선하게 보관할 수 있다고 말하고 있다. 따라서 여자가 하는 말의 주제로 가장 적절한 것은 ① '식초를 이용한 블랙베리의 신선도 유지법'이다.

**총 어휘 수** 168

## 04 의견

**소재** 젊은 사람들의 은어 사용

**듣기 대본 해석**

남: May 선생님, 괜찮으세요? 화가 나 보이세요. 무슨 일 있으세요?

여: 제가 사는 도시에서 제가 이방인처럼 느껴져요.

남: 왜 그렇게 느끼세요?

여: 음, 오늘 아침에 여기에 올 때 지하철을 탔는데 제 건너편에 한 무리의 젊은이들이 앉아 있었어요. 전 그들이 하는 말 중에서 반은 이해할 수가 없었어요.

남: 그들이 은어를 사용하고 있었다는 거죠?

여: 확실히 그랬어요. 그 젊은 사람들이 무슨 말을 하는지 정확히는 모르겠지만 모두 너무 무례하게 들렸어요.

남: 네, 제가 생각하기에 많은 어른들이 젊은 사람들의 은어를 무례하게 생각하지만, 만약에 어른들이 그것을 사용하거나 이해한다면 젊은 사람들과 더 가까워 질 수 있을 거예요.

여: 나는 이해할 수 없어요.

남: 만약에 그들이 당신이 그들의 은어를 가끔 사용하는 것을 들으면 당신을 그들과 잘 어울리는 사람으로 볼 거예요.

여: 아, 네. 이제 알겠어요.

남: 가끔 저는 아이들에게 은어를 저한테 가르쳐 달라고 하거나 제가 TV에서 들은 것을 그들에게 물어봐요.

여: 저는 당신이 젊은 사람들과 가까워지는 것을 그렇게 중요하게 여기는 줄 몰랐어요.

남: 그렇게 하는 것이 그들과의 관계에 도움이 된다고 생각해요.

**어휘**

**slang** *n.* 은어, 속어　**impolite** *a.* 무례한　**fit in with someone** ~와 잘 어울리다　**once in a while** 가끔　**big deal** 대단한 일, 큰일

**정답** ③

문제풀이
남자가 '젊은 사람들이 사용하는 은어를 자신이 가끔 사용하는 것을 그들이 들으면 그들과 잘 어울리는 사람으로 보일 것'이라는 말을 한 것으로 보아, 남자의 의견으로 가장 적절한 것은 ③ '은어 사용을 통해 젊은 사람들과 가까워질 수 있다.'이다.

총 어휘 수 188

## 05  대화자의 관계 파악

소재  부상당한 선수와 의사의 대화

듣기 대본 해석
여: Phillip, 내 말 들려요? 괜찮아요?
남: 그런 것 같은데요. 아, 내 목. 너무 아파요.
여: 그럴 거예요. 움직이지 마세요. 검사를 할 거예요. 그래서 무슨 일이 일어났는지 기억나요?
남: 제가 기억하는 마지막 일은 패스를 하려고 했는데 상대팀의 누군가가 뒤에서 태클을 걸었어요. 어깨로 넘어지면서 땅에 머리를 부딪쳤어요.
여: 그 이후에 어떤 것이라도 기억나는 것이 있나요?
남: 걸으려고 했는데 어지러웠던 게 기억나요. 제 생각에 제가 아마 다시 땅에 쓰러졌을 거예요. 제가 여기 탈의실에서 깨어날 때 까지 그 외에는 아무것도 기억이 나지 않아요.
여: 뇌진탕인 것 같아요, Phillip.
남: 정말이요? 심각한 거예요?
여: 글쎄요, 좋지 않은 건 확실해요. 얼마나 심한지 보려면 검사를 몇 개 해야돼요.
남: 감사합니다. 도와주셔서 정말 감사합니다.
여: 아니에요. 제 직업인 걸요.

어휘
**tackle** *v.* 태클을 걸다   **dizzy** *a.* 어지러운   **concussion** *n.* 뇌진탕
〈문제〉 **pedestrian** *n.* 보행자

정답 ⑤

문제풀이
남자는 아픈 곳을 말하며 패스하다가 태클을 당했다고 다친 상황을 설명하는 것으로 보아 운동선수임을 알 수 있고, 여자는 뇌진탕인 것 같은데 검사를 더 해보자고 했으므로 의사임을 알 수 있다. 따라서 정답은 ⑤ '의사 ― 운동선수'이다.

오답 보기 해석
① 경찰 ― 피해자　　　　　　② 택시 운전사 ― 보행자
③ 기자 ― 축구감독　　　　　　④ 보험 설계사 ― 고객

총 어휘 수 145

## 06  그림의 세부 내용 파악

소재  소풍 상차림

듣기 대본 해석
남: 안녕 Carrie. 소풍 식사 준비 무척 잘했네.
여: 고마워, Bob. 근데 모두가 먹을 수 있을 정도로 음식이 많지 않을까 봐 걱정돼.
남: 충분할 거야. 어쨌든, 식탁 중간에 꽃으로 장식한 것 마음에 든다.
여: 정원에서 따왔어. 또, 채식주의자들을 위해 파스타를 만들었어. 그리고 그걸 식사하는 사람들에 제일 가깝게 놨어.
남: 진짜 맛있어 보인다. 우리처럼 고기 먹는 사람들을 위해 닭 요리도 했네.
여: 맞아. 옥수수가 너무 멀리 놓여 있나?
남: 응, 더 앞쪽에 놓는 게 좋을 것 같아. 근데, 음료들은 어디 있어?
여: 음료를 위한 테이블은 따로 있어.

남: 그렇구나. 음. 손님들을 위해 건강한 후식을 준비했구나.
여: 응. 과일은 여름에 하는 소풍에 좋고 컵케이크나 파이처럼 소화가 잘 안되는 음식이 아니야.
남: 맞아. 그나저나 초대해줘서 고마워.
여: 아냐, Bob. 와줘서 기뻐.

어휘
**decorate** *v.* 장식하다　　**vegetarian** *n.* 채식주의자　　**diner** *n.*
식사하는 사람　　**out of reach** 손이 닿지 않는 곳에

정답 ④

문제풀이
여자가 음료를 위한 테이블은 따로 준비했다고 했는데 그림에서는 꽃병 뒤에 위치해 있으므로 그림과 일치하지 않는다. 따라서 정답은 ④번이다.

총 어휘 수 162

## 07  할 일

소재  보고서를 위한 설문 도와주기

듣기 대본 해석
남: 안녕, Catherine. 나 이번 주 금요일 야구 경기 표가 두 장 있어. 같이 갈래?
여: 정말 그러고 싶지만 못 갈 것 같아. 다음 주 월요일까지 학기말 리포트 두 개를 내야 해.
남: 어떤 것들인데? 내가 그걸 끝내도록 도와주면 같이 갈 수 있어?
여: 당연하지. 하나는 소설에 대한 독서 리포트이고, 다른 하나는 스마트폰이 우리 생활을 어떻게 변화시켰는가에 대한 분석 리포트야.
남: 독서 리포트는 어떻게 되어 가?
여: 그건 내일이면 다 될 것 같아. 문제는 두 번째 리포트야.
남: 스마트폰의 영향에 대한 설문 질문은 만들었어?
여: 응. 그런데 그 짧은 시간에 충분한 사람들에게 설문지를 주긴 어려울 것 같아. 도와줄 수 있어?
남: 물론. 기꺼이 그럴게. 그러면 이번 금요일에 나랑 야구 경기에 가는 거야, 그렇지?
여: 응, 약속할게. 정말 고마워.

어휘
**term paper** 학기말 보고서　　**effect** *n.* 효과　　**be willing to V**
기꺼이 ~하다　　**thanks a million** 대단히 고맙습니다

정답 ⑤

문제풀이
여자는 설문 질문은 만들었지만 짧은 시간에 혼자서 사람들에게 물어보기 어려울 것 같다면서 남자에게 도움을 청하고 있으므로 남자가 여자를 위해 할 일은 ⑤ '사람들에게 물어 설문 완성하기'이다.

오답 보기 해석
① 설문 조사 질문 만들기
② 두 장의 야구 경기 표 예매하기
③ 그녀의 두 개의 학기말 보고서 제출하기
④ 독서 리포트에 대한 조언 해주기

총 어휘 수 155

## 08  이유

소재  회의 일정 잡기

듣기 대본 해석
[전화벨이 울린다.]
남: 여보세요. Dan Brown입니다.
여: 안녕하세요, Brown 씨. Global Media의 Claudia입니다.

남: 안녕하세요, Claudia 씨. 무엇을 도와드릴까요?

여: 지난주 당신이 저희 회사와 일하는 것과 관련하여 이야기를 나눈 것에 대해 사장님께 말씀드렸습니다.

남: 그래서 자연 다큐멘터리를 허가받은 것을 이야기해주려고 전화하신 거군요, 맞죠?

여: 맞습니다. 당신이 아직도 그것을 제작해 주실 용의가 있으신지 궁금합니다.

남: 좋습니다. 그렇게 하겠습니다.

여: 감사합니다. 조만간 당신과 일하게 될 다른 프로듀서 분들과의 회의 일정을 정해야 하는데요. 목요일 저녁 7시 가능하신가요?

남: 그날은 안 되겠는데요. 그날은 제가 막 끝마친 저의 여행 다큐멘터리를 상영해야 하거든요. 금요일 낮 12시는 어떤가요?

여: 죄송하지만 금요일은 프로듀서 중 한 분이 출장을 가시고 14일이 돼서야 돌아오실 것 같아요.

남: 그렇다면 저 없이 회의하는 것이 가능할까요? 나중에 회의 내용을 간단히 알려주셔도 되니까요.

여: 그렇게 하면 될 것 같습니다. 제가 확인해 보겠습니다. 곧 다시 이야기 나누시죠, Brown 씨.

**어휘**

**get the green light** (착수) 허가를 받다    **screen** *v.* 상영하다
**brief** *v.* ~에게 (~에 대해) 알려주다(보고하다)

**정답** ④

**문제풀이**

대화의 중간쯤에서 여자가 목요일 저녁에 회의가 가능한지 물었을 때 남자는 그 날은 여행 다큐멘터리를 상영해야 해서 안 된다고 말했으므로 남자가 회의에 참석할 수 없는 이유는 ④ '다른 다큐멘터리를 상영해야 해서'이다.

**총 어휘 수** 186


# 09 숫자

**소재** 조카들의 생일선물로 테니스 라켓 구입

**듣기 대본 해석**

남: 안녕하세요. 무엇을 도와드릴까요?

여: 안녕하세요. 제 조카들에게 줄 테니스 라켓 한 세트를 찾고 있어요. 아이들이 쌍둥이인데 생일이 곧 다가오거든요.

남: 네. 몇 살이 되는데요?

여: 이제 10살이 돼요. 그렇게 어린 아이들을 위한 것이 있나요?

남: 물론이죠. 이 검은색 라켓을 한번 보세요. 70달러예요.

여: 와! 좀 비싼데요.

남: 이건 티타늄 합금으로 만들어졌고, 내구성이 좋도록 만들어졌어요. 그런데, 예산이 어느 정도 되세요?

여: 한 개에 대략 60달러씩 쓰려고요.

남: 알겠어요. 그보다 더 비싼 게 싫으시면 이 알루미늄 라켓은 어때요? 이 파란색 라켓은 제가 보여드렸던 검은색보다 20달러 더 싸답니다. 빨간 것은 40달러 밖에 안하고요.

여: 둘 다 파란색을 좋아해서요. 그걸로 할게요.

남: 잘 고르셨어요!

여: 신용카드로 계산 되죠?

남: 당연하죠. 계산대로 안내해 드릴게요.

**어휘**

**alloy** *n.* 합금    **budget** *n.* 예산, 비용    **register** *n.* 계산대

**정답** ⑤

**문제풀이**

여자는 남자가 처음에 보여준 70달러짜리 검은색 라켓보다 20달러가 더 싼 파란색 라켓을 2개 샀으므로 총 지불할 금액은 ⑤ '$100'이다.

**총 어휘 수** 151


# 10 언급 유무

**소재** 마음에 드는 정장

**듣기 대본 해석**

남: 엄마, 졸업이 다가 오고 있어서 꽤 흥분돼요.

여: 그래. 아버지께서 오늘 아침에 그것에 관해 말씀하셨어. 아버지께서는 네가 새로운 정장을 찾고 있다고 말씀하시던데.

남: 그래요. 그리고 Bowtie Suits에서 멋진 정장을 찾았어요. 거기가 어디인지 아시죠, 그렇죠?

여: 물론이지. 내가 일하고 있는 Fourth Street 근처잖아. 어떤 종류의 정장을 찾았니?

남: 그 정장은 격식을 갖추었지만 너무 과하게 격식을 갖추지는 않았거든요. 재단도 멋져요. 제 생각에는 그 정장이 저에게 완벽하게 어울려요.

여: 그래. 정장은 검은색이니 짙은 남색이니?

남: 매우 진한 짙은 남색이에요. 거의 검은색처럼 보여요.

여: 가격은 얼마니?

남: 세일해서 300달러예요. 나쁘지 않죠, 그렇죠?

여: 그건 내가 예상한 것보다는 약간 더 비싸네. 오늘 매장에 가보자꾸나. 네가 한번 입어봤으면 좋겠구나.

남: 네. 언제 저를 데려가실 시간이 날까요?

여: 아버지께서 집에 오실 때까지 기다려 보자. 우리 모두가 함께 갈 수 있을 거야.

**어휘**

**suit** *n.* 정장 *v.* 어울리다, 잘 맞다    **formal** *a.* 격식을 차린, 형식을 갖춘

**정답** ③

**문제풀이**

남자가 미리 찍어둔 정장에 대해 엄마와 이야기하는 상황이다. 매장 이름, 매장 위치, 색상, 가격에 대한 언급은 있었지만 사이즈에 대한 언급은 없었으므로 정답은 ③ '사이즈'이다.

**총 어휘 수** 156


# 11 내용 일치 · 불일치

**소재** 대학에서 열리는 겨울 캠프에 관한 안내

**듣기 대본 해석**

남: 여러분 안녕하세요. 올 겨울 Bellington University에서 제공하는 새로운 프로그램에 대해 말씀 드리고자 합니다. Bellington University는 연기와 연출을 중심으로 하는 일주일 간의 캠프를 제공할 것입니다. 그 캠프는 1월 2일부터 1월 8일까지 열릴 것이며 참가를 신청한 학생들은 캠프 기간 동안 캠퍼스 내에 머물게 될 것입니다. 참가비는 무료이나 참가할 수 있는 학생수는 제한되어 있습니다. 제한된 학생 수 때문에, 오직 최소한 평균 B학점을 보유한 고등학교 2학년과 3학년생에게만 참가 자격이 주어집니다. 또한, 관심이 있고 참가 자격이 있는 학생들은 미술이나 정보 통신 교사로부터 추천서를 받아야 합니다. 학교 홈페이지에 있는 신청서를 작성해서 지원하실 수 있습니다.

**어휘**

**acting and directing** 연기와 연출    **sign up for** ~에 지원하다,
~에 참가를 신청하다    **duration** *n.* 기간    **participate** *v.* 참가하다
**be eligible for** ~을 위한 자격이 있다    **letter of recommendation**
추천서    **application** *n.* 지원(서), 신청(서)

**정답** ③

**문제풀이**

최소한 평균 B학점을 보유한 고등학교 2학년과 3학년생에게만 참가 자격이 주어진다고 언급되어 있으므로 내용과 일치하지 않는 것은 ③ '캠프 참가비는 무료이고 고등학생 누구나 참가 가능하다.'이다.

**총 어휘 수** 133

## 12 도표

**소재** 평면 TV 선택

**듣기 대본 해석**

남: 안녕하세요. 무엇을 도와드릴까요?

여: 안녕하세요. 새 텔레비전 사려고요. 지금 것은 굉장히 오래됐어요. 브라운관이에요.

남: 와. 한동안 그 스타일을 보지 못했네요. 음. 저희는 다양한 평면 텔레비전들이 있어요. 예산이 어떻게 되시죠?

여: 600달러 이상 쓰고 싶진 않아요.

남: 특별히 생각하고 계신 브랜드가 있나요?

여: 인터넷에서 후기를 여러 개 읽어봤는데 Solo 제품이 좋은 것 같더라고요.

남: 맞아요. 여기 지점은 Solo 제품을 팔아요. 3D 기능 있는 것, 아니면 없는 것 중 어느 것이 더 좋으세요?

여: 후기에서는 3D 기능이 훌륭하다고 했어요. 그런 걸로 제 가격 범위에 있는 걸로 주세요.

남: 조건에 맞는 게 두 개 있어요. 검은색과 은색으로 나와요.

여: 검은색으로 주세요. 그래야 제 케이블 박스랑 어울리거든요.

남: 알겠습니다. 여기 기다리시면 창고에서 하나 가져 올게요.

여: 알겠습니다. 도와주셔서 감사합니다.

**어휘**

**outdated** *a.* 구식의    **specific** *a.* 구체적인, 분명한    **criterion** *n.* 표준, 기준 (복수형 criteria)    **stockroom** *n.* 창고

**정답** ⑤

**문제풀이**

600달러 이하인 Solo 제품은 ③, ④, ⑤번이고 3D기능이 있는 검정색을 원했으므로 여자가 선택한 것은 ⑤번이다.

**총 어휘 수** 175


## 13 긴 대화의 응답

**소재** 알레르기 증상에 대한 대처

**듣기 대본 해석**

남: 여보, Mike 병원 데려 갔어?

여: 응. 위에 좀 심각한 문제가 있는 것 같아.

남: 그래? 밥 먹은 다음에 계속 배가 아프다고 한 건 알고 있어.

여: 응. 의사가 Mike한테 음식 알레르기가 있을 수 있다고 했어. 이 알레르기가 배탈을 일으킬 수 있대.

남: 아! 어렸을 땐 안 그랬던 것 같은데.

여: 음. 어떤 사람들은 나중에 크고 나서 알레르기가 생길 수 있다고 의사가 그랬어.

남: 그럼 어떻게 해야 돼?

여: 걔가 뭘 먹는 지를 봐야 돼. 당분간은 쌀이나 콩 같은 단순한 음식들만 먹어야 돼.

남: 그럼 평생 동안 그렇게 먹어야 된다는 거야?

여: 아니, 알레르기 검사를 받을 때까지만. 의사가 주사 맞는 것도 추천했어.

남: ③ 그가 그걸 좋아할 것 같지는 않지만, 결국엔 도움이 될 거야.

**어휘**

**serious** *a.* 심각한, 진지한    **upset stomach** 배탈    **bother** *v.* 신경 쓰이게 하다    **stick to** ~을 고수하다, 계속하다

**정답** ③

**문제풀이**

의사가 아들에게 알레르기 주사 맞기를 추천했다고 말하는 것에 대한 응답으로 ③ '그가 그걸 좋아할 것 같지는 않지만, 결국엔 도움이 될 거야.'가 적절하다.

**오답 보기 해석**

① 나는 알레르기 주사 정말 맞고 싶지 않아.

② 응. 그가 좋아질 때까지 학교에 못 갈 거야.

④ 나는 우리가 검진을 위해 그를 의사에게 데려가야 한다고 생각해.

⑤ 나는 네가 퇴원해서 집으로 돌아와서 기뻐.

**총 어휘 수** 142


## 14 긴 대화의 응답

**소재** 작은 물고기는 풀어주기

**듣기 대본 해석**

여: 아빠. 왜 그 물고기들을 풀어주는 거예요?

남: 음, 작은 거는 잡고 싶지 않잖아.

여: 왜요? 그래도 먹을 수는 있잖아요.

남: 작은 물고기들은 아직 더 커야 돼. 우리가 다 잡아가면 이 호수에 물고기가 없을 거야.

여: 도와드릴까요? 저 물고기랑 노는 거 좋아해요.

남: 그래. 물고기를 들고 이 자로 길이를 재봐.

여: 얼마나 길어야 해요?

남: 25센티미터가 안 되면 다시 호수에 던져. 사실 그 길이보다 작은 애들을 잡아 가는 건 이 공원 규칙에도 위반돼.

여: 정말이요? 그럼 작은 물고기들을 잡아 가져 가면 우리가 곤란해질 수 있겠네요.

남: 맞아. 아, 그건 풀어줘야 될 거야. 너무 작아.

여: ① 알았어요. 이 물고기한테 행운의 날인 것 같아요.

**어휘**

**ruler** *n.* 자    **measure** *v.* 재다    **trouble** *n.* 곤란, 문제

**정답** ①

**문제풀이**

남자가 그 물고기는 너무 작으니까 풀어주라고 말했으므로 여자의 적절한 답은 ① '알았어요. 이 물고기한테 행운의 날인 것 같아요.'이다.

**오답 보기 해석**

② 우리 토요일에 같이 낚시하러 가요.

③ 물이 너무 오염되면 물고기가 죽을 거예요.

④ 엄마가 이것을 저녁 만드는 데 사용하시면 좋을 것 같아요.

⑤ 맞아요. 더 큰 물고기는 재기가 훨씬 힘들어요.

**총 어휘 수** 129


## 15 상황에 적절한 말

**소재** 공대 대회에서의 우승

**듣기 대본 해석**

남: Peter는 물리학을 전공하고 있습니다. 그의 대학교는 학생들을 위한 공학 대회를 열었는데 Peter는 대회에 참여하기 위해 롤러코스터 모델을 만들기로 합니다. 몇 주간 전 세계에서 유명한 롤러코스터들을 연구하고 나서야 Peter는 마침내 아이디어를 떠올려 작업을 끝냈습니다. 이제 그 대회에서 그의 롤러코스터 모델은 뛰어난 성능을 보여줬고 관객들을 열광시켰습니다. 그 과의 학과장인 Goldberg 교수님은 특히 깊은 인상을 받고 Peter의 노력에 칭찬을 했습니다. 그는 Peter에게 다른 교수님들도 똑같이 생각했으며 Peter가 공학 대회 우승을 하게 될 것이라고 알려주었습니다. Peter는 Goldberg 교수님의 말을 듣고 기뻤고 자신이 뽑혔다는 사실이 믿어지지가 않습니다. 이러한 상황에서 Peter가 Goldberg 교수님에게 뭐라고 말할까요?

Peter: ③ 전 정말 제가 공학 대회에서 우승할 줄은 몰랐어요.

어휘
**physics** *n.* 물리학    **major** *n.* 전공    **engineering** *n.* 공학, 공학 기술
**dean** *n.* 학장, 주임 사제    **commend** *v.* 칭찬하다    〈문제〉**flaw** *n.*
결점, 결함, 흠

정답 ③

문제풀이
Peter는 공학 대회에서 우승할 거라는 소식을 듣고 기쁘면서도 이 사실이
믿기지 않는다는 것을 표현하는 말을 해야 하므로 적절한 것은 ③ '전 정말
제가 공학 대회에서 우승할 줄은 몰랐어요.'이다.

오답 보기 해석
① 더 큰 롤러코스터는 못 만들 것 같아요.
② 설계상 결함들을 다시 작업해야 할 것 같아요.
④ 이 대학에서 공학 기술을 공부하는 것은 즐거워요.
⑤ 공학 대회에 우승한 것을 축하드립니다.

총 어휘 수  149


# 16 담화 주제 / 17 세부 내용 파악

소재  세계 곳곳에서 사용되는 영어의 차이점

듣기 대본 해석
여: 안녕하세요, 여러분. 오늘 우리는 영어에 대해 말하고자 합니다. 런던에
기반을 둔 높이 평가되는 소식통에 따르면, 영어를 말할 수 있는 사람이
세계에 20억 명이 넘습니다. 사실, 영어를 모국어로 하는 사람보다 영어를
모국어로 하지 않는 영어 사용자들이 4배나 더 많습니다. 모국어로 영어를
말하는 사람들에게도 영어는 다양한 종류가 있습니다. 예를 들어, 미국식
영어, 캐나다식 영어, 영국식 영어 그리고 호주식 영어가 있습니다. 이들
사이에 차이점은 보통 발음, 억양, 그리고 어휘에 있습니다. 종종 종류에
따라 철자의 차이도 있는데, 특히 미국식 영어와 영국식 영어 사이에 차이가
있습니다. Color와 colour, favorite과 favourite 같은 단어가 이 두
영어권 영어 차이의 보편적인 예입니다. 캐나다식 영어는 미국식 영어와
영국식 영어의 조합이지만 확실히 미국 쪽에서 더 많이 빌려왔습니다.
이런 영어를 모국어로 사용하는 나라에서의 차이점에 대한 더 많은 정보를
얻으시려면 제가 준비한 자료를 보십시오. *[잠시 후]* 이제 휴식시간 동안
여러분 각자 서로 같은 언어를 말하는 다른 나라에 대해 생각해보고 그들
사이에 차이점을 리스트로 만들어보세요. 여러분 들어주셔서 감사합니다.
휴식 후에 다시 봅시다.

어휘
**respected** *a.* 훌륭한, 높이 평가되는    **authority** *n.* 권한, 권위, 인가
**billion** *n.* 10억    **variety** *n.* 종류, 다양성    **pronunciation** *n.* 발음
**intonation** *n.* 억양    **combination** *n.* 조합    **handout** *n.* 인쇄물,
유인물

정답  16 ④  17 ③

문제풀이
16  영국식 영어와 미국식 영어의 차이를 예로 들고 캐나다식 영어의 특징을
언급하면서 영어가 모국어인 나라에서 쓰는 영어의 차이점을 말하고 있으므로
정답은 ④ '영어 원어민들이 사용하는 영어의 차이점'이 된다.

17  발음, 억양, 어휘, 철자에서 차이가 있다고는 언급했지만 강세에 대한 언급
은 하지 않았으므로 정답은 ③ '강세'이다.

오답 보기 해석
16
① 국제 영어를 규정하는 특징들
② 역사를 통해 일어난 영어의 변화
③ 어떻게 영어가 국제적인 언어가 되고 있는가
⑤ 미국 영어와 영국 영어에서 발음상의 차이점

총 어휘 수  205


## DICTATION ANSWERS

01  It's freezing out here

02  I'm starving / leftover pizza

03  keeping my blackberries fresh / extend the life / rinse the berries off / The acidity of vinegar

04  it all sounded very impolite / if adults used it or understood it / who fits in with them / getting closer to young people

05  get you checked out / tackled me from behind / felt dizzy

06  we won't have enough food / a little out of reach / There's a separate table / as heavy as cupcakes

07  term papers due next Monday / changed the way we live / made survey questions / I'm more than willing to do that

08  got the green light / schedule a meeting / I'm screening a travel documentary

09  Have a look / it's built to last / cheaper than the black one / to the register to check out

10  It's near where I work / it suits me perfectly / looks black / expensive than I expected / try it on

11  stay on campus for the duration / are eligible for this camp / get a letter of recommendation / filling out the application

12  What's your budget / spend more than six hundred dollars / fit your criteria / like it in black

13  his stomach hurting after meals / cause upset stomachs / stick to simple foods / suggested shots

14  letting those fish go / use this ruler to measure it / against park rules / we can get in trouble

15  build a model roller coaster / is particularly impressed / receive the top prize

16-17  talk about the English language / different varieties of English / spelling differences between the varieties / a combination of

# 08 수능영어듣기 실전모의고사

| | | | | | |
|---|---|---|---|---|---|
| 01 ③ | 02 ③ | 03 ① | 04 ③ | 05 ⑤ | 06 ④ |
| 07 ④ | 08 ⑤ | 09 ③ | 10 ⑤ | 11 ③ | 12 ③ |
| 13 ④ | 14 ① | 15 ② | 16 ① | 17 ④ | |

## 01 짧은 대화의 응답

**소재** 춤 대회

**듣기 대본 해석**

여: Aiden, 나 정말 긴장 돼. 내가 해낼 수 있을지 모르겠어.
남: 물론 너는 할 수 있어. 너는 모든 동작을 알고 있고 정말 열심히 노력해왔잖아.
여: 맞아. 그런데 다른 모든 댄서들은 정말 훌륭하게 춤 동작들을 해냈어.
남: ③ 다른 사람들과 비교해서 너의 능력을 판단하지 마.

**어휘**

**dedicated** *a.* 전념하는, 헌신적인    **awesome** *a.* 훌륭한
〈문제〉 **based on other people** 다른 사람들과 비교해서
**compared to** ~와 비교하여

**정답** ③

**문제풀이**

여자가 다른 댄서들의 훌륭한 모습에 위축되는 모습을 보이자 남자가 여자에게 용기를 불어넣는 응답이 가장 적절하므로 답은 ③ '다른 사람들과 비교해서 너의 능력을 판단하지 마.'이다.

**오답 보기 해석**

① 네가 이미 공연을 했다는 것에 대해 정말 감사해야 해.
② 나의 춤 동작은 다른 사람들의 동작보다 낫다고 생각했어.
④ 내 춤 동작은 너의 것에 비해 정말 좋았어.
⑤ 공연은 1시간 안에 시작할 거야.

**총 어휘 수** 45

## 02 짧은 대화의 응답

**소재** 해변의 조개

**듣기 대본 해석**

남: Lillian! 해변에 있는 조개들 놔둬. 가져가면 안 돼.
여: 하지만 정말 많은데. 왜 제가 몇 개 가져가면 안 돼요?
남: 이 해변에 오는 모든 사람들이 "몇 개씩만" 가져간다고 생각해 봐.
여: ③ 아, 이제 알겠어요. 즉시 도로 갖다 놓을게요.

**어휘**

〈문제〉 **right away** 당장, 즉시

**정답** ③

**문제풀이**

남자가 여자에게 해변의 조개를 단 몇 개라도 가져가서는 안 된다며 이유를 말하였으므로 여자의 응답은 그에 동조하는 ③ '아, 이제 알겠어요. 즉시 도로 갖다 놓을게요.'가 가장 적절하다.

**오답 보기 해석**

① 알았어요. 조개껍데기 조금만 가져갈게요.
② 그 곳을 기억해 내려고 애쓰고 있어요.
④ 멋져요! 저는 집에 더 많이 가져갈 거예요.
⑤ 우리 조만간 여기 다시 왔으면 좋겠어요.

**총 어휘 수** 51

## 03 담화 주제

**소재** 친환경적인 생활 습관의 예

**듣기 대본 해석**

남: 친환경적인 생활 습관을 갖는 것이 굉장히 중요해졌습니다. 에너지 비용의 문제 외에도, 최근 오염으로 인한 환경문제가 전국의 사람들로 하여금 더 새롭고 성실한 생활 방식을 갖게 만들었습니다. 도울 수 있는 방법이 여러 가지 있습니다. 예를 들어 승용차 이용은 꼭 필요할 때만 하는 게 좋습니다. 그렇지 않을 경우에는 자전거, 버스, 기차와 같이 더 친환경적인 교통수단을 이용하세요. 전자기기는 사용하지 않을 때 플러그를 뽑으세요. 켜져 있지 않아도 플러그가 꽂혀 있으면 텔레비전과 컴퓨터는 전기를 소모합니다. 차가운 물을 사용하면 세탁을 할 때 쓰는 에너지를 반으로 줄일 수 있습니다. 마트를 갈 때 매립 쓰레기를 줄이기 위해 가방을 챙겨 가시고 종이 컵과 접시 같은 일회용 쓰레기의 사용을 피하세요. 이렇게 솔선하셔서 친환경을 지지하는 수만 명과 함께 하세요.

**어휘**

**conscientious** *a.* 양심적인, 성실한    **opt for** ~을 선택하다
**halve** *v.* 반으로 줄이다(줄다)    **disposable** *a.* 일회용의
**initiative** *n.* 계획, 주도(권)

**정답** ①

**문제풀이**

남자는 친환경적인 생활 습관으로 대중교통 이용, 안 쓰는 가전제품 코드 뽑기, 일회용품 사용 줄이기 등을 말하고 있으므로 주제로 가장 적절한 것은 ①번이다.

**총 어휘 수** 161

## 04 의견

**소재** 도서관 신축

**듣기 대본 해석**

여: Tom, 오래된 도서관을 허물 것이라는 시의 계획에 대해 들었어요?
남: 네, 들었어요. 하지만 시에서 그 자리에 새로운 도서관을 지을 계획이라고 들었어요.
여: 정말 유감이네요. 현재 건물은 역사적인 건축물이거든요.
남: 그렇긴 하지만 새로운 자료들을 위한 공간이 충분하지 않은 게 사실이긴 해요.
여: 맞아요. 새로운 도서관이 필요하죠. 에진 도서관은 너무 불편하니까요.
남: 확실히 그래요. 거긴 여름엔 너무 덥고 겨울엔 얼 것 같이 추워요.
여: 새 건물이 그런 문제들은 확실히 해결하겠지만 적어도 원래 건물의 전면부는 살려야 해요.
남: 정말 좋은 생각이네요. 건물의 전면부는 너무 아름다워요.
여: 네, 그러면 우리는 외관은 고풍스러운 모습이고 내부는 현대적인 건물을 갖게 될 거예요.
남: 맞아요. 그것이 우리가 미래 세대를 위해 역사를 보존하는 방법이죠.

**어휘**

**tear down** (건물, 담 등을) 허물다, 헐다    **inconvenient** *a.* 불편한
**definitely** *ad.* 분명히, 틀림없이    **antique** *a.* 고풍스러운, (귀중한) 골동품인    **preserve** *v.* 지키다, 보존하다

**정답** ③

**문제풀이**

여자는 새로운 도서관을 짓되 도서관의 전면부는 살려야 한다고 말하고 있다. 따라서 정답은 ③ '현 도서관의 전면부를 살려서 새로 지어야 한다.'이다.

**총 어휘 수** 148

# 05 대화자의 관계 파악

**소재** 새 자동차에 대한 설명

**듣기 대본 해석**

남: 구매해 주셔서 감사합니다. Allen 씨. 열쇠 여기 있습니다.

여: 감사합니다. 잠깐… 이건 그냥 리모컨이잖아요. 진짜 열쇠는 어디 있어요?

남: Mondo의 최신 승용차들은 모두 스마트 열쇠로 나옵니다. 이게 주머니에 있기만 하면 손잡이에 있는 버튼을 눌러서 문을 열 수 있습니다.

여: 한번 해볼게요. *[잠시 후]* 굉장히 좋네요. 그런데 시동은 어떻게 거나요?

남: 스마트 열쇠가 차에 있는 한, 출발 버튼을 누르시기만 하면 됩니다.

여: 우왜! 굉장히 편리하네요. 무척 세련돼 보여요.

남: 맞아요! 또한, 열쇠를 절대 차에 두고 내릴 수가 없어요. 열쇠가 차에 있으면, 문이 잠기지 않거든요.

여: 제가 칠칠맞지 못하고 잘 잊어버리는데 너무 좋네요. 더 알아야 할 게 있나요?

남: 다 됐을 겁니다. 다시 한 번 저희 차를 구매해 주셔서 감사합니다. 문제가 있다면 언제든지 전화해 주세요.

여: 감사합니다.

**어휘**

**as long as** ∼하는 동안은. ∼하는 한은    **give it a try** 시도하다. 한번 해보다    **futuristic** *a.* 초현대적인. 세련된    **clumsy** *a.* 어설픈. 칠칠맞지 못한    **hesitate** *v.* 망설이다. 주저하다

**정답** ⑤

**문제풀이**

남자는 여자에게 새로운 자동차의 스마트 열쇠의 사용법에 대해 설명해주고 있고, 마지막에 구매해 주셔서 감사하다고 인사했으므로 두 사람의 관계는 ⑤ '자동차 판매원 — 자동차 구매자'임을 알 수 있다.

**총 어휘 수** 160


# 06 그림의 세부 내용 파악

**소재** 과일 가게 포스터

**듣기 대본 해석**

남: Beth, 내가 농산물 직매장 과일 가게 포스터를 만들어 봤는데 한번 봐봐.

여: 잘 만들었다. Jerry. "Hungry for apples?"라는 슬로건 맘에 든다.

남: 내가 생각해 낸 거야.

여: 네가 이렇게 창의적일 줄은 몰랐어. 왼쪽에 있는 사과는 그림이야? 진짜 같이 생겼어.

남: 그거 그리는 데 오래 걸렸어. 우리 과일 가게 이름은 어떻게 생각해? 너무 진부하지는 않지?

여: 글쎄. 난 괜찮은 것 같은데.

남: 근데 "Jerry's Fruit Stand"는 너무 평범한 것 같아. 더 창의적인 걸 생각해 내야겠어.

여: 괜찮아. 근데 글씨 크기가 좀 더 크면 좋을 것 같아. 슬로건이 포스터를 너무 많이 차지해.

남: 동감이야. 인쇄하기 전에 글씨 크기를 수정할게. 우리 아들이 사과를 몇 개 들고 있는 것도 그려봤어.

여: 너무 귀엽다. 그리고, 네가 사과로 가득 찬 바구니 들고 있는 그림 역시 잘 나왔네.

남: 정말? 내 머리가 너무 크게 나온 것 같아.

여: 전혀 그렇지 않아. 과일 가게에 딱 일 거야.

**어휘**

**farmers' market** 농산물 직매장    **slogan** *n.* 문구. 구호. 슬로건    **plain** *a.* 평범한. 소박한    **take up** 차지하다    **basket** *n.* 바구니

**정답** ④

---

**문제풀이**

남자가 아들이 사과를 몇 개 들고 있는 것도 그렸다고 했는데 그림에서는 아들이 사과를 한 개 들고 있으므로 그림과 일치하지 않는 것은 ④번이다.

**총 어휘 수** 181


# 07 할 일

**소재** 등산하기 전의 준비

**듣기 대본 해석**

남: Lucy, 나 왔어.

여: 안녕 Bobby. 일찍 와줘서 고마워. 등산하기 좋은 날씨지, 그렇지?

남: 맞아. 등산화 예쁘다.

여: 고마워. 근데 내 것이 아니야. 사촌한테 빌렸어.

남: 좋네. 갈 준비 다 된 거야?

여: 난 준비됐는데 너한테 미리 말해 둘게. 나 등산한지 꽤 됐어.

남: 괜찮아. 천천히 가자. 출발하기 전에 다 챙겼는지 보자.

여: 필요한 건 다 있는 것 같은데. 물을 너무 많이 챙겨 온 것 같아.

남: 괜찮아. 그 정도는 필요할지도 몰라. 등산스틱 가져왔어?

여: 아, 차에 두고 왔나 봐. 금방 갔다 올게.

남: 그래. 여기서 기다릴게.

**어휘**

**hike** *v.* 등산하다    **borrow** *v.* 빌리다    **warn** *v.* 경고하다    **pack** *v.* 챙기다

**정답** ④

**문제풀이**

남자가 등산스틱을 가져왔는지 물었고 여자는 차에 두고 온 것 같다며 갖고 오겠다고 했으므로 정답은 ④ '등산스틱 가져오기'이다.

**총 어휘 수** 121


# 08 이유

**소재** 인터넷 연결을 끊은 이유

**듣기 대본 해석**

남: 너 새로운 Gamebox PC 봤니? 완전 멋져 보여.

여: 왜! 정말 멋진데! 그래픽 좀 봐!

남: 사고는 싶은데. 작년에 새 컴퓨터를 샀어. 아직 비용을 다 갚지 못했어.

여: 그래. 네가 가지고 있는 컴퓨터가 여전히 잘 작동하는데 뭐 하러 새로운 PC를 사려고 해?

남: 네 말이 맞긴 한데. 이 새로운 컴퓨터가 그냥 세련되고 멋지잖아. 이 컴퓨터는 모든 최신 게임을 다 구동시킬 수 있어.

여: 너 아마도 몇몇의 수업에 낙제할 지도 모르겠어. 네가 너무 산만하게 될 거야.

남: 하하. 아마 네 말이 맞을지도. 그게 네가 너의 컴퓨터를 오랫동안 업그레이드 하지 않은 이유니?

여: 실은 난 인터넷 연결을 아예 끊었어. 내 명의를 도용당할까 봐 걱정돼서 말이야.

남: 나는 컴퓨터 사용하는 것이 점점 더 위험해진다는 것을 들었어. 그러나 나는 떨어져 있을 수는(컴퓨터를 안 쓸 수는) 없어. 나는 게임을 좋아하거든.

여: 그래. 그렇지만 나는 나의 사생활 보호가 오락보다 더 소중하다고 생각해.

남: 네가 무슨 말을 하는 건지 이해하겠어.

**어휘**

**sleek** *a.* 세련된. 윤기 있는    **distracted** *a.* 산만해진    **get rid of** ∼을 처리하다. 없애다    **identity** *n.* 신분. 신원

**정답** ⑤

여자는 컴퓨터를 오랫동안 업그레이드 하지 않은 이유가 수업에 낙제할까 봐서 그런 거냐는 남자의 질문에 사실은 명의를 도용당할까 봐 걱정돼서 인터넷을 끊었다고 답했으므로 정답은 ⑤ '명의 도용이 걱정되어서'이다.

**총 어휘 수** 149

## 09 숫자

**소재** 세탁기 구매

**듣기 대본 해석**

여: 안녕하세요. Frank's 가전 제품점입니다. 무엇을 도와드릴까요?
남: 그게, 세탁기가 고장 나서 새 것을 사려고 하고 있어요.
여: 알겠어요. 세탁기 종류가 정말 다양해요. 얼마 정도를 예상하고 계신가요?
남: 400달러 아래로 생각하고 있어요.
여: 그렇군요. 세일 상품에 어떤 것이 있는지 보도록 하지요. 이거 좋아요. 원래 500달러였는데 작은 흠집이 나 있어서 350달러에 판매하고 있어요.
남: 좋네요. 그걸로 살게요.
여: 아! 저희 매장으로부터 광고책자를 받으셨으면, 추가로 20퍼센트 할인받을 수 있는 쿠폰이 있을 거예요.
남: 네, 그거 보고 쿠폰 오려 왔어요. 여기요. 배송해주나요?
여: 그럼요. 배송비는 무료인데 설치 비용은 따로 받습니다. 추가비용은 40달러 입니다.
남: 설치해주시는 게 좋을 것 같아요. 제가 할 수 있을지 모르겠네요.
여: 알겠습니다.

**어휘**

**appliance** *n.* (가정용) 기기    **clearance** *n.* (불필요한 것) 없애기(정리)
**cosmetic** *n.* 화장품 *a.* 겉치레에 불과한    **installation fee** 설치 비용

**정답** ③

**문제풀이**

원래 500달러인 세탁기에 작은 흠집이 있어서 350달러에 파는 중이라고 했고, 쿠폰을 가져오면 20퍼센트를 추가 할인해준다고 했으므로 280달러이다. 배송비는 무료이지만 설치비가 40달러라고 했으므로 280+40=320달러가 되어 정답은 ③ '$320'이다.

**총 어휘 수** 156

## 10 언급 유무

**소재** 신혼부부를 위한 재정적 조언

**듣기 대본 해석**

여: Jiho. 너랑 Kate가 곧 결혼하니까. 너희 둘 모두 재정적인 것에 주의를 기울여야 해.
남: 그래, 나도 알아. 우리는 서로에 대한 책임을 져야 하고 우리의 모든 결정이 우리한테만 영향을 주는 게 아닐 거야.
여: 맞아. 너희는 분명 돈이 필요할 것이기 때문에 둘 다 저축을 더 하고 적게 쓰기 시작해야 해.
남: 좋은 조언이야. 나 당장 저축 계좌를 만들 거야.
여: 좋아. 그리고 그녀도 계좌를 만들어야 해. 일단 네가 결혼을 하면 너의 계좌는 공유될 거야.
남: 그녀는 지금 학생이라 파트타임으로만 일해서 계좌에 넣을 만한 많은 돈은 없을 거야.
여: 그녀는 지불해야 될 대출이 있니? 아니면 집세?
남: 아니, 없어.
여: 그러면 너희 둘이 편안해질 때까지 적어도 잠시 동안은 그녀가 버는 것의 대부분을 저축할 수 있을 거야.
남: 맞아. 그녀한테 말해보고, 이것에 대해 어떻게 생각하는지 봐야겠어.
여: 좋은 생각이야. 그 말을 들으니 기쁘다.



**financially** *ad.* 재정적으로    **impact** *v.* 영향을 주다
**savings account** 저축 예금 (계좌)

**정답** ⑤

**문제풀이**

여자가 이제 막 결혼할 남자에게 해주는 조언으로 더 많이 저축하고, 적게 쓰고, 본인과 배우자의 계좌를 개설하라고 권했지만 보험 가입에 대한 언급은 하지 않았으므로 정답은 ⑤ '보험 가입하기'이다.

**총 어휘 수** 162

## 11 내용 일치 · 불일치

**소재** Fantasy Film Festival

**듣기 대본 해석**

여: 안녕하세요, 여러분. 해마다 열리는 Fantasy Film Festival에 계속 성원해 주셔서 감사합니다. Fantasy Film Festival은 2012년부터 성장해 왔습니다. 지난해 저희는 장소가 크지 않아서 축제로 들어오는 많은 방문자의 출입을 막아야만 했습니다. 운 좋게도, 저희는 좀 더 크지만 지난 수년간 사용했던 위치의 친밀감과 개성은 여전히 가지고 있는 새로운 장소를 찾았습니다. 여러분의 친구와 가족들을 돌려보내지 않을 것이고, 훨씬 더 많은 관객들이 여러분의 영화를 볼 것이라고 장담합니다. 작년보다 더 많은 방문객을 예상하기 때문에 저희는 티켓 판매를 온라인으로 옮겼습니다. 여러분들은 여전히 박스 오피스에서 구매하실 수 있지만 웹사이트 www.fantasyfilms.com에서 구매하시는 것이 더 편리하실 겁니다. 1인 입장 가격은 60달러이고, 10명 이상의 단체는 할인이 있습니다.

**어휘**

**deny** *v.* 받아들이지 않다. 부인하다    **maintain** *v.* 유지하다
**intimacy** *n.* 친밀감    **personality** *n.* 개성. 성격    **assure** *v.* 장담하다. 확언하다    **turn somebody away** ~을 돌려보내다    **audience** *n.* 관람객. 청중

**정답** ③

**문제풀이**

티켓 판매를 온라인으로 옮겼지만 박스 오피스에서도 구매는 가능하다고 했으므로 내용과 일치하지 않는 것은 ③ '입장권은 온라인으로만 구매 가능하다.'이다.

**총 어휘 수** 149

## 12 도표

**소재** 호텔 내의 활동 프로그램

**듣기 대본 해석**

남: 안내 데스크입니다. 무엇을 도와드릴까요?
여: 안녕하세요. 오늘 비가 와서 몹시 실망했어요. 해변가로 놀러 가고 싶었는데 실내에 있을 것 같아요. 이 호텔에 우리를 즐겁게 할 수 있는 활동들이 있다고 들었어요.
남: 그렇습니다. 하루 종일 제공해 드릴 수 있는 게 많아요.
여: 일단 옆방에서 오전 11시에 영화를 볼 거예요. 한 시간 반 정도 하는 것 같아요.
남: 그렇군요. 요리 교실은 어떠세요? 오늘은 크루아상 만드는 법을 배울 거예요.
여: 재미있을 것 같은데 제 딸이 재미있어 할지 모르겠네요. 좀 쉽게 지루해 해요.
남: 그럼 오후에 어린이 그림 프로그램 두 개를 추천해드려요. 따님이 좋아할 것 같아요.
여: 그럴 수 있겠지만 그건 어린이만을 위한 거죠? 온 가족이 즐길 수 있는 걸 찾고 있어요.

남: 알겠습니다. 다른 선택지가 몇 개 더 있네요. 활동 비용은 상관있으세요?
여: 오늘이 휴가 마지막 날이라서 돈이 좀 부족해요. 제 남편, 저, 그리고 제 딸을
합해서 15달러 이상 쓰고 싶진 않아요.
남: 알겠습니다. 가족 분들을 위한 안성맞춤의 활동을 찾았습니다.

### 어휘
**hit the beach** 해변으로 가다    **croissant** *n.* 크루아상    **look for**
~을 찾다    **option** *n.* 선택권

### 정답 ③

### 문제풀이
오전 11시부터는 한 시간 반 동안 영화를 볼 것이라고 했으므로 ④번 요가는
시간이 안 맞아서 제외된다. 요리 프로그램은 아이가 지루해 할 것 같다고 했고,
그림 프로그램은 어린이만을 위한 것이라서 다른 것을 찾고 있으므로 ①번과
⑤번도 제외된다. 비용은 세 명이 15달러를 넘지 않아야 하므로 두 사람이
선택할 프로그램은 ③번이다.

### 총 어휘 수 209


# 13    긴 대화의 응답

### 소재  상대방 골키퍼의 약점

### 듣기 대본 해석
여: 주장, 뭐해?
남: FC Barcelona 비디오 좀 보고 있었어. 토요일에 얘네를 이길 수 있을지
잘 모르겠어.
여: 아! 근데 너희 팀이 제일 잘하는 축구 팀이잖아. 이길 수 있을 거야.
남: 그 쪽 골키퍼가 너무 잘해. 그는 자기한테 날아오는 공은 거의 다 막을 수 있어.
여: 그럴지 몰라도 약점을 찾으면, 너도 골을 넣을 수 있을 거야.
남: 해! 그럼 그의 약점이 뭔데?
여: 자세히 보면 골대 어느 부분을 막는 데 애를 먹는지 알 수 있어.
남: [잠시 후] 음. 그래도 아무것도 안 보이는데.
여: 그가 몸을 어떻게 움직이는지 봐봐. 왼쪽에 체중을 싣고 오른쪽으로 뛰고
있잖아.
남: 그렇네!
여: 그리고 다시 봐봐. 왼발로 밀어내면서 비슷한 행동을 하고 있어. 내가 너라면
왼쪽 코너에 슛을 할 거야.
남: ④ 네가 무슨 말 하는지 알겠어. 내가 그를 상대로 골을 넣을 수 있는 방법을
찾을 수 있을 것 같아.

### 어휘
**goalie** *n.* 골키퍼    **score on** 득점하다    **defend** *v.* 막다. 수비하다
**shift** *v.* 옮기다

### 정답 ④

### 문제풀이
여자가 상대방 골키퍼의 움직임을 보고 어디로 슛을 하면 될지 알려줬으므로
그에 적절한 남자의 응답은 ④ '네가 무슨 말 하는지 알겠어. 내가 그를 상대로
골을 넣을 수 있는 방법을 찾을 수 있을 것 같아.'이다.

### 오답 보기 해석
① 그는 오른발로 높이 점프해야 해.
② 그가 너를 향해 슛하는 거의 모든 방향을 막을 수 있을 거라고 생각해.
③ 걱정 마. 네가 열심히 하면, 그를 상대로 골을 넣을 수 있어.
⑤ 난 네가 토요일 시합에서 이길 수 없을 것 같아서 유감이야.

### 총 어휘 수 164


# 14    긴 대화의 응답

### 소재  손을 잡는 것이 결혼한 부부들에게 주는 효과

### 듣기 대본 해석
여: 여보, 뭘 읽고 있어요?
남: 인간의 신체 접촉에 관한 정말 재미있는 연구요.
여: 최근 것인가요?
남: 그래요.
여: 어떤 종류의 접촉이요?
남: 이를 테면, 손을 잡는 것과 그것이 결혼한 부부 사이에 주는 영향 같은 거죠.
여: 정말 재미있어 보이네요. 더 말해 주세요.
남: 그 연구는 두 집단의 결혼한 부부들을 살펴본 거예요. 한 집단에서, 부부들
은 서로 손을 잡은 채로 산책을 하게 해요.
여: 그럼, 다른 집단은 서로 손을 잡지 않은 채로 산책을 하게 하나요?
남: 맞아요. 산책 후에 부부들은 연구자들과 앉아서 그들이 결혼한 이후 함께
겪었던 스트레스 받은 일을 상의하도록 하죠.
여: 결과가 어땠어요?
남: 부부들이 그들의 스트레스 받은 이야기를 말하는 동안, 손을 잡고 그날
오후를 보낸 부부들은 다른 그룹의 부부들보다 훨씬 더 혈압이 낮음을
보여줬어요.
여: ① 그러니까 손을 잡는 것은 부부간의 스트레스를 낮추게 하는 것 같군요.

### 어휘
**significantly** *ad.* 상당히    **blood pressure** 혈압

### 정답 ①

### 문제풀이
두 집단의 부부들에게 한 집단은 손을 잡고, 다른 집단은 손을 잡지 않고
산책을 하도록 해서 스트레스 받는 일들을 기억나게 했을 때, 손을 잡고 산책한
집단의 혈압이 훨씬 낮았다고 한다. 이러한 연구 결과를 알려준 남자의 말에
대한 가장 적절한 여자의 대답은 ① '그러니까 손을 잡는 것은 부부간의
스트레스를 낮추게 하는 것 같군요.'이다.

### 오답 보기 해석
② 그들이 사람들 있는 곳에서 애정표현을 해서는 안 된다고 생각해요.
③ 우리가 손 잡을 때 내가 스트레스 받는 건 당연하군요.
④ 그들은 좋은 오후를 보낸 것처럼 들리네요.
⑤ 그들은 아주 최근에 결혼했어요.

### 총 어휘 수 133


# 15    상황에 적절한 말

### 소재  룸메이트와 생활 중 생긴 소음 문제

### 듣기 대본 해석
여: 주요 FPS 토너먼트 경기에서 우승한 후로 Jason은 마침내 집을 살 수 있는
돈을 마련했습니다. 그는 2개의 침실이 있는 곳을 찾았고, 친구 Ryan에게
룸메이트가 되어 줄 것을 부탁했습니다. 처음엔 모든 것이 순조로웠습니다.
Jason은 컴퓨터 게임을 같이 할 사람이 있어 즐거웠고, Ryan은 부모님과
떨어져 사는 것에 만족했습니다. 하지만, Jason이 대학에서 공부하기
시작한 후로, 재미있는 생활은 끝이 났습니다. 이제 Ryan은 게임을 하면서
늦게까지 깨어 있고, 종종 평일에 시끄러운 파티도 엽니다. 그건 매일 밤
공부를 해야 하고, 매일 아침 일찍 일어나 수업에 가야 하는 Jason에게
매우 골칫거리입니다. Jason은 이 소음 문제에 대해 Ryan과 이야기를
하고자 합니다. 이 상황에서 Jason이 Ryan에게 할 말로 가장 적절한
것은 무엇일까요?
Jason: Ryan, ② 주중에는 좀 더 조용히 해 줄래?

### 어휘
**nuisance** *n.* 성가신 일. 골칫거리. 소란 행위

### 정답 ②

## 문제풀이

Jason과 Ryan은 함께 사는 생활을 즐기다가 Jason이 학업에 열중하게 되면서 Ryan과 소음 문제로 마찰이 생기게 되었는데 이 때 Jason이 Ryan에게 할 말로 가장 적절한 것은 ② '주중에는 좀 더 조용히 해 줄래?'이다.

## 오답 보기 해석

① 내 룸메이트가 되어 주겠니?
③ 언제 내가 파티에 함께해도 될까?
④ 그 컴퓨터 게임 어떻게 하는지 가르쳐 줄래?
⑤ 컴퓨터 게임 토너먼트 하는 것은 어때?

**총 어휘 수** 132

# 16 담화 주제 / 17 세부 내용 파악

**소재** 코골이를 줄일 수 있는 방법

## 듣기 대본 해석

남: 청취자 여러분, 안녕하세요. 코골이로 인해 여러분이나 여러분의 배우자가 잠을 설친 경험을 하신 적이 있으십니까? 저는 코골이가 잠 설침, 낮 동안의 피곤함, 건강상의 문제, 그리고 배우자와의 문제를 야기할 수 있다는 얘기를 해드리기 위해 이 자리에 왔습니다. 코골이는 제가 삼십 대였을 때 많은 문제를 일으켰죠. 제 아내는 저의 코골이로 인해 잠을 자지 못했다고 불평을 했습니다. 저는 코골이에 대해 찾아보기 시작했고 인터넷에서 제가 멈출 수 있게 도와준 정보들을 찾았습니다. 제가 가장 먼저 따른 조언은 살을 빼는 것이었습니다. 비만은 목구멍 뒤쪽에 지방이 많은 조직을 만들어 코골이를 크고 자주하게 할 수 있습니다. 수면제를 먹는 것도 피해야 합니다. 이는 목에 있는 근육들이 이완되게 만들어서 호흡 곤란을 일으킬 수 있습니다. 카페인, 유제품, 그리고 밤 늦게 식사하는 것은 잠을 자기 전에는 피해야 합니다. 마지막으로 등을 대고 자는 대신 옆으로 누워서 자 보세요. 등을 대고 자면 혀가 떨어져서 기도를 막습니다. 옆으로 누워서 자면 그렇지 않습니다. 이런 모든 조언들을 따르면 당신은 분명 당신의 배우자 그리고 당신 자신을 더 행복하게 만들 수 있습니다.

## 어휘

**snore** *v.* 코를 골다  **quality** *n.* 질  **tissue** *n.* 조직  **supplement** *n.* 보충(물)  **interfere with** ~을 방해하다  **airway** *n.* 기도
〈문제〉 **physiological** *a.* 생리적인  **insomnia** *n.* 불면증

## 정답 16 ① 17 ④

## 문제풀이

16 남자는 코골이가 많은 문제를 일으킨다면서 코골이를 줄일 수 있는 정보를 제공하고 있으므로 정답은 ① '코골이를 줄일 수 있는 방법'이다.

17 코골이를 줄일 수 있는 방법으로 살 빼기, 수면제 안 먹기, 카페인이나 유제품 및 수면 전 식사 피하기를 언급했지만 흡연에 대한 언급은 없으므로 정답은 ④ '흡연'이다.

## 오답 보기 해석

16
② 코골이를 하는 생리적인 원인
③ 불면증을 없애는 자연적인 방법
④ 코골이가 일상생활에 미치는 영향
⑤ 가장 잘 맞는 취침 자세 찾기

**총 어휘 수** 186

## DICTATION ANSWERS

01 you've been really dedicated

02 take them with you

03 adopt a green lifestyle / opt for a more environmentally friendly means / You can halve the amount / Take the initiative

04 historical landmark / there just isn't enough space / preserve history for future generations

05 We appreciate your business / It seems so futuristic / pretty clumsy and forgetful

06 think of something more original / takes up so much space / turned out nice

07 are we good to go / We'll take our time / I might've even packed too much water

08 so sleek and cool / You'll be too distracted / I value my privacy over entertainment / where you're coming from

09 wide variety of washing machines / charge an installation fee

10 saving more and spending less / she's only working part-time / Does she have loans

11 Thank you for your continued support / maintains the intimacy and personality of / there are discounts for groups

12 We're pretty disappointed / wanted to hit the beach / have plenty to offer throughout / She gets bored pretty easily

13 the best soccer team around / get in front of / kicked toward / be able to score on him / pushing off his left foot

14 about human contact / the effect that has on / a stressful event they had been through / showed significantly lower blood pressure

15 had enough money to / fine in the beginning / fun came to an end / a huge nuisance to

16-17 a bad night's sleep / I'm here to tell you that / avoid taking sleeping supplements / your tongue drops and blocks your airways

| | | | | | |
|---|---|---|---|---|---|
| 01 ② | 02 ⑤ | 03 ⑤ | 04 ⑤ | 05 ④ | 06 ⑤ |
| 07 ② | 08 ① | 09 ③ | 10 ③ | 11 ④ | 12 ② |
| 13 ④ | 14 ① | 15 ⑤ | 16 ④ | 17 ④ | |

## 01 짧은 대화의 응답

**소재** 보고서 작성

**듣기 대본 해석**
남: Stacy, 시간이 늦었어. 가볍게 뭐라도 먹고 집에 가자.
여: 오늘 밤은 안 돼, Tyler. 내일 아침 전까지 이 보고서를 꼭 끝내야 하거든.
남: 거의 다 끝났으면 기다릴게.
여: ② 끝내려면 시간이 좀 걸릴 거야.

**어휘**
**grab a bite** 가볍게 먹다 〈문제〉 **a while** 잠시, 잠깐

**정답** ②

**문제풀이**
보고서 작성이 거의 끝났으면 기다리겠다는 남자의 말에 적절한 응답은 ② '끝내려면 시간이 좀 걸릴 거야.'이다.

**오답 보기 해석**
① 난 집에서 먹는 걸 좋아하지 않아.
③ 물론. 내가 보고서 끝내는 거 도와줄게.
④ 괜찮아. 네가 끝낼 때까지 기다릴게.
⑤ 배달원이 음식을 빨리 가져다 줬어.

**총 어휘 수** 44

## 02 짧은 대화의 응답

**소재** 농구 경기 티켓

**듣기 대본 해석**
여: 안녕, George. 나의 상사가 나에게 오늘 밤 농구 경기 티켓을 두 장 주었어. 너도 같이 가자.
남: 물론이지. 재미있겠는데. 자리는 좋니?
여: 팬 구역이라서 어디든지 앉을 수 있어.
남: ⑤ 앞쪽 근처에 앉을 수 있게 일찍 가자.

**어휘**
〈문제〉 **assigned a.** 할당된, 배정된

**정답** ⑤

**문제풀이**
농구 경기 티켓이 어느 자리든 앉을 수 있는 것이라고 이야기했을 때 이어지는 적절한 응답은 ⑤ '앞쪽 근처에 앉을 수 있게 일찍 가자.'이다.

**오답 보기 해석**
① 우리는 배정된 좌석에 앉아야 해.
② 미안하지만, 나는 오늘 밤에 다른 계획이 있어.
③ 매진되어서 남은 티켓이 없어.
④ 문제 없어. 너는 이 두 장의 티켓을 가져도 돼.

**총 어휘 수** 47

## 03 요지

**소재** 재택근무 제도 개발

**듣기 대본 해석**
남: 여러분, 안녕하십니까. 오늘 저는 여러분의 사업체 생산성을 증가시키는 것에 대해 얘기하고 싶습니다. 과거에는 보통의 일상이란 직원들이 아침에 와서 관리자의 감독 하에 하루 종일 일하는 것으로 이루어져 있었습니다. 그러나 매일 아침 통근에 낭비되는 시간을 생각해 보셨습니까? 아니면 직원들이 일하러 도착하기도 전에 통근 스트레스가 그들의 에너지를 얼마나 감소시킬지 생각해 보셨나요? 저는 고용주인 여러분이 직원들의 전부 혹은 일부가 집에서 일할 수 있는 시스템을 개발했으면 합니다. 매일 통근이 주는 스트레스를 줄임으로써 여러분은 직원들이 그들의 일에 더 많은 에너지를 쏟게 할 수 있습니다. 직원들이 집에서 일하도록 허락하는 것은 결국에는 여러분에게 이익이 될 것입니다.

**어휘**
**productivity n.** 생산성 **consist of** ~로 구성되다 **supervisor n.** 감독관, 관리자 **commute v.** 통근하다 **diminish v.** 줄이다 **eliminate v.** 없애다, 제거하다 **end up** 결국 (어떤 처지에) 처하게 되다

**정답** ⑤

**문제풀이**
남자는 직원들이 통근에서 오는 스트레스를 줄여서 일에 더 에너지를 쏟을 수 있도록 재택근무 제도를 개발하도록 권유하고 있으므로 정답은 ⑤ '생산성을 증가시키는 재택근무 제도를 개발해야 한다.'이다.

**총 어휘 수** 142

## 04 대화 주제

**소재** 소셜 네트워킹 사이트의 사생활 침해

**듣기 대본 해석**
남: 어제 Scott이 LookBook에 올린 Daryl 사진 봤어?
여: 그래. 봤어.
남: 그 사진 웃기다 생각했지?
여: 맞아. 꽤 웃겨. 근데 내가 생각하기에 Scott이 그 사진 올려서 Daryl이 화가 났을 것 같아.
남: 무슨 말이야?
여: 그 사진에서 Daryl이 너무 멍청해 보여.
남: 무슨 말인지 알겠어. 너는 Daryl이 그 사진을 보고, 다른 사람들이 그걸 봤다는 걸 알면 화가 날 수도 있다고 생각하는구나. 나도 그럴 경우 화날 것 같아.
여: 정말 그래. Scott이 Daryl에게 사진을 올려도 되는지 물어봤어야 했다고 생각해.
남: 나도 그렇게 생각해. LookBook 같은 소셜 네트워킹 사이트들은 네트워킹과 친구들과 지속적인 연락에는 유용하긴 한데, 사람들의 사생활이 침해되기도 해.
여: 맞아. 나는 처음에 그런 사이트들을 즐겨 이용했는데 곧 내 사생활이 얼마나 쉽게 사라질 수 있는지 깨달았어.
남: 맞아. 소셜 네트워킹 사이트에 무언가를 올릴 때는 더 주의를 기울여야 해.

**어휘**
**post v.** (글, 사진 따위를 어느 곳에) 게시하다 **social networking** 인맥 관리하기 **keep in touch with** ~과 접촉을 가지다, 연락을 취하다 **compromise v.** ~을 위태롭게 만들다 **privacy n.** 사생활 **cautious a.** 조심스러운, 신중한

**정답** ⑤

소셜 네트워킹 사이트에 동의 없이 올린 사진이 사생활 침해가 될 수 있기 때문에 주의를 기울여야 한다는 내용이므로 답은 ⑤ '소셜 네트워킹 사이트 이용 시 서로의 사생활 보호에 주의해야 한다.'이다.

**총 어휘 수** 158

## 05  대화자의 관계 파악

**소재**  Alaska에 온 관광객

**듣기 대본 해석**
여: 안녕하세요. 저는 Lilly Jones에요. 늦어서 미안해요. 비행기가 몇 시간 늦어졌어요.
남: 괜찮아요, Jones 부인. Alaska에 오신 것을 환영해요. 저는 Joseph이에요. 하지만 내 친구들은 나를 Joey라고 불러요. 제가 당신의 가이드입니다.
여: 만나서 반가워요, Joey. 다른 사람들은 모두 이미 도착했나요?
남: 네. 그룹의 나머지 사람들은 이미 도착했어요. 그들은 라운지에서 기다리고 있어요. 당신은 아마도 화장실에서 더 따뜻한 옷으로 갈아입어야 할거예요. Alaska는 Florida만큼 따뜻하지 않아요.
여: 호텔에 도착하고 나서 옷을 갈아입으면 안 되나요?
남: 저는 지금 그것을 하는 것을 정말 추천해요. 우리가 호텔에 가기 전에 전통적인 Inuit 어시장에 들를 예정이니까요. 거기는 꽤 춥거든요.
여: 알았어요. 그러면 옷을 갈아 입어야겠네요.
남: 그리고 계획에 변경이 있어요. 일기예보에서 스키 리조트에 많은 눈이 온다고 하니, 우리는 대신 Denali 국립 공원에 갈 거예요.
여: 안됐지만, 괜찮아요. 그 공원은 아름답다고 들었어요.
남: 그렇더라도 제가 사과드립니다. 이해해주셔서 감사합니다.

**어휘**
**weather forecast** 일기예보    **that's a shame** 안됐군요, 유감이에요

**정답**  ④

**문제풀이**
남자는 여자에게 자신을 가이드라고 소개하고 Alaska에 온 것을 환영한다고 말하면서, 날씨가 추우니 옷을 갈아입을 것을 권했고 일정에 대해 말해주고 있으므로 두 사람의 관계는 ④ '여행 가이드 — 관광객'임을 알 수 있다.

**총 어휘 수** 176

## 06  그림의 세부 내용 파악

**소재**  생일 파티 사진

**듣기 대본 해석**
남: 아, 이거 네 생일 파티 사진 아니니?
여: 그래, 이건 나의 일곱 번째 생일 파티였어. 내가 케이크 위에 일곱 개의 양초를 전부 불어서 끄려고 했기 때문에 기억이 나.
남: 사진에 네 옆에 있는 얘네들은 네 친구들이니?
여: 응, Jessica와 Tim이야. 그들은 당시에 나의 가장 친한 친구들이었어. 지금 그들이 무엇을 하고 있는지 궁금해.
남: 생일 모자가 마음에 드네. 너희 모두 사랑스럽구나.
여: 그건 너무 귀여운 사진이지. 모자가 모두 조금씩 다른 것을 볼 수 있어. 내 친구들은 줄무늬 모자를 썼고 나는 물방울무늬 모자를 썼어.
남: 맞아. 너는 뒤에 풍선도 3개 가지고 있어.
여: 응, 우리 부모님이 방을 꾸미기 위해 풍선을 사용하셨어.
남: 멋지다. Tim 앞에 있는 네 개의 머핀들도 맛있어 보여.
여: 사실은, Tim이 우리가 사진을 찍기 전에 머핀 하나를 먹어 버렸어. 내가 무척 화났던 게 기억나네.
남: 정말? 사진에서는 너희 모두 무척 행복해 보여.

**어휘**
**adorable** *a.* 사랑스러운    **stripe** *n.* 줄무늬    **polka dot** 물방울무늬
**decorate** *v.* 장식하다, 꾸미다    **muffin** *n.* 머핀(컵 모양의 빵)

**정답**  ⑤

**문제풀이**
대화에서는 머핀이 4개라고 하였는데 그림에서는 5개이므로 대화의 내용과 일치하지 않는 것은 ⑤번이다.

**총 어휘 수** 158

## 07  할 일

**소재**  비타민제와 영양제 주고 영화 보러 가기

**듣기 대본 해석**
여: Larry, 잠시 시간 있어?
남: 사실 지금 헬스클럽에 가고 있었어. 정오에 PT 약속이 있어.
여: 오, 맞다. 잊어버렸네. 너 매주 월요일과 수요일에 개인 훈련이 있잖아. 맞지? 맘에 들어?
남: 정말 좋아. 내 트레이너가 아는 게 정말 많고 내가 열심히 하도록 동기 부여를 해주지.
여: 굉장한데. 오늘 운동 끝나고 바빠? 시간 있으면 우리 새로 나온 Iron Man 영화 보러 가자.
남: 글쎄. 건강식품점에 가서 비타민과 영양보충제를 좀 사려 했는데.
여: 오, 집에 많아. 사실, 어떤 종류가 필요한지에 달렸지만 나한테 여분이 있어. 우리 집에 와서 살펴 봐. 그리고 네가 필요한 걸 줄게.
남: 정말? 와, 굉장한데. 그럼 그래. 영화 보러 가자.
여: 좋아. 사실 나 어제 사무실에서 공짜 티켓 두 장 얻었거든.
남: 딱 이네. 우리 영화 보고 나서 영양보충제를 확인하러 가면 되겠다. 그러고 나서 내가 커피 살게.

**어휘**
**knowledgeable** *a.* 아는 것이 많은    **motivate** *v.* 동기를 부여하다
**workout** *n.* 운동    **supplement** *n.* (영양)보충제

**정답**  ②

**문제풀이**
운동을 마친 후 건강식품점에 비타민과 영양보충제를 사러 간다는 남자의 말을 들은 여자가 집에 비타민제과 영양보충제가 많다며 남자에게 조금 주겠다고 제안 했다. 그러므로 답은 ② '비타민과 영양보충제 주기'이다.

**총 어휘 수** 173

## 08  이유

**소재**  고등학교 동창끼리의 근황

**듣기 대본 해석**
여: Paul, 나야. Lori Townsend. 우리 Markwell 고등학교 같이 다녔었잖아. 나 기억하니?
남: 맞아. 그렇구나. 어떻게 지냈어?
여: 나는 잘 지내. 나는 Green Tree financial에서 회계사 일을 시작했어. 넌 어때?
남: 난 아직 학교에 있어. Transylvania 대학에서 석사과정 중이야.
여: 그래? 무슨 공부를 하니? 고등학교에서 모두가 네가 대단한 가수가 될 거라고 생각했어.
남: 그 이후로 내 흥미가 좀 바뀌었어. 지금은 정치학을 공부하고 있어.
여: 멋지다. 왜 정치학을 선택했니?
남: 지난 선거 이후로 정치에 사로잡혔어. 넌 어때? 왜 회계사가 되었어?
여: 너 고등학교 경제학 선생님이었던 Lee 선생님 기억나지?

남: 응. 그녀는 정말 멋졌지. 카리스마도 있고 재미도 있으셨지.

여: 난 언제나 그녀를 동경했어. 고등학교 졸업 후 선생님과 나는 좋은 친구가 되었고 그녀가 내가 회계학을 공부하도록 독려하셨지.

남: 정말? 멋지다.

**어휘**

accountant *n.* 회계사　master's *n.* 석사 학위　charismatic *a.* 카리스마가 있는　adore *v.* 존경하다, 사모하다　accounting *n.* 회계

**정답** ①

**문제풀이**

대화의 마지막 부분에서 여자는 고등학교 때 경제학 선생님을 동경했고, 졸업 후 선생님과 좋은 친구가 되어 자신이 회계학을 공부하도록 독려해 주셨다고 했으므로 정답은 ① '학창 시절 매우 좋아했던 경제 선생님 때문에'이다.

**총 어휘 수** 162


# 09 숫자

**소재** 엄마 선물로 목걸이 사기

**듣기 대본 해석**

여: 야. 나 엄마 생일이 이번 주말인 거 방금 알았어.

남: 난 완전히 까먹고 있었어! 엄마한테 뭘 사다 드려야 되지?

여: 글쎄, 아까 백화점에 있었는데 엄마가 분명히 좋아하실 만한 목걸이를 봤어.

남: 정말? 비싸?

여: 그렇게 비싸지는 않아. 60달러 밖에 안하고 20퍼센트 할인을 해주고 있어.

남: 나한테는 너무 비싸. 나 22달러 밖에 없거든. 그 목걸이보다 더 싼 것은 없을까?

여: 글쎄, 귀걸이도 봤는데 내 생각엔 목걸이를 좋아하실 것 같아.

남: 근데 48달러잖아, 맞지? 반씩 낸다 해도 돈이 모자라.

여: 그럼 네가 나한테 22달러 주고 내가 나머지 낼게.

남: 좋네. 고마워.

**어휘**

mall *n.* 백화점　discount *v.* 할인하다 *n.* 할인　split *v.* 분담하다

**정답** ③

**문제풀이**

목걸이가 60달러에 20퍼센트 할인을 해서 48달러인데 남자가 22달러 밖에 없다고 하자 여자는 나머지는 자기가 내겠다고 했으므로 여자가 부담할 금액은 ③ '$26'이다.

**총 어휘 수** 117


# 10 언급 유무

**소재** 코끼리 입양과 후원

**듣기 대본 해석**

여: 안녕 Max. 뭐해?

남: 내가 입양한 아프리카에 있는 코끼리에 대해서 읽고 있었어. 이 사진 좀 봐.

여: 코끼리라고? 정말 멋지다. 이름이 뭐야?

남: Chang이야.

여: 그럼, 자선 프로그램 같은 걸 통해서 입양한 거야?

남: 맞아. 내가 최근에 아프리카에서의 밀렵과 코끼리 학대에 관한 다큐멘터리를 봤거든. 너무 인상 깊어서 내가 도움이 될 수 있는 걸 하기로 결정했어.

여: 정말 잘했구나. Chang을 돕기 위해서 뭘 하고 있는 거야?

남: 음. 난 이러한 동물들을 돌보는 야생동물 보호구역을 찾았어. 그리고 그곳이 그가 사는 곳이야. 그 사람들에게 매달 돈을 보내고 있어.

여: 얼마나 많이 보내는데?

남: 음. 내가 원하는 만큼 보낼 수 있는데. 보통 한 달에 30달러를 넘지는 않아. 너도 그 프로그램에 참가하고 싶어?

여: 그거 멋지겠는데. 지금 당장은 그럴만한 형편이 안돼.

남: 괜찮아. 나중에 돈이 생기면 도와줄 수 있을 거야.

**어휘**

adopt *v.* 입양하다　charity *n.* 자선, 자선단체　poach *v.* 밀렵하다　abuse *n.* 학대　sanctuary *n.* 보호구역　take part in ~에 참여하다　afford *v.* 여유가 되다　spare *v.* 할애하다

**정답** ③

**문제풀이**

동물을 입양한 지역, 입양한 동물의 이름, 입양하게 된 계기, 후원하는 방법에 대한 언급은 있지만, 동물을 후원해온 기간에 대해서는 언급하지 않았으므로 정답은 ③ '후원해 온 기간'이다.

**총 어휘 수** 166


# 11 내용 일치·불일치

**소재** 토네이도 대처법

**듣기 대본 해석**

남: 여러분 안녕하세요. 시청 회의에 참석해주셔서 감사합니다. 제 이름은 Jerry Mills로 Milford 소방서장입니다. 아시다시피 곧 토네이도가 닥쳐올 시기입니다. 토네이도가 올 때 여러분을 안전하게 해 줄 수 있는 조언을 몇 가지 하려고 합니다. 먼저 토네이도 경보가 울리면 바로 지하실로 대피하세요. 지하실이 없으면 화장실에 들어가 수건, 이불, 아니면 매트리스로 자신을 덮으세요. 창문과 날카로운 물건 주변은 피하세요. 날씨가 심하게 안 좋으면 밖에 나가지 마세요. 정전에 대비해서 배터리를 사용하는 라디오를 챙기는 것도 현명한 생각입니다. 그러면 날씨 상황에 대한 정보를 바로 받을 수 있습니다. 토네이도 중에 이러한 조언들을 들으면 안전할 수 있습니다. 감사합니다.

**어휘**

approach *v.* 다가오다　siren *n.* 사이렌, 경보　severe *a.* 극심한　handy *a.* 유용한, 가까운 곳에 있는　in case of ~이 발생할 시에는　power outage 정전

**정답** ④

**문제풀이**

정전을 대비해서 건전지로 작동하는 라디오를 챙기라고 했으므로 내용과 일치하지 않는 것은 ④ '정전을 대비해서 휴대폰을 챙긴다.'이다.

**총 어휘 수** 142


# 12 도표

**소재** 버스 관광 코스

**듣기 대본 해석**

남: 오, 이런. 우리 9시 정원 관광 버스를 놓쳤어!

여: 너무 아쉽다. 다음 것은 몇 시야?

남: 버스 관광 스케줄에 따르면, 그건 4시간 간격으로 운행해. 그렇게 오래 기다릴 수 없어.

여: 여기 매 시간마다 운행하는 투어가 있네. 이 투어는 어때?

남: Christine, 우리 그 투어 다녀온 거 벌써 잊었어?

여: 아, 그렇지. 그러면 10시에 출발하는 이 투어는 어때? 지금이 9시 10분이니까 그 버스 타기에 충분한 시간이 있어.

남: 비용이 너무 비싸. 한 사람에 50 달러가 넘는 돈은 쓸 수가 없어.

여: 좋아. 여기 20분 뒤에 출발하는 투어가 있네. 그걸로 하자.

남: 그건 West Terminal에서 출발해. 여기에서 West Terminal까지 가는
데 적어도 30분이 걸려.
여: 그러면 우리는 한 가지 선택밖에 없어 보이네. 다음 버스까지 얼마 동안은
기다려야겠어.
남: Central Station을 돌아다니면서 시간을 좀 때울 수 있지.
여: 괜찮은 계획 같아.

### 어휘
**run every hour** 매 시간 운행하다　**plenty of** 많은　**afford to V**
~할 여유가 있다　**depart** *v.* 떠나다. 출발하다　**kill time** 시간을 때우다

### 정답 ②

### 문제풀이
처음에 Garden Tour를 놓쳤고 다음 출발 시간은 1시라서 그때까지 오랫
동안 기다릴 수 없다고 하였다. 매 시간 출발하는 투어(City Tour)는 이미
다녀왔다고 했고, 10시에 출발하는 Castle Tour는 50달러가 넘어서 비싸다고
하였다. 다음으로 20분 안에 출발하는 투어(Shopping Tour)는 현재 위치에서
West 터미널까지 가는 시간 때문에 선택할 수 없으므로 마지막으로 조건에
맞는 투어는 ② 'Museum Tour'이다.

**총 어휘 수** 164


## 13　긴 대화의 응답

**소재** 학교 과학 축제 행사

### 듣기 대본 해석
여: 이봐 Luke, 너 Space Shooters 대회에 대해 들었어?
남: 못 들었어. 그게 뭔데?
여: 그건 해마다 하는 학교 과학 축제를 위한 행사야.
남: 그래서 네가 나한테 그것에 대해 말해줄 수 있는 게 어떤 거야?
여: 학생들은 하늘로 날려보낼 작동하는 미니어처 로켓을 만들기 위해 같이
작업해야 해. 네가 관심 있을 것 같아서.
남: 네 말이 맞아! 나 모형 로켓 만드는 거 좋아해. 내가 어렸을 때 아빠랑 나랑
항상 모형 로켓을 만들었었어.
여: 그러면 너 그것을 잘하겠구나! 너 내 파트너 할래?
남: 좋을 것 같지만 내가 참가하고 싶은지 아닌지 잘 모르겠어. 내가 다른 학생들과
경쟁하고 싶은지 아닌지 잘 모르겠거든.
여: 넌 잘할 거야! 같이 하자.
남: 음... 좋아. 우리는 팀이야. 우리가 뭐부터 시작해야 한다고 생각해?
여: 로켓 디자인들을 찾아보는 게 어떨까?
남: ④ 아이디어를 좀 얻기 위해서 인터넷을 이용하자.

### 어휘
**annual** *a.* 매년의, 연례의　**miniature** *a.* 아주 작은, 축소된
**compete** *v.* 경쟁하다　**research** *v.* 조사하다　〈문제〉**supply** *n.*
공급, 보급품

### 정답 ④

### 문제풀이
두 사람은 같이 학교 과학 축제에 나가기로 했고 먼저 로켓 디자인들을 찾아
보자고 했으므로 남자의 적절한 응답은 ④ '아이디어를 좀 얻기 위해서 인터넷을
이용하자.'이다.

### 오답 보기 해석
① 지금 바로 우리 로켓을 시험해 보자!
② 미안해. 너는 새로운 파트너를 찾아야 해.
③ 우리 충분한 물품을 가지고 있지 않아.
⑤ 로켓을 가지고 노는 것은 위험한 것 같아.

**총 어휘 수** 148


## 14　긴 대화의 응답

**소재** 병문안

### 듣기 대본 해석
여: Owen, 당신이 병원에 있다고 들어서 놀랐어요. 괜찮아요?
남: 괜찮아요. 테니스 치다가 무릎을 다쳤을 뿐이에요. 보러 와줘서 고마워요,
Nora.
여: 내가 당신이 여기 있다는 걸 들었을 때, 당신이 좋아할 만한 노래들을 다운받아
왔어요. 당신 휴대폰에 전송해 줄게요. 당신을 지루하지 않게 해 줄 거예요.
남: 당신은 정말 배려심이 있네요.
여: 그런데 어쩌다 무릎을 다쳤어요?
남: 오늘 아침에 연습하다가요. 공을 보고 뛰어올랐는데 내려올 때 무릎이
꺾였어요.
여: 오! 심각한가요?
남: 아뇨. 의사 선생님이 살짝 삔 거라고 했지만 이삼 일 정도는 쓰면 안 된대요.
여: 그러면 의사 선생님 말을 듣고 얼마 동안 쉬어요.
남: 그렇지만 저는 오는 가을에 토너먼트에 참가하려면 훈련을 계속해야 해요.
여: 그건 좋은 생각이 아닌 것 같아요. 만약 당신이 더 다치면 당신은 다시는 테
니스를 칠 수 없을지도 몰라요.
남: 의사도 같은 말을 했어요. 그렇지만 저는 토너먼트에서 정말 이기고 싶어요.
여: ① 아마 당신은 우승할 수 있겠지만 지금은 쉬어야 해요.

### 어휘
**thoughtful** *a.* 배려심 있는, 친절한　**sprain** *n.* 염좌　*v.* (손목. 발목 등을)
삐다　**stay off** 삼가다. 멀리하다　**compete** *v.* (시합 등에) 참가하다.
경쟁하다　〈문제〉**consult** *v.* 상담하다

### 정답 ①

### 문제풀이
부상을 당해 입원해 있으면서도 테니스 대회 우승을 위해 연습을 하고 싶다는
남자에게 지금은 쉬어야 한다고 충고하는 것이 적절하므로 답은 ① '아마 당신은
우승할 수 있겠지만 지금은 쉬어야 해요.'이다.

### 오답 보기 해석
② 나도 동의해요. 당신이 당신의 몸을 다른 누구보다 더 잘 알겠죠.
③ 네. 나는 당신이 다른 의사와 상담해야 한다고 생각해요.
④ 와! 나는 당신이 그렇게 테니스를 잘 치는지 몰랐어요.
⑤ 서둘러요. 그렇지 않으면 당신은 놓칠 거예요.

**총 어휘 수** 193


## 15　상황에 적절한 말

**소재** 분실한 DVD 대체

### 듣기 대본 해석
여: Andrew는 Hudson 공공 도서관에서 DVD를 빌렸습니다. 그러나, 그가
일주일 후에 그것을 반납할 준비가 되었을 때 그는 DVD가 없어진 것을
알았습니다. 그는 누군가가 DVD를 훔쳐간 것이 틀림없다고 믿습니다.
하지만 도서관 규정에는 그가 잃어버린 것을 대체하기 위해서 새로운 것을
사야 한다고 명시되어 있습니다. Andrew는 새로운 DVD를 백화점에서
사서 그것을 도서관으로 가지고 갔습니다. 사서는 그 DVD에 도서관
스티커가 없다는 것을 알아차립니다. 그녀는 그 DVD를 반납 처리할 수
없고 Andrew가 실수를 했음이 틀림없다고 말합니다. Andrew는 자신의
입장을 해명하기를 원합니다. 이러한 상황에서, Andrew가 사서에게 무슨
말을 할까요?
Andrew: ⑤ 누군가가 제 원래 DVD를 훔쳐가서 제가 대체물을 샀어요.

### 어휘
**must have p.p.** ~임이 틀림없다　**policy** *n.* 정책. 방침　**state** *v.*
말하다. 진술하다　**replace** *v.* 교체하다. 대신하다　**librarian** *n.* 사서
〈문제〉**check something out** 대출하다　**replacement** *n.* 교체.
대신할 사람

정답 ⑤

**문제풀이**

Andrew는 일주일 전 DVD를 빌렸고, 그것이 없어져서 규정대로 새것으로 샀으나, 사서는 도서관 스티커가 없다며 실수했다고 말하는 상황이므로 Andrew가 자신의 상황을 설명한 가장 적절한 응답은 ⑤ '누군가가 제 원래 DVD를 훔쳐가서 제가 대체물을 샀어요.'이다.

**오답 보기 해석**

① 제가 DVD를 제때 돌려줄 것을 약속할게요.
② 제가 DVD를 못 찾아서 늦었어요.
③ 제가 이 DVD를 좀 더 오래 대출하고 싶어요.
④ 저는 미래에 사서가 되고 싶어요. 저를 도와주시겠어요?

**총 어휘 수** 127

# 16 담화 목적 / 17 세부 내용 파악

**소재** 해외 근무의 이점

**듣기 대본 해석**

남: 안녕하세요, 신사 숙녀 여러분. 제 이름은 George Wondell이고 오늘 여기 San Jose State 취업박람회에서의 제 세미나에 여러분이 참가하게 되어 기쁩니다. 저는 해외 근무에 대해 얘기하고 싶습니다. 여러분은 다른 나라에서 일하는 기회에 대해 생각해 본 적이 있습니까? 제 이야기를 해보겠습니다. 저는 고등학교를 졸업한 후에 이 박람회와 매우 유사한 취업 박람회에 갔습니다. 한 국제 선적회사가 저를 갑판원으로 고용했습니다. 이것이 제가 세계를 보고 제 관점을 넓히는 기회가 되었습니다. 저는 많은 아름답고 흥미로운 장소들을 여행했습니다. 저는 에펠탑, 피사의 사탑, 그리고 많은 다른 유명한 랜드마크들을 보았습니다. 저는 또한 여정 중에 많은 흥미로운 사람들을 만났고 어디를 가든 친구들을 만들었습니다. 어느 날, 저는 다양한 분야에서 일할 전 세계 사람들을 고용하는 회사를 소유한 한 남자를 만났습니다. 우리는 점심을 먹었고 저는 그에게 제 여행에 대해 들려주었습니다. 그는 제 이야기에 흥미로워하며 이와 같은 세미나와 취업 박람회에서 그의 회사를 대신하여 말할 수 있는 일자리를 저에게 제공했습니다. 해외 근무는 인생의 경험이었습니다. 그것은 문을 열어주고 당신이 다른 어느 곳에서도 찾을 수 없는 기회를 제공해 주었습니다. 만약 당신이 더 많은 정보를 원한다면 우리 부스를 방문해 주세요. 들어주셔서 감사합니다.

**어휘**

**deckhand** *n.* 갑판원  **perspective** *n.* 관점  **recruit** *v.* 모집하다, 뽑다  **in a variety of** 여러 가지의 ~으로  **on behalf of** ~을 대신하여

**정답** 16 ④  17 ④

**문제풀이**

16 자신의 경험을 예로 들면서 해외 근무의 장점을 알리고 권유하는 내용이므로 남자 말의 목적은 ④ '해외 근무의 이점에 대해 말하기 위해'이다.

17 여행을 다니면서 현지에서 친구들을 사귀었다는 언급만 있으므로 정답은 ④ '그는 그의 친구들과 세계를 여행했다.'이다.

**오답 보기 해석**

16
① 기부금을 내도록 사람들을 설득하기 위해
② 채용 회사에서 새로운 직업을 찾기 위해
③ 선적 경험을 가진 사람들을 채용하기 위해
⑤ 해외 근무의 어려운 점을 논의하기 위해

17
① 그는 선적회사에서 일했다.
② 그는 피사의 사탑을 보았다.
③ 그는 많은 흥미로운 사람들을 만났다.
⑤ 그는 회사 소유주와 점심을 먹었다.

**총 어휘 수** 233

# 10 수능영어듣기 실전모의고사

| | | | | | |
|---|---|---|---|---|---|
| 01 ② | 02 ⑤ | 03 ④ | 04 ④ | 05 ② | 06 ③ |
| 07 ① | 08 ⑤ | 09 ③ | 10 ④ | 11 ④ | 12 ④ |
| 13 ① | 14 ⑤ | 15 ④ | 16 ③ | 17 ① | |

## 01 짧은 대화의 응답

**소재** 헤드라이트를 켜놓은 차주인에게 이를 알려주기

**듣기 대본 해석**
여: 저거 봐요, 아빠. 누가 헤드라이트를 켜 놓고 갔어요. 차 주변에 다른 사람은 안 보여요.
남: 끄는 걸 깜박했나 봐. 문 잠겨 있어?
여: 네. 근데 여기 전화번호가 있어요.
남: ② 지금 당장 전화해줘야 할 것 같구나.

**어휘**
**turn ~ off** ~을 끄다

**정답** ②

**문제풀이**
헤드라이트가 켜져 있고, 차에 사람이 없는 대신 전화번호가 남겨진 것을 발견한 여자에게 남자가 할 말로 적합한 것은 ② '지금 당장 전화해줘야 할 것 같구나.'이다.

**오답 보기 해석**
① 헤드라이트 끄려고 해봤니?
③ 그런가 봐. 전화 받아 봐.
④ 네 전화번호를 남기면 그들이 나중에 전화할 거야.
⑤ 네 말이 맞아. 헤드라이트 바꿀 때가 된 것 같아.

**총 어휘 수** 42

## 02 짧은 대화의 응답

**소재** 함부로 버려진 쓰레기

**듣기 대본 해석**
남: Mary, 만약에 더우면 신발 벗고 물에 발을 담그는 게 어때요? 시원하고 좋아요.
여: 좋을 것 같아요. [잠시 후] 아위! 물에 떠다니는 게 쓰레기예요?
남: 네. 사람들이 어떻게 그렇게 사려 깊지 못한지 이해할 수가 없어요. 너무 쉽게 쓰레기를 버리네요.
여: ⑤ 어떤 사람들은 환경을 전혀 신경 쓰지 않아요.

**어휘**
**take off** (옷, 신발 등을) 벗다 **float** *v.* 떠다니다 **inconsiderate** *a.* 사려 깊지 못한 〈문제〉 **trash bin** 쓰레기통

**정답** ⑤

**문제풀이**
사람들이 쓰레기를 함부로 버린다는 남자의 말에 여자도 환경을 언급하며 동조하는 것이 자연스러우므로 정답은 ⑤ '어떤 사람들은 환경을 전혀 신경 쓰지 않아요.'이다.

**오답 보기 해석**
① 우리는 쓰레기통을 하나 더 사는 게 좋겠어요.
② 나는 괜찮아요. 물이 아직 너무 차요.
③ 당신이 우리를 위해 해준 모든 것에 감사해요.
④ 쓰레기를 줍는 데 한 시간밖에 안 걸려요.

**총 어휘 수** 60

## 03 담화 목적

**소재** 예술 축제 행사 설문

**듣기 대본 해석**
남: 오늘 밤 후원자의 모임에 와주셔서 감사합니다. 후원자 위원회는 2016년 봄 예술 축제를 계획하였으며 이를 성공적인 행사로 만들기 위해 여러분의 도움을 원합니다. 예술 축제는 지금까지 우리 학교에서 아주 큰 행사였고, 우리는 올해가 이제까지 중 가장 성공적인 행사가 되었으면 합니다. 우리는 여러분 모두로부터 가능한 한 많은 의견을 기다리고 있습니다. 이 축제를 캠퍼스 혹은 다른 곳에서 개최해야 할까요? 라이브 음악을 해야 할까요? 우리가 다른 지역의 학교가 참가하도록 초대하기를 원하십니까, 안 하기를 원하십니까? 지금 돌리는 설문지에 있는 이러한 질문들 및 다른 몇 가지에 대해 답해주시면 감사하겠습니다. 작성하는 데 오래 걸리지 않을 것이고 여러분의 모든 대답과 선택은 매우 유용할 것입니다. 이것은 지역사회 행사이므로 우리는 여러분의 의견을 듣고 싶습니다. 작성이 끝나시면, 설문지를 공중으로 들어 주시기 바랍니다.

**어휘**
**booster** *n.* 후원자 **board** *n.* 위원회 **host** *v.* 개최하다 **district** *n.* 지역 **questionnaire** *n.* 설문지

**정답** ④

**문제풀이**
학교의 예술 축제 행사의 개최를 위해 축제의 장소나 내용에 관한 설문지를 작성해 줄 것을 부탁하고 있으므로, 정답은 ④ '예술 축제 개최를 위한 설문 참여를 부탁하려고'이다.

**총 어휘 수** 171

## 04 대화 주제

**소재** 학생들의 운동량을 늘리기 위한 방안

**듣기 대본 해석**
여: Baker 씨, 제 생각에는 우리 학교 학생들이 적당한 양의 운동을 하지 않는 것 같아요.
남: 저도 그것에 동의하지만, 우리가 돕기 위해 뭘 할 수 있을까요?
여: 우리가 추가 운동 프로그램을 제공하는 게 좋을 것 같아요.
남: 방과후 교실 같은 것 말씀이세요?
여: 음, 저는 사실 우리가 그것을 아침에 할 수도 있을 거라고 생각하고 있었어요.
남: 우리가 그것을 어떻게 관리할 수 있을까요?
여: 아침에 학교가 시작하기 전에, 학생들에게 마당에서 간단한 운동을 하게 할 수 있어요.
남: 그거 꽤 괜찮은 생각 같은데요. 하지만 저는 당신이 학교가 시작하기도 전에 학생들을 지치게 만들길 원한다고 생각하지 않아요.
여: 저는 아침운동이 실제로 반대 효과를 갖는다고 읽었어요. 그것은 학생들의 주의 집중에 도움을 줄 수 있어요.
남: 그런가요? 어쨌든, 저는 몇몇 학교가 학생들이 더욱 활동적이도록 격려하기 위해 방과후 프로그램을 제공하고 있다고 들었어요.
여: 그것도 좋은 생각이네요.
남: 그럼, 이것들을 시도해보고 효과가 있는지 없는지 보죠.

**어휘**
**after-school class** 방과후 교실 **manage** *v.* 처리하다, 관리하다 **courtyard** *n.* 뜰, 마당 **opposite** *a.* 반대의 **concentration** *n.* 집중 **give it a try** 시도하다

**정답** ④

**문제풀이**
남자와 여자는 학생들의 운동량을 늘려야 한다면서 그 방안에 대해 이야기하고 있으므로 정답은 ④ '학생들의 운동량을 늘리기 위한 방안'이다.

**총 어휘 수** 158

## 05 대화자의 관계 파악

**소재** 주방장과의 인터뷰

**듣기 대본 해석**

여: 만나주셔서 감사합니다. Gaines 선생님.

남: 저와 함께해주셔서 감사합니다.

여: Gaines' Eatery가 2015년 Austin의 최고 레스토랑으로 선정된 것을 먼저 축하드리고 싶습니다.

남: 감사합니다. 정말 감사드려요. 그러나 혼자서는 그것을 못했을 수도 있어요. 제 팀의 멤버들이 진정한 영웅들입니다.

여: Gaines 선생님, 제가 드리고 싶은 몇 가지 질문이 있어요. 먼저, 언제 처음으로 레스토랑 사업에 뛰어들기로 결정하셨죠?

남: 음, 제가 어렸을 때, 아버지께서 Second Street에 작은 빵집을 가지고 계셨어요. 제가 진정으로 제 사업에 대한 이해를 키워온 곳이 바로 그곳입니다.

여: 훌륭하네요. 당신의 일에서 가장 어려운 부분은 무엇인가요?

남: 저는 저녁의 혼잡한 시간대에 고객들이 만족하도록 유지하는 것이 때때로 어려워요. 그것은 스트레스 받는 일이지만 저희 팀은 혼란을 덜 수 있도록 도와줍니다.

여: 자유시간에는 무엇을 하시죠?

남: 저한테는 일이 끝나지 않습니다. 제가 일하지 않고 있을 때, 저는 항상 새로운 조리법을 찾고 새로운 방법을 시험합니다.

여: 당신은 일을 아주 진지하게 받아들이시는 것 같아요. 저희가 잡지에 사용하기 위한 당신 사진을 몇 장 찍어도 괜찮으시겠어요?

남: 물론이죠. 괜찮습니다.

**어휘**

**appreciate** *v.* 고마워하다, 인정하다    **crew** *n.* 팀, 반, 승무원 **appreciation** *n.* 감상, 공감    **rush** *n.* 혼잡, 북적거림    **ease** *v.* 덜어 주다, 덜해지다    **chaos** *n.* 혼란, 혼돈

**정답** ②

**문제풀이**

2015년 최고의 레스토랑에 선정되었다고 했고 레스토랑 사업과 조리법 연구 등에 대해 말하는 것으로 보아 남자는 주방장임을 알 수 있고, 여자는 남자를 인터뷰하면서 잡지에 실을 사진을 찍고 싶다고 했으므로 기자임을 알 수 있다. 따라서 정답은 ② '기자 — 주방장'이다.

**오답 보기 해석**

① 고객 — 점원                            ③ 기자 — 편집자

④ 사진작가 — 모델                        ⑤ 면접관 — 지원자

**총 어휘 수** 189

## 06 그림의 세부 내용 파악

**소재** Rad CraCra 광고

**듣기 대본 해석**

여: 광고는 어떻게 되고 있어, Patrick?

남: 거의 다 된 것 같아. 한번 봐줘.

여: 인상적이네. 위쪽에 'Need Energy?'라는 슬로건이 눈에 잘 띄네. 진한 대문자 글자들이 밝고 에너지가 차 있어.

남: 그게 내가 원하던 바야. 나는 또 앞으로 움직이는 것을 보여주기 위해 오른쪽을 향하는 화살표도 넣었어.

여: 좋은 생각인데.

남: 그리고, 사람들의 이목을 끌기 위해서, 손이 달린 Rad CraCra 캔도 넣었어. 그리고 그건 양손을 공중에 흔들고 있어.

여: 잘했어. 나는 공을 차고 있는 축구 선수도 좋아.

남: 그건 Phil Phillips야. 이 음료의 광고모델이지.

여: 아래에 영양상의 정보를 넣은 것도 너무 좋아. 그건 요즘 일부 사람들에게는 정말 중요하거든.

**어휘**

**stick out** 눈에 띄다, 잘 보이다    **arrow** *n.* 화살표    **include** *v.* 포함하다    **spokesmodel** *n.* 광고모델    **nutritional** *a.* 영양상의

**정답** ③

**문제풀이**

남자가 Rad CraCra 캔이 공중에서 양손을 든 채로 흔들고 있다고 했는데 그림에서는 한 손만 흔들고 있으므로 정답은 ③번이다.

**총 어휘 수** 124

## 07 할 일

**소재** 유리병 구입

**듣기 대본 해석**

*[전화벨이 울린다.]*

남: 여보세요?

여: 안녕, Bill. 저예요.

남: 여보, 무슨 일 있어요?

여: 당신이 아직 사무실에 있는지 궁금해서요.

남: 네, 아직 사무실이에요. 하지만 곧 출발할 거예요.

여: 좋아요. 집에 오는 길에 슈퍼마켓에 들를 수 있어요?

남: 물론이죠. 내가 사왔으면 하는 게 있어요?

여: 음, 제가 어제 친구 Rachel이 해야 하는 심부름을 도와줬잖아요.

남: 맞아요. 당신이 그것에 대해 말했던 거 기억해요.

여: 그녀가 저한테 여러 가지 차와 향신료가 든 상자를 줘서 그것들을 담을 예쁜 병이 필요해요.

남: 당신에게 선물을 주다니 그녀는 정말 친절하군요. 그리고 그것들을 병에 담는 것도 멋진 생각이에요. 당신은 어떤 형태의 병을 생각하고 있어요?

여: 돌려서 닫는 뚜껑이 있는 작은 유리병이요. 구식으로 보이는 그 병 알잖아요.

남: 알겠어요. 내가 슈퍼마켓에 도착하면 다시 전화할게요.

**어휘**

**stop by** ~에 들르다    **assorted** *a.* 여러 가지의    **spice** *n.* 향신료, 양념    **screw-on** *a.* 돌려서 닫는    **lid** *n.* 뚜껑    **old-fashioned** *a.* 구식의, 유행이 지난, 고풍의

**정답** ①

**문제풀이**

여자는 친구에게 여러 가지 차와 향신료를 선물로 받아서 그것들을 담을 병을 사고 싶어 한다. 남자에게 집에 오는 길에 슈퍼마켓에 들러서 병을 사 올 것을 부탁했고 남자는 그러겠다고 했으므로 남자가 여자를 위해 할 일은 ① '유리병 사기'이다.

**총 어휘 수** 160

## 08 이유

**소재** 아내의 사고

**듣기 대본 해석**

남: Amanda, 여기 차 가져왔어.

여: Nathan, 정말 고마워. 어제 어디 있었니? 회의에 안 왔던데.

남: 아내가 사고가 나서 회사에 늦게 도착했어.

여: 이런! 별 문제 없어?

남: 어, 괜찮아. 아내가 그냥 욕실에서 미끄러져 넘어졌어.

여: 큰일났구나. 네가 왜 늦었는지 알겠다.

남: 음, 그게 다가 아니야. 시간을 줄일 수 있을 것이라고 생각해서 회사에 차로 운전해서 오기로 결정했지.

여: 오, 너 보통 회사까지 지하철 타고 오잖아. 그렇지?

남: 맞아. 운전해서 오면 더 빨리 도착할 수 있을 것 같았어. 그런데 교통체증과 주차 때문에 더 오래 걸렸어.
여: 알아. 나는 여기까지 오는 데 너무 오래 걸려서 절대 운전하지 않아.
남: 음, 나는 이 지역이 처음이라 교통 상황을 몰랐어. 누군가에게 물어봤어야 했는데.
여: 괜찮아. 그래서 아내는 괜찮아?
남: 응. 발목을 좀 다쳤어. 더 심각하지 않아서 정말 다행이야.

**어휘**
slip v. 미끄러지다    turn out ~임이 드러나다    be aware of ~을 알다    traffic conditions 교통 상황

**정답** ⑤

**문제풀이**
남자는 아내의 사고로 인해 늦어서 차를 가지고 출근하다가 교통체증과 주차 때문에 늦었다고 말하고 있으므로 정답은 ⑤ '교통체증과 주차 때문에'이다.

**총 어휘 수** 169


# 09  숫자

**소재** 체리 케이크 만들 재료 구매하기

**듣기 대본 해석**
남: 안녕하세요, Crocker 부인. 오늘은 무엇을 도와드릴까요?
여: 음, 오늘 오후에 가족 모임이 있어서 제 유명한 체리 케이크를 만들려고요.
남: 알겠습니다. 필요하신 게 다 있습니다. 오늘 아침에 워싱턴에서 이 체리들이 들어왔어요. 1파운드당 6달러예요.
여: 좋네요. 2파운드 살게요. 모임에 파인애플도 있으면 좋을 것 같네요. 얼마 하나요?
남: 하나당 10달러예요.
여: 좀 비싸네요. 반만 살 수는 없나요?
남: 네. 문제 없어요.
여: 원래 파인애플 하나 가격의 반이죠?
남: 그게, 원래 파인애플 반 개에 6달러인데 저희 단골 손님이시니까 5달러에 드릴게요.
여: 고마워요. 레모네이드 1갤런도 주세요.
남: 레모네이드는 1갤런에 4달러예요. 하지만 25달러 이상 사시면 레모네이드는 공짜로 가져가실 수 있어요.
여: 괜찮아요. 체리 2파운드, 파인애플 반 개, 그리고 레모네이드 1갤런만 주세요. 나중에 청구서 보내주실 수 있죠?
남: 그럼요. 감사합니다. Crocker 부인.

**어휘**
reunion n. 재회, 모임    regular customer 단골, 단골손님
bill v. 청구서를 보내다 n. 청구서

**정답** ③

**문제풀이**
체리는 2파운드 샀으므로 12달러, 파인애플 반 통은 5달러이고, 레모네이드는 4달러이므로 정답은 ③ '$21'이다.

**총 어휘 수** 178


# 10  언급 유무

**소재** 사진 대회를 위한 전시회 개최

**듣기 대본 해석**
여: 안녕하세요, Wise 선생님. 우리가 이번 봄에 사진 대회를 위한 전시회를 개최하는 것이 어떨지 생각을 해왔습니다.
남: 좋은 생각이에요. 우리 학생들의 노고를 우리 동네에 있는 사람들에게 보여줄 수 있겠네요.

여: 맞아요. 하지만 우리는 올해의 대회의 주제를 생각해야 해요. 자연 사진에 관해서 어떻게 생각하세요?
남: 저는 좋아요. 저, 제 생각에는 우리가 시내 도서관에 있는 전시실에 공간을 좀 확보할 수 있을 것 같은데요.
여: 그렇게 생각하세요? 비용은 얼마나 드나요?
남: 글쎄요. 제가 도서관 위원회에 계신 몇몇 분들을 알아요. 저는 우리가 공간을 무료로 예약할 수 있다고 생각해요. 제가 이용 가능한지 확인해 볼게요.
여: 좋아요. 우리가 전시회를 마을에 홍보하기 위해 제가 학생들에게 포스터를 만들게 할게요.
남: 좋은 생각이에요. 부모님들을 위한 정식 초대장은 어떻게 생각하세요?
여: 그건 필요하지 않다고 생각해요. 포스터와 입소문으로 충분해요.
남: 알았어요. 음, 우리가 일에 착수해야겠군요.

**어휘**
exhibition n. 전시회    competition n. 대회, 경쟁    reserve v. 확보하다, 예약하다    formal invitation 정식 초대장
word of mouth 입소문, 구전    get to work 일에 착수하다

**정답** ②

**문제풀이**
두 사람은 전시회 주제, 장소 대여 비용, 홍보 포스터와 정식 초대장에 관한 언급은 했지만 전시회 기간에 대한 언급은 하지 않았으므로 정답은 ② '전시회 기간'이다.

**총 어휘 수** 170


# 11  내용 일치 · 불일치

**소재** 새로 문을 여는 식당 홍보

**듣기 대본 해석**
남: 올 가을, 저희는 여러분들에게 이 도시가 제공할 수 있는 가장 최고의 식사 경험을 가져다 드리려 합니다. Ricardo's on the Boardwalk은 어떤 식사 상황에도 완벽한 식당입니다. Scales Lake에 있으며, 시내에서 약 5분 정도 떨어진 곳에 자리하고 있습니다. 저희의 웅장한 식당 건축은 거의 2년이 걸렸지만 마침내 문을 열 준비가 되었답니다. 옥외 식사 공간은 놀라운 호수 전망을 제공하며, 위층의 라운지는 재즈에 재능이 있는 지역 사람들을 주말과 일부 평일 저녁에 제공합니다. 여러분은 이 지역에서 선사하는 최고의 재즈를 들으며 시사와 음료를 즐길 수 있습니다. 또한 저희는 여러분의 어린 자녀들에게 맞추어진 좀 더 가족 친화적인 식사 공간을 갖추고 있습니다. 저희 식당은 오직 최고의 요리사들만을 채용하고 있으며, 식품은 모두 현지에서 재배됩니다. 기억에 남을 만한 식사 경험을 찾고 계시다면, 올 가을에 문을 여는 Ricardo's on the Boardwalk 이외에 다른 곳은 더 알아보지 않으셔도 됩니다.

**어휘**
open-air a. 야외의, 옥외의    house v. 수용하다    cater to ~의 구미에 맞추다, ~을 충족시키다    locally ad. 근처에, 현지에서

**정답** ④

**문제풀이**
남자는 주말과 일부 평일 저녁에 지역 재즈 음악가들에게 장소가 제공되어 재즈를 들으며 식사를 할 수 있다고 말했으므로 내용과 일치하지 않는 것은 ④ '매일 평일 저녁에 재즈 공연이 있다.'이다.

**총 어휘 수** 146


# 12  도표

**소재** 알맞은 축구화 선택

**듣기 대본 해석**
여: 어서 오세요, Owen 스포츠 용품 가게입니다. 무엇을 도와드릴까요?

남: 축구화를 새로 사려고 합니다. 추천해 줄 만한 것이 있나요?
여: 여기 저희 제품 목록이 있습니다. 수비수로 활동하나요, 공격수로 활동하나요?
남: 사실 아들 주려고 사는 건데 걔는 두 포지션 모두 뛰는 것을 좋아해요.
여: 그렇군요. 그럼 다용도 축구화가 아드님께 맞을 것 같네요.
남: 그럴 것 같아요. 플라스틱과 천 중에서 어느 것을 추천해 주시겠어요?
여: 플라스틱을 추천해드립니다. 플라스틱이 훨씬 내구성이 좋아서 오래가요.
남: 알겠습니다. 플라스틱으로 살게요. 그럼 이제 두 제품만 남았네요, 저렴한 것과 비싼 것.
여: 이것은 이번 시즌 신상품이라서 더 비싸요.
남: 신상품이든 아니든 제 아들은 별로 신경 쓸 것 같지 않네요. 더 저렴한 것 5 사이즈로 살게요.
여: 선택 잘하신 것 같아요. 카운터에서 계산 도와드릴게요.
남: 좋아요. 도와주셔서 감사합니다.

### 어휘
**soccer cleat** 축구화   **suit** *v.* 어울리다   **durable** *a.* 내구성 있는, 오래가는   〈문제〉**offensive** *a.* 공격의   **defensive** *a.* 수비의

### 정답 ④

### 문제풀이
남자는 수비수와 공격수 모두에게 적합한 다목적이면서 재질은 내구성이 좋은 플라스틱, 가격은 더 저렴한 축구화를 선택하였으므로 정답은 ④번이다.

### 총 어휘 수 156


## 13  긴 대화의 응답

**소재** 태국 여행을 위한 조언

### 듣기 대본 해석
여: 안녕 Stan. 잘 지내니?
남: 음. 나는 이번 여름에 태국을 방문할 계획을 마무리 지으려고 하고 있어.
여: 정말? 태국 어디를 가려고 해? 알다시피 나는 지난 겨울에 거기에 갔잖아.
남: 그래. 나는 네가 태국에 대해 말했던 것 때문에 거기에 가려고 해. 너 방콕에 있었니 아니면 해안가로 갔었니?
여: 나는 며칠 동안 방콕에 있었고 그 다음에 Phi Phi 섬에 갔어. 너는 해변에 가봐야 해. 정말 끝내줘.
남: 그래. 내가 큰 도시는 그렇게 좋아할 것 같지 않아. 거기에서 여행하는 것에 관한 조언 좀 해 줄래?
여: 음, 너는 어디에 가더라도 가격 흥정을 해야 해.
남: 정말? 거기에는 모든 것이 비싸니?
여: 아니. 모든 것이 꽤 싸지만, 처음 가격에 절대 동의하지 마. 거의 항상 흥정을 할 수 있어.
남: 그렇구나. 내가 항상 가격에 대해 언쟁을 해야겠네.
여: 그래. 대체로, 너는 그들이 처음 너에게 말한 가격의 1/3 가격에 기념품을 살 수 있어.
남: ① 조언 고마워. 많은 도움이 되었어.

### 어휘
**finalize** *v.* 마무리 짓다, 완결하다   **make it to** ~에 이르다, 도착하다   **incredible** *a.* 믿을 수 없는, 엄청난   **haggle** *v.* 흥정을 하다   **initial** *a.* 처음의, 초기의   **bargain** *v.* 협상(흥정)하다   **souvenir** *n.* 기념품   **quote** *v.* 값을 부르다, 인용하다   〈문제〉**confirmation** *n.* 확인

### 정답 ①

### 문제풀이
여자가 남자에게 태국 여행에서 항상 가격 흥정을 하라는 조언을 해주고 있으므로 남자의 마지막 응답은 ① '조언 고마워. 많은 도움이 되었어.'가 적절하다.

### 오답 보기 해석
② 이번이 태국으로 첫 여행이야.
③ 나는 마침내 방콕으로 가는 비행기편의 확인을 받았어.
④ 내가 거기서 훨씬 더 싼 가격으로 이 기념품들을 살 수 있어.
⑤ 그거 좋은 생각이야. 나는 여기서 많은 돈을 썼어.

### 총 어휘 수 174


## 14  긴 대화의 응답

**소재** F1(자동차경주) 관람 전 간식 사기

### 듣기 대본 해석
남: 처음으로 F1 보려니까 신나지?
여: 정말 기대 돼. 앉기 전에 매점에서 간식 좀 사자.
남: 그래. 단 게 좀 끌리네. 어, 봐봐. 솜사탕 판다.
여: 솜사탕 좋아해? 애들 간식이잖아.
남: 그럴 수도 있지만 이건 F1이고 솜사탕은 즐거운 간식이 되지.
여: 그럴 수도 있지. 다 큰 남자가 솜사탕 먹는 게 좀 웃겨 보일 것 같아서.
남: 알겠어. 츄러스는 어때? 나 츄러스도 진짜 좋아해.
여: 장난치지 마. 츄러스는 너무 달아. 평범한 사람들처럼 그냥 핫도그 몇 개랑 햄버거 사면 안 될까?
남: 오, 어서! 츄러스 먹자.
여: ⑤ 고맙지만 괜찮아. 나는 너무 단 것을 먹고 싶지 않아.

### 어휘
**concession stand** 매점   **in the mood for** ~할 기분이 나서   **cotton candy** 솜사탕   **foolish** *a.* 어리석은, 바보 같은

### 정답 ⑤

### 문제풀이
여자는 솜사탕과 츄러스를 사오려는 남자에게 너무 달다면서 핫도그나 햄버거를 사오면 안 되냐고 하고 있다. 다시 한번 츄러스를 권하는 남자의 말에 대한 대답으로 적절한 것은 ⑤ '고맙지만 괜찮아. 나는 너무 단 것을 먹고 싶지 않아.'이다.

### 오답 보기 해석
① 네가 틀렸어. 나는 디저트 먹는 것 정말 좋아해.
② 모든 사람들이 F1에서 츄러스 먹는 걸 좋아해.
③ 나는 매점에서는 원하는 게 아무것도 없어.
④ 나는 우리가 이번 주말에 F1 보러 가야 한다고 생각해.

### 총 어휘 수 126


## 15  상황에 적절한 말

**소재** 폭풍우 예보로 인한 등산 연기하기

### 듣기 대본 해석
여: Kristen과 가족들은 토요일에 산으로 등산을 갈 계획을 하고 있습니다. 그녀의 아들 Gavin은 야외를 굉장히 좋아하기 때문에 특히나 더 들떠 있습니다. Kristen은 일주일 내내 등산 갈 준비를 했고 Gavin이 제일 좋아하는 간식도 몇 개 준비했습니다. 그러나 Kristen이 금요일 밤에 일기예보를 확인하자 강수확률이 80%라는 것을 알게 됩니다. 사실 일기예보에서는 주말 내내 폭풍우가 연속적으로 그 지역에 있을 것이라고 예상하였습니다. 안 좋은 날씨로 인해 기상청은 사람들이 실내에 있기를 권고하고 있습니다. Kristen은 등산을 다음 주 토요일로 미루는 것이 좋을 것이라고 생각합니다. 이러한 상황에서 Kristen이 Gavin에게 어떤 말을 할까요?
Kristen: Gavin. ④ 우리 등산을 다음 주말로 일정을 변경해야 할 것 같아.

### 어휘
**weather forecast** 일기예보   **predict** *v.* 예측하다, 예견하다   **severe** *a.* 심각한, 안 좋은   **urge** *v.* 충고하다, 권고하다   **postpone** *v.* 연기하다, 미루다

**문제풀이**

Kristen은 주말의 일기예보를 보고 등산을 연기하자고 아들에게 말하려고 하므로 적절한 말은 ④ '우리 등산을 다음 주말로 일정을 변경해야 할 것 같아.'이다.

**오답 보기 해석**
① 내일 날씨가 등산 하기에 완벽할 거야.
② 등산을 위해 마른 옷 몇 벌이 필요할 거야.
③ 내가 우리 등산을 위해 네가 가장 좋아하는 간식을 좀 준비했어.
⑤ 빗속에서 산꼭대기까지 가려면 시간이 더 걸릴 거야.

**총 어휘 수** 137

## 16 담화 주제 / 17 세부 내용 파악

**소재** 음식에 돈을 절약할 수 있는 몇 가지 조언

**듣기 대본 해석**

남: 매일 요리를 하는 것은 비용이 많이 들고 시간이 많이 소요됩니다. 요즘 사람들은 항상 정신 없이 바쁘고 스스로 요리할 시간이 없습니다. 제가 여러분들에게 음식에 돈과 시간을 절약하는 요령들을 제공하기 위해 여기에 왔습니다. 첫째, 음식물을 대량으로 구매하세요. 음식물을 개별적으로 구매하는 것보다 대량으로 사는 것이 더 저렴합니다. 둘째, 유명 브랜드를 피하고 자가 브랜드 상품을 구매하세요. 유명 브랜드 상품은 종종 자가 브랜드의 제품과 같은 종류의 재료를 포함하고 있으면서 훨씬 더 비쌉니다. 셋째, 농산물이 제철일 때에만 농산물을 구매하세요. 농산물이 제철이 아니고 그 때문에 비쌀 때는 통조림이나 냉동된 음식이 대체물이 될 수 있습니다. 또한, 제품 판촉이나 세일에 관심을 가지세요. 여러분들은 쿠폰과 세일을 이용함으로써 많은 돈을 절약할 수 있습니다. 마지막으로, 대량으로 요리 하세요. 그것이 지루하다는 것을 저도 알지만, 여러분들이 직장에 매일 점심을 싸가면 많은 돈을 절약할 수 있습니다. 예를 들면, 여러분들이 일요일 밤에 약간의 시간을 그 주의 점심을 위한 요리를 하는 데 바칠 수 있습니다. 스파게티는 다시 데워서 그 주 내내 먹을 수 있는 훌륭하고 비용 효율적인 음식입니다. 돈을 절약하기 위해 여러분들의 생활 방식을 바꾸는 것은 힘들 수 있겠지만, 그것은 확실히 가치가 있습니다.

**어휘**

**costly** *a.* 많은 돈이 드는, 비용이 드는    **time-consuming** *a.* 시간 소비가 큰    **be on the go** 정신 없이 바쁘다    **in bulk** 대량으로
**store-brand** *a.* 자가 브랜드 상품의    **produce** *n.* 농산물
**in season** 제철인, 한창인    **take advantage of** ~을 이용하다
**dedicate** *v.* 전념하다, 바치다    **worthwhile** *a.* ~할 가치가 있는

**정답** 16 ③  17 ①

**문제풀이**

16 남자는 음식에 돈을 절약하는 방법들을 몇 가지 알려주고 있다. 따라서 남자가 하는 말의 주제는 ③ '음식에 돈을 절약하는 방법에 대한 조언'이다.

17 제철 농산물, 통조림, 냉동식품, 스파게티에 대한 언급은 있었지만 즉석 요리 제품에 대한 언급은 없었으므로 정답은 ① '즉석 요리 제품'이다.

**오답 보기 해석**
16
① 집에서 식사를 요리하는 것의 이점
② 가장 신선한 농산물을 선택하는 방법
④ 맛있고 건강에 좋은 식사를 만드는 법
⑤ 바쁜 사람들을 위한 싸고 손쉬운 요리법

**총 어휘 수** 196

## DICTATION ANSWERS

01 forgot to turn them off

02 take off your shoes / people can be so inconsiderate

03 input from all of you / host the festival on campus / fill out the form / hold your questionnaire in the air

04 getting the proper amount of exercise / How could we manage that / offering after-school programs / I say we give these a try

05 have done it alone / have difficulty keeping the customers happy / researching new recipes / to use in the magazine

06 at the top really sticks out / pointing to the right / both of them in the air / nutritional information at the bottom

07 I was wondering if / on your way home / some nice jars to put them in / the ones that look old-fashioned

08 missed the meeting / take the train to work / it turns out / traffic and bad parking / wasn't aware of the traffic conditions

09 Is there any way I can / It'll be half the cost / get the lemonade for free / You can bill me later

10 held an exhibition / a theme for this year's competition / reserve the room for free / have my students make posters / word of mouth will be enough

11 about five minutes from downtown / on the weekends and some weeknights / our food is all grown locally

12 play both positions / much more durable / take the cheaper ones

13 finalize my plans / Do you have any tips / never agree to the initial price / a third of the price

14 concession stand / in the mood for something sweet / eating cotton candy looks foolish / too sweet

15 go hiking in the mountains / checks the weather forecast / Due to the severe weather / postpone the hike until next Saturday

16-17 it's in season / pay attention to promotions / taking advantage of sales

# 11 수능영어듣기 실전모의고사

| | | | | | |
|---|---|---|---|---|---|
| 01 ④ | 02 ① | 03 ① | 04 ④ | 05 ④ | 06 ② |
| 07 ④ | 08 ③ | 09 ② | 10 ④ | 11 ③ | 12 ⑤ |
| 13 ① | 14 ② | 15 ⑤ | 16 ③ | 17 ③ | |

## 01 짧은 대화의 응답

**소재** 회의에 늦은 이유

**듣기 대본 해석**
여: 안녕하세요. 무엇을 도와드릴까요?
남: 안녕하세요. 저는 Thomas Moore입니다. 저는 3시에 예정된 회의가 있는데요. 늦어서 죄송합니다.
여: 괜찮아요, Moore 씨. 우리 사무실을 찾는 것이 어려웠나요?
남: ④ 아니요, 제가 단지 지하철역을 잘못 내렸어요.

**어휘**
scheduled *a.* 예정된 〈문제〉 direction *n.* 방향, 지시

**정답** ④

**문제풀이**
남자가 회의에 늦어서 여자는 사무실을 찾는 것이 어려웠냐고 묻고 있으므로 적절한 응답은 ④ '아니요, 제가 단지 지하철역을 잘못 내렸어요.'이다.

**오답 보기 해석**
① 물론이죠. 이제 저는 회의 준비가 되었습니다.
② 죄송하지만, 저는 거기에 어떻게 가는지 잘 몰라요.
③ 네. 당신 사무실로 가는 길을 저에게 알려주세요.
⑤ 그 사무실은 길 건너편 큰 건물에 있어요.

**총 어휘 수** 46

## 02 짧은 대화의 응답

**소재** 시력 관리

**듣기 대본 해석**
남: 칠판의 글씨를 선명하게 보기가 어려워.
여: 정말이야? 시력 좋았잖아. 무슨 일이야?
남: 최근에 컴퓨터 게임을 너무 많이 하는 안 좋은 습관이 생겼어.
여: ① 네 눈을 더 잘 관리해야겠다.

**어휘**
used to V ~하곤 했다 〈문제〉 consider *v.* 고려하다

**정답** ①

**문제풀이**
최근에 컴퓨터 게임을 너무 많이 하는 안 좋은 습관이 생겼다는 남자에게 여자가 해줄 말은 ① '네 눈을 더 잘 관리해야겠다.'가 가장 적절하다.

**오답 보기 해석**
② 지금 시력 검사를 하진 않아도 돼.
③ 그런 방식으로는 습관을 고칠 수 없을 거야.
④ 책 읽기 전에 잠시 기다려야 해.
⑤ 컴퓨터를 좀 더 자주 사용할 것을 고려해 봐.

**총 어휘 수** 44

## 03 담화 주제

**소재** 온라인 쇼핑의 부정적인 면

**듣기 대본 해석**
여: 온라인으로 식품 구매를 할 수 있다는 것을 알고 있었나요? 온라인 식품 구매는 최근 몇 년 동안 꽤 대중화되었습니다. 온라인 구매는 소비자가 스마트폰, 태블릿 혹은 컴퓨터로 쇼핑을 할 수 있게 하며, 그들이 마트에 가는 시간을 절약해 줍니다. 온라인 쇼핑은 돈을 절약할 수도 있습니다. 하지만 몇 가지 부정적인 면도 있다는 것을 주의하세요. 대부분의 물건들이 상점 대신 창고에 대량으로 저장되기 때문에 더 싸지만, 이 창고들이 종종 방치되고 그래서 제품의 관리가 거의 되지 않는다는 것이 문제입니다. 이 때문에 벌레의 침입이나 부적절한 저장 방법으로 인해 제품이 손상될 수도 있습니다. 어떤 소비자들은 그들의 집으로 썩은 과일이 배송된 것을 신고 했습니다. 항의를 하고자 할 때, 그들이 할 수 있는 것은 오직 이메일을 보내고 답변을 기다리는 것뿐입니다. 온라인 구매는 시간과 돈을 절약할 수 있는 좋은 방법이지만, 온라인으로 구매하는 물건들은 그것들이 방치되었을 때 부정적인 결과를 겪지 않을 물건들로 제한해야 합니다.

**어휘**
beware *v.* 조심하다, 주의하다  aspect *n.* 측면  in bulk 대량으로  warehouse *n.* 창고  supervision *n.* 감독, 관리  goods *n.* 제품  lead to ~로 이어지다  infestation *n.* (벌레의) 침입, 침략  improper *a.* 부당한, 부적절한  file a complaint 항의를 제기하다  restrict *v.* 제한하다  neglect *v.* 방치하다

**정답** ①

**문제풀이**
여자는 온라인 쇼핑이 시간과 돈을 절약할 수 있는 좋은 방법이지만 부정적인 면도 있음을 알려주고 있다. 따라서 정답은 ① '온라인 쇼핑의 부정적인 측면'이다.

**총 어휘 수** 174

## 04 의견

**소재** 헌 샌들 기부

**듣기 대본 해석**
남: 어디 가고 있니, Amy?
여: 새 샌들을 사려고 쇼핑몰에 가.
남: 지금 신은 샌들도 괜찮아 보이는데.
여: 사실, 밑창이 너무 엉망이야(닳았어).
남: 새 신발 사면 그거 버릴 거니?
여: 아마도. 왜?
남: 그것들을 버리는 대신에 Good Will 재단에 주는 걸 고려할 수 있기 때문이야. 그들은 샌들이 필요한 누군가에게 그걸 줄 거야.
여: 정말? 그렇지만 나는 Good Will 재단이 어디에 있는지 모르는데.
남: 그건 걱정하지 마. 웹 사이트에 가서 가장 가까운 기부 센터를 찾아보면 돼.
여: 내가 기부하기 전에 내 신발을 수선해야 해?
남: 아니. 그들이 모든 것을 처리해. 그들이 밑창 수리까지 할 거야.
여: 정말 멋지구나. 그러면 새 신발 사고 나서 헌 것은 꼭 기부할래.
남: 좋아! 그러겠다니 나도 기뻐!

**어휘**
sole *n.* (신발의) 밑창  foundation *n.* 재단  donate *v.* 기부하다  definitely *ad.* 분명히

**정답** ④

**문제풀이**
신던 샌들의 밑창이 닳아서 새 샌들을 사러 가는 여자에게 남자는 여자의 헌 샌들을 버리지 말고 Good Will 재단에 기부할 것을 제안하고 있다. 따라서 ④ '헌 신발을 버리지 말고 자선 단체에 기부하라.'가 정답이다.

**총 어휘 수** 143

**소재** 태양광 에너지에 관한 인터뷰

**듣기 대본 해석**

여: 저희 프로그램에 함께해 주셔서 감사합니다. Marsh 교수님.

남: 초대해 주셔서 감사합니다.

여: 좋습니다. 바로 본론으로 들어가지요. 우선 다음 획기적인 기술이 무엇일 것이라고 생각하십니까?

남: 음. 아시겠지만 에너지가 우리나라에선 큰 문제입니다. 현재 에너지 기반시설이 비효율적일뿐더러 공기와 토지, 수질을 오염시키고 있습니다.

여: 맞습니다. 뉴스에서 항상 오염 이슈에 관한 소식을 듣죠. 그것은 덜 발달된 국가들에서는 훨씬 더 심각하지요.

남: 맞습니다. 우리는 대체에너지 자원을 개발할 필요가 있고 전통적인 방식은 버려야 합니다.

여: 어떠한 기술이 가장 탄력을 받을 것이라고 생각하십니까?

남: 태양전지입니다. 그게 바로 미래지요.

여: 그것이 풍력이나 수력과 같은 다른 재생 가능 에너지원들보다 더 나은 이점이 있나요?

남: 확실히 그렇죠. 대부분의 선진국은 태양광에 접근할 수 있지만 모두가 강에 가까이 있는 것도 아니고 바람을 이용할 수 있는 것도 아니지요. 태양광 에너지는 가격도 훨씬 싸지고 있습니다.

여: 바로 그거군요. 태양 에너지가 바로 미래군요. 함께해주셔서 감사합니다 Marsh 교수님.

남: 천만에요. 시청자분들께 이야기를 나누는 것은 언제나 좋습니다.

**어휘**

**breakthrough** *n.* 돌파구    **inefficient** *a.* 비효율적인    **pollute** *v.* 오염시키다    **alternative** *a.* 대체 가능한    **abandon** *v.* 버리다    **momentum** *n.* 탄력, 가속도    **renewable** *a.* 재생 가능한    **hydroelectric** *a.* 수력 전기의    **harness** *v.* 이용하다, 활용하다    **folks** *n.* 여러분, 얘들아(두 사람 이상의 사람들을 친근하게 부르는 말)

**정답** ④

**문제풀이**

남자가 처음에 초대해줘서 고맙다고 인사했고, 여자는 남자에게 질문을 하고 남자는 태양광 에너지에 대해 이야기해주고 있다. 마지막 부분에서 viewers (시청자)가 나오는 것으로 보아 둘의 관계는 ④ '사회자 ─ 출연자'임을 알 수 있다.

**총 어휘 수** 180

---



**소재** 새로 오픈하는 카페 전단지

**듣기 대본 해석**

남: Rose. 너 뭐 보고 있어?

여: 이거? 아. 스타디움의 새로운 카페를 위한 홍보용 전단지야. 한번 봐.

남: 재미있어 보이네. 왼쪽 뒤에 저건 빵집이야?

여: 응. 그리고 빵집 옆은 스낵바야.

남: 저 피자가 맛있어 보여. 그리고 저 사람이 카페에 있는 DJ야?

여: 응. 맞아. 그런데 카페에 DJ가 있어서 약간 이상해 보이는 것 같아. 그렇게 생각하지 않니?

남: 맞아. 이건 확실히 일반적인 카페는 아닌 것 같아.

여: 응. 카페 바깥에 어린이들을 위한 놀 거리도 좀 있어.

남: 보여. 저거 광대지?

여: 그런 것 같아. 그가 거기서 어린이들에게 동물 풍선을 만들어 주고 있어.

남: 그래. 그가 풍선을 준비하도록 돕고 있는 스태프도 보여. 이상한 카페이긴 하지만 성공할 것 같아.

여: 그랬으면 좋겠어. 개점은 이번 일요일 콘서트 전이야.

**어휘**

**promotional** *a.* 홍보의    **flyer** *n.* 전단지    **normal** *a.* 보통의, 평범한    **entertainment** *n.* 오락    **clown** *n.* 광대

**정답** ②

**문제풀이**

빵집 옆에는 스낵바가 있다며 피자가 맛있겠다고 했는데 그림에서는 요리사가 햄버거를 팔고 있으므로 일치하지 않는 것은 ②번이다.

**총 어휘 수** 150

---



**소재** 리포트 작성을 위한 DVD 찾기

**듣기 대본 해석**

남: Rachel. 나 좀 도와줄 수 있어?

여: 그래. Peter. 무슨 일인데?

남: 그게, 이미 알고 있겠지만, 내가 목요일에 수업을 못 갔어.

여: 맞아. 야구 시 대회 나갔잖아. 어떻게 됐어?

남: 잘 했어. 다음 회로 넘어 갈 수 있게 됐어.

여: 잘 됐다. 올해 너희 팀 진짜 잘하더라. 모두가 열심히 연습했잖아. 분명 너희 팀이 우승할 거야.

남: 그럴 수 있었으면 좋겠다. 하여튼 Smith 선생님 수업의 지구 온난화 보고서 끝냈어?

여: 응. 너는 끝냈어?

남: 그게, 하고 싶은데 우리가 기초로 해야 할 영화를 못 찾겠더라.

여: 그렇구나. A Troublesome Fact 말하는 거지?

남: 그거 맞아.

여: 도서관 확인해 봤어? 거기 분명히 있을 거야.

남: 도서관 확인해 볼 생각을 못했네. 지금 가서 확인할게.

**어휘**

**global warming** 지구 온난화    **be supposed to V** ~하기로 되어 있다    **troublesome** *a.* 골칫거리인, 고질적인

**정답** ④

**문제풀이**

남자는 숙제를 위해 영화를 찾고 있는데 여자가 도서관에 가면 있을 기라고 말하자 가서 확인해 보겠다고 했으므로 남자가 할 일은 ① '도서관에 기시 엉화 DVD 찻아보기'이다.

**총 어휘 수** 148

---



**소재** 일일 캠프 관리자

**듣기 대본 해석**

여: 너 이번 여름에 뭐할 거야?

남: 나는 학교에서 일일 캠프 관리자로 일할 생각이야.

여: 재미있겠는걸.

남: 사실 나 지난 5년 동안 매 여름마다 캠프 관리자로 일해 왔었어.

여: 와, 몰랐어. 그 일은 어때?

남: 일은 꽤 쉬워. 나는 아이들을 가르치고 그날 우리가 계획한 재미있는 것들을 하게 하면 돼.

여: 상당히 편안한 환경이야?

남: 음, 사실 그래. 활동에 따라 날마다 달라질 수는 있지만, 모든 사람들이 늦게 까지 일하거나 일찍 오는 데 대해서 신경 쓰지 않아. 스트레스가 거의 없지.

여: 보수는 어때?

남: 캠프 관리자로서는 보통이지만 다른 직업들보단 확실히 낮아. 그렇지만 나는 정말 돈에 별로 신경 쓰지 않아.

여: 너는 왜 그렇게 거기서 오랫동안 일해온 거니?

남: 그건 정말 나에게 이상적인 직업이야. 매일 자연을 즐기기 위해 밖으로
　　나가고 모든 일들을 직접 하거든.

#### 어휘
**supervisor** *n.* 관리자　　**fairly** *ad.* 상당히, 꽤　　**vary** *v.* 다르다, 달라지다
**depending on** ~에 따라　　**average** *a.* 보통의, 평균의　　**hands-on**
*a.* 직접 참여하는

#### 정답 ③

#### 문제풀이
대화의 마지막 부분에서 남자가 캠프 관리자로 일해 온 이유는 보수는 다른
일보다 적지만 매일 자연을 즐기기 위해 밖으로 나가고 모든 일들을 직접 하기
때문이라 말했다. 따라서 정답은 ③ '자연을 즐기며 일할 수 있어서'이다.

**총 어휘 수** 163


## 09 숫자

#### 소재 커트 후 계산

#### 듣기 대본 해석
여: 음, 다 됐어요. 가셔도 돼요.
남: 고마워요. 머리가 훨씬 보기 좋아요. 오늘 밤 회사 파티에서 멋지게 보일
　　것 같네요.
여: 제 일에 자부심이 있어요.
남: 훌륭해요. 제 친구들 모두에게 당신을 반드시 추천할게요.
여: 감사해요. 헤어 커트는 25달러가 될 겁니다. 오늘 다른 헤어 케어 제품을
　　구매하실 건가요?
남: 그럼요. 스타일링 왁스를 좀 살 거예요. 얼마죠?
여: 왁스는 20달러예요. 샴푸는 어떠세요? 알로에가 함유된 샴푸가 고객님의
　　머리 타입에 좋아요.
남: 그것도 한 병 살게요.
여: 좋아요. 그것은 한 병에 15달러예요. 다 되신 거죠?
남: 네. 저기요, 이 미용실에 첫 방문객들을 위한 어떤 할인이 있다고 언급하지
　　않으셨나요?
여: 맞아요. 고객님은 첫 방문 고객이시기 때문에 전체 가격에서 10퍼센트
　　할인을 받으십니다.
남: 좋네요. 카드 여기 있습니다.

#### 어휘
**take pride in** ~을 자랑하다　　**would like to V** ~하고 싶다
**infuse** *v.* 불어넣다

#### 정답 ②

#### 문제풀이
커트가 25달러, 왁스는 20달러, 샴푸는 15달러로 총 60달러에서 10퍼센트
할인이 적용되므로 남자는 ② '$54'를 지불해야 한다.

**총 어휘 수** 145


## 10 언급 유무

#### 소재 여행지로 갈만한 곳 소개

#### 듣기 대본 해석
남: 안녕, Sally. 이번 겨울에 좀 더 따뜻한 곳으로 여행을 갈까 생각 중이야.
　　제안할 만한 데 있니?
여: 물론이지. 내가 늘 가곤 했던 Tybee Island라고 불리는 곳이 있어. 분명히
　　네가 좋아할 거야.
남: Tybee Island라고? 한 번도 들어본 적 없는데. 어디에 있어?
여: Savannah 근처, Georgia에 있어.
남: 알겠어. 어떤 점이 그렇게 좋아?

여: 글쎄, 그 나라의 그 지역은 정말 아름다워. 식민지 시대 양식의 집들이
　　예쁘고, 해변가도 꽤 멋져.
남: 그때쯤 그곳 날씨는 어떨까?
여: 많이 덥지는 않지만, 수영을 하기에는 많이 추울 수도 있어.
남: 좋네. 그런데 난 수영을 별로 안 해서. 그곳 호텔들은 보통 얼마 정도니?
여: 글쎄, 일주일에 대략 700달러로 해변가 콘도를 빌릴 수 있어. 침실이 세 개
　　있는 방이면 너희 가족에게 딱 알맞을 것 같아.
남: 적당한 것 같네. 좀 더 역사적인 곳들을 꼭 관광하고 싶은데. 투어도 제공
　　하겠지?
여: 당연하지. 네가 참여할 만한 몇 가지 역사 투어가 있어. 저녁에 할 수 있는
　　유령 투어들도 있고.
남: 정말 재미있어 보인다. 바로 Tybee Island를 알아 봐야겠어.

#### 어휘
**colonial** *a.* 식민지의, 식민지 시대의　　**beachfront** *a.* 해안지대의,
해변가의　　**historic** *a.* 역사적인, 역사적으로 중요한

#### 정답 ④

#### 문제풀이
위치(Savannah 근처), 날씨(많이 덥지는 않지만 수영하기에는 추움), 숙박 비용
(일주일에 약 700달러), 할 만한 것들(역사 투어, 유령 투어)은 언급되었지만 '현지
가이드'는 언급되지 않았으므로 정답은 ④ '현지 가이드'이다.

**총 어휘 수** 192


## 11 내용 일치 · 불일치

#### 소재 무선 단말기 사진전

#### 듣기 대본 해석
남: 저희는 세계적으로 유명한 Mobile Device Photo Contest(무선 단말기
　　사진전)를 위한 참가 날짜를 발표하게 되어서 자랑스럽습니다. 이는 젊은
　　사람들에게 그들의 스마트폰과 태블릿을 이용한 창의적인 사용권을 주기
　　위한 것입니다. 참가자들은 16세 이하여야 합니다. 자격이 있고 참가를
　　희망하는 사람들은 다음 주제 즉, 건축, 자연 또는 상업 중 하나에 해당하는
　　사진을 제출해야 합니다. 각각의 주제에서 한 장씩 우승 사진을 뽑을 것이고
　　우승자는 500달러의 상금을 받게 될 것입니다. 기억하세요, 각 참가자는
　　대회에 참가하기 위해서 부모님의 동의를 받아야만 합니다. 온라인 등록은
　　저희 웹사이트 www.mdphoto.com에서 이번 목요일 정오부터 시작될
　　것입니다. 출품작은 2016년 10월 15일까지 제출되어야 합니다.

#### 어휘
**announce** *v.* 알리다, 발표하다　　**entry** *n.* 참가, 출품작
**contestant** *n.* 참가자　　**eligible** *a.* 자격이 있는　　**submit** *v.* 제출하다
**architecture** *n.* 건축(양식)　　**commerce** *n.* 무역, 상업　　**winning**
*a.* 이긴, 우승한　　**consent** *n.* 동의, 허락　　**registration** *n.* 등록

#### 정답 ③

#### 문제풀이
우승자는 각 주제별로 한 명씩 뽑는다고 했으므로 내용과 일치하지 않는 것은
③ '우승자는 각 분야를 합쳐서 단 한 명이다.'이다.

**총 어휘 수** 115


## 12 도표

#### 소재 공룡 장난감 고르기

#### 듣기 대본 해석
남: 여보, 뭐 보고 있어?
여: Jake에게 줄 선물을 인터넷에서 찾아 보고 있었어. 좀 있으면 걔 생일인
　　거 알지?
남: 당연하지. 뭐 사줄 생각인데?

여: 글쎄, 요즘 공룡을 많이 좋아하고 있으니까 장난감 트리케라톱스 사주려고 이거 봐봐. 엄청 귀여워.
남: 그것도 좋을 것 같기는 한데 나한테 자기가 제일 좋아하는 공룡이 티라노사우루스라고 했어.
여: 그렇구나. 일단 이 사이트의 제일 인기 있는 공룡 장난감 목록을 찾아놨어. 얼마 정도 쓰려고 생각하고 있어?
남: 200달러 넘는 건 좀 무리인 것 같아.
여: 알았어. 재질은? 나무로 사는 게 좋을 것 같아. 플라스틱은 내구성이 떨어져.
남: 나도 그렇게 생각해. 어떤 크기로 살까?
여: 음, 2피트는 너무 큰 것 같아. 당신도 그렇게 생각하지 않아?
남: 동감이야. 그럼 우리가 살 게 정해졌네. 어서 주문해.
여: 알겠어. 생일 전에 배송되면 좋겠다.

### 어휘
**browse** *v.* 둘러보다, 훑어보다  **be into** ~에 관심이 많다  **figure** *v.* 생각하다, 판단하다  **durable** *a.* 내구성이 있는, 오래가는  **place an order** 주문하다

### 정답 ⑤

### 문제풀이
공룡은 티라노사우루스를 선택했으므로 ①, ③, ⑤번 중에 고르면 되는데 200달러가 넘지 않는 것으로 하자고 했으므로 ①번은 제외된다. 크기가 2피트는 너무 크다고 했으므로 두 사람이 선택한 것은 ⑤번이 된다.

**총 어휘 수** 167

## 13  긴 대화의 응답

**소재** 다른 사람들과 함께 하는 X-Fit 운동 프로그램

### 듣기 대본 해석
남: Laura. 오랜만이네. 잘 지내?
여: 잘 지내지. 너 저번에 봤을 때랑 좀 변한 것 같아.
남: 응. 요즘 다이어트하고 운동하면서 살이 많이 빠졌어.
여: 좋네. 어떤 운동하는데?
남: 축구 조금 하긴 하는데, 일주일에 네 번 X-Fit 프로그램도 해.
여: X-Fit? 나는 집에서 Lunacy 프로그램을 했는데 별로 좋지는 않았어.
남: 집에서 보는 비디오 프로그램 같은 거지? 그런 거 한 번 해봤어. 3일 후에 그만뒀어.
여: 그럼 X-Fit은 뭐가 달라?
남: 음, X-Fit은 다른 사람들과 함께하는 운동 방법이야. 헬스장에서 만나서 일련의 운동을 해.
여: 그렇구나. 혼자 운동하는 건 별로 동기부여가 안 되는 것 같아.
남: 맞아. 여러 사람과 같이 하면 서로가 더 열심히 할 수 있도록 격려해 줄 수 있어. 정말 재미있어.
여: 다시 운동을 해야겠어. 근데 혼자 하는 건 싫어.
남: ① <u>우리 X-Fit 운동 클럽에 들어오는 건 어때?</u>

### 어휘
**quit** *v.* 그만두다  **routine** *n.* 규칙적 순서, 방법  **motivate** *v.* 동기를 부여하다

### 정답 ①

### 문제풀이
여자는 다시 운동을 시작하려 하지만 혼자 하는 것은 싫다고 했으므로 이에 대한 남자의 가장 적절한 응답은 같이 하자는 ① '우리 X-Fit 운동 클럽에 들어오는 건 어때?'이다.

### 오답 보기 해석
② 내가 갈 만한 체육관 혹시 아니?
③ 너도 살 좀 빠진 것 같은데.
④ 네가 혼자 운동하는 게 훨씬 나을 것 같아.
⑤ 혼자 운동할 때 조심해야 해.

**총 어휘 수** 166

## 14  긴 대화의 응답

**소재** 마음에 들지 않는 전공

### 듣기 대본 해석
남: 나의 전공은 너무 지루해, Sabrina. 난 무엇을 해야 할지 모르겠어.
여: 정말? 나는 너의 전공이 대학교에서 다른 어떤 전공들보다 훨씬 더 재미있다고 생각해.
남: 나는 매일 똑같은 것을 해. 나는 별로 많이 배우지 않아. 컴퓨터 공학은 나한테 맞지 않는 것 같아.
여: 너의 지도 교수님과 그것에 관해 이야기해 보았니?
남: 아니. 예전에 그녀와 얘기했을 때 별로 도움이 되지 않았거든. 게다가 학기 초라서 그녀는 신입생들과 이야기하느라 너무 바빠.
여: 그게 사실일 수도 있지만, 네가 그녀와 이야기하지 않는다면 넌 남은 일생 동안 네가 좋아하지 않는 것을 꼼짝없이 하게 될 거야.
남: 나는 그녀의 시간을 허비하고 싶지는 않아. 다른 어떤 전공을 내가 좋아할지도 확실하지 않아.
여: 나는 그것이 너의 지도 교수님께서 네가 결정하는 것을 도와 줄 수 있는 점이라고 생각해. 난 내가 뭘 하고 싶은지 확실하지 않았는데 내 지도 교수님께서 그 모든 것을 바꿔주셨어.
남: 정말? 그녀가 널 위해 무엇을 했길래?
여: ② <u>그녀는 내가 다른 무언가를 시도해 보는 것을 제안하셨어.</u>

### 어휘
**major** *n.* 전공  **academic advisor** 지도 교수  **semester** *n.* 학기  **be stuck** 꼼짝도 못 하다

### 정답 ②

### 문제풀이
여자는 남자에게 마음에 들지 않는 전공에 대해 지도 교수님과 상의하라고 조언하면서 자신의 경험을 말해주었다. 마지막에 남자가 교수님이 무엇을 해주셨는지 물었으므로 여자의 적절한 응답은 ② '그녀는 내가 다른 무언가를 시도해 보는 것을 제안하셨어.'이다.

### 오답 보기 해석
① 그녀는 네가 잘 결정하도록 도와주었음이 틀림없어.
③ 그녀는 모든 학생의 흥미를 고려해.
④ 그녀는 내가 새로운 전공을 찾는 것을 도와주기를 거절했어.
⑤ 그녀는 학생들이 전공을 선택하는 것을 도와주곤 했어.

**총 어휘 수** 169

## 15  상황에 적절한 말

**소재** 친구가 장기자랑에 참여하도록 설득하기

### 듣기 대본 해석
남: Joseph은 학년 말에 열리는 교내 장기자랑을 기획하고 있습니다. 마술, 춤, 저글링 공연이 있긴 하지만 그는 공연에서 연주를 할 음악가를 정말 찾고 싶어 합니다. 그는 Katie가 작년에 주(state) 합창 대회에서 결승 진출자였던 것을 기억하고 있습니다. Joseph은 Katie에게 전화해서 그녀에게 참여해 줄 것을 부탁합니다. 그녀는 시험 공부를 하느라 너무 바빠 연습할 수 없기 때문에 그의 요청을 거절합니다. 하지만 Joseph은 끈질기게 Katie를 장기자랑에 합류시키려고 계속 설득합니다. 그는 그녀만이 공연의 균형을 맞춰 줄 수 있는 유일한 사람이라고 말합니다. 이제 Katie는 참여하는 것을 고려 중이지만 결정을 내리지 못하고 있습니다. 이러한 상황에서, Katie가 Joseph에게 할 말로 가장 적절한 것은 무엇일까요?
Katie: ⑤ <u>그것에 대해 생각할 시간을 좀 줄래?</u>

### 어휘
**finalist** *n.* 결승 진출자  **choir** *n.* 합창단, 성가대  **participate** *v.* 참가하다  **persistent** *a.* 집요한, 끈질긴  **persuade** *v.* 설득하다  **talent show** 장기자랑  〈문제〉 **all-state** *a.* 주 대표의

정답 ⑤

## 문제풀이

Joseph은 Katie가 교내 장기자랑에서 음악 공연을 해 줄 유일한 사람이라고 생각하고 계속해서 설득을 하고 있으며, 이에 대해 Katie는 쉽게 결정을 하지 못하고 있으므로 이러한 상황에 그녀가 할 말로 가장 적절한 것은 ⑤ '그것에 대해 생각할 시간을 좀 줄래?'이다.

## 오답 보기 해석

① 네가 도와줄 수 있는 다른 사람이 있지 않니?
② 난 주 대표 합창대회에 참여할 수 없었어.
③ 장기자랑에 참여하게 돼서 너무 신난다.
④ 음악 공연을 포함시키려는 생각은 잊어버려.

**총 어휘 수** 138

# 16 담화 목적 / 17 세부 내용 파악

**소재** 부부간의 대화 시간

## 듣기 대본 해석

여: 안녕하세요, Sunday Evening Classics의 사회자 Lauren Bell입니다. 오늘 밤 시작하기 전에, 결혼한 부부와 의사소통에 관해 잠깐 말씀 드리고 싶어요. 남편과 아내 간의 대화의 양을 계산하기 위한 실험이 최근에 행해졌는데 여러분은 결과에 놀라실 거예요. 보통 사람들은 부부가 서로 꽤 자주 이야기를 나눈다고 생각할 거예요. 그런데 한 심리학자가 밝힌 것은 일반적인 부부가 사람들이 상상하는 것보다 훨씬 적게 이야기를 나눈다는 것을 보여 줍니다. 제가 지금 여러분께 알려드리고자 하는 숫자는 하루가 아니라 일주일 동안 대화를 나눈 시간입니다. 16분입니다! 충격적이지 않으세요? 여러분 자신을 보통의 부부라고 생각한다면, 대화양이 총 30분이 될 수 있게 일주일에 14분 더 배우자와 이야기하도록 해 보세요. 그리고 나서 매일 30분 대화하도록 노력해보세요. 그것이 여러분의 관계에 도움이 될까요? 저희는 그렇게 생각해요. 생각과 감정을 공유하거나 심지어 사소한 대화도 부부에게 매우 중요합니다. 저 밖에 모든 부부들을 위해 Scotty McGee의 The Modern Love Song을 들려 드리겠습니다. 감상하세요!

## 어휘

**host** *n.* (TV · 라디오 프로의) 진행자 **conduct** *v.* 수행하다
**calculate** *v.* 계산하다 **assume** *v.* 추정하다 **psychologist** *n.*
심리학자 **spouse** *n.* 배우자 **trivial** *a.* 사소한
**in the interest of** ~을 위하여 〈문제〉 **promote** *v.* 촉진하다, 고취하다
**marital** *a.* 결혼의

## 정답 16 ③ 17 ③

## 문제풀이

16 음악 프로의 사회자가 부부간의 대화 시간에 관한 실험 결과를 공개하면서 부부간의 대화 시간을 늘릴 것을 장려하고 있으므로 정답은 ③ '남편과 아내 간의 대화를 장려하려고'이다.

17 여자의 말 중간 부분에서 일반적인 부부가 일주일 동안 서로 이야기를 나누는 시간은 16분이라고 했으므로 정답은 ③ '16분'이다.

## 오답 보기 해석

16
① 음악을 통해 부부 관계를 개선하려고
② 음악 프로그램에 부부들을 초대하려고
④ 건강한 부부 관계의 중요성을 가르쳐주려고
⑤ 결혼한 커플 간의 대화 주제를 소개하려고

**총 어휘 수** 194



01 have a meeting scheduled for three o'clock

02 Your eyesight used to be good

03 allows consumers to shop from their smartphones / a few negative aspects / goods being damaged / file a complaint / save time and money

04 Where are you headed / in really bad shape / throw them away / take care of all of that

05 get right into it / pollution issues in the news / gaining the most momentum / renewable energy sources

06 promotional flyer / pizzas look delicious / making balloon animals for children

07 as you might have noticed / moving on to the next round / we're supposed to base it on / have a copy of it

08 as a day camp supervisor / for the past five years / can vary from day to day depending on / lower than most other jobs / enjoy nature

09 You're all ready to go / take pride in my work / Will that be all / a first-time customer

10 a place I used to go to / What makes it so nice / rent a beachfront condo / even have ghost tours

11 Those who are eligible / submit pictures / a winning photo from each category / consent from their parents

12 he's really into / we can afford anything over / less durable / I hope it gets delivered

13 since I last saw you / lost a lot of / four times a week / you can push one another

14 My major is so terribly boring / talked to your academic advisor / beginning of the semester / for the rest of your life / what I wanted to do

15 organizing the school talent show / asks her to participate / persuade Katie to join the talent show / is now considering joining

16-17 amount of communication / anyone would have imagined / talking to your spouse / Sharing thoughts and feelings

# 12 수능영어듣기 실전모의고사

| 01 ② | 02 ① | 03 ③ | 04 ⑤ | 05 ② | 06 ③ |
| 07 ② | 08 ④ | 09 ② | 10 ③ | 11 ① | 12 ② |
| 13 ③ | 14 ④ | 15 ③ | 16 ③ | 17 ⑤ | |

## 01 짧은 대화의 응답

**소재** Elvis 전시회 장소

**듣기 대본 해석**

남: 너 Elvis의 팬 아니니? 도시로 오는 새로운 Elvis 전시회가 있다는 것 봤어?
여: 응! 오늘 아침에 막 읽었어. 나 정말 기대돼.
남: 응, 나도 그래. 정확히 어디서 열리는데?
여: ② 그건 주립 극장에서 열릴 거야.

**어휘**

**exhibition** *n.* 전시회　**exactly** *ad.* 정확하게　〈문제〉**inspiring** *a.*
고무적인, 감격적인　**take a picture** 사진을 찍다

**정답** ②

**문제풀이**

남자가 전시회가 정확히 어디서 열리냐고 물었으므로 장소에 대한 대답이 나와야
한다. 따라서 정답은 ② '그건 주립 극장에서 열릴 거야.'이다.

**오답 보기 해석**

① 그의 음악은 전부 너무 감동적이야.
③ 충고해줘서 고마워.
④ 오, 그럼 난 못 갈 것 같아.
⑤ 사진 많이 찍는 것 잊지 마.

**총 어휘 수** 50

## 02 짧은 대화의 응답

**소재** 목적지까지 걸리는 시간과 비용

**듣기 대본 해석**

여: 안녕하세요. 제가 도심에 있는 미술관에 가야 하거든요. 시간이 얼마나
　걸릴까요?
남: 음. 이 시간이면 차가 그렇게 막히지 않아요. 30분 정도 걸릴 거예요.
여: 나쁘지 않네요. 택시타면 얼마 나오는지 알아요?
남: ① 20달러보다 적게 나올 거예요.

**어휘**

**downtown** *a.* 중심가에, 도심지에　**traffic** *n.* 교통(량)　**congested**
*a.* 붐비는, 혼잡한　〈문제〉**admission** *n.* 입장

**정답** ①

**문제풀이**

여자가 택시비가 얼마나 나올지 아는지 물었으므로 가장 적절한 남자의 응답은
① '20달러보다 적게 나올 거예요.'이다.

**오답 보기 해석**

② 입장료는 10달러예요.
③ 당신은 나에게 빨리 돈을 갚아야 해요.
④ 미술관이 저녁 9시에 닫는 것 같아요.
⑤ 저는 차가 막혀서 늦을지도 몰라요.

**총 어휘 수** 53

## 03 담화 주제

**소재** 기분과 창의성 간의 상관관계

**듣기 대본 해석**

남: 안녕하세요 여러분, 좋은 아침입니다. 저는 오늘 Minnesota 대학에서
얼마 전에 나온 흥미로운 연구에 대해 여러분께 말씀드리고 싶습니다. 연구는
행복과 창의성 간의 상관관계에 대한 것입니다. 연구자들은 사람들을 세
그룹으로 나누고 다른 상황에 두었습니다. 첫 번째 그룹은 놀이공원으로
보냈습니다. 두 번째 그룹은 공포 영화를 보러 극장에 보냈고, 세 번째 그룹은
도자기 박물관으로 보냈습니다. 각 그룹이 돌아온 후에 연구자들은 창의
성 테스트를 했습니다. 놀이공원에 갔던 그룹이 다른 그룹보다 훨씬 더 좋
은 결과를 낸 것으로 드러났습니다. 이 결과는 연구자들로 하여금 우리가
행복할 때 우리의 뇌가 이전에 얻은 지식에 더 잘 접근할 수 있고 이 지식을
(새로운 생각으로) 만들어내는 데 활용할 수 있다고 믿게 합니다. 그래서
행복한 사람들은 쉽게 다른 생각들을 합치고 그것으로부터 새로운 것을
만들어 내는 그들의 능력 때문에 더 창의적이게 됩니다.

**어휘**

**correlation** *n.* 상관관계　**horror** *n.* 공포물　**pottery** *n.* 도자기
**conduct** *v.* 수행하다　**access** *v.* 접근하다　**previously** *ad.*
이전에, 미리　**various** *a.* 여러 가지의

**정답** ③

**문제풀이**

남자는 행복한 경험을 한 사람들이 창의력 검사에서 더 좋은 결과를 냈다고
말하고 있다. 따라서 남자가 하는 말의 주제는 ③ '기분과 창의성의 상관관계'이다.

**총 어휘 수** 166

## 04 의견

**소재** 너무 많은 장난감의 부정적 효과

**듣기 대본 해석**

여: Tommy의 놀이방을 봐요. 그의 부모가 정말 장난감을 많이 사줬나 봐요.
남: 네. 그리고 그의 침실도 봐야 해요. 거긴 장난감이 천장까지 쌓여있어요.
여: 전 더 적은 장난감이 아이들에게 다른 능력을 발달시켜준다는 것에 관한
　기사를 읽었어요.
남: 정말이요? 저는 그런 건 들어본 적이 없어요. 더 많은 장난감이 더 좋다고
　알고 있었어요.
여: 음, 약간의 장난감은 아이들이 자라고 배우는 데 좋지만 너무 많은 장난감은
　실제로 해로울 수 있어요.
남: 흠… 왜 그런지 궁금해요.
여: 기사에선 너무 많은 장난감은 아이들의 상상력을 방해할 수 있다고 했어요.
남: 오? 어떻게요?
여: 더 적은 장난감을 가진 아이들은 더 많은 장난감을 가진 아이들보다 그들의
　상상력을 더 많이 사용해야만 해요. 그들은 놀 때 창의력을 더 써야만 하죠.
남: 일리가 있네요. 저는 자랄 때 장난감이 별로 없었어요. 대신 저는 저만의
　장난감을 만들거나 게임을 발명해야만 했죠.

**어휘**

**stack** *v.* 쌓다, 포개다　**ceiling** *n.* 천장　**article** *n.* 기사　**figure** *v.*
(~일 거라고) 생각하다　**harmful** *a.* 해로운　**hinder** *v* 방해(저해)하다
**imagination** *n.* 상상력　**make sense** 이해가 되다, 말이 되다

**정답** ⑤

**문제풀이**

여자는 너무 많은 장난감은 아이들에게 해로울 수 있으며, 더 적은 장난감을
가진 아이들이 상상력을 더 많이 사용한다고 말하고 있다. 따라서 여자의
의견으로 가장 적절한 것은 ⑤ '너무 많은 장난감은 아이들의 상상력에 방해가
된다.'이다.

**총 어휘 수** 145

**소재** 축구감독과의 인터뷰

**듣기 대본 해석**

여: 토요일에 Liverpool이랑 Manchester City 경기 보셨나요?

남: 네, 봤었어요.

여: Liverpool은 어땠나요?

남: 정말 잘 했어요. 골 찬스가 여러 번 있었는데 결국 이기지는 못했어요.

여: 네. 막상막하였어요. 골 하나 차이로 졌잖아요.

남: Manchester City가 그들을 잘 막았어요. 골키퍼가 아주 훌륭했어요.

여: 맞아요. 그래서 다음 주에 Liverpool이랑 경기할 때 어떤 전략을 쓸 건가요?

남: 그 슛들을 막으려면 수비를 강화해야 할 겁니다. 우리는 또한 공격을 재정비 하고 있는데 그만큼 결과가 좋기를 바라야지요.

여: 경기가 기대됩니다. 이 인터뷰를 시청하고 있는 축구 팬들께 할 말 있나요?

남: 열렬한 성원과 우리가 리그에서 성장하는 것을 지켜봐 주셔서 감사합니다. 다음 경기 꼭 이기도록 하겠습니다.

여: Charlie. 인터뷰를 위해 시간을 내주셔서 감사합니다. BCC 뉴스의 Susan Peters였습니다.

**어휘**

**shot** *n.* (슛을 하기 위한) 시도　**pull off** (힘든 것을) 해내다　**goalie** *n.* 골키퍼　**amazing** *a.* 놀라운　**strengthen** *v.* 강화하다　**defense** *n.* 수비　*a.* 수비의　**rework** *v.* 고치다　**offensive** *n.* 공격　*a.* 공격의　**appreciate** *v.* 고마워하다

**정답** ②

**문제풀이**

여자는 전략이나 팬들에게 하고 싶은 말 등을 묻고 있으므로 기자이고 남자는 다음 경기의 전략을 말하며 자신들의 경기를 지켜봐 달라고 했으므로 축구감독 임을 유추할 수 있다. 따라서 정답은 ② '기자 — 축구감독'이다.

**총 어휘 수**　180

**06**　그림의 세부 내용 파악

**소재** 중고차 팔기

**듣기 대본 해석**

*[휴대폰이 울린다.]*

남: 안녕, Megan.

여: Sam? 네가 나 좀 도와줄 수 있는지 알고 싶어.

남: 물론이지. 뭔데?

여: 음, 내 차를 팔려고 하는데 Twitter와 같은 소셜 미디어를 활용하는 것이 말을 퍼트리는 데 도움이 될 것 같아.

남: 그래. 좋은 생각이야. 난 Twitter에 팔로워가 많아. 내가 네 차에 대한 간략한 설명을 올려주길 바라니?

여: 그럼 너무 좋지. 차는 Wasp 2015 스페셜 에디션이고, 약 20,000 마일 정도 탔어.

남: 선루프는 있어?

여: 응, 스페셜 에디션은 선루프가 있는 게 기본으로 나오거든.

남: 그렇구나. 그리고 스페셜 에디션에 추가된 다른 특징들은 없는 거야?

여: 응, 옆면을 따라서 가는 세로줄 무늬가 있어.

남: 그게 다야?

여: 별 모양 휠도 있어.

남: 알았어. 차에 어떤 흠집은 없어?

여: 앞 범퍼에 작은 스크래치(긁힌 자국)가 있지만 난 그 점을 원하는 가격 결정하는 데 고려했어. 그거 말고는 내가 차를 잘 관리해 왔고, 모든 서비스 기록을 보관하고 있어.

남: 그래, 알았어. 내가 바로 Twitter에 설명을 올릴게.

여: 고마워, Sam.

**어휘**

**description** *n.* 서술, 묘사　**feature** *n.* 특징　**pinstripe** *n.* 가는 세로줄 무늬　**damage** *n.* 손상, 훼손　**factor something into** ~을 고려 요인으로 포함하다　**other than** ~외에

**정답** ③

**문제풀이**

여자는 자신의 차를 팔려고 하는데 트위터의 팔로워가 많은 남자에게 내용을 올려달라고 부탁하면서 차의 세부사항을 알려주고 있다. 여자의 차는 스페셜 에디션으로 차의 옆면에 세로줄 무늬가 있다고 했으나. 그림에서는 차의 후드 (보닛) 부분에만 줄무늬가 있으므로 정답은 ③번이다.

**총 어휘 수**　186

**07**　부탁한 일

**소재** 졸업 연설자 선정

**듣기 대본 해석**

남: 안녕하세요, Amanda.

여: 안녕하세요. John. 들어오세요.

남: 올해 졸업 연설자를 선정하는 데 도움이 필요하신지 궁금해서요.

여: 네, 도움 주시면 고맙죠. 제가 후보를 15명으로 추렸어요.

남: 좋아요. 그럼 제가 이 학생들과 무엇을 해야 하나요?

여: 저는 당신이 학생들을 개별로 만나서 대화를 하셨으면 해요. 학생 각자가 무엇을 강하게 느끼는지와 기회가 있다면 급우들과 어떤 메시지를 공유하고 싶은지 알아내 주셨으면 좋겠어요.

남: 제가 학생들과 만난 후엔 무엇을 해야 하나요?

여: 저와 다시 만나 각 학생들이 했던 이야기를 당신이 받은 전반적인 인상과 함께 자세히 알려주세요.

남: 알겠습니다. 그렇게 할게요. 그런데 학생 각자 일정이 달라서 모두와 만나기 어려울 수 있어요.

여: 당신이 일을 처리할 수 있을 거라 생각해요, John.

남: 저를 믿어주셔서 감사합니다. 좋아요, 해볼게요.

여: 고마워요, John. 이야기를 할 수 있게 끝나면 알려주세요.

**어휘**

**graduation speech** 졸업 연설　**candidate** *n.* 후보자　**handle** *v.* 다루다, 처리하다　**appreciate** *v.* 고마워하다

**정답** ②

**문제풀이**

여자가 남자에게 자신이 추린 졸업 연설 후보자들과 만나 대화를 나누고 그 세부 내용을 알려줄 것을 부탁하고 있으므로 정답은 ② '졸업 연설 후보자들과 대화하기'이다.

**총 어휘 수**　185

**08**　이유

**소재** 놀이공원에 못 가는 이유

**듣기 대본 해석**

여: Joe, 어디로 가는 거예요?

남: 딸과 함께 박물관 가는 중이에요. 여름방학 동안에 고대 이집트에 관해 해야 할 숙제가 있거든요.

여: 방학 동안에 숙제라고요? 힘들겠네요. 자, 그녀는 이번 여름 방학 때 또 뭘 해요?

남: 음. Lake Totanka에서 하는 여름캠프에 그녀를 등록시켰어요. 왜요?

여: 제 상사가 Holidayland 놀이공원 티켓 8장을 주셨거든요. 저도 가족이랑 갈 건데 당신도 우리와 함께 가고 싶으신지 궁금해서요.

남: 그거 멋지겠는걸요. 언제 갈 건데요?

여: 다음 주 일요일 20일이에요.

남: 다음 주 일요일이요? 음. 가고는 싶은데 갈 수 없어요. 다음 주에 부모님 댁에 가거든요.

여: 안됐군요.

남: 네. 일정을 변경할 수는 없어요. 왜냐하면 가족 모임이 있거든요. 꽤 성대한 파티가 될 거예요.

여: 알았어요. 그럼 다음 기회에 가요.

남: 물론이죠. 초대해 줘서 고마워요.

### 어휘

**assignment** *n.* 과제　**rough** *a.* 힘든, 골치 아픈　**sign up for** ∼에 신청하다, 등록하다　**reschedule** *v.* 일정을 변경하다　**reunion** *n.* 모임, 동창회

### 정답 ④

### 문제풀이

남자는 놀이공원에 가고 싶지만 그날 가족 모임이 있어서 부모님 댁에 가야 한다고 했으므로 정답은 ④ '가족 모임이 있어서'이다.

### 총 어휘 수 147


## 09　숫자

### 소재　모니터 구입

### 듣기 대본 해석

남: 무엇을 도와드릴까요?

여: 저는 어떤 모니터를 사야 할지 결정하려고 해요.

남: 전문가용 모니터를 원하세요, 일반용 모니터를 원하세요?

여: 음, 다른 점이 뭐죠?

남: 네. 전문가용은 비디오 편집과 그래픽 디자인과 같은 기능을 위해서 최고 해상도의 화면을 사용합니다.

여: 그렇군요. 일반용 모니터는 어때요? 그나저나, 일반용 목적은 뭔가요?

남: 일반용은 이메일 사용, 워드 프로세싱, 컴퓨터로 가끔 영화 보기가 가능해요.

여: 좋아요. 저는 그래픽 디자인이나 비디오 제작에는 관심이 없지만 화질이 좋았으면 해요.

남: 물론이죠. 모든 모니터가 정말 화질이 좋지만 일반용 모니터로 하시면 돈이 절약될 겁니다.

여: 좋아요. 얼마죠?

남: 원래 가격은 500달러이지만 현재 할인하고 있어서 10퍼센트 할인을 받으실 거예요.

여: 와, 가격 괜찮네요. 제가 웹사이트에서 가져온 쿠폰과 함께 쓸 수 있어요?

남: 물론이죠. 그래서 쿠폰이 있는걸요.

여: 좋아요. 그럼 제가 세일 가격에서 추가로 10퍼센트를 받는 거죠?

남: 맞아요. 모니터를 가지고 다시 올게요.

### 어휘

**purpose** *n.* 목적, 용도　**definition** *n.* 해상도, 선명도　**occasional** *a.* 가끔의　**on sale** 할인 판매 중인　**combine** *v.* 결합하다　**absolutely** *ad.* 틀림없이, 물론이죠, 그럼요　**additional** *a.* 추가의

### 정답 ②

### 문제풀이

모니터의 원래 가격은 500달러인데 남자가 현재 10퍼센트 할인을 받을 수 있다고 했으므로 450달러이고, 여자가 웹사이트에서 가져온 쿠폰으로 세일 가격에서 추가 10퍼센트 할인을 받을 수 있다고 했으므로 405달러에 구입할 수 있게 된다. 따라서 답은 ② '$405'이다.

### 총 어휘 수 176


## 10　언급 유무

### 소재　헌혈 자격 조건

### 듣기 대본 해석

남: 안녕하세요. 헌혈을 하기로 결정했어요. 처음이라 좀 긴장되네요.

여: 괜찮아요. 안 아프게 할게요. 그런데 몇 가지 질문을 좀 할게요. 먼저, 몇 살이세요?

남: 저 17살이에요. 문제가 되나요?

여: 음, 나이 제한이 있기는 한데 16세부터 69세까지여서 괜찮아요.

남: 그렇군요. 다른 필요조건은요?

여: 남성은 몸무게가 50킬로그램 이상이어야 하고 여성은 45킬로그램을 넘어야 해요. 당신은 괜찮을 것 같네요.

남: 당연하죠. 다른 거는요?

여: 맥박이 항상 안정적으로 분당 50비트에서 100비트 사이여야 해요. 또한, 최근에 아팠던 적이 있으세요?

남: 아니요. 아프면 헌혈 못하나요?

여: 네. 체온이 섭씨 37.5도가 넘으면 헌혈을 못해요.

남: 그렇군요. 헌혈을 하려면 좋은 건강 상태여야 하는 것이 정말 중요한 것 같네요.

### 어휘

**donate** *v.* 기부하다, 헌혈하다　**nervous** *a.* 불안해 하는　**make it easy** 편하게 해 주다　**requirement** *n.* 필요, 필요조건　**pulse** *n.* 맥박, 맥

### 정답 ③

### 문제풀이

두 사람은 헌혈의 나이제한(16∼69세), 체중(남성 50킬로그램 이상, 여성 45킬로그램 이상), 맥박(50∼100비트), 체온(37.5도 이하)은 언급하였지만 혈액형에 관해서는 언급하지 않았으므로 정답은 ③ '혈액형'이다.

### 총 어휘 수 168


## 11　내용 일치 · 불일치

### 소재　행진 악단 오디션

### 듣기 대본 해석

남: 안녕하세요 학생 여러분. Franklin 대학교 행진 악단 오디션이 곧 다가오고 있습니다. 실제 오디션은 9월 25일에서 30일까지로 신청은 9월 10일에서 15일까지 받고 있습니다. 오디션에 참가하고 싶은 음악가는 누구나 자신이 작곡한 곡이나 다른 사람이 작곡한 곡을 연주하여 오디션을 볼 수 있습니다. 각 참가자 당 최소 10분 간 연주를 해 주시기 바랍니다. 신청을 할 때 자신의 경험에 대한 짧은 자기소개서와 연주할 곡 악보도 첨부해 주시기 바랍니다. 우리 전문가 심사위원들이 누가 합류할 자격이 있는지 판단할 것입니다. 악단 정원은 100명입니다. 수상까지 한 저희 행진 악단에 관심 있는 분들은 신청을 하고 오디션을 보시기 바랍니다. 감사합니다.

### 어휘

**marching band** 행진 악단　**tryout** *n.* 오디션　**take place** 개최되다, 일어나다　**biography** *n.* 전기, 자기소개서　**permit** *v.* 허락하다　**award-winning** *a.* 상을 받은

### 정답 ①

### 문제풀이

담화의 처음 부분에서 오디션의 접수 날짜는 9월 10일에서 15일까지이고 오디션 날짜가 9월 25일에서 30일까지라고 했으므로 내용과 일치하지 않는 것은 ① '접수 날짜는 9월 25일에서 30일까지이다.'이다.

### 총 어휘 수 138


## 12　도표

### 소재　파티룸 예약

### 듣기 대본 해석

여: 안녕하세요, 선생님. 무엇을 도와드릴까요?

남: 안녕하세요. 아들의 야구팀을 위한 파티를 계획하려고 합니다. 토요일 오후에 빈자리가 있을까요?

여: 물론이죠. 오후 2시에 이용 가능한 장소가 있을 것 같아요. 여러 다른 패키지를 제안합니다. 안내책자를 봐 주세요.

남: 음, 팀은 어린이 15명입니다. 모든 패키지에 피자가 제공됩니까?

여: 그렇습니다. 얼마나 오랫동안 파티룸을 예약하고 싶으신지요? 세 가지 선택권이 있어요.

남: 이것이 그들이 서로 볼 수 있는 마지막 시간이라 좀 더 긴 파티가 좋을 거라고 생각해요.

여: 그러면 90분이나 100분으로 방을 예약하셔야 하겠네요.

남: 좋을 것 같아요. 그런데 저는 200달러 이상은 쓰고 싶지 않아요.

여: 그러면, 손님의 요구에 맞는 두 가지 다른 패키지가 있습니다. 하나는 큰 피자 두 개와 음료가 포함되어 있습니다. 다른 하나는 큰 피자 한 개와 음료가 따라옵니다.

남: 두 개의 피자가 있는 것이 적당할 것 같아요.

여: 좋아요. 토요일 2시에 파티룸을 예약하겠습니다.

### 어휘

**opening** *n.* 빈자리, 결원　　**available** *a.* 이용할 수 있는　　**reserve** *v.* 예약하다　　**put down for** ~의 예약자로서 이름을 적어 두다

### 정답 ②

### 문제풀이

남자는 참석할 어린이가 15명이라고 했으므로 ⑤번이 제외되고, 시간은 90분이나 100분이라 했으므로 ④번도 제외된다. 가격은 200달러를 넘지 않기를 바란다고 했으므로 ①번이 제외되고, 피자가 2개 나오는 패키지를 선택했으므로 정답은 ②번이다.

### 총 어휘 수 181


## 13　긴 대화의 응답

**소재** 9시 이후 소등에 관한 문제

### 듣기 대본 해석

*[전화벨이 울린다.]*

남: 안녕하세요. 세인트폴 고등학교입니다. 저는 교감 Jones입니다.

여: 안녕하세요, Jones 선생님. Raymond 엄마 되는 Grace Conroy입니다. 캠퍼스 내의 문제로 말씀드릴 게 있습니다.

남: 네. 뭐가 문제인가요?

여: 그게, 제가 어젯밤에 제 아들을 데리러 도서관에 갔는데 주차장 주변이 굉장히 어두운 걸 봤습니다.

남: 죄송하지만 9시 이후에 캠퍼스 내의 모든 불들을 끕니다. 전기를 절약하는 데에 도움이 돼요.

여: 이해해요. 전기 절약도 중요하죠. 그런데 안전상의 문제가 있지 않나요? 누가 넘어져서 다칠 수도 있습니다.

남: 그렇게 큰 문제일 줄은 몰랐네요.

여: 그리고 불을 켜는 게 나쁜 사람들이 오지 못하게 할 수도 있습니다.

남: ③ 불을 계속 켜놓는 것에 대해 제가 무엇을 할 수 있을지 볼게요.

### 어휘

**vice principal** 교감 선생님　　**electricity** *n.* 전기　　**conserve** *v.* 절약하다　　**concern** *n.* 걱정, 관심, 문제　　**undesirable** *a.* 원하지 않는, 달갑지 않은

### 정답 ③

### 문제풀이

여자가 남자에게 9시 이후로 캠퍼스에 불을 끄는 것에 대한 문제점을 이야기하며 남자를 계속 설득하고 있으므로 적절한 응답은 ③ '불을 계속 켜놓는 것에 대해 제가 무엇을 할 수 있을지 볼게요.'이다.

### 오답 보기 해석

① 어머님께서 아들을 더 빨리 데리러 오셨어야 해요.

② 학생들이 공부하기에 너무 어두울 거예요.

④ 걱정 마세요. 내일 등이 수리되도록 할게요.

⑤ Raymond가 더 주의를 기울여야 다치지 않아요.

### 총 어휘 수 132


## 14　긴 대화의 응답

**소재** 낡은 물건 리폼

### 듣기 대본 해석

남: 안녕 Amelia, 널 위해 내가 뭘 만들었어.

여: 핸드백? 나 새 것 정말 갖고 싶었는데. 네가 정말 직접 만든 거 아니지, 그렇지?

남: 글쎄, 내가 대부분의 작업을 했지만 우리 미술 선생님이 조금 도와 주셨어. 오래된 스웨터로 만든 거야.

여: 재미있네. 네가 스스로 생각해 낸 아이디어야?

남: 실은 학교에 있는 Greenback Club에 가입했어. 오래된 것들을 다른 목적에 맞게 만드는 걸 배워.

여: 정말 멋진데. "다른 목적에 맞게 만든다"는 게 무슨 뜻이니?

남: 우리는 낡고, 사용 안 하는 것들을 가지고 네 핸드백처럼 새로운 물건을 만들어.

여: 흥미로운 클럽이다. 이 핸드백 만들기 어려워 보이는데.

남: 별로, 사실 우리 프로젝트 대부분이 정말 쉬워. 다음 모임에서 우리는 낡은 병을 가지고 음료수 잔을 만드는 걸 배울 거야.

여: 재미있겠다. 어떻게 그것들을 만들지?

남: 선생님이 다음 모임에서 우리에게 보여주실 거야. 너도 같이 가자.

여: ④ 나도 그러고 싶지만 난 손으로 만드는 것에 서툴러.

### 어휘

**come up with** 생각해내다, 떠올리다　　**repurpose** *v.* 다른 목적에 맞게 만들다　　**instructor** *n.* 강사, 교사　　〈문제〉 **woodworking** *n.* 목세공

### 정답 ④

### 문제풀이

남자는 여자에게 낡은 물건들을 리폼하는 클럽 활동의 흥미로운 프로젝트들을 이야기하면서 다음에 같이 가자고 제안한다. 이에 대한 여자의 응답으로 가장 적절한 것은 ④ '나도 그러고 싶지만 난 손으로 만드는 것에 서툴러.'이다.

### 오답 보기 해석

① 이 핸드백 얼마야?

② 낡은 물건들을 낭비해서는 안돼.

③ 난 핸드백 어떻게 만드는지 몰라.

⑤ 우리 미술 선생님은 취미로 목공예를 즐기셔.

### 총 어휘 수 166


## 15　상황에 적절한 말

**소재** 할아버지한테 선물 받은 셔츠를 동생에게 주기

### 듣기 대본 해석

남: Stella의 택배가 방금 도착했습니다. Stella가 자주 뵙지 못하는 할아버지로부터 온 것입니다. 포장을 열고 감동적인 편지를 읽고 나서 Stella는 할아버지께서 Taylor Swift 티셔츠를 보내주신 것을 보고 좋아합니다. 그러나 입어보니까 Stella는 셔츠가 좀 작다는 것을 알게 됩니다. 할아버지께 다시 보내 할아버지께 말씀드려서 더 큰 사이즈로 교환하는 것을 고려해 봅니다. 그러나 심사숙고 후 그녀는 할아버지께서 셔츠를 교환하고 다시 보내시는 게 쉬운 일이 아니라는 것을 깨닫습니다. 대신에 그녀는 여동생

Clara에게 셔츠를 줍니다. Clara도 Taylor Swift를 굉장히 좋아하고 선물에 대해 고마워하지만 Stella는 할아버지께서 자신이 여동생에게 그것을 준 것을 아시는 걸 원치 않습니다. 이러한 상황에서 Stella가 Clara에게 뭐라고 말할까요?

Stella: ③ 할아버지께 내가 너에게 이 셔츠 줬다고 말하지 마.

**어휘**

**touching** *a.* 감동적인　　**deliberation** *n.* 숙고, 신중함　　**grateful** *a.* 고마워하는, 감사하는

**정답** ③

**문제풀이**

할아버지께서 Stella에게 보내주신 티셔츠가 작아서 동생에게 주기로 했다. 그러나 할아버지께는 이 사실을 알리고 싶지 않으므로 Stella가 동생에게 할 말로 적절한 것은 ③ '할아버지께 내가 너에게 이 셔츠 줬다고 말하지 마.'이다.

**오답 보기 해석**

① 할아버지께 그의 선물이 마음에 안 든다고 말씀 드리지 마.
② 우리 조만간 할아버지 뵈러 가는 게 좋을 것 같아.
④ 이 셔츠 너무 작아. 할아버지께 다시 보내드려 줘.
⑤ 이 셔츠를 교환하러 할아버지를 가게에 모시고 가 줄래?

**총 어휘 수** 161


# 16 담화 목적 / 17 세부 내용 파악

**소재** 일상생활에서 돈을 절약하는 방법

**듣기 대본 해석**

여: 여러분 안녕하세요. 저는 Baker Financial에서 일하는 Mary Anne Baker입니다. 오늘 저는 여러분들에게 일상생활에서 돈을 절약할 수 있는 방법들에 관해 이야기하고 싶습니다. 우선 교통수단이 비쌀 수 있습니다. 만약 여러분들이 매일 택시를 타고 직장에 가는 습관이 있다면, 대신 버스나 지하철을 탐으로써 많은 돈을 절약할 수 있습니다. 좀 더 일찍 일어나도록 수면 패턴을 바꿔 보세요. 둘째, 상점의 평면도(배치)는 여러분들이 사려는 것을 극대화하기 위해 만들어졌습니다. 여러분들은 왜 달걀과 우유 같은 가장 필요한 일상 용품들이 가게의 뒤편에 배치되어 있는지 궁금해 한 적 있나요? 그것은 가게를 걸으면서 세일 중인 모든 다른 상품을 보게 하기 위해서 입니다. 이러한 전략들을 의식하고 충동 구매를 억제하세요. 셋째, 온라인 쇼핑을 이용하세요. 온라인 상에서 쇼핑을 하는 것이 여러분에게 가격을 매우 쉽게 비교할 수 있게 하고 최고의 거래를 찾을 수 있게 하므로 돈을 절약하게 해줍니다. 마지막으로 생수를 사지 않도록 노력하세요. 매일 1달러나 2달러를 쓰는 대신에 물 여과기에 투자를 하고 집을 떠나기 전에 병을 채우세요. 여러분들이 이러한 간단한 조언들을 따른다면, 저는 여러분들이 돈을 절약하고 좀 더 성취감을 주는 삶을 영위하리라고 확신합니다. 들어 주셔서 감사합니다.

**어휘**

**transportation** *n.* 수송 수단, 교통 기관　　**in the habit of** ~하는 버릇이 있는　　**floor plan** 평면도　　**resist** *v.* 저항하다, 반대하다 **impulse purchase** 충동 구매　　**take advantage of** ~을 이용하다 **fulfilling** *a.* 성취감을 주는

**정답** 16 ③　17 ⑤

**문제풀이**

16 여자는 일상생활에서 어떻게 하면 돈을 절약할 수 있는지를 말해주고 있으므로 여자가 하는 말의 목적은 ③ '돈을 절약하는 방법을 알려주려고'이다.

17 여자는 대중교통 이용, 상점 평면도 의식, 온라인 쇼핑 이용, 물 여과기 사용에 대해서는 언급했지만 ⑤ '가계부 작성'에 대해서는 언급하지 않았다.

**총 어휘 수** 219

## DICTATION ANSWERS

**01** Where is it going to be held

**02** at this time of day

**03** focused on the correlation between / conducted a creativity test / easily combine various ideas

**04** They're stacked to the ceiling / the more toys, the better / hinder a child's imagination / I guess that makes sense

**05** great shots on goal / couldn't pull off the win / They only lost by one goal / strengthen our defense

**06** put up a short description / a small scratch on the front bumper / I have factored that into

**07** who would give the graduation speeches / what they feel strongly about / you can handle the task / I'll do it

**08** I'm heading over to / signed up for summer camp / That's a shame / we're having a family reunion

**09** for professional or general purposes / I'm not into / they're currently on sale / ten percent off the sale price

**10** make it easy on you / weigh more than fifty kilograms / have you been sick lately / if you're donating blood

**11** with the actual tryouts taking place / submit a short biography / who will be permitted to join

**12** organize a party for / reserve the party room / spend more than two hundred dollars / suit your needs / I'll put you down for

**13** very dark in the parking lot / It helps us save on electricity / keep undesirable people away

**14** It's made of old sweaters / come up with the idea / out of old bottles

**15** trying it on / exchange it for a bigger size / offers the shirt to her younger sister / is grateful for the gift

**16-17** are in the habit of / take advantage of online shopping / avoid buying bottled water

# 13 수능영어듣기 실전모의고사

본문 p.80

| | | | | | |
|---|---|---|---|---|---|
| 01 ① | 02 ⑤ | 03 ③ | 04 ⑤ | 05 ③ | 06 ④ |
| 07 ④ | 08 ⑤ | 09 ④ | 10 ② | 11 ② | 12 ③ |
| 13 ① | 14 ③ | 15 ③ | 16 ③ | 17 ④ | |

## 01 짧은 대화의 응답

**소재** 호텔 객실 불만

**듣기 대본 해석**
여: 좋은 아침입니다. 손님. 무엇을 도와드릴까요?
남: 음. 제 방에 문제가 있는 것 같아요.
여: 알겠습니다. 정확히 무슨 문제이신가요?
남: ① 침대 매트리스가 너무 딱딱해서 불편해요.

**어휘**
〈문제〉 **stiff** *a.* 딱딱한　**connect** *v.* 연결하다

**정답** ①

**문제풀이**
남자가 호텔 객실에 문제가 있는 것 같다고 말하고 여자는 정확히 어떤 문제인지 물었으므로 남자는 ① '침대 매트리스가 너무 딱딱하고 불편해요.'라고 대답하는 것이 가장 적절하다.

**오답 보기 해석**
② 사실 저희는 이용 가능한 방이 없습니다.
③ 당신의 방 번호를 기억 못하겠어요.
④ 저는 305호와 연락하고 싶습니다.
⑤ 당신 짐을 저희에게 맡겨두세요.

**총 어휘 수** 33

## 02 짧은 대화의 응답

**소재** 친구를 위한 깜짝 마중

**듣기 대본 해석**
남: Julia. 소식 들었어? Owen이 다음 주에 홍콩에서 돌아올 거래.
여: 들었어. 거기서 그가 지낸 이야기를 듣고 싶어서 아주 흥분돼.
남: 그가 도착할 때 공항에 그를 만나러 가자.
여: ⑤ 좋은 생각이야. 그가 그 깜짝 마중을 좋아할 거라고 생각해.

**어휘**
〈문제〉 **appreciate** *v.* 고마워하다

**정답** ⑤

**문제풀이**
남자가 다음 주에 홍콩에서 돌아오는 친구를 마중 나가자고 제안했으므로 그에 적절한 여자의 대답은 ⑤ '좋은 생각이야. 그가 그 깜짝 마중을 좋아할 거라고 생각해.'이다.

**오답 보기 해석**
① 너 언제 떠날 거야?
② 맞아. 축제는 토요일이야.
③ 너무 고마워. 나 그것이 정말 기대돼.
④ 우리 서둘러야 해. 파티가 10분 안에 시작할 거야.

**총 어휘 수** 48

## 03 담화 목적

**소재** 지식의 공유

**듣기 대본 해석**
남: 안녕하십니까. 여러분! 저희 학교에 계속 많은 관심 가져 주셔서 감사합니다. 저희가 집중하고 있는 것 중 하나는 여러분의 자녀들이 책임감 있는 사회 구성원이 되도록 준비시키고 장려하는 것입니다. 이제 여러분 모두에게 저희의 의미 있는 새 프로그램 중 하나를 소개해드리고자 합니다. 여러분 중 대부분이 "아는 것이 힘이다."라는 속담을 아실 것입니다. 그러나 지식이 공유되지 않으면 지식을 가지는 것이 무슨 소용이 있을까요? 여러분 중에 몇몇 분들은 중요한 결정에 영향을 미칠 수 있는 분들입니다. 여러분들의 지식과 전문 기술을 저희 학생들과 공유하셨으면 합니다. 참여해서 저희와 공유하고 싶으시면 다음 주 수요일에 학교로 오시면 됩니다. 여러분이 아는 것을 조금만 나눈다면 학생들의 삶에 큰 변화를 만들 수 있습니다.

**어휘**
**meaningful** *a.* 의미 있는, 중요한　**saying** *n.* 격언, 속담　**influence** *v.* 영향을 주다　**crucial** *a.* 중요한　**expertise** *n.* 전문 지식

**정답** ③

**문제풀이**
전문 분야의 지식을 가진 학부모들이 그것을 학생들과 공유하도록 촉구하는 내용이므로 남자가 하는 말의 목적은 ③ '전문 분야의 지식을 공유하도록 요청하려고'이다.

**총 어휘 수** 131

## 04 대화 주제

**소재** 식료품 영양성분 표시제

**듣기 대본 해석**
여: 너 다이어트 중인 줄 알았는데. Roy.
남: 맞아. 왜 물어보니?
여: 음. 너 방금 치즈와 랜치드레싱을 곁들인 치킨샐러드를 주문했잖아. 만약 네가 다이어트 중이라면. 아시안 샐러드가 더 나은 선택일거야.
남: 정말? 뭐가 다른데?
여: 영양 정보를 봐.
남: 아. 알겠어. 치킨샐러드는 아시안 샐러드보다 칼로리가 더 많구나. 사실. 치킨샐러드는 치즈버거 콤보만큼 많은 칼로리를 갖고 있네.
여: 맞아. 그건 샐러드라 건강해 보일지 몰라도. 사실 기름투성이의 샌드위치만큼 나빠.
남: 알겠어. 그런 정보를 볼 수 있게 되어 있는 건 참 좋다. 그들은 모든 식료품에 영양 정보를 담아야 돼. 그렇게 하면 우리는 더 좋고. 더 건강한 선택을 할 수 있어.
여: 동의해. 몇몇 나라에서는 영양상의 표시가 모든 음식과 음료에 요구되고 있어.
남: 정말? 나는 몰랐어.
여: 응. 예를 들어. 미국에서는 고기에 자세한 정보를 포함해야 해. 그들은 심지어 지방 비율까지도 포함해야만 돼.
남: 나는 우리나라가 같은 정책을 채택했으면 좋겠어. 그것은 나 같은 사람들이 건강하게 먹는 것을 더 쉽게 만들어줄 거야.
여: 맞아. 구매자들은 서로 다른 상품들이 어떤 게 더 많은 지방. 칼로리. 나트륨을 포함되어 있는지 보고 비교할 수 있어.

**어휘**
**nutritional** *a.* 영양상의　**greasy** *a.* 기름투성이의　**adopt** *v.* 채택하다　**contained** *a.* 포함된　**sodium** *n.* 나트륨

**정답** ⑤

문제풀이
여자와 남자는 영양성분 표시로 구매자들이 더 쉽게 건강한 음식을 선택할 수 있다고 말하면서 음식의 영양 정보를 필수적으로 표시하는 정책을 받아들이길 바란다고 이야기하고 있다. 따라서 두 사람이 하는 대화의 주제는 ⑤ '식료품 영양성분 표시제의 필요성'이다.

**총 어휘 수** 207


## 05  대화자의 관계 파악

**소재**  학생과 선생님의 대화

**듣기 대본 해석**
남: Tomlin 선생님, 저에게 하실 말씀이 있다고 들었습니다.
여: 맞아. Alex. 들어와서 앉거라. 맹장 수술을 받았다고 막 들었어.
남: 몇 주 전에 수술을 받았어요. 갑작스러운 일이었어요.
여: 보통 꽤 갑작스럽게 그런 일이 일어나지. 지금은 괜찮니?
남: 이제 훨씬 나아졌어요. 그 일이 일어났을 때 약간 무서웠어요.
여: 네 체육 선생님께 그 일에 대해 말씀드렸니?
남: 네, 말씀드렸어요. 선생님께서 저에게 1~2주간 쉬라고 말씀하셨어요.
여: 네가 해결할 다른 문제는 없니?
남: 특별한 건 없어요. 수술 이후로 복부 쪽이 신경이 쓰여서요.
여: 그럴 만도 하지. 내가 생각하기에 그런 느낌은 곧 사라질 거야. 그런데 그 동안 안정을 취하고 편히 쉬어야 해.
남: 조언 주셔서 감사합니다. 당분간 저는 확실히 공부를 더 많이 하고 덜 놀아야겠어요.
여: 좋아, 아마도 그렇게 하는 게 좋을 거야. 곧 밖에서 놀 수 있게 될 거야. 걱정 마.
남: 감사합니다. 이제 교실로 가봐야겠어요.

**어휘**
**appendix** *n.* 맹장    **operation** *n.* 수술    **sudden** *a.* 갑작스러운
**P.E. teacher** 체육 선생님    **fade** *v.* ~이 사라지다
**in the meantime** 그 동안에    **take it easy** 안정을 취하다
**in no time** 당장에, 곧

**정답** ③

**문제풀이**
여자는 남자가 최근 맹장 수술을 받았다는 것을 듣고 남자를 불러서 상태가 어떤지 묻는 내용이다. 그리고 남자가 대화를 마치고 교실로 돌아가야겠다고 말했으므로 둘의 관계는 ③ '학생 — 보건 교사'임을 알 수 있다.

**총 어휘 수** 165


## 06  그림의 세부 내용 파악

**소재**  Soccer Hall of Fame 방문

**듣기 대본 해석**
남: Katie, 지난주에 Soccer Hall of Fame 갔었어?
여: 갔었어. 내가 거기서 찍은 이 사진을 봐.
남: 와! 정말 인상적인걸. 벽에 있는 저 포스터들이 흥미롭네. 왜 왼쪽에 있는 사람은 장갑을 끼고 다른 유니폼을 입고 있지?
여: 음, 골키퍼는 다른 선수들과 구별되도록 항상 다른 유니폼을 입고 있어.
남: 포스터에서 그 옆에 있는 선수는 누구야? 그는 아주 진지해 보여.
여: 그는 팀의 CF, 그러니까 센터 포워드인 Conor James야.
남: 스마트폰으로 셀카를 찍고 있는 저 남자는 누구야?
여: 우리 아빠셔. 아빠 본인을 찍는 것에 아주 신나셨어. 그의 뒤에는 유명한 감독의 동상이 있어.
남: 멋지다. 오른쪽에는 너의 남동생과 엄마임에 틀림없는 것 같아.
여: 맞아. 내 남동생이 화장실을 가야 했어. 그는 여행을 그다지 즐기지 않았어.
남: 음, 적어도 너희 아버지는 즐거운 시간을 보내신 것 같아.

**어휘**
**impressive** *a.* 인상적인    **tell A apart from B** A를 B로부터 구별하다
**statue** *n.* 조각상

**정답** ④

**문제풀이**
아빠 뒤에는 유명한 감독의 동상이 있다고 했는데 트로피가 있으므로 정답은 ④번이다.

**총 어휘 수** 165


## 07  할 일

**소재**  웹사이트 알려주기

**듣기 대본 해석**
여: 안녕 Aaron, 발표에 필요한 파일들 갖고 있어?
남: 응. 지금 플래시 드라이브 갖고 있으면, 내가 거기에 파일들을 전송해 줄 수 있어.
여: 나 하나 샀어. 자 여기 있어.
남: 이게 정말 플래시 드라이브야? 이거 좀 큰데, 그렇지 않아?
여: 응, 새 거야. 한쪽 끝에는 일반적인 USB 플러그가 있고, 다른 한쪽 끝에는 소형 USB 플러그가 있어.
남: 멋지다. 그러면 네가 꽤나 쉽게 파일들을 네 스마트폰에 전송할 수 있겠는걸.
여: 맞아. 근데 나도 이걸 처음 써 보는 거야.
남: 아주 잘 작동하는 것 같아. 모든 파일들을 엄청 빠르게 전송했어. 발표에 필요한 다른 건 없어?
여: 우리가 필요한 건 모두 있어. 내일 준비가 된 것 같아.
남: 알았어. 아, 그런데 그 플래시 드라이브 어디서 샀어? 나도 내 거 하나 사고 싶어서.
여: 온라인으로 샀어. 그 사이트 주소 적어 줄게.
남: 그럼 좋지. 고마워.

**어휘**
**handy** *a.* 유용한, 가까운 곳에 있는    **transfer** *v.* 옮기다, 이송하다

**정답** ④

**문제풀이**
남자는 여자의 성능 좋은 플래시 드라이브를 보고 자신도 같은 것을 구매하고 싶어 한다. 어디서 샀냐는 남자의 질문에 여자는 온라인에서 샀다며 그 사이트 주소를 적어주겠다고 하였으므로 여자가 남자를 위해 할 일은 ④ '사이트 주소 알려주기'이다.

**총 어휘 수** 169


## 08  이유

**소재**  독서 클럽에 못 가는 이유

**듣기 대본 해석**
남: Susan, 독서 클럽 모임이 내일이야. 책 다 읽었니?
여: 다 못 읽었어. 너는?
남: 나는 주말 동안에 다 읽었어. 책에서 손을 뗄 수가 없었지. 너무 매혹적이고 흥미진진했어. 나는 네가 진짜 결말을 즐길 거라고 생각해.
여: 내가 그것을 다 읽을 수 있을 거라 생각되지가 않아. 어제 기차에 두고 내린 것 같아.
남: 네가 괜찮다면 내 책 빌려 줄게.
여: 그렇게 해 주면 좋겠네. 모임이 내일 8시지, 그렇지?
남: 아니, 사실 이번 주는 6시에 시작해.
여: 진짜로? 그러면 나는 못 갈 것 같은데.
남: 왜 못 와? 페이지가 많지 않은 책이야. 그때까지 다 읽을 수 있을 거야.

여: 그게 아니야. 내일 우리 아들 영어 선생님과 만나기로 했거든.

남: 네 남편이 갈 수는 없니?

여: 그는 (기꺼이) 가려 하겠지만 이번 주 내내 늦게까지 일해야 해. 금요일에 중요한 발표가 있거든.

남: 알았어. 음, 내가 모든 사람들에게 너의 안부를 전할게.

여: 고마워.

**어휘**

**captivating** *a.* 매혹적인  **say hello** 안부를 전하다

**정답** ⑤

**문제풀이**

대화의 마지막 부분에서 여자는 아들의 영어 선생님과의 약속이 있어서 못 간다고 했으므로 정답은 ⑤ '아들의 영어 선생님과 만나야 해서'이다.

**총 어휘 수** 161


## 09  숫자

**소재**  기념품 가게에서 물건 구매하기

**듣기 대본 해석**

남: 기념품 가게에 오신 것을 환영합니다. 경기를 즐겁게 관람하셨기를 바랍니다.

여: 네. 마지막이 환상적이었어요!

남: 맞아요. 무엇을 도와드릴까요?

여: 기념품 좀 사려고요.

남: 기념품이 아주 많아요. 티셔츠, 저지, 모자, 범퍼 스티커도 있어요.

여: 저지는 얼마예요?

남: 음. 성인용 저지는 30달러이고 아동용 저지는 25달러예요.

여: 그렇군요. 그럼 성인용 두 개랑 아동용 두 개 주세요.

남: 알겠습니다. 다른 것 필요세요?

여: 모자도 사려고요. 얼마 정도 하나요?

남: 하나당 20달러예요.

여: 네. 모자 두 개 살게요.

남: 알겠습니다. 표 아직도 갖고 계시면 추가로 10퍼센트 할인해 드려요.

여: 네, 여기 있어요.

남: 그럼. 성인용 저지 두 개, 아동용 저지 두 개, 모자 두 개 합한 금액에서 10퍼센트 할인해 드리면 되는 거죠.

여: 맞아요. 여기 카드요.

**어휘**

**souvenir** *n.* 기념품  **jersey** *n.* 저지, (운동 경기용) 셔츠  **bumper** *n.* 자동차 범퍼  **apiece** *ad.* 각각, 하나에  **stub** *n.* (표 등에서 한 쪽을 떼어 주고) 남은 부분, 토막  **additional** *a.* 추가의

**정답** ④

**문제풀이**

성인용 저지 두 개 60달러, 아동용 저지 두 개 50달러, 모자 두 개에 40달러이므로 60+50+40=150달러인데 총 금액에서 10퍼센트를 할인해준다고 했으므로 정답은 ④ '$135'이다.

**총 어휘 수** 147


## 10  언급 유무

**소재**  컴퓨터 회사에서 실시하는 여름 인턴 프로그램

**듣기 대본 해석**

여: 안녕. 너 Pear Computers에서 여름 인턴 프로그램 등록 받기 시작한 것 봤어?

남: 정말? 거기에서 인턴을 구하는 건 몰랐어.

여: 응. 네가 컴퓨터 공학을 공부하고 싶어 하니까 관심 있을 거라고 생각했어. 너한테 좋은 기회가 될 거야.

남: 물론이지. 인턴이 뭐 해야 하는지 알아?

여: 그 회사에 있는 실험실에서 일하게 될 거야. 그럼 California에서 여름을 보내게 되는 거지.

남: 멋지다. 나를 받아줄 것 같아?

여: 그럴 것 같아. 너 컴퓨터로 일해본 경험이 많잖아. 그러니까 너는 적절한 자격을 가지고 있는 거지.

남: 좋은데! 인턴십은 얼마나 오랫동안 하는데?

여: 2달 프로그램이라고 하던데.

남: 좋다. 이번 인턴십으로 돈을 받지는 않겠지?

여: 응. 네가 모든 생활비와 여행 경비 또한 내야 할 거야.

남: 음. 그게 문제구나. 어쨌든 난 흥미가 있어. 집에 가면 바로 등록할게.

**어휘**

**registration** *n.* 등록  **awesome** *a.* 멋진, 근사한  **qualification** *n.* 자격  **living expenses** 생활비  **drawback** *n.* 문제점, 결점

**정답** ②

**문제풀이**

두 사람은 인턴 프로그램의 근무 장소, 지원 자격, 근무 기간, 경비 지급에 관한 언급은 했지만 ② '지원 기한'에 관한 언급은 하지 않았다.

**총 어휘 수** 158


## 11  내용 일치 · 불일치

**소재**  사진대회 출품 안내

**듣기 대본 해석**

여: 학생 여러분 안녕하세요. Environmental Edge Photography Contest에 관하여 말할 시간을 좀 가지고 싶어요. 이 대회는 매년 개최되고 전국에 있는 모든 학생들이 참여하도록 장려합니다. 올해 대회의 주제는 환경적인 인식입니다. 사진 출품작은 환경 문제를 강조할 수 있는 사진이어야 합니다. 사진은 풀 컬러여야 하며, 가로 방향 포맷이어야 합니다. 모든 출품작은 Lopez 선생님에게 5월 15일전에 제출되어야 합니다. 이메일 출품작은 받지 않습니다. Environmental Edge는 6월 1일 대회의 우승자를 발표할 것입니다. 전국에서 가장 훌륭한 세 편의 사진 작품을 (선정하여) 시상할 것입니다. 우리 학교에는 많은 재능을 가진 학생들이 있다는 것을 알고 있기에 여러분의 많은 참여를 장려합니다. 더 많은 정보는 학교 홈페이지에서 찾을 수가 있습니다. 경청해 주셔서 감사합니다.

**어휘**

**take place** 개최되다, 일어나다  **entry** *n.* 출품작  **make an attempt** 시도하다  **landscape orientation** 가로 방향 포맷  **announce** *v.* 발표하다, 알리다  **talent** *n.* 재주, 재능있는 사람

**정답** ②

**문제풀이**

여자는 출품사진은 모두 컬러여야 한다고 했으므로 일치하지 않는 것은 ② '컬러 또는 흑백사진으로 제출 가능하다.'이다.

**총 어휘 수** 129


## 12  도표

**소재**  냉장고 구매하기

**듣기 대본 해석**

남: 여보, 이 전단지 좀 봐요. 이번 주에 냉장고 파격 할인 행사가 있네요.

여: 정말요? 우리 새 거 필요한데 잘 됐네요.

남: 전단지에 몇 가지 모델이 있어요. 돈은 얼마 정도 쓸 수 있다고 생각해요?

여: 글쎄요. 1,000달러 이상 쓰길 원하진 않아요.

남: 알겠어요. 그럼 이 모델들은 어때요?

여: 음... 저장 공간이 적어도 700리터인 거면 좋겠어요.
남: 나도 그렇게 생각해요. 700리터 이상이면 좋겠군요. 그럼 우리가 갖고
    있는 음식들이 쉽게 들어가겠죠. 문이 두 개인 거랑 네 개인 것 중에 어느
    걸 할까요?
여: 문이 두 개인 건 싫어요. 네 개짜리 문이 있는 냉장고가 물건들을 정리하기
    쉬운 듯 해서요.
남: 그럼 우리가 고를 수 있는 모델이 두 개 남네요.
여: 오, 보증기간도 꽤 중요해요. 특히 가전제품은요.
남: 알았어요. 그럼 보증기간이 더 긴 걸로 사죠.
여: 좋았어요!

### 어휘
**flyer** *n.* 전단지  **storage** *n.* 저장, 보관  **appliance** *n.* (가정용) 기기
**warranty** *n.* 보증기간, 품질 보증서

### 정답 ③

### 문제풀이
남자와 여자는 1,000달러가 넘지 않으면서, 저장 공간은 700리터 이상,
문이 네 개, 더 긴 보증기간을 제공하는 냉장고를 선택하였으므로 두 사람이
구매할 냉장고 모델은 ③번이다.

### 총 어휘 수 142


## 13  긴 대화의 응답

**소재** 자신의 버전으로 결말 써보기

### 듣기 대본 해석
남: Rachel, The Babbit 다 봤니?
여: 네, 아빠. 다 봤어요. 왜 저보고 보라고 하신 거예요?
남: 재미있지 않았어?
여: 괜찮았어요. 저한텐 너무 행복하게 끝나는 할리우드식 결말이긴 했지만요.
남: 책과는 꽤 다르지?
여: 네. 책은 굉장히 어둡고 우울하게 만드는 결말이었잖아요. 영화도 똑같을
    줄 알았어요.
남: 나도 그렇게 생각했어. 그래서 책이 더 나아, 아니면 영화가 더 나아?
여: 둘 다 별로예요. 원작은 너무 어둡고 영화는 너무 비현실적이고 밝기만 해요.
남: 그럼 무엇을 히면 이야기가 더 좋아질까?
여: 전반적으로 좀 더 밝으면서도 너무 비현실적이지 않으면 좋을 것 같아요.
남: 그럼 너의 비전으로 씨보는 게 좋겠어.
여: 무슨 말씀이세요? 이야기를 재구성해서 쓰라는 거예요?
남: ① 물론이지. 나는 네 버전으로 쓴 이야기를 읽고 싶구나.

### 어휘
**depressing** *a.* 우울하게 만드는   **care for** ~를 좋아하다
**unrealistic** *a.* 비현실적인   〈문제〉**review** *n.* 논평, 평가

### 정답 ①

### 문제풀이
책의 결말은 너무 어둡고 영화는 비현실적으로 밝다고 말하는 여자에게 남자는
자신의 버전으로 이야기를 써보라고 권하고 있는 상황이다. 이야기를 재구성
해보라는 의미인지 되묻는 여자에게 해줄 적절한 응답은 ① '물론이지. 나는
네 버전으로 쓴 이야기를 읽고 싶구나.'이다.

### 오답 보기 해석
② 주제를 생각하지 마. 내용에 초점을 맞추렴.
③ 너는 정말 원작 읽기를 즐길 것 같구나.
④ 나는 작가의 허락이 먼저 필요할 거야.
⑤ 아니, 끝난 후에 너는 논평을 써야 해.

### 총 어휘 수 151


## 14  긴 대화의 응답

**소재** 건조한 방에 대나무 들여 놓기

### 듣기 대본 해석
여: Lenny, 무슨 일이야?
남: 안녕, Sam. 괜찮아? 너 꽤 피곤해 보여.
여: 괜찮아. 근데 지난 몇 주간 잠을 잘 못 자겠더라고. 날씨 때문에 내 방 공기가
    너무 건조하거든.
남: 그렇구나. 그럼 네가 가습기를 사면 되잖아. 그리고 식물을 방에 두면 공기가
    좀 습해진다고 들었어.
여: 내가 좀 무책임해서 그 식물들에게 물 주는 걸 깜박하고 다 시들어 죽을
    거야.
남: 뭐, 그렇게 많은 관심을 안 줘도 되는 식물들도 있어. 그런 걸 키우면 되잖아.
여: 정말? 어떤 게 있는데?
남: 대나무를 물통에 넣으면 알아서 자랄 거야.
여: 아주 쉬워 보이는데.
남: 응. 나도 방에 대나무 몇 개 키우는데 물은 보통 한 달에 한 번, 통이 비어
    있을 때 물을 주면 돼.
여: 대나무는 생김새도 마음에 들어.
남: 대나무가 네 방 공기를 좀 습하게 만들 것 같아. 한번 해봐.
여: ③ 오늘 꽃집에 가서 좀 사놓아야겠다.

### 어휘
**humidifier** *n.* 가습기   **humid** *a.* 습한   **irresponsible** *a.* 무책임한
**water** *v.* (화초 등에) 물을 주다   **wither** *v.* 시들다   **attention** *n.*
관심, 집중   **bamboo** *n.* 대나무

### 정답 ③

### 문제풀이
남자는 여자에게 건조한 방에 대나무를 놓을 것을 제안하고 있으므로 이에 대한
여자의 응답으로 가장 적절한 것은 ③ '오늘 꽃집에 가서 좀 사놓아야겠다.'이다.

### 오답 보기 해석
① 병원에 가봐야겠다.
② 우리 바깥에 대나무 좀 심어야겠어.
④ 매일 대나무에 물을 줘야 해.
⑤ 매일 8잔씩 물을 마셔야 해.

### 총 어휘 수 175


## 15  상황에 적절한 말

**소재** 과제 중 끊긴 인터넷에 대한 수리 요청

### 듣기 대본 해석
남: Paul은 역사 수업의 중요한 과제를 하고 있습니다. 하지만 컴퓨터로 조사를
    하는 와중에 인터넷이 나갔습니다. 그는 인터넷을 제공하는 회사의 고객센터에
    문제를 알리려고 전화를 겁니다. 늦은 시간인데다 고객 서비스 직원이 없어
    대기 중입니다. 15분간의 대기 후에 상담원과 연결이 되었고, 상담원은
    Paul에게 모뎀을 뽑았다가 다시 꽂아보라고 말합니다. 그는 상담원의 지시를
    따랐지만 문제를 해결하지는 못했습니다. 그는 과제가 내일까지이므로
    반드시 인터넷이 고쳐져야 합니다. 이런 상황에서 Paul이 고객센터 상담원에게
    할 말로 가장 적절한 것은 무엇일까요?
Paul: ③ 최대한 빨리 인터넷을 손볼 사람을 보내주세요.

### 어휘
**go out** (불 등이) 꺼지다, 나가다   **customer service representative**
고객 서비스 상담원   **instruction** *n.* 설명, 지시   **desperately** *ad.*
필사적으로, 몹시

### 정답 ③

Paul은 기한이 내일까지인 역사 과제를 하던 중 인터넷이 끊겨 과제를 할 수 없는 처지에 놓여 있다. 이런 상황에서 그가 인터넷 서비스 제공업체의 고객 서비스 상담원에게 할 말로 가장 적절한 것은 ③ '최대한 빨리 인터넷을 손볼 사람을 보내주세요.'이다.

**오답 보기 해석**
① 문제가 해결되었어요. 도와주셔서 감사해요.
② 감사합니다만, 전 이미 (인터넷을 제공하는) 인터넷서비스 회사가 있어요.
④ 제가 어떻게 하면 고객 서비스 상담원이 될 수 있는지 알고 싶어요.
⑤ 문제가 생겨서 유감입니다. 문제를 살펴볼 사람을 보내겠습니다.

**총 어휘 수** 127

## 16 담화 주제 / 17 세부 내용 파악

**소재** 야외 활동이 아동에게 좋은 점들

**듣기 대본 해석**
남: 학부모 여러분 안녕하세요. 아이들의 건강에 대한 세미나에 오신 것을 환영합니다. 제 이름은 Dr. Jeffrey Day이고요 저는 거의 30년 동안 소아과 의사를 해 왔습니다. 우선 3세에서 12세 사이의 어린이들에 대해서 얘기를 해보도록 합시다. 이 나이대가 어린이들의 성장에 굉장히 중대한 시기입니다. 이 시기에 아이들은 자신감을 키우고, 더 활동적이게 되고, 문제해결 능력을 키우고, 평생 동안 갖고 갈 건강한 습관들을 확립하는 시기입니다. 이 때문에 저는 모든 부모가 자녀에게 최대한 많이 나가 놀도록 권고할 것을 추천합니다. 나가 노는 것은 놀라운 이점들을 갖고 있습니다. 아이들은 새로운 친구를 만날 기회를 갖게 되고 평생 갈 소꿉친구를 만들 수 있습니다. 그들은 또한 모험을 하고 야외 놀이를 함으로써 자신감도 키울 것입니다. 밖에서 노는 것이 항상 안전한 것은 아니지만, 아이가 위험을 감수하고 모험적인 행동을 하려는 의지를 키우는 것은 아이에게 새로운 능력들을 배우고 자신의 잠재력을 끝까지 끌어올릴 수 있는 기회를 줍니다. 마지막으로 나가 노는 것은 건강한 성장에 필수적인 비타민 D를 아이들에게 제공해 줍니다. 이 비타민은 아이들이 우울증, 심장병, 당뇨병 그리고 비만과 싸우는 데에 도움을 줍니다. 그래서 저는 학부모 여러분에게 아이들이 바깥에 나가 놀 수 있게 하기를 부탁드립니다. 이는 여러분에게도 도움이 될 것입니다.

**어휘**
**pediatrician** *n.* 소아과 의사    **critical** *a.* 중대한, 중요한
**development** *n.* 발달, 성장    **confidence** *n.* 자신감
**establish** *v.* 세우다, 확립하다    **willingness** *n.* 기꺼이 하는 마음, 의지
**potential** *n.* 잠재력    **depression** *n.* 우울증    **obesity** *n.* 비만

**정답 16 ③ 17 ④**

**문제풀이**
16 남자는 3세 ~ 12세의 아동들에게 가능한 한 많이 바깥에서 노는 것을 권하면서 어떠한 점이 좋은지에 대해 '새로운 친구 사귀기, 자신감과 위험을 무릅쓰려는 자세 기르기, 비타민 D공급 등'을 이야기 하고 있으므로 남자가 하는 말의 주제로 가장 적절한 것은 ③ '아이들에게 야외에서 노는 것의 장점'이다.

17 우울증(depression), 심장병(heart disease), 당뇨병(diabetes), 비만(obesity)에 비타민 D가 좋다고 언급되었지만 '피부병'은 언급되지 않았으므로 정답은 ④번이다.

**오답 보기 해석**
16
① 어린이의 건강관리에 있어 부모의 역할
② 아동기 습관의 지속적인 영향
④ 친밀한 부모–자식 관계의 중요성
⑤ 아이들이 기꺼이 모험을 해보려는 마음을 발달시킬 수 있는 활동들

**총 어휘 수** 216

## DICTATION ANSWERS

01 there seems to be a problem with

02 coming back from

03 to be responsible members of the community / influence crucial decisions / share your knowledge and expertise with our students

04 you were on a diet / They should put nutritional information / nutrition labels are required / Shoppers would be able to compare different products

05 I had the operation / I take it easy / that feeling will fade soon

06 It looks really impressive / you can tell him apart from / take a picture of himself

07 the files for the presentation / transfer things to your smartphone / write down the web address

08 captivating and exciting / I'll get a chance to finish it / to be able to make it / he has to work late

09 I hope you enjoyed the game / I'm looking to buy some souvenirs / I'll take two for adults / get an additional ten percent off

10 what the interns' duties are / experienced in working with computers / I won't get paid for / pay for all living expenses

11 This contest takes place every year / make an attempt to / Photos should be in full color / Email entries will not be accepted / on the school's website

12 spend more than one thousand dollars / More than seven hundred liters / organize stuff / get the one with a longer warranty

13 dark and depressing ending / didn't care for either of them / write your own version / rewrite the story

14 make the air more humid / they'll wither and die / it'll grow on its own / the air in your room more humid

15 is put on hold / a representative gets on the line / desperately needs to

16-17 children build their confidence / establish healthy habits / play outside as much as possible / reach their full potential

| 01 ⑤ | 02 ⑤ | 03 ③ | 04 ① | 05 ④ | 06 ⑤ |
| 07 ④ | 08 ③ | 09 ⑤ | 10 ② | 11 ③ | 12 ② |
| 13 ② | 14 ① | 15 ② | 16 ② | 17 ⑤ | |

## 01 짧은 대화의 응답

**소재** 과다한 전기요금

**듣기 대본 해석**
남: 우왜! 이번 달 전기요금 청구서 좀 봐. 거의 500달러야.
여: 왜! 너무 비싸다. 전기회사에 전화해 볼게. 분명 실수가 있었을 거야.
남: 그 사람들이 실수한 것 같진 않아. 이번 여름에 우리가 에어컨을 많이 튼 것 알잖아.
여: ⑤ 맞아. 우리가 집을 나설 때 그걸 꺼야겠어.

**어휘**
**bill** *n.* 청구서    **doubt** *v.* 확신하지 못하다, 의심하다
〈문제〉 **appliance** *n.* (가정용) 기기

**정답** ⑤

**문제풀이**
여자는 전기회사에서 실수한 것 같다고 했는데, 남자는 여름에 에어컨을 많이 켰다고 말하고 있으므로 적절한 여자의 응답은 ⑤ '맞아. 우리가 집을 나설 때 그걸 꺼야겠어.'이다.

**오답 보기 해석**
① 전기회사에 전화해서 청구서에 대해서 물어볼게.
② 내가 수리하시는 분에게 우리 에어컨을 봐달라고 부탁할게.
③ 물론. 안이 더울 때는 에어컨을 켜.
④ 네가 가전제품을 사용할 때 플러그를 뽑아선 안 돼.

**총 어휘 수** 58

## 02 짧은 대화의 응답

**소재** 책에 대한 대화

**듣기 대본 해석**
여: Liam, 뭐하고 있니? 뭔가에 매우 몰두한 것처럼 보이는데.
남: Yann Martel의 Life of Pi 읽는 중이야. 너무 재미있어서 멈출 수가 없네.
여: 영화 먼저 봤어? 좋은 영화야.
남: ⑤ 아니야. 일단 이 책을 다 읽으면, 영화를 볼 거야.

**어휘**
**immersed in** ~에 깊이 빠진, 몰두한

**정답** ⑤

**문제풀이**
Life of Pi라는 책을 읽고 있는 남자에게 여자가 영화를 먼저 봤냐고 물었다. 이에 적절한 대답은 ⑤ '아니야. 일단 이 책을 다 읽으면, 영화를 볼 거야.'이다.

**오답 보기 해석**
① 동의해. 온라인으로 그 책 주문하자.
② 알아. 그게 그 책이 읽기 쉬운 이유지.
③ 도서관에 가서 그 책을 대출하자.
④ 내 영화 DVD를 빌려줄게. 무척 재미있어.

**총 어휘 수** 48

## 03 담화 주제

**소재** 인간관계에서의 유사성

**듣기 대본 해석**
여: 안녕하세요 여러분. 저번 시간에 관계를 만들고 유지하는 것의 중요성과 그것이 우리의 성공에 어떤 영향을 미치는지에 대해서 토론했습니다. 오늘 수업에서는 '유유상종(같은 무리끼리 서로 사귐)'이란 옛말에 있는 진실에 대해 이야기할 겁니다. 인간으로서, 우리는 비슷한 사람들끼리 모이는 경향이 있습니다. 대부분의 사람들은 자신과 같은 나이, 인종, 그리고 성별을 가진 사람과 친구를 합니다. 학우들을 예로 들어볼게요. 여러분은 여러분 자신과 비슷한 특징을 가진 학우들과 친해지기 마련입니다. 이러한 특징들에는 관심사와 취미들이 포함됩니다. 물론 모두가 그런 것은 아닙니다. 어떤 사람들은 자신과 다른 인종의 사람과 연애하거나 결혼도 합니다. 그러나 이런 관계들은 일반적으로 공통된 가치관이나 교육으로부터 형성됩니다.

**어휘**
**maintain** *v.* 유지하다    **birds of a feather flock together** 유유상종
**be likely to** ~할 것 같다    **across the board** 전체에 걸쳐, 전체에 미치는    **typically** *ad.* 보통, 일반적으로    **value** *n.* 가치, 가치관

**정답** ③

**문제풀이**
사람들은 유사성을 토대로 서로 관계를 맺어간다는 것을 이야기하고 있으므로 여자가 하는 말의 주제는 ③ '인간관계에 유사성이 미치는 영향'이다.

**총 어휘 수** 128

## 04 의견

**소재** 회전문 설치

**듣기 대본 해석**
남: Sarah, 무슨 일 있어요? 괜찮아요?
여: 두통이 있고 코가 막혔어요. 아픈 것 같아요.
남: 더 따뜻한 옷을 입어야 되겠어요.
여: 맞아요. 그래야 할 것 같아요. 여기 꽤 추워지네요.
남: 이해해요. 저도 전에 프런트 데스크에서 일했었어요. 전 항상 추위가 싫었어요.
여: 네. 사람들이 건물에 들어올 때 차가운 공기가 사람들을 따라 들어와요.
남: 아마 문을 바꾸면 찬 공기가 들어오는 것을 막을 수 있을 거예요.
여: 제 생각엔 새로운 문이 필요하진 않을 것 같아요. 추가적인 난방기를 사는 게 더 낫지 않겠어요?
남: 아니요, 새로운 문이 더 효율적일 거예요. 회전문을 설치하면 건물로 들어오는 차가운 공기를 많이 줄일 수 있을 거예요.
여: 정말요? 어떻게 그게 돼요?
남: 공기가 문에 갇혀서 문이 돌기 때문에 안으로 들어올 수가 없어요.
여: 그거 좋겠네요! 효과가 있으면 좋겠어요.

**어휘**
**stuffy nose** 코막힘    **effective** *a.* 효과적인    **revolving door** 회전문    **reduce** *v.* 줄이다, 낮추다    **trap** *v.* 가두다

**정답** ①

**문제풀이**
남자는 외부의 찬 공기가 들어오는 것을 막기 위해 회전문을 설치해야 한다고 말하고 있으므로 남자의 의견으로 가장 적절한 것은 ① '출입문을 회전문으로 바꿔야 한다.'이다.

**총 어휘 수** 151

## 05 장소 파악

**소재** 간단한 아침식사 제안

**듣기 대본 해석**
남: Delgado 선생님, 다시 오신 것을 환영합니다.

여: 초대해주셔서 감사합니다. 저도 여기에 오게 되어 기뻐요.
남: 좋습니다. 프로그램을 시작해 보죠. 먼저, 관객분들에게 건강에 관한 간단한
    조언 부탁드립니다.
여: 물론이죠. 요즘에는 모든 사람들이 정신 없이 바쁘죠. 그것은 여러분의
    건강에 나쁠 수 있습니다.
남: 맞습니다. 그러면 늘 바쁜 사람이 건강하게 지내기 위해서는 무엇을 할 수
    있을까요?
여: 좋은 아침식사가 건강 유지의 핵심입니다. 아침은 다른 끼니보다 거르기 쉽죠.
    누구도 아침을 만들 시간이 없어요. 그러나 몇 가지 기본 재료들만 있다면
    당신은 적절한 아침을 드실 수 있을 겁니다.
남: 어떤 종류의 재료에 관해 이야기할까요?
여: 단백질 쉐이크로 하루를 시작하는 것은 정말 좋은 방법입니다. 필요한 것은
    단백질 파우더와 우유뿐이지요.
남: 과일이나 다른 재료는 어떤가요?
여: 좋은 의견이네요. 쉐이크를 좀 더 맛있게 하기 위해 바나나 혹은 딸기 등의
    과일을 첨가할 수 있습니다. 제 것에는 영양가를 위해 시금치를 넣는 것을
    좋아합니다.
남: 쉐이크 속에 시금치요? 맛있게 들리진 않는데요. 영양이 중요한 점이네요,
    그렇지요? 감사합니다. Delgado 선생님. 잠시 광고 시간 후 돌아오겠습니다.

어휘
**be on the go** 정신 없이 바쁘다    **decent** *a.* 괜찮은, 제대로 된
**ingredient** *n.* 재료, 성분    **spinach** *n.* 시금치    **nutritional value**
영양가

정답 ④

문제풀이
대화의 시작 부분에서 프로그램을 시작하기 전에 청중들에게 말하라고 했고,
광고 시간 후 돌아온다고 한 것으로 보아 두 사람이 대화하고 있는 장소는
④ 'TV 스튜디오'임을 추측할 수 있다.

오답 보기 해석
① 병원        ② 식당        ③ 교실        ⑤ 식료품점

총 어휘 수 192


## 06   그림의 세부 내용 파악

소재 FPS World Championship 포스터

듣기 대본 해석
여: Ryan. 나 방금 FPS World Championship의 포스터를 끝냈어. 어떤
    것 같아?
남: 너 정말 잘했구나! 난 네가 위에 있는 제목을 꾸민 게 맘에 들어. 배너 같아
    보여.
여: 고마워. 그리고 시간과 날짜를 왼쪽에 놓았어.
남: 봤어. 우리 날짜와 시간에 대해 확인을 받은 거야?
여: 받았어. 게임 협회가 오늘 아침에 확인해 줬어.
남: 좋아. 그럼 우리한테 준비할 시간이 많겠구나. 아래에 장소를 표시한 박스는
    빈칸으로 둔 게 보여.
여: 그래. 우리가 스타디움에서 이벤트를 하도록 허가증을 받으려고 계속
    노력 중이라 아직 정확하게 정해지지 않았어. 오른쪽에 너랑 Jason의
    사진은 어때?
남: 내가 제일 잘 나온 사진은 아니지만, 네가 그것을 같이 놓은 것은 좋아.
여: (웃음)
남: 나는 아래쪽에 마스코트인 공룡 그림도 좋아. 그게 뭐라고 말하고 있어?
여: 그것은 "음식과 음료 제공!"이라고 말해.

어휘
**outdo** *v.* 능가하다    **confirmation** *n.* 확인    **association** *n.* 협회
**confirm** *v.* 확인해 주다    **blank** *a.* 빈    **permit** *n.* 허가증    *v.* 허락하다,
허용하다

정답 ⑤

문제풀이
아래쪽에 공룡 마스코트가 말하고 있다고 했는데 여자 안내원이 말하고 있으므로
정답은 ⑤번이다.

총 어휘 수 158


## 07   할 일

소재 학교에 셔츠 갖다 주기

듣기 대본 해석
*[전화벨이 울린다.]*
여: 여보세요?
남: 아, 엄마. 집에 계셔서 다행이에요. 도움이 필요한 일이 있어요.
여: 무슨 일이니, Andrew?
남: 오늘 밤에 큰 야구경기가 있는 것 알고 계시리라 생각해요.
여: 물론이지. 아빠랑 내가 보러 가기로 했잖아.
남: 좋아요, 그런데 제가 오늘 아침에 집에서 제 셔츠를 깜빡했어요.
여: 오, Andrew. 너는 왜 그렇게 잘 잊어버리니? 학교 끝나고 그걸 가지러
    올 시간이 있니?
남: 없어요. 수업 후에 경기 전 저녁식사를 하고 바로 필드로 가야 해요.
여: 집에 잠깐 들러서 그걸 너한테 갖다 줄 사람은 없니?
남: 제가 알기론 없어요. 금요일 하교 후엔 모두 꽤 바빠요. 엄마가 학교에 갖다
    주실 수 있을까요?
여: 그래. 내가 할 수 있을 것 같구나.
남: 너무 감사해요, 엄마.
여: 천만에, 얘야. 곧 보자.

어휘
**forgetful** *a.* 잘 잊어 먹는, 건망증이 있는    **swing by** 잠깐 들르다

정답 ④

문제풀이
남자는 오늘 큰 야구경기가 있는데 경기 때 입을 셔츠를 집에 두고 와서 엄마에게
갖다 줄 것을 부탁했고 엄마는 그렇게 하겠다고 했으므로 여자가 남자를 위해
할 일은 ④ '학교로 셔츠 가져다 주기'이다.

총 어휘 수 145


## 08   이유

소재 화가 난 이유

듣기 대본 해석
여: Daniel. 너 화나 보인다. 무슨 일이야?
남: 신경 쓰지마. 별거 아냐. 조금 피곤할 뿐이야.
여: 어서. 마음에 있는 것을 말해봐. 그럼 한결 나을 거야.
남: 음. Jeremy와 Jane, Selena, 그리고 나는 오늘 아침 영어 수업 발표
    준비를 위해 만나기로 되어 있었어.
여: 그래, 맞아. 우리 조는 발표 파트를 나누기 위해 어제 모였어.
남: 우리도 발표를 나누고 그에 대한 자료를 수집하기로 되어있었어.
여: 그래서, 그 회의에서 무슨 일이 있었어?
남: Jeremy랑 Selena가 나타나지 않았어.
여: 와, 음, 아마도 그들도 나름의 이유가 있을 거야.
남: 아니. 둘 다 그냥 회의를 까먹었다고 말했어. 나는 화가 나. 어떻게 그들은
    이렇게 무책임할 수 있지?
여: 음. 진정해. 발표를 준비할 시간은 아직 많잖아. 그들은 분명히 미안해하고
    있을 거야.
남: 글쎄. 잘 모르겠어. 어쨌든 난 집에 가서 좀 쉬어야겠어.

어휘
**presentation** *n.* 발표    **divide** *v.* 나누다    **collect** *v.* 수집하다, 모으다
**material** *n.* 자료    **show up** 나타나다    **irresponsible** *a.* 책임감 없는

정답 ③

**문제풀이**

남자는 같이 발표 준비를 해야 하는 조원인 Jeremy와 Selena가 회의에 나오지 않아 화가 났으므로 정답은 ③ '조원들이 모임에 나오지 않아서'이다.

**총 어휘 수** 149


# 09 숫자

**소재** 캠핑장 예약

**듣기 대본 해석**

[전화벨이 울린다.]

남: Walker Mountain 캠핑장입니다. 오늘은 무엇을 도와드릴까요?

여: 안녕하세요. 다음 달 방학 동안에 우리 가족이 당신의 캠핑장에 갈 예정입니다. 하룻밤에 얼마죠?

남: 차량 한 대를 위한 자리를 포함해서 35달러입니다.

여: 음, 차량 두 대로 갈 예정이에요.

남: 그러한 경우에는 하룻밤에 10달러가 추가됩니다.

남: 알았어요. 8월 14일과 15일 이틀 밤을 예약하고 싶어요. 제 이름은 Minnie Martin이에요.

남: 알겠습니다. Martin 부인. 제가 도와드릴 다른 게 있나요?

여: 오, 야영장에서 물과 전기를 제공하나요?

남: 네, 제공합니다. 그러나, 물과 전기에 추가적인 비용을 청구합니다. 물이 나오는 야영지는 하룻밤에 5달러를 추가해야 하고 전기가 연결된 야영지는 하룻밤에 10달러를 추가해야 합니다.

여: 알겠어요. 물은 필요하지 않을 것 같은데 전기는 연결해주세요.

남: 네, 전기가 들어오는 자동차 2대용 캠프장 2일. 예약되었습니다. 다음 달에 뵙겠습니다.

**어휘**

**nightly** *a.* 야간의　**vehicle** *n.* 차량　**spot** *n.* 곳, 자리
**additional** *a.* 추가의　**reservation** *n.* 예약　**electricity** *n.* 전기
**campsite** *n.* 야영지　**hookup** *n.* 접속, 연결

정답 ⑤

**문제풀이**

차량 한 대를 포함한 자리는 하루에 35달러이고 차가 추가로 한 대 더 있으므로 10달러가 추가되어 하루에 45달러인데 이틀이므로 90달러이다. 그리고 전기가 있는 야영지는 하루에 10달러가 추가되므로 이틀에 20달러가 추가된다. 따라서 여자가 지불할 금액은 (35+10)x2+20=110달러이므로 정답은 ⑤ '$110'이다.

**총 어휘 수** 157


# 10 언급 유무

**소재** 게임 회사 인턴

**듣기 대본 해석**

여: Johnny, 너 내 이메일 받았어?

남: 아직 확인 안 했는데. 무엇에 관한 건데?

여: RD Games에서의 여름 인턴사원 근무 프로그램에 관한 거야.

남: 멋진데. 그들은 멋진 게임을 몇 개 만들었지.

여: 맞아. 그들은 Counterclockwise와 Super Doctor Brothers를 출시했어

남: 그래, 나는 그 게임들을 좋아해.

여: 그래 멋있지. 어째든 프로그래밍, 캐릭터 디자인, 베타 테스팅에 관한 인턴직에 자리가 났어.

남: 잘됐다! 나는 프로그래밍에 대해서 조금 알지만, 캐릭터 디자인을 한번 해보고 싶어. 지원 자격이 어떻게 되니?

여: 음. 그들은 몇 개의 게임 디자인 수업을 들었고, 재미있고 흥미로운 게임을 만드는 것에 대한 애정을 가지고 있는 사람을 찾고 있어.

남: 나는 어느 정도 게임 디자인 수업을 들었고, 너도 알다시피 게임 하는 것을 정말 좋아해.

여: 그들이 너를 채용할 것 같은데. 너 게임 커뮤니티에서 꽤 인기 있잖아.

남: 당장 지원해야겠어. 이걸 알려줘서 고마워.

**어휘**

**release** *v.* 출시하다　**qualification** *n.* 자격, 필요조건　**take on** ~를 채용(고용)하다

정답 ②

**문제풀이**

인턴사원을 모집하는 게임회사에서 출시된 게임으로 Counterclockwise와 Super Doctor Brothers가 언급되었고, 모집 분야(프로그래밍, 캐릭터 디자인, 베타 테스팅), 남자의 지원 분야(캐릭터 디자인), 지원 자격(게임 디자인 수업 수강. 게임에 대한 애정)은 언급이 되었지만 모집 인원에 대해서는 언급되지 않았으므로 정답은 ② '모집 인원'이다.

**총 어휘 수** 149


# 11 내용 일치 · 불일치

**소재** 캠퍼스 투어의 내용과 일정 안내

**듣기 대본 해석**

여: 여러분 안녕하세요. 저는 Williams Academy의 교감인 Jones이고 여러분이 저희 일류 학교에 오신 것을 환영합니다. 오늘 저희는 예비 학생들에게 우리 캠퍼스를 방문하고 시설을 구경할 기회를 줄 것입니다. 여러분의 가이드는 저희 시설에서의 생활에 대해 직접적인 경험을 들려드릴 학교 학생들일 것입니다. 그들은 또한 교육 프로그램에 대한 상세한 얘기와 우리 캠퍼스의 역사에 대한 얘기를 해 줄 것입니다. 투어의 첫 부분은 12시까지 진행될 것입니다. 12시에 점심을 위해 학교 식당에서 만나도록 하겠습니다. 그런 다음 한 시에 강당으로 이동하며 거기서 학생회가 연극을 공연할 것입니다. 이후 짧은 프레젠테이션을 보도록 하겠습니다. 프레젠테이션 후에 저희 학교에 대한 여러분의 질문을 학생회가 받도록 하겠습니다. 즐거운 하루를 보내시길 바라며 방문해 주셔서 감사합니다.

**어휘**

**prestigious** *a.* 일류의, 명망 있는　**potential** *a.* 가능성이 있는, 잠재적인
**facility** *n.* 기관, 시설　**first-hand** *a.* 직접적인, 직접 얻은
**auditorium** *n.* 강당

정답 ③

**문제풀이**

여자는 학교 생활에 대해 학교 학생들이 안내해 줄 것이며, 정오까지 투어의 첫 부분이 끝나면 12시에 점심을 학교 식당에서 먹고, 1시까지 강당으로 이동하여 학생들의 연극, 발표, 질의응답 시간을 갖는다고 하였으므로 정답은 ③ '투어의 첫 부분은 1시에 시작한다.'이다.

**총 어휘 수** 156


# 12 도표

**소재** 원예관련 프로그램 선택

**듣기 대본 해석**

남: Brittney, 올해 정원을 시작하는 것에 관심이 있다고 그러지 않았니?

여: 음. 채식주의자가 될 거야. 왜?

남: 음. 이번 여름에 커뮤니티 칼리지에서 제공하는 몇몇 수업에 대한 전단지를 받았거든. 하나 가져.

여: 정말? 좋다. [잠시 후] 유기농 원예 수업이 재미있어 보여.

남: 그럼 채식주의 음식 요리하는 법도 배우고 싶어?

여: 정말 재미있어 보이네. 수업 시간 때 내가 직접 요리할 수 있는 거지, 맞지?

남: 맞아. 네가 만든 걸 집에 가져 와서 내가 먹어볼 수도 있어.

여: 좋다. 그럼 그 수업도 들어야지.

남: 그래. 그럼 이제 선택할 수 있는 두 프로그램으로 좁혀졌네. 수업에서 점심 제공해 주는 걸 원해?

여: 거기서 요리할 거니까 굳이 그럴 필요는 없을 것 같아. 내가 만든 것 먹으면
되지, 맞지? 그리고 10달러 더 싸잖아.
남: 알겠어. 그럼 너한테 딱 알맞은 프로그램을 찾은 것 같아.

**어휘**
organic *a.* 유기농의　　vegan *n.* 채식주의자　　〈문제〉sustainable
*a.* 지속 가능한

**정답** ②

**문제풀이**
유기농 원에 수업과 채식주의 음식 요리를 한다고 했으므로 ①번과 ②번으로
좁혀지는데 점심은 제공되지 않은 것으로 한다고 했으므로 정답은 ②번이다.

**총 어휘 수** 160

## 13 긴 대화의 응답

**소재** 추천서 파일 부탁하기

**듣기 대본 해석**
여: 안녕하세요, Wilson 선생님.
남: 안녕, Margaret. 무슨 일이야?
여: 별일 아니에요. 저는 단지 선생님께서 저의 추천서를 끝내셨는지 궁금해서요.
제가 이번 주 말까지 저의 대학 지원서를 제출해야 해서요.
남: 맞아. 나는 월요일에 그것을 다 마쳤어. 여기 어딘가에 있을 거야. 잠깐만
기다려.
여: 천천히 찾으세요.
남: [잠시 후] 아, 여기 있네. 나는 추천서 쓰는 데 많은 시간을 보냈어. 너도
알다시피 너는 내가 가장 좋아하는 학생들 중 한 명이었지.
여: 감사해요. 추천서가 좋아 보이네요, Wilson 선생님. 제가 파일 가져가도
되나요?
남: 당연하지. 백업용이나 그런 것을 위해 필요한 거니?
여: 음. 요즘 모든 대학교 지원서가 온라인으로 제출되어서요. 그래서 제가
그것들을 이메일로 보내야 해요.
남: 내가 나의 서명이 들어간 이것을 스캔해줄게.
여: 좋아요. 스캔한 후에 저에게 이메일로 보내주실 수 있나요?
남: 그럼. 여기 종이에 너의 이메일 주소를 적어두기만 하렴.
여: 알겠습니다. 도와주셔서 감사합니다. Wilson 선생님.
남: ② 괜찮아. 준비되자마자 이 파일을 보내줄게.

**어휘**
letter of recommendation 추천장　　turn in 제출하다　　backup
*n.* 예비, 백업　　application *n.* 지원(서), 신청(서)　　submit *v.* 제출하다
signature *n.* 서명　　〈문제〉misplace *v.* 잘못 두다, 제자리에 두지 않다

**정답** ②

**문제풀이**
여자는 남자에게 추천서를 파일로 보내달라고 부탁하고 있고, 남자는 흔쾌히
허락하는 분위기이므로 남자의 마지막 대답은 ② '괜찮아. 준비되자마자 이
파일을 보내줄게.'가 적절하다.

**오답 보기 해석**
① 네가 나한테 이메일을 보내게 하는 이유를 확신할 수 없구나.
③ 천만에. 오늘 밤에 반드시 편지 쓸게.
④ 정말로 미안한데, 내가 서류를 잘못 놓아둔 것 같구나.
⑤ 그럼. 나의 이메일 주소는 gwilson@northwestacademy.edu야.

**총 어휘 수** 181

## 14 긴 대화의 응답

**소재** 아이들을 돌보는 자원봉사

**듣기 대본 해석**
남: Hailey. 오늘 봉사하는 거 재미있었어?

여: 즐거웠어. 아이들이랑 게임도 하고 노래도 불렀어.
남: 좋네. 근데 어떻게 그렇게 많은 아이들을 감당할 수 있는지 모르겠어.
여: 사실 쉬워. 아이들이랑 노는 거 재미있어.
남: 다음 번에 너랑 같이 하고 싶은데 그래야 할지 모르겠어.
여: 왜 못해?
남: 글쎄, 애들이 날 별로 안 좋아할 것 같아.
여: 왜 그렇게 생각해? 너 보통 아주 친절하고 에너지 넘치잖아.
남: 난 노래도 못하고 걔네랑 게임을 하면서 놀 인내심도 없는 것 같아. 점심
만들어 주는 것 외에는 할 수 있는 게 없을 거야.
여: 음, 네가 그 자원봉사에 지원해도 될 것 같아. 다음 번에 같이 가자.
남: 진짜 내가 도와줄 수 있을까?
여: ① 물론이지. 우리는 받을 수 있는 모든 도움이 필요해.

**어휘**
energetic *a.* 정력적인　　patience *n.* 참을성, 인내력
〈문제〉volunteer work 자원봉사

**정답** ①

**문제풀이**
남자가 아이들에게 자원봉사하는 것에 자신이 없어하면서 도움이 될 수 있을지
물었는데 여자는 할 수 있다고 용기를 주고 있으므로 적절한 대답은 ① '물론이지.
우리는 받을 수 있는 모든 도움이 필요해.'이다.

**오답 보기 해석**
② 네가 원한다면 우리가 다른 자원봉사를 찾을 수 있어.
③ 네가 나한테 아이들과 어떻게 잘 지내는지 가르쳐 주면 되겠네.
④ 네가 아이들과 노래 부르는 건 그들에게 중요해.
⑤ 게임하는 거랑 노래 부르기는 그들이 더 사교적이 되게 도와줘.

**총 어휘 수** 148

## 15 상황에 적절한 말

**소재** 직장 선택

**듣기 대본 해석**
남: Uptown 대학에서 저널리즘을 공부하는 학생인 Ryan은 이번 학기 말에
졸업할 것입니다. 그는 졸업 후 직업을 찾기 위해 열심히 일해왔고 높이
평가되는 신문사들로부터 두 개의 일자리 제안을 받았습니다. 첫 번째
제안은 Courier Crossing에서 온 것인데 대도시에 있는 큰 신문사입니다.
다른 제안은 작은 타블로이드 신문인 Hush-Hush에서 받았습니다.
Courier Crossing은 그에게 높은 봉급과 직업 안정성을 제공하지만
그의 고향으로부터 멀리 떨어져서 가야만 합니다. Hush-Hush는 훨씬
적은 봉급이지만 그는 그의 가족과 친구들로부터 떠날 필요가 없을 겁니다.
많은 숙고 끝에, Ryan은 마침내 Hush-Hush의 제안을 받아들이기로 결정
합니다. 그는 복도에서 그의 친구인 Sarah를 만났고 그녀에게 그가 결정한
것을 이야기합니다. Sarah는 왜 Ryan이 이런 결정을 했는지 이해하고
격려의 말을 해주고 싶습니다. 이런 상황에서, Sarah는 Ryan에게 뭐라고
말할까요?
Sarah: ⑤ 좋은 선택이야. 인생에서 어떤 것들은 돈보다 더 중요하니까.

**어휘**
semester *n.* 학기　　graduation *n.* 졸업　　well-respected *a.*
존경을 받는, 높이 평가되는　　tabloid *n.* 타블로이드판 (보통 신문 크기의
절반)　　security *n.* 보장, 안심　　deliberation *n.* 숙고　　hallway *n.*
복도　　encouragement *n.* 격려

**정답** ⑤

**문제풀이**
Ryan은 가족, 친구들을 떠나고 싶지 않아서 높은 급여와 안정성이 보장되는
큰 신문사를 포기하고 작은 신문사를 선택한 상황을 친구인 Sarah에게 말했고,
Sarah는 Ryan에게 격려와 지지의 말을 해주려 한다. 따라서 Sarah가
Ryan에게 해 줄 수 있는 적절한 말은 ⑤ '좋은 선택이야. 인생에서 어떤 것들은
돈보다 더 중요하니까.'이다.

① 요즘 언론계에서 직장을 찾는 것은 쉬운 일이 아니야.
② 나는 네 꿈이 Hush-Hush에서 일하는 거였다고 생각했어.
③ 너는 Courier Crossing의 제안을 받아 들여서는 안 됐어.
④ 나는 돈을 위해 이 일을 하는 게 아냐. 내가 그것을 좋아하기 때문에 하고 있어.

**총 어휘 수** 156

# 16 담화 목적 / 17 세부 내용 파악

**소재** 어버이날 선물세트에 관한 홍보

**듣기 대본 해석**

남: 부모님들 안녕하세요. Franklin 대학교의 매년 열리는 어버이날 행사에 오신 것을 환영합니다. 여러분께서는 이러한 명문 대학생들의 학부모 들이시기에 우리는 여러분들께 1927년에 이 대학교가 설립된 이후로 여기 대학교의 전통인 우리의 어버이날 선물세트를 구매할 기회를 제공합니다. 이 선물세트에서 여러분들은 여러분과 여러분의 사랑하는 사람들을 위한 범퍼 스티커, 펜, 열쇠고리를 보실 수 있을 것입니다. 학생 자치회의 회원들은 또한 올해의 축제 동안 여러분들이 즐길 수 있는 수제 쿠키를 구웠습니다. 우리의 어버이날 선물세트는 학생단체와 커뮤니티 사업에 의해 만들어 졌습니다. 이러한 선물세트들을 만드는 것을 돕는 것 이외에, 이 사업은 또한 200달러 상당의 쿠폰 책자도 준비했습니다. 이 소책자에서 여러분은 Franklin City 카페, Rainbow 제과점, Echo Lanes 볼링장, 그리고 The Downtown 식당의 유용한 쿠폰을 찾을 수 있을 것입니다. 어버이날 선물세트의 모든 수익금은 Spring Fest (축제)와 해마다 열리는 재능 대회 같은 캠퍼스 전역의 이벤트에 유익하게 사용됩니다. 만약 여러분이 어버이날 선물세트 중 하나를 구매하고 싶다면, 방문객 센터의 안내 데스크로 오세요. 우리의 멋진 캠퍼스에서 어버이날 행사에 참여해 주셔서 감사합니다.

**어휘**

**annual** *a.* 매년의, 연례의　　**kit** *n.* 선물세트　　**on top of** ~외에, ~뿐만 아니라　　**booklet** *n.* 소책자　　**proceeds** *n.* 돈(수익금)
〈문제〉 **faculty** *n.* 교수단　　**upcoming** *a.* 다가오는, 곧 있을

**정답** 16 ②　17 ⑤

**문제풀이**

16 남자는 어버이날 행사에 참여한 학부모들에게 이버이날 선물세트를 판매하기 위해 홍보하고 있다. 따라서 남자가 하는 말의 목적은 ② '어버이날 선물세트 판매를 홍보하려고'이다.

17 쿠폰이 있는 곳으로 카페, 제과점, 볼링장, 식당은 언급되었지만 수영장은 언급되지 않았으므로 정답은 ⑤ '수영장'이다.

**오답 보기 해석**

16
① 지역사회 사업들을 광고하기 위해
③ 부모님들을 교수단 멤버들에게 소개하려고
④ 다가오는 대학교 이벤트를 부모님께 알리기 위하여
⑤ 환영 선물세트를 부모님들께 판매할 자원봉사자를 모집하려고

**총 어휘 수** 195

## DICTATION ANSWERS

01 running the air conditioner

02 You look very immersed in something

03 maintain relationships / stick with our own kind / more likely to become friends / outside of their race

04 I have a headache / change the door / make more sense / install a revolving door / The air gets trapped

05 to stay healthy / you can have a decent breakfast / make the shake a little tastier / for its nutritional value

06 You've really outdone yourself / plenty of time to prepare / working on getting a permit / Food and Drinks Provided

07 you're aware / planned on coming down to watch / swing by the house / drop it off at school

08 It's no big deal / what's on your mind / what happened at the meeting

09 What's your nightly rate / be coming in two cars / we charge more for / take the electricity hookup

10 summer internship program / opened up internship positions for programming / try out character design

11 explore its facilities / give you their first-hand experience / will run until noon / perform a play

12 were interested in starting a garden / try to cook my own food

13 letter of recommendation / by the end of the week / are submitted online / email it to me

14 Did you have fun volunteering / deal with all those children / join you next time / have the patience / The only thing I could do

15 two job offers from well-respected newspapers / a small tabloid newspaper / After much deliberation / wants to offer words of encouragement

16-17 since it was founded in / valuable coupons from / pick up one of the Parents' Day kits

| | | | | | |
|---|---|---|---|---|---|
| 01 ② | 02 ② | 03 ③ | 04 ① | 05 ③ | 06 ④ |
| 07 ② | 08 ② | 09 ③ | 10 ③ | 11 ① | 12 ⑤ |
| 13 ① | 14 ⑤ | 15 ④ | 16 ② | 17 ③ | |

## 01 짧은 대화의 응답

**소재** 연회 준비

**듣기 대본 해석**

여: 안녕, Evan. 오늘 저녁 연회 준비하는 거 끝났어?
남: 대부분의 준비는 끝났는데 어떤 케이크를 만들지 정하지 못했어.
여: Jane한테 물어보지 그래? 자기가 도와줄 수 있다고 하던데.
남: ② 그거 좋은 생각이다. Jane은 정말 훌륭한 제빵사야.

**어휘**

**banquet** *n.* 연회    **preparation** *n.* 준비

**정답** ②

**문제풀이**

연회 케이크를 결정하지 못한 남자에게 여자가 Jane에게 물어보지 그러냐고 했을 때 적절한 응답은 ② '그거 좋은 생각이다. Jane은 정말 훌륭한 제빵사야.'이다.

**오답 보기 해석**

① 좋아. 그렇게 주문을 취소하면 되겠다.
③ 내가 케이크를 구우면 문제가 되지 않을 거야.
④ 그거 좋은 생각인데 난 이미 케이크를 골랐어.
⑤ 그녀가 연회에 못 온다니 정말 안타깝네.

**총 어휘 수** 49

## 02 짧은 대화의 응답

**소재** 스키장 가기 전 물건 챙기기

**듣기 대본 해석**

남: 엄마, 저 오늘 밤 Walker 산에 친구들이랑 스키 타러 가요.
여: 오늘 밤에 정말 춥대. 목도리랑 비니 꼭 챙겨.
남: 알겠어요. 제 Southback 외투를 못 찾겠어요. 혹시 보셨어요?
여: ② 방금 세탁해서 지금 (말리느라) 걸려있어.

**어휘**

**be supposed to V** ~하기로 되어 있다    《문제》**extra** *a.* 여분의
**just in case** 만일에 대비하여

**정답** ②

**문제풀이**

남자는 스키장에서 입을 외투를 못 찾고 있어 엄마에게 물어보고 있으므로 여자의 응답으로 가장 적절한 것은 ② '방금 세탁해서 지금 (말리느라) 걸려있어.'이다.

**오답 보기 해석**

① 미안한데 Southback 외투는 너무 비싸.
③ 혹시 모르니까 여분 장갑도 챙겨갈게.
④ 아빠의 스키바지 빌려 입고 가.
⑤ 아니, 거기로는 스키 타러 가면 안돼.

**총 어휘 수** 48

## 03 담화 주제

**소재** 일상생활에서 운동하기

**듣기 대본 해석**

남: 오늘 운동을 하셨나요? 모든 사람들이 운동은 건강에 좋다고 알고 있습니다. 그러나 아마 여러분은 너무 바쁘다고 그리고 단지 헬스장에 갈 시간이나 힘이 없다고 느낄 것입니다. 그러면 여러분과 같은 사람들은 무엇을 해야 할까요? 여러분의 일상의 환경을 체육관으로 바꾸도록 해보세요. 예를 들어, 가능하면 여러분은 우체국이나 식품점에 차로 가는 대신 걸어가거나 잔디를 깎기 위해 미는 잔디 깎기 기계를 사용해야 합니다. 최근의 연구는 하루의 대부분을 활동적으로 지내는 사람들이 매일 60분 체육관에서 운동하고 다른 때는 활동적이지 않게 지내는 사람들보다 10퍼센트 더 많은 에너지를 사용한다고 보여주었습니다. 하루종일 활동적으로 지내는 것이 더 쉽고 건강에 더 좋습니다. 이것은 체중감소라는 목표에 더 쉽게 도달하게 도와주기도 합니다. 여러분의 일상 생활에서 어떤 종류의 활동들이 운동이 될 수 있을까요?

**어휘**

**surroundings** *n.* 환경    **grocery store** 식료품점    **lawn mower** 잔디 깎는 기계    **indicate** *v.* 나타내다, 보여주다    **gym** *n.* (학교 등의) 체육관 (=gymnasium)    **meet** *v.* 충족시키다

**정답** ③

**문제풀이**

남자는 체육관에서 한 시간 운동하고 움직이지 않는 사람들보다 일상 생활에서 활동적으로 움직이는 것이 더 운동이 된다고 이야기하고 있으므로, 강의의 주제는 ③ '일상 생활에서 운동할 수 있는 방법을 찾아라.'이다.

**오답 보기 해석**

① 너무 많은 운동은 건강에 안 좋을 수 있다.
② 영양사에게 식이요법에 대해 말해라.
④ 식이요법과 운동을 같이 하라.
⑤ 매일 운동할 시간을 만들어라.

**총 어휘 수** 150

## 04 의견

**소재** 장난감이 가지고 있는 성 고정관념

**듣기 대본 해석**

남: 안녕, Katie. 너 크리스마스 쇼핑 했니?
여: 물론이지. 아버지 드릴 콘서트 DVD하고, 어머니 드릴 화분, 그리고 사촌한테 줄 캐릭터 인형을 샀어.
남: 멋지다. 난 어렸을 때 캐릭터 인형 좋아했었는데. 분명 그 남자아이가 아주 좋아할 거야.
여: 왜 내 사촌이 남자애라고 생각하는데?
남: 그럼 여자 사촌 주려고 캐릭터 인형을 샀다는 얘기야?
여: 그렇지. 실제로 그 여자애가 캐릭터 인형 가지고 노는 걸 좋아하거든.
남: 음… 난 남자 애들만 가지고 노는 줄 알았지. 여자 애들은 인형을 가지고 놀잖아.
여: 나도 그렇게 생각했거든. 처음에는 좀 당황스러웠는데 그 아이가 얼마나 좋아하는지 알게 되니까 성에 대한 고정관념에 대해서 마음을 열게 됐지.
남: "성에 대한 고정관념"이 뭐야?
여: 그건 사회가 남자와 여자에 대해서 정상적이라고 여기는 것들이야. 내 생각에는 남자 애들이 여자아이 장난감을 가지고 놀거나 그 반대도 괜찮아.
남: 난 여태까지 그런 생각을 전혀 해본 적이 없어.
여: 나도 그래. 하지만 내 사촌이 그걸 생각해 보게 한 거지.

**어휘**

**action figure** (영화나 만화 등에 나온) 영웅이나 캐릭터 인형    **confuse** *v.* 혼란시키다    **gender stereotype** 성 고정관념    **perceive** *v.* 인지하다    **vice versa** 거꾸로, 반대로

정답 ①

**문제풀이**

여자는 캐릭터 인형을 좋아하는 여자 사촌을 통해서 성에 대한 고정관념에 대해 마음을 열게 되었다고 했으므로 정답은 ① '장난감에 대해 가지고 있는 성 고정관념을 없애야 한다.'이다.

**총 어휘 수** 166

## 05 장소 파악

**소재** 오래된 스파게티 집

**듣기 대본 해석**

여: 우왜! 여기 되게 붐빈다. 누구 유명한 사람 왔어? 촬영 기사들 봐봐.

남: 지역 방송국에서 왔나 봐.

여: 여기가 뭐가 그렇게 특별한데?

남: 여기 스파게티가 아주 유명해. 주인 집안의 비밀 조리법을 쓴대. 증조할머니로부터 전승된 거야.

여: 왜! 그럼 여기 꽤 오래 됐나 보네?

남: 응. 4대 동안 있었으니까. 거의 100년 됐다고 들었어.

여: 굉장하다. 저 스파게티 먹어봐야겠다.

남: 여기에 대해서 좋은 소문 많이 들었어. 봐! 저기 주인이 인터뷰하는 것 같아.

여: 땀 흘리는 것 봐. 엄청 긴장했나 봐.

여: 너도 인터뷰하면 긴장되지 않겠어?

**어휘**

**recipe** *n.* 요리법, 레시피    **pass down** ~에게 물려주다, 전해주다
**generation** *n.* 세대    **incredible** *a.* 믿을 수 없는, 믿기 힘든

정답 ③

**문제풀이**

오래되고 유명한 스파게티 집에 기자들이 촬영하러 와 있는 상황이므로 두 사람이 대화하고 있는 장소는 ③ '음식점'이다.

**총 어휘 수** 123

## 06 그림의 세부 내용 파악

**소재** 파티룸 꾸미기

**듣기 대본 해석**

여: 이봐, Taylor. 네가 보고 있는 게 뭐야?

남: 우리 기관으로 오는 Ryan과 Sarah를 환영해 주기 위한 파티룸 사진이야. 이제 막 장식을 마쳤어.

여: 멋지네. 좋은 시간이 될 거야.

남: 물론이지. 그런데 이 룸에 대해 어떻게 생각해?

여: 근사해 보여. 뒤 벽에 있는 배너가 엄청 크다!

남: 그래. 나는 좀 더 작을 거라고 생각했지만, 저것도 멋있는 것 같아. 오른쪽 코너에 있는 풍선은 어떻게 생각해?

여: 멋진 솜씨인 것 같아. 난 거기에 '환영합니다'라고 쓰인 게 마음에 들어. 음식을 위해서 왼쪽에 세 개의 테이블이 있는 거니?

남: 아니야 우리는 뷔페를 하지 않아. 저것들은 손님이랑 Sarah의 지지자들을 위한 것들이야.

여: 와인병이 있는 중앙 테이블은 Sarah와 Ryan을 위한 것이 틀림없군.

남: 맞아. 난 그것들을 방 가운데 두면 좋을 거라고 생각했어.

여: 분명 좋아할 거야. 풍선 아래 단은 뭐야?

남: 그건 손님 발표자들을 위한 거야. Sarah의 친구와 가족들 몇몇이 그들의 지지를 보여주기 위해 말하고 싶어 해.

여: 좋을 것 같아.

**어휘**

**facility** *n.* 기관, 시설    **decorate** *v.* 장식하다    **podium** *n.* 단, 지휘대

정답 ④

**문제풀이**

여자가 중앙 테이블에 와인병이 있다고 했는데 그림에서는 꽃병이 있으므로 정답은 ④번이다.

**총 어휘 수** 191

## 07 할 일

**소재** 대학 합격 소식과 집 구하기

**듣기 대본 해석**

[휴대폰이 울린다.]

여: 여보세요?

남: 네, Alice. 나누고 싶은 좋은 소식이 있어서 전화했어요.

여: 좋은 소식? 네가 원하는 대학에 합격한 거니?

남: 맞아요! 막 집에 왔는데 우편함에 Princeton에서 온 입학 허가서가 있었어요.

여: 정말 훌륭하구나. 나는 네가 합격할 것이라는 것을 잠시도 의심한 적이 없단다. 축하해!

남: 정말 감사해요. Alice. 저를 도와주실 수 있으신지 궁금해요.

여: 물론이지. 내가 어떻게 도와줄까?

남: 학기가 시작하기 전에 시간은 많지 않고 해야 할 일은 많아서 제가 머물 곳을 찾지 못할 것 같아요.

여: 내가 아파트를 찾아주길 바라는 거니?

남: 그러면 좋을 것 같아요. 그 근처에 오래 사셨으니 당신의 판단을 신뢰할 수 있어요.

여: 좋아. 사실 좀 재미있을 것 같구나. 어떤 종류의 집을 원하니?

남: 침실 하나 딸린 아파트를 원해요. 저는 너무 큰 곳을 찾지는 않지만, 원룸보다는 넓은 공간이면 좋겠어요.

여: 그래, 내가 몇 군데 좋은 곳을 찾는 대로 다시 연락할게.

남: 최고예요. 도와주셔서 다시 한 번 감사드려요.

여: 나도 기쁘단다.

**어휘**

**acceptance letter** 합격통지서    **wonder** *v.* 궁금해하다
**judgment** *n.* 판단, 심사    **studio** *n.* 원룸 (아파트)    **option** *n.* 선택권
〈문제〉 **college application** 대학 지원서

정답 ②

**문제풀이**

남자는 여자에게 대학 합격 소식을 알리고 대학교 근처에 자신의 아파트를 알아봐 달라고 부탁하고 있으므로 여자가 남자를 위해 할 일은 ② '그가 아파트 찾는 것을 도와주기'이다.

**오답 보기 해석**

① 도시를 구경시켜 주기
③ 기숙사에 대해 물어보기
④ 파티 전에 집 청소하기
⑤ 대학 지원서 작성 도와주기

**총 어휘 수** 203

## 08 이유

**소재** 일찍 일어난 이유

**듣기 대본 해석**

남: 누나, 좋은 아침이야. 무슨 요리해?

여: 오믈렛을 요리하고 있어. 일찍 일어났네. 어젯밤에 늦게까지 밖에 있어서 자고 있을 줄 알았는데.

남: 응. 친구들과 함께 학년 말을 축하하러 나갔었지.

여: 피곤하겠구나. 좀 더 자지 그러니. 여름방학 첫 날이잖아.

남: 그러고 싶지만, 오늘 아빠와 산에 하이킹 가기로 했거든.

여: 아, 그래서 일찍 일어났구나.

남: 우리랑 같이 가자. 아빠와 단둘이 가는 건 좀 어색해. 둘이 무슨 이야기를 해야 할지 모르겠어.

여: 나도 도와주고 싶지만 이미 계획이 있어. Brandon과 함께 영화를 보러 가기로 했거든.

남: 오, 아냐. 괜찮아. 엄마 어디 계신지 알아? 엄마한테 등산용 지팡이를 빌려야 하는데.

여: 식료품점에 가셨어. 곧 오실 거야.

남: 알았어. 내가 찾아보는 것 보다 엄마를 기다리는 게 나을 것 같아.

### 어휘
**celebrate** *v.* 기념하다, 축하하다   **awkward** *a.* 어색한   **borrow** *v.* 빌리다

### 정답 ②

### 문제풀이
여자가 어제 늦게 잤으니 더 자라고 권유했는데, 남자는 아빠와 산에 하이킹을 가기로 해서 일찍 일어났다고 말하고 있으므로 정답은 ② '아빠와 하이킹을 가기 위해서'이다.

### 총 어휘 수 164

## 09  숫자

**소재** 여자친구를 위한 기념품 구입

### 듣기 대본 해석
여: 오, 안녕하세요. 무엇을 도와드릴까요?

남: 글쎄요, 제 여자친구를 위한 기념품을 사려고 하는데요. 저랑 이번 여행을 같이 못 와서 매우 속상해 했거든요.

여: 그렇군요. 어떤 것을 생각하고 계신가요?

남: 전 그녀가 매일 사용할 수 있으면서도 그녀가 소중히 느낄 수 있는 것을 원해요.

여: 태국 전통 등은 어때요? 20달러밖에 안 한답니다.

남: 좋긴 한데, 이건 조금 작지 않나요? 더 큰 건 얼마예요?

여: 그건 40달러예요. 태국 북부의 부족민에 의해 수작업으로 만들어진 것이랍니다.

남: 아름답군요. 더 큰 랜턴으로 할게요.

여: 네, 어머니나 할머니에게 줄 선물은 어때요? 이 전통 부채들을 좋아할 텐데요. 각각 5달러 밖에 안 해요. 그리고 45달러 넘게 사시면 전체 금액에서 10퍼센트를 할인해드려요.

남: 좋네요. 2개 주세요. 이것들을 선물용 포장해주실 수 있나요?

여: 죄송하지만 여기서 그 서비스를 제공하지는 않아요.

남: 괜찮아요.

### 어휘
**treasure** *v.* 소중히 여기다   **handcraft** *v.* 손으로 만들다
**tribesman** *n.* 부족(종족) 구성원   **giftwrap** *v.* 선물용으로 포장하다

### 정답 ③

### 문제풀이
남자는 여자친구에게 줄 선물로 40달러짜리 전통 등과 5달러짜리 부채 두 개를 사서 총 금액은 50달러이다. 여자는 구매액이 45달러를 넘으면 10퍼센트 할인을 해준다고 하였으므로 남자가 지불할 금액은 ③ '$45'이다.

### 총 어휘 수 166

## 10  언급 유무

**소재** 네팔에서의 자원봉사

### 듣기 대본 해석
여: Kyle, 여름방학 어땠니?

남: 정말 좋았어. 네팔에서 봉사자로 시간을 보냈어.

여: 멋지다. 얼마나 오래 있었니?

남: 27일.

여: 왜! 거기서 방학의 절반 이상을 보냈구나.

남: 응. 네팔에서 더 지냈으면 좋았을 텐데.

여: 거기서 무엇을 했니?

남: 너도 알다시피, 그곳은 몇 달 전 일어난 큰 지진으로 고통을 겪고 있어. 나는 병원에서 부상당한 사람들을 돌봐 줬고 변두리에 음식과 물을 전달해 줬어.

여: 멋지다. 스스로 보람을 느꼈겠구나. 다른 자원봉사자들은 모두 미국에서 왔니?

남: 아니, 우리 그룹에는 다른 미국인 한 명만 있었고, 나머지는 세계 여러 나라에서 왔어.

여: 나도 겨울방학 때는 자원봉사를 하고 싶은데, 그것을 어떻게 신청하지?

남: 내가 이메일로 관련 정보를 보내줄게. 먼저 웹사이트에 등록하고 네가 어떤 종류의 일에 자원봉사하고 싶은지 선택하면 돼.

여: 쉬워 보이네. 고마워.

### 어휘
**volunteer** *n.* 자원봉사, 자원봉사자   **suffer** *v.* 고통 받다   **outskirts** *n.* 변두리, 교외   **participate** *v.* 참가하다

### 정답 ③

### 문제풀이
두 사람은 자원봉사의 장소, 기간, 활동 내용, 신청 방법에 관해 언급했지만 주최 기관에 대한 언급은 하지 않았으므로 정답은 ③ '주최 기관'이다.

### 총 어휘 수 165

## 11  내용 일치 · 불일치

**소재** 필드하키 소개

### 듣기 대본 해석
남: 독특한 스포츠에 관심이 있으신가요? 그렇다면 필드하키를 알아보세요. 필드하키는 전 세계에서 하고 있지만 아이스 하키가 우위인 캐나다와 미국에서는 인기가 덜합니다. 그러나, 필드하키는 전 세계적으로 훨씬 더 유명합니다. 사실, 인도와 파키스탄 두 나라에서는 국민 스포츠입니다. 필드하키는 마른 땅에서 경기하는 것을 제외하면 아이스하키와 거의 비슷합니다. 경기하는 동안, 골키퍼는 몸의 어떤 부분으로든 공을 만질 수 있도록 허락되는 유일한 선수이고, 반면에 필드선수들은 스틱의 평평한 부분으로 공을 쳐야 합니다. 이 스포츠는 시작하는 데 그렇게 비싸지 않고 경기 할 스케이트장이 필요 없어서 세계 대부분의 지역에서 더 이용하기 쉽기 때문에 아이스하키의 훌륭한 대안입니다. 만약에 당신이 새로운 뭔가에 도전하고 싶으시다면, 당신의 지역에서 필드하키 클럽을 찾아보세요!

### 어휘
**unique** *a.* 독특한, 특별한   **dominate** *v.* 지배하다, 우세하다
**identical** *a.* 동일한, 똑같은   **alternative** *n.* 대안, 선택 가능한 것
**accessible** *a.* 이용 가능한, 접근 가능한

### 정답 ①

### 문제풀이
필드하키는 전 세계적으로 인기가 있지만, 캐나다와 미국에서는 인기가 덜하다고 했으므로 정답은 ① '캐나다와 미국에서 가장 인기 있는 운동이다.'이다.

### 총 어휘 수 162

## 12  도표

**소재** 가족여행을 위한 차 대여

### 듣기 대본 해석
남: Bird 자동차 대여 센터에 오신 것을 환영합니다. 제 이름은 Gabe입니다. 무엇을 도와드릴까요?

여: 안녕하세요. 차를 대여하고 싶습니다.

남: 알겠습니다. 어떤 기종을 대여하고 싶으신가요?
여: 음, 가족여행을 갈 거라서 좀 큰 게 필요할 거예요. 다섯 명이 여행을 가요.
남: 알겠습니다. 그런 경우에는 값싸고 편리한 사이즈의 차보다 큰 차를 선택하는 게 좋습니다.
여: 짐도 아주 많아요. 그래서 좀 큰 게 필요할 거예요.
남: 그럼 미니밴을 대여하는 것을 추천하고 싶네요. 자리도 충분하고 장거리 여행을 갈 때도 아주 편안해요.
여: 미니밴은 좀 비싸네요. Raven은요? 크기는 같은데 더 싸요.
남: 죄송하지만 이 기종은 지금 대여하실 수 있는 차가 없어요.
여: 그렇군요. 그럼 어쩔 수 없이 돈 좀 더 내서 이걸로 해야겠네요.
남: 잘 생각하셨습니다.

### 어휘
**rent** *v.* 대여하다  **economy-sized** *a.* 값싸고 편리한 사이즈의  **luggage** *n.* 짐  **ample** *a.* 충분한  **pricey** *a.* 값비싼  **capacity** *n.* 용량

### 정답 ⑤

### 문제풀이
다섯 명이 여행을 간다고 했으므로 ①번과 ②번은 제외되고 짐도 많아서 큰 차를 원한다고 했으므로 ④번과 ⑤번으로 좁혀진다. 남자가 미니밴을 추천하자 여자는 좀 비싸다고 ④번에 관심을 가졌지만 이용 가능한 차가 없어서 결국 미니밴을 선택하게 됐으므로 정답은 ⑤번이다.

**총 어휘 수** 154

## 13  긴 대화의 응답

**소재** 과제 주제 정하는 데 도움 받기

### 듣기 대본 해석
남: Lucy, Miller 선생님이 내 준 과제 끝냈어?
여: 어젯밤에는 할 기회가 없었어. 큰 과제인데 어디서부터 시작해야 할지 모르겠어.
남: 빨리 시작하는 게 좋을 거야. 목요일이 마감인 것 알잖아.
여: 응. 주제로 뭘 선택해야 할 지 모르겠어.
남: 내 보고서 좀 봐. 끝나지는 않았지만 아마 결정하는 데 도움이 될 거야.
여: *[잠시 후]* 이기 정말 재미있다. 미국 인구가 그렇게 빨리 늘어났는지 몰랐어.
남: 응. 시각화하기 쉽도록 선 그래프를 사용했어.
어: 정말 잘했네. 자료 정리하느라 시간 좀 걸렸겠는데.
남: 응. 주제를 정하느라 작업을 좀 했는데, 일단 결정하고 나니까 훨씬 쉬웠어.
여: 주제를 선택하고 나서 뭘 했어?
남: 가능한 많은 자료를 찾는 데 집중했어.
여: ① 도움이 많이 됐어. 이제 주제에 대한 아이디어가 떠올랐어.

### 어휘
**assignment** *n.* 과제  **be due on** ~까지 마감이다  **expand** *v.* 확대되다, 확장시키다  〈문제〉**misinterpret** *v.* 잘못 이해하다

### 정답 ①

### 문제풀이
남자는 과제 주제를 정하지 못하고 있는 여자에게 자신의 과제를 보여주며 주제 결정, 자료 정리, 절차 등을 말해주고 있다. 이에 대한 여자의 응답으로 가장 적절한 것은 ① '도움이 많이 됐어. 이제 주제에 대한 아이디어가 떠올랐어.'이다.

### 오답 보기 해석
② 내 생각에 너는 그래프를 완성하는 데 집중해야 돼.
③ 네가 분명 과제를 잘못 이해한 거 같아.
④ 네 보고서가 무엇에 관한 것인지 이해가 안 가.
⑤ 물론. 네 프로젝트 도와줄게.

**총 어휘 수** 176

## 14  긴 대화의 응답

**소재** 가습기 구입에 관한 의논

### 듣기 대본 해석
남: 여보, 기침하는 거 들었어. 괜찮아?
여: 목이 좀 건조하네. 날씨 탓인가 봐.
남: 응, 나도 코가 좀 막혀. 우리 아파트가 너무 건조한 것 같아.
여: 가습기를 사는 게 좋을 것 같아.
남: 나도 그렇게 생각해. 지난 몇 주간 하나 살까 생각하고 있었어.
여: 전에 가게에 갔을 때 몇 개를 봤어. 맘에 드는 것을 찾았어.
남: 정말? 사지 그랬어.
여: 이렇게 필요할 줄은 몰랐지.
남: 지금 가게에 가서 하나 사올게.
여: 지금은 닫았을 거야. 인터넷에서 꽤 괜찮은 것을 찾을 수 있을 거야.
남: 그렇긴 한데 인터넷으로 주문하면 올 때까지 며칠 걸릴 거잖아. 그냥 내일 가게에 가서 하나 살게.
여: 근데 우리 지금 힘들어하고 있잖아. 그때까지 어떡하지?
남: ⑤ 우리가 잠시 동안 화장실에서 샤워기를 틀어놓을 수 있어.

### 어휘
**stuffy** *a.* 답답한, 막힌  **humidifier** *n.* 가습기  **suffer** *v.* 시달리다, 고통 받다

### 정답 ⑤

### 문제풀이
지금 당장의 건조함을 해결하기 위해서 어떡하면 좋을지 묻는 여자의 말에 대한 대답으로 적절한 것은 ⑤ '우리가 잠시 동안 화장실에서 샤워기를 틀어놓을 수 있어.'이다.

### 오답 보기 해석
① 가습기를 트는 게 어떨까?
② 당신은 코가 막혀서 의사한테 가야 해.
③ 당신이 원하는 것을 온라인에서 못 찾겠어.
④ 맞아. 건조한 공기는 피부에도 너무 안 좋아.

**총 어휘 수** 161

## 15  상황에 적절한 말

**소재** 자신감을 잃은 골키퍼 친구에게 조언해주기

### 듣기 대본 해석
여: Charles와 Jack은 JLA 축구단의 공동주장으로 뽑혔습니다. 첫 경기가 조만간 있을 예정이고 축구팀은 하루에 두 시간씩 훈련합니다. Charles는 팀의 골키퍼인데 요즘 따라 훈련 중에 골을 먹히는 일이 빈번해졌습니다. 그의 팀과 학교는 그가 상대편 팀이 점수 내는 것을 막아줄 것을 기대하고 있습니다. Charles는 팀원들로부터 많은 부담을 느끼게 되고 Jack에게 팀을 탈퇴하고 싶다고 말을 합니다. Jack은 Charles에게 그가 잘할 수 있고 그 누구도 완벽하지 않다는 것을 말해주고 싶어합니다. 이러한 상황에서 Jack은 Charles에게 어떤 말을 할까요?
Jack: ④ 우리 모두는 실수를 해. 넌 이번 게임에서 잘 할 거야.

### 어휘
**goalie** *n.* 골키퍼  **lately** *ad.* 최근에, 일마 진에  **count on** ~를 믿다  **pressure** *n.* 압력, 부담  **reassure** *v.* 안심시키다

### 정답 ④

### 문제풀이
Jack은 연습 중 자꾸 골을 먹어서 팀을 탈퇴하고 싶어하는 Charles에게 잘할 수 있다고 말하려 하므로 적절한 말은 ④ '우리 모두는 실수를 해. 넌 이번 게임에서 잘 할 거야.'이다

오답 보기 해석

① 오늘 우리가 정말로 이겼다는 게 믿어지지가 않아!
② 너 도대체 왜 그래? 또 그들에게 점수를 내줬잖아!
③ 넌 더 열심히 할 필요가 있어. 우리는 이번 게임에서 질 거야.
⑤ 시즌이 거의 끝났어. 한 게임만 더 열심히 하자.

**총 어휘 수** 119

# 16 담화 주제 / 17 세부 내용 파악

**소재** 인간에게는 없는 동물의 여러 가지 감각들

**듣기 대본 해석**

남: West Town 동물원에 오신 여러분 모두를 환영합니다. 제 이름은 Frank Berger이고 저는 동물학자입니다. 저는 오늘 자연에 존재하는 감각들에 대해서 여러분들께 말씀드리고자 합니다. 누구든지 인간은 기본적으로 5가지의 감각인 시각, 후각, 촉각, 미각, 청각을 가지고 있다는 것을 압니다. 동물은 어떻습니까? 그들도 인간처럼 똑같은 감각을 가졌나요? 몇몇 동물은 인간보다 더 강력한 감각을 지니고 있고 몇몇은 인간이 지니고 있지 않은 감각을 가지고 있습니다. 비둘기를 예를 들어 보겠습니다. 비둘기는 지구의 자기장과 조화되어 있습니다. 그들은 비록 그들이 수백 마일 떨어진 곳으로 옮겨지더라도 그들의 집으로 가는 길을 찾을 수 있습니다. 그것이 전서구가 과거에 메시지를 보내는 데 사용된 이유입니다. 연어도 마찬가지로 알을 낳기 위해 그들의 출생지로 다시 돌아오는 길을 찾기 위해 지구의 자기장을 이용합니다. 바다거북도 그들이 태어난 해안가로 돌아오기 위해 비슷한 기법을 사용합니다. 몇몇의 뱀들 특히 독사는 적외선 시력을 가지고 있는데, 그들은 그들의 먹이를 식별하기 위해 적외선 시력을 사용합니다. 상어는 먹이의 근육 수축으로부터 나오는 전기를 감지할 수 있습니다. 동물계는 정말로 장대합니다. 이러한 놀라운 동물들 중 몇몇을 살펴보도록 하겠습니다.

**어휘**

**zoologist** *n.* 동물학자　**be in tune with** ~와 리듬이 맞다　**magnetic field** 자기장　**homing** *a.* 귀소성이 있는, 제 집에 돌아오는　**lay eggs** 알을 낳다　**vision** *n.* 시력　**prey** *n.* 먹이　**contraction** *n.* 수축, 축소　**animal kingdom** 동물계　**magnificent** *a.* 장대한, 훌륭한

**정답** 16 ②　17 ③

**문제풀이**

16 남자는 인간에게는 없는 여러 가지 감각을 가진 동물들의 예를 들면서 이야기를 하고 있으므로 정답은 ② '인간들에게서 발견되지 않는 동물의 감각들'이다.

17 비둘기, 연어, 바다거북, 뱀, 상어에 대한 언급은 했지만 박쥐에 대한 언급은 없으므로 정답은 ③ '박쥐'이다.

**오답 보기 해석**

16
① 동물들이 집으로 다시 돌아가는 길을 찾는 방법
③ 동물들이 먹이를 식별하기 위해 사용하는 방법들
④ 동물들에 관한 과학적 연구를 하는 것의 이점
⑤ 항해를 위해 전자기장을 이용하는 동물들

**총 어휘 수** 185

## DICTATION ANSWERS

01 finished preparing for / what kind of cake to make

02 going skiing / It's supposed to be really cold

03 Try turning your everyday surroundings into / Recent studies indicate that / your health to stay active all day

04 likes playing with action figures / about gender stereotypes / perceives as normal for males and females

05 It was passed down from / Look how much he's sweating / Wouldn't you be nervous

06 We just finished decorating it / in the right corner / it would be nice to put them

07 there was an acceptance letter / I can trust your judgment / What type of place are you looking for

08 you stayed out so late / hike the mountain / Going alone with Dad is a bit awkward

09 what do you have in mind / she can treasure / How much for the bigger one / we don't offer that service

10 That's more than half of the vacation / they suffered a major earthquake / care of the injured / do some volunteering during winter vacation

11 where ice hockey dominates / it's played on a field of grass / with the flat side of their stick / making it more accessible to

12 an economy-sized car / It has the same capacity / available at the moment

13 where to begin / the population of the United States expanded so quickly / make it easier to visualize

14 my nose is feeling stuffy / we should buy a humidifier / a great deal on the Internet

15 has been allowing a lot of goals / to keep the other team from scoring / under a lot of pressure

16-17 people have five basic senses / even if they're taken hundreds of miles away / Earth's magnetic fields / identify their prey

| | | | | | |
|---|---|---|---|---|---|
| 01 ③ | 02 ⑤ | 03 ① | 04 ③ | 05 ③ | 06 ④ |
| 07 ④ | 08 ③ | 09 ② | 10 ③ | 11 ③ | 12 ⑤ |
| 13 ④ | 14 ⑤ | 15 ④ | 16 ① | 17 ④ | |

## 01 짧은 대화의 응답

**소재** DVD 더 늦게 돌려주기

**듣기 대본 해석**

여: Dylan, 지난주에 네가 나에게 빌려준 DVD 필요하니?
남: 글쎄, 지금은 필요 없는데 이번 주말에 볼 계획이야.
여: 나는 아직 볼 기회가 없었어. 목요일에 너에게 돌려줘도 되겠니?
남: ③ 문제 없어. 토요일까지 그것을 볼 시간이 없거든.

**어휘**

〈문제〉 **highly** *ad.* 매우, 대단히　　**recommend** *v.* 추천하다

**정답** ③

**문제풀이**

여자는 남자로부터 지난주에 빌린 DVD를 아직 못 봐서 목요일에 돌려줘도 되는지 남자에게 묻고 있으므로 이에 대한 가장 적절한 남자의 응답은 ③ '문제 없어. 토요일까지 그것을 볼 시간이 없거든.'이다.

**오답 보기 해석**

① 나는 진짜 그 영화를 재미있게 봤어. 그 영화를 강력히 추천해.
② 도서관에서 빌릴 수 있는지 알아봐야 할 거야.
④ 너 벌써 봤구나. 이렇게 빨리 돌려받을지는 예상하지 못했는걸.
⑤ 정말 미안한데, 며칠 더 DVD를 가지고 있어야 할 것 같아.

**총 어휘 수** 59

## 02 짧은 대화의 응답

**소재** 조언 부탁하기

**듣기 대본 해석**

남: Wilson 선생님, 제가 사회 과목 프로젝트에 대해 조언을 부탁드려도 괜찮을까요?
여: Tim, 정말 그러고 싶지만, 나는 지금은 너무 중요한 일을 하는 중이란다.
남: 그럼 제가 이따가 다시 올까요?
여: ⑤ 그래, 오후 3시경에 다시 오렴.

**어휘**

**social studies** (학교 교과로서의) 사회　　〈문제〉 **give ~ a hand** ~를 도와주다

**정답** ⑤

**문제풀이**

사회 과목 프로젝트에 대한 조언을 구하는 남자에게 여자는 지금은 중요한 일을 하는 중이라 했다. 남자가 이따가 다시 오면 되는지 묻는 데 대한 적절한 응답은 ⑤ '그래, 오후 3시경에 다시 오렴.'이다.

**오답 보기 해석**

① 이것 좀 도와주겠니?
② 나는 사실 지금 회의를 가야 해.
③ 나는 사회 과목을 전혀 잘하지 않았어.
④ 너는 항상 좋은 충고를 해주는구나.

**총 어휘 수** 46

## 03 담화 목적

**소재** 천문대 관측 프로그램 안내

**듣기 대본 해석**

남: 여러분은 은하계와 여러분이 가장 좋아하는 별자리를 보고 싶으십니까? 그렇다면 여러분의 다음 주말 여행 목적지를 Lone Star 천문대로 잡아 보십시오. 저희 천문대는 올해 5월 31일부터 10월 1일까지 수요일부터 일요일까지, 오후 1시부터 오후 8시 30분까지 개관합니다. Lone Star 천문대에서 제공하는 모든 프로그램은 일반인들에게 개방되어 있고 완전히 무료로 참여할 수 있으며 예약을 하실 필요도 없습니다. 오후에는 태양을 관측하실 수 있고 여러 종류의 망원경 전시도 보실 수 있습니다. 저녁 시간에 방문객들은 밤하늘과 모든 별, 먼 곳에 있는 은하수를 보실 수 있는 기회를 갖습니다. 보다 즐거운 방문이 되시도록 여러분들께 천문대를 안내해 드리는 천문학자들이 항상 상주해 있습니다. 이번 여름에 여러분들을 보기를 희망합니다!

**어휘**

**constellation** *n.* 별자리, 성좌　　**observatory** *n.* 천문대
**destination** *n.* 목적지, 도착지　　**reservation** *n.* 예약　　**telescope** *n.* 망원경　　**display** *n.* 전시　　**galaxy** *n.* 은하계, 은하수
**astronomer** *n.* 천문학자

**정답** ①

**문제풀이**

남자는 천문대의 운영 시간과 프로그램 소개 및 이용 방법 등을 언급하며 천문대 관측 프로그램에 대해 안내하고 있으므로 정답은 ① '천문대의 관측 프로그램에 대해 안내하려고'이다.

**총 어휘 수** 136

## 04 대화 주제

**소재** 생체 리듬

**듣기 대본 해석**

여: Bill, 너는 오후보다 아침에 더 에너지가 넘쳐 보여.
남: 그래, 오늘 오후는 정말 힘들었어. Field 선생님의 수학 수업 시간에 집중을 할 수가 없었어.
여: 정말? 나는 네가 그분 수업을 굉장히 좋아한다고 생각했어.
남: 그래, 하지만 나는 오후에는 힘이 하나도 없어. 어떤 것에도 집중할 수가 없어.
여: 그건 생체 리듬의 문제라고 생각해. 나는 오후에 집중이 잘되고 아침에는 힘이 하나도 없어.
남: 우리 둘은 다른 리듬을 가지고 있구나.
여: 맞아. 너는 아침형 인간이야.
남: 그럼 너는 오후형 인간이겠구나.
여: 그래, 모든 사람의 생체 시계는 조금씩 달라.
남: 대단한 걸!
여: 응, 나도 그렇게 생각해. 우리 모두 자신들이 공부한 것에서 최대의 것을 얻기 위해서는 자신의 생체 시계에 맞춰서 공부를 해야 해.
남: 나도 동의해. 나는 아침에 더 많이 공부하도록 노력해야겠다.

**어휘**

**struggle** *v.* 고투하다　　**concentrate** *v.* 집중하다　　**biological rhythm** 생체 리듬, 바이오리듬　　**according to** ~에 따르면　　**benefit** *v.* ~에게 이익을 가져다 주다, 이익을 얻다

**정답** ③

**문제풀이**

남자는 오후보다 아침에 집중이 잘되고 반대로 여자는 오후에 집중이 잘된다고 하면서 그 이유가 각자 다른 생체 리듬 때문이라고 말하고 있다. 마지막에 생체 리듬에 맞춰 공부하면 최대의 것을 얻을 수 있다는 말이 있으므로 두 사람이 하는 대화의 주제로 가장 적절한 것은 ③ '생체 리듬에 따른 학습 능률'이다.

**총 어휘 수** 145

## 05 대화자의 관계 파악

**소재** 럭비팀 주장의 비행 여행

**듣기 대본 해석**

남: 안녕하세요. 마실 것 좀 드릴까요?

남: 물 한 잔만 주세요.

여: 네. *[잠시 후]* 여기 있습니다. 오! 당신은 럭비선수 아니신가요?

남: 맞아요. 저는 국가대표팀의 주장입니다.

여: 그렇게 생각했어요. 만나서 반가워요. 저는 정말 팬이에요.

남: 그래요? 지지해주셔서 감사해요.

여: 제가 당신에게 서비스를 제공하게 되다니 놀라워요. 저희는 아주 많은 유명인사 승객들을 만나진 않거든요. 저는 당신이 토너먼트에서 경기하기 위해 미국으로 가신다고 들었어요. 이게 그 여행이군요, 맞죠?

남: 맞아요. 저희는 미국에서 한 달 조금 넘게 머물 겁니다.

여: TV에서 경기를 꼭 보고 싶어요. 뭔가가 필요하시면 주저하지 말고 부르세요.

남: 감사합니다. 그런데 Los Angeles에 도착하려면 얼마나 남았나요?

여: 벌써 다섯 시니까, 약 네 시간 후에 도착할 거예요.

남: 그렇군요. 저, 만약 땅콩 있으면 좀 주셨으면 합니다.

여: 물론이죠. 여기 있습니다. 즐거운 비행 되시길 바랍니다.

**어휘**

**captain** *n.* 주장, 선장　　**celebrity** *n.* 유명인사　　**look forward to** ~을 기대하다　　**match** *n.* 경기, 시합　　**hesitate** *v.* 주저하다　　**touch down** 착륙하다　　**flight** *n.* 비행

**정답** ③

**문제풀이**

여자는 남자에게 물을 갖다 주고 비행 시간도 알려주는 것으로 보아 비행기 승무원이고, 남자는 비행기에 탄 승객으로서 국가대표팀의 주장이므로 정답은 ③ '승무원 ― 승객'이다.

**총 어휘 수** 169

## 06 그림의 세부 내용 파악

**소재** 공원으로 간 소풍

**듣기 대본 해석**

여: 너 지금 뭐 보고 있어, Jeff?

남: 그냥 지난주에 찍은 사진들을 보고 있었어. 나 소풍 갔었거든.

여: 정말 재미 있었겠다. 사진에 있는 게 너희 가족이지?

남: 물론이지.

여: 나무 아래 자고 있는 저 사람들은 누구야?

남: 잘 모르겠어. 그냥 공원에 있던 모르는 사람들이야. 벤치에서 책을 읽고 있는 분이 우리 엄마야.

여: 그렇구나. 너한테 원반을 던지는 분이 네 아버지시겠구나.

남: 맞아. 아빠랑 나는 공원에서 게임 하는 것을 좋아해.

여: 아버지랑 너랑 둘이 정말 많이 닮았어.

남: 그런 소리 많이 들었어.

여: 왼쪽에 바비큐를 담당하고 있는 사람은 누구야?

남: 우리 할아버지셔. 할아버지께서는 생선을 요리하고 계셔.

여: 또 여기 있는 사람은 누구야? 자전거를 타고 있는 네 여동생 Emma는 알겠는데 그녀를 쫓아가고 있는 게 누구지?

남: 그녀는 내 사촌이야. 그녀와 내 여동생은 서로 친해서 항상 붙어 다녀.

여: 사랑스럽다.

남: 정말 그래. 나는 소풍이 좋아. 다음 주에 또 가고 싶어.

**어휘**

**go on a picnic** 소풍가다　　**alike** *a.* (아주) 비슷한　　**man** *v.* 일하다, 담당하다　　**hang out** (~에서) 많은 시간을 보내다　　**adorable** *a.* 사랑스러운

**정답** ④

**문제풀이**

대화에서는 왼쪽에 할아버지께서 바비큐를 하고 있다고 했는데 낚시를 하고 있으므로 그림과 일치하지 않는다. 따라서 정답은 ④번이다.

**총 어휘 수** 179

## 07 부탁한 일

**소재** 부모님의 결혼기념일 이벤트 준비

**듣기 대본 해석**

여: Nate, 이번 주말에 엄마 아빠 결혼 기념일인 거 알지?

남: 완전히 잊고 있었어. 알려줘서 고마워.

여: 좀 큰 기념일이야. 결혼하신 지 30년 될 거거든. 뭔가 좀 큰 걸 해야 할 것 같아.

남: 나 선물 같은 것 잘 못 골라. 같이 가서 좀 특별하고 큰 걸 사다 드리면 되겠다.

여: 깜짝 파티가 더 나을 것 같아.

남: 그거 좋다. 레스토랑에서 하자. 파티 하기에 좋은 레스토랑 알아?

여: 글쎄. 엄마 아빠가 가장 좋아하는 데는 Turoni's Pasta야.

남: 나 거기 정말 좋아해. 네가 토요일에 파티룸 예약할래?

여: 알아볼게. 또 다른 것도 하면 좋을 것 같지 않아?

남: 지금까지 같이 찍어 온 사진으로 콜라주 만드는 건 어때?

여: 좋은 생각이야. 굉장히 좋아하실 거야.

**어휘**

**anniversary** *n.* 기념일　　**reminder** *n.* (이미 잊었거나 잊고 싶은 것을) 상기시키는(생각나게 하는) 것　　**collage** *n.* 콜라주(색종이나 사진 등의 조각들을 붙여 그림을 만드는 미술 기법)

**정답** ④

**문제풀이**

남자는 선물보다 깜짝 파티가 더 낫겠다는 여자의 의견에 동의하며 여자에게 부모님 결혼 기념일에 파티룸 예약을 부탁하였으므로 정답은 ④ '파티룸 예약 하기'이다.

**오답 보기 해석**

① 휴일 기념하기

② 콜라주 만들기

③ 새 디지털 카메라 사기

⑤ 특별한 것 사기

**총 어휘 수** 145

## 08 이유

**소재** 아빠의 심부름

**듣기 대본 해석**

여: Logan, 정말 미안하지만 도서관에 같이 못 갈 것 같아.

남: 정말? 우리 거의 다 왔는데. 무슨 일 있어?

여: 응, 아빠가 방금 전화하셨는데 내가 오늘 내 동생을 돌봐줬으면 하셔.

남: 그럼 너 지금 집으로 가야 돼?

여: 곧. 집에 가기 전에 동생을 위해서 몇 가지를 사야 돼.

남: ABC 슈퍼마켓은 어때? 가는 길에 있어.

여: 거기가 편하긴 한데 내 동생이 Jojo's 피자를 정말 좋아해. 거기서 벌써 주문해서 나는 그걸 가져가기만 하면 돼.

남: 거기 피자 정말 훌륭하지. 나도 너랑 거기로 가야겠어. 나도 페퍼로니 한 조각 먹고 싶다.

여: 잘됐다. 너랑 같이 가면 좋지.

남: 난 음료수 몇 개도 사야 해.

여: Jojo's 피자 바로 옆집에 편의점이 있어. 거기에 네가 찾는 것이 있을 거야.

남: 그럴 것 같아. 가자.

**look after** ~을 돌보다    **convenient** *a.* 편리한, 간편한
**pick something up** ~을 사다, ~을 찾아오다    **amazing** *a.* 놀라운

정답 ③

문제풀이
여자는 전화를 받고 아빠가 동생을 돌봤으면 한다며 필요한 것 몇 가지를
사서 집으로 가야 한다고 말하고 있다. 그러므로 정답은 ③ '아빠의 부탁으로
동생을 돌보기 위해'이다.

총 어휘 수 149

# 09 숫자

소재 의자 구매

듣기 대본 해석
남: 안녕하세요. 무엇을 도와드릴까요?
여: 안녕하세요. 접이식 의자를 사려고요.
남: 그렇군요. 근데 탁자 세트를 구매하시는 게 훨씬 저렴해요. 이 탁자는 의자
　　두 개랑 같이 나와요. 보통 500달러인데 40퍼센트 할인해 드릴 수 있어요.
여: 좀 비싸네요. 좀 더 할인해 줄 순 없나요?
남: 그게 제일 싼 가격입니다.
여: 전 의자만 필요하거든요. 저기 있는 것들은 얼마예요?
남: 각각 150달러이에요. 그런데 네 개를 사시면 30퍼센트 할인해 드려요.
여: 의자 두 개만 사려고요.
남: 그래도 원래 가격의 20퍼센트를 할인해 드려요.
여: 좋네요! 그러면 그걸로 하겠습니다. 배송 서비스도 해주나요?
남: 그럼요. 그런데 배송비는 20달러가 추가됩니다.
여: 괜찮네요. 토요일 오후에 배송해 주세요.

어휘
**original** *a.* 원래의    **delivery** *n.* 배달, 배송    **additional** *a.* 추가의

정답 ②

문제풀이
여자가 각 150달러인 의자를 2개 구매하는데 원래 가격의 20퍼센트를 할인
해준다고 했으므로 240달러가 된다. 여기에 배송비가 20달러 추가된다고
했으므로 여자가 지불할 총 금액은 ② '$260'이다.

총 어휘 수 152

# 10 언급 유무

소재 컨벤션 일정

듣기 대본 해석
여: 안녕하세요, Stan. 총회가 오늘이라니 믿어지지가 않아요.
남: 네, 시간이 정말 빨리 가네요. 여러 달 준비했어도 여전히 걱정돼요.
여: 긴장을 풀어요. 모든 것이 다 잘될 거예요.
남: 알아요, 하지만 다시 한번 준비사항들을 점검 해보고 싶어요.
여: 네. 부의장님이 제일 먼저 발언하시는 거죠?
남: 맞아요. 그가 첫 발언자예요. 그 다음 바로 제가 프레젠테이션을 할 차례죠.
여: 네. 프레젠테이션 이후 Paul Stevenson과 회담할 거예요, 맞죠?
남: 맞아요. 그의 비서와 이 모든 준비사항에 대해 확인했나요?
여: 그럼요. 아, 잊을 뻔 했네요. 오늘 아침에 Mary와 얘기해봤는데 그녀가
　　당신의 프레젠테이션에서 몇 가지를 수정하길 원했어요. 그녀가 리스트를
　　적어서 줬어요. 어떻게 생각하세요?
남: Mary는 정말 일을 잘하죠. 그래서 난 그녀를 믿어요.
여: 알겠어요. 이제 컨벤션 센터에 점심을 먹으러 가요.

어휘
**preparation** *n.* 준비, 대비    **go over** 점검하다, 검토하다
**vice president** 부의장, 부통령    **make an arrangement (with)**
~와 합의에 이르다

정답 ③

문제풀이
두 사람은 오늘 남자의 일정에 대해 확인하고 있다. 부의장님의 연설, 남자의
발표, Paul Stevenson과의 회의, 점심식사에 대한 언급은 했지만 청중과의
대화는 없으므로 정답은 ③ '청중과의 대화'이다.

총 어휘 수 147

# 11 내용 일치 · 불일치

소재 강좌 소개

듣기 대본 해석
여: DIY Science Museum에 오신 것을 환영합니다. 이번 여름 My Little
　　Organics라는 새롭고 신나는 프로그램을 소개하고자 합니다. 유기농
　　과일과 야채를 비싸지 않은 기술과 최소한의 공간을 이용해 재배하는
　　방법을 참가자들에게 가르쳐줄 숙련된 강사들을 초빙할 것입니다. 강좌에
　　필요한 모든 재료를 제공할 것입니다. 그러나 본인의 장갑은 가져오셔야
　　합니다. 강좌는 월요일, 수요일, 금요일 저녁 7시 그리고 일요일 오후 2시
　　이렇게 일주일에 네 번 열릴 겁니다. 이 프로그램은 모든 연령대에 제공되고
　　또한 10명이 넘는 단체는 강좌 시간을 예약해드립니다. My Little
　　Organics 프로그램에 참가하시기 위한 수업료는 한 회당 15달러이고
　　단체 강좌들은 20퍼센트 할인됩니다. My Little Organics 강좌에 대해
　　더 궁금한 것이 있으시면 홈페이지를 참조하시거나 555-251-8956으로
　　전화 주십시오.

어휘
**skilled instructor** 숙련된 강사    **on hand** 구할 수 있는, 도움을 줄 수
있는    **organic** *a.* 유기농의    **minimal** *a.* 최소한의

정답 ③

문제풀이
전 연령에게 강좌를 제공한다고 언급되었으므로 정답은 ③ '수강할 수 있는
연령에 제한이 있다.'이다.

총 어휘 수 160

# 12 도표

소재 청소대행 서비스 선정

듣기 대본 해석
여: Jeff, 뭐 보고 있어?
남: 여러 사무실 청소 서비스 가격을 보고 있어. 이곳 너무 더러워졌더라.
여: 맞아. 그래서 괜찮은 데 찾았어?
남: 음, 이게 가격도 제일 괜찮고 보증도 잘 되는 것 같아.
여: 어디 보자. [잠시 후] 아, 창문도 닦고 바닥도 왁싱 하려고 하는구나.
남: 글쎄, 잘 모르겠어. 닌 어떻게 생각해?
여: 창문은 꼭 닦아야 해.
남: 당연하지. 바닥은 어때? 왁싱 해야겠지?
여: 우리가 이 사무실로 옮긴 이후로 한 번도 한 적 없는 것 같으니까 왁싱을
　　해야 한다고 생각해.
남: 그럼 이제 이 두 개 중에서 고르면 되네.
여: 철저한 서비스와 신속한 서비스는 무슨 차이야?
남: 철저한 서비스는 청소를 조심스럽게 하고 청소의 질이 좋다는 거야. 예를
　　들어 이 서비스는 바닥을 보호하는 특별한 처리를 해줘.

여: 그렇구나. 근데 신속한 서비스보다 좀 비싸다.
남: 맞아. 음, 여기 온 이후로 한 번도 창문이나 바닥을 청소한 적 없으니까 좀 더 비싼 걸로 하는 게 좋을 것 같아.
여: 동감이야.
남: 좋아. 전화해서 날짜를 잡을게.

### 어휘
**guarantee** *n.* 보증, 보장　　**thorough** *a.* 철저한, 빈틈없는
**express** *a.* 급행의, 신속한

### 정답 ⑤

### 문제풀이
남자와 여자는 유리창 청소와 바닥 왁싱을 하기로 동의했으므로 C, E 중에서 고르면 되는데 철저한 서비스인 더 비싼 것으로 하자고 했으므로 정답은 ⑤번이다.

### 총 어휘 수 201


## 13　긴 대화의 응답

**소재** 24시간 여는 레스토랑

### 듣기 대본 해석
여: 우왜! 시간 봐봐! 그만 퇴근해야 될 거 같다.
남: 나도 그 생각하고 있었어. 뭐 먹으러 가자.
여: 좋은 생각이야. 뭐 먹고 싶은 기분이야?
남: Johnny 버거는 어때?
여: 지금 별로 버거가 먹고 싶은 기분은 아니야.
남: 글쎄, 꽤 늦어서 먹을 수 있는 데가 많지가 않아.
여: 그럼 멕시코 음식은? 이 주변에 늦게까지 하는 맛있는 멕시칸 식당 알아.
남: Walking Taco's 말하는 거지?
여: 맞아. 24시간 여는 것 같아.
남: 오, 그런데 오늘 거기 지나갔는데 닫혀 있더라.
여: 정말? 왜?
남: ④ 레스토랑을 보수하고 있는 것 같아.

### 어휘
**grab a bite** 간단히 먹다　　**in a mood for** ~에 마음이 내켜서, ~할 기분이 되어　〈문제〉 **renovate** *v.* 개조(보수)하다

### 정답 ④

### 문제풀이
24시간 여는 레스토랑인데 문이 닫혀있는 이유로 적합한 대답을 골라야 하므로 정답은 ④ '레스토랑을 보수하고 있는 것 같아.'이다.

### 오답 보기 해석
① 거기 곧 문 닫을 거라 우리가 서둘러야 한다고 생각해.
② 우리가 먹기 전에 일을 끝내야 해.
③ 나는 오후 8시 이후에는 아무것도 먹지 않으려고 노력하고 있어.
⑤ 거기는 도시에서 최고의 생선 타코를 팔아.

### 총 어휘 수 111


## 14　긴 대화의 응답

**소재** 심리학에 대한 대화

### 듣기 대본 해석
여: 안녕 Blake. 옆에 앉아도 될까?
남: 응. 앉아.
여: 고마워. 뭐하고 있는 거야?

남: 어제 Malcolm George의 Ed Talk에 관한 심리학 수업 보고서를 쓰고 있어. 너 그거 봤어?
여: 응. 나 거기 있었어. 선택에 관한 정말 놀라운 강의였어, 그렇지?
남: 맞아. 그의 통찰력은 정말 흥미로웠어.
여: 응. 강의를 들으니 Barry Schwartz가 생각나던데.
남: 그 사람 The Right Choice 쓴 사람 맞지?
여: 맞아. 너 심리학자 정말 많이 아는구나, Blake.
남: 응. 나는 의사결정 뒤에 숨겨진 힘들에 대해서 정말 관심이 있거든. 그것이 내가 깊게 공부한 분야야.
여: 우리 공통점이 꽤 있네. Malcolm George하고 Barry Schwartz를 아는 사람은 많지 않은데.
남: 나는 그들이 심리학에 있어서 아주 중요하다고 생각하는데 왜냐하면 그들은 왜 사람들이 그와 같은 결정을 하는가를 이해하기 위해서 많은 시간을 바쳐왔기 때문이지.
여: ⑤ 나도 완전히 동의해. 나는 더 많은 사람들이 그들이 하는 헌신을 하면 좋겠어.

### 어휘
**psychology** *n.* 심리학　　**insight** *n.* 통찰력
**decision-making** *n.* 의사결정　　**in common** 공통으로
〈문제〉 **put yourself in somebody's shoes** 입장 바꿔 생각해보다
**dedication** *n.* 전념, 헌신

### 정답 ⑤

### 문제풀이
두 사람은 심리학에 대해 이야기 나누고 있다. 남자가 마지막에 그들이 언급했던 심리학자들이 왜 중요하다고 생각하는지에 대해 이야기했을 때 적절한 여자의 응답은 ⑤ '나도 완전히 동의해. 나는 더 많은 사람들이 그들이 하는 헌신을 하면 좋겠어.'이다.

### 오답 보기 해석
① 네가 판단을 하기 전에 그들하고 입장을 바꿔서 생각해 봐.
② 나는 의사결정의 뒤에 있는 힘들에는 별로 관심이 없어.
③ 완전히 실망이야. 그 사람 강의는 절대 다시 안 들을 거야.
④ 난 주제는 별로 마음에 들지 않았는데 강연자가 흥미로웠어.

### 총 어휘 수 164


## 15　상황에 적절한 말

**소재** 축제를 위한 음악 연습 도움 요청

### 듣기 대본 해석
여: Mike는 최근에 Charlestown으로 이사 가서 Jefferson Academy에 다니기 시작했습니다. 그는 Charlestown에 사는 것이 좋고 학교 친구들 모두와 잘 지내지만 곤경에 처하게 됩니다. 학교는 일 년마다 하는 Spring Sprung 행사를 이번에 개최하는데 반에서 유일하게 Mike만 음악 곡을 연습하지 못한 것입니다. 나머지 학생들은 몇 달 간 연습을 했지만 Mike는 학교에 새로 전학 왔기 때문에 연습을 몇 주밖에 못했습니다. 그는 방과 후에 연습을 하고 싶지만 도움이 필요합니다. Mike는 공연의 총 책임자인 Smith 선생님께 도움을 요청하고 싶어 합니다. 이러한 상황에서 Mike는 Smith 선생님께 뭐라고 말할까요?
Mike: Smith 선생님, ④ 음악 곡 연습하는 것을 도와주실 수 있으세요?

### 어휘
**predicament** *n.* 곤경　　**annual** *a.* 매년의, 연례의

### 정답 ④

### 문제풀이
Mike는 새로 전학 온 학교에서 열리는 축제의 음악 공연 연습을 충분히 하지 못해 Smith 선생님께 도움을 요청하려고 하므로 이에 대해 할 말로 가장 적절한 것은 ④ '음악 곡 연습하는 것을 도와주실 수 있으세요?'이다.

## 오답 보기 해석

① Jefferson Academy에서 잘 지내고 계신가요?
② 행사에서 저희는 어떤 곡을 연주할 건가요?
③ 저는 행사에 있을 공연을 위한 준비가 되어 있어요.
⑤ 제가 공연의 책임자가 되고 싶어요.

**총 어휘 수** 137

# 16 담화 목적 / 17 세부 내용 파악

**소재** 대입 추천서 작성 관련 안내

## 듣기 대본 해석

남: 좋은 아침입니다. Middle Brook 고등학교 학생 여러분. 저는 학업 상담자 Michael Manson입니다. 여러분 중 많은 수가 졸업반이어서 대학 입학 시험 준비와 에세이 쓰기에 여러분 대부분의 자유시간을 사용할 것입니다. 여러분이 여러분의 모든 서류를 취합할 때 여러분의 현재 선생님들 중 한 분이나 그 이상으로부터 받는 추천서를 포함할 것을 잊지 마십시오. 이 추천서들은 작성하는 데 시간이 걸리고 아마도 당신의 선생님께서 당신 것만을 작성하는 것이 아니라는 것을 명심하십시오. 따라서 당신의 선생님께 요청드리러 가기 전에 여러분 자신에 대한 세부 정보를 준비하십시오. 우리는 이 작업을 빠르고 쉽게 하기 위해 웹 페이지를 개설했습니다. 단지 우리 학교 웹사이트에 들어가셔서 웹 페이지의 오른편 상단에 있는 "Academic Guidance" 링크를 클릭하기만 하면 됩니다. 거기서 여러분이 자기 소개서와 다른 정보를 등록할 수 있게 단계별로 안내를 해줄 것입니다. 그 정보들은 선생님께서 여러분의 추천서를 작성하시는 일을 훨씬 쉽게 만들어 줍니다. 여러분이 온라인 절차를 끝낸 후 여러분의 선생님께서 추천서를 작성하는 작업을 시작하실 것입니다. 당신의 정보를 올리는 것뿐만 아니라, 추천서와 쓰기 과정에 관해 여러분이 가질 수 있는 다른 질문들에 관해 상의하기 위해 선생님과 일대일 약속을 잡는 데에 웹사이트를 이용하실 수도 있습니다. 여러분의 자기소개서 작성과 관련된 도움이 필요하시다면 샘플 자기소개서를 보실 수 있습니다. 다른 필요한 서류에 관한 정보도 또한 얻으실 수 있습니다. 더 도움이 필요하시다면, 망설이지 말고 저를 찾아 주세요.

## 어휘

**academic advisor** 학업 상담자    **current** *a.* 현재의    **approach** *v.* 다가가다, 접촉하다    **specific** *a.* 구체적인    **process** *n.* 절차    **upload** *v.* (정보를 네트워크상에) 올리다    **personal statement** 지기 소개서    **letter of recommendation** 추천서    **regarding** *prep.* ~에 관한    **assistance** *n.* 도움    **hesitate** *v.* 주저하다

## 정답 16 ①  17 ④

## 문제풀이

16 대학 입시에 필요한 추천서와 자기소개서 작성을 도와주는 웹사이트가 생겼음을 알리고 어떻게 이용하면 되는지를 설명해주고 있으므로 남자가 하는 말의 목적은 ① '대입 추천서 작성을 위한 웹사이트 개통을 알리려고'이다.

17 웹사이트에서 할 수 있는 일로 학생의 자기소개서 등록, 선생님과 상담 예약, 자기소개서 샘플 참조, 필요한 서류에 관한 정보 수집은 언급되었으나, ④ '지원 대학의 경쟁률 확인'은 언급되지 않았다.

**총 어휘 수** 262

## DICTATION ANSWERS

**01** I haven't gotten a chance

**02** I asked you for some advice / something really important

**03** open to the public / full of stars and distant galaxies

**04** I have great focus / the two of us have different rhythms / according to their own biological clock

**05** thank you for supporting us / serve you / don't hesitate to ask / we touch down

**06** went on a picnic / throwing you the frisbee / cooking up some fish / they're always hanging out

**07** Thanks for the reminder / throw it in a restaurant / book the party room

**08** look after my little brother / It's on the way / pick it up / There's a convenience store

**09** I'm looking into buying / as cheap as it gets / buy two chairs / offer a delivery service

**10** time really flies / go over the preparations / give my big presentation / make all of the arrangements

**11** plant their own organic fruits / Classes will be held four times a week / to visitors of all ages / offer a twenty percent discount

**12** starting to get dirty / get the windows cleaned / two packages to choose from / getting an express package

**13** Let's go grab a bite to eat / not really in the mood for / You must be talking about / walked by there

**14** Have a seat / reminded me of / I'm very interested in / in depth / have quite a bit in common

**15** gets along with / found himself in a predicament / hasn't practiced the music routine / is in charge of

**16-17** you should prepare some specific information / go to our school's website / In addition to uploading your information / do not hesitate to come see me

| | | | | | |
|---|---|---|---|---|---|
| 01 ① | 02 ② | 03 ① | 04 ④ | 05 ② | 06 ⑤ |
| 07 ② | 08 ③ | 09 ② | 10 ⑤ | 11 ③ | 12 ③ |
| 13 ④ | 14 ⑤ | 15 ④ | 16 ③ | 17 ③ | |

## 01 짧은 대화의 응답

**소재** 과제 미리 받기

**듣기 대본 해석**

여: 안녕하세요, Nelson 선생님. 죄송하지만, 월요일에 수업에 못 올 것 같습니다.
남: 괜찮아. 네가 토론 팀 선수권 대회에 나가는 것을 알고 있단다.
여: 맞아요. 월요일 과제를 오늘 제가 받아갈 수 있나요?
남: ① 물론이지. 내가 지금 준비해 줄게.

**어휘**

**debate** *n.* 토론    **assignment** *n.* 과제    〈문제〉 **turn in** 제출하다

**정답** ①

**문제풀이**

남자에게 과제를 먼저 받아갈 수 있는지 물었으므로 적절한 응답은 ① '물론이지. 내가 지금 준비해 줄게.'이다.

**오답 보기 해석**

② 좋아. 그것들을 월요일에 너에게 줄게.
③ 아직 토론 주제를 선택하지 못했어.
④ 나는 토론에 관해서 그다지 많이 알지 못해. 미안해.
⑤ 문제없어. 먼저 오늘 그것을 제출 할 수 있어.

**총 어휘 수** 49

## 02 짧은 대화의 응답

**소재** 플라스틱 병 재활용

**듣기 대본 해석**

남: 저 오래된 플라스틱 병들 가지고 뭐 할거니?
여: 내가 생각해온 작은 프로젝트를 위해 병들을 전부 살펴봐서 재사용하고 싶은 것들을 고르고 있어.
남: 멋지다! 네가 생각했던 게 무슨 프로젝트인데?
여: ② 나는 그것들을 새 모이통을 만드는 데 쓸 거야.

**어휘**

**go through** ~을 살펴보다    〈문제〉 **bird feeder** 새 모이통

**정답** ②

**문제풀이**

플라스틱 병을 재활용해서 무엇을 할 것인지에 대한 남자의 질문에 가장 적절한 여자의 응답은 ② '나는 그것들을 새 모이통을 만드는 데 쓸 거야.'이다.

**오답 보기 해석**

① 네가 왜 이 프로젝트를 그렇게 흥미로워하는지 알겠다.
③ 너의 과학 프로젝트에 그것들을 사용하자.
④ 이 오래된 병들 전부 갖다 버릴 거야.
⑤ 넌 항상 헌 병들을 재활용을 해야 해.

**총 어휘 수** 51

## 03 담화 목적

**소재** 학생회장 선거의 투표 참여

**듣기 대본 해석**

남: 안녕하세요, 여러분. 저는 학생회 대표인 Tony Brown이고, Fine Arts 학교의 3학년입니다. 여러분께서 짐작하시듯이, 저는 다가오는 학생회장 선거에 대해 여러분과 이야기를 나누고자 여기 있습니다. 먼저 저는 제가 가장 관심 있는 것을 말하려 하는데요, 그것은 바로 유권자 투표율입니다. 지난해의 투표율은 고작 28%였습니다. 믿어지십니까? 그렇게 낮은 투표율 때문에 캠퍼스에서의 생활은 결코 만족스럽지 못했습니다. 여러분께서는 학교 도서관이 최신식 시설로 보수되기를 바라십니까? 학교 식당에서 좀 더 다양한 음식을 선택하고 싶으십니까? 만약에 그렇다면 그리고 많은 다른 변화들이 일어나기 바라신다면 여러분의 권리를 행사하여 투표하십오. 모두의 한 표 한 표가 중요하고 우리 모두가 학교를 더 나은 곳으로 만들 수 있다는 것을 항상 기억하십시오.

**어휘**

**representative** *n.* 대표    **election** *n.* 선거    **voter** *n.* 투표자, 유권자
**turnout** *n.* 투표율    **satisfactory** *a.* 만족스러운, 충분한    **outfit** *v.* 채비하다, 준비하다    **up-to-date** *a.* 최신의    **take place** 개최되다, 일어나다

**정답** ①

**문제풀이**

남자는 작년 학생회장 선거의 낮은 투표율 때문에 학교 생활이 만족스럽지 않았다고 말하며 학교 도서관, 학교 식당의 개선을 원한다면 투표를 해달라고 말하고 있으므로 정답은 ① '학생들의 학생회장 선거 투표를 촉구하려고'이다.

**총 어휘 수** 137

## 04 대화 주제

**소재** 등산을 취미로 시작한 친구에게 필요한 조언해주기

**듣기 대본 해석**

여: 이번 주말에 Steven's Peak로 등산 갈 생각이야.
남: Laura. 네가 등산을 좋아하는지 몰랐어.
여: 내 새로운 취미라서 조언을 구하려고 해. 조언해 줄 것 있니?
남: 물론이지. 첫 번째로 안전이 최우선이야. 그게 가장 중요한 고려 사항이지. 예를 들어 어두워지기 전에 산을 하산할 수 있도록 항상 주의해야 해.
여: 그건 알고 있었어.
남: 그렇지. 그리고 만약 네가 길을 잃어서 돌아올 수 없을 때를 대비해서 손전등이랑 라이터, 아니면 성냥을 갖고 다니는 게 좋아.
여: 아하. 내가 길을 잃었을 때 그것들로 불을 피워서 따뜻하게 있을 수 있겠구나.
남: 불은 네가 길을 잃었을 때 다른 사람들에게 신호 보낼 때도 사용할 수 있어.
여: 그건 한 번도 생각해 본 적이 없어. 다른 조언은 없어?
남: 구급상자도 하나 갖고 다니는 게 좋아. 옛말에 "나중에 후회하는 것보다 조심하는 것이 낫다"는 말이 있잖아.
여: 알겠어. 출발하기 전에 하나 꼭 챙길게. 도와줘서 고마워.
남: 아냐. 등산 즐겁게 하고 와. 이때쯤 Steven's Peak는 경치가 정말 아름다워.

**어휘**

**daylight** *n.* 햇빛, 일광    **first-aid kit** 구급상자
**better safe than sorry** [속담] 나중에 후회하는 것보다 조심하는 것이 낫다

**정답** ④

**문제풀이**

등산을 취미로 시작한 여자가 남자에게 조언을 구하고, 남자는 이에 대해 안전한 등산을 위해 필요한 물품들과 유의 사항을 말해주고 있으므로 대화의 주제는 ④ '안전한 등산을 위한 유의 사항'이다.

**총 어휘 수** 186

**소재**　배심원들에 의해 유죄가 아닌 것으로 난 판결

**듣기 대본 해석**

여: Clinton Town 법원 청사에서 속보가 있습니다. 현장에 있는 우리의 특파원 Ron Berger에게 들어보도록 하겠습니다. 안녕하세요, Ron!

남: 안녕하세요, Stacy. 저는 지금 공무원들에게 뇌물을 준 혐의로 기소된 백만장자 기업가 Pat Parker의 재판에 대해 배심원이 마침내 판결을 내린 Clinton Town 법원 청사에 나와있습니다.

여: 시민들이 결과에 대해 궁금해 합니다. 배심원들이 결론을 어떻게 냈습니까, Ron?

남: 뜻밖에 사태의 전환으로 Pat Parker는 뇌물 혐의에 대해 유죄가 아니라고 판결이 났습니다. 우리 모두에게 충격입니다.

여: 와! 놀랍네요. 그렇다면 배심원들이 모든 점에서 유죄가 아니라고 판결한 건가요?

남: 맞습니다. 배심원들은 검찰 측에서 제시한 증거들이 Parker의 유죄를 입증하는데 충분하지 않다고 결정 내린 겁니다.

여: 검찰 측의 반응이 있나요?

남: 네. 검찰 측에서 항소하겠다고 했습니다.

여: 흥미롭군요. 앞으로 어떻게 진행될지 지켜보고 있겠습니다. 보도에 감사합니다. Ron. [잠시 후] Clinton Town 법원 청사에서 배심원들이 Pat Parker의 여러 뇌물 혐의에 대해 유죄가 아니라는 판결을 내린 내용을 보도한 Channel 2의 Ron Berger였습니다. 광고 후에 이 충격적인 소식에 관한 분석과 함께 돌아오도록 하겠습니다.

**어휘**

**breaking news** 뉴스 속보　**jury** *n.* 배심원단　**trial** *n.* 재판, 공판
**guilty** *a.* 유죄의　**bribery** *n.* 뇌물수수　**prosecution** *n.* 기소, 고발,
검찰 측　**convict** *v.* 유죄를 선고하다　**file** *v.* (소송을) 제기하다
**appeal** *n.* 항소　**commercial** *n.* 광고　*a.* 상업적인

**정답**　②

**문제풀이**

여자가 속보가 있다고 전하면서 Ron에게 들어보겠다고 했고 남자에게 질문하고 있는 것으로 보아 앵커임을 알 수 있고, 남자는 법원에서 소식을 전해주고 있으므로 기자라고 추측할 수 있다. 따라서 정답은 ② '앵커 — 기자'이다.

**총 어휘 수**　197



**소재**　도서관 상황 묻기

**듣기 대본 해석**

여: Nolan. 도서관에 갔었니?

남: 응. 갔었어. Meagan을 찾는 거야? 내가 들어갔을 때 Meagan이 책을 읽고 있던데.

여: 도서관에 다른 사람도 있었니, 아니면 Meagan만 있었니?

남: Meagan외에 다른 사람들도 좀 있었어. Gianna도 거기서 책을 반납하고 있더라.

여: 내가 30분 전에 Kathy가 도서관으로 향하는 걸 본 것 같아. 그녀가 거기 있었어?

남: 맞아. 나도 그녀를 봤어. Kathy는 반납된 책을 정리하고 있어서, 난 그녀가 자원봉사를 하거나 거기서 아르바이트를 하는 것으로 생각했지.

여: 음. 그녀는 현장 실습을 해야 해서 거기서 일하고 있어.

남: 경험을 얻기 위한 좋은 방법이 되겠네.

여: Nancy는 어때? 걔 봤니? 나는 Nancy가 도서관에서 공부를 하고 있었으면 했어. 왜냐하면 그녀의 성적이 요즘 별로 좋지 않거든.

남: Nancy도 봤어. 그녀는 책상에서 공부하고 있었어.

여: 알게 돼서 정말 좋네.

남: 그리고 William도 컴퓨터로 뭔가를 읽고 있었어.

여: 그래. 사실, 나는 프로젝트를 위한 조사를 좀 해야 하거든. 사용 가능한 또 다른 컴퓨터가 있었으면 좋겠다.

남: 내 생각에는 거기 있었어.

**어휘**

**arrange** *v.* 정리하다　**available** *a.* 이용할 수 있는

**정답**　⑤

**문제풀이**

William은 컴퓨터로 뭔가를 읽고 있다고 했는데 그냥 모니터 위에 손을 대고 있는 모습이므로 ⑤번이 그림과 일치하지 않는다.

**총 어휘 수**　176



**소재**　영어캠프를 위한 준비

**듣기 대본 해석**

남: 안녕. Emma! 어디 가는 길이야?

여: 어. 안녕 Ian! 나 서점에 가고 있었어.

남: 정말? 나도 그래! 다음 주에 영어캠프를 위한 책을 좀 찾아야 해.

여: 좋겠다. 네가 찾고 있는 게 무슨 레벨이야?

남: 대부분 학생들이 상급인데 중급도 몇몇 섞여 있어.

여: 네 일이 너한테 잘 맞을 것 같구나. 두 레벨을 가르치기 어렵지 않을까?

남: 응. 그럴 것 같아. 나는 학습 안내서로 책을 이용해서 두 레벨에 동시에 유용한 활동들에 대한 생각을 얻고 싶어.

여: 그건 멋진 생각이네. 캠프를 정말 재미있고 독창적으로 만들어 줄 거야.

남: 나도 그러길 바라. 나는 학생들이 내 캠프에서 특별한 무언가를 배워가길 정말로 원해.

여: 네가 잘 준비했는지 그리고 계획대로 되지 않을 경우에 대체할 방안들이 있는지 확인해봐. 나는 네가 정말 잘할 거라고 확신해!

남: 그렇게 말해줘서 고마워.

**어휘**

**advanced** *a.* 상급의, 고급의　**cut out for** ~에 적합하여
**at the same time** 동시에, 함께　**original** *a.* 독창적인
**definitely** *ad.* 분명히, 확실히　**backup** *n.* 예비, 백업　*a.* 예비의

**정답**　②

**문제풀이**

남자는 영어캠프에서 두 레벨의 학생들을 같이 지도하기 위해 필요한 책을 찾아보러 서점에 간다고 했으므로 남자가 할 일은 ② '캠프 활동을 위한 책 찾아보기'가 정답이다.

**총 어휘 수**　158



**소재**　관심 진로가 바뀐 이유

**듣기 대본 해석**

남: 안녕. Patty. 네가 학교의 새로운 토론 우승자라는 소식을 방금 들었어. 축하해!

여: 고마워 Tommy.

남: 결승 토론 주제가 뭐였니?

여: 유럽연합이 회원국들에게 유익한지에 대한 논쟁에서 찬성 입장 쪽이었어. 그것을 위해 열심히 공부했어.

남: 그러면 너는 꽤 주제에 대해 잘 알고 있겠구나. 너는 그러면 정말 유럽 연합이 회원국들에게 혜택을 줄 거라 생각하니?

여: 응. 국경을 개방하고, 자국의 거주민을 다른 나라에서 자유롭게 일하도록 허용함으로써 유럽의 보다 가난한 국가들을 돕게 되지. 그러면 이들은 가족들에게 돈을 보내고, 이 외부에서 온 돈은 그 나라에서 순환될 수 있게 돼.

남: 그렇구나. 그럼 너는 너의 토론 기술들을 미래에 이용할 수 있을 것이라고 생각해?

여: 그럼. 난 크면 변호사가 되고 싶어.

남: 정말?

여: 응. 난 언제나 변호사와 관련된 TV쇼를 좋아했거든. 너도 법에 대해 관심이 있잖아. 맞지?

남: 그랬었지. 하지만 최근에는 은행원이 되는 공부를 하고 있어. 약간 연관이 있긴 한 것 같은데.
여: 돈과 법은 협력관계이지. 무엇이 네 생각을 바꾸게 했니?
남: 주식거래로 큰 돈을 번 은행원에 관한 책을 읽었어. 그는 그의 꿈을 쫓았고 흥미로운 삶을 살았어. 난 그게 너무 좋아서 그의 삶을 모델 삼기로 결정했어.
여: 멋지다. Tommy.

### 어휘
**pro side** 찬성 쪽　**argument** *n.* 논쟁, 언쟁　**beneficial** *a.* 유익한, 이로운　**border** *n.* 경계, 국경　**related** *a.* 관련된　**hand-in-hand** *a.* 친밀한, 협력한　**trade stock** 주식을 거래하다

### 정답 ③

### 문제풀이
대화의 마지막 부분에서 여자가 무엇이 진로를 바꾸게 했냐고 물었고, 남자는 주식거래로 큰 돈을 번 은행원에 관한 책을 읽고 삶의 모델로 삼게 되었다고 했으므로 남자의 관심 진로 분야가 바뀐 이유는 ③ '인상 깊게 읽은 책 때문에'이다.

**총 어휘 수** 226

## 09 숫자

**소재** 과수원 견학 예약

### 듣기 대본 해석
*[전화벨이 울린다.]*
여: 안녕하세요. Backwoods 과수원입니다.
남: 안녕하세요. 저는 Vanguard 고등학교의 Lewis 선생님입니다. 우리 학생들을 위한 체험 학습 예약을 하고 싶습니다.
여: 네. Lewis 선생님. 반나절 견학과 종일 견학 중 어느 것을 원하시나요?
남: 가격 차이가 얼마인가요?
여: 음. 반나절 견학은 학생당 20달러이고 종일 견학은 학생당 30달러입니다.
남: 10월 13일에 종일 견학으로 20명을 예약할 것 같습니다.
여: 네. 그날 자리가 있는지 확인해 볼게요. *[클릭하는 소리]*네. 저희가 학생들을 수용할 수 있을 것 같네요.
남: 좋아요.
여: 20명 이상의 그룹은 전체 입장료의 10퍼센트 할인을 받아요.
남: 선생님도 요금을 내나요?
여: 성인은 40달러이지만. 15명 이상의 학생을 데리고 오시는 선생님은 무료예요.
남: 좋네요. 지금 제 신용카드 정보를 원하시나요, 아니면 제가 거기에 갔을 때 드리면 되나요?
여: 여기에 왔을 때 지불하시면 돼요.
남: 좋아요. 감사해요.

### 어휘
**field trip** 체험 학습　**accommodate** *v.* 수용하다　**admission** *n.* 입장(료)　**charge** *v.* (요금, 값을) 청구하다

### 정답 ②

### 문제풀이
남자는 종일 견학으로 20명 예약하고 싶다고 했으므로 30x20=600달러이고, 20명 이상이라 전체 금액의 10퍼센트 할인이 되며, 15명 이상의 학생을 데리고 가서 선생님은 무료이므로, 남자가 지불할 금액은 ② '$540'이다.

**총 어휘 수** 166

## 10 언급 유무

**소재** 구직 인터뷰

### 듣기 대본 해석
여: 안녕하세요. 저는 Nora Stenson이에요. 만나서 반갑습니다.
남: 저는 John Ramstad입니다. 저도 만나서 반갑습니다.

여: 몇 가지 질문으로 시작해 볼까 해요. 먼저, 왜 어린이를 위한 주간캠프에서 일하는 데 관심이 있으신가요?
남: 음… 저는 여름에 아이들과 야외 활동 하는 것을 좋아하고, 본 주간캠프는 이 주변에서 가장 인기 있는 캠프입니다. 훌륭한 기관이라고 생각하고 있으며, 저는 정말 이곳의 일원이 되고 싶습니다.
여: 그렇다니 좋군요. 좋습니다. 그러면 언제 CPR과 일반 치료 자격증을 받았죠?
남: 둘 다 9달 전에 받았습니다.
여: 경험은 얼마나 되시나요?
남: 캠프 상담자로 3년의 경력이 있습니다. 일 년 동안은 Little Acorns Day 캠프에서 일했고, 지난 2년은 Young Explorers 주간캠프에서 일했습니다.
여: 당신은 Young Explorers 주간캠프에서 왜 그만두기로 결심했습니까?
남: 그곳의 커리큘럼에 동의하지 않았고 직원들이 너무 무책임하다는 것을 알게 됐습니다.
여: 좋아요, 시간 내 주셔서 감사해요. 2주 후에 연락 드릴게요.

### 어휘
**CPR** *n.* 심폐소생술　**certificate** *n.* 자격증, 면허　**counselor** *n.* 상담자　**quit** *v.* 그만두다, 중지하다　**irresponsible** *a.* 무책임한

### 정답 ⑤

### 문제풀이
지원동기(Why are you interested in working at our day camp for kids?), 자격증 취득 시기(When did you receive your CPR and general care certificates?), 근무 경력(How much experience do you have?), 전 직장을 그만 둔 이유(Why did you decide to quit your job at Young Explorers Day Camp?)는 물었지만 희망 보수에 관한 언급은 하지 않았으므로 정답은 ⑤ '희망 보수'이다.

**총 어휘 수** 186

## 11 내용 일치·불일치

**소재** 역사공원에서 주관하는 두 가지 행사

### 듣기 대본 해석
여: 안녕하세요. 제 이름은 Eston Cotton이고 저는 Angel Mounds 역사공원의 큐레이터입니다. 이번 봄 저희는 두 가지 특별 행사를 개최할 것입니다. 첫 번째 행사는 3월의 마지막 주에 진행됩니다. 해마다 열리는 미국 원주민의 날 행사가 그것이지요. 이 행사에서 우리는 미국 원주민들이 어떻게 살았는지 도구들과 집을 어떻게 만들고, 사냥을 어떻게 했는지 배웁니다. 투어 전체가 약 네 시간 소요되니 미리 예약을 하시고 일찍 오시기 바랍니다. 4월 17일에 개최되는 다른 행사는 어린이날 행사입니다. 이 행사에서 어린이들은 미국 원주민 춤을 배우고 페이스페인팅도 받고 미국 원주민들의 전통 음식을 맛볼 수 있습니다. 또한 이날 가족 전체가 즐길 수 있는 여러 가지 행사도 있습니다. 올해 행사에 꼭 오시길 바랍니다. 감사합니다.

### 어휘
**curator** *n.* 큐레이터　**reservation** *n.* 예약　**traditional** *a.* 전통적인

### 정답 ③

### 문제풀이
원주민의 날 행사에서는 원주민들이 도구들과 집을 어떻게 만들고 사냥을 했는지 배운다고 했다. 전통적인 원주민 음식을 먹는 것은 '원주민의 날 행사'가 아니라 '어린이날 행사' 내용이므로 일치하지 않는 것은 ③ '원주민의 날 행사에서는 원주민 전통 음식을 먹어볼 수 있다.'이다.

**총 어휘 수** 134

## 12 도표

**소재** 영화 편집 강좌 선택하기

### 듣기 대본 해석
남: 안녕하세요. 어떻게 도와드릴까요?
여: 영화 편집 강좌를 수강하고 싶은데요.

남: 제가 도와드릴게요. 저희 강좌를 수강하시는 것은 처음이신가요?
여: 실은 아니에요. 전에 여기 프로그램에 있는 다른 강좌들도 수강했어요.
남: 영화 편집에 관한 강좌였나요?
여: 아니요. 하지만 같은 분야의 강좌요. 영화 제작과 연출을 수강했어요.
남: 알았어요. 그렇다면 영화 편집 분야의 상급자 강좌 중 하나를 수강하시는
   게 좋겠네요. 괜찮을 것 같으세요?
여: 네, 그럴 것 같아요.
남: 좋아요, 몇 가지 중 선택하실 수 있어요.
여: Michael의 강좌 중 하나를 수강하는 것은 가능한가요? Michael이 굉장히
   좋은 강사라고 들었어요.
남: Michael이 당신의 수준에 맞는 강좌 세 개를 가르쳐요. 두 개는 학생 수가
   10명으로 제한되어있고, 나머지 하나는 15명으로 제한되어있어요. 아침
   강좌와 저녁 강좌 중에 선택하실 수 있어요.
여: 좋아요. 학생 수가 더 적은 강좌로 할게요.
남: 아침 강좌와 저녁 강좌 중에 선택하세요.
여: 아침 강좌로 할게요.
남: 아주 좋아요. 이제 등록되셨습니다.

### 어휘
**sign up for** ~을 신청하다　　**film editing** 영화 편집
**film production and directing** 영화 제작과 연출

### 정답 ③

### 문제풀이
영화 관련 강좌를 들어본 적이 있는 여자는 상급반 강좌를 듣기로 했고,
Michael의 강좌를 들으려 하므로 ②, ③, ④번이 남는다. 세 개의 Michael의
강좌 중에서도 여자는 학생 수가 적고 아침 시간대 강좌를 원했으므로 모든 조
건이 맞는 것은 ③ 'Advanced B'이다.

### 총 어휘 수 171


## 13 　긴 대화의 응답

**소재** 직원의 업무태도에 대한 상의

### 듣기 대본 해석
여: 안녕하세요, Green 씨. 시간 좀 있으세요?
남: 네. 무슨 일이에요?
여: 음. 제가 Karen에 관해 당신에게 말해야 할 것 같아서요.
남: 좋아요. Karen에 관한 어떤 거요?
여: 오해는 하지 마세요. 저는 그녀가 좋은 직원이라고 생각하지만, 요즘 그녀가
   일에 집중을 못하는 것 같아요.
남: 무슨 말씀인지 잘 모르겠네요.
여: 나는 그녀가 당신에게 말했는지는 모르겠지만, 그녀는 실제로 꽤 유명한
   소설가예요.
남: 그래요? 저는 몰랐어요. 그래서 무엇이 문제인가요?
여: 저는 그녀가 직장에서 그녀의 글쓰기에 공을 들이고 사무실에서의 임무는
   소홀히 하는 것 같아요. 그녀는 이곳 일에서 뒤처져 있어요.
남: 확실히 문제네요. 그녀가 사무실에 있을 땐 일에 집중해야 해요.
여: 동의해요. 우리가 어떻게 해야 한다고 생각하세요?
남: ④ 제가 그녀가 이것에 관심을 가지도록 하고 그녀에게 경고를 할게요.

### 어휘
**distracted** *a.* (정신이) 산만해진　　**work on** ~에 공을 들이다, 애쓰다
**get behind** (일이) 밀리다
〈문제〉 **bring something to somebody's attention** ~에 ~가
주목하게 하다

### 정답 ④

### 문제풀이
남자와 여자는 Karen의 업무태도에 문제가 있다는 생각을 가지고 대화하고
있으므로 남자의 마지막 응답은 ④ '제가 그녀가 이것에 관심을 가지도록 하고
그녀에게 경고를 할게요.'가 적절하다.

### 오답 보기 해석
① 그녀는 당신이 당신의 소설 쓰는 것을 도와 줄 수 있어서 기뻐할 거예요.
② 당신이 옳아요. 그녀는 제 시간에 직장에 도착해야 해요.
③ 음. 저는 그렇게 생각지 않아요. 저는 그녀의 소설을 그다지 좋아하지 않아요.
⑤ 잘 모르겠어요. 저는 소설 쓰는 것이 매우 시간이 많이 걸리는 일이라고
   생각해요.

### 총 어휘 수 143


## 14 　긴 대화의 응답

**소재** 축구 경기 티켓 구매

### 듣기 대본 해석
여: Devin, 너 컴퓨터로 하고 있는 게 뭐니?
남: 축구 경기 티켓을 판매할 때까지 기다리고 있어.
여: 약간 긴장되어 보이는데.
남: 나는 정말로 스탠딩 구역 티켓이 필요한데, 그들이 판매를 하자마자 버튼을
   눌러야 해.
여: 정말? 무슨 경기인데?
남: FC Barcelona가 Real Madrid와 경기를 해. 멋진 경기가 될 거야.
여: 내 생각에는 그 티켓이 너를 위한 게 아닌 것 같아. 그렇지?
남: 맞아. 티켓은 나의 아버지를 위한 것이야. 그는 FC Barcelona의 열렬한
   팬이고 그의 생신날에 그 경기가 있어.
여: 너의 아버지를 위한 멋진 선물이구나.
남: 그래. 아버지께서 이 축구 경기에 대해서 수개월 동안 말씀하셨어. 그는 그
   경기에 대해서 정말 흥분해 계셔.
여: 작년 생각이 좀 나네. 나는 Real Madrid와 경기에 대해 정말 들떠 있었는데,
   부모님께서 내가 가는 것을 허락하지 않으셨어.
남: 안 됐구나. 네가 그거 때문에 화가 났겠다.
여: ⑤ 그래. 우리 아버지께서 너희 아버지처럼 축구에 관심이 있으셨으면 좋겠어.

### 어휘
**remind A of B** A에게 B를 상기시키다　　**that's a shame** 안됐군요,
유감이에요

### 정답 ⑤

### 문제풀이
남자가 축구의 열렬한 팬인 아버지를 위해 표를 산다고 하자 여자는 작년에
부모님께서 자신을 축구 경기에 못 가게 하셨던 게 생각난다고 했다. 그래서 화가
났겠다고 말하는 남자에게 할 수 있는 여자의 적절한 대답은 ⑤ '그래. 우리
아버지께서 너희 아버지처럼 축구에 관심이 있으셨으면 좋겠어.'이다.

### 오답 보기 해석
① 걱정 마. 네가 다음 경기에는 갈 수 있을 거라 확신해.
② 문제 없어. 내가 너의 아버지를 경기에 모시고 갈 수 있어.
③ 아니. 나는 그들이 얼마나 잘 했는지 정말 깜짝 놀랐어.
④ 우리 아버지가 내가 경기에 가는 것을 허락하지 않을까 봐 걱정돼.

### 총 어휘 수 168


## 15 　상황에 적절한 말

**소재** 최근 들어 달라진 James의 학습 및 생활 태도

### 듣기 대본 해석
여: James는 인기가 많은 외향적인 학생입니다. 그는 항상 특별 활동에
   활발하게 참여하고 평균 학점도 높습니다. 그는 친구가 많고 대부분의
   학생들과 선생님들이 그를 칭찬합니다. 그러나 최근에 James는 다른
   학생들이 식당 가서 점심을 먹으러 가는 동안 교실에 있습니다. 그의
   선생님들도 그가 수업 시간에 집중을 하지 않는다는 것을 알아챕니다. 학교
   상담 교사 Towns 선생님은 James의 이상한 행동에 대해 듣게 됩니다.
   Towns 선생님은 James의 문제가 더 심각해지는 것이 우려되어 James와
   그의 문제에 대해 이야기를 나누기로 결심합니다. 이러한 상황에서
   Towns 선생님은 James에게 뭐라고 말할까요?
Mrs. Towns: ④ 난 너의 행동이 걱정돼. 괜찮니?

**outgoing** *a.* 외향적인　**extracurricular event** 특별 활동
**grade point average** 평균 학점　**admire** *v.* 존경하다
**counselor** *n.* 상담자　**bizarre** *a.* 이상한, 기이한

정답 ④

문제풀이
최근 들어 달라진 James의 학교에서의 태도가 걱정된 Mrs. Towns는
James와 그의 문제에 대해 얘기해보고자 하고 있으므로 적절한 말은 ④ '난
너의 행동이 걱정돼. 괜찮니?'이다.

오답 보기 해석
① 네가 학교에서 인기가 많다고 들었어.
② 친구들과 너의 문제에 대해서 상의를 해봐.
③ 요즘 왜 이렇게 자주 수업에 빠지는 거니?
⑤ 이 학교 특별 활동에 대해 궁금했었어.

총 어휘 수 122

# 16 담화 주제 / 17 세부 내용 파악

소재 모기에 의해 전염되는 질병

듣기 대본 해석
남: 지난 수업시간에 우리는 어떻게 일부 곤충들이 질병의 매개체가 되는지 논의
했었죠. 오늘은 여러분 모두가 친숙할거라고 자신하는 곤충. 바로 모기에
대해서 이야기할 겁니다. 모기 물림은 일시적인 간지러움보다 더 심각한
문제를 일으킬 수 있어요. 사실 모기는 세계적으로 다른 어떤 동물들을
합친 것보다도 더 많은 사람들을 죽게 합니다. 모기들은 이 사람 저 사람에게
질병을 옮김으로써 그렇게 합니다. 뎅기열과 말라리아 같은 이러한 질병들의
일부는 치명적일 수 있습니다. 뎅기열은 아이들과 노약자에게 매우 위험하고,
극단적인 경우 죽음에 이르게 합니다. 말라리아는 매년 전 세계적으로 약
2억 명에게 발병하는데 약물로 치료될 수 있습니다. 이러한 질병들은 모기들이
많이 서식하는 열대 지역에서 특히 흔하게 볼 수 있습니다. 여러분이 열대
지역으로 여행한다면 ABCD 접근법을 고려해보세요. A는 말라리아 감염의
위험성을 인식하는 것입니다. B는 물림을 예방하고, 모기 물림을 피하기 위해
예방조치를 취하는 것입니다. C는 말라리아 약을 복용해야 하는지를 점검
하는 것입니다. 그리고 D는 진단입니다. 말라리아나 뎅기열과 같은 증상을
보이기 시작한다면 곧바로 치료를 강구해야 합니다.

어휘
**carrier** *n.* 보균자, (병원체의) 매개체　**fatal** *a.* 치명적인　**affect** *v.*
영향을 미치다. (병이) 발생하다. 병이 나게 하다　**worldwide** *ad.* 전 세계에
**tropical** *a.* 열대 지방의, 열대의　**prevention** *n.* 예방
**take precautions** 예방 조치를 취하다　**diagnosis** *n.* 진단
**symptom** *n.* 증상, 징후　〈문제〉**infestation** *n.* 체내 침입

정답 16 ③　17 ③

문제풀이
16 남자는 모기에 의해 전염되는 질병의 위험성, 질병의 예, 대처 방법(ABCD
접근법) 등을 이야기하고 있으므로 남자가 하는 말의 주제로 가장 적절한
것은 ③ '모기에 의해 전염되는 질병'이다.

17 ABCD의 접근법은 A가 감염의 위험성을 인식하는 것, B는 물림 예방, C는
약 복용이 필요한지 확인하기, D는 증상 발견 시 진단받기이다. '위험
지역은 방문하지 않기'는 언급되지 않았으므로 정답은 ③번이다.

오답 보기 해석
① 말라리아 감염자들의 증상
② 열대 지역의 곤충 문제
④ 말라리아 치료에 쓰이는 약물
⑤ 모기 습격을 예방하는 방법

총 어휘 수 192

## DICTATION ANSWERS

01 debate team championships

02 reuse for a little project

03 student union representative / express my biggest
concern / that very low turnout / every single vote
counts

04 looking for a bit of advice / consider your safety / just
in case you get lost / keep warm / Better safe than
sorry

05 have breaking news / come to a decision in / found not
guilty / file an appeal / a short commercial break

06 returning a book / heading to the library / gain some
work experience / She was at the table studying

07 find some books for my English camp / Won't it be
difficult / Just make sure you prepare well

08 opening up the borders / You're also interested in law /
go hand-in-hand / read a book about a banker

09 book a field trip / price difference / be able to
accommodate you / on the total admission price /
bring more than fifteen students

10 why are you interested in working / how much
experience do you have / the staff to be very
irresponsible / be in touch in about two weeks

11 hold two special events / how they made their tools
and / takes about four hours / get their faces painted

12 sign up for a film editing class / taking one of our
advanced courses / take one of the courses with fewer
students

13 Don't get me wrong / getting very behind on her work
here / focusing on her work

14 You look a little nervous / the second they go on sale /
He's a huge fan / reminds me of last year / let me go to it

15 a high grade point average / staying in the classroom /
lost focus in class

16-17 by spreading diseases / in extreme cases / travel
in tropical regions / taking precautions to avoid
mosquito bites

# 18 수능영어듣기 실전모의고사

| 01 ② | 02 ③ | 03 ③ | 04 ⑤ | 05 ② | 06 ① |
| 07 ④ | 08 ④ | 09 ③ | 10 ⑤ | 11 ⑤ | 12 ② |
| 13 ① | 14 ② | 15 ③ | 16 ④ | 17 ⑤ | |

## 01 짧은 대화의 응답

**소재** 글쓰기 클럽 가입

**듣기 대본 해석**

여: 안녕 Austin. 네가 글쓰기 클럽에 가입했다고 들었어. 너 글을 많이 쓰니?
남: 음, 나는 더 많이 쓰고 싶은데, 지금 당장은 1주일에 대략 한 시간 정도만 글을 써.
여: 얼마나 오랫동안 글 쓰는 것에 관심이 있었니?
남: ② 내가 4학년 이래로 줄곧 관심이 있었어.

**어휘**

join v. 가입하다   〈문제〉 be better at ~을 더 잘하다

**정답** ②

**문제풀이**

여자가 얼마나 오랫동안 글쓰기에 관심 있었는지 물었으므로 적절한 남자의 대답은 ② '내가 4학년 이래로 줄곧 관심이 있었어.'이다.

**오답 보기 해석**

① 나는 학교에서 클럽 가입하는 것을 즐겼어.
③ 나는 너의 글쓰기 클럽에 가입하고 싶어.
④ 나는 1주일에 대략 2시간 동안 글을 쓰곤 했어.
⑤ 나는 초등학교 때 글을 더 잘 썼어.

**총 어휘 수** 50

## 02 짧은 대화의 응답

**소재** 잃어버린 휴내폰 찾기

**듣기 대본 해석**

남: 엄마. 제 휴대폰 어디 놓여 있는지 못 보셨죠?
여: 못 봤는데 방금 부엌을 청소했어. 잃어버린 것 같니?
남: 그런 것 같아요. 모든 곳을 찾아봤는데 아직 못 찾았어요.
여: ③ 전화해서 벨소리를 듣는 게 좋겠어.

**어휘**

search v. 수색하다, 뒤지다

**정답** ③

**문제풀이**

휴대폰을 잃어버려서 찾고 있는 아들에게 엄마가 할 말은 ③ '전화해서 벨소리를 듣는 게 좋겠어.'이다.

**오답 보기 해석**

① 내 휴대폰 좀 찾아줄래?
② 하루 종일 집 청소 했어.
④ 어떤 종류의 휴대폰을 찾고 있어?
⑤ 오늘 휴대폰으로 누구에게도 전화하지 않았어.

**총 어휘 수** 49

## 03 요지

**소재** 환경을 위한 구매 습관

**듣기 대본 해석**

남: 지난 몇 년간 여러분과 같은 젊은이들이 그전보다 더 많이 스스로 물건을 구입하고 있습니다. 하지만 여러분이 하는 모든 구매가 여러분 주변의 세상에 영향을 주고 있다는 것을 상기시키고 싶습니다. 여러분이 사는 것이 무엇이든 모든 제품이 지구에서 오는 것이기 때문에 환경에 부정적인 영향을 줄 수 있습니다. 여러분의 멋진 새 uPhone조차 직접 땅에서 나오는 물질로 만들어집니다. 여러분이 도울 수 있는 일은 구매 습관을 통제하는 것입니다. 여러분이 원하는 것을 사는 대신에 여러분이 필요한 것을 사십시오. 여러분이 무엇을 사든지 그것이 환경친화적인지 생각할 시간을 가져야 합니다. 이런 약간의 조사는 현재와 그리고 다가올 세대를 위한 지구를 보호하는 데 도움을 줄 것입니다. 이는 쉽지만 현명한 일이고 여러분은 우리가 살고 있는 세상을 모두를 위한 더 나은 세상으로 만들 것입니다.

**어휘**

purchase n. 구매   have an effect on ~에 영향을 미치다
material n. 물질, 재료   instead of ~ 대신에   friendly a. 친화적인
protect v. 보호하다, 지키다

**정답** ③

**문제풀이**

남자는 구매가 환경에 영향을 미칠 수 있으니 물건을 살 때 필요한 것만 사고 그 물건이 환경친화적인지 생각해 보라고 말하고 있다. 그러므로 정답은 ③ '환경친화적인 물건을 구입해야 한다.'이다.

**총 어휘 수** 146

## 04 대화 주제

**소재** 인터뷰 숙제에 대한 조언

**듣기 대본 해석**

남: Smith 선생님 수업은 어때, Katie?
여: 글쎄, 학기 초반에는 많은 학업량에 익숙해지는 데 정말 어려웠어.
남: 이해해. 나도 아주 힘들었어.
여: 그렇지만 이제는 모든 추가 과제들이 출판과 저널리즘에 관해 배우는 데 좋은 방법이라고 생각해.
남: 응, 그것은 흥미로운 방식의 수업이긴 하지만 나는 그것이 나한테는 매우 효과적이라고 생각하지 않아. 난 숙제에 흥미를 유지하기가 힘들어.
여: 나는 네가 과제를 잘 해오지 않고 있다는 걸 알아차렸어. 학교 신문에 너의 기사들을 많이 못 봤거든.
남: 음, 나는 학교에서 다른 학생들과 교수님들을 인터뷰하는 게 너무 부끄러워.
여: 나도 처음엔 똑같았어. 하지만 다른 사람에게 말하는 두려움을 극복한 뒤에는 내 사교 기술이 정말 향상되었어.
남: 알아. 내가 가진 두려움에 맞서서 인터뷰 요청을 시작해야 할 것 같아.
여: 그래야만 해. 나는 그것이 정말로 네가 수업을 더 즐기는 걸 도와줄 것이라고 생각해.

**어휘**

semester n. 학기   get used to ~에 익숙해지다   workload n. 업무량, 작업량   struggle v. 고투하다   publishing n. 출판
journalism n. 언론   faculty n. 교수단   social skill 사교 기술
improve v. 개선하다, 향상시키다

**정답** ⑤

**문제풀이**

남자는 인터뷰 과제가 자신에게 힘들다고 말하고 여자는 자신도 처음에는 어려웠지만 두려움을 극복해야 한다고 말해준다. 따라서 두 사람의 대화의 주제는 ⑤ '인터뷰 숙제에 대한 조언'이다.

**총 어휘 수** 171

## 05 대화자의 관계 파악

**소재** 옷 수선하기

**듣기 대본 해석**
남: 안녕하세요.
여: 안녕하세요. 무엇을 도와드릴까요?
남: 그게, 제가 지난 주말에 이 정장 바지를 샀는데 저한테 좀 길어서 수선이 필요할 것 같아요.
여: 알겠습니다. 그러면 수선할 수 있도록 치수를 잴게요. 조금 짧게, 아니면 신발에 닿게 수선되기를 원해요?
남: 보통 바지를 좀 위로 해서 입어요.
여: 알겠습니다. 문제 없습니다.
남: 그리고 이 티셔츠를 한번 봐주세요.
여: 뭐가 문제인가요?
남: 그게, 저번 주에 이탈리안 식당에서 식사를 했는데 셔츠에 스파게티 소스를 흘렸어요.
여: 지우는 데 어렵지 않을 거예요.
남: 그게, 스파게티 소스를 흘린 다음에 와인도 흘렸어요. 두 자국을 없애는 방법은 없을까요?
여: 레드 와인 자국은 빼기 어려운데 할 수 있을 것 같습니다.
남: 고맙습니다. 언제 가지러 오면 될까요? 토요일에 중요한 저녁 약속에 입고 가고 싶어요.
여: 그때까지 다 될 수 있도록 최선을 다 할게요. 목요일에 전화 주시면 제가 다 됐는지 알려드리는 건 어떤가요?
남: 좋네요. 감사합니다.

**어휘**
**hem** *v.* 단을 만들다, 올리다  **measurement** *n.* 치수  **alter** *v.* 바꾸다
**spill** *v.* 엎지르다  **stain** *n.* 얼룩  **formal** *a.* 격식을 차린, 정중한

**정답** ②

**문제풀이**
남자가 정장 바지를 줄이고 싶다고 하자 여자가 어디까지 줄일지 봐주고 있고, 남자가 다시 셔츠에 묻은 스파게티와 와인 얼룩을 제거할 수 있는지를 묻고 여자가 가능하다고 대답하고 있으므로, 두 사람의 관계는 ② '세탁소 주인 — 고객'임을 알 수 있다.

**총 어휘 수** 206

## 06 그림의 세부 내용 파악

**소재** 해변에서의 휴가

**듣기 대본 해석**
남: 마침내 휴가에서 돌아왔군요.
여: 네, 돌아와서 기쁘지만 벌써 해변이 그리워요.
남: 이해해요. 어느 해변에 갔었어요?
여: St. Petersburg 해변이요. 정말 좋았어요. 사진 찍었어요. 한번 보세요.
남: [잠시 후] 와. 사랑스러워 보여요. 나는 당신이 쓰고 있는 모자가 정말 맘에 들어요.
여: 고마워요. 저희 엄마가 저를 위해 사주셨죠. 그런데 제가 누구를 향해 손을 흔들고 있는지 모르겠어요.
남: 저 사람이 당신 남편인가요?
여: 네, 그는 파라솔 아래서 낮잠을 자고 있었어요. 휴가 대부분의 시간을 쉬면서 보냈죠.
남: 모래성을 만들고 있는 사람이 당신의 아들 Billy임이 틀림없어요.
여: 그는 꽤 창의적이에요. 그는 나를 매일 놀라게 해요.
남: 물에서 고무보트 위에 있는 사람은 누구죠?
여: 그분은 저의 시아버님인 William이에요. 아버님과 어머님은 사실 저희가 머물렀던 콘도를 가지고 계세요.
남: 배경에 있는 것이 콘도인 것 같군요.
여: 맞아요. 우리는 중간 건물의 7층에 머물렀어요.
남: 음. 저는 당신의 휴가가 정말 부럽네요. 저도 곧 가야겠어요.
여: 저도 다시 가고 싶어요.

**어휘**
**take a nap** 낮잠을 자다  **amaze** *v.* 놀라게 하다  **raft** *n.* 고무보트
**father-in-law** *n.* 장인, 시아버지  **envious** *a.* 부러워하는

**정답** ①

**문제풀이**
대화에서 손을 흔들고 있는 여자 자신이 모자를 썼다고 했는데 그림에서는 모자가 없으므로 정답은 ①번이다.

**총 어휘 수** 163

## 07 할 일

**소재** 스포츠 활동 선택

**듣기 대본 해석**
여: 안녕하세요. 무엇을 도와드릴까요?
남: 안녕하세요. 전 스포츠 활동에 참여하는 것을 생각하고 있어요.
여: 아, 좋아요. 현재 저희한테 가입되어 계신가요?
남: 아니요, 되어 있지 않아요.
여: 괜찮아요. 생각하고 계신 특정 활동이 있으신가요?
남: 딱히 없어요. 저한테 무엇이 제일 좋을지 모르겠어요.
여: 알겠습니다. 음. 여기에 저희가 이번 여름을 위해 계획한 모든 스포츠 활동의 목록이 있어요. 저희가 실내와 실외 활동들을 모두 제공한다는 것을 보실 수 있어요.
남: 와, 선택할 수 있는 활동이 정말 많네요.
여: 네. 그러면 모든 활동을 검토하시고 손님께 맞는 활동을 선택하기 위해 시간을 좀 가지세요.
남: 도움을 좀 주실 수 있으신가요?
여: 활동을 선택하는 것에서요?
남: 네, 저는 적어도 두 가지 활동에 가입하고 싶은데 어떤 것을 선택해야 할지 모르겠어요.
여: 그럼 같이 목록을 보죠. 제가 도와드릴게요.
남: 그거 좋겠어요. 대단히 감사해요.

**어휘**
**currently** *ad.* 현재, 지금  **enroll** *v.* 등록하다  **specific** *a.* 특정한, 구체적인  **go over** 검토하다  〈문제〉**assist** *v.* 돕다

**정답** ④

**문제풀이**
남자는 스포츠 활동을 등록하고 싶은데 스포츠 활동의 종류가 많고 자기한테 어떤 것이 제일 좋을지 몰라서 선택을 못하고 있다. 그래서 남자는 여자에게 스포츠 활동 선택을 도와달라고 부탁하는 중이므로 정답은 ④ '활동을 선택하는 데 그를 도와주기'이다.

**오답 보기 해석**
① 강사 만나기
② 멤버십을 위해 돈을 지불하기
③ 개인 트레이닝에 등록하기
⑤ 연례 스포츠 행사에 대해 묻기

**총 어휘 수** 151

## 08 이유

**소재** 해외 자원봉사를 위한 휴학

**듣기 대본 해석**
여: 교수님 안녕하세요?
남: Amelia, 들어와서 앉으렴. 무엇을 도와줄까?
여: 교수님과 상의할 중요한 것이 있어서요.
남: 그렇구나. 그것이 무엇이지?
여: 말씀드리기 어려운데 한 학기 휴학할까 해요.
남: 정말? 왜지? 넌 정말 좋은 학생이었잖아.
여: 감사합니다. 제 시간을 바깥에서 좀 더 의미 있는 일을 하면서 보낼까 해서요.

남: 어떤 것 말이니?
여: 봉사활동 같은 거요. 해외에 나가서 도움이 필요한 사람들에게 도움을 주고 싶어요.
남: 훌륭하구나. 어느 나라로 가는 것을 생각하고 있니?
여: 최근 네팔에 큰 지진이 있어서요. 그곳에 가서 돕고 싶습니다.
남: 너한테 좋을 것 같구나. 일이 끝나면 언제든지 돌아와서 공부해도 된단다. 행운을 빌어, Amelia.
여: 이해해 주셔서 감사합니다, 교수님.

### 어휘
**meaningful** *a.* 의미 있는, 중요한    **volunteer** *v.* 자원하다, 자원봉사하다 *n.* 자원봉사, 자원봉사자    **recently** *ad.* 최근에

### 정답 ④

### 문제풀이
여자는 해외에 나가서 도움이 필요한 사람들에게 도움을 주고 싶어서 휴학을 하고 싶다고 했으므로 정답은 ④ '해외로 봉사활동을 가기 위해'이다.

**총 어휘 수** 145


## 09  숫자

**소재**  팝콘 구매 시 할인

### 듣기 대본 해석
남: Poptastic's Gourmet Popcorn에 오신 것을 환영합니다. 무엇을 도와 드릴까요?
여: 카라멜 팝콘 큰 봉지 얼마예요?
남: 한 봉지에 10달러입니다.
여: 적당한 가격이네요. 4봉지 살게요.
남: 네. 만약 손님께서 저희 메일 리스트에 등록을 하시면, 10퍼센트 할인을 해 드립니다. 서식을 작성하는 데 몇 분밖에 안 걸립니다.
여: 그래요? 좋아요, 등록할게요. *[잠시 후]* 다 했어요. 여기 있어요.
남: 잠깐 볼게요. 좋아요. 손님의 이메일 주소는 mashimaro@leemail.com 이죠?
여: 맞아요. 다른 할인도 있나요?
남: 물론이죠. 저희는 고객의 생일인 달에 20퍼센트 할인을 해드려요. 아! 방금 작성하신 신청서를 보면, 고객님의 생일이 내일이네요!
여: 맞아요. 제 신분증을 보시겠어요?
남: 괜찮아요. 고객님을 믿습니다. 두 가지 할인을 동시에 적용해드릴 수는 없으니 더 큰 할인율을 적용해드릴게요.
여: 좋아요. 신용카드 받으시죠?

### 어휘
**reasonable** *a.* 합리적인, 적당한    **sign up** 등록하다    **complete** *v.* 기입하다, 완료하다    **trust** *v.* 신뢰하다, 믿다

### 정답 ③

### 문제풀이
여자는 한 봉지당 10달러인 팝콘을 4봉지 산다고 했고, 메일 리스트에 등록해서 10퍼센트, 생일 할인으로 20퍼센트를 할인받게 되었다. 그러나 남자가 두 할인을 동시에 받을 수 없으며, 더 큰 할인율을 적용해주겠다고 하였으므로 여자는 전체 금액의 20퍼센트를 할인받게 된다. 따라서 40달러에서 20퍼센트 할인을 받는 것이므로 여자가 지불할 금액은 ③ '$32'이다.

**총 어휘 수** 158


## 10  언급 유무

**소재**  Speech contest 참가

### 듣기 대본 해석
여: 안녕, Andrew. 복도에 있는 게시판에서 이 전단지를 봤는데 네가 관심이 있을 거라 생각했어.
남: 오, 웅변대회에 관해서구나. 전단지를 봐도 될까?
여: 그래. 자, 너 9월 22일까지 준비할 수 있을 거라 생각해?

남: 준비할 수 있을 거라 생각하지만, 약간 걱정돼. 너도 그 대회가 모든 학생들이 참여할 수 있다는 걸 알잖아. 심지어 졸업반도 참가할 수 있어. 너 등록할 계획이니?
여: 등록할 생각은 하고 있어. 내가 아주 잘할 것이라고 생각하지는 않지만 나의 발표력을 향상시키는 데 그것을 이용하려고.
남: 그건 확실해. 너 유명한 연설에 관심이 많잖아, 그렇지 않니?
여: 당연하지. 그게 바로 그 대회가 나한테 유익한 좋은 이유야. 언젠가 나는 정치가가 되고 싶어. 너는 등록할거니?
남: 그럼. 웅변대회는 Walker 강당에서 개최될 거야. 꽤 가깝지.
여: 그래. 우리는 거기에 자전거를 타고 갈 수 있어. 그런데 우리 빨리 등록해야 해. 마감일이 이번 금요일이거든.
남: 우리 집에 가서 내 컴퓨터로 등록하자.
여: 좋은 생각이야.

### 어휘
**flyer** *n.* 전단지    **billboard** *n.* 게시판, 광고판    **compete** *v.* 참여하다, 경쟁하다    **senior** *n.* 졸업반, 최상급생    **deadline** *n.* 마감 기한 **register** *v.* 등록하다, 신청하다

### 정답 ⑤

### 문제풀이
두 사람은 speech contest의 개최 일자, 참가 자격, 개최 장소, 신청 마감일에 관한 언급은 했지만 연설 제한시간에 관한 언급은 하지 않았으므로 정답은 ⑤ '연설 제한시간'이다.

**총 어휘 수** 165


## 11  내용 일치·불일치

**소재**  미술관 견학을 위한 안내

### 듣기 대본 해석
여: 안녕하세요, 여러분. Center City Art Museum에 오신 것을 환영합니다. 저는 여러분의 자녀가 미술관 방문에서 최대한의 것을 얻기 위한 좋은 방법을 조언해 드리려 합니다. 먼저, 여러분께서는 자녀들과 항상 함께 다니세요. 아이들이 혼자 돌아다니면 그들은 쉽게 길을 잃을 수 있고 무서워합니다. 그러나 아이들이 그들 스스로 미술 작품을 즐기게 해 주세요. 아이들에게 문제를 내거나 작품을 해석해 주는 것은 좋은 생각이 아닙니다. 그들이 자유롭게 생각하게 두고 가장 좋아하는 작품이 무엇인지, 왜 그런지를 물어보세요. 아이들에게 미술관의 지도와 작품 목록을 주고 그들에게 당신을 위한 투어 가이드처럼 행동해보라고 하세요. 이는 아이들에게 전체 미술관을 보게 하고 그들이 책임자인 깃처럼 느끼게 합니다. 한 번의 방문으로 모든 작품을 보는 것은 그렇게 중요하지 않습니다. 우리는 일년 내내 열려 있으니 여러 번 방문할 기회가 많습니다.

### 어휘
**make sure** 확실하게 하다    **wander off** 거닐다, 돌아다니다 **interpret** *v.* 해석하다    **artwork** *n.* 미술품    **in charge** ~을 맡은, 담당인    **multiple** *a.* 많은, 다수의

### 정답 ⑤

### 문제풀이
담화의 마지막 부분에서 한 번의 방문으로 모든 작품을 보는 것을 중요하지 않다고 했으므로 정답은 ⑤ '방문했을 때 최대한 많은 작품을 보여 주어라.'이다.

**총 어휘 수** 164


## 12  도표

**소재**  토스터 고르기

### 듣기 대본 해석
여: 여보, 곧 크리스마스야. 당신 부모님께는 뭘 선물해 드릴까?
남: 글쎄, 토스트기가 요즘 말썽이라고 엄마가 그러셨어. 토스트기 하나 찾아보자.
여: 알았어. 근데 140달러 넘게 쓰는 건 좀 아닌 것 같아.
남: 나도 그렇게 생각해. 다른 선물들도 사야 되니까.

여: 맞아. 어쨌든 어떤 크기를 사는 게 좋을 것 같아?
남: 두 조각 토스트기는 너무 작은 것 같아. 엄마는 분명히 더 큰 걸 원할 거야.
여: 당연하지. 네 조각이나 여섯 조각 토스트기로 하자. 디지털 화면은 뭐에 쓰이는 건지 알아?
남: 타이머를 써서 빵을 다 굽는 데 얼마나 시간이 남았는지 보여줘. 하지만 별로 필요하지는 않을 것 같아. 엄마가 쓰시기에는 너무 복잡할지도 몰라.
여: 맞아. 이 검은 것 봐봐. 아주 매끈하고 세련되어 보인다.
남: 우리 부엌에는 잘 어울릴 것 같은데 우리 부모님 부엌 용품은 다 하얗잖아.
여: 응. 그럼 그 색깔로 하자.
남: 이게 가장 좋을 것 같아. 주문하자.

### 어휘
**act up** 말을 안 듣다. 애를 먹이다　　**slice** *n.* 조각　　**digital display** 디지털 화면, 디지털 표시 장치　　**complicated** *a.* 복잡한　　**sleek** *a.* 윤이 나는, 매끈한　　**modern** *a.* 세련된　　**appliance** *n.* (가정용) 기기

### 정답 ②

### 문제풀이
남자와 여자는 토스터를 고르고 있다. 처음에 140달러는 넘지 않는 게 좋다고 했고, 네 조각이나 여섯 조각 토스터로 하자고 했으므로 ②, ③, ④번으로 압축된다. 그리고 디지털 표시는 없는 것이 낫다고 했으므로 ②, ④번이 가능하고 그 중에 흰색으로 하자고 했으므로 남자와 여자가 선택한 것은 ②번이 된다.

**총 어휘 수** 180

## 13  긴 대화의 응답

**소재** 갓 채용된 원어민 교사

### 듣기 대본 해석
남: JLA에 오신 것을 환영합니다. 저희는 강사 경험이 많은 영어 원어민과 일하게 되어 설레어요.
여: 고마워요, 저도 JLA 팀의 일원이 되어서 정말 기뻐요.
남: 저는 당신이 거의 4년 동안 여기 한국에서 ESL 강사를 해온 것을 봤어요.
여: 네. 저는 항상 가르치는 것을 즐겼고, 여기 서울에 있는 것이 놀라운 경험이었어요.
남: 전에 영어 학습 교재에 관해 작업해 본 적 있으세요?
여: 해보지는 않았지만 저는 새로운 프로젝트를 시작하는 데 대해 열정적이에요.
남: 그렇게 말씀하시니 기뻐요. 사실, 저희와 일하고 있는 다른 원어민이 있어요. 그는 아주 재능이 있어요.
여: 정말이요? 그를 만나보고 싶어요. 저는 우리가 공통점이 많을 거라고 확신해요.
남: 저도 그럴 것 같아요. 그가 곧 올 겁니다. 그럼 그를 만나실 수 있어요.
여: 지금까지 당신이 출판한 책은 몇 권인가요?
남: 지금까지 저희는 다섯 권만 출판했고, ESL BEST와 몇 가지 새로운 프로젝트를 함께 작업 중에 있습니다.
여: ① <u>대단해요. 저도 여기서 일할 것이 너무 기대돼요.</u>

### 어휘
**instructor** *n.* 강사　　**enthusiastic** *a.* 열정적인, 열렬한　　**talented** *a.* 재능이 있는　　**have something in common** (특징 등을) 공통적으로 지니다　　**shortly** *ad.* 얼마 안 되어, 곧

### 정답 ①

### 문제풀이
여자가 JLA에서 새로 일하게 되어 남자와 대화를 나누는 상황이다. 남자가 JLA에서 출간한 교재가 몇 권 있고 지금도 진행 중이라고 말했을 때 적절한 여자의 응답은 ① '대단해요. 저도 여기서 일할 것이 너무 기대돼요.'이다.

### 오답 보기 해석
② 당신이 대학에서 언론학을 공부했다는 걸 알아봤어요.
③ 우린 당신이 이 회사와 아주 잘 맞을 거라 생각해요.
④ 전에 ESL BEST에서 책을 출판했었어요.
⑤ 전 늘 ESL 선생님이 되고 싶었어요.

**총 어휘 수** 158

## 14  긴 대화의 응답

**소재** 여가 시간에 TV 보기

### 듣기 대본 해석
남: Stephanie, 일주일에 TV 몇 시간 봐?
여: 보통 일주일에 TV 20시간 봐.
남: 정말? 우와, 너 TV를 많이 보는구나!
여: 응. 보통 하루에 TV를 서너 시간씩 봐.
남: 하루에 네 시간? 나는 그렇게 많이 볼 시간이 없어. 학교 끝나면 공부하고 피아노 치는 걸 연습해야 하거든.
여: 나도 할 게 많아, Steve. 난 그냥 내 시간을 다르게 할애할 뿐이야.
남: 어떻게 허비할 수 있는 시간이 그렇게 많을 수 있지?
여: 음, 내가 좋아하는 TV 프로그램만 봐. 숙제랑 다른 거는 그 프로그램들 사이사이에 해.
남: 그것도 하나의 방법이긴 하겠다. 그래도 시간을 너무 많이 낭비하는 것 같아.
여: 즐기는 시간은 버리는 시간이 아냐.
남: 그렇기는 해. 근데 아직도 네가 어떻게 네가 할 일을 다 해 놓는 건지 모르겠어.
여: 보통 다른 활동들은 내 TV 스케줄에 따라 계획해. 항상 오늘 해야 할 일들 목록을 만들고 TV 보는 시간 전에 해야 할 일들에 우선순위를 매겨.
남: ② <u>나도 한번 해볼까. 보고 싶은 TV 프로그램들이 아주 많아.</u>

### 어휘
**manage** *v.* 관리하다　　**to-do list** 해야 할 일을 적은 목록　　**prioritize** *v.* 우선순위를 매기다　　〈문제〉**catch up on** ~을 따라잡다

### 정답 ②

### 문제풀이
남자가 여자에게 하루에 TV 보는 시간이 너무 많다고 하자 여자는 계획을 세워서 할 일들을 중간에 하면서 본다고 말해주고 있다. 여자가 어떻게 계획하는지에 대해 말하는 마지막 말에 대한 남자의 응답은 ② '나도 한번 해볼까. 보고 싶은 TV 프로그램들이 아주 많아.'가 적절하다.

### 오답 보기 해석
① 어젯밤에 숙제하는 걸 깜빡했어. 그래서 피아노 연습을 못했어.
③ 내가 보는 TV 프로그램들 최신편을 다 챙겨보는 게 나한테 제일 중요해.
④ 난 요즘 TV 프로그램 때문에 운동을 별로 안 해.
⑤ 네가 원한다면 우리 TV 같이 보자.

**총 어휘 수** 194

## 15  상황에 적절한 말

**소재** 친구 관계에 대한 어머니의 조언

### 듣기 대본 해석
여: Jane과 Olivia는 정말 가까운 친구였고 모든 것을 함께 합니다. 불행하게도, 그들은 최근에 특정한 그룹이나 클럽에 들어갈지 말지 같은 아주 단순한 일로 말다툼을 해 왔습니다. Jane은 말다툼을 피하고 싶었지만 그들은 계속 다투었고, 그래서 Jane은 그녀의 어머니에게 이런 상황을 이야기 했습니다. Jane의 어머니는 Jane과 Olivia가 너무 오랜 시간을 함께 보내서 다툼이 일어났다고 생각합니다. 그녀는 그들이 서로 일정 기간 떨어져 있어야 한다고 생각하고, Jane의 어머니는 Jane에게 그녀와 Olivia의 우정에 휴식 시간을 가져야 한다고 말하려 합니다. 이와 같은 상황에서 Jane의 어머니는 뭐라고 말할 것 같은가요?
Jane's mother: Jane ③ <u>몇 주 만이라도 Olivia와 어울리는 것을 그만하는 건 어떠니?</u>

### 어휘
**argue** *v.* 언쟁을 하다, 다투다　　**apart** *ad.* 떨어져　　〈문제〉**hang out** (~에서) 많은 시간을 보내다

### 정답 ③

Jane과 Olivia가 너무 붙어 다녔기 때문에 서로 떨어져 지낼 시간이 필요하다고 생각한 어머니의 조언으로 가장 적절한 것은 ③ '몇 주 만이라도 Olivia와 어울리는 것을 그만하는 건 어떠니?'이다.

오답 보기 해석
① 당사자가 없을 때 험담 당하는 것은 누구도 좋아하지 않아.
② 너는 학교에서 만나는 모두에게 왜 그렇게 부정적이니?
④ 클럽을 고르기 전에 모든 선택을 살펴볼 필요가 있어.
⑤ 새로운 학교로 전학 가는 것이 너를 외롭게 만들 수 있어.

총 어휘 수 120

# 16 담화 주제 / 17 세부 내용 파악

소재 아이들에게 건강에 좋은 음식 먹이는 방법

듣기 대본 해석
여: 여러분의 가족 중에서 식성이 까다로운 사람이 있나요? 여러분의 아이가 채소나 다른 건강에 좋은 음식을 먹으려고 하지 않기 때문에 저녁식사 시간에 매일 싸움이 벌어집니까? 자, 아이들이 싫어하는 음식을 억지로 먹이는 것은 감정적으로 부정적인 영향을 미칠 수 있습니다. 현명한 부모는 아이들을 건강한 식습관으로 이끄는 데 인내심이 있습니다. 제 아이들의 습관을 바꾸는 데 도움을 주었던 몇 가지 비법을 여러분들께 알려드리고자 합니다. 첫째로, 아이의 음식을 더 매력적으로 보이도록 장식을 하세요. 예를 들면, 아이들의 접시 위에다 채소들을 웃는 얼굴처럼 보이도록 만드세요. 브로콜리는 멋진 코가 되고, 당근을 얇게 썬 것은 멋진 눈처럼 보이고, 감자를 썬 것은 여러분의 아이에게 미소를 던져줄 수 있습니다. 둘째로, 식용색소는 단조로운 음식을 재미있게 만들 수 있습니다. 파란색, 빨간색 식용색소 몇 방울을 아이들의 오트밀에다 넣어서 생기 넘치는 모습으로 만들어 보세요. 셋째, 여러분은 별 모양, 하트 모양, 글자 모양으로 아이들이 먹는 과일이나 채소들을 자를 수 있습니다. 아이들의 이름을 쓸 수도 있습니다. 마지막으로, 저는 가끔 아이들이 좋아하는 음식에 건강에 좋은 음식을 숨길 수 있다는 걸 알았습니다. 예를 들면 시금치는 영양분이 풍부하고 피자 또는 심지어 과자나 브라우니에도 숨기기가 쉽습니다. 여러분의 생각과 약간의 창의력을 사용하면 여러분의 아이들은 곧 건강하게 식사를 할 것입니다.

어휘
**fussy eater** 편식가, 식성이 까다로운 사람    **emotional** *a.* 감정의    **impact** *n.* 영향, 충격    **sensible** *a.* 합리적인    **appealing** *a.* 흥미로운    **vibrant** *a.* 활기찬    **appearance** *n.* 모습, 외모    **nutrient** *n.* 영양소    〈문제〉**benefit** *n.* 혜택, 이득    **regularly** *ad.* 규칙적으로    **processed food** 가공된 식품    **spruce** *v.* 단장하다

정답 16 ④  17 ⑤

문제풀이
16 아이들이 채소나 다른 건강에 좋은 음식을 안 먹으려고 할 때, 그 습관을 바꿔줄 수 있는 방법을 알려주고 있으므로 이 글의 주제는 ④ '아이들의 먹는 습관을 바꾸기 위한 조언'이다.

17 브로콜리, 당근, 오트밀, 시금치는 언급했지만 토마토에 대한 언급은 없으므로 정답은 ⑤ '토마토'이다.

오답 보기 해석
16
① 규칙적으로 야채를 먹는 것의 이점
② 가공된 식품을 먹는 것의 위험
③ 아이들 건강에 해로운 음식들
⑤ 아이들의 파티를 꾸미는 창의적인 방법

17
① 브로콜리    ② 당근    ③ 오트밀    ④ 시금치

총 어휘 수 232



01 joined the writing club / How long have you been interested in

02 you might have lost it / I still haven't found it

03 have negative effects on / to control your buying habits / environmentally friendly

04 get used to the heavy workload / I'm a little too shy to interview / got over my fear / I should just face my fears

05 get your measurements / That shouldn't be a problem to get out / remove both stains

06 I don't really know who I'm waving at / He amazes me / I'm really envious of

07 Are you currently enrolled with us / any specific activities in mind / take some time to go over / I don't know which to choose

08 I'd like to take a semester off / spend a little time doing something meaningful / major earthquake in Nepal

09 That sounds reasonable / Do you have any other discounts / Do you take credit cards

10 flyer on the billboard / Even the seniors can compete / improve my public speaking skills / It's taking place at

11 wander off alone / let them enjoy the art on their own / Let their minds think freely / have them act as a tour guide / they're in charge

12 her toaster is acting up / It might be too complicated / all of my parents' appliances are white

13 Have you ever worked / He's very talented / we have a lot in common

14 just manage my time differently / you're wasting too much time / make a daily to-do list

15 whether or not to join a particular group or club / two friends spend too much time together / apart from each other / take a break from their friendship

16-17 healthy eating habits / make it look more appealing / food coloring can make dull food exciting / hide healthy food in food that my children like

# 19 수능영어듣기 실전모의고사

본문 p.116

| 01 ③ | 02 ⑤ | 03 ② | 04 ④ | 05 ① | 06 ⑤ |
| 07 ⑤ | 08 ③ | 09 ④ | 10 ② | 11 ③ | 12 ③ |
| 13 ② | 14 ④ | 15 ④ | 16 ⑤ | 17 ④ | |

## 01 짧은 대화의 응답

**소재** 예상 밖의 경기 결과

**듣기 대본 해석**

여: 지난밤에 경기 봤니? 정말 좋았어! 무슨 일이 일어났는지 알고 싶지, Steven?

남: North Stars팀이 이겼을 거라고 생각 되는데. 우리 팀은 항상 그 팀에 지거든.

여: 아냐! 어젯밤엔 우리가 이겼어.

남: ③ 와, 최곤데! 믿을 수 없어!

**어휘**

〈문제〉 **assignment** *n.* 과제

**정답** ③

**문제풀이**

남자의 추측과는 달리 우리 팀이 이겼다고 여자가 말했을 때 적절한 대답은 놀라움의 표시이므로 ③ '와, 최곤데! 믿을 수 없어!'가 적절하다.

**오답 보기 해석**

① 다른 기회가 있을 거야.

② 네가 그걸 봤으면 좋았을 텐데.

④ 문제 없어. 좀 더 연습하면 돼.

⑤ 네 과제를 잊지 마.

**총 어휘 수** 43

## 02 짧은 대화의 응답

**소재** 오페라 티켓 예매

**듣기 대본 해석**

남: 안녕, Linda. 이번 주말 오페라 티켓 남아있는지 확인해 줄 수 있어?

여: 잠깐만. [잠시 휴]다 팔린 것 같은데.

남: 정말? 지난주에 사 놓을 걸. 아내가 엄청 화낼 텐데.

여: ⑤ 아직 다음 주말 티켓은 예약할 수 있는 것 같은데.

**어휘**

**sold out** (표가) 매진된   **furious** *a.* 몹시 화가 난

〈문제〉 **book a ticket** 티켓을 예매하다

**정답** ⑤

**문제풀이**

이번 주말 티켓이 없다는 말에 남자는 지난주에 사놓을 걸 그랬다며 후회하고 있다. 이에 적절한 여자의 응답은 ⑤ '아직 다음 주말 티켓은 예약할 수 있는 것 같은데.'이다.

**오답 보기 해석**

① 그러고 싶은데 할 수 없어. 이번 주말에 계획이 있거든.

② 응. 오페라 티켓을 구하는 게 쉽지 않았어.

③ 너와 네 아내가 오페라 본다니 멋진데.

④ 걱정 마. 극장에 어떻게 가는지 알아.

**총 어휘 수** 56

## 03 담화 목적

**소재** 휘트니스 센터 홍보

**듣기 대본 해석**

여: 오늘 여러분의 기분은 어떠신가요? 여러분은 오늘 사무실에서 특별히 에너지가 넘치는 사람들을 봤을 수도 있습니다. 여러분은 또한 특별한 이유 없이 기분이 좋지 않고 우울해하는 사람들도 봤을 것입니다. 여러분께서는 어느 그룹에 속하십니까? 만약 여러분이 두 번째 그룹에 속하신다면, Heavenly Fitness에 무료 상담을 받으러 들러 보시면 어떨까요? Heavenly Fitness는 기능적인 근력 운동과 전반적인 건강관리를 위한 최첨단 휘트니스 센터입니다. 여러분 개개인의 요구에 맞는 구체적인 운동 프로그램을 짤 수 있게 도와드릴 자격증을 가진 15명의 개인 트레이너가 있습니다. 더 좋은 것은, 사물함과 화장실을 포함한 모든 시설물들이 새 것이며 운동 장비들도 모두 최고입니다. 여러분의 삶에서 더 많은 것을 얻고 싶으시다면 오늘 Heavenly Fitness에 들러주십시오.

**어휘**

**energetic** *a.* 에너지가 넘치는   **depressed** *a.* 의기소침한, 우울한

**stop by** 잠시 들르다   **consultation** *n.* 상담, 회의

**state-of-the-art** *a.* 최신식의, 최첨단의   **functional** *a.* 기능성의, 작동하는   **certified** *a.* 공인의, 자격증을 가진   **specific to** ~에 특유한, 고유한   **facility** *n.* 기관, 시설   **equipment** *n.* 장비, 설비

**정답** ②

**문제풀이**

여자는 Heavenly Fitness가 최고의 시설과 개인 트레이너를 갖추고 있다고 홍보하고 있으므로 정답은 ② '휘트니스 센터를 홍보하려고'이다.

**총 어휘 수** 134

## 04 대화 주제

**소재** 소셜 미디어 사이트의 영향

**듣기 대본 해석**

여: 안녕, Joshua. 무엇을 듣고 있니? 재미있는 거 있어?

남: 안녕, Ann. 온라인상으로 Podcast 듣고 있어.

여: 그래? 무엇에 관한 거야?

남: 소셜 미디어에 관한 거야. 2018년까지 미국에 있는 거의 모든 8살 이상의 아이들이 일종의 소셜 미디어 프로필을 가지게 될 것이라고 말하고 있어. 어떻게 생각해?

여: 음, 나는 소셜 미디어 사이트가 좋은 교육적인 가치가 있을 수 있고 온라인 보안에 대해 아이들에게 알려줄 수 있다고 생각해.

남: 좋아, 그렇지만 소셜 미디어 사이트가 아이들을 여러 가지 면에서 위험하게 한다고 생각하진 않니?

여: 어떤 면에서 그런데?

남: 미성년자들과 인터넷으로 대화하려고 어린 척 하는 위험한 어른들에 관한 기사를 읽은 적이 있어. 또한, 휴대폰 번호와 주소 같은 개인정보를 얻기 위해 어린 사용자들을 이용하는 사람들도 있어.

여: 아, 그런 점은 꽤 무섭구나.

남: 게다가, 소셜 미디어 사이트가 교육적일 수 있지만 한편으론 숙제나 아이디어를 공유하는 대신 친구들과 대화하는 데 그것을 사용하는 학생들에게는 주의 집중을 매우 방해할 수도 있어.

**어휘**

**security** *n.* 보안, 경비   **pretend to** ~인 체하다   **minor** *n.* 미성년자

**take advantage of** ~을 이용하다   **distract** *v.* 산만하게 하다

**정답** ④

**문제풀이**

여자는 소셜 미디어 사이트가 아이들에게 주는 긍정적인 면을 이야기했고 남자는 부정적인 면에 대해 언급하고 있으므로 주제로 적절한 것은 ④ '소셜 미디어 사이트가 학생들에게 끼치는 다양한 영향'이다.

**총 어휘 수** 164

## 05  대화자의 관계 파악

**소재**  인테리어 공사의 변경 사항

**듣기 대본 해석**

여: 선생님, 계약서 보셨나요?
남: 네. 근데 바꾸고 싶은 사항들이 몇 개 있더라고요.
여: 그래요? 어떤 것을 바꾸고 싶으세요?
남: 첫 번째로는 훈련 시설에 대한 것을 바꾸고 싶네요. 원래는 사우나와 온수 욕조 하나씩을 원했지만 이제는 온수 욕조 두 개를 원합니다.
여: 좋을 것 같지만 비용이 추가적으로 나올 거예요.
남: 비용은 상관 없어요. 완료되면 청구서를 보내 주세요.
여: 알겠습니다. 그리고 또 어떤 것을 바꾸고 싶으신가요?
남: 원래 체력단련실의 벽을 붉은 색으로 칠하고 싶다고 말했지만 하얀 색으로 하기로 했어요.
여: 문제 없어요. 붉은 페인트 주문을 취소하고 하얀 페인트를 주문할게요. 다른 게 또 있나요?
남: 아뇨, 그게 끝이에요. 완성된 모습이 기대되네요.
여: 아주 멋질 거예요. 그런데 언제까지 완성되어야 하나요?
남: 음. 훈련은 8월에 시작하니까 7월 말까지는 완성되었으면 좋겠네요.

**어휘**

**contract** *n.* 계약서　**tub** *n.* 욕조　**bill** *n.* 청구서　*v.* 청구서를 보내다
**complete** *a.* 완료된　**cancel an order** 주문을 취소하다

**정답**  ①

**문제풀이**

여자는 계약서를 봤는지 남자에게 물었고, 남자는 훈련시설의 온수 욕조 개수와 체력단련실 벽의 페인트 색 변경을 원한다고 말한 것으로 보아 두 사람의 관계는 ① '인테리어 업자 ― 고객'임을 알 수 있다.

**총 어휘 수**  165

## 06  그림의 세부 내용 파악

**소재**  스포츠 용품 가게에서 선물 고르기

**듣기 대본 해석**

남: 이 스포츠 용품 가게 꽤 저렴하다.
여: 응. 맞다. 곧 Jesse 삼촌 생일이잖아. 여기서 삼촌 선물 사 가자.
남: 좋은 생각이야. 저기 신반 위에 있는 운동화는 어때? 요맘때쯤 농구 많이 하시잖아.
여: 꽤 괜찮은 생각인데 어떤 사이즈 신는지 모르잖아. 혹시 아니?
남: 아니.
여: 복싱 장갑은 어때? 저기 구석에 장갑들이 아주 많다.
남: 복싱 보는 건 좋아하시는 것 같은데, 직접 하시지는 않아.
여: 응. 네 말이 맞는 것 같아. 저 긴 스케이트 보드 멋있다. 아랫면에 있는 디자인 좀 봐.
남: 멋있다. 호랑이가 그려져 있네. 근데 우리가 사기에는 너무 비싼 것 같아.
여: 맞아. 저 구석에 있는 스노우 보드도 아마 우리가 생각한 가격 범위 밖일 거야.
남: 응. 야. 탁자 위에 봐봐! 저 농구 셔츠 하나 사 드리자.
여: 좋은 생각이야! Indiana Pacers가 삼촌이 제일 좋아하는 팀이야. 삼촌이 정말 좋아하실 거야.
남: 나도 그렇게 생각해.

**어휘**

**deal** *n.* 거래　**pricey** *a.* 값비싼　**range** *n.* 범위　**jersey** *n.* 셔츠

**정답**  ⑤

**문제풀이**

탁자 위에 있는 Indiana Pacers팀의 농구 셔츠를 사드리자고 했는데, 탁자 위에 겨울 재킷이 있으므로 정답은 ⑤번이다.

**총 어휘 수**  184

## 07  할 일

**소재**  사무실에서의 대화

**듣기 대본 해석**

남: 오늘 날씨가 정말 좋네요. Wally's Waterland에 갔으면 좋겠군요.
여: 그 이름이 제 추억을 불러일으키네요. 나 어렸을 때 거기 많이 갔었어요.
남: 맞아요, 나도요. 지칠 때까지 하루 종일 미끄럼을 탔었죠.
여: 나는 파도풀도 정말 좋아했었는데.
남: 항상 좋긴 했지만 항상 사람들이 너무 많기도 했어요.
여: 네. 하지만 아직도 너무 재미있고, 이런 사무실에 갇혀 있는 것보다 훨씬 재미있죠.
남: 당신 말이 맞아요. 하지만 우리 일하러 돌아가야죠.
여: 오늘 우리 일을 빨리 마칠 수 있을 것 같아요?
남: 확실하지 않아요. 왜요?
여: 제가 오늘 친구 집에 있는 아들을 데리고 다음 주 크루즈 여행을 위한 쇼핑을 하러 갈 예정인데 할 일이 너무 많은 것 같아요.
남: 음, 내 일을 곧 마칠 거니까 오늘 오후에 당신의 보고서를 도와줄게요.
여: 당신은 너무나 친절해요, Greg. 정말 감사해요.
남: 천만에요. 언젠가 나도 당신한테 부탁을 하겠죠.

**어휘**

**ride** *v.* (~을) 타다　**stuck** *a.* 갇힌, 꼼짝 못하는

**정답**  ⑤

**문제풀이**

여자는 오늘 친구 집에서 아들을 데리고 다음 주 크루즈 여행을 위한 쇼핑을 하고 싶은데 일이 너무 많다고 했고, 남자가 자기 일을 마치고 보고서를 도와주겠다고 말했으므로 남자가 여자를 위해 할 일은 ⑤ '보고서 작성 도와주기'이다.

**총 어휘 수**  173

## 08  이유

**소재**  도서관에 온 이유

**듣기 대본 해석**

남: Melissa, 안녕. 도서관에서 뭐해?
여: Norman, 안녕, 할 게 굉장히 많아. 넌 어때? 일요일에 여긴 이떤 일이야?
남: 식물 번식에 관한 생물 리포트에 쓸 것들 좀 찾아보려고, 회요일까지야.
여: 그렇구나. 어려워 보이네. 근데 넌 무척 성실하니까 분명 잘할 거야.
남: 고마워. 아 참, 너 몸이 별로 안 좋아 보여. 괜찮아?
여: 응. 감기가 좀 있는 것 같아. 쉬어야 되는데 요 며칠 간 잠을 제대로 못 잤어.
남: 그렇구나. 다음 주 기말고사 때문에 스트레스를 많이 받고 있구나?
여: 맞아. 시험 주 전에 항상 아픈 것 같아. 심지어 성적의 40%나 되는 역사 시험도 있어.
남: 힘들겠다. 원한다면 공부하는 거 도와줄게.
여: 괜찮아. 그래도 고마워.
남: 응. 다 잘됐으면 좋겠다.

**어휘**

**research** *n.* 연구　**biology** *n.* 생물학　**reproduction** *n.* 생식, 번식
**studious** *a.* 공부를 열심히 하는　**under the weather** 몸이 안 좋은

**정답**  ③

**문제풀이**

여자가 다음 주에 있을 기말고사 때문에 스트레스를 받고 있고, 성적의 40%나 차지하는 역사 시험이 있다고 말한 것으로 미루어보아 도서관에 온 이유는 ③ '기말고사 공부를 하기 위해서'이다.

**총 어휘 수**  159

**소재** 세차 비용

**듣기 대본 해석**

남: 안녕하세요. 무엇을 도와드릴까요?

여: 제 차의 카펫을 청소하려고요.

남: 네, 일반 청소기 청소는 10달러이고 고급 샴푸 청소는 25달러입니다.

여: 어떤 것이 좋을까요? 카펫을 겨울 동안 청소하지 않았어요.

남: 샴푸 청소를 권해드리고 싶어요. 그래야 봄과 여름까지 상쾌하고 깨끗한 카펫이 될 거예요.

여: 좋아요. 그러면 고급 샴푸 청소로 할게요. 차의 외부도 세차하고 싶어요.

남: 물론이죠. 외부 세차는 15달러입니다.

여: 그래요, 좋네요. 아 그리고 바퀴도 닦아야 해요.

남: 문제 없어요. 바퀴 세차는 보통 30달러이지만 손님께서 외부 세차와 카펫 청소를 하시니 30퍼센트 할인해 드릴게요.

여: 와, 좋아요. 차를 가지러 언제 오면 되죠?

남: 차는 45분 후에 준비될 겁니다.

**어휘**

**vacuum** *n.* 진공　**deluxe** *a.* 고급　**exterior** *n.* 외부

**정답** ④

**문제풀이**

카펫을 고급 샴푸 청소하는 데 25달러, 외부 세차에 15달러이고, 바퀴 세차는 30달러인데 30퍼센트 할인해준다고 했으므로 21달러이다. 그러므로 여자가 지불해야 하는 전체 금액은 ④ '$61'이다.

**총 어휘 수** 143

## 10 언급 유무

**소재** 팔라완 섬의 발견

**듣기 대본 해석**

여: Tom, 뭐해?

남: 여행 잡지에서 필리핀의 팔라완에 대해 읽고 있어.

여: 팔라완? 무엇에 대한 이야기야?

남: 그 섬이 어떻게 그렇게 인기 있는 관광지가 되었는지에 관한 거야.

여: 난 팔라완에 대해 한 번도 들어 본 적이 없어. 거기는 경험이 풍부한 여행자들만 즐기는 그런 여행 같은데, 맞지?

남: 이 이야기에 따르면 그렇지 않아. "팔라완의 문화는 필리핀의 다른 지역이나 아시아의 문화와 매우 다르고 경관이 너무나 아름다워서 여러 곳에서 사람들이 섬으로 휴가를 즐기기 위해 모여들기 시작했다."라고 하는데.

여: 그런데 팔라완은 처음에 어떻게 대중화됐는데?

남: 그 섬은 몇 년 전에 다른 더 좋은 다이빙 지역을 찾는 다이버들을 위한 유명한 목적지였어.

여: 정말? 그럼 이젠 그 섬이 다이버들만을 위한 것이 아니란 거야?

남: 전혀. 모든 사람들이 할 만한 게 있지. El Nido 마을은 특히 커플이나 나이든 관광객들에게 인기가 많은데 매우 부드러운 분위기를 주기 때문이야.

여: 정말 멋질 것 같아. 나도 나중에 구글로 검색해서 확인해야겠다.

남: 해봐. 너의 생각은 어떤지 알려줘.

**어휘**

**tourist destination** 관광지　**experienced** *a.* 숙련된　**flock** *v.* 모이다, 떼 지어 가다　**mellow** *a.* 부드러운, 느긋한

**정답** ②

**문제풀이**

대화에서 팔라완 섬의 문화(다른 필리핀 지역과 동남아시아의 문화와 매우 다름), 사람들이 팔라완 섬을 찾는 이유(아름다움), 팔라완 섬을 처음 대중화시킨 사람들(다이버), 팔라완 섬에서 인기 있는 마을(El Nido)에 대해서는 언급되어 있지만, 팔라완 섬의 날씨에 대해서는 언급되어 있지 않으므로 정답은 ② '팔라완 섬의 날씨'이다.

**총 어휘 수** 177

## 11 내용 일치 · 불일치

**소재** 부산국제영화제 소개

**듣기 대본 해석**

여: 대한민국의 부산, 해운대 해변에서 해마다 열리는 부산국제영화제에 대해 아십니까? 그것은 아시아에서 가장 중요한 영화축제 중 하나입니다. 이 영화축제들 중 첫 번째 축제는 1996년 9월 13일부터 9월 21일에 열렸습니다. 그것은 한국에서의 첫 번째 국제 영화축제였습니다. 부산국제영화제의 초점은 특히 아시아 국가들의 새로운 영화와 신예 감독을 소개하는 것입니다. 다른 주목할 만한 특징은 영화제가 끌어들이는 많은 젊은 관객들 측면에서, 그리고 젊은 인재들을 발전시키고 알리려는 영화제의 노력 측면에서 젊은이들이 영화제에 느끼는 매력입니다. 1999년 부산 프로모션 플랜은 새로운 감독과 자금 출처를 이어주기 위해 설립되었습니다. 2011년 16번째 부산국제영화제는 새로운 영구적인 장소인 Busan Cinema Center로 옮겨졌습니다.

**어휘**

**annually** *ad.* 해마다, 일년에 한 번　**notable** *a.* 주목할 만한, 중요한　**appeal** *n.* 호소, 매력　**in terms of** ~면에서　**attract** *v.* 끌다　**promote** *v.* 촉진하다　**establish** *v.* 설립하다　**connect** *v.* 연결하다　**permanent** *a.* 영구적인

**정답** ③

**문제풀이**

부산국제영화제는 저예산 유럽 영화가 아닌 주로 아시아 출신의 신예 감독을 소개하므로 정답은 ③ '주로 유럽의 저예산 영화들을 소개한다.'이다.

**총 어휘 수** 134

## 12 도표

**소재** 스캐너 대여

**듣기 대본 해석**

남: 안녕하세요. 오늘 오후 무엇을 도와드릴까요?

여: 컬러 스캐너를 빌리고 싶은데요. 이용할 수 있는 것이 있나요?

남: 네. 도와드릴 수 있어요. 선택 가능한 네 가지 모델이 있어요. 이 책자를 보세요. 모델들이 나와있어요. 지금 가장 인기 있는 모델은 D-7이에요.

여: 좋아요. 그것에 대해 말씀해 주실래요?

남: 네. 한 달에 40달러만 내시면 정말 높은 품질의 스캐닝을 하실 수 있습니다.

여: 사실, 40달러는 제 예산에 비해 너무 비싸요. 최대 한 달에 35달러를 쓰고 싶어요.

남: 좋아요. 그럼 D-5 모델을 추천해드릴게요. 한 달에 32달러로 훌륭한 스캐닝을 제공하죠.

여: 그래요, 그게 좋네요. 제가 알아야 할 다른 특징들이 있나요?

남: 물론이죠. D-5는 컴퓨터에 선 없이 연결해서 일반 프린터로도 사용하실 수 있어요.

여: 제 사무실에 프린터는 많은데요 제가 원하는 것은 팩스기예요.

남: 그렇다면 이 모델이 당신에게 맞겠네요.

여: 좋아요. 이것으로 할게요.

**어휘**

**available** *a.* 이용할 수 있는　**at the most** 최대한　**feature** *n.* 특색, 특징　**normal** *a.* 보통의, 평범한　**hook up** 연결하다　**wirelessly** *ad.* 무선으로

**정답** ③

**문제풀이**

여자가 원하는 컬러 스캐너의 한달 대여료는 35달러 이하, 프린터의 기능보다는 팩스의 기능이 되는 것이다. 따라서 여자가 선택한 모델은 ③ 'D-3'이다.

**총 어휘 수** 180

# 13 긴 대화의 응답

**소재** 인턴십 지원에 필요한 추천서 부탁

**듣기 대본 해석**

남: Towns 선생님, 잠깐 시간 내 주실 수 있어요?

여: 물론이지, Richard. 무엇을 도와줄까?

남: Pear Computers의 여름 인턴십 프로그램에 지원하려고 해요. 제가 합격할 만한 자격이 있다고 생각하세요?

여: 그럼. 넌 올해 모든 수업과 방과후 활동에서 뛰어나게 잘 했잖아.

남: 예. 하지만 인턴십을 할 기회를 가질 수 있을지 확신이 없네요.

여: 지금 농담하는 거지? 넌 그들이 이 인턴십에서 찾고 있는 적임자야. 어쨌든 도전해봐서 손해 볼 거 없잖아.

남: 격려의 말 감사해요 Towns 선생님. 아 그런데 저한테 추천서를 써 주실 수 있으세요? 인턴십에서 요구하는 것들 중 하나거든요.

여: 나도 그러고 싶은데 더 자격을 갖춘 사람이 쓰는 게 나을 거 같은데.

남: ② 맞는 말 같아요. 제 컴퓨터 공학 교수님께 여쭤볼게요.

**어휘**

**qualification** *n.* 자격, 능력　**outdo** *v.* 능가하다　**extracurricular** *a.* 과외의　**reference letter** 추천서　〈문제〉**application** *n.* 지원(서), 신청(서)

**정답** ②

**문제풀이**

남자는 여자에게 여름 인턴십 지원에 필요한 추천서를 부탁하였는데 여자는 자신보다 더 적합한 사람이 써주는 것이 나을 것이라고 말하였다. 이에 대한 남자의 응답으로 가장 적절한 것은 ② '맞는 말 같아요. 제 컴퓨터 공학 교수님께 여쭤볼게요.'이다.

**오답 보기 해석**

① 좋아요. 그럼 바로 지원서 보낼게요.

③ 고마워요. 편지 다 쓰시면 저한테 알려주세요.

④ 신청서를 쓰는 데 시간을 내주셔서 정말 감사합니다.

⑤ 그건 문제없어요. 주말까지 쓰는 걸 끝낼게요.

**총 어휘 수** 154


# 14 긴 대화의 응답

**소재** 시골에서 자란 엄마

**듣기 대본 해석**

남: 엄마, 오늘 밤 달 봤어요? 매우 거대했어요!

여: 그래, 그렇더구나. 그것은 일년 중 가장 큰 보름달이란다. 그것은 추수 달이라고 불러.

남: 왜 그렇게 불리죠?

여: 음, 그건 추분에 가장 가까운 달이라서 그래. 그것은 농부들이 밤 늦게까지 곡식을 추수할 수 있을 정도로 충분히 밝아.

남: 이 모든 것을 어떻게 아세요?

여: 음, 내가 시골에서 자랐다는 것을 알지, 그렇지?

남: 네, 엄마가 나에게 그것에 대해 말씀하신 것을 기억해요.

여: 음, 내가 어렸을 때 가족 농장을 돕곤 했거든.

남: 오, 맞아요. 가족들이 여전히 그곳에 살고 계시나요?

여: 그럼, 많은 분들이 아직 살고 계셔.

남: 아직도 그들과 연락하세요?

여: 물론이지. 몇 달마다 나의 이모 Lucinda에게 편지를 써. 나는 지난주에 그녀로부터 편지를 받았어.

남: 엄마가 마지막으로 고향을 방문하러 간 건 언제인가요?

여: 약 10년 전에 크리스마스를 보내러 갔었지. 그들과 함께 시간을 보내는 것은 좋았어.

남: 흥미로운 곳인 것 같아요. 어렸을 때 사진 가지고 있나요?

여: ④ 당연하지. 우리가 농장에서 찍은 사진들을 보여줄게.

**어휘**

**full moon** 보름달　**harvest moon** 추분 무렵의(한가위) 보름달　**autumnal equinox** 추분　**keep in touch with** ～와 연락을 취하다

**정답** ④

**문제풀이**

아들이 엄마에게 어렸을 때 사진을 가지고 있는지 물었으므로 이어질 적절한 응답은 ④ '당연하지. 우리가 농장에서 찍은 사진들을 보여줄게.'이다.

**오답 보기 해석**

① 음. 거기에서의 보낸 시간을 그다지 많이 기억은 못해.

② 나는 나의 고향에 있는 모든 친척들과 연락이 두절되었어.

③ 아니. 크리스마스를 보내러 거기 갔을 때 나는 어떤 사진도 찍지 않았어.

⑤ 물론이지. 나는 네가 아기였을 때부터의 네 사진을 많이 가지고 있어.

**총 어휘 수** 195


# 15 상황에 적절한 말

**소재** 부모님이 자신을 아이 취급한다고 생각하는 Mike의 고민

**듣기 대본 해석**

남: 17세 고등학생인 Mike는 그를 잘 대해주시는 아주 사랑하는 부모님이 계십니다. 그러나 최근에 Mike는 그의 부모님께 불만을 느끼기 시작했습니다. 그는 자신이 좋아하는 방식으로 그의 인생을 살 정도로 나이가 들었다고 느끼지만, 그의 부모님은 여전히 마치 그가 어린아이인 것처럼 그를 대합니다. 그의 친구들은 금요일에 나가서 컴퓨터 게임을 하며 인터넷 카페에서 어울리는 반면에, Mike는 그의 부모님과 보드 게임을 하거나 오래된 영화를 보며 집에 갇혀 있습니다. 지난 주말에, Mike는 몇몇 친구들과 콘서트에 가는 것에 대해 부모에게 허락을 청했습니다. 물론 그들은 거절하셨습니다. 그러자 그는 아버지께 그를 왜 콘서트에 보내줄 수 없는지를 여쭤 보았고 그의 아버지께서는 콘서트가 너무 늦게 끝날 거라고 말씀하셨습니다. Mike는 그의 부모님이 너무 엄격하시고 그들이 자신을 어른으로서 존중하지 않는다고 믿습니다. 그는 아버지와 이에 관해 이야기하기로 결심했습니다. 이런 상황에서, Mike는 그의 아버지에게 뭐라고 말할까요?

Mike: 아빠, ④ 저를 어른처럼 대해주실 때에요. 저는 더 이상 어린아이가 아니에요.

**어휘**

**treat** *v.* 다루다, 대하다　**frustrated** *a.* 불만스러워 하는, 좌절감을 느끼는　**stuck** *a.* 갇힌, 꼼짝 못하는　**permission** *n.* 허락　**strict** *a.* 엄격한

**정답** ④

**문제풀이**

주말에도 친구들과 밖에서 놀지 못하고 콘서트도 못 가게 하는 부모께 불만이 생긴 Mike는 아버지께 자신을 더 이상 어린아이 취급하지 말하고 말씀드리려 한다. Mike가 할 말로 가장 적절한 것은 ④ '저를 어른처럼 대해주실 때에요. 저는 더 이상 어린아이가 아니에요.'이다.

**오답 보기 해석**

① 제가 아버지를 얼마나 걱정하는지 아버지는 모르시는 것 같아요.

② 제 친구들은 아버지께서 저를 그들과 가도록 해주셔서 정말 감사하고 있어요.

③ 저는 우리가 그렇게 많은 시간을 함께 보내게 돼서 너무 행복해요.

⑤ 주말에 엄마랑 같이 더 많은 시간을 보내시는 게 어때요?

**총 어휘 수** 181

# 16 담화 목적 / 17 세부 내용 파악

**소재** 소를 이용해 가난한 사람들을 돕는 방법

**듣기 대본 해석**

남: 안녕하세요, 저는 Animals for Joy의 설립자인 Noah Redman입니다. 제가 어렸을 때 아버지께서는 소를 가지고 계셨어요. 그는 소가 정말로 필요한 가족들에게 소들을 주었습니다. 여러분은 왜 아버지께서 소를 궁핍한 가정에 주었는지 궁금하실 텐데요. 가축을 소유하는 것은 자신의 사업체를 갖는 것과 같기 때문입니다. 소에서 나오는 우유, 치즈, 그리고 다른 제품들은 팔 수 있고 그 소득은 학교, 주택 개조, 부채 탕감, 즉 간단히 말해 더 나은 삶을 위해 사용될 수 있습니다. 소는 자연스럽게 미래 작물을 위한 비료도 생산할 수 있습니다. 소들은 사업이 성장하듯이 번식도 합니다. 만약에 당신이 도와주는 가족이 소의 새끼를 다른 가족에게 보내기로 하고 이러한 경향이 지역사회 안에서 계속된다면 여러분은 곧 지역사회의 빈곤이 감소하는 것을 발견할 수 있을 것입니다. 온라인 기부를 통해 Animals for Joy에 대한 여러분의 지원을 보여주세요. 그렇게 하기 위해 저희의 웹사이트 www.animals4joy.org를 방문하십시오. 여러분의 시간과 지원에 미리 감사 드립니다.

**어휘**

**livestock** *n.* 가축  **income** *n.* 수입, 소득  **home improvement** 주택 개조  **debt relief** 채무면제, 부채 탕감  **fertilizer** *n.* 비료  **offspring** *n.* 자식, 새끼  **poverty** *n.* 가난, 빈곤  〈문제〉 **caution** *v.* 주의를 주다, 경고하다  **domesticated animal** 가축

**정답** 16 ⑤  17 ④

**문제풀이**

16 남자의 아버지가 도움이 필요한 가족들에게 소를 줌으로써 어떻게 도움이 되었는지 예를 들며 기부를 촉구하고 있다. 따라서 정답은 ⑤ '가난한 사람들을 도울 수 있는 방법을 사람들에게 알려주기 위해서'이다.

17 남자는 소가 제공하는 것으로 우유, 치즈, 비료, 새끼는 언급했지만 고기는 언급하지 않았으므로 정답은 ④ '고기'이다.

**오답 보기 해석**

16
① 화장품을 위한 동물 실험에 대항하기 위해서
② 빈곤의 영향을 대중에게 경고하기 위해서
③ 새로운 축산업 기술을 소개하기 위해서
④ 가축 사육의 이점을 설명하기 위해서

**총 어휘 수** 162

# 20 수능영어듣기 실전모의고사

| 01 ④ | 02 ④ | 03 ④ | 04 ① | 05 ③ | 06 ⑤ |
| 07 ① | 08 ③ | 09 ② | 10 ① | 11 ④ | 12 ③ |
| 13 ⑤ | 14 ⑤ | 15 ④ | 16 ① | 17 ② | |

## 01 짧은 대화의 응답

**소재** 도서관 가는 날

**듣기 대본 해석**

여: Hunter, 일어나렴! 오늘 도서관 가기로 했잖니.
남: 엄마, 제가 도서관에 가야 하는 건 내일이에요. 오늘은 16일이라고요.
여: 너무 바빠서 날짜를 기억 못하는 거니? 오늘은 17일이란다.
남: ④ 정말이에요? 얼른 일어나서 바로 준비해야겠어요.

**어휘**

**wake up** 일어나다　**be supposed to V** ~하기로 되어 있다

**정답** ④

**문제풀이**

남자는 오늘이 16일이라고 착각하고 있으나 사실은 오늘이 도서관을 가야 하는 17일이라고 엄마가 말해준 상황이다. 이에 적절한 대답은 ④ '정말이에요? 얼른 일어나서 바로 준비해야겠어요.'이다.

**오답 보기 해석**

① 제가 왜 일찍 일어나야 하죠?
② 알다시피, 도서관은 오늘 휴관이에요.
③ 오, 저를 일찍 깨우지 말았어야 했어요.
⑤ 믿을 수 없어요. 16살이면 거기 혼자 가도 충분한 나이라고 생각해요.

**총 어휘 수** 47

## 02 짧은 대화의 응답

**소재** 단풍놀이

**듣기 대본 해석**

남: 가을은 내가 가장 좋아하는 계절이야. 난 가을의 바람이 좋아.
여: 맞는 말이야. 덥지도 않고 춥지도 않지.
남: 가을의 다른 좋은 점은 바로 단풍이야. 오늘 나랑 같이 단풍놀이 가는 게 어때?
여: ④ 좋은 생각이야! 내가 하고 싶었던 말이야.

**어휘**

**breeze** *n.* 산들바람, 미풍

**정답** ④

**문제풀이**

남자가 좋아하는 계절인 가을에 대해 이야기하면서 단풍놀이를 가자고 제안하였다. 이에 적절한 여자의 대답은 ④ '좋은 생각이야! 내가 하고 싶었던 말이야.'이다.

**오답 보기 해석**

① 나도야. 가을은 내가 가장 좋아하는 계절이야.
② 밖이 너무 추워서 걸을 수 없어.
③ 고마워. 하지만 나 다음 주에 바쁠 것 같아.
⑤ 초대해줘서 고맙지만 이미 저녁을 먹었어.

**총 어휘 수** 52

## 03 담화 목적

**소재** 수도관의 동파 방지

**듣기 대본 해석**

남: 실례지만, 모두 주목해주세요. 저는 여러분의 교장 선생님입니다. 지난 겨울 학교에 있는 수도관들이 동파된 것을 기억하실 것입니다. 저는 그런 일이 다시 일어날 것이라고는 생각하지 않지만, 만일을 위해 학생들과 교직원들께 특히 하루 일과를 마치고 교실을 나서면서 모든 창문을 닫을 것을 상기시켜 드립니다. 우리 학교는 자동 난방 시스템을 갖추고 있지만 창문이 열려 있다면 제대로 작동되지 않을 것입니다. 하룻밤 동안 창문이 열려 있으면 교실이 너무 추워질 것이고 난방 시스템은 파이프들이 어는 것을 막지 못할 것입니다. 파이프가 얼 경우에 물이 역류될 수 있으며 며칠 동안 학교에 아무도 없는 주말에 이 문제가 발생할 경우에 역류가 생긴 파이프가 터지고 큰 침수 피해를 일으키게 됩니다. 모든 분들께서 단순히 창문을 닫는 각자의 역할만 해 주셔도 이 상황은 쉽게 방지할 수 있습니다.

**어휘**

**interruption** *n.* 간섭, 중단　**principal** *n.* 교장 선생님　**freeze** *v.* ~이 얼다, ~을 얼리다　**faculty** *n.* 교수단　**heating system** 난방 시스템　**get backed up** ~이 밀리다, ~이 역류되다　**massive** *a.* 거대한, 엄청난　**preventable** *a.* 예방할 수 있는

**정답** ④

**문제풀이**

하루 일과를 마치고 교실을 나서며 창문을 열어 놓으면 자동 난방 시스템이 제대로 작동하지 않아 그로 인해 동파로 인한 큰 문제들이 발생할 수 있음을 알려주고 있다. 따라서 창문을 잘 닫고 다닐 것을 강조하고 있으므로 정답은 ④ '동파 방지를 위해 창문을 닫고 다닐 것을 요청하려고'이다.

**총 어휘 수** 152

## 04 대화 주제

**소재** 인터넷 사기를 피하는 방법

**듣기 대본 해석**

여: Carl, Mark에 대해 들었니?
남: 아니. 무슨 일이 있었어?
여: 음, Mark는 중고 전화기를 찾고 있었대. 마침내 온라인에서 마음에 드는 aPhone 5를 좋은 가격에 발견했지. 그런데 판매자에게 돈을 보냈는데 상품을 못 받았대.
남: 흠, 그는 판매자에게 연락을 시도해보았대?
여: 물론 그랬지. 그런데 소위 "회사"라고 하는 곳에서 가짜 연락처를 올려 놓았대.
남: 글쎄, 그가 사기 당한 것 같아. 인터넷 사기는 점점 더 흔해지고 있어.
여: 나도 중고 노트북을 사려고 찾아보고 있는데 걱정된다.
남: 근데 회사가 신뢰할 수 있는지 아닌지 알아보는 건 꽤 쉬워.
여: 정말? 내가 어떻게 확인할 수 있을까?
남: 음, 만약 판매자가 회사라면, 간단한 온라인 검색이 판매자의 이력을 알려줄 거야.
여: 그것은 하기 쉽게 들리는데.
남: 맞아. 너는 또한 판매자에게 배송 날짜와 품질 보증서가 있는지 같은 구매에 관한 질문을 할 수도 있어.
여: 너의 조언을 받아들여야겠다. 고마워, Carl.

**어휘**

**contact** *v.* 연락하다 *n.* 연락　**fake** *a.* 가짜의, 거짓의　**scam** *v.* 속이다, 사기 치다 *n.* 사기, 속임수　**fraud** *n.* 사기　**trustworthy** *a.* 신뢰할 수 있는　**purchase** *n.* 구매　**delivery** *n.* 배달, 배송　**warranty** *n.* 보증기간, 품질 보증서

**정답** ①

**문제풀이**

여자는 Mark가 온라인에서 중고 전화기를 사려고 돈을 보냈지만 물건을 받지 못했다는 이야기를 전하면서 자신도 중고 노트북을 사려고 하는데 걱정이 된다고 하자 남자는 인터넷 사기를 피하는 방법을 설명해 주고 있다. 따라서 두 사람이 하는 말의 주제는 ① '인터넷 사기를 피하는 방법'이다.

**총 어휘 수** 160

## 05 장소 파악

**소재** 인턴 주방장의 첫 출근

**듣기 대본 해석**

남: 안녕하세요. 저는 Larry입니다.

여: 안녕하세요, Larry. 저는 Tammy Smith예요. 새로 온 인턴인 것 같군요.

남: 만나게 되어서 기뻐요, Tammy.

여: 저도 당신을 만나서 기뻐요. 우리가 해야 할 일이 많기 때문에 시작해야 해요.

남: 그래요. 제가 어떻게 도와드리면 되죠?

여: 먼저, 피부를 보호하고 음식에 머리카락이 떨어지지 않게 고무장갑과 머리망을 쓰세요. 그리고 저장고에 가서 감자를 갖다 주세요.

남: 알겠습니다. [잠시 후] 자, 여기 있어요.

여: 네, 최대한 빨리 감자 껍질을 벗겨 주세요. 한 시간 후에 시작하는 연회가 있어요.

남: 그럴게요. 손님들이 몇 명이나 올 것 같아요?

여: 약 80~90명의 고객이 될 것 같아요.

남: 네. 수석 주방장님은 언제 오시는 거죠?

여: 그는 곧 오실 거예요. 그가 도착할 때까지 감자 껍질을 모두 벗겨놓도록 하세요.

**어휘**

**make somebody's acquaintance** ~를 알게 되다, 처음으로 만나다 **storage room** 저장고　**peel** *v.* 껍질을 벗기다　**banquet** *n.* 연회, 만찬　〈문제〉 **culinary** *a.* 음식의, 요리의　**commercial** *a.* 상업의, 상업적인

**정답** ③

**문제풀이**

여자가 남자에게 피부를 보호하고 머리카락이 떨어지지 않게 고무장갑과 모자를 쓰라고 했고 감자 껍질을 벗겨달라고 했으며, 수석 주방장이 등장하는 것으로 보아 대화가 일어난 장소는 ③ '상업용 주방'이다.

**오답 보기 해석**

① 슈퍼마켓

② 요리 학교

④ 사무실용 건물

⑤ 커피숍

**총 어휘 수** 147

## 06 그림의 세부 내용 파악

**소재** 지구의 날 행사 포스터

**듣기 대본 해석**

남: 엄마, 제가 그린 우리 학교 지구의 날 행사 포스터 좀 보세요.

여: 잘 그렸네. 지구의 날 때 학교에서 뭐 하는데?

남: 환경에 대해서 이야기를 나누고 어떻게 도울 수 있는지에 대해서도 얘기할 거예요.

여: 오, 좋은데. 저 포스터 왼쪽 아래에 사람들처럼 나무를 심는 것에 관해 말하려고 하는 거니?

남: 맞아요. 우린 나무를 어떻게 심는지에 관한 시범을 보려고 해요. 또 저희에게 태양 에너지를 공급해 주니까 위에 태양을 그렸어요.

여: 과연 그렇구나. 그래서 길 옆에도 풍력 터빈을 그려 놓은 거구나.

남: 네. 바람도 우리에게 에너지를 공급해 줄 수 있어요. 원래 전 터빈에 날이 네 개인 줄 알았는데 인터넷에서 본 건 다 세 개밖에 없더라고요.

여: 자전거를 타고 있는 사람은 누구야?

남: 제 친구 Frank예요. 운전을 하는 대신에 자전거를 타는 것도 환경에 도움을 주는 좋은 방법이에요.

여: 맞아. 오른쪽 아래에 애들 두 명은 뭐하고 있는 거야?

남: 길가에 있는 쓰레기를 치우고 있어요.

여: 지구를 더 살기 좋은 곳으로 만들려면 우린 모두 우리의 역할에 충실해야 하는 것 같아.

남: 맞아요, 엄마. 아, 저희 집은 재활용을 좀 더 많이 했으면 좋겠어요.

여: 알겠어. 오늘부터 그렇게 하자.

**어휘**

**environment** *n.* 환경　**solar** *a.* 태양의　**wind turbine** 풍력 발전용 터빈　**blade** *n.* 날　**garbage** *n.* 쓰레기

**정답** ⑤

**문제풀이**

오른쪽 아래에 애들 두 명은 길가에 있는 쓰레기를 치우고 있다고 했는데, 그림에서는 개를 데리고 산책을 하고 있으므로 정답은 ⑤번이다.

**총 어휘 수** 216

## 07 할 일

**소재** 시험공부 도와주기

**듣기 대본 해석**

여: Bill, Nancy한테 소식 들었어?

남: 아니. 그런데 Nancy가 오늘 아침 수업에 안 왔던데. 괜찮아?

여: Nancy는 어젯밤에 교통 사고가 나서 팔이 부러졌어.

남: 끔찍하구나. Nancy는 괜찮을까?

여: 응. 그녀는 좋아질 거야. 그런데 올해 수영 팀을 못할 거야.

남: 나쁜 소식이구나. Nancy는 아직 병원에 있어?

여: 응. 나랑 오후에 병원에 가볼래?

남: 오늘은 못 가. 다음 주 과학 시험 때문에 공부할 게 너무 많아. 내가 Nancy한테 전화해 볼게.

여: 내가 공부를 도와줄 수 있을 것 같아. 나는 작년에 시험을 잘 봤거든. 나는 괜찮으니까 그러면 함께할 시간을 더 가질 수 있을 거야.

남: 그거 좋구나. 정말 도움이 되겠어. 그럼 너 병원에 갔다가 도서관에 와서 나를 만나줄래?

여: 물론이지. 나는 가능해. 내가 Nancy 보고 나서 너한테 전화 할까?

남: 그럼. Nancy에게 내 안부도 전해줘.

**어휘**

**hang out** (~에서) 많은 시간을 보내다　**regards** *n.* 안부

**정답** ①

**문제풀이**

같이 병문안을 갈 수 있는지 물어보는 여자에게 남자는 다음 주 과학 시험 때문에 시간이 없다고 했고 여자는 공부를 도와주겠다고 말했으므로 정답은 ① '시험공부 도와주기'이다.

**총 어휘 수** 173

## 08 이유

**소재** 아르바이트를 할 수 없는 이유

**듣기 대본 해석**

여: Arthur, 어젯밤 권투경기 봤어?

남: 그래. 챔피언이 타이틀을 방어했어. 정말 대단한 싸움이었어.

여: 그래. 정말 멋졌지. 너 권투 꽤 잘 하잖아. 학교 팀에 지원해 봐.

남: 나도 하고 싶은데, 그렇게 할 수 없어.
여: 왜 못해?
남: 나는 방과 후에 극장에서 아르바이트를 하거든.
여: 오, 어떤 목표가 있어서 돈을 모으고 있는 거야?
남: 그래. 여름 방학 동안에 스페인에 수학여행을 정말로 가고 싶어.
여: 그것 참 멋지네. 나도 아르바이트를 하고 싶은데 부모님께서 허락하시지
　　않아. 내 성적이 떨어질 거라고 생각하셔.
남: 음. 그럴 수도 있어. 요즘 공부할 시간이 별로 없거든. 나의 수학 성적이
　　떨어지기 시작했어.
여: 넌 아마도 일하는 것을 그만두고 학업에 더 집중해야 할 거야.
남: 맞아. 성적이 더 중요하다고 생각하거든. 게다가, 내가 나이가 더 들었을
　　때 일할 수 있으니까.
여: 그래. 네 말이 맞아.

## 어휘

**defend** *v.* 방어하다　　**besides** *ad.* 게다가, 또한

## 정답 ③

## 문제풀이

남자의 스페인 수학여행을 위한 돈을 모으기 위해 극장에서 아르바이트를 한다는
말을 듣고, 여자는 자신도 하고 싶지만 부모님이 허락하지 않는다고 했으므로
정답은 ③ '부모님이 허락하시지 않아서'이다.

**총 어휘 수** 157


# 09　숫자

**소재** 침대와 스탠드 구매

**듣기 대본 해석**

남: 안녕하세요. Big Al의 가구 할인점에 오신 것을 환영합니다. 오늘 제가
　　무엇을 도와드릴까요?
여: 안녕하세요. 제 남편과 저는 이 침대 세트를 보고 있어요. 이건 얼마죠?
남: 이것은 가장 좋은 침대 세트 중 하나예요. 침대 프레임, 화장대, 침실용
　　스탠드와 책상을 포함해서 900달러예요.
여: 가격이 괜찮네요. 저 제품이 정말 마음에 들어요.
남: 그것은 가장 잘 팔리는 것 중에 하나고, 정가인 1,000달러에서 마침
　　10퍼센트 할인을 했는데 운이 좋으시네요.
여: 좋아요. 이것으로 실게요. 침실용 스탠드를 추가할 수 있는 방법이 있나요?
남: 문제없어요. 세트와 어울리는 것을 원하시죠?
여: 당연하죠. 이것은 얼마예요?
남: 그건 보통 하나로는 150달러이지만, 세트를 사시기 때문에 20퍼센트
　　할인해 드릴게요.
여: 좋아요. 또한 우린 이 모든 걸 옮길 트럭이 없어요. 배달받을 수 있나요?
남: 물론이죠. 저희는 보통 80달러 배송비가 있지만 운이 좋으시네요. 1,000
　　달러 이상의 구매에 관해서는 해당 사항이 없어요.
여: 좋아요. 그러면 침대 세트와 침실용 스탠드를 사겠어요.

## 어휘

**frame** *n.* 틀, 액자　　**dresser** *n.* 화장대　　**nightstand** *n.* 침실용
스탠드　　**top seller** 가장 잘 팔리는 것　　**mark down** ~의 가격을
인하하다　　**delivery fee** 배송비

## 정답 ②

## 문제풀이

침대 프레임, 화장대, 침실용 스탠드와 책상을 포함한 침대 세트가 900달러라고
했고, 침실용 스탠드가 150달러인데 세트와 같이 구매하기 때문에 20퍼센트를
할인해준다고 했으므로 120달러라서 합계는 1,020이 된다. 구매액이 1,000
달러를 넘어서 배송비는 지불할 필요가 없으므로 여자가 지불할 총 금액은
② '\$ 1,020'이다.

**총 어휘 수** 185


# 10　언급 유무

**소재** 전시회 주최자와의 인터뷰

**듣기 대본 해석**

여: 안녕하세요. 전 CBC의 Lori예요.
남: 만나서 반가워요, Lori. 전 Stan이고요, 행사에 관해 궁금해할 만한 사항에
　　답해드리려고 해요.
여: 감사합니다. 음. 일단 매우 아름다운 전시회를 개최하셨다고 말씀드리고
　　싶네요.
남: 고마워요. 이곳에는 15개국에서 온 예술가들이 그들의 작품을 전시하고
　　있어요. 150점 이상의 작품들이 있고요.
여: 와, 대단하네요. 이 전시회를 시작할 생각을 어떻게 하시게 되었나요?
남: 전 일생 동안 예술에 관심이 많았습니다. 특히 라틴 아메리카의 예술에요.
　　2~3년 전에 Boston에서 봤던 전시회를 본떠 이번 전시회를 만들었어요.
여: 이번 행사에서 기금을 모으는 목적이 무엇인지요?
남: 라틴 아메리카는 어려운 시기를 겪고 있어요. 이번 행사에서 모금된 돈은
　　도심 지역의 예술 프로그램을 지원하는데 도움을 줄 것입니다.
여: 알겠습니다. 전시회 기간이 어떻게 되나요?
남: 모든 예술 작품들은 이번 달 말까지 전시될 것입니다.
여: 잘 알겠습니다. 시간 내주셔서 감사합니다. Stan 씨.

## 어휘

**put on** 개최하다. 무대에 올리다　　**display** *v.* 전시하다
**model A after B** B를 본떠서 A를 만들다　　**fall on hard times**
어려운 시기를 겪다, 빈곤해지다　　**inner city** 도심 지역 (대도시 중심부의
저소득층 거주 지역)

## 정답 ①

## 문제풀이

작품의 수(150점 이상), 시작하게 된 계기(평생 동안 관심이 있었고, 2~3년
전에 봤던 전시회를 계기로), 기금마련의 목적(라틴 아메리카의 도심 지역 예술
프로그램 지원), 전시 기간(이번 달 말까지)은 언급되었지만, 참가 예술가의
수는 언급되지 않았으므로 정답은 ① '참가 예술가 수'이다.

**총 어휘 수** 161


# 11　내용 일치 · 불일치

**소재** 글쓰기 여름 캠프에 관한 소개

**듣기 대본 해석**

여: 학생 여러분, 안녕하세요. Aspiring Writers 여름 캠프 신청에 관한 공지를
　　하려고 합니다. 일주일 간 지속되는 이 캠프는 미래의 작가들에게 다양한
　　프로그램에 참여할 기회를 제공합니다. 이 프로그램들은 창의적인 글쓰기
　　부터 실화를 쓰는 것까지 학생들의 재능을 강화할 수 있도록 만들어
　　졌습니다. 매년 초청 작가가 와서 학생들과 대화를 나누는데 올해는 George
　　Martins께서 오셔서 이야기를 나누시고 참가자들의 질문을 받도록
　　하겠습니다. 지금 신청을 받고 있습니다. 금요일 전에 신청하시면 일찍
　　신청하는 할인을 받을 수 있습니다. 캠프 인원이 빨리 차니까 최대한 빨리
　　신청해 주세요. 신청서는 학교 홈페이지에 있습니다. 감사합니다.

## 어휘

**registration** *n.* 등록　　**a variety of** 여러 가지의　　**attendee** *n.*
참가자　　**early-bird** *a.* 이른 아침의, 일찍 오는 사람을 위한

## 정답 ④

## 문제풀이

금요일 전에 신청하면 일찍 신청하는 할인을 받을 수 있다고 했으므로 내용과
일치하지 않는 것은 ④ '한 달 전에 신청하면 할인을 받을 수 있다.'이다.

**총 어휘 수** 118

## 12 도표

**소재** 가방 선택하기

**듣기 대본 해석**

여: Andrew, 이 전단지 봤어? Rickshaw 가방을 이번 주에 백화점에서 할인한대.
남: 좋아! 나 진짜 새 가방이 필요해. 가을에 대학 들어가잖아.
여: 그렇지. 이 중 하나가 너한테 좋을 것 같아. 어떤 게 맘에 들어?
남: 글쎄. 공간이 그렇게 많이 필요할 것 같진 않고 큰 가방은 별로 안 좋아하니까 작은 게 더 나을 것 같아.
여: 나도 눈치 챘어. 지금 가방도 그렇게 크진 않잖아.
남: 맞아. 근데 어떤 스타일을 골라야 할까?
여: 모르겠어. 어깨에 메고 다닐 거야, 아니면 크로스로 매고 다닐 거야?
남: 크로스로. 그럼 메신저 가방이 나한테 더 잘 맞겠어.
여: 그렇구나. 그럼 두 개 밖에 안 남았네. 가죽 가방이 나아, 아니면 캔버스 가방이 나아?
남: 글쎄, 유행을 따르고 싶으니까 캔버스보다는 가죽으로 살래.
여: 그게 좀 더 비싸. 괜찮아?
남: 응. 괜찮아. 지금 백화점 가서 하나 사야겠다.

**어휘**

**flyer** *n.* 전단지　**mall** *n.* 백화점　**bulky** *a.* 부피가 큰, 덩치가 큰
**leather** *n.* 가죽　**waxed canvas** 캔버스　〈문제〉**satchel** *n.*
(어깨에 매는) 책가방

**정답** ③

**문제풀이**

작은 게 나을 것 같다고 했으므로 ①, ②, ③번 중에 고르면 되는데 메신저 가방이 좋고, 가죽으로 한다고 했으므로 남자가 선택할 가방은 ③번이다.

**총 어휘 수** 183

## 13 긴 대화의 응답

**소재** 장기자랑 수상자에게 줄 상품

**듣기 대본 해석**

여: 야, 이번 학기 끝날 때 학교에서 장기자랑 한대.
남: 맞아, 매년 한 번씩 해. 사실 내가 올해 장기자랑을 기획하고 있어.
여: 정말? 왜 자원했던 거야?
남: 난 새로운 거 시도하는 걸 좋아해. 그리고 이벤트 기획하는 걸 한 번도 해본적이 없어.
여: 좋네. 그럼 넌 뭘 해야 되는 거야?
남: 음, 일단 장기자랑에 참가할 사람들을 찾아야 해. 그리고 수상자들한테 줄 상품도 골라야 돼.
여: 꽤 쉽네. 어떤 상품 생각하고 있어?
남: 음, 원래 트로피를 만들려고 했는데 생각보다 너무 비싸더라고.
여: 흠... 수상자한테 리본 주는 건 어때?
남: 사실 수상자들이 오랫동안 갖고 간직할 수 있게 좀 더 값진 걸 준비하고 싶어.
여: ⑤ <u>그런 거라면, 메달은 어때?</u>

**어휘**

**talent show** 장기자랑　**semester** *n.* 학기　**volunteer** *v.* 자원하다.
자원봉사하다　**treasure** *v.* 소중히 여기다　*n.* 보물

**정답** ⑤

**문제풀이**

남자는 장기자랑 수상자에게 여자가 제안한 리본보다는 좀 더 값진 것을 주고 싶어한다. 이에 대한 여자의 응답으로 가장 적절한 것은 ⑤ '그런 거라면, 메달은 어때?'이다.

## 14 긴 대화의 응답

**소재** 지나친 콜라 섭취에 대한 친구의 조언

**듣기 대본 해석**

남: 다이어트 콜라 한 컵 더 마실 거야?
여: 응. 부엌에 있는 김에 뭐라도 가져다 줄까?
남: 난 괜찮아. 오늘 콜라 얼마나 마셨어?
여: 이게 3잔째야. 왜?
남: 너 콜라를 너무 많이 마시는 것 같아. 너한테 나쁘다고 생각하지 않아?
여: 이건 다이어트 콜라라서 실제로 나한테 훨씬 더 건강에 좋아.
남: 그렇게 생각해?
여: 설탕이 전혀 없어서 일반 콜라보다 더 좋아.
남: 그건 맞아. 근데...
여: 근데 뭐? 다이어트 콜라를 마시는 게 안 좋다는 얘기야?
남: 일반 콜라보다 더 낫다는 건 사실일지도 모르지만, 너무 많이 마시는 것은 분명 몸에 안 좋을 거야. 네가 섭취하는 모든 카페인을 생각해 봐.
여: 네 말이 맞는 것 같아. "모든 것을 적당히"라는 옛날 속담처럼 말이야.
남: ⑤ <u>바로 그거야. 내 생각에 넌 콜라를 덜 마시고 물을 더 마셔야 돼.</u>

**어휘**

**consume** *v.* 소비하다, 마시다　**in moderation** 적당히, 알맞게
〈문제〉**productive** *a.* 생산적인　**kick** *v.* (마약·습관 등을) 끊다.
극복하다　**addiction** *n.* 중독

**정답** ⑤

**문제풀이**

남자는 다이어트 콜라를 너무 많이 마시는 여자에게 양을 줄이라고 제안하고 있다. 여자는 남자의 말에 동의하며 적당히 마셔야 하겠다고 했으므로 이에 대한 남자의 응답으로 가장 적절한 것은 ⑤ '바로 그거야. 내 생각에 넌 콜라를 덜 마시고 물을 더 마셔야 돼.'이다.

**오답 보기 해석**
① 맞아. 넌 보통 어떤 브랜드를 마셔?
② 맞아. 카페인은 널 더 생산적으로 만들어 줄 수 있어.
③ 응 기억해. 나가서 콜라 좀 마시자.
④ 응. 내가 카페인 중독을 끊는 건 정말 힘들어.

**총 어휘 수** 157

## 15 상황에 적절한 말

**소재** 친구에게 컴퓨터 빌려주기

**듣기 대본 해석**

남: Seha는 Jason Lee Academy에서 세미나에 참석하고 있습니다. 그는 어제 밤새도록 준비한 캘리포니아에 대한 발표 순서를 기다리고 있습니다. 기다리면서 Seha는 옆에 Laura가 앉아 있는 것을 봅니다. 그녀는 정신 없이 가방에서 무언가를 찾고 있습니다. 그녀는 굉장히 걱정하는 것처럼 보입니다. Seha는 그녀에게 무슨 문제냐고 물어봅니다. 그녀는 자기 노트북 배터리를 다 썼는데 충전기를 집에 놔두고 왔다고 합니다. 다음이 그녀의 발표 순서인데 컴퓨터 없이 그녀는 발표를 할 수 없습니다. Seha는 그녀를 동정하여 도와주고 싶어합니다. 그는 Laura에게 자신의 컴퓨터를 빌려주고 싶습니다. 이러한 상황에서 Seha는 뭐라고 말할까요?
Seha: ④ <u>내 것을 사용해도 돼. 나는 지금 당장 사용하지 않아.</u>

어휘


**presentation** *n.* 발표    **frantically** *ad.* 정신 없이    **charger** *n.*
충전기    **sympathetic** *a.* 동정적인, 동정 어린

정답 ④

문제풀이
Seha는 바로 다음 발표 순서인 Laura에게 자신의 컴퓨터를 빌려주려고
하므로 ④ '내 것을 사용해도 돼. 나는 지금 당장 사용하지 않아.'라고 하는 것이
가장 적절하다.

오답 보기 해석
① 걱정하지 마. 다음 번엔 더 잘할 거야.
② 괜찮아. 내가 집에 가서 내 충전기를 가져올게.
③ 안됐다. 새로 하나 사는 게 어때?
⑤ 네 컴퓨터를 내가 쓰게 해줘서 고마워.

총 어휘 수 131

# 16 담화 주제 / 17 세부 내용 파악

소재 보도에 사용되는 대중 매체의 변화

듣기 대본 해석
남: 지난주 수업에서 우리는 사회에서 언론이 갖는 중요성에 대해 논의했습니다.
오늘은 대중에게 메시지를 전하는 데 쓰이는 다른 종류의 매체에 대해 이야기
할 겁니다. 먼저 우리가 이야기해볼 것은 신문을 생기게 한 인쇄기입니다.
역사상 최초로 정보는 정기적으로 대중에게 전달되었습니다. 세계 주요
도시의 글을 읽고 쓸 줄 아는 사람들은 제때에 중요 사건들에 대해 들을 수
있었습니다. 신문은 최초의 라디오 뉴스가 방송되기 전까지 거의 300년
동안 뉴스의 주요 원천이었습니다. 갑자기 언론인들은 많은 청중에게
방송을 통해 즉각적으로 뉴스를 전할 기회를 얻게 되었습니다. 텔레비전이
곧 라디오의 뒤를 이었고, 언론에 훨씬 더 많은 시각적 매체를 제공했습니다.
마지막으로, 정보화 시대는 인터넷 언론이 생기게 하였고, 이는 빠르게 전
세계에 걸쳐 뉴스의 주요 원천이 되고 있습니다. 인터넷 사용자들은 이제
거의 즉각적으로 기사를 읽고, 짧은 음성 코멘트를 들으며 영상을 볼 수
있습니다. Twitter와 같은 소셜 미디어는 즉각적인 보도를 낳았습니다.
기자들은 이제 사건이 일어나는 중일 때 보도를 방송할 수 있게 되었습니다.
이제 저는 여러분들의 생애에서 일어났던 언론의 다른 변화들에 대해
이야기하고자 합니다.

어휘
**on a regular basis** 정기적으로    **literate** *a.* 글을 읽고 쓸 줄 아는,
교양 있는    **significant** *a.* 중요한    **primary** *a.* 주요한, 기본적인, 주된
**instantly** *ad.* 즉시, 즉각    **visual** *a.* 시각적인, 시각의    **sound bite**
짧은 코멘트, 인상적인 한마디    **instantaneously** *ad.* 순간적으로,
즉석으로, 동시에    **bring about** 야기하다, 초래하다    **immediate** *a.*
즉각적인

정답 16 ⑤  17 ②

문제풀이
16 남자는 오늘의 토론 주제가 대중에게 메시지를 전달하는 데 사용되는
   매체들임을 말하였고, 과거 신문에서부터 현재의 인터넷 매체까지 소개한
   것으로 보아 남자가 하는 말의 주제로 가장 적절한 것은 ⑤ '보도에 사용되는
   대중 매체의 변화'이다.

17 남자는 신문, 라디오, 텔레비전, 소셜 미디어는 언급하였으나, 포스터는
   언급하지 않았으므로 정답은 ② '포스터'이다.

오답 보기 해석
17
① 신문      ③ 라디오      ④ 텔레비전      ⑤ 소셜 미디어

총 어휘 수 193

## DICTION ANSWERS

01 You're supposed to / you don't even remember the date

02 It's not too hot or too cold, either / Why don't we take
a trip

03 a window is left open overnight / protect the pipes
from freezing / cause massive water damage

04 did he try contacting them / Internet fraud is getting
so common / if there's a warranty

05 keep your hair from getting in the food / by the time
he arrives

06 planting trees / it provides us with solar energy /
Riding bikes instead of driving / make the Earth a
better place

07 She was in a car accident / won't be able to make the
swim / I wouldn't mind

08 try out for the school team / my grades will start
dropping / more on your schoolwork

09 finest bedroom sets / marked it down / Can we get it
delivered

10 put on quite a beautiful exhibition / How did you get
the idea / fund inner-city art programs

11 are designed to strengthen students' talent / We're
accepting applications / early-bird discount

12 what style should I choose / across your chest / that
leaves you with two options / I prefer leather to waxed
canvas

13 at the end of the semester / What made you want to
volunteer / getting some trophies made

14 This will be my third one / it's better for me than
regular cola / Think of all the caffeine / Everything in
moderation

15 he spent all last night preparing for / her laptop battery
is dead / She is next in line to present

16-17 talk about the different media / in a timely fashion /
the opportunity to report on air / as events are
happening